MW00976643

"If you are looking for a job ... before you go to the newspapers and the help-wanted ads, listen to Bob Adams, publisher of *The Metropolitan New York JobBank*."

-Tom Brokaw, *NBC*

"For those graduates whose parents are pacing the floor, conspicuously placing circled want ads around the house and typing up resumes, [*The Carolina JobBank*] answers job-search questions."

-Greensboro News and Record

"A timely book for Chicago job hunters follows books from the same publisher that were well received in New York and Boston ... A fine tool for job hunters ..."

-Clarence Peterson, *Chicago Tribune*

"Job hunting is never fun, but this book can ease the ordeal ... [*The Los Angeles JobBank*] will help allay fears, build confidence, and avoid wheel-spinning."

-Robert W. Ross, *Los Angeles Times*

"A powerful resume, *The Boston JobBank,* an aggressive job-search strategy, and a positive attitude are the keys to landing the job you want."

-Anne M. Savas, Principal
The Competitive Edge

"*The Boston JobBank* provides a handy map of employment possibilities in Greater Boston. This book can help in the initial steps of a job search by locating major employers, describing their business activities, and for most firms, by naming the contact person and listing typical professional positions. For recent college graduates, as well as experienced professionals, *The Boston JobBank* is an excellent place to begin a job search."

-Juliet F. Brudney, Career Columnist
Boston Globe

"No longer can jobseekers feel secure about finding employment just through want ads. With the tough competition in the job market, particularly in the Boston area, they need much more help. For this reason, *The Boston JobBank* will have a wide and appreciative audience of new graduates, job changers, and people relocating to Boston. It provides a good place to start a search for entry-level professional positions."

-Journal of College Placement

"*The Phoenix JobBank* provides the most convenient information source available to professionals with tight budgets and little time to waste."
-Jerry Mosqueda, President
Mosqueda & Mijas

"*The Ohio JobBank* is a very helpful tool for locating and researching potential employers. It's easy to use and even gives advice on winning the job."
-Judith G. Bishop, Manager of Employment
Barberton Citizens Hospital

"I read through the "Basics of Job Winning" and "Resumes" sections [in *The Dallas-Ft. Worth JobBank*] and found them to be very informative, with some positive tips for the job searcher. I believe the strategies outlined will bring success to any determined candidate."
-Camilla Norder, Professional Recruiter
Presbyterian Hospital of Dallas

"Through *The Dallas-Ft. Worth JobBank,* we've been able to attract high-quality candidates for several positions."
-Rob Bertino, Southern States Sales Manager
CompuServe

"One of the best sources for finding a job in Atlanta!"
-Luann Miller, Human Resources Manager
Prudential Preferred Financial Services

"This well-researched, well-edited, job-hunter's aid includes most major businesses and institutional entities in the New York metropolitan area ... Highly recommended."
-Cheryl Gregory-Pindell, *Library Journal*

"Job hunting is serious business, so don't sell yourself short. Whether you are looking for your first job or looking for a better job, *The Ohio JobBank* is a good place to start."
-Edward E. Kaufman, Director of Human Resources
Bicron

"Getting a job today means approaching a job search with research! *The Tennessee JobBank* is THE reference book of choice for career-minded professionals serious about their employment success. We use it (exclusively) because it gets results! Period!"
-Marta L. Driesslein, CPRW, Founder/President
Cambridge Career Services/Knoxville

What makes the JobBank series the nation's premier line of employment guides?

With vital employment information on thousands of employers across the nation, the JobBank series is the most comprehensive and authoritative set of career directories available today.

Each book in the series provides information on **dozens of different industries** in a given city or area, with the primary employer listings providing contact information, telephone numbers, addresses, a summary of the firm's business, and in many cases descriptions of the firm's typical professional job categories, the principal educational backgrounds sought, and the fringe benefits offered.

In addition to the **detailed primary employer listings,** the 1996 JobBank books give telephone numbers and addresses for **thousands of additional employers.**

All of the reference information in the JobBank series is as up-to-date and accurate as possible. Every year, the entire database is thoroughly researched and verified by mail and by telephone. Adams Media Corporation publishes **more local employment guides more often** than any other publisher of career directories.

In addition, the JobBank series features important information about the local job scene -- **forecasts on which industries are the hottest, overviews of local economic trends,** and **lists of regional professional associations,** so you can get your job hunt started off right.

Hundreds of discussions with job hunters show that they prefer information organized geographically, because most people look for jobs in specific areas. The JobBank series offers **20 regional titles,** from Minneapolis to Houston, and from Boston to San Francisco. Jobseekers moving to a particular area can review the local employment data not only for information on the type of industry most common to that region, but also for names of specific companies.

A condensed, but thorough, review of the entire job search process is presented in the chapter **The Basics of Job Winning**, a feature which has received many compliments from career counselors. In addition, each JobBank directory includes a section on **resumes and cover letters** the *New York Times* has acclaimed as "excellent."

The JobBank series gives job hunters the most comprehensive, timely, and accurate career information, organized and indexed to facilitate the job search. An entire career reference library, JobBank books are the consummate employment guides.

Published by Adams Media Corporation
260 Center Street, Holbrook, MA 02343

Manufactured in the United States of America.

Because addresses and telephone numbers of smaller companies change rapidly, we recommend you call each company and verify the information before mailing to the employers listed in this book. Mass mailings are not recommended.

While the publisher has made every reasonable effort to obtain and verify accurate information, occasional errors are inevitable due to the magnitude of the database. Should you discover an error, or if a company is missing, please write the editors at the above address so that we may update future editions.

"This publication is designed to provide accurate and authoritative information with regard to the subject matter covered. It is sold with the understanding that the publisher is not engaged in rendering legal, accounting, or other professional advice. If legal advice or other expert assistance is required, the services of a competent professional person should be sought."

--From a *Declaration of Principles* jointly adopted by a Committee of the American Bar Association and a Committee of Publishers and Associations

The appearance of a listing in the book does not constitute an endorsement from the publisher.

Cover photo courtesy of the Greater Miami Convention & Visitors Bureau.

ISBN: 1-55850-562-8

*This book is available at quantity discounts for bulk purchases.
For information, call 800/872-5627.*

Visit our home page at http://www.adamsonline.com

The
Florida
JobBank
1996

Managing Editor
Carter Smith

Series Editor
Steven Graber

Regional Editor
Kathryn Couzens

Associate Editor
Jennifer J. Pfalzgraf

Editorial Assistants
Marcie DiPietro
Lissa Harnish
Ernest Minks

A
ADAMS PUBLISHING
Holbrook, Massachusetts

Top career publications from Adams Media Corporation

The Atlanta JobBank, 1996 ($15.95)
The Boston JobBank, 1996 ($15.95)
The Carolina JobBank, 3rd Ed. ($15.95)
The Chicago JobBank, 1996 ($15.95)
The Dallas-Ft. Worth JobBank, 1996
    ($15.95)
The Denver JobBank, 7th Ed. ($15.95)
The Detroit JobBank, 6th Ed. ($15.95)
The Florida JobBank, 1996 ($15.95)
The Houston JobBank, 1996 ($15.95)
The Los Angeles JobBank, 1996 ($15.95)
The Minneapolis-St. Paul JobBank, 1996
    ($15.95)
The Missouri JobBank, 1st Ed. ($15.95)
The Metropolitan New York JobBank,
    1996 ($15.95)
The Ohio JobBank, 1996 ($15.95)
The Greater Philadelphia JobBank, 1996
    ($15.95)
The Phoenix JobBank, 5th Ed. ($15.95)
The San Francisco Bay Area JobBank,
    1996 ($15.95)
The Seattle JobBank, 1996 ($15.95)
The Tennessee JobBank, 2nd Ed.
    ($15.95)
The Metropolitan Washington JobBank,
    1996 ($15.95)

The National JobBank, 1996
    (Covers the entire U.S.:
    $270.00)

The JobBank Guide to Employment
    Services, 1996-1997
    (Covers the entire U.S.:
    $160.00)

Other Career Titles:

The Adams Cover Letter Almanac
    ($10.95)
The Adams Jobs Almanac, 1996 ($15.95)
The Adams Resume Almanac ($10.95)
America's Fastest Growing Employers,
    2nd Ed.($16.00)
Career Shifting ($9.95)
Careers and the College Grad ($12.95)
Careers and the Engineer ($12.95)
Careers and the MBA ($12.95)

Cold Calling Techniques (That Really
    Work!), 3rd Ed. ($7.95)
The Complete Resume & Job Search
    Book for College Students
    ($9.95)
Cover Letters That Knock 'em Dead, 2nd
    Ed. ($10.95)
Every Woman's Essential Job Hunting &
    Resume Book ($10.95)
The Harvard Guide to Careers in the
    Mass Media ($7.95)
High Impact Telephone Networking for
    Job Hunters ($6.95)
How to Become Successfully Self-
    Employed, 2nd Ed. ($9.95)
The Job Hunter's Checklist ($5.95)
The Job Search Handbook ($6.95)
Knock 'em Dead, The Ultimate
    Jobseeker's Handbook, 1996
    ($12.95)
The Lifetime Career Manager ($20.00)
The MBA Advantage ($12.95)
The Minority Career Book ($9.95)
The National Jobline Directory ($7.95)
The New Rules of the Job Search Game
    ($10.00)
Outplace Yourself ($25.00 hc)
    ($15.95 pb)
Over 40 and Looking for Work? ($7.95)
Reengineering Yourself ($12.95)
The Resume Handbook, 2nd Ed. ($5.95)
Resumes That Knock 'em Dead, 2nd Ed.
    ($10.95)
300 New Ways to Get a Better Job
    ($7.95)

To order these books or additional copies
of this book, send check or money order
(including $4.50 for postage) to:

Adams Media Corporation
260 Center Street
Holbrook MA 02343

Ordering by credit card?
Just call 800/USA-JOBS
(In Massachusetts, call 617/767-8100).
*Please check your favorite retail outlet
first.*

TABLE OF CONTENTS

SECTION ONE: INTRODUCTION

How to Use This Book/10
An introduction to the most effective way to use The Florida JobBank.

The Florida Job Market/15
An informative economic overview designed to help you understand all of the forces shaping the Florida job market.

SECTION TWO: THE JOB SEARCH

The Basics of Job Winning/22
A condensed review of the basic elements of a successful job search campaign. Includes advice on developing an effective strategy, time planning, preparing for interviews, interview techniques, etc. Special sections address unique situations faced by those jobseekers who are currently employed, those who have lost a job, and college students conducting their first job search.

Resumes and Cover Letters/39
Advice on creating a strong resume. Includes sample resumes and cover letters.

SECTION THREE: PRIMARY EMPLOYERS

The Employers/56
The Florida JobBank *is organized according to industry. Many listings include the address and phone number of each major firm listed, along with a description of the company's basic product lines and services, and, in many cases, a contact name and other relevant hiring information. Also included are hundreds of secondary listings providing addresses and phone numbers for small- and medium-sized employers.*

SECTION FOUR: EMPLOYMENT SERVICES

Temporary Employment Agencies/306
Includes addresses, phone numbers, and descriptions of companies specializing in temporary placement of clients. Also includes contact names, specializations, and a list of positions commonly filled.

Permanent Employment Agencies/307
Includes addresses, phone numbers, and descriptions of companies specializing in permanent placement of clients. Also includes contact names, specializations, and a list of positions commonly filled.

Executive Search Firms/311
Includes addresses, phone numbers, and descriptions of companies specializing in permanent placement of executive-level clients. Also includes contact names, specializations, and a list of positions commonly filled.

Resume Writing/Career Counseling Services/318
Includes addresses, phone numbers, and descriptions of companies that provide resume writing services and/or career counseling services.

SECTION FIVE: INDEX

Alphabetical Index of Primary Employers/319
Includes larger employer listings only. Does not include employers that fall under the headings "Additional Employers."

INTRODUCTION

HOW TO USE THIS BOOK

Right now, you hold in your hands one of the most effective job hunting tools available anywhere. In *The Florida JobBank*, you will find a wide array of valuable information to help you launch or continue a rewarding career. But before you open to the book's employer listings and start calling about current job openings, take a few minutes to learn how best to put the resources presented in *The Florida JobBank* to work for you.

The Florida JobBank will help you to stand out from other jobseekers. While many people looking for a new job rely solely on newspaper help-wanted ads, this book offers you a much more effective job-search method -- direct contact. The direct contact method has been proven twice as effective as scanning the help-wanted ads. Instead of waiting for employers to come looking for you, you'll be far more effective going to them. While many of your competitors will use trial and error methods in trying to set up interviews, you'll learn not only how to get interviews, but what to expect once you've got them.

In the next few pages, we'll take you through each section of the book so you'll be prepared to get a jump-start on your competition:

The Florida Job Market: An Overview

To get a feel for the state of the local job scene, read the introductory section called *The Florida Job Market*. In it, we'll recap the economy's recent performance and the steps that local governments and business leaders are taking to bring new jobs to the area.

Even more importantly, you'll learn where the local economy is headed. What are the prospects for the industries that form the core of the region's economy? Which industries are growing fastest and which ones are laying off? Are there any companies or industries that are especially hot?

To answer these questions for you, we've pored over local business journals and newspapers and interviewed local business leaders and labor analysts. Whether you are new to the area and need a source of regional information, or are a life-long resident just looking for a fresh start in a new job, you'll find this section to be a concise thumbnail sketch of where the jobs are.

This type of information is potent ammunition to bring into an interview. Showing that you're well versed in current industry trends helps give you an edge over job applicants who haven't done their homework.

Basics of Job Winning

Preparation. Strategy. Time-Management. These are three of the most important elements of a successful job search. *Basics of Job Winning* helps you address these and all the other elements needed to find the right job.

One of your first priorities should be to define your personal career objectives. What qualities make a job desirable to you? Creativity? High pay? Prestige? Use *Basics of Job Winning* to weigh these questions. Then use the rest of the chapter to design a strategy to find a job that matches your criteria.

In *Basics of Job Winning,* you'll learn which job-hunting techniques work, and which don't. We've reviewed the pros and cons of mass mailings, help-wanted ads and direct contact. We'll show you how to develop and approach contacts in your field; how to research a prospective employer; and how to use that information to get an interview and the job.

Also included in *Basics of Job Winning*: interview dress code and etiquette, the "do's and don'ts" of interviewing, sample interview questions, and the often forgotten art of what to do <u>after</u> the interview. We also deal with some of the unique problems faced by those jobseekers who are currently employed, those who have lost a job, and college students conducting their first job search.

<u>Resumes and Cover Letters</u>

The approach you take to writing your resume and cover letter can often mean the difference between getting an interview and never being noticed. In this section, we discuss different formats, as well as what to put on (and what to leave off) your resume. We review the benefits and drawbacks of professional resume writers, and the importance of a follow-up letter. Also included in this section are sample resumes and cover letters which you can use as models.

<u>The Employer Listings</u>

Employers are listed alphabetically by industry, and within each industry, by company names. When a company does business under a person's name, like "John Smith & Co.", the company is usually listed by the surname's spelling (in this case "S"). Exceptions occur when a company's name is widely recognized, like "JCPenney" or "Howard Johnson Motor Lodge." In those cases, the company's first name is the key ("J" and "H" respectively).

The Florida JobBank covers a very wide range of industries. Each company profile is assigned to one of the industry chapters listed below.

Accounting and Management Consulting
Advertising/Marketing and Public
  Relations
Aerospace
Apparel and Textiles
Architecture, Construction, and
  Engineering
Arts and Entertainment/Recreation
Automotive
Banking/Savings and Loans

Biotechnology, Pharmaceuticals and
  Scientific R&D
Business Services and Non-Scientific
  Research
Charities and Social Services
Chemicals/Rubber and Plastics
Communications: Telecommunications
  and Broadcasting
Computer Hardware, Software and
  Services
Educational Services

Electronic/Industrial Electrical
    Equipment
Environmental Services
Fabricated/Primary Metals and Products
Financial Services
Food and Beverage/Agriculture
Government
Health Care: Services, Equipment and
    Products
Hotels and Restaurants
Insurance
Legal Services

Manufacturing and Wholesaling: Misc.
    Consumer
Manufacturing and Wholesaling: Misc.
    Industrial
Mining/Gas/Petroleum/Energy Related
Paper and Wood Products
Printing and Publishing
Real Estate
Retail
Stone, Clay, Glass and Concrete Products
Transportation
Utilities: Electric/Gas/Sanitation

Many of the company listings offer detailed company profiles. In addition to company names, addresses, and phone numbers, these listings also include contact names or hiring departments, and descriptions of each company's products and/or services. Many of these listings also include a variety of additional information including:

Common positions - A list of job titles that the company commonly fills when it is hiring, organized in alphabetical order from Accountant to X-ray Technician. Note: Keep in mind that *The Florida JobBank* is a directory of major employers in the area, not a directory of openings currently available. Many of the companies listed will be hiring, others will not. However, since most professional job openings are filled without the placement of help-wanted ads, contacting the employers in this book directly is still a more effective method than browsing the Sunday papers.

Educational backgrounds sought - A list of educational backgrounds that companies seek when hiring.

Benefits - What kind of benefits packages are available from these employers? Here you'll find a broad range of benefits, from the relatively common (medical insurance) to those that are much more rare (health club membership; child daycare assistance).

Special programs - Does the company offer training programs, internships or apprenticeships? These programs can be important to first time jobseekers and college students looking for practical work experience. Many employer profiles will include information on these programs.

Parent company - If an employer is a subsidiary of a larger company, the name of that parent company will often be listed here. Use this information to supplement your company research before contacting the employer.

Number of employees - The number of workers a company employs.

Number of employees - The number of workers a company employs.

Companies may also include information on other U.S. locations and any stock exchange the firm may be listed on.

Because so many job openings are with small and mid-sized employers, we've also included the addresses and phone numbers of such employers. While none of these listings include any additional hiring information, many of them do offer rewarding career opportunities. These companies are found under each industry heading. Within each industry, they are organized by the type of product or service offered.

A note on all employer listings that appear in *The Florida JobBank*. This book is intended as a starting point. It is not intended to replace any effort that you, the jobseeker, should devote to your job hunt. Keep in mind that while a great deal of effort has been put into collecting and verifying the company profiles provided in this book, addresses and contact names change regularly. Inevitably, some contact names listed herein have changed even before you read this. We recommend you contact a company before mailing your resume to ensure nothing has changed.

At the end of each industry section, we have included a directory of other industry-specific resources to help you in your job search. These include: professional and industrial associations, many of which can provide employment advice and job search help; magazines that cover the industry; and additional directories that may supplement the employer listings in this book.

Employment Services

Immediately following the employer listings section of this book are listings of local employment services firms. Many jobseekers supplement their own efforts by contracting "temp" services, head hunters, and other employment search firms to generate potential job opportunities.

This section is a comprehensive listing of such firms, arranged alphabetically under the headings Employment Agencies, Temporary Agencies, and Executive Search Firms. Each listing includes the firm's name, address, telephone number and contact person. Most listings also include the industries the firm specializes in, the type of positions commonly filled, and the number of jobs filled annually.

Index

The Florida JobBank index is a straight alphabetical listing.

The Florida Job Market:
An Overview

Good news for Florida jobseekers: June 1995 was the 6th consecutive month that Florida's unemployment rate showed an over-the-year decline of at least one percent. That's welcome news for a state that's had a couple of difficult years. After suffering through a tumultuous period of recession, the aftermath of Hurricane Andrew, defense industry cutbacks, and major drops in tourism, Florida is finally back on track. The number of nonagricultural jobs rose 3.6 percent in June 1995 from June 1994 -- a jump of more than 200,000 jobs overall. In fact, that's more new jobs during that period than any other state besides Texas. At press time, Florida's unemployment rate was below the national average, and the 3rd lowest rate of the 11 most populous states. To a large degree, thanks go to a variety of redevelopment plans in cities around the state, a commitment to economic diversification, and an increase in international trade throughout the Southeast.

Historically, one of the keys behind the Sunshine State's economic vitality has been the steady influx of retirees moving in year after year. From 1985 to 1990, Florida was the number one destination for retirement migration with over 323,000 new retirees. Those retirees mean jobs to working-age Floridians, in that retirees need homes to live in, financial services to invest in, restaurants to dine in, and a host of other products and services. And Florida still has the highest percentage of citizens over 65. That should mean continued job growth in the health care, services, and trade industries in 1996 and beyond. *Hot retirement spots:* St. Petersburg/Clearwater and Melbourne ranked 2nd and 10th in the nation in 1995 according to *Fortune* magazine. *Other areas to watch:* The Naples area will experience the greatest citywide population growth in 1996 with a projected growth rate of 4.2 percent. On a more regional level, Central Florida's population will grow the fastest overall in 1996, with the Orlando metro area leading the way.

On the other hand, there are signs that the Florida population boom is slowing. The state's population is expected to grow more slowly over the next decade. That's because the patterns of migration may be changing. According to Charles Longino, a social gerontologist at Wake Forest University who has studied migration trends for over 20 years, "... older patterns of migration [to Florida] are plateauing. These areas have peaked." In fact, in 1996, the population is expected to grow less than 2.0 percent. The University of Florida's Bureau of Economic and Business Research expects that, by the end of the decade, the state's population to grow a mere 9.9 percent.

Services and Trade

So what does this mean for jobseekers? What was behind that 200,000 jump in jobs between 1994 and 1995? Let's take a closer look. First off, jobseekers should note that about two-thirds of Florida's new job growth in the next few years will be in trade and services industries. Between June 1994 and June 1995, the service sector accounted for 107,000 new jobs -- over half of all created. Driving this growth are a number of factors, including advances in technology, reliance on outsourcing, contractors, and temporary labor; and growing demand for services from businesses, government, and individuals due to population growth.

Best bets: business and health services. The biggest gains have been in business services, largely because of a shift of employees in other industries to contract work. New jobs created in business services between mid-'94 and mid-'95 amounted to over 62,000. Health services employers added about 17,700 new jobs. Driving the growth in health services will be improvements in medical technology as a growing and aging population increases demand for medical services. A particularly expanding field will be home health care -- aides in this field are expected to be the fastest growing occupation in the state, while social services will be the fastest growing industry due to increasing demands for child care, family social services, and residential care for the elderly.

The trade sector gained 53,700 jobs between mid-'94 and mid-'95. Eighty-three percent, or 42,500 of these jobs were in retail trade. The reason? Improvement in the tourism industry. In 1995, Apparel and accessory stores are experienced their fastest growth rates since 1989. The wholesale trade sector, on the other hand, will grow more slowly, largely because of technology -- computers taking over ordering and reordering supplies, and point-of-sale inventory systems, for example. *Another factor:* larger companies negotiating directly with suppliers, bypassing wholesalers entirely. Overall however, trade should increase its employment by over 400,000 jobs in the next decade, with over 350,000 of those in retail. Included in that group are restaurants and bars, which will add more new jobs than any other retail category.

Jobseekers should be wary of entering the construction industry in 1996, which added 8,800 jobs between mid-'94 and mid-'95, yet continues to grow more slowly than average. The slowing population growth rate is one cause of this, as well as a jump in interest rates in early 1995. Most of the growth is in special trade contracting, such as plumbers, electricians, and roofers.

Another area that has slowed is the finance/insurance/real estate sector. Over the past few years, mergers, consolidations, and closings resulting from overexpansion and competition have limited job growth. Nondepository credit institutions such as consumer finance companies and mortgage banks will expand the most as this group offers more bank-like services.

Manufacturing

While there is little growth among manufacturing companies in Florida, some sectors have brighter prospects than others. In general, the best bet for jobseekers is with durable goods manufacturers. About 60 percent of all new manufacturing jobs will be with durable goods manufacturing companies, since there is a higher concentration of high-tech companies making durable goods than in nondurable manufacturing. Industrial machinery, electronic equipment, and printing and publishing will account for more than 50 percent of new manufacturing jobs through 2005.

Many of the manufacturing jobs lost will arise in lower-skilled, labor intensive production work, which is increasingly completed by workers in Asia or Mexico. More and more, job opportunities in domestic manufacturing call for better educated and higher-skilled workers.

In the transportation, communications, and utilities sector, the number of jobs will increase as a whole over the next decade, but watch for high-tech advances to affect communications. Four out of five jobs will be generated by transportation due to a shift from rail to road freight, rising personal incomes, and growth in foreign trade. In transportation, an addition of over 70,000 jobs is anticipated by 2005.

In looking at the Florida economy, jobseekers should note that while one can learn quite a bit from statewide trends, the state should also be looked at as a number of economies, each with its own strengths and weaknesses. With that in mind, let's take a closer look at the prospects for five of Florida's major metro areas:

Miami

Although Miami's unemployment rate still lagged behind Florida's other major metro areas at 7.0 percent in June 1995, economists foresee a brighter future for Miami in 1996. The unemployment rate has fallen from 8.4 percent since June of 1994.

According to the Metro-Dade Planning Department, metro Miami's population is expected to rise steadily in the next decade, from 2,083,555 residents in 1995 to 2,234,913 in 2005.

The city, which relies heavily on the services, trade, manufacturing, transportation, and communications sectors, has benefited in the past from its port capabilities, a major airport, and free trade zones. According to *Florida Trend*'s David Poppe, "Tourists have not yet returned in force, and prospects remain uncertain, but a Fed-induced slowdown [of rising interest rates] in 1995 may inspire an economic surge in 1996."

More significantly, international trade with the Caribbean, Latin America, Europe, and Asia will grow swiftly in 1995-96. Multinational firms make up one of Greater Miami's fastest-growing business segments and are drawn by the area's location on the global trade routes. In fact, the number of air transportation businesses in Greater Miami grew by more than 40 percent between 1990 and 1994 -- an increase of 113 firms. The Port of Miami has also seen a large increase in visitors, as many cruise ship lines use the area as a gateway to the Caribbean.

The largest employers in the Miami area are **American Airlines**, which employs over 8,200; **University of Miami**, employing over 7,400; and **BellSouth Telecommunications**, with a staff of 5,800. The largest manufacturing companies are **Coulter Corporation**, **Cordis Corporation**, and **Dade International** -- all biomedical firms, and *Fortune* 500 company **Knight-Ridder**, the newspaper publishing and information services company. The largest nonmanufacturing employers are **Dade County Public Schools**, **Metropolitan Dade County**, and **Jackson Memorial Hospital**. Other major employers are **Winn-Dixie**, **Florida Power & Light**, **Burdine's Department Stores**, **Kmart**, **Ryder System**, and **Publix Supermarkets**.

Fort Lauderdale

Fort Lauderdale garnered some national attention recently when *Parade* magazine named the city among the top 10 choices for new job prospects in the year 2010. Strong industries include tourism, retail, and high-tech. Among the city's largest employers are the **Broward County School Board**, the supermarket chains **Publix** and **Winn-Dixie**, **American Express**, **Southern Bell**, **AT&T**, **Eckerd Corporation**, and **Burdine's Department Stores**.

Broward County suffered a drop in tourism in the last few years, with a large decrease in European visitors to the area. The Caribbean has become a fierce competitor as a popular vacation locale and has taken away some of Fort Lauderdale's tourists. Hotel occupancy fell 9.9 percent in 1994 but things are looking up. While 1994 occupancy rates were still 20 percent lower than they were in 1993, they rose by approximately 4.0 percent in 1995. And tourism will rise even faster if people like H. Wayne Huizenga has anything to say about it. Huizenga, the owner of **Blockbuster Entertainment**, as well as the **Miami Dolphins** football team and the **Florida Marlins** baseball team, is set to build a new arena for his hockey team, the Fort Lauderdale-based **Florida Panthers**.

Orlando

It's been several years since the *Wall Street Journal* named Orlando one of the 10 fastest growing cities of the '90s, but the fact is, it still holds this distinction. Much of the growth, of course, is directly related to tourism. In fact, no city in the world provides more hotel rooms. As the home of **Walt Disney World**, the **Epcot Center**, **Disney MGM Studios**, **Universal Studios**, **Busch Gardens**, and **Sea World**, Orlando hauls in over $2 billion a year in tourist dollars.

The city is also making a concerted effort to attract additional foreign visitors. Orlando will play host to a number of preliminary soccer games prior to the 1996 Olympic Games in Atlanta, which should help.

Heading towards 1996, the economy in Orlando and Central Florida is stable, although some analysts believe it is too reliant on the tourism and defense industries. Orlando is taking steps to diversify by strengthening other sectors, including high-tech, health care, film and television, sports, and international trade. For example, despite the fact that surrounding counties suffered from cutbacks in defense spending, Orlando has plans to create over 15,000 jobs by redeveloping the Orlando Naval Training Center, which will close in 1999 and eliminate over 3,000 positions.

In fact, metro Orlando added more jobs in the state between mid-'94 and mid-'95 than any other Florida city. The unemployment rate was 4.9 percent in June 1995, which remained one of the lowest of the major metropolitan areas in the state. Companies like **Lockheed Martin** (aerospace) and **Oracle Corporation** (software) have also added jobs recently; 1,500 and 200 respectively.

Areas surrounding Orlando had the highest occupancy rates for office space in the state in 1994. Expect new office projects to begin in 1996 in the downtown area. *Office hot spots:* Lake Mary and Heathrow. **AT&T** and **Recoton Corporation** have plans to open new facilities in Lake Mary. And other companies are relocating to Heathrow -- **Dixon Ticonderoga** and **Cincinnati Bell**, both of which plan to add several hundred jobs as well.

Jacksonville

According to Anne Johnson of *Florida Trend*, in 1995, Jacksonville's "balanced economy is expanding as pro sports and urban renewal play larger roles." The NFL's new **Jacksonville Jaguars** began their first season in 1995, while a new performing arts center and symphony hall should also boost attraction to the city and create jobs in eating and drinking places and other retail facilities. Although the unemployment rate is low in Jacksonville -- 4.5 percent in June 1995 -- and thousands of jobs are being created in the metro area, many of these jobs are relatively low-paying.

Trouble spots include health and financial services, manufacturing, and defense. **American Express** intends to close a facility in Jacksonville which would put 1,200 people out of work, although another company, **SafeCard Services** hope to take over the facility -- which would make it their headquarters and add jobs. Manufacturing companies are choosing to invest capital as opposed to hiring more workers -- **Anheuser-Busch** spent several millions of dollars on renovating its plant, while also laying off 10 percent of its employees in 1995. **The Naval Aviation Depot** was expected to yield to cutbacks by the government, thereby losing over 3,000 high-paying jobs. Jobseekers should research *Fortune* 500 companies headquartered in Jacksonville: **Winn-Dixie**, which should boom as a result of the growing retail industry, and **Barnett Banks**, which may suffer from the current trends to merge or consolidate in the financial services sector.

Tampa-St. Petersburg

During the past few years, Tampa Bay has been awarded several new sports franchises. In the Spring of 1995, Tampa finally acquired a major league baseball team, the **Devil Rays**, which will take the field in 1998. The **Tampa Bay Lightning**, a professional hockey team, hope to play in a new downtown arena built by 1996. These developments will in return attract many fans to the area and increase employment at eating and drinking places and retail facilities.

The area did, however, experience a slowdown in job growth in 1995, with more lower-paying jobs developing, but the slowdown is still nothing like the standstill that occurred in 1991-92. Many large national companies have added jobs as they opened customer service centers: **MCI** had an annual job growth rate of nearly 200 percent at the end of 1994 as the company created 375 more jobs; **Xerox**'s new facility added 700 openings; and **T. Rowe Price** and **New York Life** both developed locations with over 100 new jobs and expectations for more growth. **Beneficial Data Processing Corporation** also increased its employee count by over 100 and **Arthur Andersen Consulting** added a new office and nearly 200 employees.

Companies to watch: **Outback Steakhouse**, which was a *Fortune* Top 100 Fastest Growing company in 1995, had a job growth rate of 121.3 percent for 1994. This national restaurant chain is headquartered in Tampa. Other *Fortune* 500 companies in the Tampa Bay area include **Publix Supermarkets** in Lakeland, **Eckerd Corporation** in Largo, **Florida Progress** in St. Petersburg, and **Tech Data** in Clearwater.

Jobseekers can contact the following organizations in Florida:

The Beacon Council, One World Trade Plaza, 80 SW 8th Street, Suite 2400, Miami FL 33130. 305/536-8000.

Florida Department of Commerce, Division of Economic Development, Bureau of Economic Analysis, 107 West Gaines Street, Suite 315, Tallahassee FL 32399-2000. 904/487-2971.

Florida Department of Labor & Employment Security, Bureau of Labor Market Information, Suite 200, Hartman Building, 2012 Capital Circle SE, Tallahassee FL 32399-0674. 904/488-1048.

Greater Fort Lauderdale Chamber of Commerce, P.O. Box 14516, Fort Lauderdale FL 33302-4516. 954/462-6000.

THE JOB SEARCH

THE BASICS OF JOB WINNING:
A CONDENSED REVIEW

This chapter is divided into four sections. The first section explains the fundamentals that every jobseeker should know, especially first-time jobseekers. The following three sections deal with special situations faced by specific types of jobseekers: those who are currently employed, those who have lost a job, and college students.

THE BASICS:
Things Everyone Needs To Know

Career Planning   The first step to finding your ideal job is to clearly define your objectives. This is better known as career planning (or life planning if you wish to emphasize the importance of combining the two). Career planning has become a field of study in and of itself.

If you are thinking of choosing or switching careers, we particularly emphasize two things. First, choose a career where you will enjoy most of the day-to-day tasks. This sounds obvious, but most of us have at one point or another been attracted by a glamour industry or a prestigious job title without thinking of the most important consideration: Would we enjoy performing the everyday tasks the position entails?

> **The first step in beginning your job search is to clearly define your objectives.**

The second key consideration is that you are not merely choosing a career, but also a lifestyle. Career counselors indicate that one of the most common problems people encounter in job-seeking is that they fail to consider how well-suited they are for a particular position or career. For example, some people, attracted to management consulting by good salaries, early responsibility, and high-level corporate exposure, do not adapt well to the long hours, heavy travel demands, and constant pressure to produce. Be sure to ask yourself how you might adapt to not only the day-to-day duties and working environment that a specific position entails, but also how you might adapt to the demands of that career or industry choice as a whole.

Assuming that you've established your career objectives, the next step **Choosing** of the job search is to develop a strategy. If you don't take the time to **Your** develop a strategy and lay out a plan, you may find yourself going in **Strategy** circles after several weeks of randomly searching for opportunities that always seem just beyond your reach.

The most common job-seeking techniques are:

- following up on help-wanted advertisements
- using employment services
- relying on personal contacts
- contacting employers directly (the Direct Contact method)

Many professionals have been successful in finding better jobs using each one of these approaches. However, the Direct Contact method boasts twice the success rate of the others. So unless you have specific reasons to believe that other strategies would work best for you, Direct Contact should form the foundation of your job search.

If you prefer to use other methods as well, try to expend at least half your effort on Direct Contact, spending the rest on all of the other methods combined. Millions of other jobseekers have already proven that Direct Contact has been twice as effective in obtaining employment, so why not benefit from their experience?

With your strategy in mind, the next step is to work out the details of **Setting** your search. The most important detail is setting up a schedule. Of course, **Your** since job searches aren't something most people do regularly, it may be **Schedule** hard to estimate how long each step will take. Nonetheless, it is important to have a plan so that you can monitor your progress.

> **Job hunting is intellectually demanding work that requires you to be at your best. So don't tire yourself out working around the clock.**

When outlining your job search schedule, have a realistic time frame in mind. If you will be job-searching full-time, your search could take at least two months or more. If you can only devote part-time effort, it will probably take at least four months.

You probably know a few currently employed people who seem to spend their whole lives searching for a better job in their spare time. Don't be one of them. If you are presently working and don't feel like devoting a lot of energy to job-seeking right now, then wait. Focus on enjoying your present position, performing your best on the job, and storing up energy for when you are really ready to begin your job search.

Those of you who are currently unemployed should remember that job-hunting is tough work physically and emotionally. It is also intellectually demanding work that requires you to be at your best. So don't tire yourself out by working on your job campaign around the clock. At the same time, be sure to discipline yourself. The most logical way to manage your time while looking for a job is to keep your regular working hours.

> **The more you know about a company, the more likely you are to catch an interviewer's eye. (You'll also face fewer surprises once you get the job!)**

If you are searching full-time and have decided to choose several different contact methods, we recommend that you divide up each week, designating some time for each method. By trying several approaches at once, you can evaluate how promising each seems and alter your schedule accordingly. But be careful -- don't judge the success of a particular technique just by the sheer number of interviews you obtain. Positions advertised in the newspaper, for instance, are likely to generate many more interviews per opening than positions that are filled without being advertised.

If you are searching part-time and decide to try several different contact methods, we recommend that you try them sequentially. You simply won't have enough time to put a meaningful amount of effort into more than one method at once. Estimate the length of your job search, and then allocate so many weeks or months for each contact method, beginning with Direct Contact.

And remember that all schedules are meant to be broken. The purpose of setting a schedule is not to rush you to your goal but to help you periodically evaluate how you're progressing.

The Direct Contact Method

Once you have scheduled your time, you are ready to begin your search in earnest. If you decide to begin with the Direct Contact method, the first step is to develop a check list for categorizing the types of firms for which you'd like to work. You might categorize firms by product line, size, customer-type (such as industrial or consumer), growth prospects, or geographical location. Your list of important criteria might be very short. If it is, good! The shorter it is, the easier it will be to locate a company that is right for you.

Now you will want to use this *JobBank* book to assemble your list of potential employers. Choose firms where *you* are most likely to be able to find a job. Try matching your skills with those that a specific job demands. Consider where your skills might be in demand, the degree of competition for employment, and the employment outlook at each company.

Separate your prospect list into three groups. The first 25 percent will be your primary target group, the next 25 percent will be your secondary group, and the remaining names you can keep in reserve.

After you form your prospect list, begin work on your resume. Refer to the Resumes and Cover Letters section following this chapter to get ideas.

DEVELOPING YOUR CONTACTS: NETWORKING

Some career counselors feel that the best route to a better job is through somebody you already know or through somebody to whom you can be introduced. These counselors recommend that you build your contact base beyond your current acquaintances by asking each one to introduce you, or refer you, to additional people in your field of interest.

The theory goes like this: You might start with 15 personal contacts, each of whom introduces you to three additional people, for a total of 45 additional contacts. Then each of these people introduces you to three additional people, which adds 135 additional contacts. Theoretically, you will soon know every person in the industry.

Of course, developing your personal contacts does not work quite as smoothly as the theory suggests because some people will not be able to introduce you to anyone. The further you stray from your initial contact base, the weaker your references may be. So, if you do try developing your own contacts, try to begin with as many people that you know personally as you can. Dig into your personal phone book and your holiday greeting card list and locate old classmates from school. Be particularly sure to approach people who perform your personal business such as your lawyer, accountant, banker, doctor, stockbroker, and insurance agent. These people develop a very broad contact base due to the nature of their professions.

Once your resume is complete, begin researching your first batch of prospective employers. You will want to determine whether you would be happy working at the firms you are researching and to get a better idea of what their employment needs might be. You also need to obtain enough information to sound highly informed about the company during phone conversations and in mail correspondence. But don't go all out on your research yet! You probably won't be able to arrange interviews with some of these firms, so save your big research effort until you start to arrange interviews. Nevertheless, you should plan to spend several hours researching each firm. Do your

> **It is said that the personnel office never hires people; they screen candidates.**

research in batches to save time and energy. Start with this book, and find out what you can about each of the firms in your primary target group. Contact any pertinent professional associations that may be able to help you learn more about an employer. Read industry publications looking for articles on the firm. (Addresses of associations and names of important publications are listed after each industrial section of employer listings in this book.) Then try additional resources at your local library. Keep organized, and maintain a folder on each firm.

If you discover something that really disturbs you about the firm (they are about to close their only local office), or if you discover that your chances of getting a job there are practically nil (they have just instituted a hiring freeze), then cross them off your prospect list. If possible, supplement your research efforts by contacting individuals who know the firm well. Ideally you should make an informal contact with someone at that particular firm, but often a direct competitor, or a major supplier or customer, will be able to supply you with just as much information. At the very least, try to obtain whatever printed information the company has available -- not just annual reports, but product brochures and any other printed materials that the firm may have to offer, either about its operations or about career opportunities.

Getting The Interview

Now it is time to arrange an interview, time to make the Direct Contact. If you have read many books on job-searching, you may have noticed that most of these books tell you to avoid the personnel office like the plague. It is said that the personnel office never hires people; they screen candidates. Unfortunately, this is often the case. If you can identify the appropriate manager with the authority to hire you, you should try to contact that person directly. However, this will take a lot of time in each case, and often you'll be bounced back to personnel despite your efforts. So we suggest that initially you begin your Direct Contact campaign through personnel offices. If it seems that the firms on your prospect list do little hiring through personnel, you might consider some alternative courses of action.

DON'T BOTHER WITH MASS MAILINGS
OR BARRAGES OF PHONE CALLS

Direct Contact does not mean burying every firm within a hundred miles with mail and phone calls. Mass mailings rarely work in the job hunt. This also applies to those letters that are personalized -- but dehumanized -- on an automatic typewriter or computer. Don't waste your time or money on such a project; you will fool no one but yourself.

The worst part of sending out mass mailings, or making unplanned phone calls to companies you have not researched, is that you are likely to be remembered as someone with little genuine interest in the firm, who lacks sincerity -- somebody that nobody wants to hire.

HELP WANTED ADVERTISEMENTS

Only a small fraction of professional job openings are advertised. Yet the majority of jobseekers -- and quite a few people not in the job market -- spend a lot of time studying the help wanted ads. As a result, the competition for advertised openings is often very severe.

A moderate-sized employer told us about their experience advertising in the help wanted section of a major Sunday newspaper:

It was a disaster. We had over 500 responses from this relatively small ad in just one week. We have only two phone lines in this office and one was totally knocked out. We'll never advertise for professional help again.

If you insist on following up on help wanted ads, then research a firm before you reply to an ad. Preliminary research might help to separate you from all of the other professionals responding to that ad, many of whom will have only a passing interest in the opportunity. It will also give you insight about a particular firm, to help you determine if it is potentially a good match. That said, your chances of obtaining a job through the want ads are still much smaller than they are with the Direct Contact method.

The three obvious means of initiating Direct Contact are:

- Showing up unannounced
- Mail
- Phone calls

Cross out the first one right away. You should never show up to seek a professional position without an appointment. Even if you are somehow lucky enough to obtain an interview, you will appear so unprofessional that you will not be seriously considered.

> **Always include a cover letter if you are asked to send a resume.**

Mail contact seems to be a good choice if you have not been in the job market for a while. You can take your time to prepare a letter, say exactly what you want, and of course include your resume. Remember that employers receive many resumes every day. Don't be surprised if you do not get a response to your inquiry, and don't spend weeks waiting for responses that may never come. If you do send a letter, follow it up (or precede it) with a phone call. This will increase your impact, and because of the initial research you did, will underscore both your familiarity with and your interest in the firm.

Another alternative is to make a "Cover Call." Your Cover Call should be just like your cover letter: concise. Your first statement should interest the employer in you. Then try to subtly mention your familiarity with the firm. Don't be overbearing; keep your introduction to three sentences or less. Be pleasant, self-confident, and relaxed. This will greatly increase the chances of the person at the other end of the line developing the conversation. But don't press. When you are asked to follow up "with something in the mail," don't try to prolong the conversation once it has ended. Don't ask what they want to receive in the mail. Always send your resume and a highly personalized follow-up letter, reminding the addressee of the phone conversation. Always include a cover letter if you are asked to send a resume.

Unless you are in telephone sales, making smooth and relaxed cover calls will probably not come easily. Practice them on your own, and then with your friends or relatives.

If you obtain an interview as a result of a telephone conversation, be sure to send a thank-you note reiterating the points you made during the conversation. You will appear more professional and increase your impact. However, unless specifically requested, don't mail your resume once an interview has been arranged. Take it with you to the interview instead.

Once the interview has been arranged, begin your in-depth research. **Preparing** You should arrive at an interview knowing the company upside-down and **For The** inside-out. You need to know the company's products, types of customers, **Interview** subsidiaries, parent company, principal locations, rank in the industry, sales and profit trends, type of ownership, size, current plans, and much more. By this time you have probably narrowed your job search to one industry. Even if you haven't, you should still be familiar with the trends in the firm's industry, the firm's principal competitors and their relative performance, and the direction in which the industry leaders are headed.

BE PREPARED:
Some Common Interview Questions

Tell me about yourself...

Why did you leave your last job?

What excites you in your current job?

Where would you like to be in five years?

How much overtime are you willing to work?

What would your previous/present employer tell me about you?

Tell me about a difficult situation that you
faced at your previous/present job.

What are your greatest strengths?

What are your greatest weaknesses?

Describe a work situation where you took initiative
and went beyond your normal responsibilities.

Why do you wish to work for this firm?

Why should we hire you?

Dig into every resource you can! Read the company literature, the trade press, the business press, and if the company is public, call your stockbroker (if you have one) and ask for additional information. If

> You should arrive at an interview knowing the company upside-down and inside-out.

possible, speak to someone at the firm before the interview, or if not, speak to someone at a competing firm. The more time you spend, the better. Even if you feel extremely pressed for time, you should set aside several hours for pre-interview research.

If you have been out of the job market for some time, don't be surprised if you find yourself tense during your first few interviews. It will probably happen every time you re-enter the market, not just when you seek your first job after getting out of school.

Tension is natural during an interview, but knowing you have done a thorough research job should put you more at ease. Make a list of questions that you think might be asked in each interview. Think out your answers carefully and practice them with a friend. Tape record your responses to the problem questions. If you feel particularly unsure of your interviewing skills, arrange your first interviews at firms you are not as interested in. (But remember it is common courtesy to seem enthusiastic about the possibility of working for any firm at which you interview.) Practice again on your own after these first few interviews. Go over the difficult questions that you were asked.

Interview Attire
How important is the proper dress for a job interview? Buying a complete wardrobe of Brooks Brothers pinstripes or Donna Karan suits, donning new wing tips or pumps, and having your hair styled every morning are not enough to guarantee you a career position as an investment banker. But on the other hand, if you can't find a clean, conservative suit or won't take the time to wash your hair, then you are just wasting your time by interviewing at all.

Top personal grooming is as important as finding appropriate clothes for a job interview. Careful grooming indicates both a sense of thoroughness and self-confidence. This is not the time to make a statement -- take out the extra earrings and avoid any garish hair colors not found in nature. Women should not wear excessive makeup, and both men and women should refrain from wearing any perfume or cologne (it only takes a small spritz to leave an allergic interviewer with a fit of sneezing and a bad impression of your meeting). Men should be freshly shaven, even if the interview is late in the day, and men with long hair should have it pulled back and neat.

Men applying for any professional position should wear a suit, preferably in a conservative color such as navy or charcoal gray. It is easy to get away with wearing the same dark suit to consecutive interviews at the same company; just be sure to wear a different shirt and tie for each interview.

Women should also wear a businesslike suit. Professionalism still dictates a suit with a skirt, rather than slacks, as proper interview garb for women. This is usually true even at companies where pants are acceptable attire for female employees. As much as you may disagree with this guideline, the more prudent time to fight this standard is after you land the job.

SKIRT VS. PANTS:
An Interview Dilemma

For those women who are still convinced that pants are acceptable interview attire, listen to the words of one career counselor from a prestigious New England college:

I had a student who told me that since she knew women in her industry often wore pants to work, she was going to wear pants to her interviews. Almost every recruiter commented that her pants were "too casual," and even referred to her as "the one with the pants." The funny thing was that one of the recruiters who commented on her pants had been wearing jeans!

The final selection of candidates for a job opening won't be determined by dress, of course. However, inappropriate dress can quickly eliminate a first-round candidate. So while you shouldn't spend a fortune on a new wardrobe, you should be sure that your clothes are adequate. The key is to dress at least as formally or slightly more formally and more conservatively than the position would suggest.

What To Bring

Be complete. Everyone needs a watch, a pen, and a notepad. Finally, a briefcase or a leather-bound folder (containing extra, *unfolded*, copies of your resume) will help complete the look of professionalism.

Sometimes the interviewer will be running behind schedule. Don't be upset, be sympathetic. There is often pressure to interview a lot of candidates and to quickly fill a demanding position. So be sure to come to your interview with good reading material to keep yourself occupied and relaxed.

The Interview   The very beginning of the interview is the most important part because it determines the tone for the rest of it. Those first few moments are especially crucial. Do you smile when you meet? Do you establish enough eye contact, but not too much? Do you walk into the office with a self-assured and confident stride? Do you shake hands firmly? Do you make small talk easily without being garrulous? It is human nature to judge people by that first impression, so make sure it is a good one. But most of all, try to be yourself.

Often the interviewer will begin, after the small talk, by telling you about the company, the division, the department, or perhaps, the position. Because of your detailed research, the information about the company should be repetitive for you, and the interviewer would probably like nothing better than to avoid this regurgitation of the company biography. So if you can do so tactfully, indicate to the interviewer that you are very familiar with the firm. If he or she seems intent on providing you with background information, despite your hints, then acquiesce.

But be sure to remain attentive. If you can manage to generate a brief discussion of the company or the industry at this point, without being forceful, great. It will help to further build rapport, underscore your interests, and increase your impact.

Soon (if it didn't begin that way) the interviewer will begin the questions, many of which you will have already practiced. This period of the interview usually falls into one of two categories (or somewhere in between): either a structured interview, where the interviewer has a prescribed set of questions to ask; or an unstructured interview, where the interviewer will ask only leading questions to get you to talk about yourself, your experiences, and your goals. Try to sense as quickly as possible in which direction the interviewer wishes to proceed. This will make the interviewer feel more relaxed and in control of the situation.

> **The interviewer's job is to find a reason to turn you down; your job is to not provide that reason.**
>
> -John L. LaFevre, author, *How You Really Get Hired*
>
> Reprinted from the 1989/90 *CPC Annual*, with permission of the National Association of Colleges and Employers (formerly College Placement Council, Inc.), copyright holder.

Remember to keep attuned to the interviewer and make the length of your answers appropriate to the situation. If you are really unsure as to how detailed a response the interviewer is seeking, then ask.

As the interview progresses, the interviewer will probably mention some of the most important responsibilities of the position. If applicable, draw parallels between your experience and the demands of the position as detailed by the interviewer. Describe your past experience in the same manner that you do on your resume: emphasizing results and achievements and not merely describing activities. But don't exaggerate. Be on the level about your abilities.

The first interview is often the toughest, where many candidates are screened out. If you are interviewing for a very competitive position, you will have to make an impression that will last. Focus on a few of your greatest strengths that are relevant to the position. Develop these points carefully, state them again in different words, and then try to summarize them briefly at the end of the interview.

> **Often the interviewer will pause toward the end and ask if you have any questions. Have a list prepared of specific questions that are of real interest to you.**

Often the interviewer will pause toward the end and ask if you have any questions. Particularly in a structured interview, this might be the one chance to really show your knowledge of and interest in the firm. Have a list prepared of specific questions that are of real interest to you. Let your questions subtly show your research and your knowledge of the firm's activities. It is wise to have an extensive list of questions, as several of them may be answered during the interview.

Do not turn your opportunity to ask questions into an interrogation. Avoid reading directly from your list of questions, and ask questions that you are fairly certain the interviewer can answer (remember how you feel when you cannot answer a question during an interview).

Even if you are unable to determine the salary range beforehand, do not ask about it during the first interview. You can always ask about it later. Above all, don't ask about fringe benefits until you have been offered a position. (Then be sure to get all the details.)

Try not to be negative about anything during the interview (particularly any past employer or any previous job). Be cheerful. Everyone likes to work with someone who seems to be happy.

Don't let a tough question throw you off base. If you don't know the answer to a question, simply say so -- do not apologize. Just smile. Nobody can answer every question -- particularly some of the questions that are asked in job interviews.

Before your first interview, you may be able to determine how many rounds of interviews there usually are for positions at your level. (Of course it may differ quite a bit even within the different levels of one firm.) Usually you can count on attending at least two or three interviews, although some firms, such as some of the professional partnerships, are known to give a minimum of six interviews for all professional positions. While you should be more relaxed as you return for subsequent interviews, the pressure will be on. The more prepared you are, the better.

Depending on what information you are able to obtain, you might want to vary your strategy quite a bit from interview to interview. For instance, if the first interview is a screening interview, then be sure a few of your strengths really stand out. On the other hand, if later interviews are primarily with people who are in a position to veto your hiring, but not to push it forward, then you should primarily focus on building rapport as opposed to reiterating and developing your key strengths.

If it looks as though your skills and background do not match the position the interviewer was hoping to fill, ask him or her if there is another division or subsidiary that perhaps could profit from your talents.

> Getting a job offer is a lot like getting a marriage proposal. Someone is not going to offer it unless they're pretty sure you're going to accept it.
>
> -Marilyn Hill, Associate Director, Career Center, Carleton College

After The Interview

Write a follow-up letter immediately after the interview, while it is still fresh in the interviewer's mind (see the sample follow-up letter format found in the Resumes and Cover Letters chapter). Then, if you haven't heard from the interviewer within a week, call to stress your continued interest in the firm, and the position, and request a second interview.

THE BALANCING ACT:
Looking For A New Job While Currently Employed

For those of you who are still employed, job-searching will be particularly tiring because it must be done in addition to your normal work responsibilities. So don't overwork yourself to the point where you show up to interviews looking exhausted and start to slip behind at your current job. On the other hand, don't be tempted to quit your present job! The long hours are worth it. Searching for a job while you have one puts you in a position of strength.

Making Contact

If you're expected to be in your office during the business day, then you have an additional problem to deal with. How can you work interviews into the business day? And if you work in an open office, how can you even call to set up interviews? As much as possible you should keep up the effort and the appearances on your present job. So maximize your use of the lunch hour, early mornings, and late afternoons for calling. If you keep trying, you'll be surprised how often you will be able to reach the executive you are trying to contact during your out-of-office hours. You can catch people as early as 8 a.m. and as late as 6 p.m. on frequent occasions.

Your inability to interview at any time other than lunch just might **Scheduling** work to your advantage. If you can, try to set up as many interviews as **Interviews** possible for your lunch hour. This will go a long way to creating a relaxed atmosphere. (Who isn't happy when eating?) But be sure the interviews don't stray too far from the agenda on hand.

Lunchtime interviews are much easier to obtain if you have substantial career experience. People with less experience will often find no alternative to taking time off for interviews. If you have to take time off, you have to take time off. But try to do this as little as possible. Try to take the whole day off in order to avoid being blatantly obvious about your job

> **Try calling as early as 8 a.m. and as late as 6 p.m. You'll be surprised how often you will be able to reach the executive you want during these times of the day**

search, and try to schedule two to three interviews for the same day. (It is very difficult to maintain an optimum level of energy at more than three interviews in one day.) Explain to the interviewer why you might have to juggle your interview schedule -- he/she should honor the respect you're showing your current employer by minimizing your days off and will probably appreciate the fact that another prospective employer is interested in you.

What do you tell an interviewer who asks for references? Just say that **References** while you are happy to have your former employers contacted, you are trying to keep your job search confidential and would rather that your current employer not be contacted until you have been given a firm offer.

IF YOU'RE FIRED OR LAID OFF:
Picking Yourself Up and Dusting Yourself Off

If you've been fired or laid off, you are not the first and will not be the last to go through this traumatic experience. In today's changing economy, thousands of professionals lose their jobs every year. Even if you were terminated with just cause, do not lose heart. Remember, being fired is not a reflection on you as a person. It is usually a reflection of your company's staffing needs and its perception of your recent job performance and attitude. And if you were not performing up to par or enjoying your work, then you will probably be better off at another company anyway.

A thorough job search could take months, so be sure to negotiate a reasonable severance package, if possible, and determine what benefits, such as health insurance, you are still legally entitled to. Also, register for unemployment compensation immediately. Don't be surprised to find other professionals collecting unemployment compensation -- it is for everyone who has lost their job.

> **Be prepared for the question, "Why were you fired?", during job interviews.**

Don't start your job search with a flurry of unplanned activity. Start by choosing a strategy and working out a plan. Now is not the time for major changes in your life. If possible, remain in the same career and in the same geographical location, at least until you have been working again for a while. On the other hand, if the only industry for which you are trained is leaving, or is severely depressed in your area, then you should give prompt consideration to moving or switching careers.

Avoid mentioning you were fired when arranging interviews, but be prepared for the question, "Why were you fired?", during an interview. If you were laid off as a result of downsizing, briefly explain, being sure to reinforce that your job loss was not due to performance. If you were in fact fired, be honest, but try to detail the reason as favorably as possible and portray what you have learned from your mistakes. If you are confident one of your past managers will give you a good reference, tell the interviewer to contact that person. Do not to speak negatively of your past employer and try not to sound particularly worried about your status of being temporarily unemployed.

Finally, don't spend too much time reflecting on why you were let go or how you might have avoided it. Think positively, look to the future, and be sure to follow a careful plan during your job search.

THE COLLEGE STUDENT:
How To Conduct Your First Job Search

While you will be able to apply many of the basics covered earlier in this chapter to your job search, there are some situations unique to the college student's job search.

Gaining Experience Perhaps the biggest problem college students face is lack of experience. Many schools have internship programs designed to give students exposure to the field of their choice, as well as the opportunity to make valuable contacts. Check out your school's career services department to see what internships are available. If your school does not have a formal internship program, or if there are no available internships that appeal to you, try contacting local businesses and offering your services -- often, businesses will be more than willing to have any extra pair of hands (especially if those hands are unpaid!) for a day or two each week. Or try contacting school alumni to see if you can "shadow" them for a few days, and see what their day-to-day duties are like. Either way, try to begin building experience as early as possible in your college career.

What do you do if, for whatever reason, you weren't able to get experience directly relating to your desired career? First, look at your previous jobs and see if there's anything you can highlight. Did your duties include supervising or training other employees? Did you reorganize the accounting system, or come up with a new way to boost productivity? Accomplishments like these demonstrate leadership, responsibility, and innovation -- qualities that most companies look for in employees. And don't forget volunteer activities and school clubs, which can also showcase these traits.

Companies will often send recruiters to interview on-site at various **On-Campus** colleges. This gives students a chance to get interviews at companies that **Recruiting** may not have interviewed them otherwise, particularly if the company schedules "open" interviews, in which the only screening process is who is first in line at the sign-ups. Of course, since many more applicants gain interviews in this format, this also means that many more people are rejected. The on-campus interview is generally a screening interview, to see if it is worth the company's time to invite you in for a second interview. So do everything possible to make yourself stand out from the crowd.

The first step, of course, is to check out any and all information your school's career center has on the company. If the information seems out of date, call the company's headquarters and ask to be sent the latest annual report, or any other printed information.

THE GPA QUESTION

You are interviewing for the job of your dreams. Everything is going well: you've established a good rapport, the interviewer seems impressed with your qualifications, and you're almost positive the job is yours. Then you're asked about your GPA, which is pitifully low. Do you tell the truth and watch your dream job fly out the window?

Never lie about your GPA (they may request your transcript, and no company will hire a liar). You can, however, explain if there is a reason you don't feel your grades reflect your abilities, and mention any other impressive statistics. For example, if you have a high GPA in your major, or in the last few semesters (as opposed to your cumulative college career), you can use that fact to your advantage.

Many companies will host an informational meeting for interviewees, often the evening before interviews are scheduled to take place. DO NOT MISS THIS MEETING. The recruiter will almost certainly ask if you attended. Make an effort to stay after the meeting and talk with the company's representatives. Not only does this give you an opportunity to find out more information about both the company and the position, it also makes you stand out in the recruiter's mind. If there's a particular company that you had your heart set on, but you weren't able to get an interview with them, attend the information session anyway. You may be able to convince the recruiter to squeeze you into the schedule. (Or you may discover that the company really isn't suited for you after all.)

Try to check out the interview site beforehand. Some colleges may conduct "mock" interviews that take place in one of the standard interview rooms. Or you may be able to convince a career counselor (or even a custodian) to let you sneak a peek during off-hours. Either way, having an idea of the room's setup will help you to mentally prepare.

Be sure to be at least 15 minutes early to the interview. The recruiter may be running ahead of schedule, and might like to take you early. But don't be surprised if previous interviews have run over, resulting in your 30-minute slot being reduced to 20 minutes (or less). Don't complain; just use whatever time you do have as efficiently as possible to showcase the reasons *you* are the ideal candidate.

LAST WORDS

A parting word of advice. Again and again during your job search you will be rejected. You will be rejected when you apply for interviews. You will be rejected after interviews. For every job offer you finally receive, you probably will have been rejected a multitude of times. Don't let rejections slow you down. Keep reminding yourself that the sooner you go out and get started on your job search, and get those rejections flowing in, the closer you will be to obtaining the job you want.

RESUMES AND COVER LETTERS

When filling a position, a recruiter will often have 100-plus applicants, but time to interview only a handful of the most promising ones. As a result, he or she will reject most applicants after only briefly skimming their resumes.

Unless you have phoned and talked to the recruiter -- which you should do whenever you can -- you will be chosen or rejected for an interview entirely on the basis of your resume and cover letter. Your cover letter must catch the recruiter's attention, and your resume must hold it. (But remember -- a resume is no substitute for a job search campaign. *You* must seek a job. Your resume is only one tool.)

RESUME FORMAT:
Mechanics of a First Impression

The Basics

Recruiters dislike long resumes, so unless you have an unusually strong background with many years of experience and a diversity of outstanding achievements, keep your resume length to one page. If you must squeeze in more information than would otherwise fit, try using a smaller typeface or changing the margins.

Keep your resume on standard 8-1/2" x 11" paper. Since recruiters often get resumes in batches of hundreds, a smaller-sized resume may get lost in the pile. Oversized resumes are likely to get crumpled at the edges, and won't fit easily in their files.

First impressions matter, so make sure the recruiter's first impression of your resume is a good one. Print your resume on quality paper that has weight and texture, in a conservative color such as white, ivory, or pale gray. Use matching paper and envelopes for both your resume and cover letter.

Getting It On Paper

Modern photocomposition typesetting gives you the clearest, sharpest image, a wide variety of type styles, and effects such as italics, bold-facing, and book-like justified margins. It is also much too expensive for many jobseekers. And improvements in laser printers mean that a computer-generated resume can look just as impressive as one that has been professionally typeset.

A computer or word processor is the most flexible way to type your resume. This will allow you to make changes almost instantly and to store different drafts on disk. Word processing and desktop publishing systems also offer many different fonts to choose from, each taking up different amounts of space. (It is generally best to stay between 9-point and 12-point font size.) Many other options are also available, such as bold-facing for emphasis, justified margins, and the ability to change and manipulate spacing.

The end result, however, will be largely determined by the quality of the printer you use. You need at least "letter quality" type for your resume. Do not use a "near letter quality" or dot matrix printer. Laser printers will generally provide the best quality.

Household typewriters and office typewriters with nylon or other cloth ribbons are *not* good enough for typing your resume. If you don't have access to a quality word processor, hire a professional who can prepare your resume with a word processor or typesetting machine.

Don't make your copies on an office photocopier. Only the personnel office may see the resume you mail. Everyone else may see only a copy of it, and copies of copies quickly become unreadable. Either print out each copy individually, or take your resume to a professional copy shop, which generally use professionally-maintained, extra-high-quality photocopiers and charge fairly reasonable prices.

Proof With Care Whether you typed it yourself or paid to have it produced professionally, mistakes on resumes are not only embarrassing, but will usually remove you from further consideration (particularly if something obvious such as your name is misspelled). No matter how much you paid someone else to type, write, or typeset your resume, *you* lose if there is a mistake. So proofread it as carefully as possible. Get a friend to help you. Read your draft aloud as your friend checks the proof copy. Then have your friend read aloud while you check. Next, read it letter by letter to check spelling and punctuation.

If you are having it typed or typeset by a resume service or a printer, and you can't bring a friend or take the time during the day to proof it, pay for it and take it home. Proof it there and bring it back later to get it corrected and printed.

> The one piece of advice I give to everyone about their resume is: show it to people, show it to people, show it to people. Before you ever send out a resume, show it to at least a dozen people.
>
> -Cate Talbot Ashton,
> Associate Director,
> Career Services,
> Colby College

If you wrote your resume on a word processing program, also use that program's built-in spell checker to double-check for spelling errors. But keep in mind that a spell checker will not find errors such as "to" for "two" or "wok" for "work." It's important that you still proofread your resume, even after it has been spell-checked.

The two most common resume formats are the functional resume and the chronological resume (examples of both types can be found at the end of this chapter). A functional resume focuses on skills and de-emphasizes job titles, employers, etc. A functional resume is best if you have been out of the work force for a long time and/or if you want to highlight specific skills and strengths that your most recent jobs don't necessarily reflect. **Types Of Resumes**

Choose a chronological format if you are currently working or were working recently, and if your most recent experiences relate to your desired field. Use reverse chronological order. To a recruiter your last job and your latest schooling are the most important, so put the last first and list the rest going back in time.

Your name, phone number, and a complete address should be at the top of your resume. Try to make your name stand out by using a slightly larger font size or all capital letters. Be sure to spell out everything -- never abbreviate St. for Street or Rd. for Road. If you are a college student, you should also put your home address and phone number at the top. **Organization**

Next, list your experience, then your education. If you are a recent graduate, list your education first, unless your experience is more important than your education. (For example, if you have just graduated from a teaching school, have some business experience, and are applying for a job in business, you would list your business experience first.)

Keep everything easy to find. Put the dates of your employment and education on the left of the page. Put the names of the companies you worked for and the schools you attended a few spaces to the right of the dates. Put the city and state, or the city and country, where you studied or worked to the right of the page.

This is just one suggestion that may work for you. The important thing is simply to break up the text in some way that makes your resume visually attractive and easy to scan, so experiment to see which layout works best for your resume. However you set it up, stay consistent. Inconsistencies in fonts, spacing, or tenses will make your resume look sloppy. Also, be sure to use tabs to keep your information vertically lined up, rather than the less precise space bar.

RESUME CONTENT:
Say It With Style

You are selling your skills and accomplishments in your resume, so it is important to inventory yourself and know yourself. If you have achieved something, say so. Put it in the best possible light. But avoid subjective statements, such as "I am a hard worker" or "I get along well with my coworkers." Just stick to the facts. **Sell Yourself**

While you shouldn't hold back or be modest, don't exaggerate your achievements to the point of misrepresentation. Be honest. Many companies will immediately drop an applicant from consideration (or fire a current employee) if inaccurate information is discovered on a resume or other application material.

Keep It Brief   Write down the important (and pertinent) things you have done, but do it in as few words as possible. Your resume will be scanned, not read, and short, concise phrases are much more effective than long-winded sentences. Avoid the use of "I" when emphasizing your accomplishments. Instead, use brief phrases beginning with action verbs.

While some technical terms will be unavoidable, you should try to avoid excessive "technicalese." Keep in mind that the first person to see your resume may be a human resources person who won't necessarily know all the jargon -- and how can they be impressed by something they don't understand?

Also, try to keep your paragraphs at six lines or shorter. If you have more than six lines of information about one job or school, put it in two or more paragraphs. The shorter your resume is, the more carefully it will be examined. Remember: your resume usually has between eight and 45 seconds to catch an employer's eye. So make every second count.

Job Objective   A functional resume may require a job objective to give it focus. One or two sentences describing the job you are seeking can clarify in what capacity your skills will be best put to use.

Examples: An entry-level position in the publishing industry.
A challenging position requiring analytical thought
and excellent writing skills.

Don't include a job objective in a chronological resume. Even if you are certain of exactly what type of job you desire, the presence of a job objective might eliminate you from consideration for other positions that a recruiter feels are a better match for your qualifications. But even though you may not put an objective on paper, having a career goal in mind as you write can help give your resume a sense of focus.

Work Experience   Some jobseekers may choose to include both "Relevant Experience" and "Additional Experience" sections. This can be useful, as it allows the jobseeker to place more emphasis on certain experiences and to de-emphasize others.

Emphasize continued experience in a particular job area or continued interest in a particular industry. De-emphasize irrelevant positions. Delete positions that you held for less than four months (unless you are a very recent college grad or still in school).

USE ACTION VERBS

How you write your resume is just as important as *what* you write. The strongest resumes use short phrases beginning with action verbs. Below, we've listed a few of the action verbs you may want to use. (This list is not all-inclusive.)

accelerated	determined	interpreted	recorded
achieved	developed	interviewed	recruited
administered	devised	invented	reduced
advised	directed	launched	referred
analyzed	discovered	maintained	regulated
arranged	distributed	managed	reorganized
assembled	edited	marketed	represented
assisted	eliminated	mediated	researched
attained	established	monitored	resolved
budgeted	evaluated	motivated	restored
built	examined	negotiated	restructured
calculated	executed	obtained	reviewed
cataloged	expanded	operated	revised
charted	expedited	ordered	scheduled
circulated	facilitated	organized	selected
collaborated	formulated	oversaw	served
collected	founded	participated	sold
compiled	generated	performed	solved
completed	headed	persuaded	streamlined
computed	identified	planned	studied
conducted	implemented	prepared	summarized
consolidated	improved	presented	supervised
constructed	increased	processed	supplied
consulted	initiated	produced	supported
controlled	innovated	programmed	tested
coordinated	inspired	promoted	trained
counseled	installed	proposed	updated
created	instituted	provided	upgraded
designed	instructed	published	worked
detected	integrated	purchased	wrote

Stress your results, elaborating on how you contributed in your previous jobs. Did you increase sales, reduce costs, improve a product, implement a new program? Were you promoted? Use specific numbers (i.e., quantities, percentages, dollar amounts) whenever possible.

Mention all relevant responsibilities. Be specific, and slant your past accomplishments toward the position that you hope to obtain. For example, do you hope to supervise people? If so, then state how many people, performing what function, you have supervised.

Education

Keep it brief if you have more than two years of career experience. Elaborate more if you have less experience. If you are a recent grad with two or more years of college, you may choose to include any high school activities that are directly relevant to your career. If you've been out of school for awhile, list post-secondary education only.

Mention degrees received and any honors or special awards. Note individual courses or research projects you participated in that might be relevant for employers. For example, if you are an English major applying for a position as a business writer, be sure to mention any business or economics courses.

> **Those things [marital status, church affiliations, etc.] have no place on a resume. Those are illegal questions, so why even put that information on your resume?**
>
> -Becky Hayes, Career Counselor
> Career Services, Rice University

Highlight Impressive Skills

Be sure to mention any computer skills you may have. You may wish to include a section entitled "Additional Skills" or "Computer Skills," in which you list any software programs you know. An additional skills section is also an ideal place to mention fluency in a foreign language.

Personal Data

This section is optional, but if you choose to include it, keep it very brief (two lines maximum). A one-word mention of hobbies such as fishing, chess, baseball, cooking, etc., can give the person who will interview you a good way to open up the conversation. It doesn't hurt to include activities that are unusual (fencing, bungee jumping, snake-charming) or that somehow relate to the position or the company you're applying to (for instance, if you are a member of a professional organization in your industry). Never include information about your age, health, physical characteristics, marital status, or religious affiliation.

References

The most that is needed is the sentence, "References available upon request," at the bottom of your resume. If you choose to leave it out, that's fine.

HIRING A RESUME WRITER:
Is It The Right Choice for You?

If you write reasonably well, it is to your advantage to write your own resume. Writing your resume forces you to review your experience and figure out how to explain your accomplishments in clear, brief phrases. This will help you when you explain your work to interviewers.

If you write your resume, everything will be in your own words -- it will sound like you. It will say what you want it to say. If you are a good writer, know yourself well, and have a good idea of what parts of your background employers are looking for, you should be able to write your own resume better than anyone else can. If you decide to write your resume yourself, have as many people review and proofread it as possible. Welcome objective opinions and other perspectives.

When To Get Help

If you have difficulty writing in "resume style" (which is quite unlike normal written language), if you are unsure of which parts of your background you should emphasize, or if you think your resume would make your case better if it did not follow one of the standard forms outlined either here or in a book on resumes, then you should consider having it professionally written.

There are two reasons even some professional resume writers we know have had their resumes written with the help of fellow professionals. First, they may need the help of someone who can be objective about their background, and second, they may want an experienced sounding board to help focus their thoughts.

If You Hire A Pro

The best way to choose a writer is by reputation -- the recommendation of a friend, a personnel director, your school placement officer, or someone else knowledgeable in the field.

Important questions:
- "How long have you been writing resumes?"
- "If I'm not satisfied with what you write, will you go over it with me and change it?"
- "Do you charge by the hour or a flat rate?"

There is no sure relation between price and quality, except that you are unlikely to get a good writer for less than $50 for an uncomplicated resume and you shouldn't have to pay more than $300 unless your experience is very extensive or complicated. There will be additional charges for printing.

Few resume services will give you a firm price over the phone, simply because some resumes are too complicated and take too long to do for a predetermined price. Some services will quote you a price that applies to almost all of their customers. Once you decide to use a specific writer, you should insist on a firm price quote before engaging their services. Also, find out how expensive minor changes will be.

COVER LETTERS:
Quick, Clear, and Concise

Always mail a cover letter with your resume. In a cover letter you can show an interest in the company that you can't show in a resume. You can also point out one or two skills or accomplishments the company can put to good use.

Make It Personal The more personal you can get, the better. If someone known to the person you are writing has recommended that you contact the company, get permission to include his/her name in the letter. If you have the name of a person to send the letter to, address it directly to that person (after first calling the company to verify the spelling of the person's name, correct title, and mailing address). Be sure to put the person's name and title on both the letter and the envelope. This will ensure that your letter will get through to the proper person, even if a new person now occupies this position. But even if you don't have a contact name and are simply addressing it to the "Personnel Director" or the "Hiring Partner," definitely send a letter.

Type cover letters in full. Don't try the cheap and easy ways, like using a computer mail merge program, or photocopying the body of your letter and typing in the inside address and salutation. You will give the impression that you are mailing to a host of companies and have no particular interest in any one.

Cover letter dos and don'ts

- *Do* keep your cover letter brief and to the point.
- *Do* be sure it is error-free.
- *Don't* just repeat information verbatim from your resume.
- *Don't* overuse the personal pronoun "I."
- *Don't* send a generic cover letter -- show your personal knowledge of and interest in that particular company.
- *Do* accentuate what you can offer the company, not what you hope to gain from them.

FUNCTIONAL RESUME
(Prepared on a word processor and laser printed.)

PENELOPE FRANCES PANZ
430 Miller's Crossing
Essex Junction VT 05452
802/555-9354

Objective
A position as a graphic designer commensurate with my acquired skills and expertise.

Summary
Extensive experience in plate making, separations, color matching, background definition, printing, mechanicals, color corrections, and personnel supervision. A highly motivated manager and effective communicator. Proven ability to:

- **Create Commercial Graphics**
- **Produce Embossed Drawings**
- **Color Separate**
- **Control Quality**
- **Resolve Printing Problems**
- **Analyze Customer Satisfaction**

Qualifications

Printing:
Knowledgeable in black and white as well as color printing. Excellent judgment in determining acceptability of color reproduction through comparison with original. Proficient at producing four or five color corrections on all media, as well as restyling previously reproduced four-color artwork.

Customer Relations:
Routinely work closely with customers to ensure specifications are met. Capable of striking a balance between technical printing capabilities and need for customer satisfaction through entire production process.

Specialties:
Practiced at creating silk screen overlays for a multitude of processes including velo bind, GBC bind, and perfect bind. Creative design and timely preparation of posters, flyers, and personalized stationery.

Personnel Supervision:
Skillful at fostering atmosphere that encourages highly talented artists to balance high-level creativity with maximum production. Consistently meet or beat production deadlines. Instruct new employees, apprentices, and students in both artistry and technical operations.

Experience
Graphic Arts Professor, University of Vermont, Burlington VT (1987-1993).
Manager, Design Graphics, Barre VT (1993-present).

Education
Massachusetts Conservatory of Art, Ph.D. 1987
University of Massachusetts, B.A. 1984

CHRONOLOGICAL RESUME
(Prepared on a word processor and laser printed.)

MAURICE DUPETREAUX
412 Maple Court
Seattle, WA 98404
(206) 555-6584

EXPERIENCE

THE CENTER COMPANY   Seattle, WA
Systems Programmer   1993-present
- Develop and maintain over 100 assembler modules.
- Create screen manager programs, using Assembler and Natural languages, to trace input and output to the VTAM buffer.
- Install and customize Omegamon 695 and 700 on IBM mainframes.
- Develop programs to monitor complete security control blocks, using Assembler and Natural.
- Produce stand alone IPLs and create backrests on IBM 3380 DASD.

INFO TECH, INC.   Seattle, WA
Technical Manager   1991-1993
- Designed and managed the implementation of a network providing the legal community with a direct line to Supreme Court cases, using Clipper on IBM 386s.
- Developed a system which catalogued entire library inventory, using Turbo Pascal on IBM AT.
- Used C to create a registration system for university registrar on IBM AT.

EDUCATION

SALEM STATE UNIVERSITY   Salem, OR
    B.S. in Computer Science.   1989
    M.S. in Computer Science.   1991

COMPUTER SKILLS

- Programming Languages: C, C++, Assembler, COBOL, Natural, Turbo Pascal, dBASE III+, and Clipper.
- Software: VTAM, Complete, TSO, JES 2, ACF 2, Omegamon 695 and 700, and Adabas.
- Operating Systems: MVS/XA, MVS/SP, MS-DOS, AND VMS.

FUNCTIONAL RESUME
(Prepared on an office-quality typewriter)

LORRAINE AVAKIAN
70 Monback Avenue
Oshkosh, WI 54901
(608) 586-1243

OBJECTIVE:
To contribute over eight years experience in promotion, communications, and administration to an entry-level position in advertising.

SUMMARY OF QUALIFICATIONS:
- Performed advertising duties for small business.
- Experience in business writing and communications skills.
- General knowledge of office management.
- Demonstrated ability to work well with others, in both supervisory and support staff roles.
- Type 75 words per minute.

SELECTED ACHIEVEMENTS AND RESULTS:

Promotion:
Composing, editing, and proofreading correspondence and PR materials for own catering service. Large-scale mailings.

Communication:
Instruction; curriculum and lesson planning; student evaluation; parent-teacher conferences; development of educational materials. Training and supervising clerks.

Computer Skills:
Proficient in MS Word, Lotus 1-2-3, Excel, and Filemaker Pro.

Administration:
Record-keeping and file maintenance. Data processing and computer operations, accounts receivable, accounts payable, inventory control, and customer relations. Scheduling, office management, and telephone reception.

WORK HISTORY:
Teacher; Self-Employed (owner of catering service); Floor Manager; Administrative Assistant; Accounting Clerk.

EDUCATION:
Beloit College, Beloit, WI, BA in Education, 1986

CHRONOLOGICAL RESUME
(Prepared on a word processor and laser printed)

T. WILLIAM MAGUIRE
16 Charles Street #3
Marlborough CT 06447
203/555-9641

EDUCATION

Keene State College, Keene NH
Bachelor of Arts in Elementary Education, 1994
- Graduated *magna cum laude*
- English minor
- Kappa Delta Pi member, inducted 1991

EXPERIENCE
September 1994-
Present

Elmer T. Thienes Elementary School, Marlborough CT
Part-time Kindergarten Teacher
- Instruct kindergartners in reading, spelling, language arts, and music.
- Participate in the selection of textbooks and learning aids.
- Organize and supervise class field trips and coordinate in-class presentations.

Summers
1992-1994

Keene YMCA, Youth Division, Keene NH
Child-care Counselor
- Oversaw summer program for low-income youth.
- Budgeted and coordinated special events and field trips, working with Program Director to initiate variations in the program.
- Served as Youth Advocate in cooperation with social worker to address the social needs and problems of participants.

Spring 1994

Wheelock Elementary School, Keene NH
Student Teacher
- Taught third-grade class in all elementary subjects.
- Designed and implemented a two-week unit on Native Americans.
- Assisted in revision of third-grade curriculum.

Fall 1993

Child Development Center, Keene NH
Daycare Worker
- Supervised preschool children on the playground and during art activities.
- Created a "Peter Rabbit Corner," where children could quietly look at books or take a voluntary "time-out."

ADDITIONAL INTERESTS
Martial arts, skiing, politics, reading, writing.

GENERAL MODEL FOR A COVER LETTER

Your mailing address
Date

Contact's name
Contact's title
Company
Company's mailing address

Dear Mr./Ms. _____:

Immediately explain why your background makes you the best candidate for the position that you are applying for. Describe what prompted you to write (want ad, article you read about the company, networking contact, etc.). Keep the first paragraph short and hard-hitting.

Detail what you could contribute to this company. Show how your qualifications will benefit this firm. Describe your interest in the corporation. Subtly emphasizing your knowledge about this firm and your familiarity with the industry will set you apart from other candidates. Remember to keep this letter short; few recruiters will read a cover letter longer than half a page.

If possible, your closing paragraph should request specific action on the part of the reader. Include your phone number and the hours when you can be reached. Mention that if you do not hear from the reader by a specific date, you will follow up with a phone call. Lastly, thank the reader for their time, consideration, etc.

Sincerely,

(signature)

Your full name (typed)

Enclosure (use this if there are other materials, such as your resume, that are included in the same envelope)

COVER LETTER SAMPLE

16 Charles Street
Marlborough CT 06447
November 16, 1995

Ms. Lia Marcusson
Assistant Principal
Jonathon Daniels Elementary School
43 Mayflower Drive
Keene NH 03431

Dear Ms. Marcusson:

Janet Newell recently informed me of a possible opening for a third grade teacher at Jonathon Daniels Elementary School. With my experience instructing third-graders, both in schools and in summer programs, I feel I would be an ideal candidate for the position. Please accept this letter and the enclosed resume as my application.

Jonathon Daniels' educational philosophy that every child can learn and succeed interests me, since it mirrors my own. My current position at Elmer T. Thienes Elementary has reinforced this philosophy, heightening my awareness of the different styles and paces of learning and increasing my sensitivity toward special needs children. Furthermore, as a direct result of my student teaching experience at Wheelock Elementary School, I am comfortable, confident, and knowledgeable working with third-graders.

I look forward to discussing the position and my qualifications for it in more detail. I can be reached at 203/555-9641 evenings or 203/555-0248 weekdays. If I do not hear from you before Tuesday of next week, I will call to see if we can schedule a time to meet. Thank you for your time and consideration.

Sincerely,

T. William Maguire

T. William Maguire

GENERAL MODEL FOR A FOLLOW-UP LETTER

Your mailing address
Date

Contact's name
Contact's title
Company
Company's mailing address

Dear Mr./Ms._____:

Remind the interviewer of the reason (i.e., a specific opening, an informational interview, etc.) you were interviewed, as well as the date. Thank him/her for the interview, and try to personalize your thanks by mentioning some specific aspect of the interview.

Confirm your interest in the organization (and in the opening, if you were interviewing for a particular position). Use specifics to re-emphasize that you have researched the firm in detail and have considered how you would fit into the company and the position. This is a good time to say anything you wish you had said in the initial meeting. Be sure to keep this letter brief; a half-page is plenty.

If appropriate, close with a suggestion for further action, such as a desire to have an additional interview, if possible. Mention your phone number and the hours that you can be reached. Alternatively, you may prefer to mention that you will follow up with a phone call in several days. Once again, thank the person for meeting with you, and state that you would be happy to provide any additional information about your qualifications.

Sincerely,

(signature)

Your full name (typed)

ACCOUNTING AND MANAGEMENT CONSULTING

 As the number of accounting grads drops and the economy strengthens, all kinds of accounting professionals will benefit. According to the BLS, the number of accounting jobs may grow by as much as 40 percent by 2005. In fact, a recent survey conducted by Robert Half International found that the best opportunities for accountants were in the financial, insurance, and real estate sector, followed by the retail and wholesale industries. The best states in the country for accountants are Arkansas, Louisiana, Oklahoma, and Texas.

Even faster growth is projected for the management consulting industry, where the number of jobs is expected to grow almost three times faster than the rate for all industries. The increasing complexity of business will contribute to industry growth. Among other things, today's managers must worry about rapid technological innovations, changes in government regulation, growing environmental concerns, continuing reduction of trade barriers, and globalization of markets. Because it has become difficult to keep abreast of these changes, corporations, institutions, and governments will increasingly need the aid of well-trained, well-informed management consulting professionals.

ARTHUR ANDERSEN & COMPANY LLP
One South Biscayne Tower, Suite 2100, Miami FL 33131. 305/374-3700. **Contact:** Human Resources. **Description:** Arthur Andersen LLP is a global provider of professional services in 74 countries, with over 72,000 personnel in 358 member offices. Business is conducted through two business units: Arthur Andersen for audit, tax, and other consulting services; and Andersen Consulting for systems integration, change management services, and advanced systems. **Other U.S. locations:** Nationwide.

ARTHUR ANDERSEN & COMPANY LLP
101 East Kennedy Boulevard, Suite 2200, Tampa FL 33602-5150. 813/222-4600. **Contact:** Human Resources. **Description:** Arthur Andersen LLP is a global provider of professional services in 74 countries, with over 72,000 personnel in 358 member offices. Business is conducted through two business units: Arthur Andersen for audit, tax, and other consulting services; and Andersen Consulting for systems integration, change management services, and advanced systems. **Other U.S. locations:** Nationwide.

COOPERS & LYBRAND
200 Biscayne Boulevard, Suite 1900, Miami FL 33131. 305/375-7400. **Contact:** Human Resources. **Description:** One of the largest certified public accounting firms, providing a broad range of services in the areas of accounting and auditing; taxation; management consulting; and actuarial, benefits, and compensation consulting. Operates 100 offices in the United States; more than 700 offices in 112 foreign locations. **Other U.S. locations:** Nationwide.

DELOITTE & TOUCHE
One Independent Drive, Suite 2801, Jacksonville FL 32202-5022. 904/356-0011. **Contact:** Human Resources. **Description:** An international firm of certified public accountants, providing professional accounting, auditing, tax, and management consulting services to widely diversified clients. More than 500 offices throughout the world. Deloitte & Touche has a specialized program consisting of some 25 national

industry groups and 50 functional (technical) groups that cross industry lines. Groups are involved in various disciplines, including accounting, auditing, taxation management advisory services, small and growing businesses, mergers and acquisitions, and computer applications. **Other locations:** Worldwide.

DELOITTE & TOUCHE
500 East Broward Boulevard, Suite 900, Fort Lauderdale FL 33394-3002. 954/778-3800. **Contact:** Human Resources. **Description:** An international firm of certified public accountants, providing professional accounting, auditing, tax, and management consulting services to widely diversified clients. More than 500 offices throughout the world. Deloitte & Touche has a specialized program consisting of some 25 national industry groups and 50 functional (technical) groups that cross industry lines. Groups are involved in various disciplines, including accounting, auditing, taxation management advisory services, small and growing businesses, mergers and acquisitions, and computer applications. **Other locations:** Worldwide.

DELOITTE & TOUCHE
201 East Kennedy Boulevard, Suite 1200, Tampa FL 33602-5821. 813/223-7591. **Contact:** Human Resources. **Description:** An international firm of certified public accountants, providing professional accounting, auditing, tax, and management consulting services to widely diversified clients. More than 500 offices throughout the world. Deloitte & Touche has a specialized program consisting of some 25 national industry groups and 50 functional (technical) groups that cross industry lines. Groups are involved in various disciplines, including accounting, auditing, taxation management advisory services, small and growing businesses, mergers and acquisitions, and computer applications. **Other locations:** Worldwide.

ERNST & YOUNG
390 North Orange Avenue, Suite 1700, Orlando FL 32801. 407/872-6600. **Contact:** Human Resources. **Description:** A worldwide certified public accounting organization, with operations in three main areas: Auditing and Accounting; Tax Services; and Management Consulting. Ernst & Young has approximately 5,000 professionals and 600 partners and directors in offices throughout the United States and abroad. **Other locations:** Worldwide.

ERNST & YOUNG
100 North Tampa Street, Suite 2200, Tampa FL 33601. 813/225-4800. **Contact:** Human Resources. **Description:** A worldwide certified public accounting organization, with operations in three main areas: Auditing and Accounting; Tax Services; and Management Consulting. Ernst & Young has approximately 5,000 professionals and 600 partners and directors in offices throughout the United States and abroad. **Other locations:** Worldwide.

KPMG PEAT MARWICK
One South Biscayne Tower, Suite 2800, Miami FL 33131-1802. 305/358-2300. **Contact:** Human Resources. **Description:** A large certified public accounting firm providing auditing, management consulting, and tax services, with more than 1,000 partners and principals in the United States. Operates approximately 100 offices in the United States, and 233 offices in 89 countries abroad. **Other locations:** Worldwide.

KPMG PEAT MARWICK
110 East Broward Boulevard, Fort Lauderdale FL 33301-3503. 954/524-6000. **Contact:** Human Resources. **Description:** A large certified public accounting firm providing auditing, management consulting, and tax services, with more than 1,000 partners and principals in the United States. Operates approximately 100 offices in the United States, and 233 offices in 89 countries abroad. **Other locations:** Worldwide.

PRICE WATERHOUSE
Suite 3000, One Union Financial Center, Miami FL 33131-2330. 305/381-9400. **Contact:** Human Resources. **Description:** An accounting firm.

PRICE WATERHOUSE
400 North Ashley Street, Suite 2800, Tampa FL 33602. 813/223-7577. **Contact:** Human Resources. **Description:** An accounting firm.

PRICE WATERHOUSE
NATIONAL ADMINISTRATIVE CENTER
3109 West Dr. Martin Luther King Boulevard, Tampa FL 33607. 813/348-7000. **Fax:**
813/348-7002. **Contact:** Personnel Department. **Description:** An accounting firm.

Note: Because addresses and telephone numbers of smaller companies change rapidly,
we recommend you call each company to verify the information below before inquiring
about job opportunities. Mass mailings are not recommended.

Additional employers with under 250 employees:

**ACCOUNTING, AUDITING,
AND BOOKKEEPING
SERVICES**

Deloitte & Touche
100 SE 2nd St, Suite 2500,
Miami FL 33131-2146.
305/358-4141.

**Matson Driscoll & Damico
CPA**
1900 Summit Tower Blvd,
Orlando FL 32810-5939.
407/875-9955.

Paychex
1501 Corporate Dr, Boynton
Beach FL 33426-6649.
407/369-0201.

Better Business Service
1430 Royal Palm Square
Blvd, Fort Myers FL 33919-
1071. 941/936-1904.

Bill Med
6550 N Federal Hwy, Ft
Lauderdale FL 33308-1404.
954/776-6707.

Central Patient Billing
231 N Kentucky Ave,
Lakeland FL 33801-4977.
941/682-2500.

MANAGEMENT SERVICES

Barton Malow Company
5570 Bee Ridge Rd, Sarasota
FL 34233-1505. 941/379-
0334.

CMD
200 S Hoover Blvd #219-
170, Tampa FL 33609-
3540. 813/254-9110.

Hanscomb Associates
2500 Maitland Center Pkwy,
Suite 3, Maitland FL 32751-
7224. 407/875-0707.

Ogden Cisco
5100 S Alafaya Trail,
Orlando FL 32831-2000.
407/281-6265.

Sovereign Management Corp.
7571 W Irlo Bronson
Memorial Hwy, Kissimmee FL
34747-1725. 407/396-
4998.

Callander and Companies
2300 Palm Beach Lakes
Blvd, West Palm Beach FL
33409-3303. 407/687-
5155.

**BUSINESS CONSULTING
SERVICES**

Alexander Proudfoot Co.
1700 Palm Beach Lakes
Blvd, West Palm Beach FL
33401-2008. 407/697-
9600.

ARA DevCon
2121 Killarney Way,
Tallahassee FL 32308-3401.
904/668-2519.

Asset Management Group
1645 Palm Beach Lakes Blvd
400, West Palm Beach FL
33401-2216. 407/478-
0080.

Brooks International
7108 Fairway Dr, Palm
Beach Gardens FL 33418-
3767. 407/626-7117.

Colortyme
399 NW 2nd Ave, Suite
150, Boca Raton FL 33432-
3765. 407/395-0412.

Developmental Services
1095 W Morse Blvd, Winter
Park FL 32789-3711.
407/645-3211.

**Maria Elena Torano &
Associates**
1000 Brickell Ave Fl 4,
Miami FL 33131-3013.
305/579-2180.

MD Carlisle Management
1701 Lee Rd, Winter Park FL
32789-2161. 407/628-
4295.

Morgan Parsons
2455 E Sunrise Blvd, Ft
Lauderdale FL 33304-3118.
954/563-2900.

Power Factor Correction
480 Shady Ln, Bartow FL
33830-3354. 941/533-
6685.

**Schreiber Management
Consulting**
1680 Varner Ct, Bartow FL
33830-9360. 941/533-
9343.

Strategic Solutions
11251 Harbour Villa Rd,
Orlando FL 32821-9302.
407/238-1300.

The Kendrick Company
382 State Road 434 W,
Longwood FL 32750-5116.
407/260-2555.

Atec Associates
5555 W Waters Ave, Tampa
FL 33634-1230. 813/886-
0907.

**Personal Performance
Consultants**
3452 Lake Lynda Dr, Orlando
FL 32817-1430. 407/380-
6518.

Beverly Enterprises
1120 W Donegan Ave,
Kissimmee FL 34741-2241.
407/846-8520.

Kaset International
221 SE Osceola St, Stuart FL
34994-2206. 407/283-
2878.

Florida Worldwide
3900 N Washington Blvd,
Sarasota FL 34234-4835.
941/355-6985.

Master Research Services
2990 Mission Oaks Trail,
Bartow FL 33830-7456.
941/533-7905.

Builders Service Group
495 W Stuart St, Bartow FL
33830-6258. 941/533-
1643.

Caldera Corporation
P.O. Box 1632, Daytona
Beach FL 32115-1632.
904/254-2920.

Easley McCaleb & Stallings
400 N Ashley Dr, Tampa FL
33602-4300. 813/223-
1788.

Hanley Company
2313 Bowers Rd, Bartow FL
33830-8722. 941/534-
1433.

Harmon H. Jones
11540 E US Highway 92,
Seffner FL 33584-7346.
813/623-5400.

James P Latimore
8600 Hidden River Pkwy,
Suite 100, Tampa FL 33637-
1012. 813/971-2701.

Janus Information Services
16310 Bonneville Dr, Tampa
FL 33624-1115. 813/960-
5164.

Joseph Bonanno
3030 N Rocky Point Dr W,
Suite 30, Tampa FL 33607-
5803. 813/289-0040.

Madsen/Barr Corp.
109 Applewood Dr,
Longwood FL 32750-3450.
407/260-9668.

Michael A Peters
101 E Kennedy Blvd, Suite
2700, Tampa FL 33602-
5148. 813/223-7474.

Poole & Dent Co.
7041 Grand National Dr,

Orlando FL 32819-8381.
407/351-2852.

Steven R Sanders
8507 Sunstate St, Tampa FL
33634-1311. 813/885-
5811.

Norton Lilly International
9485 Regency Square Blvd,
Suite 215, Jacksonville FL
32225-8119. 904/724-
1988.

Elden Enterprises
31 Ocean Reef Dr, Key Largo
FL 33037-5210. 305/367-
3321.

Barton-Aschman Associates
3550 W Busch Blvd, Tampa
FL 33618-4402. 813/932-
5220.

Barton-Aschman Associates
5310 NW 33rd Ave, Suite
206, Ft Lauderdale FL
33309-6300. 954/733-
4220.

Lodestar Site Management
630 US Highway 1, No Palm
Beach FL 33408-4606.
407/863-5605.

**Telecom Engineering
Consultants**
9400 NW 25th St, Miami FL

33172-1401. 305/592-
4328.

A-1 Teletronics
2600 118th Ave N, St
Petersburg FL 33716-1921.
813/572-9933.

Bosek Gibson & Associates
2014 University Blvd W,
Jacksonville FL 32217-2016.
904/730-8011.

Ardaman & Associates
1017 SE Holbrook Ct, Port
St Lucie FL 34952-3430.
407/337-1200.

AWD Technologies
8509 Benjamin Rd, Tampa
FL 33634-1224. 813/886-
3099.

Golder Associates
8933 Western Way, Suite
12, Jacksonville FL 32256-
8395. 904/448-0605.

**Woodward-Clyde
Consultants**
9950 Princess Palm Ave,
Suite 232, Tampa FL 33619-
8347. 813/626-0047.

Argenbright & Associates
800 W Cypress Creek Rd, Ft
Lauderdale FL 33309-2075.
954/771-1036.

For more information on career opportunities in accounting and management consulting:

Associations

AMERICAN ACCOUNTING ASSOCIATION
5717 Bessie Drive, Sarasota FL 34233.
813/921-7747. An academically-oriented
accounting association that offers two
quarterly journals, a semi-annual journal, a
newsletter, and a wide variety of continuing
education programs.

**AMERICAN INSTITUTE OF CERTIFIED
PUBLIC ACCOUNTANTS**
1211 Avenue of the Americas, New York
NY 10036. 212/596-6200. A national
professional organization for all CPAs.
AICPA offers a comprehensive career
package to students.

AMERICAN MANAGEMENT ASSOCIATION
Management Information Service, 135 West
50th Street, New York NY 10020.
212/586-8100. Provides a variety of
publications, training videos, and courses,
as well as an Information Resource Center,
which provides management information,
and a library service.

**ASSOCIATION OF GOVERNMENT
ACCOUNTANTS**
2200 Mount Vernon Avenue, Alexandria VA
22301. 703/684-6931.

**ASSOCIATION OF MANAGEMENT
CONSULTING FIRMS**
521 Fifth Avenue, 35th Floor, New York NY
10175. 212/697-9693. Offers certification
programs.

FEDERATION OF TAX ADMINISTRATORS
444 North Capital Street NW, Washington
DC 20001. 202/624-5890.

INSTITUTE OF INTERNAL AUDITORS
49 Maitland Avenue, Altamont Springs FL
32701. 407/830-7600. Publishes
magazines and newsletters. Provides
information on current issues, a network of
more than 50,000 members in 100
countries, and professional development
and research services.

**INSTITUTE OF MANAGEMENT
ACCOUNTANTS**
10 Paragon Drive, Box 433, Montvale NJ
07645-1760. 201/573-9000. Offers a
Certified Management Accountant Program,
periodicals, seminars, educational programs,
a research program, a financial management
network, and networking services.

**INSTITUTE OF MANAGEMENT
CONSULTANTS**
521 Fifth Avenue, 35th Floor, New York NY
10175. 212/697-8262. Offers certification
and professional development and a
directory of members.

NATIONAL ASSOCIATION OF TAX CONSULTORS
454 North 13th Street, San Jose CA 95112. 408/298-1458.

NATIONAL ASSOCIATION OF TAX PRACTITIONERS
720 Association Drive, Appleton WI 54914. 414/749-1040. Offers seminars, research, newsletters, preparer worksheets, state chapters, insurance, and other tax-related services.

NATIONAL SOCIETY OF PUBLIC ACCOUNTANTS
1010 North Fairfax Street, Alexandria VA 22314. 703/549-6400. Offers professional development services, government representation, a variety of publications, practice aids, low-cost group insurance, and annual seminars.

Directories

AICPA DIRECTORY OF ACCOUNTING EDUCATION
American Institute of Certified Public Accountants, 1211 Avenue of the Americas, New York NY 10036. 212/596-6200. $150.00. Only available to AICPA members.

ACCOUNTING FIRMS AND PRACTITIONERS
American Institute of Certified Public Accountants, 1211 Avenue of the

Americas, New York NY 10036. 212/596-6200. $150.00. Only available to AICPA members.

Magazines

CPA JOURNAL
530 Fifth Avenue, New York NY 10136. 212/719-8300. Published monthly by The New York State Society.

CPA LETTER
American Institute of Certified Public Accountants, 1211 Avenue of the Americas, New York NY 10036. 212/596-6200.

JOURNAL OF ACCOUNTANCY
American Institute of Certified Public Accountants, 1211 Avenue of the Americas, New York NY 10036. 212/596-6200.

MANAGEMENT ACCOUNTING
Institute of Management Accounting, 10 Paragon Drive, Montvale NJ 07645. 201/573-9000.

WENDELL'S REPORT FOR CONTROLLERS
Warren, Gorham, and Lamont, Inc., 210 South Street, Boston MA 02111. 617/423-2020.

ADVERTISING, MARKETING AND PUBLIC RELATIONS

Due to several trends shaping the industry, finding a job in advertising is as tough today as it ever has been. To remain competitive, the industry's largest firms are downsizing to save money for larger campaigns. On the other hand, smaller agencies are increasingly specializing in fields such as direct marketing and public relations in order to gain a stronger presence in the market. Meanwhile, the growing cable industry has opened the door to new business opportunities, as has the Internet. Increasingly, advertisers are using the Information Highway to conduct business, as well as to target specific "digital" audiences.

In the public relations field, there has been an explosion in the number and range of consultants in the marketplace. Partially as a result of the recession of the early '90s, many senior executives who were released from their contracts at major firms have launched companies of their own.

AT&T AMERICAN TRANSTECH
8000 Baymeadows Way, Jacksonville FL 32256. 904/636-1000. **Contact:** Kathy Schuler, Director of Personnel. **Description:** A customer care company specializing in customer servicing, employee servicing, and selective telemarketing.

ANSON-STONER, INC.
111 East Fairbank Winter Park, Winter Park FL 32789. **Contact:** Human Resources. **Description:** An advertising agency.

BARKER & ASSOCIATES
P.O. Box 533562, Orlando FL 32853. 407/894-0010. **Contact:** Mark Barker, President. **Description:** An advertising agency.

CATALINA MARKETING
11300 Ninth Street North, St. Petersburg FL 33716. 813/579-5000. **Fax:** 813/570-8507. **Contact:** Human Resources. **Description:** Catalina Marketing provides consumer product manufacturers and supermarket retailers with a cost effective method of implementing a targeted consumer marketing strategy. Catalina's point-of-scan electronic marketing network delivers checkout coupons directly to targeted consumers at supermarket checkouts based on their purchases. **Common positions include:** Accountant/Auditor; Buyer; Clerical Supervisor; Computer Programmer; Computer Systems Analyst; Customer Service Representative; Electronics Technician; General Manager; Human Resources Specialist; Marketing Research Analyst; Operations/Production Manager; Purchasing Agent and Manager; Quality Control Supervisor; Services Sales Representative. **Educational backgrounds include:** Accounting; Business Administration; Computer Science. **Benefits:** 401K; Dental Insurance; Disability Coverage; Life Insurance; Medical Insurance; Savings Plan. **Special Programs:** Internships. **Operations at this facility include:** Administration; Research and Development. **Listed on:** New York Stock Exchange. **Number of employees at this location:** 120. **Number of employees nationwide:** 403.

CHARNEY PALACIOS AND COMPANY
9200 Dayland Boulevard, Suite 307, Miami FL 33156. 305/670-9450. **Contact:** Charles Charney, Vice President. **Description:** An advertising representative for Latin America.

THE WILLIAM COOK AGENCY
225 Water Street, Suite 1600, Jacksonville FL 32202. 904/353-3911. **Contact:** Char Adamsons, Personnel Manager. **Description:** The William Cook Agency is an advertising and public relations agency. **Common positions include:** Account Executive; Advertising Clerk; Art Director; Commercial Artist; Copywriter; Marketing Specialist; Media Planner/Specialist; Public Relations Specialist. **Educational backgrounds include:** Advertising; Art/Design; Business Administration; Communications; Marketing; Public Relations. **Benefits:** 401K; Dental Insurance; Disability Coverage; Life Insurance; Medical Insurance; Stock Option. **Special Programs:** Internships. **Corporate headquarters location:** This Location. **Other U.S. locations:** Charlotte NC. **Listed on:** Privately held. **Number of employees at this location:** 81. **Number of employees nationwide:** 86.

CRISP & HARRISON AGENCY
9210 Cypress Green Drive, Jacksonville FL 32256. 904/731-3674. **Contact:** Darryl Crisp, President. **Description:** An advertising agency.

DENTON FRENCH INC.
3817 West Humphrey, Suite 202, Tampa FL 33614. 813/933-1810. **Contact:** Robert Denton, President. **Description:** An advertising firm.

W.B. DONER AND COMPANY
6200 Courtney Campbell Causeway Turnpike, Suite 150, Tampa FL 33607. 813/289-6909. **Contact:** General Manager. **Description:** An advertising agency.

EARLE PALMER BROWN
260 First Avenue South, Suite 300, St. Petersburg FL 33701. 813/821-5155. **Contact:** Personnel. **Description:** An advertising agency. **Common positions include:** Account Executive; Account Manager; Advertising Account Executive; Advertising Clerk; Advertising Sales; Artist; Marketing Specialist; Marketing/Advertising/PR Manager; Public Relations Specialist.

FRY/HAMMOND/BAR INCORPORATED
600 East Washington Street, Orlando FL 32801. 407/849-0100. **Contact:** Executive Assistant. **Description:** An advertising agency.

GOUCHENOUR AND ASSOCIATES, INC.
455 South Orange Avenue, 6th Floor, Orlando FL 32801. 407/841-8585. **Fax:** 407/425-5297. **Contact:** Personnel Department. **Description:** A full-service advertising, marketing, research, sales promotion, and public relations firm. Operating since 1969. Services local, regional, and national accounts. A member of the American Association of Advertising Agencies (AAAA). **Common positions include:** Advertising Clerk; Commercial Artist; Computer Operator; Designer; Marketing/Advertising/PR Manager; Media Planner/Specialist; Public Relations Specialist; Purchasing Agent and Manager; Typist/Word Processor. **Educational backgrounds include:** Art/Design; Communications; Marketing. **Benefits:** 401K; Bonus Award/Plan; Dental Insurance; Medical Insurance; Profit Sharing. **Special Programs:** Internships. **Corporate headquarters location:** This Location. **Operations at this facility include:** Administration; Sales. **Number of employees at this location:** 22.

GRAPHIC PERSUASION, INC.
500 Australian Avenue, Suite 710, West Palm Beach FL 33401. 407/833-8075. **Contact:** David Robinson, President. **Description:** An advertising agency.

HEALTH CARE PROS
6015 Morrow Street, Jacksonville FL 32217. 904/737-5040. **Contact:** Human Resources. **Description:** A marketing company for the health care industry.

HIT PROMOTIONAL PRODUCTS
P.O. Box 10200, St. Petersburg FL 33733. 813/541-5561. **Contact:** Bobbye Spencer, Personnel Director. **Description:** A manufacturer of advertising specialty items.

HUSK JENNINGS
50 North Laura Street, Suite 2600, Jacksonville FL 32202. 904/354-2600. **Fax:** 904/354-7226. **Contact:** Mary McDonald, Office Manager. **Description:** An advertising, marketing, and public relations agency. **Common positions include:** Administrative Services Manager; Public Relations Specialist. **Educational backgrounds include:** Art/Design; Marketing. **Benefits:** 401K; Dental Insurance; Life Insurance;

Medical Insurance; Profit Sharing. **Corporate headquarters location:** This Location. **Number of employees at this location:** 16.

JILOTY COMMUNICATIONS
1510 Ridgewood Avenue, Holly Hill FL 32117. 904/677-0673. **Contact:** President. **Description:** An advertising agency. **NOTE:** This company does not accept unsolicited resumes. Please apply for advertised positions only.

LANDERS AND PARTNERS, INC.
7901 4th Street North, Suite 306, St. Petersburg FL 33702. 813/577-6868. **Contact:** Personnel Department. **Description:** An advertising firm.

MARKET DEVELOPMENT GROUP OF FLORIDA
1053 Maitland Center Commons, Maitland FL 32751. 407/875-1770. **Contact:** Pam Mosley, Office Manager. **Description:** An advertising and consulting firm.

NATIONWIDE ADVERTISING SERVICE, INC.
3510 Bay to Bay Boulevard, Tampa FL 33629. 813/831-1085. **Contact:** Sue Katalines, Office Manager. **Description:** With offices in 36 major U.S. and Canadian cities, Nationwide Advertising Service is the largest and oldest independent, full-service advertising agency exclusively specializing in human resource communications, promotions, and advertising. The company offers consultation, campaign planning, ad placement, research, and creative production.

RY&P
1900 Summit Tower Boulevard, Suite 600, Orlando FL 32810. 407/875-1111. **Contact:** Julie Gochnour, Personnel Director. **Description:** An advertising agency.

SHAKER ADVERTISING AGENCY
4920 Cypress Street West, Suite 104, Tampa FL 33607. 813/289-1100. **Contact:** Morrie Skall, Office Manager. **Description:** An advertising agency.

TULLY-MENARD, INC.
4919 Bayshore Boulevard, Tampa FL 33611. 813/832-6602. **Contact:** J.E. Tully, President. **Description:** An advertising agency.

VAL PAK DIRECT MARKETING
8605 Largo Lakes Drive, Largo FL 34643. 813/393-1270. **Contact:** Human Resources. **Description:** Provides direct marketing services, including printing coupons and mailing them to consumers' homes.

WEST GROUP
1 Independent Drive, Suite 3201, Jacksonville FL 32202. 904/354-5601. **Contact:** Personnel. **Description:** An advertising and marketing agency.

Note: Because addresses and telephone numbers of smaller companies change rapidly, we recommend you call each company to verify the information below before inquiring about job opportunities. Mass mailings are not recommended.

Additional employers with under 250 employees:

MISC. ADVERTISING SERVICES

Burson-Marsteller
201 S Biscayne Blvd, Suite 2900, Miami FL 33131-4330. 305/372-1513.

Crown Marketing
900 N Maitland Ave, Maitland FL 32751-4429. 407/647-6757.

Earle Palmer Brown Co.
345 S Magnolia Dr, Tallahassee FL 32301-2968. 904/656-6550.

Moore Communication Group
3333 S Congress Ave, Delray Beach FL 33445-7322. 407/272-4990.

Scott-McRae Advertising
701 Fisk St, Suite 111, Jacksonville FL 32204-3339. 904/354-4900.

Yunker Industries
2744 Summerdale Dr, Clearwater FL 34621-2935. 813/799-2467.

United Grafix
11229 Astronaut Blvd,
Orlando FL 32837-9203. 407/857-7331.

Cable TV & Ads
1595 SW 4th Ave, Delray Beach FL 33444-8133. 407/738-1788.

Russell Johns Associates
1001 S Myrtle Ave, Suite 7, Clearwater FL 34616-3930. 813/443-3047.

Rustin International Marketing
8001 N Dale Mabry Hwy,

Tampa FL 33614-3290.
813/935-7388.

**Bellsouth Advertising &
Publishing**
3230 W Commercial Blvd,
Suite 400, Ft Lauderdale FL
33309. 954/497-4005.

**Show & Sell Of Broward
County**
1799 W Oakland Park Blvd,
Ft Lauderdale FL 33311-
1537. 954/739-7355.

**Show & Sell Photo
Advertising**
10028 S US Highway 1, Port
St Lucie FL 34952-5625.
407/335-7355.

For Rent Magazine
9116 Cypress Green Dr,
Jacksonville FL 32256-7779.
904/737-4181.

Moore Epstein Moore
7900 SW 24th St, Ft
Lauderdale FL 33021 5921
954/424-9476.

United Services
1720 S Orange Ave, Orlando
FL 32806. 407/839-1274.

**DIRECT MAIL ADVERTISING
SERVICES**

Harte Hanks Direct Marketing
11700 Central Pkwy,

Jacksonville FL 32224-2600.
904/642-6000.

Advo
1903 Cypress Lake Dr,
Orlando FL 32837-8459.
407/857-1271.

Lannom
6601 NW 14th Ct, Ft
Lauderdale FL 33313-4579.
954/321-6655.

Response Media
7823 N Dale Mabry Hwy,
Tampa FL 33614-3281.
813/931-4600.

**For more information on career opportunities in advertising, marketing, and public
relations:**

Associations

ADVERTISING RESEARCH FOUNDATION
641 Lexington Avenue, New York NY
10022. 212/751-5656.

**AFFILIATED ADVERTISING AGENCIES
INTERNATIONAL**
2280 South Xanadu Way, Suite 300,
Aurora CO 80014. 303/671-8551.

**AMERICAN ASSOCIATION OF
ADVERTISING AGENCIES**
666 Third Avenue, New York NY 10017.
212/682-2500. Offers educational and
enrichment benefits such as publications,
videos, and conferences.

AMERICAN MARKETING ASSOCIATION
250 South Wacker Drive, Suite 200,
Chicago IL 60606. 312/648-0536.

DIRECT MARKETING ASSOCIATION
1120 Avenue of Americas, New York NY
10036-6700. 212/768-7277. Offers
monthly newsletters, seminars, and
conferences.

**INTERNATIONAL ADVERTISING
ASSOCIATION**
521 Fifth Avenue, Suite 1807, New York
NY 10075. 212/557-1133.

LEAGUE OF ADVERTISING AGENCIES
2 South End Avenue #4C, New York NY
10280. 212/945-4991. Seminars available.

MARKETING RESEARCH ASSOCIATION
2189 Silas Deane Highway, Suite #5,
Rocky Hill CT 06067. 203/257-4008.
Publishes several magazines and
newsletters.

PUBLIC RELATIONS SOCIETY OF AMERICA
33 Irving Place, New York NY 10003.
212/995-2230. Publishes three magazines
for public relations professionals.

TELEVISION BUREAU OF ADVERTISING
850 3rd Avenue, 10th Floor, New York NY
10022-5892. 212/486-1111.

Directories

AAAA ROSTER AND ORGANIZATION
American Association of Advertising
Agencies, 666 Third Avenue, 13th Floor,
New York NY 10017. 212/682-2500.

**DIRECTORY OF MINORITY PUBLIC
RELATIONS PROFESSIONALS**
Public Relations Society of America, 33
Irving Place, New York NY 10003.
212/995-2230.

**O'DWYER'S DIRECTORY OF PUBLIC
RELATIONS FIRMS**
J. R. O'Dwyer Company, 271 Madison
Avenue, Room 600, New York NY 10016.
212/679-2471.

**PUBLIC RELATIONS CONSULTANTS
DIRECTORY**
American Business Directories, Division of
American Business Lists, 5711 South 86th
Circle, Omaha NE 68127. 402/593-4500.

**PUBLIC RELATIONS JOURNAL -- REGISTER
ISSUE**
Public Relations Society of America, 33
Irving Place, New York NY 10003.
212/995-2230.

**STANDARD DIRECTORY OF ADVERTISING
AGENCIES**
Reed Reference Publishing Company, P.O.
Box 31, New Providence NJ 07974.
800/521-8110.

Magazines

ADVERTISING AGE
Crain Communications, 740 North Rush
Street, Chicago IL 60611. 312/649-5316.

ADWEEK
BPI, 1515 Broadway, 12th Floor, New York
NY 10036-8986. 212/536-5336.

BUSINESS MARKETING
Crain Communications, 740 North Rush
Street, Chicago IL 60611. 312/649-5260.

JOURNAL OF MARKETING
American Marketing Association, 250 South
Wacker Drive, Suite 200, Chicago IL
60606. 312/648-0536.

THE MARKETING NEWS
American Marketing Association, 250 South
Wacker Drive, Suite 200, Chicago IL
60606. 312/648-0536.

PR REPORTER
PR Publishing Company, P.O. Box 600,
Exeter NH 03833. 603/778-0514.

PUBLIC RELATIONS JOURNAL
Public Relations Society of America, 33
Irving Place, New York NY 10003.
212/995-2230.

PUBLIC RELATIONS NEWS
Phillips Publishing Inc., 1202 Seven Locks
Road, Suite 300, Potomac MD 20854.
301/340-1520.

AEROSPACE

The aerospace industry, which was wracked by layoffs throughout the early '90s, has yet to pull out of its tailspin. As ever, the slump is being fueled by declining commercial aircraft orders and further defense cuts. As a result, research and development dollars have been trimmed and more industry mergers are expected. Many companies are trying to shift to commercial production, reducing their dependence on dwindling defense contracts.

Although the industry depends less on defense spending than in the past, defense purchases still support a significant number of aerospace workers. Employment in aerospace production occupations are projected to decline in the next few years, as manufacturers increase productivity by improving organizational and manufacturing techniques. Over the long haul, the industry's focus on advanced technology will mean more professional and technical positions -- with engineers leading the way.

AAI CORPORATION
2801 Professional Parkway, Ocoee FL 34761-2965. 407/877-4400. **Contact:** Human Resources. **Description:** A manufacturer of helicopter simulators for the United States Navy.

ABA INDUSTRIES
10260 U.S. 19 North, Pinellas Park FL 34666. **Contact:** Human Resources. **Description:** A manufacturer of aircraft engines.

A.M.R. COMBS, INC.
4050 South West 11th Terrace, Fort Lauderdale FL 33315. 954/359-0000. **Contact:** Personnel Department. **Description:** A.M.R. Combs is a supplier and distributor of machine parts for corporate jets. The company is also involved in refueling, avionics repair, and installation and offers maintenance and inspections of corporate jets. **Common positions include:** Customer Service Representative; Mechanic. **Benefits:** 401K; Dental Insurance; Life Insurance; Medical Insurance; Profit Sharing. **Corporate headquarters location:** Ft. Worth TX. **Other U.S. locations:** Denver CO; Windsor Locks CT; Indianapolis IN; Memphis TN. **Parent company:** AMR Services. **Operations at this facility include:** Administration; Service. **Listed on:** New York Stock Exchange. **Number of employees at this location:** 98.

AERO COMPONENT TECHNOLOGIES
630 Anchors Street NW, Ft. Walton Beach FL 32548. 904/244-7684. **Contact:** Human Resources. **Description:** Repairs turbine jet engine component parts. **Common positions include:** Ceramics Engineer; Materials Engineer; Mechanical Engineer; Metallurgical Engineer. **Operations at this facility include:** Administration; Manufacturing.

AERO CORPORATION
P.O. Box 1909, Lake City FL 32056-1909. 904/752-7911. **Contact:** Genia McNair, Personnel Director. **Description:** An aircraft manufacturer.

AEROSONIC CORPORATION
1212 North Hercules Avenue, Clearwater FL 34625. 813/461-3000. **Fax:** 813/447-5926. **Contact:** Kathy Woodling, Manager of Human Resources. **Description:** A manufacturer of aircraft instruments and clocks. **Common positions include:** Accountant/Auditor; Buyer; Cost Estimator; Customer Service Representative; Draftsperson; Electrical/Electronics Engineer; Human Resources Specialist; Industrial Engineer; Machinist; Mechanical Engineer; Purchasing Agent and Manager; Quality Control Supervisor; Receptionist; Secretary; Stock Clerk; Technical Writer/Editor;

Truck Driver. **Educational backgrounds include:** Accounting; Engineering; Finance; Marketing. **Benefits:** 401K; Dental Insurance; Disability Coverage; Life Insurance; Medical Insurance; Pension Plan. **Corporate headquarters location:** This Location. **Other U.S. locations:** Wichita KS. **Operations at this facility include:** Administration; Manufacturing; Research and Development; Sales; Service. **Listed on:** American Stock Exchange. **Number of employees at this location:** 200. **Number of employees nationwide:** 220.

AIRCRAFT POROUS MEDIA, INC.
6301 49th Street North, Pinellas Park FL 34665. 813/522-3111. **Contact:** Susan Gonzalez, Personnel Director. **Description:** Aircraft Porous Media is engaged in fluid clarification through high-technology filtration. The company is also engaged in the field of filtration for hydraulic systems, fuel systems, and lubrication systems. **Common positions include:** Accountant/Auditor; Administrator; Aerospace Engineer; Buyer; Computer Programmer; Draftsperson; Human Resources Specialist; Machinist; Mechanical Engineer; Operations/Production Manager; Purchasing Agent and Manager; Quality Control Supervisor; Systems Analyst. **Educational backgrounds include:** Accounting; Business Administration; Communications; Computer Science; Engineering; Marketing. **Benefits:** Dental Insurance; Disability Coverage; Employee Discounts; Life Insurance; Medical Insurance; Pension Plan; Profit Sharing; Savings Plan; Tuition Assistance. **Corporate headquarters location:** Glen Cove NY. **Parent company:** Pall Corporation. **Listed on:** New York Stock Exchange.

ALLIEDSIGNAL AEROSPACE
2100 Northwest 62nd Street, Fort Lauderdale FL 33309. 954/928-2100. **Fax:** 954/928-3003. **Recorded Jobline:** 800/638-7816. **Contact:** Pamela Gant, Staffing Specialist. **Description:** The parent company, AlliedSignal Corporation, serves a broad spectrum of industries through more than 40 strategic businesses, which are grouped into three sectors: Aerospace, Automotive, and Engineered Materials. AlliedSignal Aerospace business units include Engines, Air Transport Avionics, General Aviation Avionics, Aerospace Systems and Equipment, Controls and Accessories, Fluid Systems, Aircraft Landing Systems, Technical Services Corporation, and Government Electronics Systems. AlliedSignal Engineered Materials does business in fibers, chemicals, plastics, and advanced materials. AlliedSignal Automotive business units include Braking Systems, Safety Restraint Systems, AlliedSignal Truck Brake Systems Company (alliance with Knorr-Bremse AG), Filters and Spark Plugs, Automotive Aftermarket, and Aftermarket Europe. As part of the Aerospace sector, operations at this location include the design and manufacture of airborne electronic equipment for the commercial airline and military markets. **Common positions include:** Buyer; Computer Systems Analyst; Draftsperson; Electrician; Industrial Engineer; Mechanical Engineer; Purchasing Agent and Manager; Software Engineer; Typist/Word Processor. **Educational backgrounds include:** Business Administration; Computer Science; Engineering; Finance. **Benefits:** Dental Insurance; Disability Coverage; Employee Discounts; Life Insurance; Medical Insurance; Pension Plan; Savings Plan; Tuition Assistance. **Special Programs:** Internships. **Corporate headquarters location:** Redmond WA. **Other U.S. locations:** Nationwide. **Parent company:** AlliedSignal Corporation. **Operations at this facility include:** Administration; Manufacturing; Research and Development; Sales; Service. **Listed on:** New York Stock Exchange. **Number of employees at this location:** 950. **Number of employees nationwide:** 85,000.

B/E AEROSPACE
1300 Corporate Center Way, Wellington FL 33414. 407/791-1266. **Fax:** 407/791-3966. **Contact:** Joseph A. Piegari, Vice President. **Description:** B/E Aerospace manufactures commercial aircraft cabin interior products through the strategic acquisitions of seating, passenger entertainment and service systems (PESS), and galley structures and inserts. The company was incorporated in July 1987 to acquire the assets of Bach Engineering, Inc., and in August 1989 acquired the assets of EECO Avionics; both of which were engaged exclusively in the assembly and sale of PESS products. In 1993, B/E Aerospace acquired all of the capital stock in Inventum, Nordskog Industries, and Acurex Corporation, and the assets of Airvision. The company supplies its products to a majority of the world's airlines and airframe manufacturers. **Common positions include:** Accountant/Auditor; Attorney; Credit Manager; Designer; Electrical/Electronics Engineer; Human Resources Specialist; Industrial Engineer; Paralegal; Purchasing Agent and Manager; Technical Writer/Editor. **Educational backgrounds include:** Accounting; Engineering; Finance. **Benefits:** 401K; Dental Insurance; Disability Coverage; Life Insurance; Medical Insurance; Profit Sharing; Stock Option; Tuition Assistance. **Special Programs:** Internships. **Corporate headquarters location:** This Location. **Other U.S. locations:** London, England;

Singapore; CA; CT; FL; MN; WA. **Operations at this facility include:** Administration; Sales. **Listed on:** NASDAQ. **Number of employees at this location:** 30. **Number of employees nationwide:** 1,500.

B/E AEROSPACE
NORDSKOG GALLEY DIVISION
11710 Central Parkway, Jacksonville FL 32224-7626. 904/641-4900. **Contact:** Personnel Department. **Description:** A manufacturer of flight galleys. **Corporate headquarters location:** 1300 Corporate Center Way, Wellington FL 33414. **Listed on:** NASDAQ.

COLLINS AVIONICS
P.O. Box 1060, Melbourne FL 32902-1060. 407/725-0800. **Contact:** David Ashwell, Personnel Director. **Description:** Manufacturers of radio transmitters for use on aircraft. **Parent company:** Rockwell International.

CRESTVIEW AEROSPACE CORPORATION
5486 Fairchild Road, Crestview FL 32539. 904/682-2746. **Contact:** Douglas Weeks, Director, Employee Relations. **Description:** Crestview Aerospace Corporation manufactures aircraft components. The company is also engaged in aircraft modification. **Common positions include:** Accountant/Auditor; Administrator; Aerospace Engineer; Blue-Collar Worker Supervisor; Buyer; Computer Programmer; Department Manager; Draftsperson; Electrical/Electronics Engineer; Financial Analyst; Human Resources Specialist; Industrial Engineer; Marketing Specialist; Operations/Production Manager; Purchasing Agent and Manager; Quality Control Supervisor; Systems Analyst. **Educational backgrounds include:** Accounting; Business Administration; Computer Science; Engineering; Finance. **Benefits:** Dental Insurance; Disability Coverage; Life Insurance; Medical Insurance; Pension Plan; Retirement Plan; Savings Plan; Tuition Assistance. **Corporate headquarters location:** Chantilly VA. **Parent company:** Fairchild Aircraft Corporation. **Operations at this facility include:** Divisional Headquarters; Manufacturing.

DAYTON-GRANGER, INC.
3299 SW 9th Avenue, JAME, Fort Lauderdale FL 33315. 954/463-3451. **Fax:** 954/761-3172. **Contact:** Karen Kucsak, Manager of Human Resources. **Description:** A manufacturer of aviation communication products. **Common positions include:** Accountant/Auditor; Electrical/Electronics Engineer; Mechanical Engineer. **Educational backgrounds include:** Accounting; Engineering. **Benefits:** Dental Insurance; Disability Coverage; Employee Discounts; Life Insurance; Medical Insurance; Profit Sharing; Savings Plan; Tuition Assistance. **Corporate headquarters location:** This Location. **Operations at this facility include:** Administration; Manufacturing; Sales; Service. **Number of employees at this location:** 230.

EG&G FLORIDA, INC.
412 High Point Drive, Cocoa FL 32926-6698. 407/631-7300. **Contact:** Earl E. Patrick, Manager of Employment. **Description:** The company is the base operations contractor for the Kennedy Space Center, which is involved in all phases of the space program from maintenance, security, fire protection, and environmental health to technical, administrative, and computer support. **Common positions include:** Accountant/Auditor; Chemical Engineer; Civil Engineer; Computer Engineer; Draftsperson; Electrical/Electronics Engineer; Mechanical Engineer; Purchasing Agent and Manager; Systems Analyst; Technical Writer/Editor. **Educational backgrounds include:** Computer Science; Engineering; Mathematics. **Benefits:** Dental Insurance; Disability Coverage; Employee Discounts; Life Insurance; Medical Insurance; Pension Plan; Savings Plan; Tuition Assistance. **Special Programs:** Training Programs. **Corporate headquarters location:** Wellesley MA. **Operations at this facility include:** Service. **Listed on:** New York Stock Exchange. **Number of employees nationwide:** 43,000.

EATON CORPORATION
2250 Whitfield Avenue, Sarasota FL 34243. 941/758-7726. **Contact:** Personnel Department. **Description:** A manufacturer of airplane switches.

GABLES ENGINEERING, INC.
247 Greco Avenue, Coral Gables FL 33146. 305/442-2578. **Fax:** 305/446-5902. **Contact:** Cary Reyes, Human Resources Manager. **Description:** Engaged in the engineering, design, configuration, and manufacture of aircraft communication and navigation control systems. EOE. **Common positions include:** Electrical/Electronics Engineer; Electronics Technician; Software Engineer; Technical Writer/Editor.

Educational backgrounds include: Engineering. **Benefits:** Dental Insurance; Disability Coverage; Life Insurance; Medical Insurance; Pension Plan; Profit Sharing. **Corporate headquarters location:** This Location. **Operations at this facility include:** Manufacturing; Research and Development. **Number of employees at this location:** 180.

GREENWICH AIR SERVICES
P.O. Box 522187, Miami FL 33152. 305/526-7000. **Contact:** Personnel Manager. **Description:** An aircraft engine repair company. **Common positions include:** Accountant/Auditor; Aircraft Mechanic/Engine Specialist; Blue-Collar Worker Supervisor; Computer Programmer; Financial Analyst; Systems Analyst. **Benefits:** 401K; Dental Insurance; Employee Discounts; Life Insurance. **Operations at this facility include:** Service.

GRUMMAN ST. AUGUSTINE CORPORATION
P.O. Drawer 3447, St. Augustine FL 32085. 904/825-3300. **Contact:** Personnel Manager. **Description:** An aircraft overhaul and modification facility. **Educational backgrounds include:** Accounting; Business Administration; Computer Science; Engineering. **Benefits:** Disability Coverage; Employee Discounts; Life Insurance; Medical Insurance; Retirement Plan; Savings Plan; Tuition Assistance. **Corporate headquarters location:** Bethpage NY. **Parent company:** Northrop Grumman Corporation. **Operations at this facility include:** Administration; Manufacturing; Service. **Listed on:** New York Stock Exchange.

HEICO CORPORATION
3000 Taft Street, Hollywood FL 33021. 954/987-6101. **Contact:** Human Resources. **Description:** Heico Corporation manufactures and distributes jet aircraft engine parts, aviation, and defense component parts, and repairs and overhauls engine components.

HONEYWELL INC.
AEROSPACE DIVISION
13350 US Highway 19 North, Clearwater FL 34623-7226. 813/531-4611. **Contact:** Human Resources. **Description:** An international computer corporation serving customer needs for automation and control through five businesses: Aerospace and Defense, Control Products, Control Systems, Information Systems, and International. This location, part of the Aerospace and Defense division, launches vehicles and space systems. The company's manufacturing facilities can be found on six continents in 26 countries. **Other locations:** Worldwide.

HOOVER INDUSTRIES INC.
P.O. Box 522337, Miami FL 33166. 305/888-9791. **Fax:** 305/887-4632. **Contact:** Gloria Garcell, Director of Human Resources. **Description:** A manufacturing company founded in 1955. The company produces interiors (seat covers, cushions, etc.) and inflatable survival equipment for the aircraft industry. **Common positions include:** Accountant/Auditor; Blue-Collar Worker Supervisor; Buyer; Computer Systems Analyst; Cost Estimator; Draftsperson; Human Resources Specialist; Purchasing Agent and Manager; Quality Control Supervisor; Software Engineer; Transportation/Traffic Specialist. **Educational backgrounds include:** Accounting; Business Administration; Computer Science; Engineering; Finance; Marketing. **Benefits:** Dental Insurance; Disability Coverage; Life Insurance; Medical Insurance. **Corporate headquarters location:** This Location. **Listed on:** Privately held. **Number of employees at this location:** 200.

INTERNATIONAL RECOVERY CORPORATION
700 South Royal Poinciana Boulevard, Suite 800, Miami Springs FL 33166. 305/884-2001. **Contact:** Ileana Garcia, Director of Personnel. **Description:** International Recovery Corporation (IRC) is engaged in aviation fuel services for air carriers and is a large used-oil recycler in the southeastern United States. **Common positions include:** Accountant/Auditor; Biological Scientist/Biochemist; Chemist; Credit Manager; Geologist/Geophysicist; Petroleum Engineer; Services Sales Representative. **Educational backgrounds include:** Accounting; Business Administration; Chemistry. **Benefits:** Dental Insurance; Life Insurance; Medical Insurance. **Corporate headquarters location:** This Location. **Operations at this facility include:** Administration; Divisional Headquarters; Regional Headquarters. **Listed on:** New York Stock Exchange.

JOHNSON CONTROLS WORLD SERVICES INC., REF: NJB
P.O. Box 4608, Mail Unit LBS6135, Patrick Air Force Base, Cape Canaveral FL 32925. 407/853-7761. **Fax:** 407/853-7979. **Contact:** Donald K. Mosby, Manager/Employment. **Description:** Launch Base Support contractor to the U.S. Air Force with

responsibility for the engineering, management, operation and maintenance of Cape Canaveral Air Force Station. **Common positions include:** Civil Engineer; Computer Programmer; Electrical/Electronics Engineer; Mechanical Engineer; Systems Analyst. **Educational backgrounds include:** Computer Science; Engineering. **Benefits:** Dental Insurance; Employee Discounts; Life Insurance; Medical Insurance; Pension Plan; Savings Plan; Stock Option; Tuition Assistance. **Corporate headquarters location:** Milwaukee WI. **Parent company:** Johnson Controls. **Operations at this facility include:** Administration; Service. **Listed on:** New York Stock Exchange. **Number of employees at this location:** 2,000.

LOCKHEED MARTIN
CANAVERAL BRANCH
P.O. Box 321399, Cocoa Beach FL 32932-1399. 407/853-6066. **Contact:** Manager of Human Resources. **Description:** An aerospace and technology company engaged in the design, manufacture, and management of systems and products in the fields of space, defense, electronics, communications, information management, energy, and materials.

LOCKHEED MARTIN
OCALA BRANCH
498 Oak Road, Ocala FL 34472. 352/687-2163. **Contact:** Personnel Department. **Description:** An aerospace and technology company engaged in the design, manufacture, and management of systems and products in the fields of space, defense, electronics, communications, information management, energy, and materials.

METRIC SYSTEMS CORPORATION
645 Anchors Street, Ft. Walton Beach FL 32548. 904/244-9600. **Contact:** Director of Human Resources. **Description:** Designs, develops, and manufactures aerospace defense products. **Common positions include:** Accountant/Auditor; Blue-Collar Worker Supervisor; Buyer; Clerical Supervisor; Computer Operator; Computer Programmer; Computer Systems Analyst; Cost Estimator; Department Manager; Designer; Draftsperson; Electrical/Electronics Engineer; Employment Interviewer; Financial Manager; General Manager; Human Resources Specialist; Human Service Worker; Industrial Engineer; Industrial Production Manager; Inspector/Tester/Grader; Machinist; Marketing/Advertising/PR Manager; Mechanical Engineer; Payroll Clerk; Precision Assembler; Purchasing Agent and Manager; Quality Control Supervisor; Receptionist; Sheet-Metal Worker; Software Engineer; Stenographer; Stock Clerk; Systems Analyst; Technical Writer/Editor; Tool and Die Maker; Typist/Word Processor; Welder. **Educational backgrounds include:** Accounting; Computer Science; Engineering; Marketing. **Benefits:** 401K; Dental Insurance; Disability Coverage; Employee Discounts; Life Insurance; Medical Insurance; Pension Plan; Tuition Assistance. **Special Programs:** Training Programs. **Corporate headquarters location:** Houston TX. **Parent company:** Tech-Sym Corporation. **Operations at this facility include:** Administration; Manufacturing; Research and Development; Sales; Service. **Listed on:** New York Stock Exchange. **Number of employees at this location:** 700.

THE NEW PIPER AIRCRAFT INC.
2926 Piper Drive, Vero Beach FL 32960. 407/507-4361. **Contact:** Human Resources. **Description:** Manufactures aircraft.

PRATT & WHITNEY AIRCRAFT
P.O. Box 109600, West Palm Beach FL 33410-9600. 407/796-2000. **Contact:** Human Resources. **Description:** A manufacturer of aircraft engines and space propulsions for the government. **Corporate headquarters location:** East Hartford CT.

REFLECTONE, INC.
P.O. Box 15000, 4908 Tampa West Boulevard, Tampa FL 33684-5000. 813/885-7481. **Contact:** Employment Department. **Description:** The company designs, manufactures, and sells flight simulators; weapon system, tactical air defense, small arms, maintenance and part-task trainers; and other sophisticated training devices for the U.S. Government, commercial and international customers, as well as simulation-based entertainment devices for the entertainment industry. The company also provides a variety of simulator-related training services at customer-owned facilities, its Tampa training center, and the British Aerospace-owned Dulles training facility. Reflectone's business is conducted through its three primary operating segments: the Training Devices Segment, the Training Services Segment, and the Systems Management Segment. In 1993, the company acquired British Aerospace Simulation,

Ltd. which has been renamed Reflectone UK limited (RUKL). **Common positions include:** Accountant/Auditor; Administrator; Aerospace Engineer; Buyer; Draftsperson; Electrical/Electronics Engineer; Industrial Designer; Mechanical Engineer; Purchasing Agent and Manager; Quality Control Supervisor. **Educational backgrounds include:** Accounting; Engineering; Finance; Marketing; Mathematics; Physics. **Benefits:** Dental Insurance; Disability Coverage; Employee Discounts; Life Insurance; Medical Insurance; Pension Plan; Profit Sharing; Savings Plan; Stock Option; Tuition Assistance. **Corporate headquarters location:** This Location. **Number of employees at this location:** 400. **Number of employees nationwide:** 980.

ROCKWELL INTERNATIONAL CORPORATION
P.O Box 21105, Orlando FL 32815-0105. 407/799-6800. **Contact:** Human Resources. **Description:** A contractor for the NASA Space Center.

SIKORSKY AIRCRAFT
FLORIDA DIVISION
P.O. Box 109610, West Palm Beach FL 33410-9610. 407/775-5200. **Contact:** Manager/Human Resources. **Description:** An aircraft manufacturing company.

UNISON INDUSTRIES
7575 Bay Meadows Way, Jacksonville FL 32256. 904/739-4000. **Contact:** Personnel Manager. **Description:** A manufacturer of aircraft parts.

Note: Because addresses and telephone numbers of smaller companies change rapidly, we recommend you call each company to verify the information below before inquiring about job opportunities. Mass mailings are not recommended.

Additional employers with over 250 employees:

AIRCRAFT

Advanced Aero Marine
27518 County Road 561, Tavares FL 32778-9460. 352/742-8122.

Boeing Commercial Airplane Group
9424 Baymeadows Rd, Jacksonville FL 32256-0149. 904/367-0309.

Composite Aircraft Designs
3900 Dow Rd #J, Melbourne FL 32934-9255. 407/459-3200.

Tepper Aviation
5486 Fairchild Rd, Crestview FL 32536-6141. 904/682-8411.

Ultra Efficient Products
2590 17th St, Sarasota FL 34234-1905. 813/366-0883.

Velocity Aircraft
9354 Fleming Grant Rd, Sebastian FL 32976-2712. 407/589-1860.

Coleman Research Corp.
5950 Lakehurst Dr, Orlando FL 32819-8343. 407/352-3700.

East Europe Ventures
246 E Eau Gallie Blvd, Satellite Beach FL 32937-4874. 407/773-3459.

AIRCRAFT EQUIPMENT AND PARTS

Garrett Hydraulic Controls
2150 NW 62nd St, Ft Lauderdale FL 33309-1823. 954/492-8400.

Additional employers with under 250 employees:

AIRCRAFT

Stewart 51
3120 Airport West Dr, Vero Beach FL 32960-1924. 407/778-0051.

Coleman Research Corp.
7675 Municipal Dr, Orlando FL 32819-8930. 407/354-0047.

AIRCRAFT EQUIPMENT AND PARTS

Advanced Technology & Research
14201 Myerlake Circle, Clearwater FL 34620-2824. 813/539-8585.

Chipola Aerotronics
3787 Industrial Park Dr, Marianna FL 32446-8096. 904/526-5911.

Eastern Aero Marine
3580 NW 25th St, Miami FL 33142-6210. 305/871-4050.

AAR Landing Gear Center
9371 NW 100th St, Miami FL 33178-1420. 305/887-4027.

Accudyne Corporation
P.O. Box 1059, Melbourne FL 32902-1059. 407/724-6500.

Aircraft Modular Products
4000 NW 36th Ave, Miami FL 33142-4248. 305/633-6817.

Aircraft Products Co.
12807 Lake Dr, Delray Beach FL 33447. 407/276-6083.

Airfoil Textron
2287 Premier Row, Orlando FL 32809-6211. 407/859-0632.

Aviall Accessory Services
3950 NW 28th St, Miami FL 33142-5610. 305/871-3383.

Britt Metal Processing
15800 NW 49th Ave,

Hialeah FL 33014-6307.
305/621-5200.

**Chromalloy Gas Turbine
Corporation**
630 Anchors St NW, Ft
Walton Beach FL 32548-
3801. 904/244-7684.

Embraer Aircraft Corp.
276 SW 34th St, Ft
Lauderdale FL 33315-3603.
954/359-3700.

Grimes Aerospace Co.
1900 NE 25th Ave, Ocala FL

34470-4849. 352/622-
1101.

Growth Industries
1100 Lee Wagener Blvd, Ft
Lauderdale FL 33315-3570.
954/359-9946.

**Honeycomb Company Of
America**
1950 Limbus Ave, Sarasota
FL 34243-3900. 941/756-
8781.

Lundy Technical Center
3901 NE 12th Ave,

Pompano Beach FL 33064-
5129. 954/943-1500.

AEROSPACE PRODUCTS

Horizons Technology
1800 Penn St, Suite 6,
Melbourne FL 32901-2625.
407/728-0481.

**McDonnell Douglas
Aerospace**
P.O. Box 833, Cape
Canaveral FL 32920-0833.
407/730-0790.

For more information on career opportunities in aerospace:

<u>Associations</u>

**AIR TRANSPORT ASSOCIATION OF
AMERICA**
1301 Pennsylvania Avenue NW, Suite
1100, Washington DC 20004. 202/626-
4000.

**AMERICAN INSTITUTE OF AERONAUTICS
AND ASTRONAUTICS**
85 John Street, 4th Floor, New York NY
10038. 212/349-1120. Membership
required. Publishes six journals and books.

**FUTURE AVIATION PROFESSIONALS OF
AMERICA**
4959 Massachusetts Boulevard, Atlanta GA
30337. 404/997-8097. Publishes a
monthly newsletter which monitors the job
market for flying jobs; a pilot employment

guide, outlining what is required to become
a pilot; and a directory of aviation
employers.

**NATIONAL AERONAUTIC ASSOCIATION
OF USA**
1815 North Fort Meyer Drive, Suite 700,
Arlington VA 22209. 703/527-0226.
Publishes a magazine. Membership required.

**PROFESSIONAL AVIATION MAINTENANCE
ASSOCIATION**
500 NW Plaza, Suite 1016, St. Ann MO
63074. 314/739-2580. Members' resumes
are distributed to companies who advise the
organization of employment opportunities.
Many local chapters also provide job
referrals. Members also can have access to
the Worldwide Membership Directory.

APPAREL AND TEXTILES

 *The apparel industry is looking toward an uncertain future. Women's apparel prices dropped 4.4 percent in 1994, and many experts expect continued deflation through 1996. Consumers have remained uninterested in new fashions and refuse to pay higher prices. Textile and apparel mills are under pressure from the other end of the supply chain as well -- the cost of cotton and other raw materials has remained at close-to-record highs, with raw cotton prices jumping 35 percent in 1994. As a result, many textile producers have recently reported significant drops in earnings. However, improved consumer confidence, more attractive fashions, and lower prices may prod consumers into buying after going without for the past four years, and this will eventually increase business for mills. Also, the sales of men's suits soared by 20 percent in 1994, and this trend is expected to continue, though at a somewhat slower pace, as men look for upscale casual wear to accommodate more relaxed dress codes. The highest demand in both men's and women's apparel will probably be for lower priced clothing produced for discount stores.*

AMERICAN WOOLEN COMPANY
P.O. Box 521399, Miami FL 33152-1399. 305/635-4000. **Fax:** 305/633-4997. **Contact:** Richard Marcus, President. **Description:** Manufactures blankets.

CHICO'S
11215 Metro Parkway, Fort Meyers FL 33912. 941/277-6200. **Contact:** Personnel. **Description:** A manufacturer and retailer of women's apparel. **Number of employees at this location:** 325. **Corporate headquarters location:** This location.

DECORATOR INDUSTRIES, INC.
10011 Pines Boulevard, Suite 201, Pembroke Pines FL 33024. 954/436-8909. **Contact:** Employment. **Description:** Manufactures draperies, bedspreads, and accessory products.

FRAYNE FASHION
6402 West Linebaugh Avenue, Tampa FL 33625. 813/961-7171. **Contact:** Personnel Department. **Description:** A garment manufacturer.

GATOR INDUSTRIES
1000 Southeast 8th Street, Hialeah FL 33010. 305/888-5000. **Contact:** Carmen Romero, Personnel Director. **Description:** A shoe manufacturing and exporting company.

HOLLANDER HOME FASHIONS CORPORATION
6560 West Rogers Circle, Boca Raton FL 33487-2705. 407/997-6900. **Fax:** 407/997-8738. **Contact:** Bonnie M. George, Corporate Personnel Manager. **Description:** Hollander Home Fashions manufactures bed pillows, comforters, mattress pads, comforter sets, and specialty bedding products. The company's locations include nine manufacturing facilities, a showroom, and the corporate office. **Common positions include:** Accountant/Auditor; Administrative Services Manager; Blue-Collar Worker Supervisor; Clerical Supervisor; Computer Programmer; Credit Manager; Customer Service Representative; Designer; Financial Analyst; General Manager; Human Resources Specialist; Industrial Engineer; Industrial Production Manager; Manufacturer's/Wholesaler's Sales Rep.; Mechanical Engineer; Purchasing Agent and Manager; Quality Control Supervisor. **Educational backgrounds include:** Accounting; Art/Design; Business Administration; Computer Science; Engineering; Liberal Arts; Marketing. **Benefits:** 401K; Disability Coverage; Life Insurance; Medical Insurance.

Corporate headquarters location: This Location. Other U.S. locations: Nationwide. Operations at this facility include: Administration; Manufacturing; Research and Development; Sales. Listed on: Privately held. Number of employees at this location: 42. Number of employees nationwide: 1,200.

INJECTION FOOTWEAR CORPORATION
8730 North West 36th Avenue, Miami FL 33147. 305/696-4611. Contact: Brian Tewes, Assistant Controller. Description: Manufacturer of shoes. Common positions include: Accountant/Auditor; Administrator; Computer Programmer; Credit Manager; Customer Service Representative; General Manager; Industrial Designer; Manufacturer's/Wholesaler's Sales Rep.; Marketing Specialist; Purchasing Agent and Manager; Quality Control Supervisor; Systems Analyst. Educational backgrounds include: Accounting; Business Administration; Computer Science; Engineering; Marketing. Benefits: Employee Discounts; Life Insurance; Tuition Assistance. Corporate headquarters location: This Location. Operations at this facility include: Manufacturing; Sales.

NUTMEG MILLS
4408 West Linebaugh Avenue, Tampa FL 33624. 813/963-6153. Contact: Human Resources. Description: Manufactures licensed sportswear.

RUSSELL CORPORATION
4215 Kelson Avenue, Marianna FL 32446-8211. 904/526-3695. Contact: Human Resources. Description: Russell Corporation, formerly Russell Mills, is a vertically integrated international designer, manufacturer, and marketer of activewear, athletic uniforms, knit shirts, leisure apparel, licensed sports apparel, sports and casual socks, and a comprehensive line of lightweight, yarn-dyed woven fabrics. The company's manufacturing operations include the entire process of converting raw fibers into finished apparel and fabrics. Russell's products are marketed principally through five sales divisions -- Knit Apparel, Athletic, Licensed Products, International, and Fabrics -- as well as through Cross Creek Apparel, Inc. and DeSoto Mills, Inc. two wholly-owned subsidiaries. Products are marketed to sporting goods dealers, department and specialty stores, mass merchandisers, golf pro shops, college bookstores, screen printers, distributors, mail-order houses, and other apparel manufacturers. Major brand names include Jerzee's (knit apparel) and Russell Athletic (teamwear and knit activewear). Corporate headquarters location: Alexander City AL. Other U.S. locations: Crestview FL; Niceville FL. Number of employees nationwide: 16,640.

RUSSELL CORPORATION
5680 John Givens Road, Crestview FL 32539-7018. 904/682-1286. Contact: Human Resources. Description: Russell Corporation, formerly Russell Mills, is a vertically integrated international designer, manufacturer, and marketer of activewear, athletic uniforms, knit shirts, leisure apparel, licensed sports apparel, sports and casual socks, and a comprehensive line of lightweight, yarn-dyed woven fabrics. The company's manufacturing operations include the entire process of converting raw fibers into finished apparel and fabrics. Russell's products are marketed principally through five sales divisions -- Knit Apparel, Athletic, Licensed Products, International, and Fabrics -- as well as through Cross Creek Apparel, Inc. and DeSoto Mills, Inc. two wholly-owned subsidiaries. Products are marketed to sporting goods dealers, department and specialty stores, mass merchandisers, golf pro shops, college bookstores, screen printers, distributors, mail-order houses, and other apparel manufacturers. The company's brand names include Jerzee's (knit apparel) and Russell Athletic (teamwear and knit activewear). Corporate headquarters location: Alexander City AL. Other U.S. locations: Marianna FL; Niceville FL. Number of employees nationwide: 16,640.

RUSSELL CORPORATION
100 Hart Street, Niceville FL 32578-1039. 904/678-2212. Contact: Human Resources. Description: Russell Corporation, formerly Russell Mills, is a vertically integrated international designer, manufacturer, and marketer of activewear, athletic uniforms, knit shirts, leisure apparel, licensed sports apparel, sports and casual socks, and a comprehensive line of lightweight, yarn-dyed woven fabrics. The company's manufacturing operations include the entire process of converting raw fibers into finished apparel and fabrics. Russell's products are marketed principally through five sales divisions -- Knit Apparel, Athletic, Licensed Products, International, and Fabrics -- as well as through Cross Creek Apparel, Inc. and DeSoto Mills, Inc. two wholly owned subsidiaries. Products are marketed to sporting goods dealers, department and specialty stores, mass merchandisers, golf pro shops, college bookstores, screen printers, distributors, mail-order houses, and other apparel manufacturers. Major brand

names include Jerzee's (knit apparel) and Russell Athletic (teamwear and knit activewear). **Corporate headquarters location:** Alexander City AL. **Other U.S. locations:** Marianna FL; Crestview FL. **Number of employees nationwide:** 16,640.

SUAVE SHOE CORPORATION
P.O. Box 4828, Hialeah FL 33014. 305/822-7880. **Contact:** Director of Personnel. **Description:** A shoe manufacturer and importer. **Common positions include:** Computer Programmer; Industrial Engineer. **Educational backgrounds include:** Computer Science; Engineering.

SUPERIOR SURGICAL MANUFACTURING COMPANY, INC.
P.O. Box 4002, 10099 Seminole Boulevard, Seminole FL 34642. 813/397-9611. **Fax:** 813/391-5401. **Contact:** John H. Lord, Corporate Manager of Human Resources. **Description:** A manufacturer and wholesale distributor of uniforms, career apparel, and accessories for the hospital and health care fields; hotels and restaurants; and the public safety, industrial, transportation, and commercial markets. Through a variety of catalogs, flyers, sales bulletins, product releases and trade advertising, Superior Surgical Manufacturing Company, Inc. offers its products from eight divisions. Fashion Seal Uniforms is its largest division and a prime supplier to the health care market. Other divisions include Worklon, Martin's Uniforms, Appel uniforms, Universal Laundry Bags, Lamar Caribbean Sales, D'Armigene Design Center, and Superior Surgical International. **Common positions include:** Accountant/Auditor; Buyer; Commercial Artist; Computer Programmer; Credit Manager; Customer Service Representative; Human Resources Specialist; Industrial Engineer; Industrial Production Manager; Manufacturer's/Wholesaler's Sales Rep.; Quality Control Supervisor; Systems Analyst. **Educational backgrounds include:** Accounting; Business Administration; Computer Science; Marketing. **Benefits:** Disability Coverage; Life Insurance; Medical Insurance; Pension Plan. **Corporate headquarters location:** This Location. **Listed on:** American Stock Exchange.

TROPICAL SPORTSWEAR INTERNATIONAL
4902 West Waters Avenue, Tampa FL 33634. 813/249-4900. **Contact:** Personnel Department. **Description:** A garment manufacturer.

VANITY FAIR MILLS, INC.
SANTA ROSA
P.O. Box 584, Milton FL 32572. 904/623-3813. **Contact:** Alan Williams, Personnel Director. **Description:** A manufacturer of women's lingerie.

WEAVEXX
P.O. Box 979, Quincy FL 32353-0979. 904/627-7141. **Contact:** Olivia Goodwin, Personnel Manager. **Description:** Weavexx manufactures forming fabrics.

WESTPOINT STEVENS
P.O. Box 625, Chipley FL 32428. 904/638-4956. **Contact:** Human Resources. **Description:** WestPoint Stevens manufactures a variety of bedding products, including comforters, bedspreads, curtains, duvets, and other products.

Note: Because addresses and telephone numbers of smaller companies change rapidly, we recommend you call each company to verify the information below before inquiring about job opportunities. Mass mailings are not recommended.

Additional employers with over 250 employees:

APPAREL WHOLESALE

Embassy Apparel
6363 NW 6th Way #200, Ft Lauderdale FL 33309-6119. 954/484-7229.

KNITTING MILLS

Sherry Manufacturing Co.
3287 NW 65th St, Miami FL 33147. 305/693-7000.

Kuppenheimer Manufacturing
3900 E 10th Ct, Hialeah FL 33013-2924. 305/691-7256.

BROADWOVEN FABRIC MILLS

Niagara Lockport Industries
P.O. Box 979, Quincy FL 32353. 904/627-7141.

CHILDREN'S AND INFANTS' CLOTHING

Gepetto
425 E 10th Ct, Hialeah FL 33010. 305/887-0380.

CANVAS PRODUCTS

Foot Tec Industries
15750 NW 59th Ave, Hialeah FL 33014-6716. 305/556-2300.

Additional employers with under 250 employees:

BROADWOVEN FABRIC MILLS

Skandia Industries
270 Crossway Rd,
Tallahassee FL 32310-7462.
904/878-1144.

TEXTILE FINISHING

Team Edition Apparel
4208 19th Street Ct E,
Bradenton FL 34208-7336.
941/747-5300.

Tinter
13000 NW 45th Ave, Opa
Locka FL 33054-4304.
305/685-7543.

CARPETS AND RUGS

Aladdin Mills
1320 NW 163rd St, Miami
FL 33169-5709. 305/624-
8787.

TEXTILE GOODS

Fiberwebb North America
610 Chemstrand Rd,
Cantonment FL 32533-
6857. 904/968-0100.

MEN'S AND BOYS' CLOTHING

L&M Fashions
940 W 19th St, Hialeah FL
33010-2309. 305/883-
0681.

Sunstate Sportswear
2102 S MacDill Ave, Tampa
FL 33629-5934. 813/254-
9710.

Kantor Brothers Neckwear
575 E 10th Ave, Hialeah FL
33010-4639. 305/885-
4056.

Steinberg Neckwear
Corporation
7875 W 20th Ave, Hialeah
FL 33014-3228. 305/822-
3591.

Martin's Uniforms
5201 N Armenia Ave, Tampa
FL 33603-1492. 813/877-
0511.

Max-E Corporation
RR 1 Box 287A, Hawthorne
FL 32640-8115. 352/481-
4361.

Happy Fella
3710 E 10th Ct, Hialeah FL
33013-2920. 305/836-
4130.

Kariss
772 NW 76th Ave, Miami FL
33126-2917. 305/262-
6766.

Raymel Corporation
275 E 10th Ave, Hialeah FL
33010-5141. 305/885-
9660.

Starter Sportswear
8821 Grove Dr, Pensacola FL
32514. 904/484-7777.

WOMEN'S AND MISSES' CLOTHING

Gilmor Trading Corp.
2190 E 11th Ave, Hialeah FL
33013-4308. 305/835-
0101.

Command Enterprises
Corporation
P.O. Box 520, Monticello FL
32345-0520. 904/997-
3589.

Jo-Joel
301 E 10th Ave, Hialeah FL
33010-5142. 305/883-
9599.

Lake Butler Apparel Co.
255 SE 6th Ave, Lake Butler
FL 32054-2225. 904/496-
3601.

New Ponce Shirt Co.
Hwy 90 W, Ponce De Leon
FL 32455. 904/836-4429.

RB Apparel
3522 E 10th Ct, Hialeah FL
33013-2916. 305/691-
8857.

Regal Fashions
915 W 18th St, Hialeah FL
33010-2322. 305/884-
8555.

Ronar Dress Manufacturing
601 SW 71st Ave, Miami FL
33144-2724. 305/261-
6011.

Ross Of Florida
2765 US Highway 92 E,
Lakeland FL 33801-9223.
941/686-3855.

Suburban Manufacturing
Company
1589 102nd Ave N, St
Petersburg FL 33716-5049.
813/577-3389.

Sun State Manufacturing
Company
RR 13 Box 839, Lake City FL
32055-9026. 904/755-
0820.

Tail Active Sportswear
3300 NW 41st St, Miami FL
33142-4306. 305/638-
2650.

Piba Industries
1100 E 41st St, Hialeah FL
33013-2518. 305/836-
5890.

HEAD WEAR

Bernard Cap Co.
9800 NW 79th Ave, Hialeah
FL 33016-2425. 305/822-
4800.

Forget-Me-Not Of Delaware
6550 NE 4th Ct, Miami FL
33138-6112. 305/756-
7711.

CHILDREN'S AND INFANTS' CLOTHING

Bend 'N Stretch
7905 W 20th Ave, Hialeah
FL 33014-3229. 305/362-
2229.

Dorrissa Of Miami
2751 N Miami Ave, Miami FL
33127-4439. 305/573-
3600.

Sylvia Whyte Manufacturing
67 NE 17th Terrace, Miami
FL 33132-1113. 305/379-
7365.

Arlene Designs
313 Ansin Blvd, Hallandale
FL 33009-3108. 954/458-
5333.

Brookstex
19363 Oliver St, Brooksville
FL 34601-6537. 352/796-
1461.

Girls Will Be Girls
9907 NW 79th Ave, Hialeah
FL 33016-2412. 305/822-
6262.

Holiday Sportswear Of Miami
537 NW 24th St, Miami FL
33127-4327. 305/573-
6710.

Ibiley Manufacturing
Corporation
1927 W Flagler St, Miami FL
33135-1614. 305/643-
6385.

MISC. APPAREL AND ACCESSORIES

Angelica Corporation
9119 NW 105th Way, Miami
FL 33178-1221. 305/883-
6145.

Holloway Sportswear
550 State Road 207, St
Augustine FL 32095-0161.
904/824-4411.

Jasper Textile Corp.
RR 2 Box 35, Jasper FL
32052-9618. 904/792-
2562.

Peter Popovitch
13200 N W 45th Ave, Miami
FL 33175. 305/687-8383.

Speedline Athletic Wear
1804 N Habana Ave, Tampa
FL 33607-3345. 813/876-
1375.

**Starke Uniform
Manufacturing Co.**
P.O. Box 1150, Starke FL
32091-1150. 904/964-
5090.

CURTAINS AND DRAPERIES

Decorama Cortley Desley
685 W 25th St, Hialeah FL
33010-2148. 305/884-
3100.

Sultan & Sons
650 SW 9th Terrace,
Pompano Beach FL 33069-
4520. 954/782-6600.

CANVAS PRODUCTS

Aldon Industries
1900 47th Terrace E,
Bradenton FL 34203-3701.
941/747-1900.

York Manufacturing
2350 31st St S, St
Petersburg FL 33712-3348.
813/321-3149.

TRIMMINGS, APPAREL FINDINGS, AND RELATED PRODUCTS

Breakaway
18524 NW 67th Ave #256,
Hialeah FL 33015-3302.
305/625-5500.

Harlequin Nature Graphics
16145 Old US Highway 41,
Fort Myers FL 33912-2297.
941/489-1620.

Joy Silkscreen Products
3555 E 11th Ave, Hialeah FL
33013-2927. 305/691-
7240.

Wise Company
2420 New Tampa Hwy,
Lakeland FL 33801-3457.
941/688-8183.

FABRICATED TEXTILE PRODUCTS

Brooklyn Bow & Ribbon Co.
2010 Seabird Way, Riviera
Beach FL 33404-5009.
407/840-8801.

Lake Butler Apparel Co.
U S Hwy 19 S, Cross City FL
32628. 352/498-3204.

SI Cutting Services
13290 NW 45th Ave, Opa
Locka FL 33054-4308.
305/687-0388.

FOOTWEAR

Asahi
15750 NW 59th Ave,
Hialeah FL 33014-6716.
305/557-6981.

LUGGAGE

**Mercury Luggage
Manufacturing**
4843 Victor St, Jacksonville
FL 32207-7963. 904/733-
9595.

MISC. LEATHER GOODS

Morris Corporation
7150 114th Ave, Largo FL
34643-5311. 813/545-
9009.

APPAREL WHOLESALE

Good Buy Sportswear
2400 31st St S, St
Petersburg FL 33712-3350.
813/327-3773.

Partex Industries
11700 NW 102nd Rd, Miami
FL 33178-1029. 305/889-
0600.

Roma Industries
7150 114th Ave N, St
Petersburg FL 33716.
813/545-9009.

Karlink
3570 Consumer St, Riviera
Beach FL 33404-1740.
407/842-2568.

For more information on career opportunities in the apparel and textiles industries:

Associations

**AMERICAN APPAREL MANUFACTURERS
ASSOCIATION**
2500 Wilson Boulevard, Suite 301,
Arlington VA 22201. 703/524-1864.
Publishes numerous magazines,
newsletters, and bulletins for the benefit of
employees in the apparel manufacturing
industry.

**AMERICAN TEXTILE MANUFACTURERS
INSTITUTE**
Office of the Chief Economist, 1801 K
Street NW, Suite 900, Washington DC
20006. 202/862-0500.

THE FASHION GROUP
597 5th Avenue, 8th Floor, New York NY
10017. 212/593-1715. A nonprofit
organization for professional women in the
fashion industries (apparel, accessories,
beauty, and home). Offers career counseling
workshops 18 times per year.

**INTERNATIONAL ASSOCIATION OF
CLOTHING DESIGNERS**
475 Park Avenue South, 17th Floor, New
York NY 10016. 212/685-6602.

Directories

AAMA DIRECTORY
American Apparel Manufacturers
Association, 2500 Wilson Boulevard, Suite
301, Arlington VA 22201. 703/524-1864.
A directory of publications distributed by
the American Apparel Manufacturers
Association.

APPAREL TRADES BOOK
Dun & Bradstreet Inc., 430 Mountain
Avenue, New Providence NJ 07974.
908/665-5000.

**FAIRCHILD'S MARKET DIRECTORY OF
WOMEN'S AND CHILDREN'S APPAREL**
Fairchild Publications, 7 West 34th Street,
New York NY 10001. 212/630-4000.

Magazines

ACCESSORIES
Business Journals, 50 Day Street, P.O. Box
5550, Norwalk CT 06856. 203/853-6015.

AMERICA'S TEXTILES
Billiam Publishing, 37 Villa Road, Suite 111,
P.O. Box 103, Greenville SC 29615.
803/242-5300.

APPAREL INDUSTRY MAGAZINE
Shore Communications Inc., 6255 Barfield
Road, Suite 200, Atlanta GA 30328-4893.
404/252-8831.

BOBBIN
Bobbin Publications, P.O. Box 1986, 1110
Shop Road, Columbia SC 29202. 803/771-
7500.

TEXTILE HILIGHTS
American Textile Manufacturers Institute,
Office of the Chief Economist, 1801 K
Street NW, Suite 900, Washington DC
20006.

WOMEN'S WEAR DAILY (WWD)
Fairchild Publications, 7 West 34th Street,
New York NY 10001. 212/630-4000.

ARCHITECTURE, CONSTRUCTION AND ENGINEERING

The U.S. Department of Labor anticipates 1.2 million new construction jobs from 1992 through 2005, due to the need to replace aging experienced workers. Residential construction will grow slowly, as a result of the expected decline in population growth. Industrial construction, however, will be stronger because of an increase in exports by manufacturers. Heavy construction is growing faster than the industry average, with much activity in highway, bridge, and street construction.

Job prospects for engineers have been good for a number of years, and will continue to improve into the next century. Employers will need more engineers as they increase investment in equipment in order to expand output. In addition, engineers will find work improving the nation's deteriorating infrastructure.

A.J.T. & ASSOCIATES
101 George King Boulevard, Cape Canaveral FL 32920-3305. 407/783-7989. **Contact:** Debbi Autery, Office Manager. **Description:** Provides environmental science and architectural engineering services. **Common positions include:** Architect; Civil Engineer; Electrical/Electronics Engineer; Environmental Engineer; Mechanical Engineer.

ARMSTRONG WORLD INDUSTRIES INC.
P.O. Box 1991, Pensacola FL 32589-1991. 904/433-8321. **Contact:** Human Resources. **Description:** A manufacturer of acoustical ceiling tile.

BAKER BROTHERS, INC.
P.O. Box 2954, Jacksonville FL 32203. 904/733-9633. **Contact:** Doris Spears, Employee Services Manager. **Description:** A wholesale heating and cooling equipment company.

CELOTEX CORPORATION
4010 Boy Scout Boulevard, Tampa FL 33607. 813/873-4252. **Fax:** 813/873-4430. **Contact:** Ms. Jean Galleher, Human Resources. **Description:** Celotex manufactures building products. **Common positions include:** Accountant/Auditor; Assistant Manager; Attorney; Budget Analyst; Buyer; Clerical Supervisor; Computer Operator; Computer Programmer; Computer Systems Analyst; Credit Manager; Department Manager; Economist/Market Research Analyst; Employment Interviewer; Human Resources Specialist; Marketing Research Analyst; Marketing/Advertising/PR Manager; Paralegal; Payroll Clerk; Purchasing Agent and Manager; Quality Control Supervisor; Sales/Marketing Director; Secretary; Systems Analyst; Transportation/Traffic Specialist; Typist/Word Processor. **Educational backgrounds include:** Accounting; Business Administration; Computer Science; Economics; Finance; Liberal Arts; Marketing. **Benefits:** Daycare Assistance; Dental Insurance; Disability Coverage; Employee Discounts; Life Insurance; Medical Insurance; Pension Plan; Retirement Plan; Savings Plan; Tuition Assistance. **Other U.S. locations:** AL; AR; CA; IA; IN; KY; LA; MI; NC; NJ; OH; PA; TN; TX; WY. **Parent company:** Jim Walter Corporation. **Operations at this facility include:** Administration. **Number of employees at this location:** 264. **Number of employees nationwide:** 2,764.

CENTEX ROONEY
6300 NW Fifth Way, Fort Lauderdale FL 33309. 954/771-7122. **Contact:** Personnel Department. **Description:** A construction and general contracting company.

EDWARD M. CHADBOURNE, INC.
4375 McCoy Drive, Pensacola FL 32503. 904/433-3001. **Contact:** Vice President. **Description:** A road building contractor.

J.W. CONNER & SONS, INC.
P.O. Box 2522, Tampa FL 33601-2522. 813/247-4441. **Contact:** Ms. Jan Guerard, Director of Personnel. **Description:** A road and highway contractor.

ELECTRICAL MACHINERY ENTERPRISES
2515 East Hanna, Tampa FL 33610-5010. 813/251-2444. **Contact:** Personnel. **Description:** An electrical contractor.

FAILURE ANALYSIS ASSOCIATES, INC.
1501 Venera Avenue, Coral Gables FL 33146. 305/661-7726. **Contact:** Human Resources. **Description:** Founded in 1967, Failure Analysis Associates has performed the scientific analysis of thousands of cases, from headline-making multimillion-dollar disasters to small accident investigations and routine risk assessments. The company's expertise is used in areas such as accident reconstruction, biomechanics, construction and structural engineering, aviation and marine investigations, environmental assessment, materials and product testing, warnings and labeling issues, accident statistic data analysis and risk prevention and mitigation. Failure Analysis Associates is a subsidiary of The Failure Group, Inc.

FILBERT CORPORATION
P.O. Box 161909, Altamonte Springs FL 32716-1909. 407/862-1011. **Contact:** Ken Johnson, General Manager. **Description:** A contractor for industrial refrigeration. **Common positions include:** Accountant/Auditor; Draftsperson; General Manager; Mechanical Engineer; Services Sales Representative. **Educational backgrounds include:** Accounting; Engineering. **Benefits:** Dental Insurance; Disability Coverage; Life Insurance; Medical Insurance; Pension Plan; Savings Plan; Stock Option; Tuition Assistance. **Corporate headquarters location:** Milwaukee WI. **Parent company:** Vitler Manufacturing Corporation. **Operations at this facility include:** Regional Headquarters.

FLORIDA ENGINEERED CONSTRUCTION PRODUCTS
P.O. Box 24567, Tampa FL 33623. 813/621-4641. **Fax:** 813/621-0671. **Contact:** Larry Toll, Personnel Director. **Description:** A manufacturer of building materials including precast lintels and sills, prestressed concrete beams and joints, roof trusses, and architectural precast slabs. **Common positions include:** Accountant/Auditor; Civil Engineer; Draftsperson; Management Trainee; Manufacturer's/Wholesaler's Sales Rep.; Operations/Production Manager; Quality Control Supervisor. **Educational backgrounds include:** Business Administration; Engineering; Finance; Marketing. **Benefits:** Dental Insurance; Life Insurance; Medical Insurance; Savings Plan. **Corporate headquarters location:** This Location. **Other U.S. locations:** Kissimmee FL; Odessa FL; Sarasota FL; West Palm Beach FL; Winter Springs FL. **Operations at this facility include:** Administration; Divisional Headquarters; Manufacturing; Regional Headquarters; Sales; Service. **Listed on:** Privately held. **Number of employees at this location:** 250. **Number of employees nationwide:** 350.

GLASSALUM ENGINEERING CORPORATION
7933 North West 71st Street, Miami FL 33166. 305/592-1212. **Contact:** Personnel Department. **Description:** A curtain wall manufacturer.

HARPER BROTHERS
14860 Six-Mile Cypress Parkway, Fort Meyers FL 33912. 941/481-2350. **Contact:** Personnel Department. **Description:** A contractor specializing in road construction.

THE HASKELL COMPANY
P.O. Box 44100, Jacksonville FL 32231-4100. 904/791-4500. **Contact:** Nancy F. Williams, Human Resources Administrator. **Description:** A design and construction firm. **Common positions include:** Accountant/Auditor; Administrator; Architect; Civil Engineer; Computer Programmer; Draftsperson; Electrical/Electronics Engineer; Human Resources Specialist; Management Trainee; Mechanical Engineer; Operations/Production Manager; Quality Control Supervisor; Systems Analyst. **Educational backgrounds include:** Accounting; Business Administration; Engineering; Finance; Marketing. **Benefits:** Dental Insurance; Disability Coverage; Employee Discounts; Life Insurance; Medical Insurance; Pension Plan; Profit Sharing; Savings Plan; Tuition Assistance. **Corporate headquarters location:** This Location. **Operations at this facility include:** Regional Headquarters.

C.H. HEIST CORPORATION
810 North Belcher Road, Clearwater FL 34625. 813/461-5656. **Contact:** Human Resources Department. **Description:** Provides sandblasting, high-pressure water cleaning, and painting services.

HOMES OF MERIT, INC.
P.O. Box 1606, Building 121, Bartow FL 33831. 941/533-0593. **Contact:** Michael Taylor, Director of Human Resources. **Description:** A builder and manufacturer of residential homes.

HUBBARD CONSTRUCTION COMPANY
P.O. Box 547217, Orlando FL 32854-7217. 407/645-5500. **Contact:** Director of Personnel. **Description:** A contractor specializing in heavy and highway construction. **Common positions include:** Blue-Collar Worker Supervisor; Civil Engineer; Estimator. **Educational backgrounds include:** Engineering. **Benefits:** 401K; Dental Insurance; Disability Coverage; Life Insurance; Medical Insurance; Profit Sharing; Tuition Assistance. **Corporate headquarters location:** This Location. **Operations at this facility include:** Administration. **Number of employees at this location:** 750. **Number of employees nationwide:** 1,000.

JJW CONSTRUCTION
P.O. Box 16298, Plantation FL 33318. 954/587-5597. **Contact:** Personnel. **Description:** A commercial and office building construction company. **Number of employees at this location:** 305.

McDONALD CONSTRUCTION CORPORATION
P.O. Box 5109, Lakeland FL 33807. 941/646-5763. **Contact:** Wiley Johnson, Vice President. **Description:** A heavy-construction firm.

MISENER MARINE CONSTRUCTION INC.
P.O. Box 13427, Tampa FL 33681. 813/839-8441. **Contact:** Bert Potts, Personnel Director. **Description:** Engaged in heavy marine construction of bridges, docks and piers, subaqueous pipeline and cable, and foundation piling. **Common positions include:** Accountant/Auditor; Civil Engineer; Computer Programmer; Draftsperson; Geologist/Geophysicist; Purchasing Agent and Manager. **Educational backgrounds include:** Accounting; Business Administration; Engineering. **Benefits:** Disability Coverage; Life Insurance; Medical Insurance; Profit Sharing; Tuition Assistance. **Corporate headquarters location:** This Location.

NOBILITY HOMES, INC.
P.O. Box 5128, Ocala FL 34478. 352/732-5157. **Contact:** John Cramer, Treasurer. **Description:** A manufacturer of mobile homes.

ORIOLE HOMES CORPORATION
1690 South Congress Avenue, Delray Beach FL 33445. 407/274-2000. **Contact:** Personnel Department. **Description:** Oriole Homes builds and sells homes and condominiums.

PLUMBING BY GUS, INC.
P.O. Box 9, Dunedin FL 34697. 813/734-8804. **Contact:** Personnel Director. **Description:** A plumbing contracting business.

POST, BUCKLEY, SCHUH, AND JERNIGAN, INC.
2001 Northwest 107th Avenue, Miami FL 33166. 305/592-7275. **Contact:** Recruiting Coordinator. **Description:** A national engineering, planning and architectural consulting firm. **Common positions include:** Architect; Chemical Engineer; Chemist; Civil Engineer; Draftsperson; Electrical/Electronics Engineer; Mechanical Engineer; Structural Engineer; Technical Writer/Editor; Transportation/Traffic Specialist. **Educational backgrounds include:** Engineering. **Benefits:** Dental Insurance; Disability Coverage; Employee Discounts; Life Insurance; Medical Insurance; Profit Sharing; Tuition Assistance. **Operations at this facility include:** Administration; Regional Headquarters; Sales; Service.

POWER ENGINEERING INTERNATIONAL
4205 Salzedo Street, Coral Gables FL 33146. 305/567-2630. **Contact:** George Scopetta, Personnel Manager. **Description:** Corporate office for an engineering company.

REYNOLDS, SMITH, AND HILLS, INC.
P.O. Box 4850, Jacksonville FL 32201. 904/296-2000. **Contact:** Connie Norsworthy, Recruitment Manager. **Description:** Offers architectural, engineering, and planning/ design consulting services. **Common positions include:** Architect; Architectural Engineer; Chemical Engineer; Civil Engineer; Electrical/Electronics Engineer; Energy Engineer; Environmental Engineer; Geologist/Geophysicist; Mechanical Engineer; Transportation/Traffic Specialist. **Educational backgrounds include:** Bachelor of Arts; Engineering. **Benefits:** 401K; Dental Insurance; Disability Coverage; Life Insurance; Medical Insurance; Stock Option; Tuition Assistance. **Other U.S. locations:** Merritt Island FL; Orlando FL; Tampa FL; Greensboro NC. **Number of employees nationwide:** 375.

SCOTTY'S, INC.
P.O. Box 939, Winter Haven FL 33882-0939. 941/299-1111. **Contact:** Julie Martin, Human Resources Administrator. **Description:** A wholesale construction supply company.

TRI CITY ELECTRICAL CONTRACTORS
430 West Drive, Altamonte Spring FL 32714. 407/788-3500. **Contact:** Human Resources. **Description:** Performs electrical contracting work for both commercial and residential clients.

U.S. GYPSUM COMPANY
P.O. Box 9579, Jacksonville FL 32208. 904/768-2501. **Contact:** Bob Harry, Human Resources Manager. **Description:** A manufacturer of assorted building materials.

WALTER INDUSTRIES
1500 North Dale Mabry, Tampa FL 33607. 813/871-4811. **Contact:** Employment Manager. **Description:** Walter Industries is one of the nation's largest industrial companies, with interests in homebuilding and financing, natural resources, building materials, and industrial manufacturing.

WATKINS ENGINEERS AND CONSTRUCTION
P.O. Box 2194, Tallahassee FL 32316. 904/576-7181. **Contact:** Personnel Director. **Description:** A contractor specializing in industrial buildings and warehouses.

WATSCO COMPONENTS, INC.
1800 West Fourth Avenue, Hialeah FL 33010. 305/885-1911. **Fax:** 305/887-0372. **Contact:** Ray Koneicke, Vice President, Human Resources. **Description:** Watsco Components, Inc. primarily manufactures and distributes climate control equipment. The company is a large independent distributor of air conditioner components nationwide. **Common positions include:** Accountant/Auditor; Blue-Collar Worker Supervisor; Buyer; Computer Operator; Computer Programmer; Computer Systems Analyst; Credit Clerk and Authorizer; Credit Manager; Customer Service Representative; Department Manager; Draftsperson; Electrical/Electronics Engineer; Electrician; Employment Interviewer; Financial Manager; Heating/AC/Refrigeration Technician; Human Resources Specialist; Inspector/Tester/Grader; Machinist; Marketing/Advertising/PR Manager; Mechanical Engineer; Millwright; Payroll Clerk; Precision Assembler; Production Manager; Purchasing Agent and Manager; Quality Control Supervisor; Receptionist; Secretary; Statistician; Stock Clerk; Tool and Die Maker; Truck Driver; Typist/Word Processor; Welder. **Educational backgrounds include:** Accounting; Business Administration; Engineering. **Benefits:** Dental Insurance; Life Insurance; Medical Insurance; Pension Plan; Profit Sharing; Tuition Assistance. **Special Programs:** Training Programs. **Corporate headquarters location:** Miami FL. **Parent company:** Watsco, Inc. **Operations at this facility include:** Administration; Manufacturing; Regional Headquarters; Research and Development; Sales; Service. **Listed on:** American Stock Exchange. **Number of employees at this location:** 312.

Note: Because addresses and telephone numbers of smaller companies change rapidly, we recommend you call each company to verify the information below before inquiring about job opportunities. Mass mailings are not recommended.

Additional employers with under 250 employees:

GENERAL CONTRACTORS

Aetna Construction
3063 NW 23rd Terrace, Ft Lauderdale FL 33311-1402. 954/731-2311.

Bill Carpenter Roofing Contractors
700 Old Dixie Hwy, Riviera Beach FL 33404. 407/848-8886.

Clancy & Theys Construction
4201 Vineland Rd, Suite I-9, Orlando FL 32811-6626. 407/648-2275.

Davis Brothers Construction
951 Broken Sound Pkwy NW, Boca Raton FL 33487-3528. 407/998-0500.

Davis Homes
1314 Neptune Dr, Boynton Beach FL 33426-8404. 407/731-1777.

Davis Nelson Construction
3483 Alt 19, Palm Harbor FL 34683-1414. 813/228-8616.

Evergreen Homes
114 S Hampton Dr, Jupiter FL 33458-8101. 407/575-1727.

Federal Construction Company
1355 Snell Isle Blvd NE, St Petersburg FL 33704-2426. 813/821-8000.

Glenn Wright Construction
112 Rose Dr, Ft Lauderdale FL 33316-1044. 954/761-3472.

GT McDonald Enterprises
7951 SW 6th St, Suite 112, Ft Lauderdale FL 33324-3211. 954/475-8332.

Halliburton Services
Hwy 30 E, Perry FL 32347. 904/584-5967.

International Steel Industries
P.O. Box 560489, Orlando FL 32856-0489. 407/649-9784.

JB Cochran & Sons Contractors
1149 NE 35th St, Ocala FL 34479-2840. 352/732-8589.

L&L Builders Of Vero Beach
9350 101st Ave, Vero Beach FL 32967-3165. 407/589-6600.

Landstar Homes
2533 Boggy Creek Rd, Kissimmee FL 34744-3806. 407/422-2252.

Martin K. Eby Construction Company
7285 Estapona Circle, Fern Park FL 32730-2356. 407/331-3100.

Morganti Florida
4362 Northlake Blvd, Palm Beach Gardens FL 33410-6275. 407/624-8104.

Olen Construction
4511 N Himes Ave, Tampa FL 33614-7074. 813/874-1992.

Paulsen Builders
560 Pinto Trail, Englewood FL 34223-3952. 941/475-3410.

Penco Construction Of Orlando
4305 Vineland Rd, Suite G14, Orlando FL 32811-7373. 407/426-7712.

Pulte Tampa Division
12973 N Telecom Pkwy, Tampa FL 33637-0907. 813/971-4801.

Rodeh
6610 W Linebaugh Ave, Tampa FL 33625-4955. 813/265-1200.

The Hardaway Company
6215 E Sligh Ave, Tampa FL 33617-9104. 813/623-5877.

TL Wingate
350 W Blue Heron Blvd, Riviera Beach FL 33404-4433. 407/845-5343.

Tropic Supply
1124 N G St, Lake Worth FL 33460-2166. 407/684-3997.

US Home Corp. North Florida Division
6860 Timber Pines Blvd, Spring Hill FL 34606-3641. 352/683-7634.

Venters Construction
3003 S Atlantic Ave, Daytona Beach FL 32118-6149. 904/788-5663.

Weddle Brothers Construction Co.
5533 Force Four Pkwy, Orlando FL 32839-2920. 407/851-1781.

WG Mills
4716 W Montgomery Ave, Tampa FL 33616-1042. 813/835-1605.

A-1 Builders
801 W State Road 436 #W, Altamonte Spring FL 32714-3054. 407/788-7866.

Acreage Aluminum & Screen
12860 56th Place N, West Palm Beach FL 33411-8536. 407/798-5489.

Sun Technical Systems
520 Clifton St, Orlando FL 32808-8160. 407/295-7486.

First General Service Sarasota
2052 Princeton St, Sarasota FL 34237-3424. 941/365-6661.

Inrecon
1471 SW 30th Ave, Boynton Beach FL 33426-9022. 407/428-7788.

Biltmore Construction Co.
1000 36th St, Vero Beach FL 32960-4862. 407/778-0082.

Calton Homes Of Florida
111 Madrona Dr, Eustis FL 32726-2021. 352/383-2355.

Harborlite Construction
9617 125th St, Seminole FL 34642-2048. 813/398-4552.

Mercedes Homes
7667 Greenboro Dr, Melbourne FL 32904-1669. 407/726-6511.

Timber Pines
2368 Fairskies Dr, Spring Hill FL 34606-7259. 352/446-4114.

Abbey Custom Builders
2060 Massachusetts Ave NE, St Petersburg FL 33703-3404. 813/526-0296.

Colony Homes
403 Lancers Dr, Winter Springs FL 32708-3337. 407/696-7795.

Donner Partners
2260 N Dixie Hwy, Boca Raton FL 33431-8003. 407/367-8618.

Holiday Builders Model Center
1431 Emerson Dr NE, Palm Bay FL 32907-3219. 407/729-6627.

Mercedes Home
947 Sabal Grove Dr, Rockledge FL 32955-4159. 407/633-6400.

Poinciana New Township
24 Doverplum Ave, Poinciana
FL 34759-3423. 407/933-
5000.

Pulte Home Corporation
7615 Savannah Ln, Tampa
FL 33637-6534. 813/989-
2994.

Robert Kraus Homes
1601 Tiverton St, Winter
Springs FL 32708-6125.
407/366-3901.

Auchter Company
1021 Oak St, Jacksonville FL
32204-3905. 904/355-
3536.

**Williams Company Of
Orlando**
2301 Silver Star Rd, Orlando
FL 32804-3309. 407/295-
2530.

OPERATIVE BUILDERS

Engle Homes
123 NW 13th St, Suite 300,
Boca Raton FL 33432-1624.
407/391-4012.

Palm House Condominiums
2707 Hill St, New Smyrna FL
32169-3484. 904/426-
1595.

**L Gaskins Construction
Company**
7016 Davis Creek Rd,
Jacksonville FL 32256-3026.
904/260-6000.

Mathews Corporation
3514 W Arch St, Tampa FL
33607-4902. 813/871-
3710.

Stellar Group
2900 Hartley Rd,
Jacksonville FL 32257-8221.
904/260-2900.

Elkins Constructors
4501 Beverly Ave,
Jacksonville FL 32210-2006.
904/384-6455.

Widell Associates
5850 Orange Dr, Ft
Lauderdale FL 33314-3618.
954/587-0520.

Robin Builders
4100 N Washington Blvd,
Sarasota FL 34234-4839.
941/351-9002.

ROAD CONSTRUCTION

Amick Construction Ltd.
401 Ferguson Dr, Orlando FL
32805-1009. 407/293-
6562.

Bergeron Land Development
2155 NW 184th Ave,

Pembroke Pines FL 33029-
3855. 954/431-1500.

JB Coxwell Contracting
6741 Lloyd Rd W,
Jacksonville FL 32254-1249.
904/786-1120.

Overstreet Paving Company
1390 Donegan Rd, Largo FL
34641-3007. 813/585-
4786.

Anderson Columbia Co.
N Highway 349, Old Town
FL 32680. 352/542-7942.

John Carlo
10589 Tradeport Dr, Orlando
FL 32827-5320. 407/850-
9423.

Pavex Corporation
2501 NW 48th St, Miami FL
33142-3612. 305/949-
3650.

OR Colan Associates
4050 SW 14th Ave, Ft
Lauderdale FL 33315-3516.
954/359-7662.

LG Defelice
1786 Dunlawton Ave,
Daytona Beach FL 32127-
4756. 904/322-9227.

**BRIDGE, TUNNEL, AND
HIGHWAY CONSTRUCTION**

Cappelti Brothers
P.O. Box 4944, Hialeah FL
33014-0944. 305/823-
9500.

Jamco
1630 Clare Ave, West Palm
Beach FL 33401-6914.
407/655-3634.

HEAVY CONSTRUCTION

**Advanced Technology
Systems**
7641 Currency Dr, Orlando
FL 32809-6924. 407/856-
8770.

**Belvedere Construction
Company**
P.O. Box 15107, Ft
Lauderdale FL 33318-5107.
954/683-5344.

Burnup & Sims
125 Commerce Way,
Sanford FL 32771-7206.
407/324-9299.

HC Connell
400 McCormack St,
Leesburg FL 34748-4733.
352/787-6732.

Voltelcon
1325 N Congress Ave, West
Palm Beach FL 33401-2005.
407/640-6291.

Ecology & Environment
1415 E Sunrise Blvd, Ft
Lauderdale FL 33304-2339.
954/779-2771.

Ecology & Environment
1203 Governors Square Blvd
4th, Tallahassee FL 32301-
2980. 904/877-1978.

**Contech Construction
Products**
1343 Main St, Sarasota FL
34236-5637. 941/366-
2102.

**PLUMBING, HEATING, AND
A/C**

Bared & Company
7841 NW 56th St, Miami FL
33166-3523. 305/592-
4710.

Farmer & Irwin Corp.
3300 Avenue K #10117,
Riviera Beach FL 33404-
2138. 407/842-5316.

Nagelbush
P.O. Box 32, Hollywood FL
33022. 954/748-7893.

**Zicaros Plumbing & Sewer
Service**
2960 NW Commerce Park
Dr, Boynton Beach FL
33426-8773. 407/547-
1600.

Roto-Rooter Service
2028 W 21st St,
Jacksonville FL 32209-4746.
904/350-9111.

Blue Heron Irrigation
114 Corporation Way,
Venice FL 34292-3525.
941/484-3485.

Bared & Company
406 Reo St, Suite 136,
Tampa FL 33609-1014.
813/287-5755.

Environmental Mechanical
5509 Interbay Blvd, Tampa
FL 33611-4734. 813/960-
3165.

Foster Wheeler
4141 Pine Forest Rd,
Cantonment FL 32533-
6545. 904/478-2558.

**WW Gay Mechanical
Contractors**
3220 39th St, Orlando FL
32839-8605. 407/841-
4670.

Air Flow Designs
5615 Saint Augustine Rd,
Jacksonville FL 32207-8029.
904/398-0831.

Carrier Of Florida
850 Maguire Rd, Ocoee FL

34761-2916. 407/656-
1014.

Pameco Corp.
3029 E Thomas St,
Inverness FL 34453-3222.
352/344-8883.

R&R Supply
6170 Idlewild St, Fort Myers
FL 33912-1216. 941/936-
9595.

The Waldinger Corporation
4801 George Rd, Suite 160,
Tampa FL 33634-6200.
813/884-0037.

**PAINTING AND PAPER
HANGING**

JL Manta
4825 Palm Tree Ct,
Windermere FL 34786-8805.
407/876-6559.

Service Painting Corp.
910 E 127th Ave, Tampa FL
33612-3548. 813/972-
1400.

Spartan Painting Company
1410 Atlanta Ave, Orlando
FL 32806-3917. 407/649-
0034.

**Surface Technologies
Corporation**
2275 Atlantic Blvd,
Jacksonville FL 32207-3567.
904/241-1501.

ELECTRICAL WORK

Amber Electric
P.O. Box 737, Ocoee FL
34761-0737. 407/656-
2335.

Ferran Engineering Group
530 Grand St, Orlando FL
32805-4795. 407/422-
3551.

Goldfield Corporation
100 Rialto Place, Suite 500,
Melbourne FL 32901-3073.
407/724-1700.

Paxson Electric Co.
P.O. Box 5769, Jacksonville
FL 32247-5769. 904/398-
1101.

Adkins Electric
10477 New Kings Rd,
Jacksonville FL 32219-2417.
904/765-1622.

Allstate Electric Contractors
7447 Salisbury Rd,
Jacksonville FL 32256-6909.
904/296-2700.

**Bay Area Electric &
Refrigeration**
4501 W Ohio Ave, Tampa FL
33614-7715. 813/879-
8685.

Dale C Rossman
2810 N 34th St, Tampa FL
33605-3120. 813/247-
5676.

Energy Electric
8112 N 9th St, Tampa FL
33604-3112. 813/932-
7146.

Enertech Electric Co.
1001 N US Highway 1,
Jupiter FL 33477-4482.
407/743-5537.

Regency Electric Company
1500 NW 49th St, Ft
Lauderdale FL 33309-3700.
954/771-2797.

Terry's Electric
600 Thacker Ave, Kissimmee
FL 34741. 407/846-4252.

Tri City Electrical Contractors
2118 Corporate Dr, Boynton
Beach FL 33426-6655.
407/369-8490.

**MASONRY, STONEWORK,
AND PLASTERING**

Pyramid Masonry Contractors
7649 Commerce Center Dr,
Orlando FL 32819-8923.
407/351-5700.

Passeri Marble
111 S Congress Ave, Delray
Beach FL 33445-4615.
407/243-3356.

Summitville Pompano
1330 S Andrews Ave, Ft
Lauderdale FL 33316-1838.
954/782-3522.

**CARPENTRY AND FLOOR
WORK**

Pete M. Bertolotti Carpenters
3856 Edgewood Ave, Fort
Myers FL 33916-1004.
941/694-9772.

P&P Cabinets
1621 Palm Ave, Fort Myers
FL 33916-1827. 941/337-
1884.

Florida Flooring Installers
10815 US Highway 19 N,
Clearwater FL 34624-7442.
813/571-1722.

**ROOFING, SIDING, AND
SHEET METAL WORK**

Dennies Contracting Co.
2501 Rockfill Rd, Fort Myers
FL 33916-4823. 941/337-
5515.

General Roofing Industries
1251 Seminola Blvd,
Casselberry FL 32707-3520.
407/695-1212.

Amre
8416 Laurel Fair Circle,
Tampa FL 33610-7360.
813/626-2040.

CONCRETE WORK

Capform
2141 Main St, Suite I,
Dunedin FL 34698-5660.
813/733-9200.

Jim's Concrete Of Brevard
1434 Norman St NE, Suite
2, Palm Bay FL 32907-2285.
407/725-3971.

Fosroc
3820 Gunn Hwy, Tampa FL
33624-4720. 813/265-
8784.

Ceco Corporation
7021 E Broadway Ave,
Tampa FL 33619-1830.
813/621-0025.

Hayward Baker
6850 Benjamin Rd, Tampa
FL 33634-4416. 813/884-
3441.

**MISC. SPECIAL TRADE
CONTRACTORS**

Hewitt Contracting Company
3839 County Road 48,
Okahumpka FL 34762-3202.
352/787-5651.

Lowell Dunn Company
P.O. Box 2577, Hialeah FL
33012-0577. 305/821-
8300.

Ryan Inc. Eastern Shop
1071 SW 30th Ave,
Deerfield Beach FL 33442-
8104. 954/570-9871.

Howard Fox Builders
17 Sycamore Circle, Ormond
Beach FL 32174-3411.
904/673-4881.

Pools By Andrews
440 E Altamonte Dr,
Altamonte Springs FL
32701-4602. 407/834-
7946.

**SPG Lock Scaffolding &
Equipment**
2110 US Highway 1 S,
Rockledge FL 32955-3727.
407/631-1852.

Spider Staging Corporation
225 Pineda St, Unit 159,
Longwood FL 32750-6452.
407/339-0387.

Sears Cabinet Refacing
6011 Benjamin Rd, Tampa
FL 33634-5173. 813/884-
4700.

AJ Johns
3225 Anniston Rd,

Jacksonville FL 32246-4605.
904/641-2055.

MOBILE HOMES

Fleetwood Homes Of Florida
70 S Bartow Ave,
Auburndale FL 33823.
941/967-7575.

Fleetwood Homes Of Florida
2433 Az Park Rd, Lakeland
FL 33801-6801. 941/665-
5526.

Jacobsen Manufacturing
901 4th St N, Safety Harbor
FL 34695-3404. 813/726-
1138.

Linman
Hwy 100 E, Lake City FL
32056. 904/755-6800.

Palm Harbor Homes
605 S Frontage Rd, Plant
City FL 33566-1901.
813/752-1368.

**Skyline Corporation Homette
Division**
P.O. Box 2648, Ocala FL
34478-2648. 352/629-
7571.

Skyline Homes
P.O. Box 2168, Ocala FL
34478-2168. 352/622-
5111.

CONSTRUCTION MATERIALS WHOLESALE

Alpha Tile Distributors
3868 Bengert St, Orlando FL
32808-4604. 407/293-
3993.

Gulf Coast Paving
3751 University Pkwy,
Sarasota FL 34243-4210.
941/355-4323.

Road Material Supply
14013 Tiny Morse Blvd,
Clermont FL 34711-8751.
407/877-3777.

Florida Rock Industries
1975 University Pkwy,
Sarasota FL 34243-2735.
941/351-9611.

Florida Rock Industries
1920 Dobbs Rd, St
Augustine FL 32086-5245.
904/829-6461.

**Coastal Construction
Products**
4901 W Grace St, Tampa FL
33607-3805. 813/289-
8949.

Gulfside Supply
P.O. Box 11475, Tampa FL
33680-1475. 813/247-
4560.

Ashley Aluminum
2853 Kirby Ave NE, Suite
12, Palm Bay FL 32905-
3429. 407/723-0051.

Dietrich Industries
721 Industrial Dr, Wildwood
FL 34785-4704. 904/748-
7200.

Eagle Supply
P.O. Box 75305, Tampa FL
33675-0305. 813/248-
4911.

Seven D Wholesale
1761 W Hillsboro Blvd,
Deerfield Beach FL 33442-
1530. 954/427-7798.

Glass Depot
4720 Distribution Dr, Tampa
FL 33605-5979. 813/247-
2156.

All Interior Supply
4000 N Orange Blossom
Trail, Orlando FL 32804-
2765. 407/291-8024.

PLUMBING, HEATING, AND A/C EQUIPMENT WHOLESALE

Crane Plumbing
1497 Forest Hill Blvd, West
Palm Beach FL 33406-6013.
407/641-5259.

**Raymond James &
Associates**
3385 Tamiami Trail N,
Naples FL 33940-4166.
941/649-0900.

Insituform Southeast
4302 E 10th Ave, Tampa FL
33605-4631. 813/247-
7139.

Symmons Industries
4075 LB McLeod Rd,
Orlando FL 32811-5661.
407/425-5004.

American Cast Iron
2910 Sammonds Rd, Plant
City FL 33567-4561.
813/752-6521.

**Davis Meter & Supply
Company**
3333 Old Winter Garden Rd,
Orlando FL 32805-1181.
407/297-6147.

**McWane Cast Iron Pipe
Company**
1730 NE 23rd Terrace, Ocala
FL 34470-4790. 352/351-
2111.

Gemaire Distributors
2151 W Hillsboro Blvd, Suite
400, Deerfield Beach FL
33442-1275. 954/426-
0814.

Bryant Of Florida
3071 N Orange Blossom
Trail, Orlando FL 32804-
3455. 407/299-0411.

R&R Supply Company
212 N Orange St, New
Smyrna FL 32168-7030.
904/428-3020.

R&R Supply Company
3602 W Spruce St, Tampa
FL 33607-2505. 813/877-
9421.

Sid Harvey Industries
4808 Trouble Creek Rd, New
Port Richey FL 34652-4827.
813/845-1234.

Tom Barrow Co.
6818 Benjamin Rd, Tampa
FL 33634-4416. 813/442-
3564.

Totaline
11301 47th St N,
Clearwater FL 34622-4963.
813/573-9433.

ENGINEERING SERVICES

**Applied Measurement
Systems**
1 Oakwood Blvd, Suite 180,
Hollywood FL 33020-1937.
954/925-0200.

CDI Marine Company
9487 Regency Square Blvd,
Jacksonville FL 32225-8126.
904/724-9700.

General Offshore Corp.
P.O. Box 21726, Ft
Lauderdale FL 33335-1726.
954/989-2188.

Kimley-Horn & Associates
4431 Embarcadero Dr, West
Palm Beach FL 33407-3297.
407/845-0665.

King Engineering Associates
24945 US Highway 19 N,
Clearwater FL 34623-3927.
813/791-1441.

King Engineering Associates
5010 W Kennedy Blvd, Suite
200, Tampa FL 33609-
1827. 813/886-0111.

Law Companies
4919 W Laurel St, Tampa FL
33607-3811. 813/289-
0750.

**National Inspection &
Consultants**
3949 Evans Ave, Suite 207,
Fort Myers FL 33901-9343.
941/939-4313.

Tilden Lobnitz & Cooper
1717 S Orange Ave, Orlando
FL 32806-2944. 407/841-
9050.

Ayres Associates
3901 Coconut Palm Dr, Suite 100, Tampa FL 33619-8362. 813/628-0742.

Brown & Caldwell
5130 Eisenhower Blvd, Suite 166, Tampa FL 33634-6312. 813/889-9515.

Florida Testing and Engineering Company
877 NW 61st St, Ft Lauderdale FL 33309-2037. 954/938-4400.

G&E Engineering
425 Cheney Hwy # R 50, Titusville FL 32780-7265. 407/269-9891.

GPS Technologies
5095 S Washington Ave, Suite 201, Titusville FL 32780-7333. 407/267-5253.

KBN Engineering & Applied Sciences
5405 W Cypress St, Tampa FL 33607-1772. 813/287-1717.

Tilden Lobnitz & Cooper
874 Dixon Blvd, Cocoa FL 32922-5809. 407/636-0274.

Tri-Duct Corporation
6399 142nd Ave N, Clearwater FL 34620-2760. 813/532-0696.

Dames & Moore
1211 Governors Square Bld, Tallahassee FL 32301-2959. 904/942-5617.

Greiner
25910 US Highway 19 N, Clearwater FL 34623-2049. 813/799-4424.

Martin Paving Company
9436 N US Highway 1, Sebastian FL 32958-6395. 407/562-8800.

Universal Engineering Sciences
381 Hibiscus Ave, Merritt Is FL 32953-4750. 407/452-1008.

Tom Arnold & Associates
536 E Tarpon Ave, Tarpon

Springs FL 34689-4344. 813/942-1657.

Kimley-Horn and Associates
9280 Bay Plaza Blvd, Tampa FL 33619-4453. 813/620-1460.

Ebon Research Systems
1173 Spring Centre South Blvd, Altamonte Springs FL 32714-1942. 407/682-1511.

Camp Dresser & McKee
1 Tampa City Center, Tampa FL 33602. 813/221-2833.

Camp Dresser & McKee
19345 US Highway 19 N, Clearwater FL 34624-3162. 813/530-9984.

Camp Dresser & McKee
201 Montgomery Ave, Sarasota FL 34243-1510. 941/351-7100.

D&Z
1819 Main St, Sarasota FL 34236-5951. 941/955-1388.

Frederic R Harris
4115 E Fowler Ave, Tampa FL 33617-2011. 813/971-4117.

Gannett Fleming
4902 Eisenhower Blvd, Tampa FL 33634-6310. 813/882-4366.

Greenhorne & O'Mara
1850 Forest Hill Blvd, West Palm Beach FL 33406-6064. 407/968-9222.

Gresham Smith & Partners
1660 Prudential Dr, Suite 201, Jacksonville FL 32207-8185. 904/346-3300.

ICF Kaiser Engineers
5486 Jet Port Industrial Blvd, Tampa FL 33634-5222. 813/884-5848.

JKH Mobility
3450 E Lake Rd, Palm Harbor FL 34685-2411. 813/787-6818.

Post Buckley Schuh & Jernigan
1560 Orange Ave, Suite

700, Winter Park FL 32789-5542. 407/647-7275.

SEA
6101 Johns Rd, Suite 2, Tampa FL 33634-4425. 813/885-7477.

Stone & Webster Engineering Corp.
150 S Pine Island Rd, Plantation FL 33324-2669. 954/476-1800.

Walker Park Consultants Engineers
4902 Eisenhower Blvd, Tampa FL 33634-6310. 813/888-5800.

Wilbur Smith Associate
2100 Centerville Rd, Tallahassee FL 32308-4314. 904/385-2229.

Wilbur Smith Associates
3535 Lawton Rd, Suite 100, Orlando FL 32803-3729. 407/896-5851.

ARCHITECTURAL SERVICES

Candela Spillis & Partners
200 S Orange Ave, Orlando FL 32801-3410. 407/422-4220.

Gee & Jenson Architects
1900 Summit Tower Blvd, Orlando FL 32810-5939. 407/660-1660.

Candela Spillis & Partners
800 Douglas Entrance North Tower, Coral Gables FL 33134. 305/444-4691.

The Ritchie Organization
3050 Bee Ridge Rd, Sarasota FL 34239-7140. 941/923-4911.

SURVEYING SERVICES

Bowyer Singleton & Associates
3700 N Harbor City Blvd, Melbourne FL 32935-5756. 407/253-2522.

Devino & Associates
3505 US Highway 1 S, St Augustine FL 32086-6492. 904/797-1867.

For more information on career opportunities in architecture, construction and engineering:

Associations

AMERICAN ASSOCIATION OF COST ENGINEERS
209 Prairie Avenue, Suite 100, Morgantown WV 26505-1550. 304/296-8444. 800/858-2678. Toll-free number

provides information on scholarships for undergraduates.

AMERICAN CONSULTING ENGINEERS COUNCIL
1015 15th Street NW, Suite 802, Washington DC 20005. 202/347-7474.

AMERICAN INSTITUTE OF ARCHITECTS
1735 New York Avenue NW, Washington
DC 20006. 202/626-7300. 800/365-2724.
Contact toll-free number for brochures.

AMERICAN SOCIETY FOR ENGINEERING EDUCATION
1818 N Street NW, Suite 600, Washington
DC 20036. 202/331-3500. Promotes
engineering education. Publishes monthly
magazines.

AMERICAN SOCIETY OF CIVIL ENGINEERS
345 East 47th Street, New York NY
10017. 212/705-7496.

AMERICAN SOCIETY OF HEATING, REFRIGERATING AND AIR CONDITIONING ENGINEERS
1791 Tullie Circle NE, Atlanta GA 30329.
404/636-8400. Non-profit. Publishes
several books.

AMERICAN SOCIETY OF LANDSCAPE ARCHITECTS
4401 Connecticut Avenue NW, Fifth Floor,
Washington DC 20008. 202/686-2752.

AMERICAN SOCIETY OF MECHANICAL ENGINEERS
345 East 47th Street, New York NY
10017. 212/705-7722.

AMERICAN SOCIETY OF NAVAL ENGINEERS
1452 Duke Street, Alexandria VA 22314.
703/836-6727.

AMERICAN SOCIETY OF PLUMBING ENGINEERS
3617 Thousand Oaks Boulevard, Suite 210,
Westlake CA 91362-3694. 805/495-7120.
Provides technical and educational
information.

AMERICAN SOCIETY OF SAFETY ENGINEERS
1800 East Oakton Street, Des Plaines IL
60018-2187. 708/692-4121. Jobline
service available at ext. 243.

ASSOCIATED BUILDERS AND CONTRACTORS
1300 North 17th Street, Rosslyn VA
22209. 703/812-2000.

ASSOCIATED GENERAL CONTRACTORS OF AMERICA, INC.
1957 E Street NW, Washington DC 20006.
202/393-2040.

ILLUMINATING ENGINEERING SOCIETY OF NORTH AMERICA
120 Wall Street, 17th Floor, New York NY
10005. 212/248-5000.

JUNIOR ENGINEERING TECHNICAL SOCIETY
1420 King Street, Suite 405, Alexandria VA
22314. 703/548-JETS.

NATIONAL ACTION COUNCIL FOR MINORITIES IN ENGINEERING
3 West 35th Street, New York NY 10001.
212/279-2626. Offers scholarship
programs for students.

NATIONAL ASSOCIATION OF HOME BUILDERS
1201 15th Street NW, Washington DC
20005. 202/822-0200.

NATIONAL ASSOCIATION OF MINORITY ENGINEERING
435 North Michigan Avenue, Suite 1115,
Chicago IL 60611. 312/670-2095, ext.
744.

NATIONAL SOCIETY OF BLACK ENGINEERS
1454 Duke Street, Alexandria VA 22314.
703/549-2207. A non-profit organization
run by college students. Offers scholarships,
editorials, and magazines.

NATIONAL SOCIETY OF PROFESSIONAL ENGINEERS
1420 King Street, Alexandria VA 22314-
2794. 703/684-2800. 703/684-2830. This
number provides scholarship information for
students.

SOCIETY OF FIRE PROTECTION ENGINEERS
1 Liberty Square, Boston MA 02109-4825.
617/482-0686.

UNITED ENGINEERING TRUSTEES
345 East 47th Street, New York NY
10017. 212/705-7000.

Directories

DIRECTORY OF ENGINEERING SOCIETIES
American Association of Engineering
Societies, 1111 19th Street NW, Suite
608, Washington DC 20036. 202/296-
2237. $185.00. Lists other engineering
association members, publications, and
convention exhibits.

DIRECTORY OF ENGINEERS IN PRIVATE PRACTICE
National Society of Professional Engineers,
1420 King Street, Alexandria VA 22314.
703/684-2800. $50.00. Lists members and
companies.

ENCYCLOPEDIA OF PHYSICAL SCIENCES & ENGINEERING INFORMATION SOURCES
Gale Research Inc., 835 Penobscot Building,
Detroit MI 48226. 313/961-2242.
$155.00. Offers online databases, several
topics on physical engineering, and different
ways to obtain information on physical
engineering.

Magazines

THE CAREER ENGINEER
National Society of Black Engineers, 1454
Duke Street, Alexandria VA 22314.
703/549-2207.

CAREERS AND THE ENGINEER
Adams Media Corporation, 260 Center
Street, Holbrook MA 02343. 617/767-
8100.

CHEMICAL & ENGINEERING NEWS
American Chemical Society 1155 16th
Street NW, Washington DC 20036.
202/872-4600.

COMPUTER-AIDED ENGINEERING
Penton Publishing, 1100 Superior Avenue,
Cleveland OH 44114. 216/696-7000.

EDN CAREER NEWS
Cahners Publishing Company, 275
Washington Street, Newton MA 02158.
617/964-3030.

ENGINEERING TIMES
National Society of Professional Engineers,
1420 King Street, Alexandria VA 22314.
703/684-2800.

NAVAL ENGINEERS JOURNAL
American Society of Naval Engineers, 1452
Duke Street, Alexandria VA 22314.
703/836-6727. Subscription: $48.

ARTS AND ENTERTAINMENT/RECREATION

Job opportunities in the entertainment and recreation industries are projected to increase 39 percent through the year 2005, faster than the average for all industries. Higher incomes, growth of leisure time, and increasing awareness of the health benefits of physical fitness will effect employment growth.

The market for leisure activities is changing. In the past, amusement and recreation services catered to those in their 20s and 30s who had steadily growing incomes. Now that those baby boomers have grown up, companies are targeting adults between 50 and 75 years old.

The performing arts sector will increase with growing population and rising interest in the arts. Producing, acting, directing, and entertaining jobs will grow much faster than average through 2005. Even so, competition will be as intense as ever.

Amusement and theme parks should experience steady growth and offer many seasonal and part-time job opportunities. Virtually all jobs in the industry should experience job growth, with the exception of communications equipment operators, and typists and word processors. The decline in these jobs will result from new technology that will allow fewer workers to do more work.

BUSCH GARDENS
P.O. Box 9158, Tampa FL 33674. 813/987-5171. **Contact:** Personnel Department. **Description:** An amusement park, offering a petting zoo and tours of the Busch brewery among its many recreational activities and facilities.

CASINO AMERICA INC.
2200 Corporate Boulevard, Suite 310, Boca Raton FL 33434-4150. 407/995-6660. **Contact:** Human Resources. **Description:** Casino America Inc. develops, owns, and operates riverboat, dockside casinos, and related facilities. The company also provides riverboat and dockside casino consulting and management services. **Other U.S. locations:** Biloxi MS.

DISCOVERY ZONE FUN CENTER
205 University Park Drive, Winter Park FL 32792-4435. 407/671-4386. **Contact:** Store Manager. **Description:** An indoor fitness center for small children and their families. Discovery Zone's Fun Center offers activities for children accompanied by an adult including tubes, tunnels, turbo slides, and obstacle courses. The facility also houses a private party room for birthdays and offers various packages including the 'megablast' and other theme parties. The center provides special events on a daily and monthly basis and organizes group trips. **Corporate headquarters location:** Chicago IL. **Other U.S. locations:** Dallas TX.

FLORIDA CYPRESS GARDENS, INC.
P.O. Box 1, Cypress Gardens FL 33884. 941/324-2111. **Contact:** Human Resources Manager. **Description:** A theme park.

INTERNATIONAL SPEEDWAY CORPORATION
P.O. Box 2801, Daytona Beach FL 32120-2801. 904/254-2700. **Contact:** Linda Marvel, Director of Personnel. **Description:** International Speedway Corporation and its subsidiaries are predominantly sports-oriented, producing and conducting motor sport

activities in the form of stock car, sports car, motorcycle, and go-cart racing events for spectators at six locations, including two in Daytona Beach, Florida. The company also conducts the food, beverage, and souvenir operations at most of these facilities through its wholly-owned subsidiary, Amercrown Service Corporation, and produces and syndicates race and race-related radio broadcasts through MRN Radio. Among the major events conducted by the company are late-model stock car races sanctioned by the National Association for Stock Car Auto Racing, Inc. (NASCAR). **Benefits:** Stock Option. **Other U.S. locations:** Talladega County AL; Pima County AZ; Watkins Glen NY; Darlington SC. **Number of employees nationwide:** 4,620.

MODERN TALKING PICTURE SERVICE, INC.
5000 Park Street North, St. Petersburg FL 33709. 813/541-7571. **Contact:** Personnel. **Description:** Distributes sound motion pictures sponsored by companies, trade associations, and governments.

PINE FOREST NUTRITION CENTER
3856 Grant Road, Jacksonville FL 32207. 904/398-2096. **Contact:** Human Resources. **Description:** An activity center for senior citizens offering various recreational and exercise programs.

SEA WORLD OF FLORIDA
7007 Sea World Drive, Orlando FL 32821. 407/351-3600. **Recorded Jobline:** 407/363-2612. **Contact:** Professional Staffing Department. **Description:** A marine-life park located in central Florida.

TILT
3201 East Colonial Drive, Orlando FL 40789-4410. 407/894-4190. **Contact:** Human Resources. **Description:** An arcade amusement center. **Other U.S. locations:** Arlington VA. **Number of employees at this location:** 250.

WALT DISNEY WORLD
Casting Center, 1515 Buena Vista Drive, Lake Buena Vista FL 32830-1000. 407/824-2222. **Recorded Jobline:** 407/345-5701. **Contact:** Professional Staffing Department. **Description:** Administrative offices for the theme park. **Corporate headquarters location:** Los Angeles CA.

Note: Because addresses and telephone numbers of smaller companies change rapidly, we recommend you call each company to verify the information below before inquiring about job opportunities. Mass mailings are not recommended.

Additional employers with over 250 employees:

AMUSEMENT AND RECREATION SERVICES

Fun-N-Games
8001 S Orange Blossom Trl, Orlando FL 32809-7654. 407/857-5887.

Goldenrod Bingo
3020 N Goldenrod Rd, Winter Park FL 32792-8708. 407/657-5393.

International Game Room
818 Formosa Ave, Winter Park FL 32789-4527. 407/644-0457.

Jai-Alai Fronton Of Tampa
5125 S Dale Mabry Hwy, Tampa FL 33611-3505. 813/831-1411.

Orlando Kartworld
5370 International Dr, Orlando FL 32819-9427. 407/352-7879.

Orlando Scottish Highland Games
8829 Aspen Ave, Orlando FL 32817. 407/672-1682.

Paintball City
7215 Rose Ave, Orlando FL 32810. 407/294-2627.

Q-Zar At Fashion Village
3855 E Colonial Dr, Orlando FL 32803. 407/895-8297.

Radical Sensation Adventures
5767 Major Blvd, Orlando FL 32819. 407/352-4559.

Ripley's Believe It or Not
8201 International Dr, Orlando FL 32819-9326. 407/363-4418.

Scenic Boat Tour
312 E Morse Blvd, Winter Park FL 32789-3823. 407/644-4056.

Top Gun Entertainment
3851 E Colonial Dr, Orlando FL 32803-5254. 407/896-0212.

Tourist Information Center
7232 Sand Lake Rd, Orlando FL 32819. 407/345-0013.

Manatees
835 Bennett Rd, Orlando FL 32803. 407/896-6033.

Wet N Wild
6200 International Dr, Orlando FL 32819-8290. 407/351-1800.

Additional employers with under 250 employees:

TRAILER PARKS AND CAMPSITES

Arbor Terrace Travel Trailer Park
405 57th Ave W, Bradenton FL 34207-3848. 941/755-6494.

Heritage Plantation
3550 NE Hwy 70, Arcadia FL 33821. 941/494-1744.

Kissimmee Orlando KOA
4771 W Bronson Memorial Hwy, Kissimmee FL 34746. 407/396-2400.

Winter Paradise RV Park
16108 US Highway 19, Hudson FL 34667-4303. 813/868-2285.

Lake Manatee State Recreation Area
20007 E State Road 64, Bradenton FL 34202-9431. 941/741-3028.

Three Flags RV Resort
1755 E State Road 44, Wildwood FL 34785-8410. 904/748-3870.

SPORTING AND RECREATIONAL CAMPS

Florida Sheriffs Youth Camp
P.O. Box 1000, Barberville FL 32105-1000. 904/749-9999.

MOTION PICTURE AND VIDEO TAPE PRODUCTION AND DISTRIBUTION

Arrowhead Productions International
100 Sunport Ln, Orlando FL 32809-7871. 407/826-2350.

Indigo Productions
9829 Terrace Trail Ln, Tampa FL 33637-5058. 813/989-8667.

F&B Productions
309 Oakwood Ct, Lake Mary FL 32746-5909. 407/330-2900.

Ceco International Corp.
7625 Currency Dr, Orlando FL 32809-6924. 407/859-4017.

Time Warner Cable
3767 All American Blvd, Orlando FL 32810-4728. 407/291-2500.

MOTION PICTURE THEATERS

Galleria 4 GCC Theatres
2630 E Sunrise Blvd, Ft Lauderdale FL 33304-3206. 954/565-1883.

Southchase Cinema 7
12441 S Orange Blossom Trail, Orlando FL 32837-6508. 407/856-9409.

THEATRICAL PRODUCERS AND SERVICES

Tod Booth Production
11990 Beach Blvd, Jacksonville FL 32246. 904/642-9307.

PGA Tour Productions
8160 Baymeadows Way W, Jacksonville FL 32256-7441. 904/737-7001.

Discount Ticket Shack
5730 Bronson Memorial Highway, Kissimmee FL 34746-4715. 407/396-8826.

Florida VIP
3490 Polynesian Isle Blvd, Kissimmee FL 34746-4655. 407/397-1800.

Gateway Marketing Group
5075 Bronson Memorial Highway, Kissimmee FL 34746-5345. 407/397-4998.

Linda Rigo Marketing
4519 Bronson Memorial Highway, Kissimmee FL 34746-5303. 407/397-0844.

New Age Marketing
5001 Bronson Memorial Highway, Kissimmee FL 34746-5344. 407/397-7664.

Ticketmaster
1511 N Westshore Blvd, Tampa FL 33607-4523. 813/287-8844.

Ticketmaster
225 E Robinson St, Suite 355, Orlando FL 32801-4326. 407/839-0900.

U All Enjoy
4900 W Irlo Bronson Memorial H, Kissimmee FL 34746-5306. 407/397-4933.

ENTERTAINERS AND ENTERTAINMENT GROUPS

Emigdio Ortiz Y Su Orquesta
2100 Coral Way, Coral Gables FL 33145. 305/859-8066.

The New World Symphony
541 Lincoln Rd, Miami Beach FL 33139-2913. 305/673-3330.

Emery Deutsch Orchestras
1200 West Ave, Miami Beach FL 33139-4311. 305/672-6511.

The Florida Orchestra
1211 N Westshore Blvd, Tampa FL 33607-4600. 813/447-3975.

Celebrity Circle
2001 Pan Ann Circle, Tampa FL 33607. 813/229-9401.

M&M Promotions
4023 N Armenia Ave, Tampa FL 33607-1017. 813/875-9905.

PROFESSIONAL SPORTS CLUBS AND PROMOTERS

Houston-Osceola Astros
1000 Bill Beck Blvd, Kissimmee FL 34744-4401. 407/933-5500.

Orlando Magic Basketball Team
1 Magic Place, Orlando FL 32801-1116. 407/649-3200.

Tampa Bay Buccaneers
4201 N Dale Mabry Hwy, Tampa FL 33607-6103. 813/879-2827.

Advanced Promotion Concepts
2802 N Howard Ave, Tampa FL 33607-2623. 813/254-6600.

Neptune Racing & Promotion
2640 Algonquin Dr, Melbourne FL 32935-8806. 407/724-0540.

RACING AND TRACK OPERATION

Flagler Greyhound Track
401 NW 38th Ct, Miami FL 33126-5638. 305/649-3000.

Naples Ft Myers Greyhound
10601 Bonita Beach Rd, Bonita Springs FL 33923-5620. 941/992-2411.

PHYSICAL FITNESS FACILITIES

Bally's Health Clubs
4850 Lawing Ln, Orlando FL

32811-3657. 407/297-8400.

GOLF COURSES

Emerald Bay Pro Shop
40001 Emerald Coast Pkwy, Destin FL 32541-3885. 904/837-5197.

Emerald Hills Golf & Country
4100 N Hills Dr, Hollywood FL 33021-2400. 407/625-5767.

Kings Point Golf Courses
7000 W Atlantic Ave, Delray Beach FL 33446-1699. 407/499-0140.

Poinciana Golf & Racquet Resort
500 Cypress Pkwy, Kissimmee FL 34759-3310. 407/933-7202.

Sandestin Golf Resort
E Hwy 98, Santa Rosa Beach FL 32459. 904/267-8144.

Special Tee Golf
614 E Altamonte Dr, Altamonte Springs FL 32701-4803. 407/834-1000.

The Links Golf Club
8706 Pavilion Dr, Hudson FL 34667-6500. 813/868-1091.

AMUSEMENT PARKS

Recreation Center Playground
6039 Hanley Rd, Tampa FL

33634-4913. 813/554-5002.

Party Land
2622 E Fowler Ave, Tampa FL 33612. 813/972-4373.

MEMBERSHIP SPORTS AND RECREATION CLUBS

Plantation Golf-Country Club
500 Rockley Blvd, South Venice FL 34293-4300. 941/493-0047.

Tournament Players Club
110 TPC Blvd, Ponte Vedra FL 32082. 904/273-3230.

Admirals Cove
200 Admirals Cove Blvd, Jupiter FL 33477-4046. 407/744-1700.

Coral Ridge Country Club
3801 Bayview Dr, Ft Lauderdale FL 33308-5800. 954/564-1271.

Hideaway Beach Association
403 Gate House Ct, Marco Island FL 33937-1901. 941/642-6301.

Lost Tree Golf Course
Lost Tree Village, No Palm Beach FL 33408. 407/626-2047.

AMUSEMENT AND RECREATION SERVICES

Grand Cypress Equestrian Center
1 Equestrian Dr, Orlando FL 32836. 407/239-1938.

Sportservice Corporation
12400 SW 152nd St, Miami FL 33177-1402. 305/233-8389.

THI Florida
5770 W Irlo Bronson Memorial Hwy, Kissimmee FL 34746-4732. 407/396-4888.

Pavo Real Gallery
495 Town Center, Boca Raton FL 33431-7272. 407/392-5521.

Wentworth Galleries
1118 NW 159th Dr, Miami FL 33169-5808. 305/624-0715.

Bonaventure Town Center Club
16690 Saddle Club Rd, Ft Lauderdale FL 33326-1808. 954/384-8330.

MUSEUMS AND ART GALLERIES

Haas Museum St Petersburg Historical Society
3511 2nd Ave S, St Petersburg FL 33711-1309. 813/327-1437.

BOTANICAL AND ZOOLOGICAL GARDENS

Lowry Park Zoo
7530 North Blvd, Tampa FL 33604-4756. 813/935-8552.

For more information on career opportunities in arts, entertainment and recreation:

Associations

ACTOR'S EQUITY ASSOCIATION
165 West 46th Street, New York NY 10036. 212/869-8530.

AMERICAN ALLIANCE FOR THEATRE AND EDUCATION
Division of Performing Arts, Virginia Tech, Blacksburg VA 24061-0141. 703/231-5335.

AMERICAN ASSOCIATION OF MUSEUMS
1225 I Street NW, Suite 200, Washington DC 20005. 202/289-1818.

AMERICAN COUNCIL FOR THE ARTS
1 East 53rd Street, New York NY 10022. 212/223-2787.

AMERICAN CRAFTS COUNCIL
72 Spring Street, New York NY 10012. 212/274-0630.

AMERICAN DANCE GUILD
31 West 21st Street, New York NY 10010. 212/627-3790.

AMERICAN FEDERATION OF MUSICIANS
1501 Broadway, Suite 600, New York NY 10036. 212/869-1330.

AMERICAN FEDERATION OF TELEVISION AND RADIO ARTISTS
260 Madison Avenue, New York NY 10016. 212/532-0800. Membership required.

AMERICAN FILM INSTITUTE
John F. Kennedy Center for the Performing Arts, Washington DC 20566. 202/828-4000.

AMERICAN GUILD OF MUSICAL ARTISTS
1727 Broadway, New York NY 10019. 212/265-3687.

AMERICAN MUSIC CENTER
30 West 26th Street, Suite 1001, New York NY 10010. 212/366-5260.

AMERICAN SOCIETY OF COMPOSERS, AUTHORS, AND PUBLISHERS (ASCAP)
1 Lincoln Plaza, New York NY 10023. 212/595-3050.

AMERICAN SYMPHONY ORCHESTRA LEAGUE
1156 15th Street NW, Suite 4800, Washington DC 20005. 202/628-0099.

AMERICAN ZOO AND AQUARIUM ASSOCIATION
Oglebay Park, Wheeling WV 26003. 304/242-2160. Produces a monthly newspaper.

ASSOCIATION OF INDEPENDENT VIDEO AND FILMMAKERS
625 Broadway, 9th Floor, New York NY 10012. 212/473-3400.

NATIONAL ARTISTS' EQUITY ASSOCIATION
P.O. Box 28068, Central Station, Washington DC 20038-8068. 202/628-9633.

NATIONAL DANCE ASSOCIATION
1900 Association Drive, Reston VA 22091. 703/476-3436.

NATIONAL ENDOWMENT FOR THE ARTS
1100 Pennsylvania Avenue NW, Washington DC 20506. 202/682-5400.

NATIONAL ORGANIZATION FOR HUMAN SERVICE EDUCATION
Brookdale Community College, Newman Springs Road, Lyncroft NJ 07738. 908/842-1900, ext. 546.

NATIONAL RECREATION AND PARK ASSOCIATION
2775 South Quincy Street, Suite 300, Arlington VA 22206. 703/820-4940.

PRODUCERS GUILD OF AMERICA
400 South Beverly Drive, Suite 211, Beverly Hills CA 90212. 310/557-0807.

SCREEN ACTORS GUILD
5757 Wilshire Boulevard, Los Angeles CA 90036-3600. 213/954-1600.

THEATRE COMMUNICATIONS GROUP
355 Lexington Avenue, New York NY 10017. 212/697-5230.

WOMEN'S CAUCUS FOR ART
Moore College of Art, 20th & The Parkway, Philadelphia PA 19103. 215/854-0922.

Directories

ARTIST'S MARKET
Writer's Digest Books, 1507 Dana Avenue, Cincinnati OH 45207. 513/531-2222.

CREATIVE BLACK BOOK
866 3rd Avenue, 3rd Floor, New York NY 10022. 212/254-1330.

PLAYERS GUIDE
165 West 46th Street, New York NY 10036. 212/869-3570.

ROSS REPORTS TELEVISION
Television Index, Inc., 40-29 27th Street, Long Island City NY 11101. 718/937-3990.

Magazines

AMERICAN ARTIST
One Astor Place, 1515 Broadway, New York NY 10036. 212/764-7300. 800/346-0085, ext. 477.

AMERICAN CINEMATOGRAPHER
American Society of Cinematographers, P.O. Box 2230, Hollywood CA 90028. 213/969-4333.

ART BUSINESS NEWS
Myers Publishing Company, 19 Old Kings Highway South, Darien CT 06820. 203/656-3402.

ART DIRECTION
10 East 39th Street, 6th Floor, New York NY 10016. 212/889-6500.

ARTFORUM
65 Bleecker Street, New York NY 10012. 212/475-4000.

ARTWEEK
12 South First Street, Suite 520, San Jose CA 95113. 408/279-2293.

AVISO
American Association of Museums, 1225 I Street NW, Suite 200, Washington DC 20005. 202/289-1818.

BACK STAGE
1515 Broadway, New York NY 10036. 212/764-7300.

BILLBOARD
Billboard Publications, Inc., 1515 Broadway, New York NY 10036. 212/764-7300.

CASHBOX
157 West 57th Street, Suite 503, New York NY 10019. 212/245-4224.

CRAFTS REPORT
300 Water Street, Wilmington DE 19801. 302/656-2209.

DRAMA-LOGUE
P.O. Box 38771, Los Angeles CA 90038. 213/464-5079.

HOLLYWOOD REPORTER
5055 Wilshire Boulevard, 6th Floor, Los Angeles CA 90036. 213/525-2000.

VARIETY
249 West 17th Street, New York NY 10011. 212/779-1100. 800/323-4345.

WOMEN ARTIST NEWS
300 Riverside Drive, New York NY 10025. 212/666-6990.

AUTOMOTIVE

 *The automotive industry saw a big turnaround in 1994, with the sales of new cars and trucks reaching a six-year high. The good news is expected to continue through 1995 and 1996 -- Business Week predicted a 4 percent gain in U.S. car sales in 1995. In fact, potential sales seemed to be limited only by the ability of car companies to produce enough to meet market demand. On the downside, increasing interest rates and rising steel prices are putting pressure on the Big Three automakers to cut costs and boost productivity, so that job increases won't be quite as dramatic as the increases in sales. According to Ronald Glantz, an analyst at Dean Witter, the overall effect on the automotive industry should be a boost in industry profits from $14.6 billion in 1994 to $19.7 billion in 1995 and $26.8 billion in 1996.*

BREED TECHNOLOGIES, INC.
P.O. Box 33050, 5300 Old Tampa Highway, Lakeland FL 33807-3050. 941/284-6000. **Contact:** Human Resources. **Description:** A designer, developer, manufacturer, and seller of crash sensors and automotive airbag systems. Breed Technologies estimates that in the 1994 model year magnetically-biased electromechanical ball-in-tube sensors supplied by the company were used in approximately two-thirds of all airbag-equipped vehicles produced in the United States. Products based on the company's technology are also installed in cars produced and sold in Japan and Europe. Breed Technologies also sells all-mechanical airbag systems (AMS systems) that contain all necessary airbag components in a self-contained unit installed in the steering wheel. Breed has expanded its product line to include driver- and passenger-side electrically initiated airbag inflators, electronic sensing diagnostic modules, and electrically initiated airbag systems. **Common positions include:** Buyer; Chemical Engineer; Chemist; Computer Systems Analyst; Designer; Draftsperson; Electrical/Electronics Engineer; Financial Analyst; Mechanical Engineer. **Educational backgrounds include:** Business Administration; Chemistry; Computer Science; Engineering. **Benefits:** 401K; Dental Insurance; Disability Coverage; EAP; Life Insurance; Medical Insurance; Stock Option; Tuition Assistance. **Corporate headquarters location:** This Location. **Other U.S. locations:** Southfield MI; Boonton NJ; Dayton OH; Brownsville TX. **Operations at this facility include:** Administration; Manufacturing; Research and Development. **Listed on:** New York Stock Exchange.

EMERGENCY ONE INC.
P.O. Box 2710, Ocala FL 34478-2710. 352/237-1122. **Fax:** 352/237-1151. **Contact:** Dan D. Wombold, Vice President of Human Resources. **Description:** Engaged in the manufacturing and sale of fire trucks and emergency response vehicles. **Common positions include:** Accountant/Auditor; Administrative Services Manager; Automotive Mechanic/Body Repairer; Blue-Collar Worker Supervisor; Budget Analyst; Buyer; Ceramics Engineer; Computer Programmer; Computer Systems Analyst; Cost Estimator; Customer Service Representative; Designer; Draftsperson; Education Administrator; Electrical/Electronics Engineer; Electrician; Emergency Medical Technician; Financial Analyst; General Manager; Health Services Manager; Human Resources Specialist; Industrial Engineer; Industrial Production Manager; Licensed Practical Nurse; Materials Engineer; Mechanical Engineer; Metallurgical Engineer; Operations/Production Manager; Purchasing Agent and Manager; Quality Control Supervisor; Registered Nurse; Services Sales Representative; Technical Writer/Editor; Transportation/Traffic Specialist. **Educational backgrounds include:** Accounting; Business Administration; Computer Science; Engineering; Liberal Arts; Marketing. **Benefits:** 401K; Dental Insurance; Disability Coverage; Employee Discounts; Life Insurance; Medical Insurance; Profit Sharing; Savings Plan; Tuition Assistance. **Corporate headquarters location:** Oak Brook IL. **Parent company:** Federal Signal Corporation. **Operations at this facility include:** Administration; Manufacturing; Research and Development; Sales; Service. **Listed on:** New York Stock Exchange. **Number of employees at this location:** 1,300.

EXCEL INDUSTRIES
9444 Florida Mining Boulevard, Jacksonville FL 32257. 904/268-8300. **Contact:** Human Resources. **Description:** Manufactures automobile windows.

HI-STAT MANUFACTURING COMPANY
7290 26th Court East, Sarasota FL 34243. 941/355-9761. **Contact:** Human Resources. **Description:** Manufactures automobile sensors.

MARK III INDUSTRIES INC.
P.O. Box 2525, Ocala FL 34478-2525. 352/732-5878. **Contact:** Human Resources. **Description:** A van conversion company.

S&H FABRICATING & ENGINEERING
2660 Jewett Lane, Sanford FL 32771. 407/323-2780. **Contact:** Human Resources. **Description:** Manufactures air conditioning hoses for vehicles.

WHEELED COACH INDUSTRIES, INC.
P.O. Box 677339, Orlando FL 32867-7339. 407/677-7777. **Fax:** 407/677-8948. **Contact:** Richard Magill, Manager of Human Resources. **Description:** Wheeled Coach is one of the world's largest manufacturer of ambulances. The company also manufactures buses and other specialty vehicles. **Common positions include:** Accountant/Auditor; Automotive Mechanic/Body Repairer; Blue-Collar Worker Supervisor; Buyer; Computer Programmer; Computer Systems Analyst; Designer; Draftsperson; Electrical/Electronics Engineer; Emergency Medical Technician; Mechanical Engineer; Painter; Quality Control Supervisor; Welder. **Educational backgrounds include:** Accounting; Business Administration; Computer Science; Engineering; Marketing. **Benefits:** 401K; Dental Insurance; Disability Coverage; Life Insurance; Medical Insurance; Tuition Assistance. **Corporate headquarters location:** Hutchinson KS. **Other U.S. locations:** KS; TX. **Parent company:** Collins Industries. **Operations at this facility include:** Administration; Divisional Headquarters; Manufacturing; Sales; Service. **Listed on:** NASDAQ. **Number of employees at this location:** 450. **Number of employees nationwide:** 1,100.

Note: Because addresses and telephone numbers of smaller companies change rapidly, we recommend you call each company to verify the information below before inquiring about job opportunities. Mass mailings are not recommended.

Additional employers with under 250 employees:

AUTOMOTIVE STAMPINGS

Caravan International
2504 Countryside Pines Dr, Clearwater FL 34621-4921. 813/796-2202.

INDUSTRIAL VEHICLES AND MOVING EQUIPMENT

Hi-Way
4190 Ben Durrance Rd, Bartow FL 33830-8432. 941/533-1118.

MOTOR VEHICLES AND EQUIPMENT

Combat Vehicle Operations
550 Cidco Rd, Cocoa FL 32926-5810. 407/636-1791.

National Atlantic Ambulance
230 N Ortman Dr, Orlando FL 32805-1941. 407/299-0064.

AlliedSignal Brake Systems Division
1006 Arthur Dr, Lynn Haven FL 32444-1683. 904/265-6993.

Escod Industries
2800 Alt 27 N, Lake Wales FL 33853. 941/676-9416.

Filko-Cobra
2050 47th Terrace E, Bradenton FL 34203-3701. 941/746-6263.

Florida Detroit Diesel Allison
2277 NW 14th St, Miami FL 33125-2101. 305/638-5300.

Pylon Manufacturing
1341 W Newport Center Dr, Deerfield Beach FL 33442-7734. 954/428-7373.

Rally Manufacturing
5255 NW 159th St, Hialeah FL 33014-6217. 305/628-2886.

RT Industries
2001 NW 15th Ave, Pompano Beach FL 33069-1432. 954/970-4518.

Eager Beaver
4425 US Highway 27 S, Lake Wales FL 33853-8788. 941/638-1421.

TRAVEL TRAILERS AND CAMPERS

Chariot Eagle
931 NW 37th Ave, Ocala FL 34475-5683. 352/629-7007.

MOTOR VEHICLE EQUIPMENT WHOLESALE

Greater Tampa Bay Auto Auction
401 S US Highway 301, Tampa FL 33619-4341. 813/247-1666.

Gulf Coast Auto Auction
6005 24th St E, Bradenton
FL 34203-5032. 941/756-
8478.

**Southeast Toyota
Distributors**
120 NW 12th Ave, Deerfield
Beach FL 33442-1702.
954/429-2000.

Florida Auto Auction
1100 Marshall Farms Rd,
Ocoee FL 34761-3315.
407/656-6201.

Bennett Car Sales
19995 US Highway 19 N,
Clearwater FL 34624-5013.
813/791-1300.

Discount Auto Parts
4677 W Atlantic Ave, Delray
Beach FL 33445-3858.
407/272-4267.

IPW Of Orlando
806 W Washington St,
Orlando FL 32805-1643.
407/849-0180.

**Keystone Automotive
Industries**
940 W 13th St, Riviera
Beach FL 33404-6712.
407/845-3700.

Motor Parts
250 W Van Fleet Dr, Bartow
FL 33830. 941/533-0788.

Parts Depot Company
725 W Central Blvd, Orlando
FL 32805. 407/843-1170.

Walker Manufacturing
4949 Distribution Dr, Tampa
FL 33605. 813/247-5215.

Sandy Sansing Chevy Geo
6200 Pensacola Blvd,
Pensacola FL 32505-2214.
904/476-2480.

Crown Auto Top
340 SW 21st Terrace, Ft
Lauderdale FL 33312-1427.
954/581-1881.

Heafner Tires & Products
3780 Hartsfield Rd,
Tallahassee FL 32303-1121.
904/422-2600.

Big T Tire Man
1109 W Main St, Avon Park
FL 33825-3348. 941/452-
2031.

**Don Olson Tire & Auto
Centers**
16125 N Dale Mabry Hwy,
Tampa FL 33618-1340.
813/960-7997.

**Don Olson Tire & Auto
Centers**
2901 W Hillsborough Ave,
Tampa FL 33614-6054.
813/870-0021.

**AUTOMOTIVE REPAIR
SHOPS**

Dacco
4901 W Rio Vista Ave,
Tampa FL 33634-5338.
813/884-4898.

**Tampa Brake & Supply
Company**
1419 E 4th Ave, Tampa FL
33605-5097. 813/247-
3444.

**Tampa Brake & Supply
Company**
2141 Whitfield Park Loop,
Sarasota FL 34243-4014.
941/758-8282.

Bob's Harmon Glass
1210 Dyer Blvd, Kissimmee
FL 34741-3723. 407/239-
7111.

Brake Shop 4
7501 N Dale Mabry Hwy,
Tampa FL 33614-3225.
813/930-9072.

Canoe Creek Chevron
229 Sunshine State Pkwy,
Saint Cloud FL 34769.
407/892-8081.

Gary's Transmissions
3908 NE 5th Ave, Oakland
Park FL 33334-2232.
954/561-2679.

Vehicare
6015 Benjamin Rd, Suite
321, Tampa FL 33634-
5179. 813/888-9200.

Xpert Tune
315 North St #17 92,
Longwood FL 32750-7642.
407/696-7744.

Ring Power Corporation
2920 S Byron Butler Pkwy,
Perry FL 32347-6314.
904/584-2800.

Harmon Glass
535 W Central Blvd, Orlando
FL 32801-2540. 407/841-
6350.

Lube Express
6482 Forest Hill Blvd, West
Palm Beach FL 33415-6106.
407/966-3944.

Reality Auto
7189 48th Ave N, St
Petersburg FL 33709-2703.
813/544-6466.

Zinn Companies
2300 N State Road 7,
Hollywood FL 33021-3202.
954/966-2150.

Tire Kingdom
3550 S Washington Ave,
Suite 40, Titusville FL
32780-5662. 407/268-
5772.

B&F Auto Repair
1412 S US Highway 1, Fort
Pierce FL 34950-5138.
407/466-1205.

Gulf Coast Thermo King
7802 Highway 301 N,
Tampa FL 33637-6774.
813/985-8502.

For more information on career opportunities in the automotive industry:

Associations

**ASSOCIATION OF INTERNATIONAL
AUTOMOBILE MANUFACTURERS**
1001 19th Street North, Suite 1200,
Arlington VA 22209. 703/525-7788.

**AUTOMOTIVE AFFILIATED
REPRESENTATIVES**
25 Northwest Point Boulevard, Suite 425,
Elk Grove Village IL 60007-1035. 708/228-
1310.

AUTOMOTIVE SERVICE ASSOCIATION
1901 Airport Freeway, Suite 100, P.O. Box
929, Bedford TX 76095. 817/283-6205.

**MOTOR VEHICLE MANUFACTURERS
ASSOCIATION**
7430 2nd Avenue, Suite 300, Detroit MI
48202. 313/872-4311.

**NATIONAL AUTOMOTIVE PARTS
ASSOCIATION**
2999 Circle 75 Parkway, Atlanta GA
30339. 404/956-2200.

**NATIONAL INSTITUTE FOR AUTOMOTIVE
SERVICE EXCELLENCE**
13505 Dulles Technology Drive, Herndon
VA 22071. 703/713-3800.

Directories

AUTOMOTIVE NEWS MARKET DATA BOOK
Crain Communications, Automotive News, 1400 Woodbridge Avenue, Detroit MI 48207-3187. 313/446-6000.

WARD'S AUTOMOTIVE YEARBOOK
Ward's Communications, 3000 Town Center, Suite 2750, Southville MI 48075. 810/357-0800.

Magazines

AUTOMOTIVE INDUSTRIES
Chilton Book Company, 201 King of Prussia Road, Radnor PA 19089. 800/695-1214.

AUTOMOTIVE NEWS
1400 Woodbridge Avenue, Detroit MI 48207. 313/446-6000.

WARD'S AUTO WORLD
Ward's Communications, Inc., 3000 Town Center, Suite 2750, Southville MI 48075. 810/357-0800.

WARD'S AUTOMOTIVE REPORTS
Ward's Communications, Inc., 3000 Town Center, Suite 2750, Southville MI 48075. 810/357-0800.

BANKING/SAVINGS AND LOANS

The banking industry has fared well for the past three years. Banks reported record earnings from 1992 to 1995, as low interest rates kept the number of bad loans falling and investment profits rising. The early '90s were also a good time for banking professionals, who, despite numerous mergers and consolidations throughout the industry, avoided the large layoffs that hit workers in other industries. As a result of rising interest rates, however, times had changed by 1995. Analysts argue that there are simply too many banks clogging the market. This glut of banks (over 10,000 in the United States as compared to 60 in Canada), an emphasis on multi-branch banking, and a decline in traditional transactions, have forced banks to consolidate and close branches, which in turn is shrinking employment. Dramatic layoffs, involving tellers, bank office workers, and managers, will continue to take place into the next century.

Banks are also facing increasing competition from brokerage houses, mutual fund groups, and other financial service companies, resulting in a drop in commercial lending. Competition will most likely take the form of innovation, with new technology and delivery systems; of securitization, including the conversion of assets into marketable certificates; and of internationalization, with the elimination of geographic barriers.

AMERICAN NATIONAL BANKS OF FLORIDA, INC.
P.O. Box 10129, Jacksonville FL 32207. 904/396-8111. **Contact:** Sandra Hayes, Personnel Officer. **Description:** A full-service banking institution.

AMERICAN SAVINGS OF FLORIDA FSB
17801 NW 2nd Avenue, Miami FL 33169-5003. 305/653-5353. **Recorded Jobline:** 305/770-2019. **Contact:** Human Resources. **Description:** American Savings of Florida was formed in 1988 through a merger of the American Savings and Loan Association of Florida and a subsidiary of the Enstar Group. The company is a federal savings bank which conducts mostly residential mortgage business through 29 branches and seven mortgage offices.

AMSOUTH BANK
16120 U.S. Highway 19 North, Clearwater FL 34624. 813/538-1000. **Contact:** Ms. Mel Lewis, Director of Human Resources. **Description:** A commercial bank holding company. **Other U.S. locations:** AL; GA; TN.

AMSOUTH BANK
P.O. Box 12790, Pensacola FL 32575. 904/434-1361. **Contact:** Sharon Hensel, Personnel Director. **Description:** A commercial bank. **Other U.S. locations:** AL; GA; TN.

AMSOUTH BANK
3300 South West 34th Avenue, Suite 101, Ocala FL 34474. 352/854-0177. **Contact:** Barbara Fitos, Personnel Director. **Description:** A commercial bank. **Other U.S. locations:** AL; GA; TN.

BANKATLANTIC
1750 East Sunrise Boulevard, Fort Lauderdale FL 33304. 954/760-5480. **Fax:** 954/760-5489. **Recorded Jobline:** 954/760-5550. **Contact:** Human Resources. **Description:** A federal savings and loan bank whose principal business is checking and savings deposits and consumer and commercial loans. **Common positions include:** Accountant/Auditor; Branch Manager; Customer Service Representative; Securities Sales Rep. **Benefits:** 401K; Bonus Award/Plan; Dental Insurance; Disability Coverage;

Employee Discounts; Life Insurance; Medical Insurance; Pension Plan; Tuition Assistance. **Parent company:** BankAtlantic Financial Corporation. **Listed on:** NASDAQ. **Number of employees at this location:** 640.

BARNETT BANK OF JACKSONVILLE, N.A.
P.O. Box 990, Jacksonville FL 32231. 904/791-7945. **Contact:** Kristin Jackson, Human Resource Specialist. **Description:** An affiliate bank of Barnett Banks, Inc., which operates 34 offices. **Common positions include:** Accountant/Auditor; Bank Officer/Manager; Credit Clerk and Authorizer; Loan Officer; Management Trainee. **Educational backgrounds include:** Accounting; Business Administration; Economics; Finance; Liberal Arts. **Benefits:** Dental Insurance; Disability Coverage; Employee Discounts; Life Insurance; Medical Insurance; Pension Plan; Savings Plan; Tuition Assistance. **Corporate headquarters location:** P.O. Box 40789, Jacksonville FL 32203-0789. **Parent company:** Barnett Banks, Inc. **Operations at this facility include:** Regional Headquarters.

BARNETT BANK OF LEE COUNTY, N.A.
P.O. Box 338, Fort Meyers FL 33902. 941/936-6666. **Contact:** Dawn Ellis, Director of Personnel. **Description:** An affiliate bank of Barnett Banks, Inc., operating 20 offices. **Corporate headquarters location:** Jacksonville FL. **Parent company:** Barnett Banks, Inc. **Operations at this facility include:** Regional Headquarters.

BARNETT BANK OF MARION COUNTY, N.A.
P.O. Box 550, Ocala FL 34478. 352/620-1111. **Contact:** Human Resources. **Description:** An affiliate bank of Barnett Banks, Inc., operating 13 offices. **Corporate headquarters location:** Jacksonville FL. **Parent company:** Barnett Banks, Inc.

BARNETT BANK OF PINELLAS COUNTY, N.A.
P.O. Box 12288, St. Petersburg FL 33733-2288. 813/535-0711. **Contact:** Personnel Department. **Description:** An affiliate bank of Barnett Banks, Inc., operating 54 offices. **Corporate headquarters location:** Jacksonville FL. **Parent company:** Barnett Banks, Inc.

BARNETT BANK OF SOUTH FLORIDA, N.A.
701 Brickell Avenue, Miami FL 33131. 305/350-7100. **Recorded Jobline:** 305/374-4473. **Contact:** Human Resources. **Description:** An affiliate bank of Barnett Banks, Inc., operating 46 offices. **Corporate headquarters location:** Jacksonville FL. **Parent company:** Barnett Banks, Inc.

BARNETT BANK OF SOUTHWEST FLORIDA, N.A.
P.O. Box 1478, Sarasota FL 34230. 941/366-1500. **Contact:** Sandy Dalton, Senior Vice President. **Description:** An affiliate bank of Barnett Banks, Inc., operating 26 offices. **Corporate headquarters location:** Jacksonville FL. **Parent company:** Barnett Banks, Inc.

BARNETT BANK OF TALLAHASSEE, N.A.
P.O. Box 5257, Tallahassee FL 32314. 904/561-1700. **Contact:** Senior Vice President. **Description:** An affiliate bank of Barnett Banks, Inc., operating 10 offices. **Corporate headquarters location:** Jacksonville FL. **Parent company:** Barnett Banks, Inc.

BARNETT BANK OF TAMPA, N.A.
101 East Kennedy Boulevard, Suite 210, Tampa FL 33602. 813/225-8376. **Fax:** 813/225-8742. **Contact:** Anita Tefft, Senior Vice President and Human Resources Director. **Description:** An affiliate bank of Barnett Banks, Inc., operating 40 offices.

BARNETT BANKS INC.
P.O. Box 40789, Jacksonville FL 32203-0789. 904/791-7720. **Recorded Jobline:** 904/464-2426. **Contact:** Human Resources. **Description:** Barnett Banks, Inc., Florida's largest bank holding company, operates over 600 offices in Florida and Georgia (610 in Florida, 18 in Georgia). Barnett has 31 affiliate bank systems in Florida and Georgia, in addition to nonbanking affiliates providing support services and specialized financial services such as trust, full-service brokerage, credit card, mortgage banking, and consumer finance. The company holds a market share in Florida in most banking lines of business, including ranking first, second, or third in deposit share in the 45 Florida counties in which it operates. Barnett is one of the largest bank holding companies in the United States. **Corporate headquarters location:** This location. **Listed on:** New York Stock Exchange.

FEDERAL RESERVE BANK OF MIAMI
9100 NW 36th Street, Miami FL 33178. 305/471-6434. **Recorded Jobline:** 305/471-6480. **Contact:** Human Resources. **Description:** One of 12 regional Federal Reserve banks that, along with the Federal Reserve Board of Governors in Washington, DC, and the Federal Open Market Committee (FOMC), comprise the Federal Reserve System, the nation's central bank. The Federal Reserve Bank is charged with three major responsibilities: monetary policy, banking supervision and regulation, and processing payments.

FIDELITY FEDERAL SAVINGS BANK OF FLORIDA
218 Datura Street, West Palm Beach FL 33401. 407/659-9900. **Contact:** Jan Newlands, Personnel Director. **Description:** A savings bank.

FIRST NATIONAL BANK OF SOUTH MIAMI
5750 Sunset Drive, South Miami FL 33143. 305/667-5511. **Contact:** Marjorie Matthes, Human Resources Director. **Description:** A banking institution.

FIRST OF AMERICA
6701 Crosswind Drive North, St. Petersburg FL 33710. 813/344-7757. **Fax:** 813/344-7724. **Contact:** Linda Allen, Human Resources Assistant. **Description:** A banking institution. **Common positions include:** Bank Officer/Manager; Branch Manager; Customer Service Representative; Department Manager; Services Sales Representative. **Educational backgrounds include:** Business Administration. **Benefits:** Dental Insurance; Disability Coverage; Employee Discounts; Life Insurance; Medical Insurance; Pension Plan; Savings Plan; Tuition Assistance. **Special Programs:** Training Programs. **Corporate headquarters location:** This Location.

FIRST STATE BANK OF THE FLORIDA KEYS
P.O. Box 1579, Key West FL 33041. 305/296-8535. **Contact:** Patricia Lucas, Personnel Officer. **Description:** A banking institution. **Common positions include:** Accountant/Auditor; Bank Officer/Manager; Bank Teller; Branch Manager; Customer Service Representative; Marketing/Advertising/PR Manager; Payroll Clerk; Secretary. **Number of employees at this location:** 100.

FIRST UNION NATIONAL BANK OF FLORIDA
125 North Airport Road, Naples FL 33942. 941/435-3100. **Contact:** Human Resources. **Description:** A full-service bank. The parent company, First Union Corporation, is an interstate bank holding company with assets of $72.6 billion, and banking operations at 266 offices in North Carolina. Other banking subsidiaries are located in Georgia (163), Florida (488), Tennessee (63), South Carolina (67), Virginia (193), Maryland (32), and Washington D.C. (30). The company also conducts mortgage banking operations through 53 offices in 16 states, and home equity lending in 151 offices. Other activities include consumer finance services and trust operations. **Parent company:** First Union Corporation.

FIRST UNION NATIONAL BANK OF FLORIDA
225 Water Street, Jacksonville FL 32202. 904/361-2265. **Recorded Jobline:** 904/361-6971. **Contact:** Personnel Department. **Description:** A full-service bank. The parent company, First Union Corporation, is an interstate bank holding company with assets of $72.6 billion, and banking operations at 266 offices in North Carolina. Other banking subsidiaries are located in Georgia (163), Florida (488), Tennessee (63), South Carolina (67), Virginia (193), Maryland (32), and Washington D.C. (30). The company also conducts mortgage banking operations through 53 offices in 16 states, and home equity lending in 151 offices. Other activities include consumer finance services and trust operations. **Parent company:** First Union Corporation.

FIRST UNION NATIONAL BANK OF FLORIDA
203 Avenue A NW, Winter Haven FL 33881. 941/294-3101. **Contact:** Human Resources. **Description:** A full-service bank. The parent company, First Union Corporation, is an interstate bank holding company with assets of $72.6 billion, and banking operations at 266 offices in North Carolina. Other banking subsidiaries are located in Georgia (163), Florida (488), Tennessee (63), South Carolina (67), Virginia (193), Maryland (32), and Washington D.C. (30). The company also conducts mortgage banking operations through 53 offices in 16 states, and home equity lending in 151 offices. Other activities include consumer finance services and trust operations. **Parent company:** First Union Corporation.

MEMORIAL EMPLOYEES CREDIT UNION
3195 Ponce De Leon Boulevard, Hollywood FL 33021. 954/987-2000. **Contact:** Human Resources. **Description:** A credit union.

NATIONSBANK
2400 First Street, Fort Meyers FL 33901. 941/335-1225. **Contact:** Personnel Department. **Description:** In addition to a complete selection of financial accounts, NationsBank offers a variety of other banking services. NationsBank also offers an automatic savings transfer program, allowing regular transfer of money from checking to savings, and direct deposit. **NOTE:** Please send resumes to: 6010 Royal Palm Avenue, Fort Meyers, FL 33901. **Corporate headquarters location:** Charlotte NC. **Number of employees nationwide:** 2,000.

NATIONSBANK
400 North Ashley, 13th Floor, Tampa FL 33602. 813/224-5241. **Recorded Jobline:** 813/224-5921. **Contact:** Personnel. **Description:** A banking corporation. In addition to a complete selection of financial accounts, NationsBank offers a variety of other banking services. NationsBank also offers an automatic savings transfer program, allowing regular transfer of money from checking to savings, and direct deposit. **Common positions include:** Bank Officer/Manager; Management Trainee. **Educational backgrounds include:** Business Administration. **Benefits:** Daycare Assistance; Dental Insurance; Disability Coverage; Employee Discounts; Life Insurance; Medical Insurance; Pension Plan; Profit Sharing; Savings Plan; Stock Option; Tuition Assistance. **Special Programs:** Training Programs. **Corporate headquarters location:** Charlotte NC. **Operations at this facility include:** Administration; Sales; Service. **Number of employees nationwide:** 2,000.

NEW SENTINEL FEDERAL CREDIT UNION
500 Northeast 4th Street, Fort Lauderdale FL 33301. 954/522-5626. **Contact:** Human Resources. **Description:** A credit union.

REGIONS BANK
P.O. Drawer 608, Milton FL 32572. 904/623-3846. **Contact:** Personnel. **Description:** A savings and loan association. **Parent company:** Great Western Holding Company.

REPUBLIC NATIONAL BANK OF MIAMI
10 NW 42nd Avenue, Miami FL 33126. 305/441-7300. **Recorded Jobline:** 305/250-5051. **Contact:** Human Resources. **Description:** Operates national commercial banks.

SOCIETY FIRST FEDERAL SAVINGS BANK
FORT MEYERS
P.O. Box 940, Fort Meyers FL 33902. 941/334-4106. **Contact:** Human Resources. **Description:** A savings and loan association.

SUNTRUST BANKS, INC.
777 Brickell Avenue, Miami FL 33131. 305/592-0800. **Recorded Jobline:** 305/579-7001. **Contact:** Human Resources. **Description:** SunTrust Banks provide a range of financial services including traditional deposit and credit services, and trust and investment services. The company also provides corporate finance, mortgage banking, factoring, credit cards, discount brokerage, credit-related insurance, and data processing and information services.

SUNTRUST BANKS, INC.
1777 Main Street, Sarasota FL 34236. 941/366-7000. **Contact:** Vice President. **Description:** SunTrust Banks provide a range of financial services including traditional deposit and credit services, and trust and investment services. The company also provides corporate finance, mortgage banking, factoring, credit cards, discount brokerage, credit-related insurance, and data processing and information services. **Common positions include:** Accountant/Auditor; Advertising Clerk; Branch Manager; Department Manager; Human Resources Specialist; Public Relations Specialist; Purchasing Agent and Manager; Services Sales Representative; Underwriter/Assistant Underwriter. **Educational backgrounds include:** Accounting; Business Administration; Communications; Computer Science; Economics; Finance; Marketing. **Benefits:** Dental Insurance; Disability Coverage; Life Insurance; Medical Insurance; Pension Plan. **Special Programs:** Internships; Training Programs.

SUNTRUST BANKS, INC.
501 South Flagler Drive, West Palm Beach FL 33401. 407/659-2265. **Contact:** Personnel Director. **Description:** SunTrust Banks provide a range of financial services including traditional deposit and credit services, and trust and investment services. The company also provides corporate finance, mortgage banking, factoring, credit cards, discount brokerage, credit-related insurance, and data processing and information services.

SUNTRUST BANKS, INC.
P.O. Box 3303, Tampa FL 33601-3303. 813/224-2121. **Recorded Jobline:** 813/224-2001. **Contact:** Personnel Department. **Description:** SunTrust Banks provide a range of financial services including traditional deposit and credit services, and trust and investment services. The company also provides corporate finance, mortgage banking, factoring, credit cards, discount brokerage, credit-related insurance, and data processing and information services.

SUNTRUST BANKS, INC.
515 East Las Olas Boulevard, Fort Lauderdale FL 33301. 954/467-5000. **Recorded Jobline:** 954/765-7100. **Contact:** Personnel Annex. **Description:** SunTrust Banks provide a range of financial services including traditional deposit and credit services, and trust and investment services. The company also provides corporate finance, mortgage banking, factoring, credit cards, discount brokerage, credit-related insurance, and data processing and information services.

SUNTRUST BANKS, INC.
P.O. Box 3833, Orlando FL 32802. 407/237-4216. **Recorded Jobline:** 407/237-6878. **Contact:** Holly Conley, Recruiting Coordinator. **Description:** Statewide bank holding company with over 15 local unit banks. Operates a total of 333 branches in Florida that are full-service banks. **Educational backgrounds include:** Accounting; Business Administration; Finance. **Benefits:** Dental Insurance; Employee Discounts; Fitness Program; Life Insurance; Medical Insurance; Pension Plan; Savings Plan; Stock Option; Tuition Assistance. **Special Programs:** Training Programs.

TRANSCAPITAL FINANCIAL CORPORATION
1221 Brickell Avenue, Miami FL 33131. 305/536-1475. **Contact:** Human Resources. **Description:** A credit union.

WOMETCO ENTERPRISES CREDIT UNION
P.O. Box 141609, Coral Gables FL 33134. 305/529-1400. **Contact:** Human Resources. **Description:** A credit union.

Note: Because addresses and telephone numbers of smaller companies change rapidly, we recommend you call each company to verify the information below before inquiring about job opportunities. Mass mailings are not recommended.

Additional employers with over 250 employees:

COMMERCIAL BANKS

Citizens Federal Bank
999 Brickell Ave, Miami FL 33131-3012. 305/577-0430.

City National Bank Of Florida
25 W Flagler St, Miami FL 33130-1712. 305/577-7333.

Southeast Bank NA
200 S Biscayne Blvd, Miami FL 33131-2310. 305/375-7500.

Intercontinental Bank
200 SE 1 St 4th Floor, Miami FL 33131-1903. 305/377-6900.

Northern Trust Bank Of Florida NA
700 Brickell Ave, Miami FL 33131-2804. 305/372-1000.

SAVINGS INSTITUTIONS

Coral Gables Federal Savings & Loan
2511 Ponce De Leon Blvd, Miami FL 33134-6019. 305/447-4711.

Coral Gables Federal Savings & Loan
5600 P G A Blvd, Palm Beach Gardens FL 33418. 407/622-0445.

Financial Federal Savings & Loan Assn.
6625 Miami Lakes Dr, Hialeah FL 33014-2799. 305/557-7409.

CREDIT UNIONS

Shea Credit Union
1000 SW 84th Ave, Hollywood FL 33025-1419. 954/983-4321.

Dupont Mining Employee Credit Union
P.O. Box 753, Starke FL 32091-0753. 352/964-1233.

Additional employers with under 250 employees:

COMMERCIAL BANKS

First National Bank & Trust Co. Treasury
P.O. Box 9012, Stuart FL 34995-9012. 407/287-4000.

American Bank Remote
4210 University Blvd S, Jacksonville FL 32216-4995. 904/731-5553.

Citibank Latino
2703 Gateway Dr #A, Pompano Beach FL 33069-4323. 954/975-5200.

Citizens National Bank Naples
P.O. Box 413031, Naples FL 33941-3031. 941/261-5522.

City National Bank
P.O. Box 900, Tallahassee FL 32302-0900. 904/841-1300.

Comerica Bank & Trust
1800 Corporate Blvd NW, Boca Raton FL 33431-7341. 407/994-6801.

Compass Bank
3560 University Blvd N, Jacksonville FL 32277-2423. 904/744-4990.

Enterprise National Bank
P.O. Box 550537, Jacksonville FL 32255-0537. 904/296-2265.

First Federal/Osceola
1115 Bermuda Ave, Kissimmee FL 34741. 407/846-2171.

First Federal/Osceola
1300 E Vine St, Kissimmee FL 34744-3620. 407/847-5566.

Fort Brooke Bank
510 Vonderburg Dr, Brandon FL 33511-5970. 813/685-2000.

Founders National Trust Bank
P.O. Box 60219, Fort Myers FL 33906-6219. 941/433-3600.

Island National Bank & Trust Company
180 Royal Palm Way, Palm Beach FL 33480-4254. 407/832-7766.

Orange Bank
7800 South Highway 17-92, Fern Park FL 32730. 407/331-1961.

Palm Beach National Bank & Trust Co.
11760 US Highway 1, No Palm Beach FL 33408-3013. 407/627-1776.

Riverside National Bank Of Florida
5053 Sunshine Pkwy Feeder Dr, Fort Pierce FL 34951. 407/461-3000.

Southtrust Bank Jacksonville
51 W Bay St, Jacksonville FL 32202-3642. 904/798-6960.

United National Bank
1399 SW First Ave, Miami FL 33130-4327. 305/557-5471.

United Southern Bank
10021 County Road 44, Leesburg FL 34788-2461. 352/728-0077.

First Federal Savings & Loan Association Palm
95 NE 5th Ave, Delray Beach FL 33483-5492. 407/278-6261.

First National Bank & Trust Co. Treasury
11711 SE US Hwy 1, Hobe Sound FL 33455. 407/546-5097.

First Nationwide Bank A Federal Savings Bank
35098 US Highway 19 N, Palm Harbor FL 34684-1927. 813/786-1689.

First Performance National Bank
1695 US Highway 1 S, St Augustine FL 32086-4236. 904/824-0101.

Fifth Third Trust Co. & Savings Bank
P.O. Box 413021, Naples FL 33941-3021. 941/261-3911.

American Bank Of Hollywood
6600 Taft St #6879, Hollywood FL 33024-4040. 954/966-9810.

Boca Bank
7000 W Palmetto Park Rd, Suite 10, Boca Raton FL 33433-3479. 407/368-5050.

Citibank International
1 SE 3rd Ave, Miami FL 33131-1704. 305/377-6800.

Coconut Grove Bank
2701 S Bayshore Dr, Miami FL 33133-5309. 305/858-6666.

Community Bank Of Homestead
28801 SW 157th Ave, Homestead FL 33033-2437. 305/245-2211.

Community Savings
3950 S US Highway 1, Jupiter FL 33477-1199. 407/627-3220.

Community Savings
11400 SE Federal Hwy, Hobe Sound FL 33455-5209. 407/546-2700.

Community Savings
660 US Highway 1, No Palm Beach FL 33408-4697. 407/881-4800.

Coral Gables Federal Savings & Loan
4576 Okeechobee Blvd, West Palm Beach FL 33417-4622. 407/471-4202.

Coral Gables Federal Savings & Loan
3355 SE Federal Hwy, Stuart FL 34997-4913. 407/288-3443.

Coral Gables Federal Savings & Loan
1238 US Highway 1, Vero Beach FL 32960-5730. 407/778-1898.

Eagle National Bank Of Miami
P.O. Box 12281, Miami FL 33101-2281. 305/358-5300.

Equity Bank
5030 Linton Blvd, Delray Beach FL 33484-6526. 407/496-1301.

First Federal Savings Bank
2889 Green St, Marianna FL 32446-3307. 904/526-2300.

First Florida Savings Bank
4343 W Flagler St Fl 2, Miami FL 33134-1586. 305/448-7979.

Florida First Federal Savings Bank
P.O. Box 670, Panama City FL 32402-0670. 904/872-7000.

Financial Federal Savings & Loan Association Dade
6625 Miami Lakes Dr E, Hialeah FL 33014-2705. 305/827-7444.

Fortune Bank A Savings Bank
1500 Pinehurst Dr, Spring
Hill FL 34606-4555.
352/683-6385.

Great Western Bank
10523 US Highway 19, Port
Richey FL 34668-2857.
813/868-9451.

**Harbor Federal Savings &
Loan Association**
75 N Nova Rd, Ormond
Beach FL 32174-5119.
904/673-2021.

**Harbor Federal Savings &
Loan Association**
4156 Okeechobee Rd, Fort
Pierce FL 34947-5497.
407/461-2600.

**Harbor Federal Savings &
Loan Association**
1700 S A-1-A, Vero Beach
FL 32963. 407/231-0181.

**Key Biscayne Bank and Trust
Company**
95 W McIntyre St, Key
Biscayne FL 33149-1845.
305/361-9100.

**Nationsbank Of Florida
National Association**
777 E Merritt Island Cswy,
Merritt Is FL 32952-3576.
407/452-9500.

Nationsbank Of Florida
1 Financial Plaza, Ft
Lauderdale FL 33394-0029.
954/465-2000.

**Northern Trust Bank Of
Florida NA**
440 Royal Palm Way, Palm
Beach FL 33480-4138.
407/655-9770.

**Northern Trust Bank Of
Florida NA**
4001 Tamiami Trail N, Suite
105, Naples FL 33940-
3591. 941/262-8800.

Peoples Bank Of Lakeland
P.O. Box 1607, Lakeland FL
33802-1607. 941/687-
6500.

**Riverside National Bank Of
Florida**

989 S Federal Hwy, Stuart
FL 34994-3734. 407/287-
7600.

**Security Federal Savings
Association**
2392 Commercial Way,
Spring Hill FL 34606-3569.
352/769-3232.

Suburban Bank
6801 Lake Worth Rd, Lake
Worth FL 33467-2996.
407/964-6100.

Sun Commercial Bank
Caller Box 2180, Panama
City FL 32402. 904/769-
4811.

**Suncoast Savings & Loan
Association**
4000 Hollywood Blvd,
Hollywood FL 33021-6751.
954/963-2448.

The Bank Of Inverness
330 US Highway 41 S,
Inverness FL 34450-4956.
352/726-1221.

Hernando County Bank
1187 S Broad St, Brooksville
FL 34601-3111. 352/799-
2265.

**Wilmington Trust Florida
National Association**
4725 Highway A1A, Vero
Beach FL 32963-5401.
407/286-3686.

SAVINGS INSTITUTIONS

Citizens Federal Bank
1862 W Hillsboro Blvd,
Deerfield Beach FL 33442-
1402. 954/428-3022.

**General Federal Savings &
Loan Association**
P.O. Box 350636, Miami FL
33135. 305/662-6801.

Great Western Bank
500 E Altamonte Dr,
Altamonte Springs FL
32701. 407/831-0320.

**Savings America A Division
Home Savings**
225 US Hwy 1, Tequesta FL
33469. 407/747-2222.

**Savings America A Division
Home Savings**
2050 US Highway 1, Vero
Beach FL 32960-5480.
407/569-3700.

Floridabank
4655 Salisbury Rd,
Jacksonville FL 32256-0902.
904/281-7600.

FFO Financial Group
2200 Live Oak Blvd, Saint
Cloud FL 34771-8441.
407/892-1200.

CREDIT UNIONS

McCoy Federal Credit Union
1900 McCoy Rd, Orlando FL
32809-7896. 407/855-
5452.

**Sarasota Coastal Credit
Union**
5433 Fruitville Rd, Sarasota
FL 34232-6418. 941/378-
5654.

Diesel Electric Credit Union
3545 New Kings Rd,
Jacksonville FL 32209-3349.
904/282-4896.

**Local 606 Electrical Workers
Credit Union**
820 Virginia Dr, Orlando FL
32803-2530. 407/896-
7271.

POC Credit Union
3443 First Ave N, St
Petersburg FL 33713-8516.
813/327-8690.

**Tampa Longshoremen's
Credit Union**
707 E Harrison St, Tampa FL
33602-3424. 813/229-
1192.

**OFFICES OF BANK HOLDING
COMPANIES**

**South Trust Bank Vollusia
County**
400 W Granada Blvd,
Ormond Beach FL 32174-
5102. 904/756-6000.

**For more information on career opportunities in the banking/savings and loans
industry:**

Associations

AMERICAN BANKERS ASSOCIATION
1120 Connecticut Avenue NW, Washington
DC 20036. 202/663-5221. Provides
banking education and training services,
sponsors industry programs and
conventions, and publishes articles,
newsletters, and the ABA Service Member
Directory.

**INDEPENDENT BANKERS ASSOCIATION
OF AMERICA**
900 19th Street NW, Suite 400,
Washington DC 20006. 202/857-3100.

**U.S. LEAGUE OF SAVINGS AND LOAN
INSTITUTIONS**
900 19th Street NW, Suite 400,
Washington DC 20006. 202/857-3100.

Directories

AMERICAN BANK DIRECTORY
Thomson Financial Publications, 6195
Crooked Creek Road, Norcross GA 30092.
404/448-1011.

AMERICAN SAVINGS DIRECTORY
McFadden Business Publications, 6195
Crooked Creek Road, Norcross GA 30092.
404/448-1011.

**BUSINESS WEEK/TOP 200 BANKING
INSTITUTIONS ISSUE**
McGraw-Hill, Inc., 1221 Avenue of the
Americas, 39th Floor, New York NY 10020.
212/512-4776.

MOODY'S BANK AND FINANCE MANUAL
Moody's Investors Service, Inc., 99 Church
Street, First Floor, New York NY 10007.
212/553-0300.

POLK'S BANK DIRECTORY
R.L. Polk & Company, P.O. Box 305100,
Nashville TN 37320-5100. 615/889-3350.

RANKING THE BANKS/THE TOP NUMBERS
American Banker, Inc., 1 State Street Plaza,
New York NY 10004. 212/943-6700.

Magazines

ABA BANKING JOURNAL
American Bankers Association, 1120
Connecticut Avenue NW, Washington DC
20036. 202/663-5221.

BANK ADMINISTRATION
1 North Franklin, Chicago IL 60606.
800/323-8552.

BANKERS MAGAZINE
Warren, Gorham & Lamont, Park Square
Building, 31 St. James Avenue, Boston MA
02116-4112. 617/423-2020.

**JOURNAL OF COMMERCIAL BANK
LENDING**
Robert Morris Associates, P.O. Box 8500 S-
1140, Philadelphia PA 19178. 215/851-
9100.

BIOTECHNOLOGY, PHARMACEUTICALS, AND SCIENTIFIC R&D

 The pharmaceutical industry was characterized by a mass of mergers and acquisitions in 1994, with more of the same expected for 1995 and 1996. Drug companies have also been concentrating on cutting costs, in order to boost profit margins. Many R&D budgets have been slashed as a result. And industry watchers don't expect the arrival of many big-selling new products in the near future. As more patents continue to expire on some of the industry's top-selling drugs, the large pharmaceutical companies that held those patents will see a negative impact on their sales growth. Conversely, the expired patents mean more opportunity for generic drug manufacturers, who should continue to gain market share through 1996.

ABC RESEARCH
3437 Southwest 24th Avenue, Gainesville FL 32607. 352/372-0436. **Contact:** Human Resources. **Description:** A testing laboratory.

FOX PHARMACAL, INC.
6420 NW Fifth Way, Fort Lauderdale FL 33309. 954/772-7487. **Contact:** Personnel Department. **Description:** A distributor of private label pharmaceuticals.

GULF DISTRIBUTION INC.
5959 Northwest 37th Avenue, Miami FL 33142. 305/634-6800. **Contact:** Human Resources. **Description:** A wholesaler of pharmaceuticals.

IVAX CORPORATION
8800 Northwest 36th Street, Miami FL 33178. 305/590-2200. **Contact:** Human Resources. **Description:** IVAX Corporation is a holding company with subsidiaries involved in specialty chemicals, pharmaceuticals, personal care products, and medical diagnostics. Its principal business is the research, development, manufacture, marketing, and distribution of health care products. Pharmaceutical operations, which include the development and acquisition of brand-name and generic pharmaceutical products, as well as veterinary products, account for approximately three-quarters of the consolidated net revenues of the company. Brand-name products, marketed under the 'Baker Norton' trade name, include the urological medications Bicitra, Polycitra, Polycitra-K, Polycitra-LC, Neutra-Phos, Neutra-Phos-K, Prohim, Urotrol, Lubraseptic Jelly, and Pro-Banthine; and cardiovascular medicines Cordilox, Triam-Co, Amil-Co, Spiro-Co, and Fru-Co. Other drugs include Proglycem, used to treat hyperinsulinemia; Serenance, a neuroleptic used for psychiatric disorders; the respiratory medications Cromogen, Salamol, and Beclazone metered dose inhalers; the Steri-Nebs line of nebulization products; and the opthalmic medications Eye-Crom and Glaucol. IVAX also markets generic drugs, which are therapeutically equivalent to brand name drugs but lower priced. Through DVM Pharmaceuticals, Inc. (acquired in 1992), the IVAX Corporation formulates, packages, and distributes veterinary products, including DermCaps, a daily dietary supplement; a line of topical therapeutics, including ChlorhexiDerm Flush and Shampoo, OxyDex Shampoo and Gel, HyLyt Shampoo and Rinse, Relief Shampoo, Rinse and Spray; two groups of optic products known as Clear and OtiCalm; the DuraKyl and SynerKyl line of ectoparasiticidals; and the wound dressing BioDres. **Number of employees nationwide:** 2,910.

MONTICELLO DRUG COMPANY
P.O. Box 61749, Jacksonville FL 32236. 904/384-3666. **Contact:** Personnel Department. **Description:** A manufacturer of drugs.

NORTH AMERICAN BIOLOGICALS, INC.
16500 North West 15th Avenue, Miami FL 33169. 305/628-0080. **Contact:** Bill Vandervalk, Human Resources Director. **Description:** Involved in the collection, sale, processing, testing, and distribution of plasma and blood derivatives. **Common positions include:** Accountant/Auditor; Biological Scientist/Biochemist; Blue-Collar Worker Supervisor; Buyer; Chemical Engineer; Clerical Supervisor; Clinical Lab Technician; Computer Programmer; Computer Systems Analyst; Customer Service Representative; Emergency Medical Technician; Financial Analyst; Human Resources Specialist; Licensed Practical Nurse; Management Trainee; Medical Technologist; Purchasing Agent and Manager; Quality Control Supervisor; Registered Nurse. **Educational backgrounds include:** Biology; Business Administration; Chemistry; Liberal Arts; Medical Technology. **Benefits:** Dental Insurance; Life Insurance; Medical Insurance; Savings Plan; Tuition Assistance. **Corporate headquarters location:** This Location. **Operations at this facility include:** Administration; Manufacturing. **Listed on:** NASDAQ. **Number of employees at this location:** 250. **Number of employees nationwide:** 1,700.

RX MEDICAL SERVICES CORPORATION
888 East Las Olas Boulevard, Third Floor, Fort Lauderdale FL 33301. 954/462-1711. **Contact:** Human Resources. **Description:** Owns and operates medical laboratories.

REXALL GROUP
851 Broken Sound Parkway NW, Boca Raton FL 33487. **Toll free phone:** 800/255-7399. **Contact:** Human Resources. **Description:** A manufacturer and distributor of pharmaceutical products.

ROUX LABORATORIES
P.O. Box 37557, Jacksonville FL 32236-7557. 904/693-1200. **Fax:** 904/693-1259. **Contact:** James M. House, Human Resources Manager. **Description:** A laboratory. **Common positions include:** Accountant/Auditor; Blue-Collar Worker Supervisor; Buyer; Chemist; Computer Programmer; Computer Systems Analyst; Credit Manager; Electrician; Human Resources Specialist; Industrial Engineer; Industrial Production Manager. **Educational backgrounds include:** Business Administration; Chemistry; Engineering. **Benefits:** 401K; Dental Insurance; Disability Coverage; Life Insurance; Medical Insurance; Pension Plan; Savings Plan; Tuition Assistance. **Operations at this facility include:** Administration; Manufacturing; Regional Headquarters.

SCHERING LABORATORIES
13900 North West 57th Court, Miami Lakes FL 33014. 305/364-9100. **Contact:** Manager of Human Resources. **Description:** Schering Laboratories manufactures physician-recommended and prescribed products. Schering Laboratories supplies these products to pharmacies, hospitals, and physicians' office suppliers. **Common positions include:** Blue-Collar Worker Supervisor; Chemist; Operations/Production Manager; Quality Control Supervisor. **Educational backgrounds include:** Business Administration; Chemistry; Pharmacology. **Benefits:** Credit Union; Dental Insurance; Disability Coverage; Employee Discounts; Life Insurance; Medical Insurance; Pension Plan; Profit Sharing; Savings Plan; Tuition Assistance.

SMITHKLINE BEECHAM CLINICAL LABORATORIES
4225 East Fowler, Tampa FL 33617. 813/972-7100. **Contact:** Human Resources Department. **Description:** SmithKline Beecham Clinical Laboratories collects and analyzes biological specimens and reports the results to client physicians, hospitals, laboratories, and businesses. **Common positions include:** Chemist; Clinical Lab Technician; Customer Service Representative; Medical Technologist. **Educational backgrounds include:** Business Administration; Chemistry; Medical Technology. **Benefits:** 401K; Dental Insurance; Disability Coverage; Employee Discounts; Life Insurance; Medical Insurance; Pension Plan; Profit Sharing; Savings Plan; Tuition Assistance. **Corporate headquarters location:** Collegeville PA. **Other U.S. locations:** Leesburg FL; Miami FL; Orlando FL; Tallahassee FL. **Parent company:** SmithKline Beecham. **Operations at this facility include:** Sales; Service. **Listed on:** New York Stock Exchange. **Number of employees at this location:** 400. **Number of employees nationwide:** 10,000.

SMITHKLINE BEECHAM CORPORATION
13955 Southwest 144th Street, Miami FL 33186. 305/253-6601. **Contact:** Human Resources. **Description:** A health care company engaged in the research, development, manufacture and marketing of ethical pharmaceuticals, animal health products, ethical and proprietary medicines and eye care products. The company's principal divisions

include SmithKline Beecham Pharmaceuticals, SmithKline Beecham Animal Health, SmithKline Beecham Consumer Healthcare, and SmithKline Beecham Clinical Laboratories. The company is also engaged in many other aspects of the health care field, including the production of medical instruments and electronic instruments used in the health care field. Manufactures proprietary medicines through its subsidiary, Menley & James Laboratories, including such nationally known products as Contac Cold Capsules, Sine-Off sinus medicine, Love cosmetics, and Sea & Ski outdoor products. **Corporate headquarters location:** Philadelphia PA. **Number of employees nationwide:** 20,000.

ZENITH GOLDLINE PHARMACEUTICALS
1900 West Commercial Boulevard, Fort Lauderdale FL 33309. 954/491-4002. **Contact:** Human Resources. **Description:** Manufactures generic pharmaceuticals.

Note: Because addresses and telephone numbers of smaller companies change rapidly, we recommend you call each company to verify the information below before inquiring about job opportunities. Mass mailings are not recommended.

Additional employers with under 250 employees:

PHARMACEUTICAL PREPARATIONS

Belmac Corporation
4830 W Kennedy Blvd, Suite 550, Tampa FL 33609-2562. 813/286-4401.

Noven Pharmaceuticals
11960 SW 144th St, Miami FL 33186-6109. 305/253-5099.

BIOLOGICAL PRODUCTS

Viragen
2343 W 76th St, Hialeah FL 33016-1842. 305/557-6000.

DRUGS, DRUG PROPRIETARIES, AND DRUGGISTS' SUNDRIES

Foxmeyer Drug Co.
6100 Phillips Hwy, Jacksonville FL 32216-5921. 904/730-8299.

Mason Distributors
5105 NW 159th St, Hialeah FL 33014-6336. 305/624-5557.

McKesson Drug Company
915 Chad Ln, Tampa FL 33619-4331. 813/620-0621.

Model Imperial Supply
1201 Clint Moore Rd, Boca Raton FL 33487-2718. 407/241-8244.

McKesson Drug Co.
8226 Phillips Hwy, Jacksonville FL 32256-8202. 904/733-7750.

Superior Wholesale
7901 Woodland Center Blvd,

Tampa FL 33614-2408. 813/885-2725.

MEDICAL AND DENTAL LABORATORIES

Allied Clinical Laboratories
224 Southpark Circle E, St Augustine FL 32086-5135. 904/824-7792.

Allied Clinical Laboratories
811 S Orlando Ave, Winter Park FL 32789-7102. 407/629-2441.

Continental Medical Laboratory
1790 SW 22nd St, Ft Lauderdale FL 33315-1837. 954/763-1770.

Florida Institute Of Health
4850 W Oakland Park Blvd, Ft Lauderdale FL 33313-7260. 954/739-3030.

Genetrix
10770 N 46th St, Tampa FL 33617-3442. 813/979-9442.

Integrated Genetics
14502 N Dale Mabry Hwy, Carrollwood FL 33618-2072. 813/963-6024.

Metpath Damon Clinical Labs
2150 Collier Ave, Suite L, Fort Myers FL 33901-8129. 941/939-0561.

Metpath
106 Manatee Ave E, Bradenton FL 34208-1930. 941/748-8050.

Metpath
2010 59th St W, Bradenton FL 34209-4616. 941/792-4033.

National Health Laboratories
1444 Biscayne Blvd, Miami FL 33132-1430. 305/374-0525.

Pathologists Ref Lab SW Florida
7041 Grand National Dr, Orlando FL 32819-8381. 407/351-4872.

Roche Biomedical Labs
705 W Sanlando Springs Dr, Longwood FL 32750. 407/332-8151.

Roche Biomedical Labs
331 N Maitland Ave, Maitland FL 32751-4762. 407/645-1710.

Smithkline Beecham Clinic Labs
1045 Riverside Ave, Suite G45, Jacksonville FL 32204-4126. 904/354-6866.

SmithKline Beecham Clinic Labs
85 W Miller St, Suite 105, Orlando FL 32806-2026. 407/423-1420.

SmithKline Beecham Clinic Labs
400 Tamiami Trail S, Suite 180, Venice FL 34285-2623. 941/484-4624.

Associated Dental Tech
14333 58th St N, Clearwater FL 34620-2817. 813/530-9444.

Volusia Dentalcare
1630 W International Speedway, Daytona Beach FL 32114-1446. 904/253-6634.

Denturecare
6001 Argyle Forest Blvd,

Jacksonville FL 32244-5705. 904/771-6838.

COMMERCIAL PHYSICAL AND BIOLOGICAL RESEARCH

Automation Research Systems
1000 N Ashley Dr, Suite 510, Tampa FL 33602-3717. 813/228-8711.

Badger Design
1401 N Westshore Blvd Fl 2, Tampa FL 33607-4511. 813/289-1991.

Hill Top Research
6699 13th Ave N, St Petersburg FL 33710-5401. 813/344-7602.

Mar
1800 Eller Dr #110, Ft Lauderdale FL 33316-4200. 954/525-1379.

Marc Analysis Research
498 Palm Springs Dr, Suite 100, Altamonte Springs FL 32701-7805. 407/260-0090.

National Health Laboratories
685 Palm Springs Dr, Suite 2D, Altamonte Springs FL 32701-7853. 407/834-0804.

Bionomics Laboratory
4310 Anderson Rd, Orlando FL 32812-7304. 407/851-2560.

Carter & Burgess
10770 N 46th St, Tampa FL 33617-3442. 813/971-4859.

DME Corporation
12889 Ingenuity Dr, Orlando FL 32826-3001. 407/381-6062.

Tasc The Analytic Sciences
1992 Lewis Turner Blvd Bldg, Ft Walton Beach FL 32547-1255. 904/863-8000.

TESTING LABORATORIES

Continental-Viking Lab
6120 Hanging Moss Rd, Orlando FL 02807-3701. 407/671-3600.

Feisco Risk Management Services
200 W College Ave Fl 3, Tallahassee FL 32301-7710. 904/224-9994.

Naval Research Lab
3909 S Summerlin Ave, Orlando FL 32806-6905. 407/875-5100.

Pace
5460 Beaumont Center Blvd, Tampa FL 33634-5215. 813/884-8268.

For more information on career opportunities in biotechnology, pharmaceuticals, and scientific R&D:

Associations

AMERICAN ASSOCIATION FOR CLINICAL CHEMISTRY
2101 L Street NW, Suite 202, Washington DC 20037-1526. 202/857-0717 or 800/892-1400. International scientific/medical society of individuals involved with clinical chemistry and other clinical labscience-related disciplines.

AMERICAN ASSOCIATION OF COLLEGES OF PHARMACY
1426 Prince Street, Alexandria VA 22314-2841. 703/739-2330. An organization composed of all U.S. pharmacy colleges and over 2,000 school administrators and faculty members. Career publications include: *Shall I Study Pharmacy?*, *Pharmacy A Caring Profession*, and *A Graduate Degree in the Pharmaceutical Sciences: An Option For You?*

AMERICAN COLLEGE OF CLINICAL PHARMACY (ACCP)
3101 Broadway, Suite 380, Kansas City MO 64111. 816/531-2177. Operates ClinNet jobline at 412/648-7893 for both members and nonmembers, for a fee.

AMERICAN PHARMACEUTICAL ASSOCIATION
2215 Constitution Avenue NW, Washington DC 20037. 202/628-4410. Operates a resume referral service for all members.

AMERICAN SOCIETY FOR BIOCHEMISTRY AND MOLECULAR BIOLOGY
9650 Rockville Pike, Bethesda MD 20814-3996. 301/530-7145. A nonprofit scientific and educational organization whose primary scientific activities are in the publication of the *Journal of Biological Chemistry* and holding an annual scientific meeting. Also publishes a career brochure entitled

Unlocking Life's Secrets: Biochemistry and Molecular Biology.

AMERICAN SOCIETY OF HOSPITAL PHARMACISTS
7272 Wisconsin Avenue, Bethesda MD 20814. 301/657-3000.

BIOMEDICAL INDUSTRY COUNCIL
225 Broadway, Suite 1600, San Diego, CA 92101. 619/236-1322.

BIOTECHNOLOGY INDUSTRY ORGANIZATION
1625 K Street NW, Suite 1100, Washington DC 20006-1604. 202/857-0244.

NATIONAL ASSOCIATION OF PHARMACEUTICAL MANUFACTURERS
747 Third Avenue, New York NY 10017. 212/838-3720.

NATIONAL PHARMACEUTICAL COUNCIL
1894 Preston White Drive, Reston VA 22091. 202/620-6390. Fax: 703/476-0904. Fax requests to the attention of Pat Adams, Vice President of Finance and Administration. Organization of leading research-based pharmaceutical companies.

Directories

DRUG TOPICS RED BOOK
Medical Economics Company, 5 Paragon Drive, Montvale, NJ 07645. 201/358-7200.

Magazines

DRUG TOPICS
Medical Economics Company, 5 Paragon Drive, Montvale NJ 07645. 201/358-7200.

PHARMACEUTICAL ENGINEERING
International Society of Pharmaceutical
Engineers, 3816 West Linebaugh Avenue,
Suite 412, Tampa FL 33624. 813/960-
2105.

BUSINESS SERVICES AND NON-SCIENTIFIC RESEARCH

 *The business services sector, which includes 16 of the 20 fastest growing industries, covers a broad spectrum of careers, including everything from adjustment and collection services to data processing companies. While the job outlook varies upon which service is being discussed, in general, the business services sector is among the fastest-growing in the nation. Increasingly, American companies are "outsourcing" functions like data processing to outside firms. Often large organizations will go so far as to hand over the management of their entire data center to an outside service provider. This trend is expected to boost opportunities for those who work for data processing services.*

Other types of services that benefit from this trend include security, and personnel services firms. Many businesses are using temporary workers instead of hiring new permanent staffers, thus avoiding the much higher overhead costs such as health insurance. Companies that supply these temporary workers, as well as those that place permanent workers, are among the fastest-growing in the nation. While one third of the jobs available are administrative support occupations, there is a growing trend toward specialization which will open up more positions for highly-skilled workers, such as engineers or managers.

CAPITAL CREDIT CORPORATION
8000 Arlington Expressway, Suite 200, Jacksonville FL 32211. 904/725-3641. **Contact:** Diane Bishop, Director of Human Resources. **Description:** A collection agency. **Corporate headquarters location:** This Location.

EQUIFAX PAYMENT SERVICES
5301 West Idlewild Avenue, Tampa FL 33634. 813/886-5000. **Contact:** Bob Kemph, Manager of Employment. **Description:** Divisional headquarters of a payment authorization service for financial institutions and retail establishments nationwide. National online computer systems enable authorization of check and credit card transactions. **Common positions include:** Accountant/Auditor; Computer Programmer; Financial Analyst; Operations/Production Manager; Systems Analyst. **Educational backgrounds include:** Accounting; Computer Science. **Benefits:** Dental Insurance; Disability Coverage; Employee Discounts; Life Insurance; Medical Insurance; Pension Plan; Savings Plan; Tuition Assistance. **Corporate headquarters location:** Tampa FL. **Operations at this facility include:** Administration; Divisional Headquarters; Regional Headquarters; Research and Development; Sales; Service. **Listed on:** NASDAQ.

GEONEX CORPORATION
8950 9th Street North, St. Petersburg FL 33702. 813/578-0100. **Fax:** 813/577-6946. **Contact:** Trinka Burdick, Human Resources Director. **Description:** Provides international mapping services, AM/FM-GIS. **Common positions include:** Agricultural Engineer; Biological Scientist/Biochemist; Computer Programmer; Computer Systems Analyst; Draftsperson; Electrical/Electronics Engineer; Financial Analyst; General Manager; Geographer; Geologist/Geophysicist; Mechanical Engineer; Mining Engineer; Software Engineer; Surveyor. **Educational backgrounds include:** Biology; Computer Science; Engineering; Geology; Marketing; Mathematics. **Benefits:** Dental Insurance; Disability Coverage; Life Insurance; Medical Insurance. **Corporate headquarters**

location: This Location. **Other U.S. locations:** Los Angeles CA; Chicago IL. **Operations at this facility include:** Administration; Divisional Headquarters; Manufacturing; Regional Headquarters; Research and Development; Sales; Service. **Number of employees at this location:** 300. **Number of employees nationwide:** 1,480.

MULTI ENTERTAINMENT
2000 Southwest 30th Avenue, Pembrook Park FL 33009. 954/458-4000. **Fax:** 954/458-4003. **Contact:** Jim Etkin, Vice President. **Description:** Multi Entertainment is a convention production corporation -- including sets, lighting, staging, floral, decor, audiovisual, entertainment and music. **Common positions include:** Commercial Artist; Computer Programmer; Construction Contractor and Manager; Cost Estimator; Department Manager; Designer; Draftsperson; Electrician; General Manager; Manufacturer's/Wholesaler's Sales Rep.; Marketing/Advertising/PR Manager; Public Relations Specialist; Secretary; Sheet-Metal Worker; Travel Agent; Typist/Word Processor. **Educational backgrounds include:** Accounting; Art/Design; Business Administration; Communications; Computer Science; Marketing. **Benefits:** Disability Coverage; Medical Insurance. **Special Programs:** Apprenticeships; Internships; Training Programs. **Corporate headquarters location:** This Location. **Operations at this facility include:** Administration; Manufacturing; Sales. **Number of employees at this location:** 60.

NATIONAL LINEN
1828 Evans Avenue, Fort Meyers FL 33901. 941/332-1165. **Contact:** Debi Bryn, Employment Relations Manager. **Description:** A commercial laundry service. **Common positions include:** Industrial Engineer; Operations/Production Manager. **Benefits:** Employee Discounts; Life Insurance; Medical Insurance; Profit Sharing; Tuition Assistance. **Corporate headquarters location:** This Location. **Operations at this facility include:** Regional Headquarters; Sales; Service.

PALM COAST DATA LTD.
11 Commerce Boulevard, Palm Coast FL 32164. 904/445-4662. **Contact:** Human Resources. **Description:** A subscription fulfillment company. Palm Coast Data manages subscription lists for publishing companies.

THE WACKENHUT CORPORATION
1319 Naldo Avenue, Jacksonville FL 32207. 904/398-1640. **Contact:** Janet Rowe, Secretary. **Description:** A security services company. **Common positions include:** Security Officer. **Corporate headquarters location:** Coral Gables FL.

THE WACKENHUT CORPORATION
1500 San Remo Avenue, Coral Gables FL 33146. 305/662-7415. **Fax:** 305/662-7485. **Contact:** Mr. Jan P. Vandersluis, Manager of Corporate Recruiting. **Description:** Wackenhut provides physical security services, correction services, and products to businesses, governments, and individuals from more than 150 domestic and foreign offices. Specific services include security guard services; corrections staffing; private investigative services; the assembly and sale of electronic security equipment and systems; the training of security guards and fire and crash rescue personnel; providing fire protection and emergency ambulance service to municipalities; security consulting; planning, designing, and implementing integrated security systems; and providing specialized services to the nuclear power industry. Wackenhut has 90 offices located in most major United States cities. International opportunities exist in foreign countries. **Common positions include:** Accountant/Auditor; Administrative Services Manager; Branch Manager; Clerical Supervisor; Computer Programmer; Computer Systems Analyst; Customer Service Representative; General Manager; Human Resources Specialist; Management Trainee; Services Sales Representative. **Educational backgrounds include:** Accounting; Business Administration; Computer Science; Criminal Justice; Law Enforcement. **Benefits:** 401K; Dental Insurance; Disability Coverage; Life Insurance; Medical Insurance; Pension Plan; Savings Plan. **Corporate headquarters location:** This Location. **Other U.S. locations:** Nationwide. **Subsidiaries include:** Wackenhut Corrections, Inc.; Wackenhut International. **Operations at this facility include:** Administration; Divisional Headquarters; Service. **Listed on:** NASDAQ; New York Stock Exchange. **Number of employees at this location:** 275. **Number of employees nationwide:** 40,000.

Note: Because addresses and telephone numbers of smaller companies change rapidly, we recommend you call each company to verify the information below before inquiring about job opportunities. Mass mailings are not recommended.

Additional employers with under 250 employees:

LINEN SUPPLY

Angelica Healthcare Service Group
1950 NW First Ave, Miami FL 33136-1302. 305/573-1544.

Angelica Healthcare Service Group
2420 Florida Ave, West Palm Beach FL 33401-7812. 407/832-5742.

Angelica Healthcare Service Group
1250 State Ave, Holly Hill FL 32117-2752. 904/672-3931.

Angelica Rental Services
614 N McDuff Ave, Jacksonville FL 32254-3256. 904/384-2390.

Angelica Rental Services
1929 NW First Ave, Miami FL 33136-1301. 305/945-9952.

Jacksonville Linen Service
354 Park St, Jacksonville FL 32204-2342. 904/354-6675.

Pensacola Linen Service
2900 W Navy Blvd, Pensacola FL 32505-8022. 904/433-3106.

Athletic Towel Service
2101 W Cypress St, Tampa FL 33606-1019. 813/251-2483.

G&K Services
1290 Beverly St, Ft Walton Beach FL 32547-1434. 904/863-4019.

Guy's Dust Control Service
2101 W Cypress St, Tampa FL 33606-1019. 813/877-3336.

ADJUSTMENT AND COLLECTION SERVICES

General Accounts Service
221 W Prospect Rd, Ft Lauderdale FL 33309-3925. 407/655-8766.

HH&L Financial Services
3000 Langley Ave, Pensacola FL 32504-4702. 904/479-9477.

Merchants Association
146 2nd St N, St Petersburg FL 33701-3361. 813/892-3300.

CREDIT REPORTING SERVICES

All-Credit Reports
7545 Central Industrial Dr, Riviera Beach FL 33404-3429. 407/842-2229.

Credit Bureau Affiliates
7325 Alderwood Dr, Sarasota FL 34243-1707. 941/355-1664.

Equifax
3001 Executive Dr, Clearwater FL 34622-2260. 813/573-2522.

Merchants Association Credit Bureau
1300 Executive Center Dr, Tallahassee FL 32301. 904/878-9918.

DISINFECTING AND PEST CONTROL SERVICES

Massey Services
1051 Winderley Place, Suite 201, Maitland FL 32751-7269. 407/875-3939.

Arab Pest Control
6410 Ridge Rd, Port Richey FL 34668-6748. 904/796-2951.

Clements Getz Pest Control
1539 NW 65th Ave, Ft Lauderdale FL 33313-4542. 954/584-6744.

Orkin Exterminating Co.
4133 US Highway 301 N, Ellenton FL 34222-2409. 941/747-5780.

Prism-Bugs Burger
226 Wilshire Blvd, Casselberry FL 32707-5371. 407/331-1881.

Rentokil Pest Control
3195 N Powerline Rd, Pompano Beach FL 33069-1015. 954/979-9000.

Sears Authorized Treatment & Pest Control
812 Chestnut St, Clearwater FL 34616-5642. 813/447-4718.

Sears Termite & Pest Control
1611 Jaydell Circle, Tallahassee FL 32308-5401. 904/747-8780.

Terminix International
4406 Enterprise Ave, Naples FL 33942-7011. 941/643-6692.

Truly Nolen Pest Control Corporation
5455 Spring Hill Dr, Spring Hill FL 34606-4598. 352/686-9400.

Terra Asgrow Florida Co.
122 N 11th Ave, Arcadia FL 33821-8905. 941/494-4400.

CLEANING AND MAINTENANCE SERVICES

Unified Services
P.O. Box 21082, Orlando FL 32815-0082. 407/875-1414.

Action Kleen Systems
156 NW 37th St, Miami FL 33127-3111. 305/573-6655.

American Building Maintenance
129 NW 13th St, Suite 32, Boca Raton FL 33432-1636. 407/394-9429.

American Building Maintenance
5871 Saint Augustine Rd, Jacksonville FL 32207-8024. 904/737-2755.

Coverall Of South Florida
915 Middle River Dr, Ft Lauderdale FL 33304-3544. 954/565-9885.

Crystal Clean Janitor Service
328 N Park Ave, Apopka FL 32703-4150. 407/647-4229.

ISS International Service Systems
4461 Parkbreeze Ct, Orlando FL 32808-1043. 407/298-2440.

Royal Services
958 S Orange Ave, Orlando FL 32806-1263. 407/422-6979.

Tri Angle Maintenance Service
12031 31st Ct N, St Petersburg FL 33716-1810. 813/573-9519.

Versatech Industries
433 Plaza Real, Suite 275,
Boca Raton FL 33432-3945.
407/395-6434.

Servicemaster
3104 S Andrews Ave, Ft
Lauderdale FL 33316-4112.
954/525-1414.

Rochester Midland Corp.
5311 W Crenshaw St,
Tampa FL 33634-2406.
813/885-5079.

**COMPUTER PROCESSING
AND DATA PREPARATION
SERVICES**

**Florida Informanagement
Service**
401 S Magnolia Ave, Orlando
FL 32801-3331. 407/841-
1712.

Business Records Corp.
1431 Tallevast Rd, Sarasota
FL 34243-5035. 941/351-
4981.

Computer Task Group
5300 NW 33rd Ave, Suite
115, Ft Lauderdale FL
33309-6356. 954/486-
7105.

Medical Business Services
3049 Cleveland Ave, Fort
Myers FL 33901-7049.
941/337-3199.

Paradyne
604 Courtland St, Orlando FL
32804-1361. 407/644-
0624.

**COMPUTER RENTAL AND
LEASING**

Bay Resources
4307 Vineland Rd, Orlando
FL 32811-7374. 407/423-
4140.

**DETECTIVE, GUARD, AND
ARMORED CAR SERVICES**

Allied Security
5151 Adanson St, Suite 98,
Orlando FL 32804-1315.
407/629-6064.

Allied Security
2880 W Oakland Park Blvd,
Suite 111, Ft Lauderdale FL
33311-1362. 954/486-
5608.

Allied Security
4511 N Himes Ave, Suite
191, Tampa FL 33614-
7005. 813/878-2911.

Vickers Security Service
1205 E Hillsborough Ave,
Tampa FL 33604-7207.
813/237-0300.

Granada Security
2526 Park St #872 2,
Jacksonville FL 32204-4518.
904/389-1880.

Onguard Systems
403 E Beacon Rd, Lakeland
FL 33803-2609. 941/646-
1327.

Nation Wide Security
1000 N Ashley Dr, Tampa FL
33602-3716. 813/221-
5577.

Pinkerton Security Services
500 Fairway Dr, Suite 201,
Deerfield Beach FL 33441-
1877. 954/428-3008.

Polygem Security
13640 NW 19th Ave, Opa
Locka FL 33054-4234.
305/687-0465.

**Russell Security
Services/Esco**
1107 Myra St, Jacksonville
FL 32204-3321. 904/355-
1122.

Chain Investigation
979 W Montrose St,
Clermont FL 34711-2055.
904/242-0721.

**Crescent Lake Information
Service**
210 Division St, Clermont FL
34711-7701. 904/394-
6544.

**Richard J Hudson
Investigator**
30 Areca Dr, Orlando FL
32807-5032. 407/277-
3684.

**SECURITY SYSTEMS
SERVICES**

Advance Security Systems
2642 Palm Bay Rd NE, Palm
Bay FL 32905-3524.
407/725-7277.

Samco Enterprises
8710 N 48th St, Tampa FL
33617-6022. 813/988-
0197.

Alarmforce
7740 SW 104th St, Miami
FL 33156-3149. 305/665-
1111.

Arius
4951 Adamo Dr #B, Tampa
FL 33605. 813/248-5110.

Emergency Networks
4207 Vineland Rd, Suite M-
14, Orlando FL 32811-6629.
407/872-3350.

Network Multi-Family
2901 W Busch Blvd, Tampa

FL 33618-4523. 813/932-
3411.

**Rollins Protective Services
Company**
5031 Savarese Circle,
Tampa FL 33634-2480.
813/885-5881.

Scott Security Systems
385 Whooping Loop,
Altamonte Springs FL
32701-3443. 407/834-
3733.

Security Data Group
4960 SW 52nd St, Davie FL
33314-5530. 954/321-
8696.

Wells Fargo Alarm Services
10235 SW 53rd St, Cooper
City FL 33328-5613.
954/680-0140.

MISC. BUSINESS SERVICES

Applied Benefits Research
34125 US Highway 19 N,
Suite 300, Palm Harbor FL
34684-2159. 813/785-
2819.

**Orlando/Orange County
Convention**
7208 Sand Lake Rd, Suite
300, Orlando FL 32819-
5279. 407/363-5800.

**Payment Systems For Credit
Unions**
100 Carillon Pkwy, St
Petersburg FL 33716-1207.
813/572-8822.

Home Pro Of Mid Florida
1000 Savage Ct, Suite 208,
Longwood FL 32750-4988.
407/767-2462.

CICB
5874 S Semoran Blvd,
Orlando FL 32822-4817.
407/277-0884.

Hyde Park Interiors
11724 N Dale Mabry Hwy,
Tampa FL 33618-3504.
813/264-4425.

Telecheck
4902 Eisenhower Blvd,
Tampa FL 33634-6310.
813/884-1900.

**All Exchange Answering
Service**
1221 N Florida Ave, Tampa
FL 33602-3305. 813/229-
7994.

Smith Appraisal Service
2013 Jorome Dr, Tampa FL
33612-5051. 813/935-
7557.

RGIS Inventory Specialists
3450 W Busch Blvd, Tampa
FL 33618. 813/930-9042.

RGIS Inventory Specialists
370 Whooping Loop,
Altamonte Springs FL
32701-3451. 407/331-
1128.

**Washington Inventory
Service**
4241 Baymeadows Rd,
Jacksonville FL 32217-4689.
904/733-0381.

Dataplex
6011 Benjamin Rd, Suite
101B, Tampa FL 33634-
5173. 813/888-7821.

Infocopy
8095 NW 98th St, Hialeah
FL 33016-2332. 305/822-
0244.

Lanier Worldwide
2114 Airport Blvd, Pensacola
FL 32504. 904/478-3071.

Congress Center
1325 S Congress Ave,
Boynton Beach FL 33426-
5876. 407/369-5772.

The DSJ Companies
3020 Mercy Dr, Orlando FL
32808-3139. 407/843-
3030.

RG Systems
5008 W Linebaugh Ave,
Tampa FL 33624-5095.
813/963-7878.

**For more information on career opportunities in miscellaneous business services and
non-scientific research:**

<u>Associations</u>

AMERICAN SOCIETY OF APPRAISERS
P.O. Box 17265, Washington DC 20041.
703/478-2228.

**EQUIPMENT LEASING ASSOCIATION OF
AMERICA**
1300 17th Street, Suite 1010, North
Arlington VA 22209. 703/527-8655.

**NATIONAL ASSOCIATION OF PERSONNEL
SERVICES**
3133 Mt. Vernon Avenue, Alexandria VA
22305. 703/684-0180.

CHARITIES AND SOCIAL SERVICES

The outlook for social service workers is better than average. In fact, opportunities for qualified applicants are expected to be excellent, partly due to the rapid turnover in the industry due as a result of lower wages offered.

Note: Because of the high turnover rate and the continuous need for social services, the outlook for this industry has remained constant over the past few years.

AMERICAN RED CROSS
220 Hospital Drive NE, Walton Beach FL 32548-5068. 904/243-3322. **Contact:** Human Resources. **Description:** A social services organization committed to providing relief to victims of disasters and helping people to prevent, prepare for, and respond to emergencies. **Corporate headquarters location:** Washington DC.

YMCA
500 Pope Road, St. Augustine FL 32084-5931. 904/471-9622. **Contact:** Human Resources. **Description:** The YMCA provides a variety of programs that develop a healthy body, mind, and spirit for all, regardless of race, sex, age, religion, or ability to pay. Programs include child care, youth leadership, and recreational sports and fitness programs for children and adults.

Note: Because addresses and telephone numbers of smaller companies change rapidly, we recommend you call each company to verify the information below before inquiring about job opportunities. Mass mailings are not recommended.

Additional employers with under 250 employees:

JOB TRAINING AND VOCATIONAL REHABILITATION SERVICES

Career & Personal Counseling Center
4200 54th Ave S, St Petersburg FL 33711-4744. 813/867-1166.

MISC. SOCIAL SERVICES

Goodwill Industries Of Central Florida
10601 US Highway 441, Leesburg FL 34788-7237. 352/728-3488.

Goodwill Industries-Gulfstream
885 SE Monterey Rd, Stuart FL 34994-4506. 407/287-3666.

American Cancer Society
3901 NW 79th Ave, Miami FL 33166-6554. 305/594-4363.

Bert Road Group Home
1010 Bert Rd, Jacksonville FL 32211-5817. 904/723-3527.

Cystic Fibrosis Foundation
1211 N Westshore Blvd, Suite 602, Tampa FL 33607-4605. 813/286-0266.

Family Resources
3160 5th Ave N, St Petersburg FL 33713-7630. 813/321-5554.

Family Resources
3821 5th Ave N, St Petersburg FL 33713-7547. 813/323-2244.

Human Services Foundation
677 N Washington Blvd #38, Sarasota FL 34236-4241. 941/954-1124.

Jewish Federation Palm Beach County
4601 Community Dr, West Palm Beach FL 33417-2716. 407/478-0700.

Larc Residential Services
95 W North Shore Ave, Fort Myers FL 33903-4403. 941/995-7710.

Palm Beach Habilitation Center
4522 S Congress Ave, Lake Worth FL 33461-4797. 407/965-8500.

Parent To Parent Palm Beach County
1201 Australian Ave, Riviera Beach FL 33404-6635. 407/863-3310.

Tampa Hillsborough County Dacco
4422 E Columbus Dr, Tampa FL 33605-3233. 813/623-3500.

Volunteers Of America North & Central Florida
3550 W Waters Ave, Tampa FL 33614-2711. 813/915-0706.

YMCA
116 5th St S, St Petersburg FL 33701-4112. 813/895-9622.

Haven Of Life Center
1506 18th St W, Bradenton FL 34205-4735. 941/378-5433.

For more information on career opportunities in charities and social services:

Associations

AMERICAN COUNCIL OF THE BLIND
1155 15th Street NW, Suite 720,
Washington DC 20005. 202/467-5081.
Membership. Offers an annual conference, a
monthly magazine, and scholarships.

CATHOLIC CHARITIES USA
1731 King Street, Suite 200, Alexandria VA
22314. 703/549-1390. Membership.

**FAMILY SERVICE ASSOCIATION OF
AMERICA**
11700 West Lake Park Drive, Park Place,
Milwaukee WI 53224. 414/359-1040.
Membership.

**NATIONAL COUNCIL ON FAMILY
RELATIONS**
3989 Central Avenue NE, Suite 550,
Minneapolis MN 55421. 612/781-9331.

Fax: 612/781-9348. Membership. Publishes
two quarterly journals. Offers an annual
conference and newsletters.

**NATIONAL FEDERATION OF SOCIETIES
FOR CLINICAL SOCIAL WORK, INC.**
P.O. Box 3740, Arlington VA 22203.
703/522-3866. A lobbying organization.
Offers newsletters and a conference every
two years to membership organizations.

NATIONAL FEDERATION OF THE BLIND
1800 Johnson Street, Baltimore MD
21230. 410/659-9314. Membership of
50,000 in 600 local chapters. Monthly
magazine.

NATIONAL MULTIPLE SCLEROSIS SOCIETY
733 Third Avenue, New York NY 10017.
212/986-3240. Toll-free: 800/344-4867.
Publishes a quarterly magazine.

CHEMICALS/RUBBER AND PLASTICS

 *First the good news: overall growth in the chemical industry is on the upswing. Sales were expected to rise as much as eight percent in 1995. Chemical products and services are currently in high demand, thus creating a demand for more workers, and recent price increases are holding steady. During 1994, the U.S. chemical trade surplus grew four percent.*

Now the bad news: costs for pollution reduction are rising. Factories are running at 85 percent capacity, and if companies increase spending on plant and equipment, an oversupply could result if economic growth slows too quickly.

Growth prospects for the domestic synthetic rubber industry remain mixed, reflecting the industry's dependence on tire manufacturing. The tire industry shows signs of stabilizing after undergoing a period characterized by massive restructuring, the effects of recession in the domestic market, and consistently high levels of imports.

In the plastics industry, greater reliance on computer-aided design and manufacturing is expected in the last half of the 1990s, as production is streamlined. These measures will be aimed at strengthening the industry's competitiveness in the areas of quality control and improved client relations.

ARIZONA CHEMICAL
Caller Box 2447, Panama City FL 32402. 904/785-8521. **Contact:** Andy Tomasik, Personnel Director. **Description:** A gum and wood chemicals company. **Common positions include:** Chemical Engineer; Chemist.

ATLANTIS PLASTICS
2665 South Bayshore Drive, 8th Floor, Miami FL 33133. 305/858-2200. **Contact:** David Velmosky, Human Resources. **Description:** The holding company for a manufacturer of various plastic products, including injection-molded plastics and plastic film.

BETZ PAPERCHEM INC.
7510 Baymeadows Way, Jacksonville FL 32256. 904/733-7110. **Contact:** Tom Burke, Human Resources. **Description:** Develops, sells, and services specialty process chemicals for the pulp and paper industry. **Common positions include:** Chemical Engineer; Chemist; Computer Programmer; Manufacturer's/Wholesaler's Sales Rep. **Educational backgrounds include:** Chemistry; Computer Science; Engineering. **Benefits:** 401K; Credit Union; Dental Insurance; Disability Coverage; Life Insurance; Medical Insurance; Pension Plan; Profit Sharing; Tuition Assistance. **Special Programs:** Internships. **Parent company:** Betz Laboratories, Inc. **Operations at this facility include:** Administration; Divisional Headquarters; Research and Development; Sales; Service. **Listed on:** NASDAQ.

BUSCH BOLLE ALLEN
2051 North Lane Avenue, Jacksonville FL 32254. 904/783-2180. **Contact:** R.R. Ohmer, Human Resources Management. **Description:** A manufacturer and distributor of chemicals. **Common positions include:** Accountant/Auditor; Blue-Collar Worker Supervisor; Buyer; Chemical Engineer; Chemist; Computer Programmer; Customer Service Representative; Electrical/Electronics Engineer; Human Resources Specialist; Manufacturer's/Wholesaler's Sales Rep.; Operations/Production Manager; Purchasing Agent and Manager. **Educational backgrounds include:** Accounting; Chemistry; Computer Science; Engineering. **Benefits:** Life Insurance; Medical Insurance; Pension Plan; Savings Plan; Tuition Assistance. **Special Programs:** Training Programs.

Corporate headquarters location: Wayne NJ. Operations at this facility include: Administration; Manufacturing; Research and Development; Sales. Listed on: New York Stock Exchange. Number of employees at this location: 167.

CF INDUSTRIES, INC.
PLANT CITY BRANCH
P.O. Drawer L, Plant City FL 33564. 813/782-1591. Contact: Tom Pitt, Personnel Director. Description: Branch office of the producer of phosphate fertilizers.

CF INDUSTRIES, INC.
TAMPA BRANCH
2520 Guy Verger Boulevard, Tampa FL 33605. 813/247-5531. Contact: Personnel Department. Description: A chemical company specializing in the production of phosphates for use in fertilizer.

CARGILL FERTILIZER
8813 Highway 41 South, Riverview FL 33569-4866. 813/677-9111. Contact: Tony Farraj, Human Resources Manager. Description: A chemical company specializing in the production of phosphates for use in fertilizer.

CARGILL FERTILIZER
P.O. Box 9002, Bartow FL 33831. 941/533-2171. Contact: Personnel Manager. Description: A chemical company specializing in the production of phosphates for use in fertilizer. Operations at this facility include: Regional Headquarters.

DAYCO PRODUCTS
3100 Mericamp Road, Ocala FL 34471. 352/732-6191. Contact: Kent Foster, Human Resources Manager. Description: Manufactures braided and woven molded rubber hose.

FARMLAND HYDRO
Stock Road 640, P.O. Box 960, Bartow FL 33830. 941/533-1141. Contact: John McGarrity, Personnel Director. Description: A producer of acids for use in fertilizers.

W.R. GRACE & COMPANY
One Town Center Road, Boca Raton FL 33486. 407/362-2000. Fax: 407/362-2306. Contact: Terry Fleites, Manager of Staff Support. Description: W.R. Grace is a producers of specialty chemicals, as well as a provider of specialized health care products. The major divisions of W.R. Grace include Grace Packaging, Grace Davison, Grace Construction Products, Grace Dearborn, Grace Container & Specialty Polymers, and Grace Health Care. Grace Packaging specializes in flexible packaging systems for meat, poultry, cheese, and other perishable food products, as well as shrink packaging materials for consumer and industrial products. Grace Davison catalysts 'crack' crude oil into fuel and related by-products. Davison polyolefin catalysts are involved in polyethylene production, and its silica and zeolite adsorbents are ingredients in industrial and consumer applications. Grace Construction products include concrete and cement additives, fireproofing, and waterproofing systems which protect structures from nature by strengthening concrete, fighting corrosion, stopping water damage, and protecting structural steel from fire damage. Grace Dearborn water treatment and process chemicals inhibit scale, corrosion, and fouling in water systems, treat wastewater, and enhance operating efficiency and environmental performance. Grace Container & Specialty Polymers include container sealant systems that keep food and beverages protected from bacteria and other contaminants, extend shelf-life, and preserve flavor, while specialty polymers are used in the manufacture of printed circuit board and electronic components assembly. Common positions include: Accountant/Auditor; Attorney; Computer Systems Analyst; Financial Analyst; Human Resources Specialist; Management Analyst/Consultant. Educational backgrounds include: Accounting; Business Administration; Finance. Benefits: 401K; Dental Insurance; Life Insurance; Medical Insurance; Pension Plan; Tuition Assistance. Corporate headquarters location: This Location. Operations at this facility include: Administration; Divisional Headquarters. Listed on: New York Stock Exchange. Number of employees at this location: 440. Number of employees nationwide: 34,000.

IMC FERTILIZER, INC.
NEW WALES OPERATIONS
P.O. Box 2000, Mulberry FL 33860. 941/428-2500. Contact: Kurt W. Wickland, Supervisor of Labor Relations. Description: A manufacturer of chemical fertilizer.

Common positions include: Accountant/Auditor; Blue-Collar Worker Supervisor; Buyer; Chemist; Civil Engineer; Computer Programmer; Draftsperson; Electrical/Electronics Engineer; Industrial Engineer; Laboratory Technician; Machinist; Mechanical Engineer; Supervisor. **Educational backgrounds include:** Chemistry; Computer Science; Engineering. **Benefits:** Dental Insurance; Disability Coverage; Employee Discounts; Life Insurance; Medical Insurance; Pension Plan; Savings Plan; Tuition Assistance. **Corporate headquarters location:** Mundelin IL. **Other U.S. locations:** Barton FL; Carlsbad NM. **Operations at this facility include:** Manufacturing. **Number of employees nationwide:** 1,150.

McNEEL INTERNATIONAL CORPORATION
5401 West Kennedy Boulevard, Suite 751, Tampa FL 33609. 813/286-8680. **Contact:** Human Resources. **Description:** McNeel International Corporation manufactures rubber and plastics products.

MONSANTO COMPANY
P.O. Box 97, Gonzalez FL 32560. 904/968-7000. **Contact:** Human Resources. **Description:** Manufactures chemicals and fibers.

REICHHOLD CHEMICAL INC.
P.O. Box 1433, Pensacola FL 32596-1433. 904/433-7621. **Contact:** Ross Moses, Personnel Administrator. **Description:** A chemical plant manufacturing coating resins, epoxy, epoxy hardeners, acrylic, and co-polymer resins. **Common positions include:** Accountant/Auditor; Blue-Collar Worker Supervisor; Buyer; Chemical Engineer; Chemist; Electrician; General Manager; Human Service Worker; Industrial Production Manager; Mechanical Engineer; Plant Manager; Purchasing Agent and Manager. **Educational backgrounds include:** Accounting; Business Administration; Chemistry; Engineering. **Benefits:** 401K; Dental Insurance; Life Insurance; Medical Insurance; Tuition Assistance. **Corporate headquarters location:** Durham NC. **Operations at this facility include:** Manufacturing. **Listed on:** Privately held. **Number of employees at this location:** 85.

SECURITY PLASTICS INC.
P.O. Box 4723, Miami Lakes FL 33014. 305/364-7700. **Contact:** Personnel Department. **Description:** A manufacturer of plastic components for the OEM market. **Common positions include:** Accountant/Auditor; Administrator; Computer Programmer; Credit Manager; Customer Service Representative; Department Manager; Manufacturer's/Wholesaler's Sales Rep.; Marketing Specialist; Mechanical Engineer; Operations/Production Manager; Plastics Engineer; Quality Control Supervisor. **Educational backgrounds include:** Business Administration; Computer Science; Engineering; Marketing; Mathematics. **Benefits:** Dental Insurance; Disability Coverage; Employee Discounts; Life Insurance; Medical Insurance; Pension Plan; Savings Plan; Tuition Assistance. **Corporate headquarters location:** This Location. **Operations at this facility include:** Manufacturing.

SHELL CHEMICAL
2525 South Combee Road, Lakeland FL 33801. 941/665-6226. **Contact:** Personnel Director. **Description:** A manufacturer of chemical products for coatings and adhesives, textiles, construction and mineral processing.

UNIROYAL TECHNOLOGY CORPORATION
2 North Tamiami Trail, Suite 900, Sarasota FL 34236. 941/366-5282. **Contact:** Human Resources. **Description:** Manufactures naughahyde and a variety of plastic products, including foam and molded plastic products.

Note: Because addresses and telephone numbers of smaller companies change rapidly, we recommend you call each company to verify the information below before inquiring about job opportunities. Mass mailings are not recommended.

Additional employers with over 250 employees:

MANMADE FIBERS

American Cyanamid Co.
1801 Cyanamid Rd, Milton FL 32571. 904/994-5311.

PLASTICS PRODUCTS

Clairson International
720 SW 17th St, Ocala FL 34474. 352/351-6100.

Seamless
1909 NE 25th Ave, Ocala FL 34470-4848. 352/732-0600.

Sun Coast Plastics
P.O. Box 4700, Sarasota FL
34230-4700. 813/355-
7166.

**INDUSTRIAL INORGANIC
CHEMICALS**

Conserv
4891 Angus Rd, Polk City FL
33868. 813/425-1164.

Mobil Mining & Minerals
P.O. Box 311, Nichols FL
33863-0311. 813/425-
6200.

Additional employers with under 250 employees:

**INDUSTRIAL INORGANIC
CHEMICALS**

Theochem Laboratories
7373 Rowlett Park Dr,
Tampa FL 33610-1141.
813/237-6463.

**PAINTS, VARNISHES, AND
RELATED PRODUCTS**

**Color Wheel Paint
Manufacturing Co.**
2814 Silver Star Rd, Orlando
FL 32808-3941. 407/293-
6810.

Coronado Paint Co.
308 S Old County Rd,
Edgewater FL 32132-1812.
904/428-6461.

Flex Bon Paint
2131 Andrea Ln, Fort Myers
FL 33912-1903. 941/489-
2332.

Scott Paint Corporation
7839 Fruitville Rd, Sarasota
FL 34240-9280. 941/371-
0005.

**INDUSTRIAL ORGANIC
CHEMICALS**

PCR
P.O. Box 1466, Gainesville
FL 32602-1466. 352/376-
8246.

PCR
8570 Phillips Hwy,
Jacksonville FL 32256-1225.
904/730-7511.

QO Chemicals
Airport Rd, Belle Glade FL
33430. 407/996-6576.

SCM Glidco Organics
P.O. Box 389, Jacksonville
FL 32201-0389. 904/768-
5800.

**AGRICULTURAL
CHEMICALS**

Piney Point Phosphates
13300 US Highway 41 N,
Palmetto FL 34221-8661.
941/722-4555.

Sunniland Corp.
US 17-92 & Hwy 419,
Sanford FL 32772. 407/322-
2421.

Sureco
10008 N Dale Mabry Hwy,
Tampa FL 33618-4424.
813/960-8333.

**MISC. RUBBER AND
PLASTICS PRODUCTS**

**Townley Manufacturing
Company**
10551 S E 110th St, Candler
FL 32111. 904/687-3001.

RUBBER PRODUCTS

TSE Industries
5260 113th Ave N,
Clearwater FL 34620-4838.
813/573-7676.

Atco Rubber Products
3007 Central Dr, Plant City
FL 33567-1158. 813/752-
3044.

Mold-Ex Rubber Co.
8052 Armstrong Rd, Milton
FL 32583-8712. 904/626-
7211.

**UNSUPPORTED PLASTICS
PRODUCTS**

Essex Plastics
1531 NW 12th Ave,
Pompano Beach FL 33069-
1730. 954/941-6333.

Master Packaging
6932 S Manhattan Ave,
Tampa FL 33616-1829.
813/837-1575.

PLASTICS PRODUCTS

Taylor Distributors
3071 Warehouse Rd, Fort
Myers FL 33916-7614.
941/337-3211.

JM Manufacturing Co.
P.O. Box 185, Green Cove
Springs FL 32043-0185.
904/284-3091.

River City Plastics
7167 Old Kings Rd,
Jacksonville FL 32219-3795.
904/783-1980.

Sewell Plastics
4020 N 29th Terrace,
Hollywood FL 33020-1045.
954/925-0236.

US Container Corp.
753 Central Florida Pkwy,
Orlando FL 32824-8501.
407/859-7560.

A&M Engineering Plastics
10521 75th St, Largo FL
34647-1419. 813/541-
4482.

CKS Rigal Plastics
333 W Michigan St, Orlando
FL 32806-4422. 407/423-
0333.

Command Medical Products
15 Signal Ave, Ormond
Beach FL 32174-2984.
904/672-8116.

**Continental Plastic Card
Company**
3651 NW 120th Ave, Coral
Springs FL 33065-2530.
305/753-0670.

Dart Container Corp.
4610 Airport Rd, Plant City
FL 33567-1114. 813/752-
1990.

Echo Plastic Systems
P.O. Box 694217, Miami FL
33269-1217. 305/931-
8405.

Flo-Control
1251 NE 48th St, Pompano
Beach FL 33064-4910.
954/428-8703.

Granutec
8601 Somerset Dr, Largo FL
34643-2714. 813/536-
5502.

Hamilton Products
P.O. Box 770069, Ocala FL
34477-0069. 352/237-
6188.

Mercer Products Co.
37235 Hwy 19, Eustis FL
32727. 904/357-4119.

Pac Tec
4820 Middle Ave, Sarasota
FL 34234-3128. 941/351-
9950.

Polyplastex United
6200 49th St, Pinellas Park
FL 34665-5718. 813/525-
2173.

Servotech Industries
8900 NW 77th Ct, Medley
FL 33166-2102. 305/888-
3555.

Sun Coast Closures
7350 26th Ct E, Sarasota FL
34243-3947. 941/355-
7166.

Thermotech
3200 Tyrone Blvd N, St
Petersburg FL 33710-2338.
813/347-2191.

**Tredegar Molded Products
Company**
2701 75th St N, St
Petersburg FL 33710-2938.
813/384-2600.

Zone Fabricators
825 South Village Dr, St
Petersburg FL 33716.
813/577-7773.

Advanced Dial Company
552 NW 77th St, Boca
Raton FL 33487-1324.
407/241-3964.

**PLASTICS MATERIALS
WHOLESALE**

General Plastic Corp.
8900 NW 77th Ct, Ft
Lauderdale FL 33321-2058.
954/760-4479.

**CHEMICALS AND ALLIED
PRODUCTS WHOLESALE**

Caremark
317 S North Lake Blvd, Suite

1020, Altamonte Springs FL
32701-5263. 407/830-
1505.

**Clearwater Chemical
Corporation**
8051 N Tamiami Trail, Suite
18, Sarasota FL 34243-
2016. 941/355-8815.

Craft America
4340 W Hillsborough Ave,
Tampa FL 33614-5522.
813/872-7238.

Devoe & Reynolds Co.
4200 Commercial Way,
Spring Hill FL 34606-2325.
352/686-0240.

Shipley Company
9500 Koger Blvd N, St
Petersburg FL 33702-2483.
813/576-3532.

Stuart Hatteras Ltd.
2401 P G A Blvd, West Palm
Beach FL 33410. 407/775-
3531.

Parkway Research Corp.
2501 NW 75th St, Miami FL
33147-6009. 305/691-
1922.

Zep Manufacturing Co.
7322 Exchange Dr, Orlando
FL 32809-6243. 407/851-
5610.

**PAINTS, VARNISHES, AND
SUPPLIES WHOLESALE**

Glidden Paints
35 S Wickham Rd,
Melbourne FL 32904-1129.
407/728-7872.

MCI-Wattyl Paints
4539 26th St W, Bradenton
FL 34207-1295. 941/755-
7773.

MCI-Wattyl Paints
20070 Cortez Blvd,
Brooksville FL 34601-3834.
352/796-2622.

Porter Paints
9500 Satellite Blvd, Suite
110, Orlando FL 32837-
8461. 407/438-2320.

**Sherwin-Williams Co.
District Office**
6741 W Sunrise Blvd, Suite
1, Ft Lauderdale FL 33313-
6029. 954/321-8688.

Sherwin-Williams Co.
3721 N Florida Ave, Tampa
FL 33603-4907. 813/227-
9264.

Sherwin-Williams Co.
136 US Highway 1, No Palm
Beach FL 33408-5402.
407/848-2866.

**For more information on career opportunities in the chemicals/rubber and plastics
industries:**

Associations

**AMERICAN ASSOCIATION FOR CLINICAL
CHEMISTRY**
2101 L Street NW, Suite 202, Washington
DC 20037-1526. 202/857-0717 or
800/892-1400. International
scientific/medical society of individuals
involved with clinical chemistry and other
clinical labscience-related disciplines.

AMERICAN CHEMICAL SOCIETY
Career Services, 1155 16th Street NW,
Washington DC 20036. 202/872-4600.

**AMERICAN INSTITUTE OF CHEMICAL
ENGINEERS**
345 East 47th Street, New York NY
10017. 212/705-7338 or 800/242-4363.
Provides leadership in advancing the
chemical engineering profession as it meets
the needs of society.

AMERICAN INSTITUTE OF CHEMISTS, INC.
7315 Wisconsin Avenue, Suite 502 E,
Bethesda MD 20814. 301/652-2447. A
professional organization supporting the
social, economic, and career objectives of
the individual scientist.

**CHEMICAL MANAGEMENT RESEARCH
ASSOCIATION**
60 Bay Street, Suite 702, Staten Island NY
10301. 718/876-8800.

**CHEMICAL MANUFACTURERS
ASSOCIATION**
2501 M Street NW, Washington DC
20037. 202/887-1100. A trade association
that develops and implements programs and
services and advocates public policy that
benefits the industry and society.

THE ELECTROCHEMICAL SOCIETY
10 South Main Street, Pennington NJ
08534-2896. An international educational
society dealing with electromechanical
issues. Also publishes monthly journals.

SOAP AND DETERGENT ASSOCIATION
475 Park Avenue South, 27th Floor, New
York NY 10016. 212/725-1262. A trade
association and research center.

SOCIETY OF PLASTICS ENGINEERS
14 Fairfield Drive, P.O. Box 403, Brookfield
CT 06804-0403. 203/775-0471.
Dedicated to helping members attain higher
professional status through increased
scientific, engineering, and technical
knowledge.

**THE SOCIETY OF THE PLASTICS
INDUSTRY, INC.**
1275 K Street NW, Suite 400, Washington
DC 20005. 202/371-5200. Promotes the
development of the plastics industry and
enhances public understanding of its

contributions while meeting the needs of society.

Directories

CHEMICAL INDUSTRY DIRECTORY
State Mutual Book and Periodical Service, Order Department, 17th Floor, 521 5th Avenue, New York NY 10175. 516/537-1104.

CHEMICALS DIRECTORY
Cahners Publishing, 275 Washington Street, Newton MA 02158. 617/964-3030.

DIRECTORY OF CHEMICAL ENGINEERING CONSULTANTS
American Institute of Chemical Engineering, 345 East 47th Street, New York NY 10017. 212/705-7338.

DIRECTORY OF CHEMICAL PRODUCERS
SRI International, 333 Ravenswood Avenue, Menlo Park CA 94025. 415/326-6200.

Magazines

CHEMICAL & ENGINEERING NEWS
American Chemical Society 1155 16th Street NW, Washington DC 20036. 202/872-4600.

CHEMICAL MARKETING REPORTER
Schnell Publishing Company, 80 Brot Street, 23rd Floor, New York NY 10004. 212/248-4177.

CHEMICAL PROCESSING
Putnam Publishing Company, 301 East Erie Street, Chicago IL 60611. 312/644-2020.

CHEMICAL WEEK
888 7th Avenue, 26th Floor, New York NY 10106. 212/621-4900.

COMMUNICATIONS: TELECOMMUNICATIONS & BROADCASTING

Telecommunications: Business is booming with the dramatic acceleration in telecommunications to reach new ground and more customers, especially in wireless phone service. Regulations are changing, causing doors to open and companies to come together in the cable and local and long distance phone business. Nearly all of the top-rated companies in the industry have experienced an increase in sales and revenues in the past year.

Broadcasting: Competition is high in this industry, especially for high-profile positions such as newscasters and dee-jays. In television, the hottest industry is cable. Cable companies are rapidly expanding requiring a need for people in the industry, more so in technical fields. In radio, syndicated radio shows are tearing up the air waves. Larger stations with more money, experience, and bigger names are producing shows which smaller stations are picking up to save money. This increase in syndication will result in even higher competition in the radio industry.

AT&T PARADYNE CORPORATION
8545 126th Avenue North, P.O. Box 2826, MS LG222, Largo FL 34649-2826. 813/530-2000. **Contact:** Steve Oakman, Human Resources. **Description:** A data communications manufacturer. **Common positions include:** Accountant/Auditor; Computer Programmer; Computer Systems Analyst; Electrical/Electronics Engineer; Software Engineer. **Educational backgrounds include:** Communications; Computer Science; Engineering; Finance; Marketing. **Benefits:** Daycare Assistance; Dental Insurance; Disability Coverage; Employee Discounts; Life Insurance; Medical Insurance; Pension Plan; Profit Sharing; Savings Plan; Tuition Assistance. **Special Programs:** Internships; Training Programs. **Operations at this facility include:** Administration; Divisional Headquarters; Manufacturing; Sales; Service. **Listed on:** New York Stock Exchange. **Number of employees at this location:** 2,150.

AEROTRON REPCO SALES INC.
2400 Sand Lake Road, Orlando FL 32809. 407/856-1953. **Fax:** 407/856-1960. **Contact:** Ted McDonald, Personnel Manager. **Description:** A manufacturer of communications equipment. **Corporate headquarters location:** This Location. **Listed on:** Privately held. **Number of employees at this location:** 115.

ALLTEL FLORIDA, INC.
P.O. Box 550, Live Oak FL 32060. 904/364-2400. **Contact:** Human Resources. **Description:** A telephone utility company.

AMNEX (AMERICAN NETWORK EXCHANGE)
100 West Lucerne Circle, Orlando FL 32801. 407/246-1234. **Contact:** Human Resources. **Description:** Provides long distance telephone service.

ASCOM TIMEPLEX INC.
16255 Bay Vista Drive, Clearwater FL 34620. 813/530-9475. **Contact:** Human Resources. **Description:** Offers commercial telecommunications services to businesses.

DICTAPHONE
3900 West Sarno Road, Melbourne FL 32934. 407/259-4524. **Contact:** Cecil Prentis, Personnel Director. **Description:** Regional office of the manufacturers of office dictation machines.

DYCOM INDUSTRIES INC.
450 Australian Avenue S, Suite 860, West Palm Beach FL 33401-5005. 407/659-6301. **Contact:** Human Resources. **Description:** Dycom Industries Inc. is a holding company for subsidiaries which manufacture mobile phones and provide communication services.

ELCOTEL, INC.
6428 Parkland Drive, Sarasota FL 34243. 941/758-0389. **Contact:** Carol Ziebell, Personnel Director. **Description:** Markets and services privately-owned pay telephones.

MICRODYNE CORPORATION
P.O. Box 7213, Ocala FL 34472. 352/687-4633. **Contact:** Personnel Director. **Description:** A manufacturer of radio and television transmitters.

NOKIA-MOBIRA INC.
P.O. Box 30370, Tampa FL 33630. 813/288-3800. **Contact:** Human Resources. **Description:** A manufacturer of mobile phones.

JOHN H. PHIPPS, INC.
P.O. Box 3048, Tallahassee FL 32315. 904/668-0842. **Fax:** 904/668-0546. **Contact:** Kim Rogers, Employee Relations. **Description:** A television station.

SCIENTIFIC-ATLANTA PRIVATE NETWORKS, INC.
420 North Wickham Road, Melbourne FL 32935. 407/255-3000. **Contact:** Human Resources. **Description:** Scientific-Atlanta is a provider of communications equipment, electronics, instrumentation products, and satellite-based network systems. The company was founded in 1951 to develop and manufacture electronic test equipment for antennas used in the space and defense industries. Today, the company considers itself to be a global communications innovator, bringing customers cable, telephone, computer, and consumer technology. The company develops, manufactures, and supports a line of equipment and systems for broadband terrestrial network delivery of cable television, telephony, and electric utility services. Products and systems are used by cable operations in more than 100 countries, as well as in 9,000 local cable sites in the United States. Scientific-Atlanta is also involved in satellite-based communications, with more than 45,000 earth station systems in 135 countries. The company designs, manufactures, installs, operates, and services earth station systems and networks that provide audio, video, and data communication services.

SIEMENS CORPORATION
5500 Broken Sound Boulevard, Building 3, Boca Raton FL 33487. 407/997-3100. **Contact:** Personnel Department. **Description:** Suppliers of telecommunications equipment and office printers to small- and medium-sized businesses, as well as to Bell Telephone operating companies.

SONY PROFESSIONAL PRODUCTS COMPANY
6500 Congress Avenue, Boca Raton FL 33487. 407/998-9922. **Contact:** Human Resources Manager. **Description:** Manufactures professional analog recorders, digital recorders, and mixing consoles for recording and broadcasting, as well as for the television and teleproduction markets. **Common positions include:** Accountant/Auditor; Administrator; Buyer; Computer Programmer; Department Manager; Electrical/Electronics Engineer; Financial Analyst; General Manager; Human Resources Specialist; Industrial Engineer; Instructor/Trainer; Mechanical Engineer; Operations/Production Manager; Purchasing Agent and Manager; Quality Control Supervisor; Systems Analyst; Teacher; Technical Writer/Editor; Transportation/Traffic Specialist. **Educational backgrounds include:** Accounting; Business Administration; Computer Science; Engineering; Finance; Mathematics; Physics. **Benefits:** Disability Coverage; Employee Discounts; Life Insurance; Profit Sharing; Savings Plan; Stock Option; Tuition Assistance. **Special Programs:** Internships; Training Programs. **Corporate headquarters location:** Park Ridge NJ. **Parent company:** Sony Electronics, Inc. **Operations at this facility include:** Administration; Manufacturing; Research and Development; Service. **Number of employees at this location:** 200.

STROMBERG-CARLSON
400 Rinehart Road, Lake Mary FL 32746. 407/942-5000. **Contact:** Garth Shoemaker, Personnel. **Description:** A telecommunications firm.

TCI

9825 SW 77th Street, Miami FL 33173. 305/595-0766. **Contact:** Personnel. **Description:** TCI manages cable television communications. The Cable Communications Division has more than 1.6 million subscribers. **Common positions include:** Accountant/Auditor; Advertising Clerk; Claim Representative; Customer Service Representative; Department Manager; Financial Analyst; General Manager; Marketing Specialist; Services Sales Representative. **Educational backgrounds include:** Accounting; Business Administration; Communications; Finance; Liberal Arts; Marketing. **Benefits:** Dental Insurance; Disability Coverage; Life Insurance; Medical Insurance; Tuition Assistance. **Corporate headquarters location:** This Location. **Operations at this facility include:** Administration. **Number of employees nationwide:** 3,100.

WTVJ

316 North Miami Avenue, Miami FL 33128. 305/379-4444. **Contact:** Ellen S. Gorringe, Employee Relations Manager. **Description:** WTVJ, a television station owned and operated by NBC, employs individuals in the areas of engineering, television production, operations, general administration, news gathering and reporting. An Equal Opportunity Employer M/F/H/V. **Common positions include:** Account Executive; Editor; Graphic Artist; Reporter. **Educational backgrounds include:** Art/Design; Business Administration; Communications; Liberal Arts; Marketing; Radio; Television. **Benefits:** Dental Insurance; Disability Coverage; Employee Discounts; Life Insurance; Medical Insurance; Pension Plan; Savings Plan. **Parent company:** General Electric.

WOMETCO CABLE CORPORATION

9500 South Dadeland Boulevard, Miami FL 33456. 305/662-2205. **Contact:** Human Resources. **Description:** The company offers cable television services.

Note: Because addresses and telephone numbers of smaller companies change rapidly, we recommend you call each company to verify the information below before inquiring about job opportunities. Mass mailings are not recommended.

Additional employers with under 250 employees:

COMMUNICATIONS EQUIPMENT

Atlantic Teleconnect
5445 Williamsburg Dr, Punta Gorda FL 33982-1717.
941/637-4777.

Precision Systems
11800 30th Ct N, St Petersburg FL 33716-1846.
813/572-9300.

RS Telephones
8512 Hamster Dr, Zephyrhills FL 33540-6842. 813/780-7677.

Starcom
3303 N Dixie Hwy, Boca Raton FL 33431-6047.
407/392-7001.

DME Corporation
6830 NW 16th Terrace, Ft Lauderdale FL 33309-1518.
954/463-5066.

Don's Two-Way Radio Service
5215 NW 33rd Ave, Ft Lauderdale FL 33309-6302.
954/493-9086.

Fischer International Systems
4073 Mercantile Ave, Naples

FL 33942-3343. 941/643-1500.

Mnemonics
3900 Dow Rd, Suite J, Melbourne FL 32934-9291.
407/254-7300.

Res-Net Microwave
12449 Enterprise Blvd, Largo FL 34643-2710. 813/530-9555.

Sunair Electronics
3101 SW 3rd Ave, Ft Lauderdale FL 33315-3317.
954/525-1505.

Tallahassee Communications
1720 W Paul Dirac St, Tallahassee FL 32310.
904/576-6684.

Advantor Corporation
6101 Lake Ellenor Dr, Orlando FL 32809-4660.
407/859-3350.

Edwards System Technology
6411 Parkland Dr, Sarasota FL 34243-4037. 941/756-3278.

Protel
4150 Kidron Rd, Lakeland FL

33811-1274. 941/644-5558.

Repco
2400 Sand Lake Rd, Orlando FL 32809-7642. 407/856-1953.

TELEPHONE COMMUNICATIONS

General Telephone
1011 E Lemon St, Lakeland FL 33801-5122. 941/688-5757.

General Telephone Company Of Florida
120 E Lime St, Lakeland FL 33801-4606. 941/688-5333.

Mobilnet GTE
694 Tamiami Trail N, Naples FL 33940-8131. 941/262-4465.

Southern Bell
5528 Jammes Rd, Jacksonville FL 32244-1898.
904/778-4703.

Allnet Communication Service
201 E Kennedy Blvd, Tampa FL 33602. 813/273-0210.

American Digital Access
135 W Central Blvd, Orlando
FL 32801-2430. 407/422-
9998.

**Best Communications Of
Tampa**
1818 E Busch Blvd, Tampa
FL 33612-8664. 813/933-
8798.

BTI
6622 Southpoint Dr S,
Jacksonville FL 32216-8014.
904/296-1411.

Cable & Wireless
6622 Southpoint Dr S,
Jacksonville FL 32216-8014.
904/296-2340.

Commercial Pay Phones
8510 NW 56th St, Miami FL
33166-3329. 305/716-
4910.

EF&I Services
109 Falkenburg Rd, Tampa
FL 33619. 813/654-6411.

HAS
4709 Barrett Ct, Tampa FL
33617-6930. 813/985-
0998.

ICC
7359 NW 54th St, Miami FL
33166-4831. 305/888-
0361.

Intermedia Communications
201 S Orange Ave, Orlando
FL 32801-3413. 407/648-
2200.

**International Telecom Data
Systems**
10014 N Dale Mabry Hwy,
Carrollwood FL 33618-4426.
813/265-2661.

ITM Communications
208 Margaret St, Neptune
Beach FL 32266-4829.
904/249-1510.

National Telecommunications
6650 Southpoint Pkwy,
Jacksonville FL 32216-0922.
904/296-9300.

Phone One
135 W Central Blvd, Suite
1050, Orlando FL 32801-
2437. 407/425-3333.

RTI Telecom
47 E Robinson St, Orlando FL
32801-1630. 407/426-
6868.

Southern Bell
666 NW 79th Ave, Miami FL
33126-4018. 305/263-
3020.

Southern Bell
500 N Orange Ave #568,

Orlando FL 32801-1341.
407/237-3325.

Sprint
7560 W Courtney Campbell
Cswy, Tampa FL 33607.
813/282-7700.

Star Datacom
3502 Riga Blvd, Suite C,
Tampa FL 33619-8349.
813/621-0681.

Tel-Com Support Services
9481 Highland Oak Dr,
Tampa FL 33647. 813/973-
7922.

Teleco Plus
12932 NW 7th Ave, Miami
FL 33168-2726. 305/688-
2825.

United Telephone Company
P.O. Box 1028, Avon Park FL
33825-1028. 941/452-
3111.

Universal Technology
1273 SW 114th Way, Ft
Lauderdale FL 33325-4547.
954/370-4600.

**Advance Communication
Network**
320 Newburyport Ave,
Altamonte Springs FL
32701-3645. 407/332-
5343.

Excel Training Center
4077 W Oak Ridge Rd,
Orlando FL 32809-3604.
407/354-3322.

**JJ Central
Telecommunication**
700 NW 108th St, Miami FL
33168-2130. 305/757-
6144.

MCI
6650 Southpoint Pkwy,
Jacksonville FL 32216-0922.
904/281-9044.

Phone Zone
1429 Massaro Blvd, Tampa
FL 33619-3005. 813/664-
1256.

Save-U-Systems
3650 Stephen Rd, Lady Lake
FL 32159-5327. 352/753-
6485.

Suntel Communications
127 N Magnolia Ave,
Orlando FL 32801-2301.
407/872-0470.

Tel-America
333 N Tamiami Trail,
Sarasota FL 34236-4806.
941/957-3633.

Teleco Plus
8222 Biscayne Blvd, Miami

FL 33138-4124. 305/758-
7768.

Teleco Plus
7804 NE 2nd Ave, Miami FL
33138-4805. 305/757-
4491.

Telenvia Communication
1687 SW 107th Ave, Miami
FL 33165-7344. 305/223-
5440.

Voicecom Systems
512 Tivoli Ct, Altamonte
Springs FL 32701-6826.
407/331-6777.

MCI
406 Sarasota Quay #26,
Sarasota FL 34236-4844.
941/955-1743.

Accessplus
7880 N University Dr, Ft
Lauderdale FL 33321-2124.
954/722-9696.

**AT&T USA Europe & Latin
America**
6405 NW 36th St, Suite
102, Miami FL 33166-6977.
305/871-4771.

Comtel Industries
17090 NW 3rd Ave, Miami
FL 33169-5905. 305/948-
9116.

Dial One
1650 Prudential Dr, Suite
300, Jacksonville FL 32207-
8150. 904/396-1171.

EEA Of Florida
283 N North Lake Blvd,
Altamonte Springs FL
32701-3437. 407/331-
1191.

Eunetcom
500 Winderley Place,
Maitland FL 32751-7247.
407/660-1116.

Excel Center
8576 Arlington Expy,
Jacksonville FL 32211-8003.
904/724-4000.

**Excel Center Independent
Reps**
7907 W McNab Rd, Ft
Lauderdale FL 33321-8428.
954/726-9003.

First Coast Cable
6932 Blanding Blvd,
Jacksonville FL 32244-4421.
904/772-7176.

**Florida Network
Communications**
4995 NW 72nd Ave, Miami
FL 33166. 305/599-1473.

Global Discount Telephone
7900 Glades Rd, Boca Raton

FL 33434-4167. 407/852-4438.

H&W Communications
20039 NW 34th Ct, Opa Locka FL 33056-1760. 305/621-3505.

Hispanic Telecom Service
8370 W Flagler St, Miami FL 33144-2030. 305/225-4011.

Hyman Enterprises
4949 Sunbeam Rd, Jacksonville FL 32257-6170. 904/733-2308.

Intermedia Communications
6800 Southpoint Pkwy, Jacksonville FL 32216-6219. 904/296-9235.

International Communication Systems
701 S J St, Pensacola FL 32501-5239. 904/435-7505.

Leader Communications
5750 Major Blvd, Orlando FL 32819-7946. 407/345-0478.

MRA
4456 El Mar Dr, Ft Lauderdale FL 33308-3606. 954/771-6871.

National Telephone Message Company
10001 W Oakland Park Blvd, Suite 30, Ft Lauderdale FL 33351-6925. 954/742-5520.

One 800/900
200 N Laura St #1200, Jacksonville FL 32202-3500. 904/355-9000.

Pay Phone Consultants
1111 Island Shores Dr, West Palm Beach FL 33413-2116. 407/966-9066.

Pride Electrical Contractors
4711 SW 26th St, Hollywood FL 33023-4315. 954/961-8720.

Spectracom
363 2 Prestwick Circle, West Palm Beach FL 33418. 407/625-3654.

Startel
1212 Palmer St, Orlando FL 32801-4119. 407/894-2085.

Stonebraker & Wilson
4214 San Amaro Dr, South Miami FL 33146-1043. 305/661-6422.

Tel Con Resources
19501 NE 10th Ave, Miami

FL 33179-3576. 305/654-1456.

Telcom Services Of America
1636 Shadowood Ln, Suite 106, Jacksonville FL 32207-2187. 904/399-5860.

Tele Difference
8350 40th Ave N, St Petersburg FL 33709-3935. 813/341-2111.

Teleco International Services
6909 Biscayne Blvd, Miami FL 33138-5733. 305/754-0405.

Telelink Communications USA
7859 NW 15th St, Miami FL 33126-1109. 305/599-2002.

Telenex
1915 N Dale Mabry Hwy, Tampa FL 33607-2555. 813/877-1608.

Telymas
7471 SW 8th St, Miami FL 33144-4547. 305/267-6150.

Vic Transfer & General Service
1232 N Krome Ave, Homestead FL 33030-4205. 305/248-3911.

TELEGRAPH AND OTHER MESSAGE COMMUNICATIONS

Faxcast USA
14502 N Dale Mabry Hwy, Carrollwood FL 33618-2072. 813/264-1399.

RADIO BROADCASTING STATIONS

WAMR AM
282 N Auburn Rd, Venice FL 34292-1601. 941/484-2636.

WCFB
220 S Ridgewood Ave, Daytona Beach FL 32114-4318. 904/239-0945.

WFTI FM
360 Central Ave, Suite 1240, St Petersburg FL 33701-3838. 813/823-1140.

WGLF FM
1310 N Paul Russell Rd, Tallahassee FL 32301-4825. 904/878-1104.

WJNO AM
1500 N Flagler Dr, West Palm Beach FL 33401-3402. 407/838-4300.

WKGF AM
P.O. Box 632, Arcadia FL 33821-0632. 941/494-2427.

WKSJ FM Business Office
744 E Burgess Rd, Pensacola FL 32504-6227. 904/477-9600.

WRMF FM
1000 Corporate Dr, Ft Lauderdale FL 33334-3655. 954/771-2273.

WSNI FM
3360 Capital Circle NE, Suite D, Tallahassee FL 32308-1575. 904/422-3107.

TELEVISION BROADCASTING STATIONS

WCIX
8900 NW 18th Terrace, Miami FL 33172-2623. 305/593-0606.

WCPX
4466 N John Young Pkwy, Orlando FL 32804-1699. 407/291-6000.

WFTV
490 E South St, Orlando FL 32801-2816. 407/841-9000.

WFTX
621 SW Pine Island Rd, Fort Myers FL 33991-1950. 941/574-3636.

WPTV
622 N Flagler Dr, West Palm Beach FL 33401-4007. 407/655-5455.

WTLV
1070 E Adams St, Jacksonville FL 32202-1998. 904/354-1212.

WTSP
11450 Gandy Blvd N, St Petersburg FL 33702-1908. 813/577-1010.

WTVT
3213 W Kennedy Blvd, Tampa FL 33609-3092. 813/876-1313.

Telemundo Productions
2470 W 8th Ave, Hialeah FL 33010-2020. 305/884-8200.

CABLE/PAY TELEVISION SERVICES

Cablevision Industries
2019 13th St, Saint Cloud FL 34769-4205. 407/892-8466.

Cox Cable University City
1115 NW 4th St, Gainesville
FL 32601-4256. 352/377-
2368.

Continental Cablevision
2101 NW 33rd St, Pompano
Beach FL 33069-1068.
954/978-1218.

Discovery Cable TV
3023 US 1, Mims FL 32754-
3000. 407/268-1724.

For more information on career opportunities in the communications industries:

Associations

ACADEMY OF TELEVISION ARTS & SCIENCES
5220 Lankershim Boulevard, North
Hollywood CA 91601. 818/754-2800.

AMERICAN WOMEN IN RADIO AND TV, INC.
1650 Tysons Boulevard, Suite 200, McLean
VA 22102. 703/506-3290.

BROADCAST PROMOTION AND MARKETING EXECUTIVES
2029 Century Park East, Suite 555, Los
Angeles CA 90028. 310/788-7600. Fax:
310/788-7616.

INTERACTIVE SERVICES ASSOCIATION
Suite 865, 8403 Colesville Road, Silver
Springs MD 20910. 301/495-4955.

INTERNATIONAL TELEVISION ASSOCIATION
6311 North O'Connor Road, Suite 230,
Irving TX 75309. 214/869-1112.
Membership required.

NATIONAL ASSOCIATION OF BROADCASTERS
1771 N Street NW, Washington DC 20036.
202/429-5300, ext. 5490. 202/429-5343
Provides employment information.

NATIONAL CABLE TELEVISION ASSOCIATION
1724 Massachusetts Avenue NW,
Washington DC 20036. 202/775-3550.

UNITED STATES TELEPHONE ASSOCIATION
900 19th Street NW, Suite 800,
Washington DC 20006. 202/326-7300.

Magazines

BROADCASTING AND CABLE
Broadcasting Publications Inc., 1705
DeSales Street NW, Washington DC 20036.
202/659-2340.

ELECTRONIC MEDIA
Crain Communications, 220 East 42nd
Street, New York NY 10017. 212/210-
0100.

COMPUTER HARDWARE, SOFTWARE AND SERVICES

 *Hardware and Software: Companies are starting to invest more in corporate technology after several years of lean spending. Network servers have been the hot business product recently -- anticipate spending to jump nearly 30 percent in 1995. Expect a revival in big machines -- parallel computers, mainframes, and minicomputers -- to support a growing interest in online databases, accessing the Internet, and e-mail. PCs will remain the strongest part of the hardware market. Employment numbers were expected to level off during 1995 after tumbling 90,000 since 1990. The composition of the software industry is shrinking with many firms merging or acquiring others. Expect to see cable television and telephone companies move to acquire a greater foothold in the software market. Despite consolidation in the industry, the overall number of software jobs is still rising.*

What's hot on the market? Strong PC sales have fueled demand for multimedia CD-ROM titles. Sales of CD-ROMs were expected to grow 25 percent in 1995. Also, the commercial online services and the Internet are creating new opportunities for software companies.

Services: Computer services professionals perform three activities: systems integration, custom programming, and consulting/training. Consulting and integration servers will be among the fastest-growing segments in computing, due to the demand for networking. And with more computer power made available, more computer support will be needed.

CBIS
851 Trafalger Court, Maitland FL 32751. 407/661-8000. **Contact:** Jerry Lerner, Staffing Manager, Human Resources. **Description:** A computer software company specializing in the telecommunications industry. **Common positions include:** Computer Programmer; Computer Systems Analyst. **Educational backgrounds include:** Computer Science. **Benefits:** Dental Insurance; Disability Coverage; Employee Discounts; Life Insurance; Medical Insurance; Pension Plan; Tuition Assistance. **Special Programs:** Internships; Training Programs. **Corporate headquarters location:** Cincinnati OH. **Parent company:** Cincinnati Bell, Inc. **Operations at this facility include:** Regional Headquarters; Research and Development; Sales; Service. **Listed on:** New York Stock Exchange.

CPA SOFTWARE
One Pensacola Plaza, Suite 500, Pensacola FL 32501. 904/434-2685. **Contact:** J.J. Todd, Administrative Manager. **Description:** CPA Software sells professional software to certified public accountants. **Common positions include:** Computer Programmer; Customer Service Representative; Marketing Specialist; Public Relations Specialist; Purchasing Agent and Manager; Services Sales Representative; Systems Analyst; Technical Writer/Editor. **Educational backgrounds include:** Accounting; Business Administration; Communications; Computer Science; Marketing. **Benefits:** Dental Insurance; Disability Coverage; Life Insurance; Medical Insurance; Profit Sharing; Tuition Assistance. **Special Programs:** Training Programs. **Corporate headquarters location:** This Location. **Parent company:** Fenimore Software Group, Inc. **Number of employees at this location:** 80.

ENCORE COMPUTER CORPORATION
6901 West Sunrise Boulevard, MS-111, Plantation FL 33313. 954/587-2900. **Contact:** Staffing Representative. **Description:** Encore specializes in mini-computers for aerospace, defense, simulation, energy, and information systems. **Common positions include:** Computer Systems Analyst; Electrical/Electronics Engineer; Software Engineer; Technical Writer/Editor. **Educational backgrounds include:** Computer Science; Engineering. **Benefits:** 401K; Dental Insurance; Disability Coverage; Life Insurance; Medical Insurance; Savings Plan; Tuition Assistance. **Special Programs:** Internships. **Corporate headquarters location:** This Location. **Operations at this facility include:** Administration; Research and Development; Service. **Listed on:** NASDAQ. **Number of employees at this location:** 450. **Number of employees nationwide:** 720.

HARRIS COMPUTER SYSTEMS CORPORATION
2101 West Cypress Creek Road, Fort Lauderdale FL 33309. 954/973-5300. **Fax:** 954/973-5301. **Contact:** C. Dean Hitsos, Senior Human Resources Representative. **Description:** Harris Computer Systems Corporation supplies high performance real-time and multilevel secure computer systems, and provides support, software, and related services for the commercial and government markets. Services include simulation and training, data acquisition and control, and trusted computing. The company serves aerospace and defense, academic, engineering, scientific, and computer-aided design clients. **Common positions include:** Software Engineer. **Educational backgrounds include:** Computer Science; Engineering; Marketing. **Special Programs:** Internships. **Operations at this facility include:** Administration; Divisional Headquarters; Manufacturing; Research and Development; Sales; Service. **Listed on:** American Stock Exchange. **Number of employees at this location:** 300. **Number of employees nationwide:** 425.

IBM CORPORATION
HUMAN RESOURCES U.S.A.
3109 West Dr. Martin Luther King Boulevard, Tampa FL 33607. 813/872-1646. **Contact:** Central Employment. **Description:** International Business Machines (IBM) is a developer, manufacturer, and marketer of advanced information processing products, including computers and microelectronic technology, software, networking systems and information technology-related services. The company strives to offer value worldwide, through its United States, Canada, Europe/Middle East/Africa, Latin America and Asia Pacific business units, by providing comprehensive and complete product choices. **Common positions include:** Chemical Engineer; Computer Operator; Computer Programmer; Data Entry Clerk; Electrical/Electronics Engineer; Manufacturing Engineer; Mechanical Engineer; Sales Representative; Secretary; Software Engineer; Systems Analyst; Technical Writer/Editor; Technician.

IBM CORPORATION
HUMAN RESOURCES U.S.A.
100 Northtrust 51st Street, Boca Raton FL 33431. 407/443-0075. **Contact:** Central Employment. **Description:** International Business Machines (IBM) is a developer, manufacturer, and marketer of advanced information processing products, including computers and microelectronic technology, software, networking systems and information technology-related services. The company strives to offer value worldwide, through its United States, Canada, Europe/Middle East/Africa, Latin America and Asia Pacific business units, by providing comprehensive and complete product choices. **Common positions include:** Chemical Engineer; Computer Operator; Computer Programmer; Data Entry Clerk; Electrical/Electronics Engineer; Manufacturing Engineer; Mechanical Engineer; Sales Representative; Secretary; Software Engineer; Systems Analyst; Technical Writer/Editor; Technician.

MODULAR COMPUTER SYSTEMS, INC.
1650 West McNab Road, Fort Lauderdale FL 33309. 954/974-1380. **Contact:** Personnel Department. **Description:** Manufactures computers designed for industrial automation, energy transportation and communication systems.

NATIONAL DATA PRODUCTS, INC.
2145 Calumet Street, Clearwater FL 34625. 813/562-2336. **Fax:** 813/562-2565. **Contact:** Dave Costel, Human Resources Director. **Description:** A provider of information systems, which offers network design, consulting services, and educational products. **Number of employees at this location:** 92.

RACAL-DATACOM INC.
1601 North Harrison Parkway, Sunrise FL 33323. 954/846-5250. **Fax:** 954/846-5025 or 954/846-5235 **Contact:** Brenda Benoit, Senior Employment Representative. **Description:** Racal-Datacom Inc. manufactures data communications equipment including WANs, LANs, and access products. The company also offers related services including project management, installation, consultation, network integration, maintenance, disaster recovery, and training. **Common positions include:** Electrical/Electronics Engineer; Marketing/Advertising/PR Manager; Software Engineer. **Educational backgrounds include:** Accounting; Business Administration; Communications; Computer Science; Engineering; Finance; Marketing. **Benefits:** 401K; Dental Insurance; Disability Coverage; Employee Discounts; Life Insurance; Medical Insurance; Tuition Assistance. **Corporate headquarters location:** This Location. **Other locations:** Nationwide; Asia; Europe; Canada; Australia; France. **Parent company:** The Racal Corporation. **Operations at this facility include:** Administration; Divisional Headquarters; Manufacturing; Research and Development; Sales; Service. **Number of employees at this location:** 900. **Number of employees nationwide:** 2,500.

SYSTEMHOUSE
950 South Winter Park Drive, Suite 200, Casselberry FL 32707. 407/767-8704. **Contact:** Mr. Jan Ackerman, Recruiter. **Description:** Systemhouse offers systems integration computer services, combining hardware, software, and network communications for large companies. The company also offers telecommunications, client server architecture, rapid applications development, Unix-based applications development, and large-scale network management. In addition, Systemhouse supports voice and data technologies worldwide; provides a blend of technical support and professional services to assist in the development, testing, and deployment of software and hardware products for the communications industry; and offers expertise in computer interface technology and software development. **Common positions include:** Accountant/Auditor; Computer Programmer; Computer Systems Analyst; Electrical/Electronics Engineer; Systems Analyst; Technical Writer/Editor. **Educational backgrounds include:** Accounting; Computer Science; Engineering; Marketing; Mathematics. **Benefits:** Dental Insurance; Disability Coverage; Life Insurance; Medical Insurance; Pension Plan; Savings Plan; Tuition Assistance. **Special Programs:** Internships; Training Programs. **Corporate headquarters location:** Dallas TX. **Other U.S. locations:** Los Angeles CA; Boulder CO; Washington DC; Chicago IL; New York NY. **Operations at this facility include:** Service. **Listed on:** New York Stock Exchange. **Number of employees at this location:** 150. **Number of employees nationwide:** 2,000.

TECH DATA CORPORATION
5350 Tech Data Drive, Vay Vista Complex, Clearwater FL 34620. 813/539-7429. **Contact:** Human Resources. **Description:** A distributor of microcomputer-related hardware and software products to value-added resellers (VARs) and computer retailers throughout the United States, Canada, Europe, Latin America, and the Caribbean. Tech Data Corporation purchases its products directly from manufacturers and publishers in large quantities, maintains stocking inventory of more than 25,000 products and sells to an active base of over 50,000 customers. The company offers manufacturers of microcomputer hardware and publishers of software the ability to reach low-volume customers on a cost-efficient basis. Tech Data Corporation provides its customers with products in networking, mass storage, peripherals, software, and systems from more than 600 manufacturers and publishers including Adobe, Aldus, Apple, Borland, Corel, Hewlett-Packard, IBM, Intel, Lotus, Microsoft, and Novell. The company also maintains a staff of technical advisers who assist customers by telephone. **Common positions include:** Accountant/Auditor; Budget Analyst; Buyer; Clerical Supervisor; Computer Operator; Computer Programmer; Computer Systems Analyst; Credit Manager; Customer Service Representative; Department Manager; Economist/Market Research Analyst; Editor; Education Administrator; Employment Interviewer; Financial Analyst; General Manager; Human Resources Specialist; Management Trainee; Manufacturer's/Wholesaler's Sales Rep.; Marketing Specialist; Operations/Production Manager; Purchasing Agent and Manager; Quality Control Supervisor; Services Sales Representative; Software Engineer; Systems Analyst; Technical Writer/Editor; Wholesale and Retail Buyer. **Educational backgrounds include:** Accounting; Business Administration; Computer Science; Finance; Marketing. **Benefits:** 401K; Daycare Assistance; Dental Insurance; Disability Coverage; Employee Discounts; Life Insurance; Medical Insurance; Savings Plan; Tuition Assistance. **Corporate headquarters location:** This Location. **Operations at this facility include:** Administration; Divisional Headquarters; Regional Headquarters; Sales; Service. **Listed on:** NASDAQ. **Number of employees at this location:** 300. **Number of employees nationwide:** 1,500.

TELEMATICS INTERNATIONAL, INC.
1201 West Cyprus Creek Road, Fort Lauderdale FL 33309. 954/772-3070. **Contact:** Human Resources Department. **Description:** Telematics International Inc. provides computer equipment, programs, and other software services. **Common positions include:** Computer Systems Analyst; Electrical/Electronics Engineer. **Educational backgrounds include:** Computer Science; Engineering. **Benefits:** 401K; Dental Insurance; Disability Coverage; Life Insurance; Medical Insurance; Tuition Assistance. **Corporate headquarters location:** This Location. **Other U.S. locations:** Calabasas CA. **Parent company:** ECI Telecom. **Operations at this facility include:** Administration; Manufacturing; Research and Development. **Number of employees at this location:** 220.

Note: Because addresses and telephone numbers of smaller companies change rapidly, we recommend you call each company to verify the information below before inquiring about job opportunities. Mass mailings are not recommended.

Additional employers with under 250 employees:

COMPUTERS AND RELATED EQUIPMENT

Boca Research
1377 Clint Moore Rd, Boca Raton FL 33487-2722. 407/997-6227.

Boca Research
430 Commerce Dr, Suite 35F, Delray Beach FL 33445-4655. 407/997-8621.

Core International
6500 E Rogers Circle, Boca Raton FL 33487-2699. 407/997-6044.

Distributed Processing
140 Candace Dr, Maitland FL 32751-3331. 407/830-5522.

WPI Sarasota Division
2651 Whitfield Ave, Sarasota FL 34243-3923. 941/753-6756.

XI Vision/Hetra
10300 102nd Terrace, Sebastian FL 32958-7823. 407/589-7331.

COMPUTERS AND COMPUTER EQUIPMENT WHOLESALE

Romart Computer Corp.
8615 S Bay Dr, Orlando FL 32819-4948. 407/876-0026.

Amdahl Corporation
1900 Summit Tower Blvd, Orlando FL 32810-5939. 407/875-8505.

Data Switch Corp.
2301 Maitland Center Pkwy #1, Maitland FL 32751-4128. 407/875-8335.

MR CD-ROM
123 S Woodland St, Winter Garden FL 34787-3545. 407/877-3807.

XI Datacomp
600 Fairway Dr, Deerfield Beach FL 33441-1811. 954/360-0300.

COMPUTER SOFTWARE, PROGRAMMING, AND SYSTEMS DESIGN

Allen Systems Group
750 11th St S, Naples FL 33940-6775. 941/263-6700.

Concord Management Systems
5301 W Cypress St #T, Tampa FL 33607-1700. 813/281-2200.

Software Technology
1225 Evans Rd, Melbourne FL 32904-2314. 407/723-3999.

Tybrin Corporation
1283 Eglin Pkwy, Shalimar FL 32579-1256. 904/651-1150.

Cutler/Williams
1407 Piedmont Dr E, Tallahassee FL 32312-2943. 904/386-7388.

Future Tel
124 Robin Rd, Altamonte Springs FL 32701-5026. 407/331-0110.

Insight Industries
3900 Dow Rd, Melbourne FL 32934-9255. 407/254-8815.

Telecommunication Systems
2909 W Bay To Bay Blvd, Tampa FL 33629-8100. 813/831-6353.

Computer Horizons Corp.
3710 Corporex Park Dr, Suite 250, Tampa FL 33619-1160. 813/626-6366.

Bertrand Computer Network
195 Cypress Way E, Naples FL 33942-1266. 941/566-8235.

CCS Technology Group
900 Winderley Place, Suite 200, Maitland FL 32751-7231. 407/660-0343.

Clarion Software Corp.
150 E Sample Rd #200, Pompano Beach FL 33064-3550. 954/785-4555.

Coaxis
600 S Barracks St, Pensacola FL 32501-6000. 904/469-9940.

Computer Task Group
1995 W Nasa Blvd, Melbourne FL 32904-2310. 407/725-1300.

FDP Corporation
2140 S Dixie Hwy, Miami FL 33133-2424. 305/858-8200.

HSB Reliability Technologies
2000 E Edgewood Dr, Suite 215, Lakeland FL 33803-3658. 941/666-2330.

Caci Field Services
4302 Henderson Blvd, Tampa FL 33629-5608. 813/253-2620.

Computerized Lodging Systems
498 Palm Springs Dr, Altamonte Springs FL

32701-7805. 407/767-0150.

Edunectics
7515 Long Meadow Ln, Pensacola FL 32506-3851. 904/455-1484.

Elke Corporation
14502 N Dale Mabry Hwy, Tampa FL 33618-2072. 813/969-2062.

Gateway Conversion Tech
3452 Lake Lynda Dr, Orlando FL 32817-1430. 407/382-3499.

Infotec Development
1333 Gateway Dr, Suite 1012, Melbourne FL 32901-2623. 407/951-2000.

Jefferson Pilot Data Service
1650 Winding Creek Rd, Palm Harbor FL 34683-6552. 813/789-0469.

Loadstar Systems
12017 Chervil Ct, Orlando FL 32837-6743. 407/850-1072.

Metro Information Services
1200 S Pine Island Rd, Plantation FL 33324-4413. 954/476-9746.

MRX Computer Services
1224 Windsor Ave, Longwood FL 32750-6824. 407/331-3355.

Openconnect Systems
7600 Southland Blvd, Orlando FL 32809-6975. 407/851-5515.

Stingray Software Co.
16702 Foothill Dr, Carrollwood FL 33624-1053. 813/264-4116.

Rnet Computer Services
1400 Commerce Blvd, Sarasota FL 34243-5023. 941/359-2111.

COMPUTER MAINTENANCE AND REPAIR

Alpha Microsystems
1287 E Newport Center Dr 201, Deerfield Beach FL 33442-7706. 954/427-6703.

Ameridata
500 Fairway Dr, Suite 108, Deerfield Beach FL 33441-1877. 954/421-3484.

Comp U Ware
8723 Del Rey Ct Apt 13E, Tampa FL 33617-7082. 813/963-2289.

Concurrent Computer Corp. Service
2486 Sand Lake Rd, Orlando FL 32809-7686. 407/850-1021.

Delta Business Systems
5440 Beaumont Blvd Suite 400, Tampa FL 33634-5208. 813/888-7710.

For more information on career opportunities in the computer industry:

Associations

ASSOCIATION FOR COMPUTING MACHINERY
1515 Broadway, 17th Floor, New York NY 10036. 212/869-7440. Membership required.

INFORMATION AND TECHNOLOGY ASSOCIATION OF AMERICA
1616 North Fort Myer Drive, Suite 1300, Arlington VA 22209. 703/522-5055.

Directories

INFORMATION INDUSTRY DIRECTORY
Gale Research Inc., 835 Penobscot Building, Detroit MI 48226. 313/961-2242.

Magazines

COMPUTER-AIDED ENGINEERING
Penton Publishing, 1100 Superior Avenue, Cleveland OH 44114. 216/696-7000.

COMPUTERWORLD
IDG, 375 Cochituate Road, P.O. Box 9171, Framingham MA 01701-9171. 508/879-0700.

DATA COMMUNICATIONS
McGraw-Hill, 1221 Avenue of the Americas, New York NY 10020. 212/512-2000.

DATAMATION
Cahners Publishing, 275 Washington Street, Newton MA 02158. 617/964-3030.

IDC REPORT
International Data Corporation, Five Speen Street, Framingham MA 01701. 508/872-8200.

EDUCATIONAL SERVICES

Job prospects for college and university faculty, elementary school teachers, counselors, and education administrators should show moderate improvement throughout the '90s, although most of the openings will result from retirements. Among kindergarten and elementary school teachers, the best opportunities await those with training in special education. The employment outlook is also good for teacher aides, as many assist special education teachers, as school reforms call for more individual attention to students, and as the number of students who speak English as a second language rises. Adult education and secondary school teachers, and sports and physical fitness instructors and coaches are other occupations expected to grow faster than average.

BREVARD COMMUNITY COLLEGE
1519 Clearlake Road, Cocoa FL 32922. 407/632-1111. **Recorded Jobline:** 407/632-1111x2561. **Contact:** Human Resources. **Description:** A medium-sized, state-supported, two-year college.

BROWARD COMMUNITY COLLEGE
Broward Community College, 225 East Las Olas Boulevard, Fort Lauderdale FL 33301. 954/475-6500. **Recorded Jobline:** 954/761-7503. **Contact:** Human Resources. **Description:** A large, state-supported, two-year college.

EDISON COMMUNITY COLLEGE
P.O. Box 60210, Fort Meyers FL 33906-6210. 941/489-9280. **Fax:** 941/489-0941. **Recorded Jobline:** 941/489-9120. **Contact:** Jackie House, Human Resources Director. **Description:** Edison Community College is a two-year college serving the five southwestern counties of Florida including Charlotte, Collier, Glades, Hendry, and Lee. It offers AA and AS degrees as well as certification in four programs and noncredit continuing education courses. The three campuses are located in Charlotte, Collier, and Lee counties. **Common positions include:** Computer Programmer; Computer Systems Analyst; Education Administrator; Human Resources Specialist; Library Technician; Purchasing Agent and Manager; Teacher. **Educational backgrounds include:** Accounting; Art/Design; Biology; Business Administration; Chemistry; Computer Science; Economics; Engineering; Finance; Geology; Mathematics; Physics. **Benefits:** 403B; Dental Insurance; Disability Coverage; Life Insurance; Medical Insurance; Pension Plan; Tuition Assistance. **Corporate headquarters location:** This Location. **Other U.S. locations:** Port Charlotte FL; Naples FL. **Operations at this facility include:** Administration; Divisional Headquarters. **Number of employees at this location:** 200. **Number of employees nationwide:** 350.

EMBRY-RIDDLE AERONAUTICAL UNIVERSITY
600 South Clyde Morris Boulevard, Daytona Beach FL 32114-3900. 904/226-6145. **Contact:** Human Resources. **Description:** Embry-Riddle University is a private, four-year coeducational undergraduate institution committed to studies in aviation, aerospace, and engineering. **Common positions include:** Accountant/Auditor; Administrator; Blue-Collar Worker Supervisor; Buyer; Computer Programmer; Counselor; Department Manager; Electrical/Electronics Engineer; Financial Analyst; General Manager; Human Resources Specialist; Management Trainee; Marketing Specialist; Physicist/Astronomer; Purchasing Agent and Manager; Statistician; Systems Analyst; Technical Writer/Editor; Transportation/Traffic Specialist. **Educational backgrounds include:** Accounting; Business Administration; Chemistry; Communications; Computer Science; Economics; Engineering; Finance; Liberal Arts; Marketing; Mathematics. **Benefits:** Dental Insurance; Disability Coverage; Employee Discounts; Life Insurance; Medical Insurance; Pension Plan; Tuition Assistance. **Special Programs:** Internships; Training Programs. **Other U.S. locations:** Prescott AZ. **Number of employees nationwide:** 1,200.

FLORIDA AGRICULTURAL AND MECHANICAL UNIVERSITY
211 Foote-Hilyer Building, Tallahassee FL 32307. 904/599-3000. **Recorded Jobline:** 904/561-2436. **Contact:** Personnel. **Description:** A university specializing in agriculture, business, education, journalism, engineering, arts and sciences, pharmacy, allied health sciences, architecture, and nursing.

FLORIDA ATLANTIC UNIVERSITY
777 Glades Road, Boca Raton FL 33431. 407/367-3070. **Recorded Jobline:** 407/367-3506. **Contact:** Personnel Department. **Description:** A university.

FLORIDA INTERNATIONAL UNIVERSITY
NORTH MIAMI CAMPUS
Personnel Office, 3000 NE 145th Street, Miami FL 33199. 305/940-5545. **Recorded Jobline:** 305/348-2500. **Contact:** Personnel. **Description:** A university. **NOTE:** Florida International hires only U.S. citizens. Jobseekers must fill out an FIU application and provide proof of education. EOE/AA.

FLORIDA MEMORIAL COLLEGE
15800 Northwest 42nd Avenue, Miami FL 33054. 305/626-3622. **Fax:** 305/626-3700. **Contact:** Eleanor L. Hatton, Human Resources Manager. **Description:** A liberal arts college. **Common positions include:** Accountant/Auditor; Budget Analyst; Buyer; Computer Programmer; Computer Systems Analyst; Counselor; Education Administrator; Financial Analyst; Human Resources Specialist; Librarian; Library Technician; Mathematician; Physicist/Astronomer; Psychologist; Public Relations Specialist; Purchasing Agent and Manager; Statistician; Teacher. **Educational backgrounds include:** Accounting; Biology; Business Administration; Chemistry; Communications; Computer Science; Economics; Engineering; Finance; Liberal Arts; Marketing; Mathematics; Physics. **Benefits:** 403B; Dental Insurance; Disability Coverage; Employee Discounts; Life Insurance; Medical Insurance; Tuition Assistance. **Special Programs:** Internships. **Operations at this facility include:** Administration. **Listed on:** Privately held. **Number of employees at this location:** 220.

FLORIDA STATE UNIVERSITY
5632 University Center (A), Tallahassee FL 32306-1001. 904/644-6034. **Recorded Jobline:** 904/644-6066. **Contact:** Personnel Department. **Description:** A state university. **Common positions include:** Accountant/Auditor; Budget Analyst; Computer Programmer; Computer Systems Analyst; Library Technician; Radio/TV Announcer/Newscaster; Registered Nurse. **Educational backgrounds include:** Accounting; Business Administration; Finance. **Benefits:** Dental Insurance; Life Insurance; Medical Insurance; Pension Plan; Savings Plan; Tuition Assistance. **Operations at this facility include:** Administration; Research and Development. **Number of employees at this location:** 2,500.

HILLSBOROUGH COMMUNITY COLLEGE
P.O. Box 31127, Tampa FL 33631-3127. 813/253-7000. **Fax:** 813/253-7034. **Recorded Jobline:** 813/253-7185. **Contact:** Personnel Analyst, Employment Office. **Description:** Hillsborough Community College is a multicampus, state-supported community college fully accredited by the Southern Association of Colleges and Schools. HCC is an equal access/equal opportunity institution committed to affirmative action. The school seeks qualified and diverse candidates with multicultural experience including members of protected class groups. Staffing of all positions is contingent upon funding and the Board of Trustees approval. **Common positions include:** Accountant/Auditor; Administrative Worker/Clerk; Administrator; Buyer; Cashier; Clinical Lab Technician; Computer Programmer; Education Administrator; Human Resources Specialist; Instructor/Trainer; Library Technician; Security Officer; Teacher. **Educational backgrounds include:** Accounting; Biology; Business Administration; Chemistry; Computer Science; Education; Mathematics; Radiologic Technology; Sonography. **Benefits:** Dental Insurance; Disability Coverage; Employee Discounts; Life Insurance; Medical Insurance; Retirement Plan; Tuition Assistance. **Corporate headquarters location:** This Location. **Operations at this facility include:** Administration. **Number of employees at this location:** 1,500.

INTERNATIONAL NETWORK FOR CHILDREN AND FAMILIES
P.O. Box 7236, Gainesville FL 32605. 352/377-2176. **Toll free phone:** 800/257-9002. **Contact:** Kathryn Kvols, President. **Description:** A worldwide parent training network that teaches skill-building strategies to families. The classes emphasize

teamwork, creating win-win situations, and effectively avoiding power struggles using kind-but-firm methods promoted by Alfred Adler and Dr. Rudof Dreikurs. **Common positions include:** Accountant/Auditor; Customer Service Representative; Education Administrator; General Manager. **Educational Backgrounds include:** Business Administration; Education. **Operations at this facility:** Regional Headquarters; Research and Development; Sales; Service. **Corporate headquarters location:** This Location. **Other U.S. locations:** Nationwide. **Listed on:** Privately held. **Number of employees nationwide:** 700.

MIAMI-DADE COMMUNITY COLLEGE
11011 SW 104 Street, Miami FL 33176. 305/237-2051. **Fax:** 305/237-2928. **Recorded Jobline:** 305/237-2050. **Contact:** Gilda Crocker, Human Resources. **Description:** A two-year state college committed to providing access to a very diverse population while at the same time maintaining high academic standards and a goal of excellence for all. **Common positions include:** Buyer; Clerical Supervisor; Computer Programmer; Computer Systems Analyst; Counselor; Draftsperson; Electrician; Emergency Medical Technician; Librarian; Library Technician; Registered Nurse; Teacher. **Educational backgrounds include:** Biology; Business Administration; Chemistry; Computer Science; Economics; Engineering; Mathematics; Physics. **Benefits:** Dental Insurance; Disability Coverage; Life Insurance; Medical Insurance; Tuition Assistance. **Corporate headquarters location:** This Location. **Other U.S. locations:** 11380 NW 27th Avenue, Miami FL 33167; 500 College Terrace, Miami FL 33030; 300 NE 2nd Avenue, Miami FL 33132; and 950 NW 20th Street, Miami FL 33127. **Operations at this facility include:** Administration. **Number of employees at this location:** 5,600.

MIAMI-DADE COMMUNITY COLLEGE
MEDICAL CENTER CAMPUS
950 NW 20th Street, Miami FL 33127. 305/237-4247. **Recorded Jobline:** 305/237-0985. **Contact:** Human Resources. **Description:** A two-year state college committed to providing access to a very diverse population while at the same time maintaining high academic standards.

MIAMI-DADE COMMUNITY COLLEGE
NORTH CAMPUS
11380 NW 27th Avenue, Miami FL 33167. 305/237-2051. **Recorded Jobline:** 305/237-0955. **Contact:** Human Resources. **Description:** A two-year state college committed to providing access to a very diverse population while at the same time maintaining high academic standards.

MIAMI-DADE COMMUNITY COLLEGE
MITCHELL WOLFSON CAMPUS
300 NE 2nd Avenue, Miami FL 33132. 305/237-3036. **Recorded Jobline:** 305/237-0975. **Contact:** Human Resources. **Description:** A two-year state college committed to providing access to a very diverse population while at the same time maintaining high academic standards.

NOVA UNIVERSITY
3301 College Avenue, Fort Lauderdale FL 33314. 954/475-7491. **Contact:** Human Resources. **Description:** A university.

PALM BEACH COMMUNITY COLLEGE
4200 Congress Avenue, Lake Worth FL 33461. 407/439-8017. **Fax:** 407/439-8202. **Contact:** Arnease Johnson, Manager of Employment. **Description:** A community college. **Common positions include:** Accountant/Auditor; Buyer; Computer Programmer; Computer Systems Analyst; Counselor; Education Administrator; Human Resources Specialist; Librarian; Library Technician; Occupational Therapist; Registered Nurse; Respiratory Therapist; Teacher. **Educational backgrounds include:** Master of Arts; MBA. **Benefits:** Life Insurance; Pension Plan. **Corporate headquarters location:** This Location.

ROLLINS COLLEGE
1000 Holt Avenue-2718, Winter Park FL 32779. 407/646-2102. **Fax:** 407/646-2188. **Recorded Jobline:** 407/646-2300. **Contact:** Human Resources Department. **Description:** A private liberal arts college. **Benefits:** 401K; Dental Insurance; Disability

Coverage; Employee Discounts; Life Insurance; Medical Insurance; Savings Plan;Tuition Assistance. **Corporate headquarters location:** This Location. **Operations at this facility include:** Administration. **Listed on:** Privately held. **Number of employees at this location:** 530.

ST. PETERSBURG JUNIOR COLLEGE
P.O. Box 13489, St. Petersburg FL 33733. **Fax:** 813/341-3368. **Recorded Joblines:** Clerical, Office and Maintenance positions: 813/341-3220; Instructional and Professional positions: 813/341-3311. **Contact:** Human Resources. **Description:** St. Petersburg Junior College is a multicampus higher education institution serving the population of Pinellas County, Florida. The school awards associate's degrees in the arts and sciences and prepares students for transferring to other institutions for further educational enrichment. **Common positions include:** Accountant/Auditor; Buyer; Clerical Supervisor; Clinical Lab Technician; Computer Programmer; Counselor; Education Administrator; Electrician; Human Resources Specialist; Librarian; Library Technician; Public Relations Specialist; Purchasing Agent and Manager; Teacher. **Educational backgrounds include:** Accounting; Biology; Business Administration; Chemistry; Communications; Computer Science; Engineering; Mathematics; Physics. **Benefits:** 403B; Dental Insurance; Disability Coverage; Employee Discounts; Life Insurance; Medical Insurance; Pension Plan; Tuition Assistance. **Operations at this facility include:** Administration; Service. **Number of employees at this location:** 940.

UNIVERSITY OF CENTRAL FLORIDA
P.O. Box 16040, Orlando FL 32816. 407/823-2771. **Recorded Jobline:** 407/823-2778. **Contact:** Personnel. **Description:** A university.

UNIVERSITY OF FLORIDA
P.O. Box 115002, Fourth Floor, Stadium West, Gainesville FL 32611-2033. 352/392-4621. **Fax:** 352/392-7094. **Recorded Jobline:** 352/392-4631. **Contact:** Human Resources. **Description:** A university. **Common positions include:** Accountant/Auditor; Agricultural Scientist; Biological Scientist/Biochemist; Chemist; Civil Engineer; Computer Programmer; Computer Systems Analyst; Dental Assistant/Dental Hygienist; Human Service Worker; Library Technician; Licensed Practical Nurse. **Educational backgrounds include:** Accounting; Biology; Business Administration; Chemistry; Computer Science; Economics; Engineering; Finance; Liberal Arts; Mathematics. **Benefits:** 401K; Daycare Assistance; Dental Insurance; Disability Coverage; Employee Discounts; Life Insurance; Medical Insurance; Tuition Assistance. **Corporate headquarters location:** This Location. **Number of employees at this location:** 11,500.

UNIVERSITY OF MIAMI
P.O. Box 248106, Coral Gables FL 33124. 305/284-3798. **Recorded Jobline:** 305/284-6918. **Contact:** Human Resources. **Description:** A university.

UNIVERSITY OF NORTH FLORIDA
4567 St. Johns Bluff Road South, Jacksonville FL 32224. 904/646-2903. **Contact:** Human Resources. **Description:** A university. **Common positions include:** Accountant/Auditor; Blue-Collar Worker Supervisor; Broadcast Technician; Clerical Supervisor; Computer Programmer; Computer Systems Analyst; Human Resources Specialist; Library Technician; Purchasing Agent and Manager. **Educational backgrounds include:** Accounting; Business Administration; Computer Science; Finance; Marketing; Mathematics. **Benefits:** 401K; Dental Insurance; Disability Coverage; Employee Discounts; Life Insurance; Medical Insurance; Pension Plan; Savings Plan; Tuition Assistance. **Corporate headquarters location:** Tallahassee FL. **Number of employees at this location:** 1,700.

UNIVERSITY OF SOUTH FLORIDA
4202 East Fowler Avenue, SSB 2172, Tampa FL 33620-6980. 813/974-2011. **Recorded Jobline:** 813/974-2879. **Contact:** Personnel Department. **Description:** A state university.

UNIVERSITY OF WEST FLORIDA
11000 University Parkway, Pensacola FL 32514. 904/474-2694. **Recorded Jobline:** 904/474-2842. **Contact:** Human Resources Department. **Description:** A university.

Note: Because addresses and telephone numbers of smaller companies change rapidly, we recommend you call each company to verify the information below before inquiring about job opportunities. Mass mailings are not recommended.

Additional employers with over 250 employees:

**ELEMENTARY AND
SECONDARY SCHOOLS**

Braddock High School
3601 SW 147th Ave, Miami
FL 33185-4336. 305/220-
9400.

Colonial High School
6100 Oleander Dr, Orlando
FL 32807-3493. 407/277-
5431.

**COLLEGES, UNIVERSITIES,
AND PROFESSIONAL
SCHOOLS**

Barry University
11300 NE 2nd Ave, Miami
FL 33161-6695. 305/899-
3000.

Bethune Cookman College
640 2nd Ave, Daytona
Beach FL 32114-3099.
904/255-1401.

**Florida Institute Of
Technology**
150 W University Blvd,
Melbourne FL 32901-6967.
407/768-8000.

Florida Southern College
111 Lake Hollingsworth Dr,
Lakeland FL 33801-5607.
813/680-4111.

Lynn University
3601 N Military Trl, Boca
Raton FL 33431-5598.
407/994-0770.

Orlando College
5500 Diplomat Cir, Orlando
FL 32810. 407/628-5870.

St. Leo College
P.O. Box 2008, Saint Leo FL
33574. 904/588-8218.

Stetson University
421 N Woodland Blvd,
Deland FL 32720-3799.
904/822-7000.

University Of Tampa
401 W Kennedy Blvd, Tampa
FL 33606. 813/253-3333.

**JUNIOR COLLEGES AND
TECHNICAL INSTITUTES**

Polk Community College
999 Avenue H NE, Winter

Haven FL 33881-4299.
813/297-1000.

**Florida Community College
Jacksonville**
501 W State St, Jacksonville
FL 32202-4030. 904/632-
3000.

**Pasco Hernando Community
College**
2401 State Hwy 41 North,
Dade City FL 33525.
904/567-6701.

Valencia Community College
P.O. Box 3028, Orlando FL
32802-3028. 407/299-
5000.

**Gulf Coast Community
College**
5230 W Highway 98,
Panama City FL 32401-
1041. 904/769-1551.

**Okaloosa Walton Community
College**
100 College Blvd E Bldg,
Niceville FL 32578-1347.
904/678-5111.

Additional employers with under 250 employees:

**ELEMENTARY AND
SECONDARY SCHOOLS**

Bishop Kenny High School
P.O. Box 5544, Jacksonville
FL 32247-5544. 904/398-
7545.

Berkeley Preparatory School
4811 Kelly Rd, Tampa FL
33615-5020. 813/885-
1673.

Hillel Community Day School
19000 NE 25th Ave, Miami
FL 33180-3209. 305/931-
2831.

**Lake Highland Preparatory
School**
901 Highland Ave, Orlando
FL 32803-3295. 407/425-
8686.

Miami Country Day School
P.O. Box 380608, Miami FL
33238-0608. 305/759-
2843.

Pine Crest School
1501 NE 62nd St, Ft
Lauderdale FL 33334-5199.
954/492-4100.

**Shorecrest Preparatory
School**
5101 First St NE, St
Petersburg FL 33703-3009.
813/522-2111.

St Andrew's School
3900 Jog Rd, Boca Raton FL
33434. 407/483-8900.

The Benjamin School
11000 Ellison Wilson Rd, No
Palm Beach FL 33408-3108.
407/626-3744.

The Bolles School
7400 San Jose Blvd,
Jacksonville FL 32217-3430.
904/733-9292.

Gulliver Academy
12595 S Red Rd, Miami FL
33156-6397. 305/665-
3593.

Oak Leaf Alternative School
6601 Central Florida Pkwy,
Orlando FL 32821-8064.
407/345-5000.

Taravella Community School
10600 Riverside Dr,

Pompano Beach FL 33071-
7900. 954/344-2304.

Deland High School
800 N Hill Ave, Deland FL
32724-3726. 904/738-
8000.

**River Ridge Middle-High
School**
11646 Town Center Rd,
New Port Richey FL 34654-
6201. 813/836-7777.

**Little River Elementary
School**
514 NW 77th St, Miami FL
33150-2853. 305/754-
7531.

**Middleburg Elementary
School**
P.O. Box 148, Middleburg FL
32050-0148. 904/282-
5187.

Sheppard Elementary School
5700 W 24th Ave, Hialeah
FL 33016-4424. 305/556-
2204.

Dario Middle School
350 NW 97th Ave, Miami FL

33172-4107. 305/226-0179.

Eisenhower Junior High School
7620 Big Bend Rd,
Gibsonton FL 33534-5700.
813/671-5121.

Hammocks Middle School
9889 Hammocks Blvd,
Miami FL 33196-1539.
305/385-0896.

Hunter's Creek Middle School
13400 Town Loop Blvd,
Orlando FL 32837-5511.
407/858-4620.

Landmark Middle School
101 Kernan Blvd N,
Jacksonville FL 32225-5302.
904/221-7125.

Mandarin Middle School
5100 Hood Rd, Jacksonville
FL 32257-1122. 904/292-0555.

Miami Edison Middle School
6101 NW 2nd Ave, Miami FL
33127-1211. 305/754-4683.

Sixteenth Street Middle School
701 16th St S, St Petersburg
FL 33705-2135. 813/893-2400.

American High School
18350 NW 67th Ave,
Hialeah FL 33015-3496.
305/556-9563.

Anderson High School
3050 NW 41st St, Ft
Lauderdale FL 33309-4317.
954/497-3800.

Apopka High School
555 Martin St, Apopka FL
32712-3598. 407/889-4194.

Armwood High School
12000 E US Highway 92,
Seffner FL 33584-3418.
813/744-8040.

Atlantic High School
2501 Seacrest Blvd, Delray
Beach FL 33444-4392.
407/243-1500.

Auburndale High School
1 Bloodhound Trail,
Auburndale FL 33823-2607.
941/965-6200.

Bay High School
1200 Harrison Ave, Panama
City FL 32401-2433.
904/872-4600.

Bloomingdale High School
1700 Bloomingdale Ave,
Valrico FL 33594-6220.
813/744-8018.

Boca Ciega High School
924 58th St S, St Petersburg
FL 33707-2597. 813/893-2780.

Boca Raton High School
1501 NW 15th Ct, Boca
Raton FL 33486-1198.
407/338-1400.

Boone High School
2000 S Mills Ave, Orlando
FL 32806-4199. 407/898-5491.

Cape Coral High School
2300 Santa Barbara Blvd,
Cape Coral FL 33991-4399.
941/574-6766.

Chamberlain High School
9401 North Blvd, Tampa FL
33612-7893. 813/975-7677.

Charlotte High School
1250 Cooper St, Punta
Gorda FL 33950-6203.
941/639-2118.

Choctawatchee Senior High School
110 Racetrack Rd NW, Ft
Walton Beach FL 32547-1604. 904/833-3614.

Clearwater High School
540 S Hercules Ave,
Clearwater FL 34624-6399.
813/298-1620.

Coconut Creek High School
1400 NW 44th Ave,
Pompano Beach FL 33066-1399. 954/977-2100.

Cooper City High School
9401 Stirling Rd, Cooper
City FL 33328-5899.
954/680-7200.

Coral Springs High School
7201 W Sample Rd, Coral
Springs FL 33065-2299.
954/344-3400.

Cypress Creek High School
1101 Bear Crossing Dr,
Orlando FL 32824-6004.
407/859-0203.

Deltona High School
100 Wolf Pack Run, Deltona
FL 32725-2924. 904/789-9653.

Dixie Hollins High School
4940 62nd St N, St
Petersburg FL 33709-3336.
813/547-7876.

Doctor Phillips High School
6500 Turkey Lake Rd,
Orlando FL 32819-4718.
407/352-4040.

Dunedin High School
1651 Pinehurst Rd, Dunedin

FL 34698-3897. 813/469-4100.

East Bay High School
7710 Big Bend Rd,
Gibsonton FL 33534-5706.
813/671-5134.

Edgewater High School
3100 Edgewater Dr, Orlando
FL 32804-3798. 407/849-0130.

Escambia High School
1310 N 65th Ave, Pensacola
FL 32506-3999. 904/453-3221.

Fletcher High School
700 Seagate Ave, Neptune
Beach FL 32266-3576.
904/247-5905.

Forest High School
1614 SE Fort King St, Ocala
FL 34471-2599. 352/629-8711.

Forest Hill High School
6901 Parker Ave, West Palm
Beach FL 33405-4599.
407/540-2400.

Forrest High School
5530 Firestone Rd,
Jacksonville FL 32244-1599.
904/573-1170.

Fort Pierce-Westwood High School
1801 Angle Rd, Fort Pierce
FL 34947-7021. 407/468-5400.

Fort Walton Beach High School
400 Hollywood Blvd SW, Ft
Walton Beach FL 32548-4599. 904/833-3300.

Gainesville High School
1900 NW 13th St,
Gainesville FL 32609-3494.
352/955-6707.

George Jenkins High School
6000 Lakeland Highlands Rd,
Lakeland FL 33813-3877.
941/648-3566.

Gibbs High School
850 34th St S, St Petersburg
FL 33711-2297. 813/893-5452.

Gulf High School
5355 School Rd, New Port
Richey FL 34652-4399.
813/842-8485.

Hillsborough High School
5000 N Central Ave, Tampa
FL 33603-2214. 813/276-5620.

Hollywood Hills High School
5400 Stirling Rd, Hollywood
FL 33021. 954/985-5225.

Jefferson High School
4401 W Cypress St, Tampa
FL 33607-4097. 813/872-
5241.

John I Leonard High School
4701 10th Ave N, Lake
Worth FL 33463-2297.
407/641-1200.

Jupiter High School
500 Military Trail, Jupiter FL
33458-5797. 407/744-
7900.

Lake Brantley High School
991 Sand Lake Rd,
Altamonte Springs FL
32714-7099. 407/862-
1776.

Lake Gibson High School
7007 N Socrum Loop Rd,
Lakeland FL 33809-2280.
941/853-6100.

Lake Howell High School
4200 Dike Rd, Winter Park
FL 32792-6399. 407/678-
5565.

Lake Weir High School
10351 SE Maricamp Rd,
Ocala FL 34472-6778.
352/687-4040.

Lake Worth High School
1701 Lake Worth Rd, Lake
Worth FL 33460-3699.
407/533-6300.

Lakeland High School
726 Hollingsworth Rd,
Lakeland FL 33801-5818.
941/499-2900.

Lakewood High School
1400 54th Ave S, St
Petersburg FL 33705-5099.
813/893-2916.

Largo High School
410 Missouri Ave N, Largo
FL 34640-1598. 813/588-
3758.

Leto High School
4409 W Sligh Ave, Tampa
FL 33614-3697. 813/872-
5300.

Lincoln High School
3838 Trojan Trail,
Tallahassee FL 32311-3899.
904/487-2110.

Lyman High School
1141 County Road 427 S,
Longwood FL 32750-6462.
407/831-5600.

Mainland High School
125 S Clyde Morris Blvd,
Daytona Beach FL 32114-
3954. 904/252-0401.

Manatee High School
1000 32nd St W, Bradenton

FL 34205-3299. 941/746-
7181.

Mandarin High School
4831 Greenland Rd,
Jacksonville FL 32258-1500.
904/260-3911.

Martin County High School
2801 S Kanner Hwy, Stuart
FL 34994-4898. 407/287-
0710.

**Miami Central Senior High
School**
1781 NW 95th St, Miami FL
33147-3199. 305/696-
4161.

Miami Edison High School
6161 NW 5th Ct, Miami FL
33127-1259. 305/751-
7337.

Miami Jackson High School
1751 NW 36th St, Miami FL
33142-5495. 305/634-
2621.

**Miami Killian Senior High
School**
10655 SW 97th Ave, Miami
FL 33176-2808. 305/271-
3311.

Miami Norland High School
1050 NW 195th St, Miami
FL 33169-3040. 305/653-
1416.

**Miami Northwestern High
School**
7007 NW 12th Ave, Miami
FL 33150-3824. 305/836-
0991.

**Miami Palmetto Senior High
School**
7460 SW 118th St, Miami
FL 33156-4599. 305/235-
1360.

Miami Senior High School
2450 SW First St, Miami FL
33135-1402. 305/649-
9800.

**Miami Southridge High
School**
19355 SW 114th Ave,
Miami FL 33157-8107.
305/238-6110.

Milton High School
103 Stewart Street, Milton
FL 32570. 904/623-0341.

Miramar High School
3601 S Douglas Rd, Miramar
FL 33025-3299. 954/437-
0600.

Mosley High School
501 Mosley Dr, Lynn Haven
FL 32444-5628. 904/872-
4400.

Niceville High School
800 John Sims Pkwy E,

Niceville FL 32578-1210.
904/833-4113.

North Marion High School
151 W Hwy 329, Citra FL
32113. 904/620-7587.

**North Miami Beach High
School**
1247 NE 167th St, Miami FL
33162-2723. 305/949-
8381.

Northeast High School
700 NE 56th St, Oakland
Park FL 33334-3499.
954/928-0300.

Oak Ridge High School
6000 Winegard Rd, Orlando
FL 32809-4895. 407/855-
2911.

Orange Park High School
2300 Kingsley Ave, Orange
Park FL 32073-4299.
904/272-8110.

Oviedo High School
601 King St, Oviedo FL
32765-9712. 407/365-
5671.

Palatka High School
302 Mellon Rd, Palatka FL
32177-4099. 904/329-
0577.

Palm Bay High School
101 Pirate Ln, Melbourne FL
32901. 407/952-5900.

**Palm Beach Lakes High
School**
3505 Shiloh Dr, West Palm
Beach FL 33407-6898.
407/640-5000.

Parker High School
7301 Parker School Rd,
Jacksonville FL 32211-5105.
904/720-1650.

Pensacola High School
500 W Maxwell St,
Pensacola FL 32501-1699.
904/433-8291.

Pine Forest High School
2500 Longleaf Dr, Pensacola
FL 32526-8924. 904/944-
1121.

Pinellas Park High School
6305 118th Ave, Largo FL
34643-3795. 813/538-
7410.

Plant City High School
1 Raider Place, Plant City FL
33566-7199. 813/757-
9370.

Plantation High School
6901 NW 16th St, Ft
Lauderdale FL 33313-5399.
954/797-4400.

Port Charlotte High School
18200 Toledo Blade Blvd,
Port Charlotte FL 33948-
3398. 941/625-9000.

Port St. Lucie High School
1201 SE Jaguar Ln, Port St
Lucie FL 34952-8127.
407/337-6770.

Ridgewood High School
7650 Orchid Lake Rd, New
Port Richey FL 34653-1399.
813/836-3900.

Riverdale High School
2815 Buckingham Rd, Fort
Myers FL 33905-2499.
941/694-4141.

Riverview High School
1 Ram Way, Sarasota FL
34231-5141. 941/923-
1484.

Rutherford High School
1000 School Ave, Panama
City FL 32401-5199.
904/872-4500.

**Sandalwood Senior High
School**
2750 John Prom Blvd,
Jacksonville FL 32246-3921.
904/646-5100.

Sarasota High School
1000 S School Ave,
Sarasota FL 34237-8044.
941/955-0181.

Seminole High School
2701 Ridgewood Ave,
Sanford FL 32773-4999.
407/322-4352.

Seminole High School
8401 131st St, Seminole FL
34646-3199. 813/547-
7536.

**South Miami Senior High
School**
6856 SW 53rd St, Miami FL
33155-5716. 305/666-
5871.

Southeast High School
1200 37th Ave E, Bradenton
FL 34208-4599. 941/741-
3366.

Spanish River High School
5100 Jog Rd, Boca Raton FL
33496-2299. 407/241-
2200.

Springstead High School
3300 Mariner Blvd, Spring
Hill FL 34609-2799.
352/666-2525.

St Augustine High School
3205 Varella Ave, St
Augustine FL 32095-2096.
904/829-3471.

St Petersburg High School
2501 5th Ave N, St

Petersburg FL 33713-6901.
813/323-4100.

**Stoneman Douglas High
School**
5901 Pine Island Rd,
Pompano Beach FL 33076-
2306. 954/345-4900.

Taravella High School
10600 Riverside Dr, Coral
Springs FL 33071-7901.
954/344-2300.

Tate High School
P.O. Box 68, Gonzalez FL
32560-0068. 904/968-
9522.

Titusville High School
150 Terrier Trail, Titusville FL
32780. 407/264-3100.

University High School
11501 Eastwood Dr, Orlando
FL 32817-3500. 407/275-
7627.

Vanguard High School
7 NW 28th St, Ocala FL
34475-3487. 352/620-
7201.

**Vero Beach Senior High
School**
1707 16th St, Vero Beach
FL 32960-3626. 407/778-
7077.

Wakulla County High School
RR 2 Box 4800,
Crawfordville FL 32327-
9802. 904/926-7125.

Washington High School
6000 College Pkwy,
Pensacola FL 32504-7997.
904/478-8134.

Western High School
1200 SW 136th Ave, Ft
Lauderdale FL 33325-4399.
954/370-1600.

White High School
1700 Old Middleburg Rd,
Jacksonville FL 32210-1232.
904/693-7620.

Winter Haven High School
600 6th St SE, Winter Haven
FL 33880-3737. 941/291-
5330.

Wolfson High School
7000 Powers Ave,
Jacksonville FL 32217-3398.
904/739-5265.

**Wakulla County School
District**
P.O. Box 100, Crawfordville
FL 32326-0100. 904/926-
7131.

VOCATIONAL SCHOOLS

Marine Mechanics Institute
9751 Delegates Dr, Orlando

FL 32837-8353. 407/240-
2422.

Miami Technical Institute
7601 W Flagler St, Miami FL
33144-2405. 305/263-
9832.

JS&T Nursing Studies
7402 N 56th St, Tampa FL
33617-7733. 813/980-
1092.

**COLLEGES, UNIVERSITIES,
AND PROFESSIONAL
SCHOOLS**

Edward Waters College
1658 Kings Rd, Jacksonville
FL 32209. 904/355-3030.

Flagler College
P.O. Box 1027, St Augustine
FL 32085. 904/829-6481.

Fort Lauderdale College
1040 Bayview Dr, Ft
Lauderdale FL 33304-2522.
954/568-1600.

Jones College
5353 Arlington Expy,
Jacksonville FL 32211-5540.
904/743-1122.

**Southeastern College
Assembly Of God**
1000 Longfellow Blvd,
Lakeland FL 33801-6099.
941/665-4404.

Tampa College
3319 W Hillsborough Ave,
Tampa FL 33614-5801.
813/879-6000.

Tampa College - Lakeland
1200 US Highway South,
Suite 45, Lakeland FL
33801. 941/686-1444.

**JUNIOR COLLEGES AND
TECHNICAL INSTITUTES**

Chipola Junior College
3094 Indian Circle Bldg A,
Marianna FL 32446-1701.
904/526-2761.

Lake City Community College
RR 3 Box 7, Lake City FL
32055. 904/752-1822.

**Lake Sumter Community
College**
9501 US Highway 441,
Leesburg FL 34788-3950.
352/787-3747.

**Lewis M. Lively Vocational-
Tech Center**
500 Appleyard Dr,
Tallahassee FL 32304-2810.
904/487-7555.

**South Florida Community
College**
600 W College Dr, Avon Park

FL 33825-9356. 941/453-6661.

St Johns River Community College
5001 Saint Johns Ave, Palatka FL 32177-3807. 904/328-1571.

MISC. SCHOOLS AND EDUCATIONAL SERVICES

Comair Aviation Academy
2700 Flightline Ave, Sanford FL 32773-9683. 407/330-7020.

Kaset International
8875 Hidden River Pkwy, Suite 400, Tampa FL 33637-1017. 813/962-7830.

CHILD DAYCARE SERVICES

Alpi Wabassa Child Development Center
8445 64th Ave, Vero Beach FL 32967. 407/589-7437.

Another Generation Preschool II
1250 Dykes Rd, Ft Lauderdale FL 33326-1901. 954/389-0488.

Childtime Child Care
9950 Saint Augustine Rd, Jacksonville FL 32257-7584. 904/268-1933.

Kindercare Learning Centers
12307 S Orange Blossom Trail, Orlando FL 32837-6506. 407/240-6640.

La Petite Academy
9005 Regents Park Dr,

Tampa FL 33647-2460. 813/973-4524.

Mims Parent & Child Development
2333 Palmetto Ave, Mims FL 32754. 407/269-2173.

Paga Private Schools
10250 University Blvd, Orlando FL 32817-1905. 407/657-7277.

RCMA Childcare Research & Referral
30435 Commerce Dr, San Antonio FL 33576-8084. 904/588-4252.

Samoset Head Start
3124 17th St E, Bradenton FL 34208-4304. 941/748-6670.

Sarasota Family YMCA Childcare
1075 S Euclid Ave, Sarasota FL 34237-8124. 941/952-9533.

Sarasota Family YMCA Childcare
1819 Main St, Sarasota FL 34236-5951. 941/954-8960.

Sarasota Memorial Hospital Child Care
1935 Hyde Park St, Sarasota FL 34239-3612. 941/953-1477.

Southwind Child Enrichment Center
8951 Stirling Rd, Cooper City FL 33328-5166. 954/434-5555.

Sunrise Child Care
2618 E Robinson St, Orlando FL 32803-5824. 407/894-3717.

The Carol Center
112 NW 3rd St, Miami FL 33128-1708. 305/375-3222.

The Children's Center
8900 N Kendall Dr, Miami FL 33176-2118. 305/596-6523.

Winter Springs Child Care Center
6 N Devon Ave, Winter Springs FL 32708-2515. 407/327-4110.

YMCA Day Care-Palm Beaches
2085 S Congress Ave, West Palm Beach FL 33406-7601. 407/967-1978.

Manatee Opportunity Council
1707 15th St E, Bradenton FL 34208-3423. 941/748-0137.

Gingerbread Schools
1480 74th St N, St Petersburg FL 33710-4530. 813/343-9890.

Northside Christian Schools
6000 38th Ave N, St Petersburg FL 33710-1720. 813/381-4999.

Westside Village Child Care Center
3102 Sammonds Rd, Plant City FL 33567-4410. 813/754-3040.

For more information on career opportunities in educational services:

Associations

AMERICAN ASSOCIATION OF SCHOOL ADMINISTRATORS
1801 North Moore Street, Arlington VA 22209. 703/528-0700.

AMERICAN FEDERATION OF TEACHERS
555 New Jersey Avenue NW, Washington DC 20001. 202/879-4400.

COLLEGE AND UNIVERSITY PERSONNEL ASSOCIATION
1233 20th Street NW, Suite 301, Washington DC 20036. 202/429-0311. Membership required.

NATIONAL ASSOCIATION OF BIOLOGY TEACHERS
11250 Roger Bacon Drive, #19, Reston VA 22090. 703/471-1134.

NATIONAL ASSOCIATION OF COLLEGE ADMISSION COUNSELORS
1631 Prince Street, Alexandria VA 22314. 703/836-2222. An education association of secondary school counselors, college and

university admission officers, and related individuals who work with students as they make the transition from high school to post-secondary education.

NATIONAL ASSOCIATION OF COLLEGE AND UNIVERSITY BUSINESS OFFICERS
1 DuPont Circle, Suite 500, Washington DC 20036. 202/861-2500. Association for those involved in the financial administration and management of higher education. Membership required.

NATIONAL SCIENCE TEACHERS ASSOCIATION
1840 Wilson Boulevard, Arlington VA 22201-3000. 703/243-7100. Organization committed to the improvement of science education at all levels, preschool through college. Publishes five journals, a newspaper, and a number of special publications. Also conducts national and regional conventions.

Books

ACADEMIC LABOR MARKETS
Falmer Press, Taylor & Francis, Inc., 1900
Frost Road, Suite 101, Bristol PA 19007.
800/821-8312.

HOW TO GET A JOB IN EDUCATION
Adams Media Corporation, 260 Center
Street, Holbrook MA 02343. 617/767-
8100.

Directories

**WASHINGTON HIGHER EDUCATION
ASSOCIATION DIRECTORY**
Council for Advancement and Support of
Education, 11 DuPont Circle NW, Suite
400, Washington DC 20036 202/328-
5900.

ELECTRONIC/INDUSTRIAL ELECTRICAL EQUIPMENT

 *Heading into 1995, industry analysts expected productivity in the fast-paced electronics industry to spiral, even as the number of production workers in the industry declined. Intense competition from overseas has companies cutting costs by sending labor-intensive operations to low-wage regions like the Far East and Mexico. On the other hand, the increased computerization of the industry is increasing the demand for highly-trained knowledge workers.*

Semiconductor manufacturers, in particular, are on a roll. This sector far exceeded growth projections in 1993 and 1994 with a robust growth rate of 29 percent. Many chipmakers predicted that 1995 growth would surpass the 15 percent growth rate forecast by the Semiconductor Industry Association. Factors spawning a high demand for semiconductors: a surging PC market; new Information Highway markets; and a stronger telecommunications and consumer electronics market -- bolstered by a recovering Japanese economy. All told, the number of jobs in the semiconductor industry in 1995 was expected to hit 240,000 for the first time since 1990.

ACR ELECTRONICS
5757 Ravenswood Road, Fort Lauderdale FL 33312. 954/981-3333. **Contact:** Gary Van Arsdale, Director of Human Resources. **Description:** Producers of survival and safety electronics equipment for government and marine consumers.

ANILAM ELECTRONICS
5625 NW 79th Avenue, Miami FL 33166. 305/592-2727. **Contact:** Larry Mize, Controller. **Description:** Anilam Electronics produces digital readouts and computer controls for machine tools. The company serves the aerospace and machine tool and die industries.

C-MAC OF AMERICA, INC.
1601 Hill Avenue, West Palm Beach FL 33407. 407/845-8455. **Fax:** 407/881-2342. **Contact:** Human Resources. **Description:** A manufacturer of microcircuits, multiclip modules, complex backpanels, and card cage assemblies used in the electronics industry. **Common positions include:** Accountant/Auditor; Administrator; Blue-Collar Worker Supervisor; Buyer; Ceramics Engineer; Chemical Engineer; Computer Programmer; Computer Systems Analyst; Cost Estimator; Customer Service Representative; Department Manager; Electrical/Electronics Engineer; Environmental Engineer; General Manager; Health Services Worker; Human Resources Specialist; Industrial Engineer; Mechanical Engineer; Process Engineer; Quality Assurance Engineer; Quality Control Supervisor; Test Engineer. **Educational backgrounds include:** Business Administration; Chemistry; Engineering; Finance; Marketing; Physics. **Benefits:** Dental Insurance; Disability Coverage; Life Insurance; Medical Insurance; Savings Plan; Tuition Assistance. **Corporate headquarters location:** Sherbrooke, Quebec. **Parent company:** C-MAC Industries, Inc. **Operations at this facility include:** Manufacturing. **Listed on:** Canadian Stock Exchange. **Number of employees at this location:** 400. **Number of employees nationwide:** 2,100.

COMPUTER PRODUCTS, INC.
7900 Glades Road, Suite 500, Boca Raton FL 33434. 407/451-1000. **Fax:** 407/451-1050. **Contact:** Human Resources. **Description:** Computer Products is a designer and producer of electronic products and subsystems. The company manufactures both standard and custom products used in an array of applications including powering communications networks, controlling the manufacture of fiber optics, enabling voice

messaging, multimedia power for global Internet servers, and operating traffic signals with real-time embedded computers. The company consists of three business segments: Power Conversion, a supplier of power systems technology to the communications industry; RTP Corporation, an industrial automation business that delivers input/output products and intelligent controllers; and Heurikon Corporation, a computer systems business that designs and provides real-time computers and subsystems tailored to the markets of voice messaging, graphics, video-on-demand, machine vision, and simulation. **Common positions include:** Aerospace Engineer; Computer Programmer; Electrical/Electronics Engineer. **Educational backgrounds include:** Computer Science; Engineering; Marketing. **Benefits:** Dental Insurance; Disability Coverage; Life Insurance; Medical Insurance; Savings Plan; Tuition Assistance. **Corporate headquarters location:** This Location. **Other U.S. locations:** Fremont CA; Pompano Beach FL; Boston MA; Madison WI. **Operations at this facility include:** Administration. **Listed on:** NASDAQ. **Number of employees nationwide:** 1,600.

CUTLER HAMMER
110 Douglas Road East, P.O. Box 819, Oldsmar FL 34677. 813/855-4621. **Fax:** 813/855-4626. **Contact:** Human Resources. **Description:** Cutler Hammer produces high technology products and various services within several divisions. The Broadcasting Division operates as Group W, and primarily owns and operates radio and television stations. The Electronic Systems Group produces advanced electronic systems for the U.S. Department of Defense and other government agencies. Environmental Systems provides environmental services, including toxic, hazardous, and radioactive waste services. Power Systems includes businesses involving electrical power generation, Knoll Group provides office furniture, and WCI develops residential communities. This location manufactures smart drives (computer units that run air conditioners).

DBA SYSTEMS, INC.
P.O. Drawer 550, Melbourne FL 32902-0550. 407/727-0660. **Contact:** Human Resources. **Description:** Develops and manufactures advanced imaging technology systems for military and intelligence applications. **Common positions include:** Computer Programmer; Electrical/Electronics Engineer; Systems Analyst. **Educational backgrounds include:** Computer Science; Engineering. **Benefits:** 401K; Dental Insurance; Disability Coverage; Employee Discounts; Life Insurance; Medical Insurance; Profit Sharing; Tuition Assistance. **Corporate headquarters location:** This Location. **Other U.S. locations:** Fairfax VA. **Listed on:** NASDAQ. **Number of employees at this location:** 130. **Number of employees nationwide:** 230.

DYNALCO CONTROLS
P.O. Box 5328, Fort Lauderdale FL 33310. 954/739-4300. **Contact:** Ms. Lee Mellon, Human Resources Manager. **Description:** Produces electronic monitors, controls, sensors, and displays, primarily for stationary engines. The parent company is a major producer of industrial valves, liquid temperature control devices for industrial and commercial applications, and controls for large stationary engines. **Common positions include:** Accountant/Auditor; Buyer; Electrical/Electronics Engineer; Operations/Production Manager; Technical Writer/Editor. **Educational backgrounds include:** Accounting; Computer Science; Engineering; Finance; Marketing. **Benefits:** Dental Insurance; Disability Coverage; Life Insurance; Medical Insurance; Pension Plan; Savings Plan; Stock Option; Tuition Assistance. **Corporate headquarters location:** Skokie IL. **Other U.S. locations:** Long Beach CA; Billerica MA; Tulsa OK. **Parent company:** Mark Controls Corporation. **Operations at this facility include:** Administration; Manufacturing; Research and Development; Sales; Service. **Number of employees at this location:** 80.

ECC INTERNATIONAL CORPORATION
P.O. Box 598022, Orlando FL 32859-8022. 407/859-7410. **Contact:** Personnel Department. **Description:** Designs and manufactures simulation training devices, primarily for the United States military. **Common positions include:** Accountant/Auditor; Commercial Artist; Computer Programmer; Computer Systems Analyst; Cost Estimator; Draftsperson; Electrical/Electronics Engineer; Graphic Artist; Industrial Engineer; Machinist; Mechanical Engineer; Precision Assembler; Purchasing Agent and Manager; Receptionist; Secretary; Sheet-Metal Worker; Software Engineer; Technical Writer/Editor; Typist/Word Processor; Welder. **Educational backgrounds include:** Accounting; Computer Science; Engineering; Mathematics; Physics. **Benefits:** Dental Insurance; Disability Coverage; Life Insurance; Medical Insurance; Pension Plan; Profit Sharing; Savings Plan; Tuition Assistance. **Corporate headquarters location:**

Wayne PA. **Operations at this facility include:** Administration; Manufacturing; Research and Development; Service. **Listed on:** New York Stock Exchange. **Number of employees at this location:** 780. **Number of employees nationwide:** 810.

ELECTRO CORPORATION
1845 57th Street, Sarasota FL 34243. 941/355-8411. **Contact:** Personnel Director. **Description:** A manufacturer of magnetic sensing devices, tachometers, proximity switches, and circuit and control systems. **Common positions include:** Accountant/Auditor; Blue-Collar Worker Supervisor; Buyer; Computer Programmer; Customer Service Representative; Draftsperson; Electrical/Electronics Engineer; Human Resources Specialist; Industrial Engineer; Marketing Specialist; Mechanical Engineer; Operations/Production Manager; Purchasing Agent and Manager; Quality Control Supervisor; Services Sales Representative; Systems Analyst. **Educational backgrounds include:** Accounting; Computer Science; Engineering; Finance; Marketing. **Benefits:** Disability Coverage; Life Insurance; Medical Insurance; Profit Sharing; Savings Plan; Tuition Assistance. **Corporate headquarters location:** This Location. **Operations at this facility include:** Manufacturing.

ELTEC INSTRUMENTS INC.
P.O. Box 9610, Daytona Beach FL 32120. 904/252-0411. **Contact:** Samuel D. Mollenkof, Director of Personnel. **Description:** Develops, manufactures, and markets infrared sensors, industrial control systems, and high-meg ohm resistors. Primary customers include intruder alarm manufacturers, building automation systems, heating air conditioning and lighting control marketers, and process control systems developers. **Common positions include:** Accountant/Auditor; Administrator; Buyer; Draftsperson; Electrical/Electronics Engineer; Human Resources Specialist; Operations/Production Manager; Purchasing Agent and Manager; Sensors Engineer; Systems Engineer. **Educational backgrounds include:** Accounting; Business Administration; Engineering; Marketing. **Benefits:** Dental Insurance; Life Insurance; Medical Insurance; Tuition Assistance. **Corporate headquarters location:** This Location. **Operations at this facility include:** Administration; Manufacturing; Research and Development; Sales; Service.

GROUP TECHNOLOGY
10901 McKinnley Drive, Tampa FL 33612. 813/972-6002. **Contact:** Personnel Department. **Description:** An electronics manufacturer.

HARRIS CORPORATION
1025 West NASA Boulevard, Melbourne FL 32919. 407/727-9100. **Contact:** Robert Stovall, Director of Human Resources. **Description:** Harris Corporation is focused on four major businesses: advanced electronic systems, semiconductors, electronic systems, and Lanier office systems. The company uses advanced technologies to provide innovative and cost-effective solutions for commercial and government customers. Electronic systems includes advanced information processing and communication systems and software for defense applications, air traffic control, avionics, satellite communications, space exploration, mobile-radio networks, simulation, energy management, law enforcement, electronic systems testing, and newspaper composition. The semiconductor sector includes advanced analog, digital, and mixed-signal integrated circuits and discrete semiconductors for power, signal processing, data-acquisitions, and logic applications. Markets include automotive systems, wireless communications, telecommunication line cards, video and imaging systems, industrial equipment, computer peripherals, and military and aerospace systems. The communications sector includes broadcast, radio communication, and telecommunications products and systems, including transmitters and equipment for TV and radio; HF, VHF, and UHF radio communication equipment; microwave radios; digital telephone switches; telephone subscriber-loop equipment; and in-building paging equipment. Lanier Worldwide sells, services, and provides supplies for copying, facsimile, dictation, optical-based information management, continuous recording, and PC-based health care management systems through 1,600 locations in 80 countries. **Common positions include:** Accountant/Auditor; Computer Programmer; Computer Systems Analyst; Electrical/Electronics Engineer; Financial Analyst; Software Engineer. **Educational backgrounds include:** Computer Science; Engineering. **Corporate headquarters location:** This Location. **Listed on:** New York Stock Exchange. **Number of employees nationwide:** 28,000.

HARRIS CORPORATION
SEMICONDUCTOR SECTOR
P.O. Box 883, Melbourne FL 32902. 407/724-7000. **Contact:** Director of Human Resources. **Description:** The semiconductor sector includes advanced analog, digital, and mixed-signal integrated circuits and discrete semiconductors for power, signal processing, data-acquisitions, and logic applications. Markets include automotive systems, wireless communications, telecommunication line cards, video and imaging systems, industrial equipment, computer peripherals, and military and aerospace systems. This location manufactures semiconductors. **Common positions include:** Accountant/Auditor; Administrator; Attorney; Blue-Collar Worker Supervisor; Computer Programmer; Customer Service Representative; Department Manager; Editor; Electrical/Electronics Engineer; Financial Analyst; General Manager; Human Resources Specialist; Industrial Engineer; Manufacturer's/Wholesaler's Sales Rep.; Marketing Specialist; Mechanical Engineer; Metallurgical Engineer; Operations/Production Manager; Public Relations Specialist; Purchasing Agent and Manager; Quality Control Supervisor; Reporter; Systems Analyst. **Educational backgrounds include:** Accounting; Business Administration; Communications; Computer Science; Economics; Engineering; Finance; Marketing; Physics. **Benefits:** Dental Insurance; Disability Coverage; Employee Discounts; Life Insurance; Medical Insurance; Pension Plan; Profit Sharing; Savings Plan; Tuition Assistance. **Special Programs:** Training Programs. **Corporate headquarters location:** Melbourne FL. **Operations at this facility include:** Administration; Divisional Headquarters; Manufacturing; Research and Development; Sales; Service. **Listed on:** New York Stock Exchange.

HERCULES DEFENSE ELECTRONICS SYSTEMS INC.
P.O. Box 4648, Clearwater FL 34618. 813/572-3319. **Contact:** Human Resources. **Description:** A defense electronics contractor for the Department of Defense. The company's products include automatic test equipment, decision support systems, electronic countermeasures, millimeter wave guidance, radar and fire control, systems integration. **Corporate headquarters location:** Wilmington DE. **Parent company:** Hercules, Inc.

INFRARED INDUSTRIES, INC.
12151 Research Parkway, Orlando FL 32826. 407/282-7700. **Contact:** Cathy Walls, Personnel Director. **Description:** Manufacturers of infrared detector systems and related products.

INSTRUMENT CONTROL SERVICE, INC.
P.O. Box 7126, Pensacola FL 32534. 904/968-2191. **Contact:** Tom Alexander, Director of Human Resources. **Description:** A manufacturer of industrial control instruments. **Common positions include:** Blue-Collar Worker Supervisor; Branch Manager; Chemical Engineer; Civil Engineer; Computer Programmer; Draftsperson; Electrical/Electronics Engineer; Industrial Engineer; Manufacturer's/Wholesaler's Sales Rep.; Purchasing Agent and Manager; Systems Analyst; Technical Writer/Editor. **Educational backgrounds include:** Accounting; Business Administration; Computer Science; Engineering; Marketing. **Benefits:** Disability Coverage; Life Insurance; Medical Insurance; Pension Plan; Savings Plan. **Corporate headquarters location:** This Location. **Operations at this facility include:** Administration; Manufacturing; Sales; Service.

INTERWORLD ELECTRONICS, INC.
47 32nd Street, Miami FL 33172. 305/592-9506. **Contact:** Personnel Department. **Description:** A distributor of electronics for consumer companies.

LIGHTING COMPONENTS AND DESIGN
692 South Military Trail, Deerfield FL 33442. 954/425-0123. **Contact:** John Cooper, President. **Description:** A manufacturer of pre-wired electrical devices, indicator lights, and lamp holders for small appliances. **Corporate headquarters location:** This Location.

LITTON LASER, INC.
LASER SYSTEMS DIVISION
P.O. Box 547300, Orlando FL 32854. 407/295-4010. **Contact:** Deborah Yates, Senior Human Resources Administrator. **Description:** Engaged in the design, development, and manufacturing of military and commercial laser systems. **Common positions include:** Accountant/Auditor; Aerospace Engineer; Buyer; Cashier; Chef/Cook/Kitchen Worker; Draftsperson; Electrical/Electronics Engineer; Financial Manager; Food and Beverage Service Worker; Human Resources Specialist; Industrial Engineer; Inspector/Tester/Grader; Librarian; Machinist; Mechanical Engineer; Payroll Clerk; Purchasing Agent and Manager; Secretary; Stock Clerk; Typist/Word Processor.

Educational backgrounds include: Accounting; Business Administration; Engineering; Finance; Mathematics; Physics. **Benefits:** Dental Insurance; Disability Coverage; Employee Discounts; Life Insurance; Medical Insurance; Pension Plan; Savings Plan; Tuition Assistance. **Corporate headquarters location:** Beverly Hills CA. **Operations at this facility include:** Administration; Divisional Headquarters; Manufacturing; Research and Development. **Listed on:** New York Stock Exchange. **Number of employees at this location:** 400.

LOCKHEED MARTIN ELECTRONICS AND MISSILES
5600 Sand Lake Road, MP-9, Orlando FL 32819. 407/356-5682. **Contact:** Bruce Czarniak, Chief of Staffing. **Description:** Engaged in the design, development, testing, and manufacture of defense systems for military applications. The company's products include missiles, guided projectiles, anti-armor weapons, weapon delivery systems, and tactical communications systems. **Common positions include:** Accountant/Auditor; Aerospace Engineer; Attorney; Buyer; Chemical Engineer; Computer Programmer; Computer Systems Analyst; Electrical/Electronics Engineer; Environmental Engineer; Human Resources Specialist; Industrial Engineer; Industrial Production Manager; Manufacturing Engineer; Mechanical Engineer; Optical Engineer; Quality Control Supervisor; Technical Writer/Editor. **Educational backgrounds include:** Accounting; Computer Science; Engineering; Finance; Microelectronics. **Benefits:** Credit Union; Dental Insurance; Disability Coverage; Employee Discounts; Life Insurance; Medical Insurance; Pension Plan; Profit Sharing; Savings Plan; Tuition Assistance. **Corporate headquarters location:** Bethesda MD. **Operations at this facility include:** Manufacturing; Research and Development. **Listed on:** New York Stock Exchange. **Number of employees at this location:** 4,000.

MOTOROLA, INC.
COMMUNICATIONS SECTOR
1500 Gateway Boulevard, Boynton Beach FL 33426. 407/364-2000. **Contact:** Employment. **Description:** The company provides applied research, development, manufacturing, and marketing of high-technology electronic systems and components for industry and government in communications, automotive, controls, semiconductor, information systems, and office information fields. Motorola, Inc.'s primary products include two-way radios and pagers. **Corporate headquarters location:** Schaumburg IL. **Listed on:** New York Stock Exchange. **Number of employees nationwide:** 98,000.

MOTOROLA, INC.
COMMUNICATIONS SECTOR
8000 West Sunrise Boulevard, Plantation FL 33322. 954/723-5700. **Fax:** 954/723-4490. **Contact:** Jerry Vetter, Staffing Manager. **Description:** The company provides applied research, development, manufacturing, and marketing of high-technology electronic systems and components for industry and government markets in communications, automotive, controls, semiconductor, information systems, and office information fields. Motorola, Inc.'s primary products include two-way radios, special applications products, and pagers. **Common positions include:** Accountant/Auditor; Chemical Engineer; Computer Programmer; Electrical/Electronics Engineer; Financial Analyst; Human Resources Specialist; Industrial Designer; Industrial Engineer; Marketing Specialist; Mechanical Engineer; Metallurgical Engineer; Purchasing Agent and Manager; Systems Analyst; Technical Writer/Editor. **Educational backgrounds include:** Accounting; Chemistry; Computer Science; Engineering; Finance; Marketing. **Benefits:** Dental Insurance; Disability Coverage; Employee Discounts; Life Insurance; Medical Insurance; Pension Plan; Profit Sharing; Savings Plan; Tuition Assistance. **Corporate headquarters location:** Schaumburg IL. **Operations at this facility include:** Administration; Divisional Headquarters; Manufacturing; Research and Development. **Listed on:** New York Stock Exchange.

NOVATRONICS
P.O. Box 878, Pompano Beach FL 33061. 954/942-5200. **Contact:** Director of Human Resources. **Description:** A manufacturer of power supplies, avionics and precision equipment, supplying the defense and electronics industries. **Common positions include:** Aerospace Engineer; Electrical/Electronics Engineer; Industrial Engineer; Mechanical Engineer. **Educational backgrounds include:** Business Administration; Engineering. **Benefits:** Dental Insurance; Disability Coverage; Life Insurance; Medical Insurance; Pension Plan; Profit Sharing; Savings Plan; Tuition Assistance. **Corporate headquarters location:** Melville NY. **Parent company:** Lambda Electronics. **Number of employees at this location:** 240.

PHILIPS COMPONENTS
1440 Indiantown Road, P.O. Box 689605, Jupiter FL 33468-9605. 407/881-3200.
Contact: Tim Atzinger, Human Resources Director. **Description:** A manufacturer of electronic components for industrial, telecommunications, and computer companies. **Common positions include:** Blue-Collar Worker Supervisor; Marketing Specialist; Mechanical Engineer; Quality Control Supervisor. **Educational backgrounds include:** Engineering. **Benefits:** Dental Insurance; Life Insurance; Medical Insurance; Pension Plan; Savings Plan; Tuition Assistance. **Operations at this facility include:** Manufacturing; Sales. **Listed on:** New York Stock Exchange.

PIEZO TECHNOLOGY, INC.
P.O. Box 547859, Orlando FL 32854-7859. 407/298-2000. **Contact:** Ms. Huong Nguyen, Personnel Director. **Description:** A manufacturer of frequency control systems for defense industry communications systems.

S.T. KELTEC
84 Hill Avenue, Ft. Walton Beach FL 32548. 904/244-0043. **Contact:** Pat Tuthill, Director of Personnel. **Description:** A designer and manufacturer of power conversion equipment.

SENSORMATIC ELECTRONICS CORPORATION
500 North West 12th Avenue, Deerfield Beach FL 33442-1795. 954/420-2000. **Contact:** Human Resource Department. **Description:** Sensormatic produces and services electronic security solutions to retail and commercial businesses worldwide. The company's products include AC500 Access Control System, which integrates hands-free access control with video imaging; SpeedDome programmable dome camera; Alligator anti-shoplifting tags; AisleKeeper, SekurPost, and SuperTag anti-shoplifting systems; Electronic Asset Protection systems; and SekurNed systems, which monitor and track hospital patients. **Common positions include:** Accountant/Auditor; Computer Programmer; Customer Service Representative; Draftsperson; Electrical/Electronics Engineer; Financial Analyst; Industrial Engineer; Marketing Specialist; Mechanical Engineer; Operations/Production Manager; Purchasing Agent and Manager; Quality Control Supervisor; Services Sales Representative; Systems Analyst. **Educational backgrounds include:** Accounting; Business Administration; Computer Science; Engineering; Finance; Liberal Arts; Marketing. **Benefits:** Dental Insurance; Disability Coverage; Life Insurance; Medical Insurance; Pension Plan; Profit Sharing; Retirement Plan; Salary Continuation; Savings Plan; Stock Option; Tuition Assistance. **Corporate headquarters location:** This Location. **Operations at this facility include:** Administration; Manufacturing; Research and Development. **Listed on:** New York Stock Exchange. **Number of employees nationwide:** 5,500.

SOLITRON DEVICES, INC.
3301 Electronics Way, West Palm Beach FL 33407. 407/848-4311x255. **Fax:** 407/881-5652. **Contact:** Linda M. Petteruti, Human Resources Administrator. **Description:** A manufacturer of semiconductors. **Common positions include:** Accountant/Auditor; Advertising Clerk; Budget Analyst; Buyer; Chemical Engineer; Clerical Supervisor; Computer Systems Analyst; Cost Estimator; Credit Clerk and Authorizer; Credit Manager; Customer Service Representative; Department Manager; Designer; Draftsperson; Electrical/Electronics Engineer; Electrician; Financial Manager; General Manager; Human Resources Specialist; Industrial Engineer; Machinist; Manufacturer's/Wholesaler's Sales Rep.; Marketing/Advertising/PR Manager; Mechanical Engineer; Order Clerk; Payroll Clerk; Precision Assembler; Purchasing Agent and Manager; Quality Control Supervisor; Receptionist; Secretary; Stock Clerk; Tool and Die Maker. **Educational backgrounds include:** Accounting; Business Administration; Chemistry; Engineering; Finance; Marketing; Physics. **Benefits:** 401K; Dental Insurance; Disability Coverage; Life Insurance; Medical Insurance; Pension Plan; Profit Sharing; Tuition Assistance. **Corporate headquarters location:** This Location. **Other U.S. locations:** Nationwide. **Operations at this facility include:** Administration; Divisional Headquarters; Manufacturing; Regional Headquarters; Research and Development; Sales. **Listed on:** NASDAQ. **Number of employees at this location:** 120.

SPARTON ELECTRONICS
P.O. Box 788, DeLeon Springs FL 32130. 904/985-4631. **Fax:** 904/985-5845. **Contact:** Elizabeth C. Dempsey, Director of Human Resources. **Description:** Sparton Electronics offers electronics engineering and manufacturing services. Services include design engineering, development engineering, manufacturing, and test engineering. Capabilities include DFMA, box build, board layout, rapid prototyping, mechanical design, system integration, full environmentals, design from concept, board level

assembly, software development, and concurrent engineering. Sparton technical design skills include electronics (analog, digital, solid-state devices, hybrid circuits, VHF transmitters, UHF receivers, custom integrate circuits, and signal processing); mechanics (die casting, injection molding, stamping, extrusions, blow molding, and flotation systems); sensors (hydrophones, transducers, magnetics, acoustics, ultrasonics, and pressure); computers (programming, modeling, automatic test, design analysis, statistical analysis, finite element analysis, and algorithms); chemistry (electrochemistry, batteries, polymers, adhesives, and encapsulants); and environmental (hi-g shock, random vibration, humidity, temperature, altitude, high pressure, and shelf life). **Common positions include:** Blue-Collar Worker Supervisor; Budget Analyst; Buyer; Draftsperson; Electrical/Electronics Engineer; Financial Analyst; General Manager; Industrial Engineer; Materials Engineer; Operations/Production Manager; Software Engineer. **Educational backgrounds include:** Engineering; Finance. **Corporate headquarters location:** Jackson MS. **Other U.S. locations:** Brooksville FL. **Operations at this facility include:** Administration; Divisional Headquarters; Manufacturing. **Number of employees at this location:** 300. **Number of employees nationwide:** 700.

SPARTON ELECTRONICS
30167 Power Line Road, Brooksville FL 34602. 352/799-6502. **Fax:** 352/796-7482. **Contact:** Human Resources. **Description:** Sparton Electronics offers electronics engineering and manufacturing services. Services include design engineering, development engineering, manufacturing, and test engineering. Capabilities include DFMA, box build, board layout, rapid prototyping, mechanical design, system integration, full environmentals, design from concept, board level assembly, software development, and concurrent engineering. Sparton technical design skills include electronics (analog, digital, solid-state devices, hybird circuits, VHF transmitters, UHF receivers, custom integrate circuits, and signal processing); mechanics (die casting, injection molding, stamping, extrusions, blow molding, and flotation systems); sensors (hydrophones, transducers, magnetics, acoustics, ultrasonics, and pressure); computers (programming, modeling, automatic test, design analysis, statistical analysis, finite element analysis, and algorithms); chemistry (electrochemistry, batteries, polymers, adhesives, and encapsulants); and environmental (hi-g shock, random vibration, humidity, temperature, altitude, high pressure, and shelf life).

TRAK MICROWAVE CORPORATION
4726 Eisenhower Boulevard, Tampa FL 33634-6391. 813/884-1411. **Fax:** 813/886-2794. **Contact:** Linda Reynolds, Manager of Human Resources. **Description:** TRAK Microwave is a supplier of active and passive electronic microwave components, microwave subsystems, ferrite products, and precision timing equipment for use in communications and radar products. The microwave components include energy sources (oscillators and amplifiers), frequency multipliers, filters, ferrite isolators and circulators, and a broad range of passive components for modulation and control of microwave energy. The microwave subsystems consist of synthesizers, frequency converters, and microwave receiver assemblies. TRAK's microwave components and subsystems can be found in defense products such as electronic warfare equipment, defense radars, communications equipment, and missile guidance systems. Space applications include components for communication, television broadcast, meteorological, earth resource, and intelligence gathering satellites. Commercial applications include Transponder Collision Avoidance Systems (TCAS), Microwave Landing Systems (MLS), radar altimeters, distance measuring equipment, and airborne weather radar. TRAK also builds timing systems for use by government and commercial organizations. Timing products are used to provide signals to time or initiate events by extracting time information from the NAVSTAR satellites of the Global Positioning System (operated by the United States Government), and in the synchronizing of communication carrier signals between sites. Customers of timing systems include NASA, telephone companies, and electric power utilities. **Common positions include:** Accountant/Auditor; Buyer; Computer Programmer; Draftsperson; Electrical/Electronics Engineer; Mechanical Engineer; Registered Nurse. **Educational backgrounds include:** Business Administration; Communications; Engineering; Marketing. **Benefits:** 401K; Dental Insurance; Disability Coverage; Employee Discounts; Life Insurance; Medical Insurance; Savings Plan; Tuition Assistance. **Corporate headquarters location:** Houston TX. **Parent company:** Tech-Sym Corporation. **Operations at this facility include:** Administration; Manufacturing; Sales. **Listed on:** Privately held. **Number of employees at this location:** 350.

Note: Because addresses and telephone numbers of smaller companies change rapidly, we recommend you call each company to verify the information below before inquiring about job opportunities. Mass mailings are not recommended.

Additional employers with over 250 employees:

AEROSPACE AND/OR NAUTICAL SYSTEMS AND INSTRUMENTS

Brunswick Corporation
2000 Brunswick Ln, Deland FL 32724-2001. 904/736-1700.

ELECTRICAL INDUSTRIAL APPARATUS

ABB Power T&D Co.
4300 Coral Ridge Dr, Pompano Beach FL 33065-7617. 954/752-6700.

ELECTRONIC COMPONENTS AND ACCESSORIES

American Radionic Co.
P.O. Box 352919, Palm Coast FL 32135-2919. 904/445-6000.

Electronics & Space
1201 Silver Lake Dr, Sanford FL 32773. 407/330-5300.

Inex Vision Systems
13327 US Highway 19 N,Clearwater FL 34624-7225. 813/535-5502.

TRANSFORMERS

Central Moloney Transformers
211 W Palmetto St, Arcadia FL 33821-3815. 813/494-1727.

Instrument Transformers
1907 Calumet St, Clearwater FL 34625. 813/442-0414.

Additional employers with under 250 employees:

SWITCHGEAR AND SWITCHBOARD APPARATUS

ABB Power T&D
201 Hickman Dr, Sanford FL 32771-8201. 407/323-8220.

Micro Pneumatic Logic
2890 W Cypress Creek Rd, Ft Lauderdale FL 33309-1786. 954/973-6166.

ELECTRICAL INDUSTRIAL APPARATUS

Beckwith Electric Co.
6190 118th Ave, Largo FL 34643-3724. 813/535-3408.

Radiation Systems
6200 118th Ave, Largo FL 34643-3726. 813/541-6681.

Deltona Transformer Corporation
P.O. Box 3430, Deland FL 32723-3430. 904/736-7900.

Square D Company
1700 Sunshine Dr, Clearwater FL 34625-1320. 813/447-2511.

ELECTRIC LIGHTING AND WIRING EQUIPMENT

Interconnection Products
1601 N Powerline Rd, Pompano Beach FL 33069-1622. 954/979-2050.

Molex-ETC
4650 62nd Ave, Pinellas

Park FL 34665-5944. 813/521-2700.

Award Lighting Products
16333 NW 54th Ave, Hialeah FL 33014-6108. 305/625-8100.

ELECTRONIC COMPONENTS AND ACCESSORIES

Continental Circuit
1150 Belle Ave, Winter Springs FL 32708-2998. 407/699-5000.

KBS
1498 NW 3rd St, Deerfield Beach FL 33442-1647. 954/360-7200.

Marlo Electronics
4007 NE 6th Ave, Ft Lauderdale FL 33334-2208. 954/565-4839.

Printed Circuits Of America
5443 115th Ave N, Clearwater FL 34620-4842. 813/573-0707.

Square D Company
1771 N Hercules Ave, Clearwater FL 34625-1112. 813/449-0055.

Universal Circuits
950 Sunshine Ln, Altamonte Springs FL 32714-3892. 407/869-6500.

AG Associates
504 Roy Blvd, Altamonte Springs FL 32701-6850. 407/339-5648.

Chip Supply
7725 N Orange Blossom

Trail, Orlando FL 32810-2653. 407/298-7100.

Cirrus Logic
5201 Congress Ave, Boca Raton FL 33487-3627. 407/241-5777.

National Semiconductor Corporation
7850 NW 146th St, Hialeah FL 33016-1564. 305/822-5350.

PCSI
5201 Congress Ave, Boca Raton FL 33487-3627. 407/241-7030.

Cantex
101 Gandy Rd, Auburndale FL 33823-2733. 941/967-4161.

Hytronics Corporation
15401 Roosevelt Blvd, Clearwater FL 34620-3509. 813/536-7861.

Precision Econowind
8940 N Fork Dr, Fort Myers FL 33903-1421. 941/997-3860.

ABB Ceag Power Supplies
1 Pine Lakes Pkwy N, Palm Coast FL 32137-3607. 904/445-0311.

Acopian Technical Co.
2001 W Nasa Blvd, Melbourne FL 32904-2321. 407/727-1172.

Automation Intelligence
850 Trafalgar Ct Fl 2, Maitland FL 32751-4141. 407/661-7000.

Caribean Assemblies
404 State Road 434 E,
Winter Springs FL 32708-
2626. 407/327-0602.

MC Assembly & Test
751 North Dr, Melbourne FL
32934-9289. 407/253-
0541.

**Paramount Electronic
Manufacturing Co.**
1020 SW 10th Ave,
Pompano Beach FL 33069-
4632. 954/781-3755.

PEC Ltd.
5780 Carrier Dr, Orlando FL
32819-8311. 407/351-
3400.

Protek Electronics
1781 Independence Blvd,
Suite 2, Sarasota FL 34234-
2114. 941/351-4399.

Q Bit Corporation
2144 Franklin Dr NE, Palm
Bay FL 32905-4021.
407/727-1838.

Sawtek
1818 S Hwy 441, Apopka
FL 32703. 407/886-8860.

Sawtek
P.O. Box 609501, Orlando
FL 32860-9501. 407/886-
8860.

**ELECTRICAL ENGINE
EQUIPMENT**

**East Coast Starter Drive
Nobro**
1000 SW 12th Ave,
Pompano Beach FL 33069-
4688. 954/946-1030.

Web Wire Products
5602 NW 161st St, Hialeah
FL 33014-6129. 305/621-
1033.

**ELECTRICAL EQUIPMENT,
MACHINERY, AND SUPPLIES**

M-R-S Power Systems
16228 Flight Path Dr,
Brooksville FL 34609-6875.
352/544-4000.

**ELECTRICAL EQUIPMENT
WHOLESALE**

Ace Electric Supply Co.
5911 Phillips Hwy,
Jacksonville FL 32216-5916.
904/731-5900.

FWC Supply
450 Lane Ave N,
Jacksonville FL 32254-2819.
904/786-0944.

Graybar Electric Company
P.O. Box 970709, Miami FL
33197. 305/232-1530.

**Southern Electric Supply
Company**
672 Old Dixie Hwy, Vero
Beach FL 32962-1619.
407/562-3032.

**Southern Electric Supply
Company**
500 E Donegan Ave,
Kissimmee FL 34744-1928.
407/846-1611.

JK Kessler & Associates
3906 E 11th Ave, Tampa FL
33605-4522. 813/248-
5078.

Ace Electric Supply Co.
7902 Anderson Rd, Tampa
FL 33634-3038. 813/884-
7860.

American Electric
10008 N Dale Mabry Hwy,
Tampa FL 33618-4424.
813/968-6223.

AMJ Equipment
400 Commerce Way,
Longwood FL 32750-6396.
407/339-7022.

Consolidated Electric Supply
3055 Dixie Hwy NE, Palm
Bay FL 32905-2513.
407/723-6531.

Graybar Electric Co.
2475 17th St, Sarasota FL
34234-1904. 941/955-
0905.

Graybar Electric Co.
6952 Sonny Dale Dr, W
Melbourne FL 32904-2262.
407/768-7661.

Hughes Supply
259 N Industrial Dr, Orange
City FL 32763-7412.
904/775-8222.

Landis & Gyr Powers
5602 Thompson Center Ct,
Tampa FL 33634-4301.
813/882-8338.

Raybro/CED Electric Supply
323 23rd St S, St Petersburg
FL 33712-1251. 813/327-
4201.

Hughes Supply
5285 Highway Ave, Suite 1,
Jacksonville FL 32254-3695.
904/783-4567.

Ademco Distribution
2109 Corporate Dr, Boynton
Beach FL 33426-6645.
407/738-9781.

**ELECTRONIC PARTS AND
EQUIPMENT WHOLESALE**

Able Telcom Holding
800 W Cypress Creek Rd, Ft
Lauderdale FL 33309-2075.
954/776-0667.

Allied Electronics
4241 Baymeadows Rd,
Jacksonville FL 32217-4689.
904/739-5920.

Allied Electronics
100 E Sybelia Ave, Suite
327, Maitland FL 32751-
4758. 407/539-0055.

Bell Industries
650 S North Lake Blvd, Suite
400, Altamonte Springs FL
32701-6176. 407/339-
0078.

**Electronic Maintenance
Supply Company**
1230 W Central Blvd,
Orlando FL 32805-1815.
407/849-6362.

Elreha Control Corp.
2232 5th Ave S, St
Petersburg FL 33712-1259.
813/327-4811.

Future Electronics-FAI
1451 NE 62nd St, Ft
Lauderdale FL 33334-5133.
954/776-0177.

ISI Integrated Solutions
8100 Chancellor Dr, Suite
135, Orlando FL 32809-
7664. 407/851-6800.

MC Gems Electronics
1326 N Dixie Hwy, Suite 11,
Lake Worth FL 33460-1839.
407/547-2639.

Newark Electronics
1080 Woodcock Rd, Suite
111, Orlando FL 32803-
3514. 407/896-8350.

Powell Electronics
3540 NW 56th St, Ft
Lauderdale FL 33309-2260.
954/484-8377.

Thermotron Industries
400 Commerce Way, Suite
124, Longwood FL 32750-
6396. 407/830-0001.

**Victors Electronic Disc
Center**
4690 W Irlo Bronson
Memorial H, Kissimmee FL
34746-5319. 407/239-
7590.

Pairgain Technologies
1232 Apache Dr, Geneva FL
32732-9162. 407/349-
1075.

Voicecom Systems
3710 Corporex Park Dr,
Tampa FL 33619-1160.
813/664-0630.

Wiltel
1103 N 22nd St, Tampa FL
33605-5309. 813/248-
2862.

Gabriel Contact
1400 NW 23rd Ave, Ft Lauderdale FL 33311-5147. 954/792-1234.

Xicor
100 E Sybelia Ave, Suite 355, Maitland FL 32751-4758. 407/740-8282.

Sentry Security
7520 NW 5th St, Ft Lauderdale FL 33317-1613. 954/797-7703.

For more information on career opportunities in the electronic/industrial electrical equipment industry:

Associations

AMERICAN CERAMIC SOCIETY
735 Ceramic Place, Westerville OH 43081. 614/890-4700. 800/837-1804. Provides ceramics futures information. Membership required.

ELECTROCHEMICAL SOCIETY
10 South Main Street, Pennington NJ 08534-2896. 609/737-1902.

ELECTRONIC INDUSTRIES ASSOCIATION
25000 Wilshire Boulevard, Arlington VA 22201. 202/457-4900.

ELECTRONICS TECHNICIANS ASSOCIATION
602 North Jackson Street, Greencastle IN 46135. 317/653-8262. Offers published job-hunting advice from the organization's officers and members. Also offers educational material and certification programs.

INSTITUTE OF ELECTRICAL AND ELECTRONICS ENGINEERS (IEEE)
345 East 47th Street, New York NY 10017. 212/705-7900. Toll-free customer service line: 800/678-4333.

INSTITUTE OF ELECTRICAL AND ELECTRONICS ENGINEERS (IEEE)
1828 Elm Street NW, Suite 1202, Washington DC 20036-5104. Professional activities line: 202/785-0017. National information line: 202/785-2180.

INTERNATIONAL BROTHERHOOD OF ELECTRICAL WORKERS
1125 15th Street NW, Washington DC 20005. 202/833-7000. Has over 1,000 apprenticeship programs.

INTERNATIONAL SOCIETY OF CERTIFIED ELECTRONICS TECHNICIANS
2708 West Berry Street, Ft. Worth TX 76109. 817/921-9101.

NATIONAL ELECTRONICS SALES AND SERVICES ASSOCIATION
2708 West Berry, Ft. Worth TX 76109. 817/921-9061. Provides newsletters and directories to members.

ROBOTICS INTERNATIONAL OF THE SOCIETY OF MANUFACTURING ENGINEERS (SME)
P.O. Box 930, One SME Drive, Dearborn MI 48121. 313/271-1500.

ENVIRONMENTAL SERVICES

According to the Environmental Protection Agency, the increase in environmental awareness over recent decades is more than just a trend. State and national legislation, such as the 1990 amendments to the Clean Air Act, have generated a new range of opportunities in skilled administrative, professional, and technical areas. However, the most critical positions needing to be filled are for scientists and engineers. These two groups develop new solutions to old problems, and therefore are instrumental in the research and development stages.

On the other hand, the current climate in the Congress is significantly cooler towards environmental regulation than in years past. Many members of Congress argue that American business is already overburdened by the Federal government, and some propose that the Environmental Protection Agency itself be disbanded.

ANALYTICAL TECHNOLOGIES, INC. (ATI)
11 East Olive Road, Pensacola FL 32514. 904/474-1001. **Contact:** Personnel. **Description:** An environmental testing laboratory.

ENVIRONMENTAL SCIENCE & ENGINEERING, INC.
P.O. Box 1703, Gainesville FL 32602-1703. **Toll free phone:** 800/874-7872. **Contact:** Nathan E. Weeks, Human Resources Assistant. **Description:** Environmental Science & Engineering, Inc., a national multidisciplinary consulting firm, possesses a full range of capabilities in environmental and engineering consulting, laboratory analysis, asbestos management, industrial hygiene, engineering, and architecture for governmental, industrial, and commercial clients. **Common positions include:** Accountant/Auditor; Administrative Services Manager; Architect; Biological Scientist/Biochemist; Blue-Collar Worker Supervisor; Branch Manager; Buyer; Chemical Engineer; Chemist; Civil Engineer; Computer Programmer; Computer Systems Analyst; Cost Estimator; Department Manager; Designer; Division Manager; Draftsperson; Ecologist; Electrical/Electronics Engineer; Environmental Engineer; Forester/Conservation Scientist; Geologist/Geophysicist; Human Resources Specialist; Industrial Hygienist; Marketing Specialist; Metallurgical Engineer; Meteorologist; Mining Engineer; Nuclear Engineer; Office Manager; Petroleum Engineer; Physicist/Astronomer; Quality Control Supervisor; Services Sales Representative; Software Engineer; Systems Analyst; Technical Writer/Editor; Travel Agent. **Educational backgrounds include:** Accounting; Art/Design; Biology; Business Administration; Chemistry; Communications; Computer Science; Ecology; Engineering; Finance; Geology; Hydrogeology; Marketing; Meteorology; Physics. **Benefits:** 401K; Dental Insurance; Disability Coverage; Employee Discounts; Life Insurance; Medical Insurance; Tuition Assistance. **Corporate headquarters location:** Peoria IL. **Other U.S. locations:** Nationwide. **Parent company:** Cilcorp. **Subsidiaries include:** Keck Instruments, Inc. **Operations at this facility include:** Administration; Divisional Headquarters; Service. **Number of employees at this location:** 420. **Number of employees nationwide:** 1,500.

KIMMINS ENVIRONMENTAL SERVICE CORPORATION
1501 2nd Avenue, Tampa FL 33605. 813/248-3878. **Contact:** Personnel. **Description:** A provider of hazardous and nonhazardous waste remediation services. **Number of employees at this location:** 580.

MUNTERS CORPORATION
P.O. Box 6428, Fort Meyers FL 33911. 941/936-1555. **Contact:** Sherri Thompson, Human Resources Administrator. **Description:** An environmental technology and pollution control company. **Common positions include:** Accountant/Auditor; Blue-Collar Worker Supervisor; Draftsperson; Electrician; Industrial Production Manager;

Mechanical Engineer; Purchasing Agent and Manager. **Educational backgrounds include:** Accounting; Engineering; Finance. **Benefits:** 401K; Dental Insurance; Disability Coverage; Life Insurance; Medical Insurance; Profit Sharing; Tuition Assistance. **Operations at this facility include:** Administration; Manufacturing; Research and Development; Sales. **Number of employees at this location:** 120. **Number of employees nationwide:** 420.

QUANTERRA ENVIRONMENTAL SERVICES
5910 Breckinridge Parkway, Suite H, Tampa FL 33610. 813/621-0784. **Fax:** 813/623-6021. **Contact:** Human Resources. **Description:** In June, 1994, Cornings Enseco division and IT Analytical Services, the two largest commercial environmental analytical companies in the world, merged to form Quanterra, a completely new, independent company. Quanterra provides a complete range of environmental testing services to private industry, engineering consultants, and government agencies in support of major federal and state environmental regulations. The company also possesses a variety of special analytical capabilities, including specializations in the following areas: Air Toxins; Field Analytical Services, Radiochemistry/Mixed Waste; and Advanced Technology. The company is owned jointly by Corning Incorporated and International Technology Corporation. The company's goal is to provide customers with the highest level of service in the environmental analytical testing industry.

VIROGROUP INC.
428 Pine Island Road SW, Cape Coral FL 33991. 941/574-1919. **Contact:** Human Resources. **Description:** An environmental consulting engineering group.

Note: Because addresses and telephone numbers of smaller companies change rapidly, we recommend you call each company to verify the information below before inquiring about job opportunities. Mass mailings are not recommended.

Additional employers with under 250 employees:

MISC. ENVIRONMENTAL SERVICES

Decon Environmental
230 Power Ct, Suite 116, Sanford FL 32771-9401. 407/330-9612.

Siebe Environmental
7101 Presidents Dr, Suite 250, Orlando FL 32809-5687. 407/859-6802.

Environmental Consulting & Technology
5405 Cypress Center Dr, Tampa FL 33609-1052. 813/289-9338.

Pollution Prevention Services
308 South Blvd, Tampa FL 33606-2151. 813/258-3981.

Environmental Science & Engineering
1575 Main St, Sarasota FL 34236-5802. 941/371-1716.

Environmental Science & Engineering
5840 W Cypress St, Tampa FL 33607-1787. 813/287-2755.

For more information on career opportunities in environmental services:

<u>Associations</u>

AIR AND WASTE MANAGEMENT ASSOCIATION
One Gateway Center, Third Floor, Pittsburgh PA 15222. 412/232-3444. A nonprofit, technical and educational organization providing a neutral forum where all points of view of an environmental management issue can be addressed.

ASSOCIATION OF STATE & INTERSTATE WATER POLLUTION CONTROL ADMINISTRATORS
750 First Street NE, Suite 910, Washington DC 20002. 202/898-0905.

ENVIRONMENTAL INDUSTRY ASSOCIATION
4301 Connecticut Avenue N, Suite 300,
Washington DC 20008. 202/659-4613. Fax 202/966-4818.

INSTITUTE OF CLEAN AIR COMPANIES
1707 L Street NW, Suite 570, Washington DC 20036. 202/457-0911-4201. National association of companies involved in stationary source air pollution control.

U.S. ENVIRONMENTAL PROTECTION AGENCY
401 M Street SW, Washington DC 20460. 202/260-2090. Provides EPA background career information.

WATER ENVIRONMENT FEDERATION
601 Wythe Street, Alexandria VA 22314. 703/684-2400. Subscription to jobs newsletter required for career information.

Magazines

CAREERS AND THE ENGINEER
Adams Media Corporation, 260 Center Street, Holbrook MA 02343. 617/767-8100.

ENVIRONMENTAL CAREER OPPORTUNITIES
1776 Eye Street NW, Suite 710,

Washington DC 20006. Publication listing career opportunities in the environmental fields. $67 for 12 issues; $127 for 26 issues.

JOURNAL OF AIR AND WASTE MANAGEMENT ASSOCIATION
One Gateway Center, Third Floor, Pittsburgh PA 15222. 412/232-3444.

FABRICATED/PRIMARY METALS AND PRODUCTS

Nineteen Ninety-Four brought a surge in demand for steel, with U.S. steel consumption growing 8 percent. The biggest push came from U.S. automakers, particularly from the increased sales of minivans and other light trucks, which use more steel than cars. Residential and road and bridge construction also contributed to the higher steel sales. The U.S. steel industry even began to expand its exports to satisfy a growing foreign market. In fact, industry demand was so high that, despite steel mills operating at near full capacity, orders still exceeded deliveries by at least 5 percent. This caused a jump in steel prices (an average hike of about 5 percent in 1994, with a similar increase expected in 1995), which in turn led to increased profits for integrated steel companies. However, while higher prices are good news for the big companies, they have the opposite effect on minimills. Higher steel prices cause parallel rises in the price of scrap, the main raw material for minimills. In addition to the increases in scrap prices, minimills will also have to deal with rapidly rising competition, with about ten new minimills scheduled to open between 1995 and 1998.

ALPINE ENGINEERED PRODUCTS, INC.
P.O. Box 2225, Pompano Beach FL 33061. 954/781-3333. **Contact:** Kris Tubridy, Personnel Director. **Description:** A manufacturer of metal connector plates for floors and roofs.

ALUMAX EXTRUSIONS, INC.
1650 Alumax Circle, Plant City FL 33567. 813/752-4117. **Contact:** Diane Knox, Personnel Director. **Description:** An aluminum factory.

AMERICAN NATIONAL CAN COMPANY
3331 West 12th Street, Jacksonville FL 32254-1701. 904/353-5694. **Contact:** Human Resources. **Description:** American National Can Company manufactures metal cans. **Other U.S. locations:** St. Paul MN; St. Louis MO; Cleveland OH.

ASHLEY ALUMINUM, INC.
P.O. Drawer 15398, Tampa FL 33684. 813/884-0444. **Contact:** Jim Decker, Director of Personnel. **Description:** A manufacturer and distributor of aluminum and vinyl building products. **Common positions include:** Accountant/Auditor; Blue-Collar Worker Supervisor; Branch Manager; Buyer; Claim Representative; Clerical Supervisor; Computer Programmer; Computer Systems Analyst; Credit Manager; Financial Analyst; General Manager; Human Resources Specialist; Industrial Engineer; Industrial Production Manager; Management Trainee; Manufacturer's/Wholesaler's Sales Rep.; Operations/Production Manager; Wholesale and Retail Buyer. **Educational backgrounds include:** Accounting; Business Administration; Computer Science; Liberal Arts; Marketing. **Other U.S. locations:** Georgia; Alabama; Louisiana; Texas; Kentucky. **Listed on:** NASDAQ. **Number of employees at this location:** 100. **Number of employees nationwide:** 420.

BETHLEHEM STEEL CORPORATION
9428 Baymeadows Road, Jacksonville FL 32256-0190. **Contact:** Human Resources. **Description:** A manufacturer of iron and steel products. The company's operations also include marine construction and repair; and the mining and sale of raw materials. **Corporate headquarters location:** Bethlehem PA. **Listed on:** New York Stock Exchange.

LORAL AMERICAN BERYLLIUM CORPORATION
P.O. Box 1087, Tallevast FL 34270. 941/355-5105. **Contact:** Vicki Derriberry, Industrial Relations Manager. **Description:** Engaged in ultra-precision machining and assembly of beryllium alloys and other traditional aerospace materials for aerospace and electronic applications.

SONOCO PRODUCTS
1854 Central Florida Parkway, Orlando FL 32837. 407/851-5800. **Contact:** Human Relations. **Description:** A manufacturer of composite corrugated cans.

VAW OF AMERICA INC
P.O. Box 3887, St. Augustine FL 32085. 904/794-1500. **Fax:** 904/794-1508. **Contact:** David Black, Corporate Director of Human Resources. **Description:** Producer of aluminum billets, drawn tubes, extrusions and fabricated and finished products in three plants in the United States. **Common positions include:** Blue-Collar Worker Supervisor; Designer; Draftsperson; Industrial Production Manager; Maintenance Supervisor; Manufacturer's/Wholesaler's Sales Rep.; Mechanical Engineer; Metallurgical Engineer; Quality Control Supervisor. **Educational backgrounds include:** Business Administration; Engineering. **Benefits:** 401K; Dental Insurance; Disability Coverage; Life Insurance; Medical Insurance; Pension Plan; Profit Sharing; Tuition Assistance. **Corporate headquarters location:** This Location. **Other U.S. locations:** Phoenix AZ; Ellenville NY. **Operations at this facility include:** Administration; Manufacturing; Sales. **Listed on:** Privately held. **Number of employees at this location:** 525. **Number of employees nationwide:** 1,400.

Note: Because addresses and telephone numbers of smaller companies change rapidly, we recommend you call each company to verify the information below before inquiring about job opportunities. Mass mailings are not recommended.

Additional employers with over 250 employees:

STEEL PIPE AND TUBES

Berg Steel Pipe Corp.
P.O. Box 2029, Panama City
FL 32402. 904/769-2273.

FABRICATED STRUCTURAL
METAL PRODUCTS

Aluminum Building Systems
1107 Thomas Rd, Leesburg
FL 34748. 352/787-7766.

Southeastern Metals
Manufacturing Co.
P.O. Box 26347,
Jacksonville FL 32226-6347.
904/757-4200.

FABRICATED WIRE
PRODUCTS

Cleaners Hanger Co.
P.O. Box 9100, Palm Harbor

FL 34682-9100. 813/789-
3000.

METAL FASTENERS

Stimpson Company
1515 SW 13th Ct, Pompano
Beach FL 33069-4710.
954/946-3500.

Additional employers with under 250 employees:

STEEL WORKS, BLAST
FURNACES, AND ROLLING
MILLS

Avesta Sandvik Tube
1101 N Main St, Wildwood
FL 34785-3432. 904/748-
1313.

Crown Products Co.
6390 Phillips Hwy,
Jacksonville FL 32216-6050.
904/737-7144.

Exceletech
901 12th St, Clermont FL
34711. 904/394-2155.

Looney & Son Inc.
5795 John Givens Rd,

Crestview FL 32539-7019.
904/682-0293.

STEEL SHEET, STRIP, AND
BARS

ALRO Metals Service Center
6200 Park Of Commerce
Blvd, Boca Raton FL 33487-
8201. 407/997-6766.

Tampa Tank & Welding
5205 Adamo Dr, Tampa FL
33619. 813/623-2675.

STEEL PIPE AND TUBES

Enviroq Corporation
11811 Phillips Hwy,
Jacksonville FL 32256-1650.
904/262-5802.

IRON AND STEEL
FOUNDRIES

US Foundry & Manufacturing
8351 NW 93rd St, Miami FL
33166-2025. 305/885-
0301.

ALUMINUM

Tri City Aluminum Products
7175 N US Highway 441,
Ocala FL 34475-1215.
352/622-8658.

NONFERROUS ROLLING
AND DRAWING OF METALS

Florida Extruders
2540 Jewett Ln, Sanford FL
32771. 407/323-3300.

METAL CONTAINERS

Ball Metal Beverage Container
4700 E Whiteway Dr, Tampa FL 33617-3424. 813/980-6073.

Crown Cork & Seal
Rte 437 Box 1328, Plymouth FL 32768. 407/889-4116.

Metal Container Corp.
1100 Ellis Rd S, Jacksonville FL 32205-6219. 904/695-7600.

Metal Container Corp.
5909 NW 18th Dr, Gainesville FL 32653-1639. 352/378-8800.

Reynolds Metals Co.
10420 Malcolm McKinley Dr, Tampa FL 33612-6402. 813/972-7303.

FABRICATED STRUCTURAL METAL PRODUCTS

Addison Steel
7351 Overland Rd, Orlando FL 32810-3409. 407/295-6434.

Allstate Steel Co.
8202 W Beaver St, Jacksonville FL 32220-2381. 904/781-6040.

Downey Industries
P.O. Box 10307, Pompano Beach FL 33061-6307. 954/974-3200.

Florida Miscellaneous Steel
2710 E 5th Ave, Tampa FL 33605-5522. 813/248-5222.

Owen Steel Company Of Florida
10483 General Ave, Jacksonville FL 32220-2103. 904/781-4780.

Steel Fabricators
721 NE 44th St, Ft Lauderdale FL 33334-3150. 954/772-0440.

Alcan Building Products
4504 30th St W, Bradenton FL 34207-1099. 941/755-1591.

Allied Steel Products
3201 NE 167th St, Miami FL 33160-3847. 305/624-3333.

Alumco Industries
5100 140th Ave N, Clearwater FL 34620-3753. 813/530-5435.

Aluminum Building Systems
1107 Thomas Rd, Leesburg FL 34748-3631. 352/787-7766.

American Metal Products
1315 Neptune Dr, Boynton Beach FL 33426-8403. 407/732-8118.

Binnings Pan American
2805 NE 185th St, Miami FL 33180-2994. 305/931-2350.

Frameco
326 Cypress Rd, Ocala FL 34472-3102. 352/680-1801.

Howard Industries
8130 NW 74th Ave, Miami FL 33166-7402. 305/888-1521.

JW Window Components
215 SE 10th Ave, Hialeah FL 33010-5536. 305/888-3641.

Nu-Air Manufacturing Co.
8105 Anderson Rd, Tampa FL 33634-2396. 813/885-1654.

Rollix International
975 Aurora Rd, Melbourne FL 32935-5968. 407/259-2406.

Wrono Enterprises
211 NW 5th Ave, Hallandale FL 33009-4019. 954/456-6979.

RDS Manufacturing
300 Industrial Park Dr, Perry FL 32347-6323. 904/584-6898.

Atlas Metal Industries
1135 NW 159th Dr, Miami FL 33169-5807. 305/625-2451.

Daniel & Jones Sheet Metal
12951 49th St N, Clearwater FL 34622-4014. 813/885-3388.

Exact
5323 Highway Ave, Jacksonville FL 32254-3634. 904/783-6640.

Ferber Sheet Metal Works
4121 Evergreen Ave, Jacksonville FL 32206-1500. 904/354-3219.

Groff Industries
9507 N Trask St, Tampa FL 33624-5136. 813/961-1331.

Metal Industries
8409 W Crystal St, Crystal River FL 34428-4508. 904/795-5717.

Miami Decking Corp.
25 SE 2nd Ave, Suite 919, Miami FL 33131-1604. 305/558-2315.

SCREW MACHINE PRODUCTS

Vico Manufacturing
2363 Industrial Blvd, Sarasota FL 34234-3131. 941/355-8481.

METAL STAMPINGS

Better Built Co.
8811 Grow Dr, Pensacola FL 32514-7051. 904/478-3298.

Hughes Manufacturing
11910 62nd St, Largo FL 34643-3705. 813/536-7891.

COATING, ENGRAVING, AND ALLIED SERVICES

Metalplate Galvanizing
7123 Moncrief Rd W, Jacksonville FL 32219-3313. 904/768-6330.

FABRICATED WIRE PRODUCTS

Florida Wire & Cable
825 Lane Ave S, Jacksonville FL 32205-4704. 904/781-9224.

Reid Co. Inc.
P.O. Box 352440, Palm Coast FL 32135-2440. 904/445-2000.

SEMCO Southeastern Manufacturing Co.
P.O. Box 1899, Ocala FL 34478-1899. 352/732-7330.

Ivy Steel & Wire Co.
3050 Melson Ave, Jacksonville FL 32254-1858. 904/354-8552.

FABRICATED METAL PRODUCTS

Collier Safe Co.
13331 Byrd Dr, Odessa FL 33556-5309. 813/920-5091.

Electroform Machine
12155 NW 39th St, Coral Springs FL 33065-2518. 954/344-8380.

Metal Fab Corp.
P.O. Box 2611, Ormond Beach FL 32175-2611. 904/677-2140.

Metal Industries
8610 W Crystal St, Crystal River FL 34428-4469. 904/795-6611.

Metallic Engineering Co.
5150 NW 72nd Ave, Miami
FL 33166. 305/592-3440.

**WHOLESALE METALS
SERVICE CENTERS AND
OFFICES**

McNichols Company
P.O. Box 30300, Tampa FL
33630. 813/289-4100.

Master-Halco
5035 W Tharpe St,
Tallahassee FL 32303-7811.
904/575-0615.

ML Service
1025 S Semoran Blvd,
Winter Park FL 32792 5511.
407/671-7911.

Thyssen Steel
1 Tampa City Center, Tampa
FL 33602. 813/221-1600.

**Kraus Enterprises
International**
113 Gull Ct, Casselberry FL
32707 5107. 407/000-
6527.

**For more information on career opportunities in the fabricated/primary metals and
products industries:**

Associations

**ASM INTERNATIONAL: THE MATERIALS
INFORMATION SOCIETY**
Materials Park OH 44073. 800/336-5152.
Gathers, processes, and disseminates
technical information to foster the
understanding and application of engineered
materials.

AMERICAN FOUNDRYMEN'S SOCIETY
505 State Street, Des Plaines IL 60016-
708/824-0181.

AMERICAN WELDING SOCIETY
550 LeJeune Road NW, Miami FL 33126.
305/443-9353.

Directories

**DIRECTORY OF STEEL FOUNDRIES IN THE
UNITED STATES, CANADA, AND MEXICO**
Steel Founder's Society of America, 455
State Street, Des Plaines IL 60016.
708/299-9160.

Magazines

AMERICAN METAL MARKET
25 7th Avenue, New York NY 10019.
212/887-8580.

IRON & STEEL ENGINEER
Association of Iron and Steel Engineers,
Three Gateway Center, Suite 2350,
Pittsburgh PA 15222. 412/281-6323.

IRON AGE NEW STEEL
191 South Gary, Carol Stream IL 60188.
708/462-2285.

MODERN METALS
625 North Michigan Avenue, Suite 2500,
Chicago IL 60611. 312/654-2300.

FINANCIAL SERVICES

 During 1994, the financial services sector has seen higher interest rates, increased regulation, and corporate consolidation. Rising rates in 1994 and 1995 have led to large trading losses for securities firms. Analysts expected that consolidations due to mergers, coupled with globalization, would mean 10,000 layoffs industry-wide in 1995. Other financial instruments have also been slumping, including bonds and the once-hot mutual funds. New investments in mutual funds dropped better than 50 percent in 1994. Because of losses in bond funds, many investors sought out safer money-market funds and bank certificates of deposit.

On the bright side: Some dominant U.S investment banks have successfully gone global, and those professionals specializing in consulting and underwriting are in great demand. Naturally, those with expertise in mergers and acquisitions consulting will also benefit.

ALLIANCE MORTGAGE COMPANY
P.O. Box 2109, Jacksonville FL 32232. 904/281-6475. **Fax:** 904/281-6145. **Recorded Jobline:** 904/281-6000. **Contact:** Human Resources Department. **Description:** Engaged in the origination, purchase, sale, and servicing of residential first mortgages. **Common positions include:** Accountant/Auditor; Clerical Supervisor; Customer Service Representative; Loan Officer; Loan Processor. **Educational backgrounds include:** Business Administration; Finance; Liberal Arts. **Benefits:** 401K; Dental Insurance; Disability Coverage; Life Insurance; Medical Insurance; Profit Sharing; Tuition Assistance. **Corporate headquarters location:** This Location. **Operations at this facility include:** Administration; Service. **Listed on:** Privately held. **Number of employees at this location:** 180. **Number of employees nationwide:** 205.

CITICORP SERVICES, INC.
6700 Citicorp Drive, Tampa FL 33619. 813/621-6700. **Contact:** Annie Horne, AVP of Staffing. **Description:** Provides financial services including customer and operations support for global cash management, global trade, and worldwide securities. **Common positions include:** Accountant/Auditor; Adjuster; Administrative Services Manager; Claim Representative; Computer Programmer; Computer Systems Analyst; Customer Service Representative; Financial Analyst; Quality Control Supervisor. **Educational backgrounds include:** Accounting; Business Administration; Computer Science; Finance. **Benefits:** 401K; Dental Insurance; Disability Coverage; Employee Discounts; Life Insurance; Medical Insurance; Pension Plan; Savings Plan; Tuition Assistance. **Corporate headquarters location:** New York NY. **Other U.S. locations:** Nationwide. **Operations at this facility include:** Divisional Headquarters; Service. **Listed on:** New York Stock Exchange. **Number of employees at this location:** 1,000. **Number of employees nationwide:** 75,000.

EQUICREDIT CORPORATION
P.O. Box 53077, Jacksonville FL 32201. 904/398-7581. **Fax:** 904/396-6112. **Contact:** Constance D. Halford, Vice President. **Description:** EquiCredit Corporation originates, sells, and services fixed rate and variable rate consumer loans secured by first and second mortgages, substantially all of which are on owner-occupied single family residences. The company operates through a network of 102 branch offices in 34 states. **Common positions include:** Accountant/Auditor; Attorney; Branch Manager; Computer Programmer; Computer Systems Analyst; Customer Service Representative; Paralegal. **Educational backgrounds include:** Accounting; Computer Science. **Benefits:** 401K; Dental Insurance; Disability Coverage; Life Insurance; Medical Insurance; Profit Sharing; Tuition Assistance. **Corporate headquarters location:** This Location. **Operations at this facility include:** Administration. **Number of employees at this location:** 250. **Number of employees nationwide:** 634.

ALLEN C. EWING & COMPANY
50 North Flora Street, Suite 3625, Jacksonville FL 32202. 904/354-5573. **Contact:** Human Resources. **Description:** A securities brokerage.

INVESTMENT MANAGEMENT AND RESEARCH
4417 Beach Boulevard, Suite 101, Jacksonville FL 32207. 904/396-3290. **Contact:** Branch Manager. **Description:** A securities firm. **NOTE:** This company does not accept unsolicited resumes. Please apply for advertised positions only.

RAYMOND JAMES AND ASSOCIATES
880 Carillon Parkway, St. Petersburg FL 33716. 813/573-3800. **Contact:** Human Resources Department. **Description:** An investment brokerage firm. **Common positions include:** Accountant/Auditor; Administrator; Advertising Clerk; Customer Service Representative; Financial Analyst; Technical Writer/Editor. **Educational backgrounds include:** Accounting; Business Administration; Finance; Marketing. **Benefits:** Dental Insurance; Disability Coverage; Life Insurance; Medical Insurance; Pension Plan; Profit Sharing; Savings Plan; Tuition Assistance. **Operations at this facility include:** Administration; Divisional Headquarters; Regional Headquarters; Research and Development; Sales; Service. **Listed on:** New York Stock Exchange.

MERRILL LYNCH
BRADENTON BRANCH
1401 Manatee Avenue West, 7th Floor, Bradenton FL 34205. 941/746-1123. **Contact:** Kris Seeger, Manager's Secretary. **Description:** A diversified financial service organization. The company is a major broker in securities, option contracts, commodities and financial futures contracts, and insurance, which also deals with corporate and municipal securities and investment banking. **NOTE:** Please call for specific information on where to mail resume. **Common positions include:** Financial Consultant. **Educational backgrounds include:** Economics; Finance; Mathematics. **Benefits:** 401K; Daycare Assistance; Dental Insurance; Disability Coverage; Life Insurance; Medical Insurance; Profit Sharing; Savings Plan; Tuition Assistance. **Corporate headquarters location:** New York NY. **Listed on:** New York Stock Exchange. **Number of employees at this location:** 30.

MERRILL LYNCH
CLEARWATER BRANCH
601 Cleveland Street, Suite 900, Clearwater FL 34615. 813/462-2300. **Contact:** Personnel Office. **Description:** A diversified financial service organization. The company is a major broker in securities, option contracts, commodities and financial futures contracts, and insurance, which also deals with corporate and municipal securities and investment banking. **NOTE:** Please call for specific information on where to mail resume. **Corporate headquarters location:** New York NY.

MERRILL LYNCH
JACKSONVILLE BRANCH
50 North Laura Street, Suite 3700, Jacksonville FL 32202. 904/634-6000. **Contact:** David Middleton, District Director. **Description:** A diversified financial service organization. The company is a major broker in securities, option contracts, commodities and financial futures contracts, and insurance, which also deals with corporate and municipal securities and investment banking. **NOTE:** Please call for specific information on where to mail resume. **Corporate headquarters location:** New York NY.

PAINE WEBBER INCORPORATED
One Independent Drive, Second Floor, Jacksonville FL 32202. 904/354-6000. **Contact:** Marty Karvelis, Branch Manager. **Description:** Regional office of the well-known securities brokerage firm. Paine Webber assists corporations, governments, and individuals in meeting their long-term financial needs. The company also has operations in equity and fixed-income securities. **Common positions include:** Services Sales Representative. **Educational backgrounds include:** Business Administration; Economics; Finance; Liberal Arts; Marketing. **Benefits:** Disability Coverage; Employee Discounts; Life Insurance; Medical Insurance; Pension Plan; Savings Plan; Tuition Assistance. **Special Programs:** Internships; Training Programs. **Corporate headquarters location:** New York NY. **Operations at this facility include:** Sales; Service. **Listed on:** New York Stock Exchange.

PRUDENTIAL SECURITIES, INC.
P.O. Box 45049, Jacksonville FL 32232-5049. 904/391-3400. **Contact:** Joe Grippi, Branch Manager. **Description:** Branch office of the securities brokerage firm. **Corporate headquarters location:** New York NY.

QUICK AND REILLY
230 South County Road, Palm Beach FL 33480. 407/655-8000. **Contact:** Human Resources. **Description:** Quick and Reilly is a holding company engaged in providing discount brokerage services through its subsidiaries primarily to retail customers throughout the United States, clearing securities transactions for its own customers and for other brokerage firms and banks, and acting as a specialist on the floor of the New York Stock Exchange. **Number of employees nationwide:** 848.

ROBINSON-HUMPHREY COMPANY
SMITH BARNEY, INC.
50 North Laura Street, Suite 2500, Jacksonville FL 32202. 904/366-6400. **Fax:** 904/354-5926. **Contact:** Branch Administrator. **Description:** The local office of a regional securities brokerage firm. **Common positions include:** Brokerage Clerk; Customer Service Representative; Securities Sales Rep. **Educational backgrounds include:** Economics; Finance. **Benefits:** 401K; Dental Insurance; Disability Coverage; Employee Discounts; Life Insurance; Medical Insurance; Pension Plan; Savings Plan; Tuition Assistance. **Special Programs:** Internships. **Corporate headquarters location:** Atlanta GA. **Parent company:** The Travelers. **Operations at this facility include:** Sales. **Listed on:** New York Stock Exchange. **Number of employees at this location:** 48. **Number of employees nationwide:** 45,000.

TRANSMEDIA NETWORK
11900 Biscayne Boulevard, Miami FL 33181-2726. 305/892-3300. **Contact:** Human Resources. **Description:** Acquires rights to receive goods and services from restaurants, which are then sold to cardholders for cash. **Number of employees at this location:** 25.

Note: Because addresses and telephone numbers of smaller companies change rapidly, we recommend you call each company to verify the information below before inquiring about job opportunities. Mass mailings are not recommended.

Additional employers with under 250 employees:

CREDIT AGENCIES AND INSTITUTIONS

Alliance Funding Co.
18830 US Highway 19 N, Clearwater FL 34624-3165. 813/536-1661.

American General Finance
9850 San Jose Blvd, Jacksonville FL 32257-5457. 904/824-4093.

Commercial Credit Corp.
7136 N University Dr, Tamarac FL 33321-2916. 954/720-8433.

Florida Home Loan Corp.
1320 S Federal Hwy, Suite 104, Stuart FL 34994-3409. 407/220-2264.

Kentucky Finance
456 E Burleigh Blvd, Tavares FL 32778-5257. 352/343-2676.

Margaretten and Company
201 N Riverside Dr,

Indialantic FL 32903-4248. 407/728-9555.

Mercury Finance Co.
3590 N Highway 17-92, Sanford FL 32773. 407/328-7799.

Mercury Finance Co.
6003-4 Roosevelt Blvd, Jacksonville FL 32244. 904/779-0700.

Mercury Finance Co.
670 N Orlando Ave, Suite 202, Maitland FL 32751-4465. 407/539-2233.

Nationscredit Financial Service Corporation
1674 S Congress Ave, Lake Worth FL 33461-2142. 407/968-9605.

Transouth Financial Corp.
8056 N 56th St, Tampa FL 33617-7620. 813/988-9148.

Transouth Financial Corp.
5104 W Colonial Dr, Orlando

FL 32808-7604. 407/299-8060.

Beneficial Management Corporation
400 N Bumby Ave, Orlando FL 32803-6028. 407/895-6360.

Offshore Financial
2190 SE 17th St, Ft Lauderdale FL 33316-3109. 954/462-7773.

Auto Credit Of Florida
4819 San Juan Ave, Jacksonville FL 32210-3231. 904/387-9800.

Discover Card Services
140 Intracoastal Point Dr, Jupiter FL 33477-5096. 904/407-8048.

First USA
1725 Palm Cove Blvd, Delray Beach FL 33445-6771. 407/265-0314.

Nabanco
195 Wekiva Springs Rd,

Longwood FL 32779-6199.
407/865-5490.

MORTGAGE BANKERS

Aabco Mortgage
7850 Ulmerton Rd, Largo FL
34641-4015. 813/536-
9999.

Aabco Mortgage
4605 S Tamiami Trail,
Sarasota FL 34231-3457.
941/925-9999.

**Bancboston Mortgage
Corporation**
3230 W Commercial Blvd, Ft
Lauderdale FL 33309-3400.
954/733-5200.

Collateral Mortgage Ltd.
2727 NW 43rd St, Suite 3,
Gainesville FL 32606-6632.
352/378-1666.

Norwest Mortgage
1300 SE 17th St, Ft
Lauderdale FL 33316-1721.
954/768-9113.

**Community Mortgage
Corporation**
7845 Baymeadows Way,
Jacksonville FL 32256-7511.
904/737-5155.

Allen Molton & Williams
1890 Semoran Blvd, Winter
Park FL 32792-2285.
407/671-4663.

**American Residential
Mortgage Corporation**
3550 W Busch Blvd, Tampa
FL 33618-4402. 813/932-
1005.

**Atlantic Mortgage &
Investment Corp.**
4348 Southpoint Blvd,
Jacksonville FL 32216-0986.
904/296-1400.

**Bancboston Mortgage
Corporation**
3550 W Busch Blvd, Suite
100, Tampa FL 33618-
4402. 813/932-7690.

Countrywide Funding
14315 N Dale Mabry Hwy,
Carrollwood FL 33618-2017.
813/265-3139.

**Fortune Bank Mortgage
Division**
3333 W Commercial Blvd,
Suite 105, Ft Lauderdale FL
33309-3407. 954/484-
4404.

Holliday Fenoglio Dockerty
2500 N Military Trail, Suite
450, Boca Raton FL 33431-
6342. 407/241-6500.

Huntington Home Mortgage
3450 Buschwood Park Dr,

Tampa FL 33618-4455.
813/933-1788.

**Independence Mortgage
Corp. of America**
780 S Apollo Blvd, Suite
107, Melbourne FL 32901-
1423. 407/984-3344.

JDL Mortgage Corp.
1500 NE 62nd St, Suite
108, Ft Lauderdale FL
33334-5138. 954/772-
3877.

**Loan America Financial
Corporation**
1500 NE 62nd St, Ft
Lauderdale FL 33334-5138.
954/351-8091.

Margaretten & Company
4010 W Boy Scout Blvd,
Suite 78, Tampa FL 33607-
5727. 813/879-4000.

Mizner Mortgage Corporation
1600 Sarno Rd, Melbourne
FL 32935. 407/259-7856.

**North American Mortgage
Company**
11300 4th St N, Suite 147,
St Petersburg FL 33716-
2939. 813/577-9939.

NVR Mortgage LP
222 S Westmonte Dr, Suite
100, Altamonte Springs FL
32714. 407/774-1684.

**Pinnacle Financial Mortgage
Corp.**
1500 Lee Rd, Suite 200,
Orlando FL 32810-5344.
407/578-2000.

Princeton Financial Corp.
1750 S Volusia Ave, Suite 1,
Orange City FL 32763-7344.
904/774-0550.

Ryland Mortgage Co.
13907 N Dale Mabry Hwy,
Tampa FL 33618-2411.
813/969-4100.

Ryland Mortgage Co.
8380 Baymeadows Rd,
Jacksonville FL 32256-7433.
904/448-8114.

**Source One Mortgage
Services**
6462 NW 5th Way, Ft
Lauderdale FL 33309-6112.
954/493-8168.

**Source One Mortgage
Services**
801 N Magnolia Ave,
Orlando FL 32803-3851.
407/839-4748.

Sunbelt National Mortgage
2194 Highway A1A, Indian
Harbor Beach FL 32937-
4930. 407/777-4302.

Transouth Financial Corp.
10601 US Highway 441,
Suite C17, Leesburg FL
34788-7240. 352/787-
2232.

**Universal American Mortgage
Company**
2826 N University Dr,
Sunrise FL 33322-2450.
954/748-2826.

**Universal American Mortgage
Company**
1110 Douglas Ave, Suite
2000, Altamonte Springs FL
32714-2004. 407/682-
7110.

Chemical Mortgage Co.
6900 Southpoint Dr N,
Jacksonville FL 32216-8007.
904/296-6000.

SECURITY BROKERS AND DEALERS

Biltmore Securities
6700 N Andrews Ave, Suite
500, Ft Lauderdale FL
33309-2165. 954/351-
4200.

Carnes Capital Corp.
3003 Tamiami Trail N,
Naples FL 33940-2714.
941/261-2112.

Carney Group
1101 N Congress Ave,
Boynton Beach FL 33426-
3308. 407/369-1400.

**Corporate Management
Group**
980 N Federal Hwy, Boca
Raton FL 33432-2740.
407/338-2860.

Corporate Securities Group
20801 Biscayne Blvd, Suite
100, Miami FL 33180-1422.
305/935-3737.

First Miami Securities
20660 W Dixie Hwy, Miami
FL 33180-1130. 305/937-
0660.

Marcus Stowell & Beye
4875 N Federal Hwy Fl 3, Ft
Lauderdale FL 33308-4610.
954/772-3800.

BC Ziegler and Company
500 N Maitland Ave, Suite
111, Maitland FL 32751-
4440. 407/628-5845.

Donald & Co. Securities
2536 Countryside Blvd
#410, Clearwater FL 34623-
1633. 813/530-9655.

Edward D Jones & Co.
121 E Marion Ave Unit
1116, Punta Gorda FL
33950-3635. 941/639-
1170.

Edward D Jones & Co.
1790 Highway A1A, Satellite
Beach FL 32937-5438.
407/777-9766.

Edward D Jones & Co.
1905 NE Ricou Ter, Jensen
Beach FL 34957-4130.
407/334-1119.

Edward D Jones & Co.
104A N Evers St, Plant City
FL 33566-3330. 813/752-
9400.

Edward D Jones & Co.
10377 Southern Blvd, Royal
Palm Beach FL 33411-4339.
407/795-7753.

Humphrey Robinson Co.
50 N Laura St, Jacksonville
FL 32202-3664. 904/366-
6400.

Ibis Realty Associates
8850 Ibis Blvd, West Palm
Beach FL 33412-1303.
407/624-8000.

Invest Financial Corp.
701 W Cypress Creek Rd,
Suite 300, Ft Lauderdale FL
33309. 954/568-0042.

JC Bradford & Co.
1200 Riverplace Blvd,
Jacksonville FL 32207-9046.
904/396-2480.

JW Charles Securities
1856 W Hillsboro Blvd,
Deerfield Beach FL 33442-
1402. 954/481-9404.

JW Charles Securities
2810 E Oakland Park Blvd
#10, Ft Lauderdale FL
33306. 954/561-4501.

Keegan Morgan & Co.
316 S Baylen St, Pensacola
FL 32501. 904/434-2207.

Meridian Associates
9501 US Highway 19, Port
Richey FL 34668-4641.
813/846-9766.

Offerman & Company
5750 Major Blvd, Orlando FL
32819. 407/351-6188.

Olde Discount Stockbrokers
11141 US Highway 1, No
Palm Beach FL 33408-3219.
407/627-6100.

Olde Discount Stockbrokers
11230 Park Blvd, Largo FL
34642. 813/391-0228.

Salomon Brothers
8800 Hidden River Pkwy,
Tampa FL 33637-1028.
813/558-7000.

Shocet Securities
5875 N University Dr,
Tamarac FL 33321-4617.
954/721-3000.

**COMMODITY CONTRACTS
BROKERS AND DEALERS**

Global Futures Holdings
1451 NE 62nd St, Fort
Lauderdale FL 33334-5133.
954/771-4160.

INVESTMENT ADVISORS

**Legend Investment
Management**
3920 RCA Blvd, Palm Beach
Gardens FL 33410-4220.
407/694-0110.

Concord Holding Corp.
150 2nd Ave N, St
Petersburg FL 33701-3327.
813/821-7722.

**Wells Fargo Nikko
Investment**
2180 State Road 434 W,
Longwood FL 32779-5041.
407/862-0570.

Avco Financial Services
3802 Ehrlich Rd, Suite 205,
Tampa FL 33624-2331.
813/961-8338.

**Fairburn Investment Banking
Group**
902 Oak St, Melbourne
Beach FL 32951-2223.
407/724-1973.

Invest Financial Corp.
3000 N University Dr,
Sunrise FL 33322-1611.
954/572-0641.

Norwest Financial America
751 S State Road 7,
Plantation FL 33317-4000.
954/583-5151.

For more information on career opportunities in financial services:

Associations

FINANCIAL EXECUTIVES INSTITUTE
P.O. Box 1938, Morristown NJ 07962-
1938. 201/898-4600. Fee and membership
required. Publishes biennial member
directory. Provides member referral service.

INSTITUTE OF FINANCIAL EDUCATION
111 East Wacker Drive, Chicago IL 60601.
312/946-8800. Offers career development
program.

**NATIONAL ASSOCIATION OF BUSINESS
ECONOMISTS**
1233 20th Street NW, Suite 505,
Washington DC 20036. 202/463-6223.
Bulletin board number: 216/241-6254.
Newsletter and electronic bulletin board list
job openings. Members can upload resumes
and listed positions desired to bulletin
board.

**NATIONAL ASSOCIATION OF CREDIT
MANAGEMENT**
8815 Centre Park Drive, Suite 200,
Columbia MD 21045-2158. 410/740-5560.
Contact: Delores Richman. Publishes a
business credit magazine.

**NATIONAL ASSOCIATION OF REAL
ESTATE INVESTMENT TRUSTS**
1129 20th Street NW, Suite 305,
Washington DC 20036. 202/785-8717.
Contact: Donna Smith, Membership.

PUBLIC SECURITIES ASSOCIATION
40 Broad Street, 12th Floor, New York NY
10004. 212/809-7000. Contact: Caroline
Binn x427. Publishes an annual report and
several newsletters.

SECURITIES INDUSTRY ASSOCIATION
120 Broadway, 35th Floor New York NY
10271. 212/608-1500. Contact: Phil
Williams/Membership. Publishes a security
industry yearbook.

TREASURY MANAGEMENT ASSOCIATION
7315 Wisconsin Avenue, Suite 1250-W,
Bethesda MD 20814. 301/907-2862.

Directories

**DIRECTORY OF AMERICAN FINANCIAL
INSTITUTIONS**
Thomson Business Publications, 6195
Crooked Creek Road, Norcross GA 30092.
404/448-1011. Sales 800/321-3373.

MOODY'S BANK AND FINANCE MANUAL
Moody's Investor Service, 99 Church
Street, New York NY 10007. 212/553-
0300.

Magazines

**BARRON'S: NATIONAL BUSINESS AND
FINANCIAL WEEKLY**
Dow Jones & Company, 200 Liberty Street,
New York NY 10281. 212/416-2700.

FINANCIAL PLANNING
40 West 57th Street, 11th Floor, New York
NY 10019. 212/765-5311.

FINANCIAL WORLD
Financial World Partners, 1328 Broadway,
3rd Floor, New York NY 10001. 212/594-
5030.

**FUTURES: THE MAGAZINE OF
COMMODITIES AND OPTIONS**
250 South Wacker Drive, Suite 1150,
Chicago IL 60606. 312/977-0999.

INSTITUTIONAL INVESTOR
488 Madison Avenue, 12th Floor, New
York NY 10022. 212/303-3300.

FOOD AND BEVERAGES/AGRICULTURE

 Employment in food processing is expected to fall slightly through 2005. Although the industry's output should grow, increasing automation and productivity will mean food can be produced with fewer workers. However, some food processing industries are likely to remain fairly labor intensive. For example, meat packing and poultry processing are difficult to fully automate because each animal processed is different. Professional specialty occupations, although small in number, are also expected to grow. The growth of these occupations -- including engineers, systems analysts, and food scientists -- reflects the industry's emphasis on scientific research to improve food products and production processes. Demand for food scientists will also grow in response to expanding government inspection and regulation of food production.

Several factors may slow the decline in food processing employment. As consumers increasingly seek 'ready-to-heat' foods, the food processing industry has introduced many new products. Many of these new goods, which require more processing than the items they are replacing, will help maintain the demand for food processors in the future. In addition, the food processing industry is taking advantage of new technology to perform much of the processing formerly done by retailers. One other factor that may help stem employment decline is growing international trade in food products. Food processing firms expect growing trade to provide new markets for their products. The emerging field of biotechnology and other new food science technologies may also provide new jobs.

AFFILIATED OF FLORIDA INC.
1102 North 28th Street, Tampa FL 33605. 813/248-5781. **Contact:** Harry Britton, Director of Personnel. **Description:** Producers of wholesale groceries.

ANHEUSER-BUSCH, INC.
111 Busch Drive, Jacksonville FL 32218. 904/751-0700. **Contact:** Supervisor/Plant Personnel. **Description:** A beer producer with a high-tech brewing process and high-speed packaging lines. Anheuser-Busch, Inc. began operations in 1852 as the Bavarian Brewery and now ranks as one of the world's largest brewers, holding the position of industry leader in the United States since 1957. More than four out of every 10 beers sold in the United States are Anheuser-Busch products. Brand names include Budweiser, Michelob, and Busch beers. **Common positions include:** Accountant/Auditor; Buyer; Chemist; Computer Programmer; Electrical/Electronics Engineer; Human Resources Specialist; Mechanical Engineer; Purchasing Agent and Manager; Quality Control Supervisor; Supervisor; Systems Analyst. **Educational backgrounds include:** Accounting; Business Administration; Engineering; Food Science; Microbiology. **Benefits:** Dental Insurance; Disability Coverage; Employee Discounts; Life Insurance; Medical Insurance; Pension Plan; Savings Plan; Tuition Assistance; Vision Insurance. **Corporate headquarters location:** St. Louis MO. **Operations at this facility include:** Manufacturing. **Listed on:** New York Stock Exchange.

ANHEUSER-BUSCH, INC.
P.O. Box 9245, Tampa FL 33674. 813/988-4111. **Contact:** Manager/Employee Relations. **Description:** A regional plant of the beer distributor and producer. Anheuser-Busch, Inc., which began operations in 1852 as the Bavarian Brewery, ranks as one of the world's largest brewers and has held the position of industry leader in the United States since 1957. More than four out of every 10 beers sold in the United States are

Anheuser-Busch products. Brand names include Budweiser, Michelob, and Busch beers. **Corporate headquarters location:** St. Louis MO.

ARAMARK
1301 Gulf Life Drive, Jacksonville FL 32207-9047. 904/396-5037. **Contact:** Human Resources. **Description:** A food services contractor.

ATLANTIC SUGAR
P.O. Box 1570, Belle Glade FL 33430. 407/996-6541. **Contact:** Human Resources. **Description:** A sugar manufacturer.

BACARDI IMPORTS, INC.
2100 Biscayne Boulevard, Miami FL 33137. 305/573-8511. **Contact:** Personnel Department. **Description:** An importer, seller, and distributor of wine and rum.

BASIC FOOD INTERNATIONAL
P.O. Box 22948, Fort Lauderdale FL 33335. 954/467-1700. **Contact:** Mr. Bauer, President. **Description:** International traders of food products. **Common positions include:** Services Sales Representative. **Special Programs:** Apprenticeships.

BEE GEE SHRIMP
P.O. Box 3709, Lakeland FL 33802. 941/687-4411. **Contact:** Human Resources. **Description:** A shrimp processing plant.

BEN HILL GRIFFIN, INC.
P.O. Box 127, Frostproof FL 33843. 941/635-2251. **Contact:** Personnel Director. **Description:** A citrus fruit grower.

BERRY CITRUS, INC.
P.O. Box 459, Labelle FL 33935. 941/675-2769. **Contact:** Donna Wieland, Personnel. **Description:** A citrus grower. **Common positions include:** Accountant/Auditor; Computer Programmer. **Educational backgrounds include:** Accounting; Computer Science. **Benefits:** Dental Insurance; Disability Coverage; Life Insurance; Medical Insurance.

BURGER KING DISTRIBUTION SERVICES
P.O. Box 020783, T4-S, Miami FL 33102. 305/378-7011. **Contact:** Human Resources Manager. **Description:** A distributor of food products nationwide to Burger King restaurants. **Common positions include:** Accountant/Auditor; Administrator; Customer Service Representative; Department Manager; Driver; Financial Analyst; General Manager; Operations/Production Manager; Transportation/Traffic Specialist; Warehouse/Distribution Worker. **Educational backgrounds include:** Accounting; Business Administration; Finance; Transportation/Logistics. **Benefits:** Dental Insurance; Disability Coverage; Employee Discounts; Life Insurance; Medical Insurance; Pension Plan; Profit Sharing; Savings Plan; Tuition Assistance. **Special Programs:** Training Programs. **Corporate headquarters location:** This Location. **Parent company:** Grand Metropolitan plc. **Operations at this facility include:** Administration; Service.

BUTTER KRUST BAKERIES
P.O. Box 1707, Lakeland FL 33802. 941/682-1155. **Contact:** Jenny Brockston, Manager of Human Resources. **Description:** A bakery.

CARGILL CORPORATION
5421 West Beaver Street, Jacksonville FL 32254. 904/693-5633. **Contact:** Ed Bullard, Director of Personnel. **Description:** A poultry processing plant. Nationally, Cargill, its subsidiaries, and its affiliates are involved in nearly 50 individual lines of business. The company has 130 years of service and international expertise in commodity trading, handling, transporting, processing, and risk management, employing more than 70,000 people in plants and offices all over the world. Cargill is a major trader of grains and oilseeds, as well as a marketer of many other agricultural and nonagricultural commodities. As a transporter, it uses a complex network of rail and road systems, inland waterways, and ocean-going routes, combining its own fleet and transportation services purchased from outside sources to find the most efficient and economical modes of transport to move bulk commodities from point of origin to point of consumption. As an agricultural supplier, Cargill is a leader in developing high-quality, competitively priced farm products and in supplying them to growers. Agricultural products include a wide variety of feed, seed, fertilizers, and other goods and services needed by producers worldwide. Cargill is also a leader in producing and

marketing seed varieties and hybrids. Cargill Central Research, located at Cargill headquarters, is dedicated to developing new agricultural products to address the needs of customers around the world. The company also provides financial and technical services. Cargill's Financial Markets Division (FMD) supports Cargill and its subsidiaries with financial products and services that address the full spectrum of market conditions. These include financial instrument trading, emerging markets instrument trading, value investing, and money management. Cargill's worldwide food processing businesses supply products ranging from basic ingredients used in food production to recognized name brands. Cargill also operates a number of industrial businesses, including the production of steel, industrial-grade starches, ethanol, and salt products.

CITRUS WORLD, INC.
P.O. Box 1111, Lake Wales FL 33859-1111. 941/676-1411. **Fax:** 941/676-0494. **Contact:** Director of Human Resources. **Description:** A processor of citrus products. **Common positions include:** Accountant/Auditor; Buyer; Chemist; Computer Programmer; Department Manager; Electrical/Electronics Engineer; Human Resources Specialist; Mechanical Engineer; Operations/Production Manager; Purchasing Agent and Manager; Quality Control Supervisor; Systems Analyst; Transportation/Traffic Specialist. **Educational backgrounds include:** Accounting; Business Administration; Computer Science; Engineering; Finance; Marketing. **Benefits:** Disability Coverage; Employee Discounts; Medical Insurance; Pension Plan; Tuition Assistance. **Operations at this facility include:** Manufacturing.

COCA-COLA BOTTLING COMPANY OF MIAMI
3350 Pembroke Road, Hollywood FL 33021. 954/985-5000. **Contact:** Lori Welch, Director of Human Resources. **Description:** A bottling facility for the local soft-drink supplier.

B.C. COOK AND SONS ENTERPRISES
P.O. Box 1597, Haines City FL 33845. 941/422-1121. **Contact:** Controller. **Description:** A citrus grower.

DIXIE PACKERS INC.
P.O. Box 622, Madison FL 32341. 904/973-4101. **Contact:** Human Resources. **Description:** A meat-packing plant.

ENTENMANN'S BAKERY OF FLORIDA
3325 Northwest 62nd Street, Miami FL 33147. 305/836-4900. **Contact:** Human Resources. **Description:** Bakes cakes, cookies, pies, and doughnuts. This location is the headquarters for the Southeast Region. **Operations at this facility include:** Regional Headquarters.

FLAV-O-RICH, INC.
4711 34th Street North, P.O. Box 60189, St. Petersburg FL 33784. 813/526-9191. **Contact:** Nancy Hansford, Personnel Manager. **Description:** A processor of assorted dairy products.

FLORIDA GLOBAL CITRUS LIMITED
P.O. Box 37, 625 West Bridgers Avenue, Auburndale FL 33823. 941/967-4431. **Fax:** 941/965-2480. **Contact:** Beverly Joines, Vice President of Industrial Relations. **Description:** Florida Global Citrus Limited processes citrus fruits and citrus fruit by-products for bulk concentrate sales. The company is also engaged in warehousing. **Common positions include:** Accountant/Auditor; Blue-Collar Worker Supervisor; Clerical Supervisor; Computer Programmer; Human Resources Specialist; Payroll Clerk; Production Manager; Purchasing Agent and Manager; Quality Control Supervisor; Receptionist; Secretary; Truck Driver; Typist/Word Processor; Welder. **Educational backgrounds include:** Accounting; Business Administration; Computer Science; Engineering; Finance; Marketing. **Benefits:** 401K; Dental Insurance; Disability Coverage; Life Insurance; Medical Insurance; Pension Plan; Scholarship Program. **Corporate headquarters location:** This Location. **Operations at this facility include:** Administration; Manufacturing; Sales. **Number of employees at this location:** 200.

FLORIDA JUICE, INC.
P.O. Drawer 3628, Lakeland FL 33802-2004. 941/686-1173. **Contact:** Sandy Sexton, Personnel Manager. **Description:** Offices of the food processing company.

FLOWERS BAKING COMPANY
17800 North West Miami Court, Miami FL 33169. 305/652-3416. **Contact:** Ken Simmons, Personnel Director. **Description:** A bread baking facility.

FLOWERS BAKING COMPANY
P.O. Box 12579, Jacksonville FL 32209. 904/354-3771. **Contact:** Rick Hancock, Director of Human Resources. **Description:** A bread baking facility.

GOLD KIST POULTRY PROCESSING
FLORIDA DIVISION
P.O Drawer 1000, Live Oak FL 32060. 904/362-2544. **Contact:** David Mullis, Division Human Resources Manager. **Description:** A poultry grow-out and processing complex. **Common positions include:** Food Service Manager; Management Trainee. **Educational backgrounds include:** Agricultural Science; Business Administration. **Benefits:** 401K; Disability Coverage; Life Insurance; Medical Insurance; Pension Plan; Tuition Assistance. **Corporate headquarters location:** Atlanta GA. **Operations at this facility include:** Divisional Headquarters. **Number of employees at this location:** 1,200. **Number of employees nationwide:** 14,000.

GOLDEN GEM GROWERS, INC.
P.O. Drawer 9, Umatilla FL 32784-0009. 352/669-2101. **Contact:** Debra D. Fontaine, Personnel Manager. **Description:** Processors of fresh and frozen citrus fruits. **Benefits:** Disability Coverage; Employee Discounts; Life Insurance; Medical Insurance; Savings Plan; Tuition Assistance. **Corporate headquarters location:** This Location. **Operations at this facility include:** Administration; Manufacturing.

HOLLY HILL FRUIT PRODUCTS COMPANY
P.O. Box 708, Davenport FL 33837. 941/422-1131. **Contact:** Georgia Elam, Personnel Director. **Description:** Produces canned and frozen juices and citrus fruits.

HOLSUM BAKING COMPANY
8700 North West 77th Court, Miami FL 33166. 305/888-3441. **Contact:** Oren Tomlisen, Personnel Director. **Description:** A bakery.

INTERSTATE BRANDS CORPORATION
P.O. Box 233, Orlando FL 32802. 407/843-5110. **Contact:** Personnel Manager. **Description:** A bakery. **Common positions include:** Blue-Collar Worker Supervisor; Manufacturer's/Wholesaler's Sales Rep. **Benefits:** Dental Insurance; Disability Coverage; Employee Discounts; Life Insurance; Medical Insurance; Pension Plan; Savings Plan.

INTERSTATE BRANDS CORPORATION
MERITA DIVISION
P.O. Box 28489, Jacksonville FL 32226. 904/696-1400. **Contact:** Steve Butler, Director of Personnel. **Description:** A bakery.

JUICE BOWL PRODUCTS
P.O. Box 1048, Lakeland FL 33802. 941/665-5515. **Fax:** 941/667-7152. **Contact:** Brenda Hall, Vice President of Human Resources. **Description:** A canned fruit processing company. **Common positions include:** Accountant/Auditor; Buyer; Clinical Lab Technician; Computer Programmer; Credit Manager; Customer Service Representative; Electrician; Human Resources Specialist; Mechanical Engineer; Operations/Production Manager; Public Relations Specialist; Purchasing Agent and Manager. **Educational backgrounds include:** Accounting; Biology; Business Administration; Engineering; Finance; Marketing; Mathematics. **Benefits:** Dental Insurance; Disability Coverage; Employee Discounts; Life Insurance; Medical Insurance; Pension Plan; Profit Sharing; Tuition Assistance. **Operations at this facility include:** Administration; Manufacturing; Research and Development; Sales; Service. **Listed on:** Privately held. **Number of employees at this location:** 175.

LAKE WALES CITRUS GROWERS ASSOCIATION
P.O. Box 672, Lake Wales FL 33859-0672. 941/676-3497. **Contact:** Mary Schaal, Office Manager. **Description:** Fresh citrus fruit shipping company.

LYKES BROTHERS, INC.
SUBSIDIARY & AFFILIATED COMPANIES
P.O. Box 31244, Tampa FL 33631-3244. 813/223-3981. **Contact:** Ken Bricker, Manager/Recruitment Services. **Description:** One of the world's largest packers of

private-label citrus products and one of Florida's largest privately-held corporations. The company's diversified interests include: citrus, meats, and coffee processing.

MAXWELL HOUSE COFFEE COMPANY
P.O. Box 2010, Jacksonville FL 32203. 904/366-3400. **Contact:** Personnel Department. **Description:** A producer of regular and instant coffee products. **Common positions include:** Chemical Engineer; Electrical/Electronics Engineer; Mechanical Engineer. **Educational backgrounds include:** Engineering. **Benefits:** Dental Insurance; Disability Coverage; Life Insurance; Medical Insurance; Pension Plan; Profit Sharing; Stock Option; Thrift Plan; Tuition Assistance. **Corporate headquarters location:** White Plains NY. **Parent company:** Philip Morris. **Operations at this facility include:** Manufacturing.

McARTHUR DAIRY
2451 NW 7th Avenue, Miami FL 33127. 305/576-2880. **Contact:** Rick Robles, Personnel Director. **Description:** A dairy. **NOTE:** Please send your resume to 500 Sawgrass Corporate Parkway, Sunrise, FL 33325.

NATIONAL BEVERAGE CORPORATION
One North University Drive, Fort Lauderdale FL 33324. 954/581-0922. **Contact:** Personnel Department. **Description:** National Beverage Corporation is an integrated producer and distributor of multiflavored soft drink products. The company's brand names include Shasta, Shasta Plus, Mt. Shasta Water, Faygo, Faygo Iced Teas, Faygo Sparkling Waters, Spree, a Sante, Body Works, Big Shot, mr., Frolic, and nuAnce. **Benefits:** Bonus Award/Plan; Profit Sharing; Retirement Plan; Stock Option. **Other U.S. locations:** Nationwide. **Listed on:** NASDAQ.

OKEELANTA CORPORATION
P.O. Box 86, South Bay FL 33493. 407/996-9072. **Contact:** Oscar Schneider, Personnel Director. **Description:** A producer of nonrefined cane sugar.

PEPSI-COLA COMPANY/MIAMI
7777 Northwest 41st Street, Miami FL 33166. 305/592-1980. **Contact:** Abelardo R. de Guzman, Employee Relations Manager. **Description:** Manufactures, sells, and distributes Pepsi-Cola products, as well as Dr. Pepper, 7-Up, Sunkist, and Barq's. The parent company operates on a worldwide basis within three industry segments: beverages, snack foods, and restaurants. The beverage segment markets its brands worldwide and manufactures concentrates for its brands for sale to franchised bottlers worldwide. The beverage segment also operates bottling plants and distribution facilities of its own located in the United States and key international markets and distributes ready-to-drink Lipton tea products under a joint-venture agreement. In addition, under separate distribution and joint-venture agreements, Pepsi-Cola distributes certain previously existing, as well as jointly developed, Ocean Spray juice products. **Benefits:** Dental Insurance; Disability Coverage; Life Insurance; Medical Insurance; Pension Plan. **Special Programs:** Internships.

PEPSI-COLA COMPANY/ORLANDO
1700 Directors Row, Orlando FL 32809. 407/826-5942. **Fax:** 407/826-5999. **Contact:** Irma Widman, Human Resources Manager. **Description:** A regional bottling plant. The parent company operates on a worldwide basis within three industry segments: beverages, snack foods, and restaurants. The beverage segment markets its brands worldwide and manufactures concentrates for its brands for sale to franchised bottlers worldwide. The beverage segment also operates bottling plants and distribution facilities of its own located in the United States and key international markets and distributes ready-to-drink Lipton tea products under a joint-venture agreement. In addition, under separate distribution and joint-venture agreements, the segment distributes certain previously existing, as well as jointly developed, Ocean Spray juice products. **Common positions include:** Computer Operator; Department Manager; Human Resources Specialist; Industrial Production Manager; Manufacturer's/Wholesaler's Sales Rep.; Payroll Clerk; Quality Control Supervisor; Secretary; Truck Driver. **Educational backgrounds include:** Accounting; Business Administration; Chemistry; Finance; Marketing. **Benefits:** Dental Insurance; Disability Coverage; Employee Discounts; Life Insurance; Medical Insurance; Pension Plan; Savings Plan; Stock Option; Tuition Assistance. **Special Programs:** Internships; Training Programs. **Corporate headquarters location:** Somers NY. **Parent company:** PepsiCo. **Operations at this facility include:** Manufacturing; Regional Headquarters; Sales; Service. **Listed on:** New York Stock Exchange. **Number of employees at this location:** 400. **Number of employees nationwide:** 26,000.

QUAKER OATS COMPANY
ARDMORE FARMS, INC.
P.O. Box 183, Deland FL 32721. 904/734-4634. **Contact:** Michael A. Tenney, Director of Human Resources. **Description:** A grocery products company with 81 percent of sales produced by brands holding the number-one or number-two positions in their respective categories. The Quaker Oats Company is best known for its Old Fashioned Quaker Oats. This location is engaged in juice processing.

QUINCY FARMS
Route 4, Box 245, Quincy FL 32351. 904/875-1600. **Contact:** Sandy Pearsall, Personnel Director. **Description:** A fresh fruit and vegetable company.

ROYAL CROWN COMPANY
1000 Corporate Drive, Fort Lauderdale FL 33334. 954/351-5600. **Contact:** Suzanne Acosta, Director of Human Resources. **Description:** A manufacturer of soft drink concentrates and syrups. **Common positions include:** Accountant/Auditor; Administrative Services Manager; Attorney; Budget Analyst; Computer Programmer; Computer Systems Analyst; Human Resources Specialist. **Educational backgrounds include:** Accounting; Finance; Marketing. **Benefits:** 401K; Dental Insurance; Disability Coverage; Life Insurance; Medical Insurance; Tuition Assistance. **Corporate headquarters location:** This Location. **Other U.S. locations:** LaMirada CA; Cincinnati OH; Columbus OH. **Parent company:** TRIAC. **Operations at this facility include:** Administration; Divisional Headquarters. **Listed on:** New York Stock Exchange. **Number of employees at this location:** 70. **Number of employees nationwide:** 210.

SHOWELL FARMS, INC.
P. O. Box 1040, De Funiak Springs FL 32433. 904/892-3151. **Contact:** Joyce Szilvasy, Personnel Director. **Description:** A poultry plant. **Common positions include:** Accountant/Auditor; Blue-Collar Worker Supervisor; General Manager; Human Resources Specialist; Industrial Production Manager; Management Trainee; Mechanical Engineer; Purchasing Agent and Manager; Quality Control Supervisor; Sales Associate. **Benefits:** Dental Insurance; Life Insurance; Medical Insurance; Pension Plan. **Corporate headquarters location:** Showell MD. **Operations at this facility include:** Administration; Manufacturing; Sales.

SINGLETON SEAFOOD COMPANY
5024 Uceta Road, Tampa FL 33619. 813/241-1500. **Contact:** Personnel Department. **Description:** A seafood processor.

SOUTH FLORIDA GROWERS ASSOCIATION INC.
P.O. Box 458, Goulds FL 33170. 305/258-1631. **Contact:** Harold E. Kendall, President. **Description:** Engaged in the growing, processing, and marketing of tropical fruits including avocados, limes, mangos, and papayas. **Common positions include:** Accountant/Auditor; Administrator; Agricultural Engineer; Blue-Collar Worker Supervisor; Buyer; Chemist; Credit Manager; Food Scientist/Technologist; Industrial Engineer; Marketing Specialist; Operations/Production Manager; Purchasing Agent and Manager; Quality Control Supervisor; Sales Associate. **Educational backgrounds include:** Accounting; Business Administration; Marketing. **Benefits:** Dental Insurance; Disability Coverage; Employee Discounts; Medical Insurance; Tuition Assistance. **Corporate headquarters location:** This Location. **Parent company:** Kendall Foods Corporation. **Operations at this facility include:** Administration; Divisional Headquarters; Manufacturing; Regional Headquarters; Research and Development; Sales; Service.

SOUTHERN WINE AND SPIRITS
1600 North West 163rd Street, Miami FL 33169. 305/625-4171. **Contact:** Ileana Ricart, Personnel Director. **Description:** Wholesalers of wine, spirits, beer, and water.

SUN CITY INDUSTRIES INC.
5545 Northwest 35th Avenue, Fort Lauderdale FL 33309. 954/730-3333. **Contact:** Human Resources. **Description:** A food distribution company. **Corporate headquarters location:** This Location.

SWISHER INTERNATIONAL

P.O. Box 2230, Jacksonville FL 32203. 904/353-4311. **Contact:** John Kenny, Personnel Manager. **Description:** A tobacco products manufacturer.

TROPICANA PRODUCTS, INC.

P.O. Box 338, Bradenton FL 34206. 941/747-4461. **Contact:** Tom Vorpahl, Director of Human Resources. **Description:** Offices of a consumer foods and beverage manufacturer. **Common positions include:** Accountant/Auditor; Biological Scientist/Biochemist; Blue-Collar Worker Supervisor; Buyer; Chemical Engineer; Chemist; Computer Programmer; Draftsperson. **Educational backgrounds include:** Accounting; Biology; Business Administration; Chemistry; Computer Science; Engineering; Marketing. **Benefits:** Dental Insurance; Disability Coverage; Employee Discounts; Life Insurance; Medical Insurance; Pension Plan; Profit Sharing; Tuition Assistance. **Corporate headquarters location:** This Location. **Parent company:** Seagram. **Operations at this facility include:** Administration; Divisional Headquarters; Manufacturing; Regional Headquarters; Research and Development; Sales; Service.

UNITED STATES SUGAR CORPORATION

P.O. Drawer 1207, Clewiston FL 33440. 941/983-8121. **Contact:** Mike Dobrow, Personnel Officer. **Description:** A producer of sugar products. **Common positions include:** Accountant/Auditor; Agricultural Engineer; Biological Scientist/Biochemist; Blue-Collar Worker Supervisor; Buyer; Chemical Engineer; Chemist; Claim Representative; Computer Programmer; Department Manager; Electrical/Electronics Engineer; General Manager; Human Resources Specialist; Industrial Engineer; Mechanical Engineer; Operations/Production Manager; Systems Analyst. **Educational backgrounds include:** Accounting; Biology; Business Administration; Chemistry; Communications; Computer Science; Economics; Engineering; Finance. **Benefits:** Dental Insurance; Life Insurance; Medical Insurance; Pension Plan; Stock Option; Tuition Assistance. **Corporate headquarters location:** This Location. **Operations at this facility include:** Administration; Divisional Headquarters; Manufacturing; Regional Headquarters; Research and Development; Sales; Service.

WAVERLY GROWERS CO-OP, INC.

P.O. Box 287, Waverly FL 33877-0287. 941/439-3602. **Contact:** Personnel Department. **Description:** A citrus fruit grower.

Note: Because addresses and telephone numbers of smaller companies change rapidly, we recommend you call each company to verify the information below before inquiring about job opportunities. Mass mailings are not recommended.

Additional employers with over 250 employees:

FOOD WHOLESALE

City Provisioners
P.O. Box 2246, Daytona Beach FL 32115-2246. 904/677-2240.

DAIRY PRODUCTS

Isaly-Klondike Co.
5400 118th Ave N, Clearwater FL 34620-4315. 813/572-7088.

PRESERVED FRUITS AND VEGETABLES

Florida Select Citrus
P.O. Box 98, Groveland FL 34736-0098. 904/429-2101.

SUGAR AND CONFECTIONERY PRODUCTS

Osceola Farms Co.
P.O. Box 679, Pahokee FL 33476-0679. 407/924-7156.

BEVERAGES

Stroh Brewery Co.
11111 N 30th St, Tampa FL 33612. 813/972-8500.

SEAFOOD

Kitchens Of The Ocean
104 SE 5th Ct, Deerfield Beach FL 33441. 954/421-2192.

Beaver Street Fisheries
P.O. Box 41430, Jacksonville FL 32203-1430. 904/354-5661.

Tampa Maid
4816 N Hesperides St, Tampa FL 33614-6408. 813/876-4181.

Variety Seafoods
P.O. Box 15751, Tampa FL 33684-5751. 813/872-4411.

CHIPS AND SNACKS

Frito-Lay
2800 Silver Star Rd, Orlando FL 32808. 407/295-1810.

Additional employers with under 250 employees:

**FLORICULTURE AND
NURSERY PRODUCTS**

International Foliage Corp.
P.O. Box 2249, Apopka FL
32704-2249. 407/886-
3255.

Mace Sod Service
275 SW 3rd Ave, South Bay
FL 33493-2294. 407/996-
6716.

Polk Nursery Co.
890 Lake Myrtle Rd,
Auburndale FL 33823-9317.
941/967-6641.

VEGETABLES AND MELONS

Bernard Egan & Co.
1900 Old Dixie Hwy, Vero
Beach FL 32960-3578.
407/567-8331.

DNE World Fruit Sales
1900 Old Dixie Hwy, Vero
Beach FL 32960-3578.
407/567-8335.

FRUITS AND TREE NUTS

Alico
P.O. Box 338, Labelle FL
33935-0338. 941/675-
2966.

Via Tropical Fruits
15950 SW Kanner Hwy,
Indiantown FL 34956-3138.
407/597-2126.

FIELD CROPS

Alger Farms
950 NW 8th St, Homestead
FL 33030. 305/247-4334.

CROP FARMS

United Agri Products
12120 US Highway 301 N,
Parrish FL 34219-8658.
941/776-3238.

DAIRY FARMS

Larson Dairy
Hilolo Rd, Okeechobee FL
34972. 941/467-2728.

**Tampa Independent Dairy
Farmers Association**
3725 E 10th Ave, Tampa FL
33605-4512. 813/247-
3961.

TG Lee Foods
2205 NW Pine Ave, Ocala FL
34475-9256. 352/622-
4666.

TG Lee Foods
3302 W 20th St,
Jacksonville FL 32254-1704.
904/781-4143.

Velda Farms Dairy
3634 Vineland Rd, Orlando
FL 32811-6436. 407/843-
9360.

POULTRY AND EGGS

Zephyr Egg Co.
4622 Gall Blvd, Zephyrhills
FL 33541-6237. 813/782-
1521.

CROP SERVICES

Central Coast Harvesting
1009 N 29th St, Immokalee
FL 33934-2639. 941/657-
3919.

Sunpure Ltd.
18999 SE US Highway 70,
Arcadia FL 33821-7763.
941/494-7780.

**Consolidated-Tomoka Land
Company**
600 State Road 70 W, Lake
Placid FL 33852-8702.
941/465-2511.

**FARM MANAGEMENT AND
LABOR SERVICES**

Graves Brothers Co.
25690 Orange Ave, Fort
Pierce FL 34945-4323.
407/489-2161.

**MEAT AND POULTRY
PROCESSING**

Blue Ribbon Meats
3340 E 3rd Ave, Hialeah FL
33013-3209. 305/887-
7534.

Central Florida Finer Foods
5582 Commercial Blvd,
Winter Haven FL 33880-
1008. 941/967-0623.

Central Packing Co.
Hwy 48, Center Hill FL
33514. 904/793-3671.

Deep South Products
210 Century Blvd, Bartow FL
33830-7704. 941/533-
2111.

DAIRY PRODUCTS

Borden Dairy
17707 NW Miami Ct, Miami
FL 33169-5014. 305/652-
4411.

Rich Ice Cream Co.
2915 S Dixie Hwy, West
Palm Beach FL 33405-1503.
407/833-7585.

Gustafson's Dairy
P.O. Box 338, Green Cove

Springs FL 32043-0338.
904/284-3750.

**Long Life Dairy Products
Company**
2198 W Beaver St,
Jacksonville FL 32209-7590.
904/354-8256.

Superbrand Dairy Products
3304 Sydney Rd, Plant City
FL 33567-1181. 813/754-
1847.

Velda Farms
909 5th St SW, Winter
Haven FL 33880-3315.
941/293-4152.

**PRESERVED FRUITS AND
VEGETABLES**

Beef Stake Tomato Growers
440 S Shelfer St, Quincy FL
32351-3549. 904/875-
4020.

Deep South Products
110 N Hwy 434, Orlando FL
32854. 407/862-1230.

Gracewood Fruit Co.
1626 90th Ave, Vero Beach
FL 32966-6614. 407/567-
1151.

**Mims Citrus Growers
Association**
2455 Folsom Rd, Mims FL
32754-3499. 407/267-
4661.

Ocean Spray Cranberries
925 74th Ave SW, Vero
Beach FL 32968-9755.
407/562-0800.

Riverfront Groves
4889 US Highway 1, Vero
Beach FL 32967-1505.
407/562-4155.

**Caulkins Indiantown Citrus
Company**
19100 SW Warfield Blvd,
Indiantown FL 34956-9704.
407/597-3511.

**Dundee Citrus Growers
Association**
111 1st St S, Dundee FL
33838-4230. 941/439-
1574.

Sunpure Ltd.
3200 US Highway 27 N,
Avon Park FL 33825-9572.
941/453-2222.

**Winter Garden Citrus
Products**
355 9th St, Winter Garden
FL 34787-3651. 407/656-
1000.

PREPARED FEEDS AND INGREDIENTS FOR ANIMALS

Coronet Industries
P.O. Box 760, Plant City FL
33564-0760. 813/752-
1161.

BAKERY PRODUCTS

A&C Italian Bakery
10777 NW 36th Ave, Miami
FL 33167-3705. 305/681-
7000.

Bagelmania
7562 W Commercial Blvd, Ft
Lauderdale FL 33319-2132.
954/748-5077.

Best Foods Baking Group
2300 Old Dixie Hwy, Riviera
Beach FL 33404-5456.
407/848-9705.

Fuchs Baking Co.
330 N Federal Hwy, Fort
Pierce FL 34950. 407/461-
3700.

Wonder Hostess
3351 58th Ave N, St
Petersburg FL 33714-1334.
813/526-4777.

Dad's Cookies
1 Cookie Cutter Ln, Plant
City FL 33566. 813/754-
5565.

SUGAR AND CONFECTIONERY PRODUCTS

Pioneer Products
P.O. Box 279, Ocala FL
34478-0279. 352/622-
3134.

BEVERAGES

Stephens Distributing
185 Ravenswood Rd, Ft
Lauderdale FL 33312-6605.
954/989-4350.

Southeast-Atlantic Corp.
3860 W Columbus Dr,
Tampa FL 33607-5719.
813/877-9511.

Southeast-Atlantic Corp.
3700 Avenue F, Fort Pierce
FL 34947-5832. 407/461-
3383.

SEAFOOD

Lombardi's Seafood
7491 Brokerage Dr, Orlando
FL 32809-5623. 407/859-
1015.

Florida Sea
1804 Turkey Creek Rd, Plant
City FL 33567-1915.
813/754-3954.

Peninsular Seafoods
4709 N Lauber Way, Tampa
FL 33614-6917. 813/875-
1086.

Raffield Fisheries
101-3 Canal Dr, Port St Joe
FL 32456. 904/229-8229.

Shaw Southern Belle Frozen
821 Virginia St, Jacksonville
FL 32208. 904/765-4487.

CHIPS AND SNACKS

Tom's Foods
700 W Toms Dr, Perry FL
32347. 904/584-7574.

FOOD PREPARATIONS

K'Jun Food Products
1163 Scotten Rd,
Jacksonville FL 32205-5240.
904/387-6376.

Lo-An Foods
6002 Benjamin Rd, Tampa
FL 33634-5104. 813/886-
3590.

Quality Bakery Products
888 E Las Olas Blvd #700,
Ft Lauderdale FL 33301-
2272. 954/779-3663.

TOBACCO PRODUCTS

In Fiesta Cigar Factory
59 Saint George St, St
Augustine FL 32084-3607.
904/824-6922.

Villazon & Co.
3104 N Armenia Ave, Tampa
FL 33607-1634. 813/879-
2291.

FOOD WHOLESALE

B&R Foods
3150 N Gallagher Rd, Dover
FL 33527-4730. 813/659-
0811.

Bari Italian Foods
7300 Technology Dr, Suite
A, W Melbourne FL 32904-
1520. 407/727-7619.

Bass & Swaggerty
330 Carswell Ave, Holly Hill
FL 32117-4437. 904/255-
0423.

BHF Associates
809 Belvedere Rd, West
Palm Beach FL 33405-1109.
407/833-5602.

Garcia Family Vegetables
427 El Prado, West Palm
Beach FL 33405-1966.
407/655-9075.

Movsovitz Produce Co.
3661 S Pine Ave, Ocala FL
34471-6610. 352/372-
5361.

National Fisheries
7104 E 9th Ave, Tampa FL
33619-3336. 813/621-
1234.

Seneca Foods Corp.
1605 Main St, Suite 1010,
Sarasota FL 34236-5861.
941/366-9707.

Sysco Food Services-South Florida
3931 RCA Blvd, Palm Beach
Gardens FL 33410-4236.
407/622-1225.

Budd Mayer Co. Of Tampa
3840 N 50th St, Tampa FL
33619-1002. 813/621-
4991.

Budd Mayer Companies
2930 Biscayne Blvd, Miami
FL 33137-4122. 305/576-
7000.

Southeast Frozen Foods
18770 NE 6th Ave, Miami FL
33179-3916. 305/652-
4622.

Haagen-Dazs Company
4504 W Kentucky Ave,
Tampa FL 33614-7708.
813/875-0538.

Cypress Foods
702 42nd St NW, Winter
Haven FL 33881-2869.
941/967-0775.

Sun City Egg Marketing
8600 NW 36th St, Suite
304, Miami FL 33166-6688.
305/593-2355.

Golden Flake Snack Foods
8916 Maislin Dr, Tampa FL
33637-6707. 813/988-
7314.

Golden Flake Snack Foods
2900 Shader Rd, Orlando FL
32808-3920. 407/297-
0041.

Blue Ribbon Meats
2340 W 3rd Ave, Hialeah FL
33010-1435. 305/887-
7534.

Colorado Boxed Beef Co.
P.O. Box 899, Winter Haven
FL 33882-0899. 941/967-
0636.

Mapelli Food Distributing Company
636 US Highway 1, No Palm
Beach FL 33408-4606.
407/848-1606.

Parkway Food Service
5160 140th Ave N,
Clearwater FL 34620-3750.
813/530-1611.

Cheney's Premier Produce
516 Monceaux Rd, West
Palm Beach FL 33405-1533.
407/848-9200.

Florida Citrus Commission
1115 E Memorial Blvd,
Lakeland FL 33801-2021.
941/682-0171.

Newbern Groves
P.O. Box 17237, Tampa FL
33682-7237. 813/971-
0440.

**PPI Del Monte Tropical Fruit
Company**
800 S Douglas Rd Fl N, Coral
Gables FL 33134-3125.
305/520-8400.

Center State Harvesting
336 US Highway 27 S, Lake
Wales FL 33853-4561.
941/676-5165.

Fort Meade Citrus Co.
7 7th St NE, Fort Meade FL
33841-2039. 941/285-
6900.

William G Roe & Sons
1000 Detour Rd, Haines City
FL 33844-9350. 941/422-
5902.

John Owens Co.
592 Ellis Rd S, Suite 100,
Jacksonville FL 32254-3574.
904/781-2410.

**Canada Dry Bottling Co. Of
Florida**
4895 Park Ridge Blvd,
Boynton Beach FL 33426-
8316. 407/732-7395.

Southeast-Atlantic Corp.
605 Gus Hipp Blvd,
Rockledge FL 32955-4808.
407/635-5554.

Universal Source
5106 Arthur St, Hollywood
FL 33021-5226. 954/989-
0323.

**Merita Bakery & Surplus
Stores**
388 N Nova Rd, Daytona
Beach FL 32114-3002.
904/255-4774.

Sunshine Biscuits
9940 Currie Davis Dr #C,
Tampa FL 33619-2669.
813/626-2606.

ALCOHOL WHOLESALE

Brown Distributing
1300 Allendale Rd, West
Palm Beach FL 33405-1085.
407/655-3791.

Galan Cueto Enterprises
3505 NW 107th St, Miami
FL 33167-3716. 305/688-
4286.

**Grantham Distributing
Company**
2685 Hansrob Rd, Orlando
FL 32804-3317. 407/299-
6446.

Pepin Distributing Co.
6401 N 54th St, Tampa FL
33610-4014. 813/626-
6176.

Wayne Densch
75 W Holden Ave, Orlando
FL 32839-2099. 407/851-
7100.

Anthony Distributors
201 S Caesar St, Tampa FL
33602-5511. 813/224-
0438.

Double Eagle Distributing
50 Lock Rd, Deerfield Beach
FL 33442-1513. 954/426-
2970.

Schenck Company
4161 N John Young Pkwy,
Orlando FL 32804-2717.
407/298-2424.

N Goldring Corp.
675 S Pace Blvd, Pensacola
FL 32501-5026. 904/438-
4053.

National Distributing Co.
4901 Savarese Circle,
Tampa FL 33634-2413.
813/855-3200.

National Distributing Co.
9423 N Main St,
Jacksonville FL 32218-5749.
904/751-0090.

Premier Beverage
216 Kelsey Ln, Tampa FL
33619-4300. 813/623-
6161.

Carbo Distributors
5210 16th Ave S, Tampa FL
33619-5385. 941/366-
2104.

FARM SUPPLIES
WHOLESALE

Lesco Service Center
300 Sunshine Rd, West Palm
Beach FL 33411-3616.
407/791-9971.

Lesco Service Center
2940 NW Commerce Park
Dr, Boynton Beach FL
33426-8773. 407/588-
0394.

Lesco Service Center
1805 6th Avenue North
Annex, Lake Worth FL
33461-3815. 407/582-
4488.

Lesco Service Center
5039 Tampa West Blvd,
Tampa FL 33634-2414.
813/887-5055.

FLOWERS AND FLORAL
PRODUCTS WHOLESALE

Carlstedt's Wholesale Florist
410 27th St, Orlando FL
32806-4451. 407/849-
0970.

Floramor USA
2980 NW 74th Ave, Miami
FL 33122-1426. 305/594-
9077.

Nordlie-Tampa Bay
1421 Massaro Blvd, Tampa
FL 33619-3005. 813/626-
0599.

Oscar G Carlstedt Co.
3116 N Florida Ave, Tampa
FL 33603. 813/224-9731.

Oglesby Plant Laboratory
3714 SW 52nd Ave,
Hollywood FL 33023-6915.
954/983-2970.

**For more information on career opportunities in the food and beverage, and agriculture
industries:**

Associations

**AMERICAN ASSOCIATION OF CEREAL
CHEMISTS (AACC)**
3340 Pilot Knob Road, St. Paul MN 55121.
612/454-7250. Contact: Marla Meyers.
Dedicated to the dissemination of technical
information and continuing education in
cereal science.

AMERICAN FROZEN FOOD INSTITUTE
1764 Old Meadow Lane, Suite 350.
McLean VA 22102. 703/821-0770.
National trade association representing the
interests of the frozen food industry.

AMERICAN SOCIETY OF AGRICULTURAL ENGINEERS
2950 Niles Road, St. Joseph MI 49085. 616/429-0300. Contact: Julie Swim.

AMERICAN SOCIETY OF BREWING CHEMISTS ASSOCIATION
3340 Pilot Knob Road, St. Paul MN 55121. 612/454-7250. Founded in 1934 to improve and bring uniformity to the brewing industry on a technical level.

CIES - THE FOOD BUSINESS FORUM
3800 Moore Plaza, Alexandria VA 22305. 703/549-4525. A global food business network. Membership is on a company basis. Members learn how to manage their businesses more effectively and gain access to information and contacts.

DAIRY AND FOOD INDUSTRIES SUPPLY ASSOCIATION (DFISA)
1451 Dolley Madison Boulevard, McLean VA 22101-3850. 703/761-2600. Contact: Dorothy Brady. A trade association whose members are suppliers to the food, dairy, liquid processing, and related industries.

MASTER BREWERS ASSOCIATION OF THE AMERICAS (MBAA)
2421 North Mayfair Road, Suite 310, Wauwatosa, WI 53226. 414/774-8558. Promotes, advances, improves, and protects the professional interests of brew and malt house production and technical personnel. Disseminates technical and practical information.

NATIONAL AGRICULTURAL CHEMICALS ASSOCIATION
1156 15th Street NW, Suite 900, Washington DC 20005. 202/296-1585.

NATIONAL BEER WHOLESALERS' ASSOCIATION
1100 South Washington Street, Alexandria VA 22314-4494. 703/683-4300. Fax: 703/683-8965. Contact: Karen Craig.

NATIONAL FOOD PROCESSORS ASSOCIATION
1401 New York Avenue NW, Suite 400, Washington DC 20005. 202/639-5900. Contact: Ned Endler.

NATIONAL SOFT DRINK ASSOCIATION
1101 16th Street NW, Washington DC 20036. 202/463-6732.
UNITED DAIRY INDUSTRY ASSOCIATION (UDIA)
10255 West Higgins Road, Suite 900, Rosemont IL 60018. 708/803-2000. A federation of state and regional dairy promotion organizations that develop and execute effective programs to increase consumer demand for U.S.-produced milk and dairy products.

Directories

FOOD ENGINEERING'S DIRECTORY OF U.S. FOOD PLANTS
Chilton Book Company, Chilton Way, Radnor PA 19089. 800/695-1214.

THOMAS FOOD INDUSTRY REGISTER
Thomas Publishing Company, Five Penn Plaza, New York NY 10001. 212/695-0500.

Magazines

BEVERAGE WORLD
Keller International Publishing Corporation. 150 Great Neck Road, Great Neck NY 11021. 516/829-9210.

FOOD PROCESSING
301 East Erie Street, Chicago IL 60611. 312/644-2020.

FROZEN FOOD AGE
Maclean Hunter Media, #4 Stamford Forum, Stamford CT 06901. 203/325-3500.

PREPARED FOODS
Gorman Publishing Company, 8750 West Bryn Mawr, Chicago IL 60631. 312/693-3200.

GOVERNMENT

Local government is projected to be the fastest-growing government sector in Florida, in 1996 and beyond. In 1995 alone, 19,600 of the 22,000 government jobs added were in the local sector. According to the state's Bureau of Labor Market Information, this trend will continue -- more than 75 percent of new government jobs will be added in that sector with strong growth in education. Of the 220,000 jobs that Florida expects to add to its workforce between 1992 and 2005, nearly 170,000 of those positions will be with the local government.

The outlook for the state and federal sectors in Florida is less than encouraging. As a result of cutbacks by the Department of Defense, federal and state jobs in the Sunshine State declined in 1995, resulting in a direct loss of over 3,000 jobs. Jobseekers should note that although the government sector has experienced declines on the federal and state levels, the Bureau of Labor Market Information still expects an addition of 50,000 state jobs and 2,400 federal jobs by the year 2005.

BROWARD COUNTY
115 South Andrews Avenue, Fort Lauderdale FL 33301. 954/357-7585. **Recorded Jobline:** 954/357-6450. **Contact:** Human Resources. **Description:** Provides county services such as sheriffs, courts, motor vehicle registration, and social services.

COASTAL SYSTEMS STATION
Human Resources Office Code PC90, 6703 West Highway 98, Panama City FL 32407-7001. 904/235-5554. **Contact:** Ms. Deborah Weaver, Personnel Staffing Specialist. **Description:** The Navy's principal research and development laboratory.

DADE COUNTY
CENTER FOR EMPLOYMENT
140 West Flagler Street, Suite 105, Miami FL 33130. **Recorded Jobline:** 305/375-1871. **Contact:** Personnel Recruitment. **Description:** Provides county government services.

DADE COUNTY FIRE DEPARTMENT
6000 SW 87th Avenue, Miami FL 33173. 305/596-8591. **Recorded Jobline:** 305/596-8645. **Contact:** Human Resources. **Description:** Provides firefighting services for Dade County.

FLORIDA DEPARTMENT OF AGRICULTURE AND CONSUMER SERVICES
408 Mayo Building, Tallahassee FL 32399-0800. 904/487-2785. **Recorded Jobline:** 904/487-2474. **Contact:** Human Resources. **Description:** Provides agricultural and consumer services.

FLORIDA DEPARTMENT OF COMMERCE
408 Collins Building, Tallahassee FL 32399-2000. 904/487-2431. **Recorded Jobline:** 904/488-0869. **Contact:** Human Resources. **Description:** Provides state commerce programs and services.

FLORIDA DEPARTMENT OF COMMUNITY AFFAIRS
152 Rhyne Building, 2740 Centerview Drive, Tallahassee FL 32399-2100. 904/487-4627. **Recorded Jobline:** 904/488-4776. **Contact:** Human Resources. **Description:** Provides community services.

FLORIDA DEPARTMENT OF CORRECTIONS
Region 1, 4610 Highway 90 East, Marianna FL 32446. 904/482-9533. **Recorded Jobline:** 904/482-3531. **Contact:** Human Resources. **Description:** Provides correctional services.

FLORIDA DEPARTMENT OF CORRECTIONS
Region 3, 400 West Robinson Street, Suite N-909, Orlando FL 32801. 407/423-6125. **Recorded Jobline:** 407/423-6600. **Contact:** Human Resources. **Description:** Provides correctional services.

FLORIDA DEPARTMENT OF CORRECTIONS
Region 5, 5422 West Bay Center Drive, Tampa FL 33609. 813/554-2300. **Fax:** 813/873-4899. **Recorded Jobline:** 813/871-7142. **Contact:** Robert J. Hinson, Regional Personnel Officer. **Description:** Provides correctional services and programs. **Common positions include:** Accountant/Auditor; Human Resources Specialist; Licensed Practical Nurse; Medical Record Technician; Physician; Psychologist; Purchasing Agent and Manager; Registered Nurse; Teacher. **Educational backgrounds include:** Accounting; Business Administration; Health Care. **Benefits:** Dental Insurance; Disability Coverage; Employee Discounts; Life Insurance; Medical Insurance; Savings Plan; Tuition Assistance. **Special Programs:** Internships. **Corporate headquarters location:** Tallahassee FL. **Operations at this facility include:** Administration; Regional Headquarters.

FLORIDA DEPARTMENT OF EDUCATION
101 Florida Education Center, 325 West Gaines Street, Tallahassee FL 32399-0400. 904/488-8652. **Recorded Jobline:** 904/487-2367. **Contact:** Human Resources. **Description:** Provides educational services and programs to the state of Florida.

FLORIDA DEPARTMENT OF ENVIRONMENTAL PROTECTION
353 Douglas Building, 3900 Commonwealth Building, Tallahassee FL 32399-3000. 904/488-0450. **Recorded Jobline:** 904/487-0436. **Contact:** Human Resources. **Description:** Provides environmental protection programs for the state of Florida.

FLORIDA DEPARTMENT OF HEALTH AND REHABILITATIVE SERVICES
223 Building D, Winewood Office Complex, 1317 Winewood Boulevard, Tallahassee FL 32399-0700. 904/488-2840. **Recorded Jobline:** 904/488-2255. **Contact:** Human Resources. **Description:** Provides health and rehabilitative programs and services for the state of Florida. **Corporate headquarters location:** This Location.

FLORIDA DEPARTMENT OF HEALTH AND REHABILITATIVE SERVICES
P.O. Box 8420, 160 Governmental Center, Pensacola FL 32505-2949. 904/444-8180. **Recorded Jobline:** 904/444-8037. **Contact:** Human Resources. **Description:** Provides health and rehabilitative programs and services for the state of Florida.

FLORIDA DEPARTMENT OF HEALTH AND REHABILITATIVE SERVICES
170-Cedars Executive Center, 2739 North Monroe Street, Tallahassee FL 32399-2949. 904/487-2800. **Recorded Jobline:** 904/488-0831. **Contact:** Human Resources. **Description:** Provides health and rehabilitative services and programs for the state of Florida. Corporate headquarters is located at 223 Building D, Winewood Office Complex, 1317 Winewood Boulevard, Tallahassee FL 32399-0700.

FLORIDA DEPARTMENT OF HEALTH AND REHABILITATIVE SERVICES
P.O. Box 62, Gainesville FL 32601. 352/955-5074. **Recorded Jobline:** 352/955-5190. **Contact:** Human Resources. **Description:** Provides health and rehabilitative services and programs for the state of Florida. **Corporate headquarters location:** Tallahassee FL.

FLORIDA DEPARTMENT OF HEALTH AND REHABILITATIVE SERVICES
5920 Arlington Expressway, Jacksonville FL 32211. 904/723-2177. **Recorded Jobline:** 904/723-2024. **Contact:** Human Resources. **Description:** Provides health and rehabilitative services and programs for the state of Florida. **Corporate headquarters location:** Tallahassee FL.

FLORIDA DEPARTMENT OF HEALTH AND REHABILITATIVE SERVICES
11351 Ulmerton Road, Largo FL 34648. 813/588-6630. **Recorded Jobline:** 813/588-6628. **Contact:** Human Resources. **Description:** Provides health and rehabilitative services and programs for the state of Florida. **Corporate headquarters location:** Tallahassee FL.

FLORIDA DEPARTMENT OF HEALTH AND REHABILITATIVE SERVICES
111 Georgia Avenue, Suite 104, West Palm Beach FL 33401. 407/837-5091. **Recorded Jobline:** 407/467-4279. **Contact:** Human Resources. **Description:** Provides health and rehabilitative services and programs for the residents of Florida. **Corporate headquarters location:** Tallahassee FL.

FLORIDA DEPARTMENT OF HEALTH AND REHABILITATIVE SERVICES
201 West Broward Boulevard, Fort Lauderdale FL 33301-1885. 954/467-4240. **Fax:** 954/468-2742. **Recorded Jobline:** 954/467-4279. **Contact:** C.B. Durrett, Senior Personnel Manager. **Description:** Provides health and rehabilitative services and programs for the state of Florida. **Common positions include:** Accountant/Auditor; Administrative Services Manager; Attorney; Budget Analyst; Buyer; Civil Engineer; Clerical Supervisor; Clinical Lab Technician; Computer Programmer; Computer Systems Analyst; Construction Contractor and Manager; Cost Estimator; Counselor; Dental Assistant/Dental Hygienist; Dental Lab Technician; Dentist; Dietician/Nutritionist; Environmental Engineer; General Manager; Health Services Manager; Human Resources Specialist; Human Service Worker; Librarian; Library Technician; Management Analyst/Consultant; Management Trainee; Medical Record Technician; Occupational Therapist; Paralegal; Pharmacist; Physician; Property and Real Estate Manager; Psychologist; Purchasing Agent and Manager; Radiologic Technologist; Recreational Therapist; Registered Nurse; Respiratory Therapist; Social Worker; Teacher; Technical Writer/Editor. **Educational backgrounds include:** Accounting; Business Administration; Computer Science; Health Care; Liberal Arts; Social Work. **Corporate headquarters location:** Tallahassee FL. **Number of employees at this location:** 3,000.

FLORIDA DEPARTMENT OF INSURANCE
200 Gaines Street, Tallahassee FL 32399-0525. 904/922-3182. **Recorded Jobline:** 904/487-2644. **Contact:** Human Resources. **Description:** Regulates insurance for the state.

FLORIDA DEPARTMENT OF LAW ENFORCEMENT
P.O. Box 1489, Tallahassee FL 32302. 904/488-4814. **Recorded Jobline:** 904/488-0797. **Contact:** Human Resources. **Description:** Provides law enforcement services and programs for the state of Florida.

FLORIDA DEPARTMENT OF MANAGEMENT SERVICES
Koger Executive Center, 2737 Centerview Drive, Suite 114, Knight Building, Tallahassee FL 32399-0950. 904/488-2707. **Recorded Jobline:** 904/487-3988. **Contact:** Human Resources. **Description:** Provides management services for the state of Florida.

FLORIDA DEPARTMENT OF REVENUE
118 Carlton Building, 501 South Calhoun Street, Tallahassee FL 32399-0100. 904/488-6800. **Recorded Jobline:** 904/488-3895. **Contact:** Human . Resources. **Description:** Compiles and calculates state income taxes and other related state revenues.

FLORIDA DEPARTMENT OF STATE
1902 Capitol Building, Tallahassee FL 32399-0252. 904/488-1177. **Recorded Jobline:** 904/488-1179. **Contact:** Human Resources. **Description:** Manages elections, library services, cultural affairs, corporate filings, and other functions.

FLORIDA DEPARTMENT OF STATE
DIVISION OF LIBRARY AND INFORMATION SERVICES
500 South Bronough Street, Tallahassee FL 32399-0252. 904/487-2651. **Recorded Jobline:** 904/488-5232. **Contact:** Human Resources. **Description:** Provides information and library services and programs.

FLORIDA DEPARTMENT OF TRANSPORTATION
605 Suwannee Street, Mail Stop #50, Tallahassee FL 32399-0450. 904/488-6816. **Fax:** 904/922-3867. **Recorded Jobline:** 904/922-9867. **Contact:** Walter R. Mitchell, Employment Manager. **Description:** The Florida Department of Transportation is the state agency responsible for developing and maintaining the state's transportation systems. **Common positions include:** Accountant/Auditor; Administrative Services Manager; Attorney; Budget Analyst; Civil Engineer; Clerical Supervisor; Computer Programmer; Computer Systems Analyst; Draftsperson; Electrician; Environmental Engineer; Human Resources Specialist; Landscape Architect; Management

Analyst/Consultant; Management Trainee; Materials Engineer; Paralegal; Property and Real Estate Manager; Public Relations Specialist; Purchasing Agent and Manager; Structural Engineer; Surveyor; Transportation/Traffic Specialist. **Educational backgrounds include:** Accounting; Business Administration; Computer Science; Engineering; Finance; Geology. **Benefits:** Dental Insurance; Disability Coverage; Life Insurance; Medical Insurance; Tuition Assistance. **Corporate headquarters location:** This Location. **Operations at this facility include:** Administration. **Number of employees at this location:** 2,000. **Number of employees nationwide:** 10,000.

FLORIDA GAME AND FRESHWATER FISH COMMISSION
138 Farris Bryant Building, 620 South Meridian Street, Tallahassee FL 32399-1600. 904/488-6411. **Recorded Jobline:** 904/488-5805. **Contact:** Mona L. Pearson, Recruitment and Training Specialist. **Description:** Manages and conserves game and freshwater fish resources. **Common positions include:** Police/Law Enforcement Officer; Science Technologist. **Educational backgrounds include:** Biology; Criminal Justice. **Benefits:** Dental Insurance; Disability Coverage; Employee Discounts; Life Insurance; Medical Insurance; Pension Plan; Tuition Assistance. **Corporate headquarters location:** This Location. **Operations at this facility include:** Administration; Divisional Headquarters; Research and Development. **Number of employees at this location:** 180. **Number of employees statewide:** 900.

FLORIDA STATE COURT SYSTEM
Supreme Court Building, 500 South Duval Street, Tallahassee FL 32399-1900. 904/487-0778. **Recorded Jobline:** 904/488-2556. **Contact:** Human Resources. **Description:** Provides judicial services.

FLORIDA STATE LOTTERY
250 Marriott Drive, Tallahassee FL 32301. 904/487-7721. **Recorded Jobline:** 904/487-7731. **Contact:** Human Resources. **Description:** Provides lottery programs and services.

HOLLYWOOD, CITY OF
2600 Hollywood Boulevard, Room 215, Hollywood FL 33020. 954/921-3216. **Fax:** 954/921-3487. **Recorded Jobline:** 954/921-3292. **Contact:** Human Resources. **Description:** Provides municipal services.

JACKSONVILLE, CITY OF
220 East Bay Street, Room 113, Jacksonville FL 32202. 904/630-3069. **Recorded Jobline:** 904/630-3095. **Contact:** Human Resources. **Description:** Provides municipal services.

JACKSONVILLE PORT AUTHORITY
P.O. Box 3005, Jacksonville FL 32206. 904/630-3069. **Fax:** 904/630-3076. **Recorded Jobline:** 904/630-3095. **Contact:** Manager of Human Resources. **Description:** Manages the port of Jacksonville's commercial activities, including the operation of the Blount Island and Talleyrand Docks Marine Terminals, as well as the Jacksonville International Airport and two General Aviation Airports. **Common positions include:** Accountant/Auditor; Automotive Mechanic/Body Repairer; Cargo Handler. **Educational backgrounds include:** Accounting; Business Administration. **Benefits:** Dental Insurance; Disability Coverage; Life Insurance; Medical Insurance; Pension Plan; Tuition Assistance. **Corporate headquarters location:** This Location. **Operations at this facility include:** Administration; Sales; Service. **Number of employees at this location:** 350.

LEON COUNTY
BOARD OF COUNTY COMMISSIONERS
301 South Monroe Street, Suite 108, Tallahassee FL 32301. 904/487-2220. **Fax:** 904/488-6293. **Recorded Jobline:** 904/922-4944. **Contact:** Human Resources. **Description:** Provides county government services. **Educational backgrounds include:** Business Administration. **Benefits:** Dental Insurance; Disability Coverage; Employee Discounts; Life Insurance; Medical Insurance; Tuition Assistance. **Special Programs:** Internships. **Operations at this facility include:** Administration. **Number of employees at this location:** 600.

MIAMI, CITY OF
300 Biscayne Boulevard, 2nd Floor, Miami FL 33131. 305/579-2411. **Recorded Jobline:** 305/579-2400. **Contact:** Human Resources. **Description:** Provides municipal services.

MONROE COUNTY
5100 West College Road, Room 204, Wing 2, Key West FL 33040. 305/292-4557.
Contact: Human Resources. **Description:** Provides county government services.

NORTH MIAMI, CITY OF
776 NE 125th Street, North Miami FL 33161. 305/893-6511. **Recorded Jobline:**
305/895-8095. **Contact:** Human Resources. **Description:** Provides municipal services.

NORTH MIAMI BEACH, CITY OF
17011 NE 19th Avenue, North Miami Beach FL 33162. 305/948-2918. **Recorded
Jobline:** 305/947-7581x37. **Contact:** Human Resources. **Description:** Provides
municipal services.

PEMBROKE PINES, CITY OF
10100 Pine Boulevard, Pembroke Pines FL 33026. 954/431-4566. **Recorded Jobline:**
954/437-1108. **Contact:** Human Resources. **Description:** Provides municipal services.

PINELLAS PARK, CITY OF
5141 78th Avenue North, Pinellas Park FL 34665. 813/541-0803. **Recorded Jobline:**
813/541-0703. **Contact:** Human Resources. **Description:** Provides municipal services.

ST. PETERSBURG, CITY OF
175 5th Street North, Room 107, St. Petersburg FL 33701. 813/898-7171. **Fax:**
813/893-7712. **Recorded Jobline:** 813/893-7033. **Contact:** Employment Office.
Description: Provides municipal services.

TALLAHASSEE, CITY OF
300 South Adams Street, Tallahassee FL 32301. 904/891-8219. **Recorded Jobline:**
904/891-8219. **Contact:** Human Resources. **Description:** Provides municipal services.

UNITED STATES POSTAL SERVICE
5201 West Spruce Street, Sectional Center, Tampa FL 33630. 813/877-0746.
Contact: Personnel Department. **Description:** Tampa's postal service.

For more information about career opportunities in the government:

Directories

ACCESS...FCO ON-LINE
Federal Research Service, Inc., P.O. Box 1059,
243 Church Street, Vienna VA 22183-1059.
703/281-0200. This is the online service of
the *Federal Career Opportunities* publication.
To join online, the cost is $25 for the set-up
and $45 for one hour, payable by credit card
over the phone.

HEALTH CARE: SERVICES, EQUIPMENT AND PRODUCTS

With no time to worry about the failure of government-proposed health care reforms, the health care industry is surging ahead with its own solutions, pressured by a competitive marketplace to cut costs. HMOs and insurance providers are looking to nursing homes and home care companies as an alternative to long-term hospital stays, and shifting from inpatient to less expensive outpatient care. Hospitals are streamlining operations and consolidating, with cutback efforts targeting staff, as well as unnecessary tests and laboratory fees. Hospital cost-cutting has also hurt medical equipment suppliers, as many hospitals form networks to share expensive equipment.

Even so, from 1990 to 1995, the number of health care workers in the United States grew from 8.86 million 10.5 million. Despite pressure to cut back, the health care industry remains a growth area. As the elderly population continues to grow faster than the population as a whole and the survival rate of the severely ill continues to improve, the need for new workers will continue to increase, and the large employment base will create replacement needs.

ALTHIN MEDICAL, INC.
14620 North West 60th Avenue, Miami Lakes FL 33014-2811. 305/823-5240. **Contact:** Ms. Araceli Harrison, Senior Human Resources Administrator. **Description:** A multinational medical device manufacturer and distributor of medical products. **Common positions include:** Accountant/Auditor; Biomedical Engineer; Blue-Collar Worker Supervisor; Buyer; Chemical Engineer; Chemist; Computer Programmer; Credit Manager; Customer Service Representative; Human Resources Specialist; Marketing Specialist; Mechanical Engineer; Operations/Production Manager; Purchasing Agent and Manager; Quality Control Supervisor; Systems Analyst. **Educational backgrounds include:** Accounting; Biology; Business Administration; Chemistry; Computer Science; Engineering; Marketing. **Benefits:** Dental Insurance; Disability Coverage; Employee Discounts; Life Insurance; Medical Insurance; Profit Sharing; Savings Plan; Tuition Assistance. **Corporate headquarters location:** This Location. **Other U.S. locations:** Portland OR. **Operations at this facility include:** Administration; Manufacturing; Research and Development; Sales. **Number of employees at this location:** 250.

BAPTIST HOSPITAL OF MIAMI
8900 North Kendall Drive, Miami FL 33176. 305/596-1960. **Fax:** 305/598-5999. **Contact:** Human Resources. **Description:** Not-for-profit hospital with more than 400 beds.

BAPTIST MEDICAL CENTER
800 Prudential Drive, Jacksonville FL 32207. 904/393-2000. **Contact:** Human Resources. **Description:** A medical center.

BAUSCH & LOMB
2040 Whitfield Avenue, Sarasota FL 34243. 941/756-5521. **Contact:** Terry Kibler, Personnel Director. **Description:** A regional office of the eyewear company. Bausch & Lomb competes in selected segments of global health care and optical markets. The Healthcare Segment consists of three sectors: Personal Health, Medical, and Biomedical. The Personal Health Sector is comprised of branded products purchased directly by consumers in health and beauty aid sections of pharmacies, food stores and mass merchandise outlets. Products include lens care solutions; oral care, eye

care, and skin care products; and nonprescription medications. The Medical Sector consists of contact lenses, ophthalmic pharmaceuticals, hearing aids, dental implants and other products sold to health care professionals, or which are obtained by consumers only through a prescription. The Biomedical Sector includes products and services supplied to customers engaged in the research and development of pharmaceuticals and the production of genetically engineered materials. These include purpose-bred research animals, bioprocessing services and products derived from specific pathogen-free eggs. The Optics Segment consists primarily of premium-priced sunglasses sold under such internationally recognized brand names as Ray-Ban and Revo. Manufacturing or marketing organizations have been established in 34 countries, and the company's products are distributed in more than 70 other nations. **Number of employees worldwide:**14,400.

BAUSCH & LOMB PHARMACEUTICALS, INC.
8500 Hidden River Parkway, Tampa FL 33637. 813/975-7700. **Fax:** 813/572-1064. **Contact:** Human Resources. **Description:** Bausch and Lomb Pharmaceuticals, Inc. makes contact lenses and related solutions and accessories, ophthalmic drugs, dental plaque removal devices, and optical items. Health care products include personal health, medical, and biomedical products. Personal health items consist of solutions used for the care of contact lenses and relief of eye irritation sold under Sensitive Eyes, ReNu, and other names; contact lenses accessories; over-the-counter drugs; and oral care products, which include the Interplank line of home plaque removal devices, Interjet oral irrigator, and Clear Choice alcohol-free mouthwash. Medical products include contact lenses and lens material, prescription pharmaceuticals, periodontal diagnostic items and hearing aids. Therapeutic skin care products are also sold. A vision care service plan and other contact lens service programs are also offered.

BAYFRONT MEDICAL CENTER
701 6th Street S, St. Petersburg FL 33701. 813/823-1234. **Contact:** Human Resources. **Description:** A hospital.

BON SECOURS-ST. JOSEPH HOSPITAL
2500 Harbor Boulevard, Port Charlotte FL 33952. 941/624-7638. **Fax:** 941/624-7697. **Recorded Jobline:** 941/764-2006. **Contact:** Cyndi Ingala, Employment Specialist. **Description:** A JCAHO-accredited 212-bed acute care facility with an affiliated 104-bed long-term care facility located on the gulf coast of southwestern Florida. Bon Secours is part of the Bon Secours Health System. **Common positions include:** Computer Systems Analyst; Licensed Practical Nurse; Medical Record Technician; Nuclear Engineer; Nuclear Medicine Technologist; Pharmacist; Radiologic Technologist; Registered Nurse; Respiratory Therapist; Surgical Technician. **Educational backgrounds include:** Business Administration; Computer Science; Nursing. **Benefits:** Daycare Assistance; Dental Insurance; Disability Coverage; Employee Discounts; Life Insurance; Medical Insurance; Pension Plan; Tuition Assistance. **Special Programs:** Internships. **Corporate headquarters location:** Mariottsville MD. **Other U.S. locations:** Miami FL; St. Petersburg FL; St. Clair Shores MI; Charlotte SC; Richmond VA. **Operations at this facility include:** Administration; Service. **Number of employees at this location:** 1,000.

CHARLOTTE REGIONAL MEDICAL CENTER
809 East Marion Avenue, Punta Gorda FL 33950. 941/637-2552. **Fax:** 941/637-2469. **Recorded Jobline:** 941/637-3166. **Contact:** Jean Juchnowicz, Director of Human Resources. **Description:** Charlotte Regional Medical Center (CRMC) is a 208-bed, private acute care hospital with specialized services including the following: cardiac care, a sports medicine and wellness program (physical fitness, aerobics, and aquatic programs and rehabilitative services), a behavioral center (mental health and addictions treatment), sleep disorder programs, a pulmonary rehabilitation program (breathing disorder treatment), home health services, occupational medicine (offered through an outpatient clinic in North Port), an emergency department, an ambulatory care center, a critical care recovery unit (recovery from open heart surgery), a diabetes center, and a lifeline emergency response system. The parent company, Health Management Associates, Inc., operates 21 hospitals in 11 states across the Southeast, focusing on acquiring underperforming community health care facilities with turn-around potential. **Common positions include:** Accountant/Auditor; Adjuster; Administrative Services Manager; Blue-Collar Worker Supervisor; Buyer; Clerical Supervisor; Clinical Lab Technician; Compliance Analyst; Computer Programmer; Counselor; Dietician/Nutritionist; Education Administrator; EEG Technologist; EKG Technician; Electrician; Emergency Medical Technician; Financial Analyst; Food Scientist/Technologist; Health Services Manager; Human Resources Specialist;

Licensed Practical Nurse; Management Analyst/Consultant; Management Trainee; Medical Record Technician; Nuclear Engineer; Occupational Therapist; Pharmacist; Physical Therapist; Physician; Psychologist; Public Relations Specialist; Purchasing Agent and Manager; Quality Control Supervisor; Radiologic Technologist; Recreational Therapist; Registered Nurse; Respiratory Therapist; Services Sales Representative; Social Worker; Speech-Language Pathologist; Surgical Technician. **Benefits:** 401K; Daycare Assistance; Dental Insurance; Disability Coverage; Employee Discounts; Life Insurance; Medical Insurance; Pension Plan; Profit Sharing; Savings Plan; Tuition Assistance. **Special Programs:** Internships. **Corporate headquarters location:** Naples FL. **Parent company:** Health Management Associates, Inc. **Operations at this facility include:** Administration; Service. **Listed on:** New York Stock Exchange. **Number of employees at this location:** 818.

CORAL SPRINGS MEDICAL CENTER
3000 Coral Hills Drive, Coral Springs FL 33065. 954/344-3000. **Contact:** Human Resources. **Description:** A medical center serving Coral Springs, Tamarac, Parkland, Margate, and other surrounding cities.

CORDIS CORPORATION
14201 North West 60th Avenue, Miami Lakes FL 33014. 305/824-2000. **Contact:** Recruiting Representative. **Description:** Cordis Corporation is a producer of medical devices including anglographics and neuro products. The company also acts as a supplier for hospitals and physicians. **Common positions include:** Administrator; Biomedical Engineer; Blue-Collar Worker Supervisor; Buyer; Chemical Engineer; Customer Service Representative; Financial Analyst; Industrial Engineer; Marketing Specialist; Mechanical Engineer; Operations/Production Manager; Production Manager; Quality Control Supervisor; Sales Representative; Technical Writer/Editor. **Educational backgrounds include:** Engineering. **Benefits:** Medical Insurance. **Number of employees nationwide:** 3,370.

COULTER CORPORATION
11800 Southwest 147th Avenue, MC/31-1302, Miami FL 33196. 305/380-3215. **Fax:** 305/380-3689. **Contact:** Jack S. Greenblott, Principal Staffing Representative. **Description:** Suppliers of blood cell counters and assorted instrumentation, serving hospitals, clinics, and physicians' offices. **Common positions include:** Accountant/Auditor; Biological Scientist/Biochemist; Computer Programmer; Computer Systems Analyst; Designer; Electrical/Electronics Engineer; Financial Analyst; Software Engineer; Technical Writer/Editor. **Educational backgrounds include:** Accounting; Biology; Computer Science; Engineering; Finance. **Benefits:** 401K; Dental Insurance; Disability Coverage; Life Insurance; Medical Insurance; Pension Plan; Savings Plan; Tuition Assistance. **Corporate headquarters location:** This Location. **Operations at this facility include:** Administration; Manufacturing; Regional Headquarters; Research and Development; Sales; Service. **Listed on:** Privately held. **Number of employees at this location:** 3,500.

DADE INTERNATIONAL INC.
P.O. Box 520672, Miami FL 33152. 305/592-2311. **Contact:** Human Resources. **Description:** Manufacturers of diagnostic reagents, controls, instrument systems, and labware, which serves the clinical laboratory market worldwide. **Common positions include:** Accountant/Auditor; Biological Scientist/Biochemist; Blue-Collar Worker Supervisor; Buyer; Chemical Engineer; Chemist; Computer Programmer; Customer Service Representative; Draftsperson; Electrical/Electronics Engineer; Industrial Engineer; Mechanical Engineer. **Educational backgrounds include:** Accounting; Biochemistry; Business Administration; Chemistry; Computer Science; Engineering; Medical Technology. **Benefits:** Dental Insurance; Disability Coverage; Life Insurance; Medical Insurance; Pension Plan; Savings Plan; Stock Option; Tuition Assistance. **Corporate headquarters location:** Deerfield IL. **Parent company:** Baxter Travenol Labs. **Operations at this facility include:** Divisional Headquarters; Manufacturing; Research and Development. **Listed on:** New York Stock Exchange.

DAYTONA MEDICAL CENTER
P.O. Box 9000, Daytona Beach FL 32120. 904/239-5018. **Fax:** 904/239-5025. **Contact:** Susan Castello, R.N., Professional Recruiter. **Description:** Daytona Medical Center is a 214-bed JCAHO-accredited general acute care hospital. **Corporate headquarters location:** Nashville TN. **Parent company:** Columbia/HCA Healthcare Corporation. **Number of employees at this location:** 530. **Number of employees nationwide:** 310,000.

ESSILOR OF AMERICA
MANUFACTURING DIVISION
4900 Park Street N, St. Petersburg FL 33709-2228. 813/541-5733. **Contact:** Human Resources. **Description:** A manufacturer of optical lenses.

FLORIDA AGENCY FOR HEALTH CARE ADMINISTRATION
Ft. Knox Building 1, 2727 Mahan Drive, Tallahassee FL 32308. 904/922-8435. **Recorded Jobline:** 904/488-8356. **Contact:** Human Resources. **Description:** Provides access to affordable health care services.

FLORIDA HOSPITAL MEDICAL CENTER
601 East Rollins Street, Orlando FL 32803. 407/896-6611. **Recorded Jobline:** 407/331-8000x6125. **Contact:** Human Resources. **Description:** A non-profit 1,200 bed hospital.

FLORIDA STATE HOSPITAL
P.O. Box 1000, Chattahoochee FL 32324-1000. 904/663-7258. **Contact:** Tom Carpenter, Recruitment Coordinator. **Description:** Florida State Hospital is a mental health institution that rehabilitates persons with mental illnesses, and with persons with other mental and addictive illnesses. **Common positions include:** Accountant/Auditor; Computer Programmer; Counselor; Dental Assistant/Dental Hygienist; Dentist; Dietician/Nutritionist; Electrical/Electronics Engineer; Electrician; Food Scientist/Technologist; Human Resources Specialist; Human Service Worker; Landscape Architect; Librarian; Library Technician; Licensed Practical Nurse; Medical Record Technician; Occupational Therapist; Paralegal; Pharmacist; Physical Therapist; Physician; Psychologist; Quality Control Supervisor; Recreational Therapist; Registered Nurse; Respiratory Therapist; Restaurant/Food Service Manager; Social Worker; Teacher; Transportation/Traffic Specialist. **Educational backgrounds include:** Accounting; Biology; Computer Science; Engineering; Finance; Nursing. **Benefits:** Daycare Assistance; Dental Insurance; Disability Coverage; Life Insurance; Medical Insurance; Pension Plan; Tuition Assistance. **Special Programs:** Internships. **Corporate headquarters location:** Tallahassee FL. **Parent company:** State of Florida. **Operations at this facility include:** Administration; Regional Headquarters. **Number of employees at this location:** 3,000.

W.R. GRACE & COMPANY
One Town Center Road, Boca Raton FL 33486. 407/362-2000. **Fax:** 407/362-2306. **Contact:** Terry Fleites, Manager of Staff Support. **Description:** W.R. Grace is a provider of specialized health care products, as well as one of the largest producers of specialty chemicals. The major divisions of W.R. Grace include Grace Health Care, Grace Packaging, Grace Davison, Grace Construction Products, Grace Dearborn, and Grace Container & Specialty Polymers. Through its subsidiary National Medical Care, Grace Health Care is involved in the specialized health care markets of dialysis services, medical products, and home health care. Grace Packaging specializes in flexible packaging systems for meat, poultry, cheese, and other perishable food products, as well as shrink packaging materials for consumer and industrial products. Grace Davison catalysts 'crack' crude oil into fuel and related by-products. Davison polyolefin catalysts are involved in polyethylene production, and its silica and zeolite adsorbents are ingredients in industrial and consumer applications. Grace Construction products include concrete and cement additives, fireproofing, and waterproofing systems which protect structures from nature by strengthening concrete, fighting corrosion, stopping water damage, and protecting structural steel from fire damage. Grace Dearborn water treatment and process chemicals inhibit scale, corrosion, and fouling in water systems, treat wastewater, and enhance operating efficiency and environmental performance. Grace Container & Specialty Polymers include container sealant systems that keep food and beverages protected from bacteria and other contaminants, extend shelf-life, and preserve flavor, while specialty polymers are used in the manufacture of printed circuit board and electronic components assembly. **Common positions include:** Accountant/Auditor; Attorney; Computer Systems Analyst; Financial Analyst; Human Resources Specialist; Management Analyst/Consultant. **Educational backgrounds include:** Accounting; Business Administration; Finance. **Benefits:** 401K; Dental Insurance; Life Insurance; Medical Insurance; Pension Plan; Tuition Assistance. **Corporate headquarters location:** This Location. **Operations at this facility include:** Administration; Divisional Headquarters. **Listed on:** New York Stock Exchange. **Number of employees at this location:** 440. **Number of employees nationwide:** 34,000.

HCA NORTH FLORIDA REGIONAL MEDICAL CENTER
P.O. Box 147006, Gainesville FL 32614-7006. 352/333-4100. **Contact:** Human Resources. **Description:** A hospital which is part of the Columbia Healthcare System.

HCA TALLAHASSEE COMMUNITY HOSPITAL
2626 Captial Medical Boulevard, Tallahassee FL 32308. 904/656-5000. **Contact:** Human Resources. **Description:** A hospital which is part of the Columbia Healthcare System.

HARBORVIEW HOSPITAL
1861 NW South River Drive, Miami FL 33125. 305/642-3555. **Contact:** Human Resources. **Description:** A hospital.

HEALTH CENTRAL
P.O. Box 614007, Orlando FL 32861. 407/296-1000. **Contact:** Human Resources. **Description:** A medical center.

HEALTH MANAGEMENT ASSOCIATION
5811 Pelican Bay Boulevard, Suite 500, Naples FL 33963. 941/598-3131. **Contact:** Personnel Department. **Description:** Provides a broad range of general acute-care health services to rural communities. Health Management Association also operates psychiatric hospitals. **Number of employees nationwide:** 5,300.

HEALTHINFUSION, INC.
1905 NW 82nd Avenue, Miami FL 33126. 305/267-1177. **Contact:** Human Resources. **Description:** HealthInfusion, Inc. provides home infusion therapy services and supplies to patients in their homes in 26 states, through 32 regional facilities located in Arizona, California, Florida, Georgia, Illinois, Indiana, Maryland, New York, New Jersey, North Carolina, Ohio, Oklahoma, Oregon, Pennsylvania, and Texas. Infusion therapy is the administering of nutrients, antibiotics, or other drugs and fluids to a patient either intravenously or through a feeding tube. Home infusion therapy generally offers cost-savings and quality of life advantages to the patient in comparison with hospital care. Patients are typically referred to the company in connection with their discharge from a hospital, in order to continue at home infusion initiated in the hospital. **Number of employees nationwide:** 287.

HEALTHSOUTH MIAMI HOSPITAL
7031 SW 62nd Avenue, Miami FL 33143. 305/284-7700. **Contact:** Human Resources. **Description:** A hospital.

HOLMES REGIONAL MEDICAL CENTER
1350 South Hickory Street, Melbourne FL 32901. 407/676-7110. **Fax:** 407/722-8587. **Contact:** Monia Yust, Director of Employment. **Description:** A medical center. **Common positions include:** Clinical Lab Technician; EKG Technician; Occupational Therapist; Physical Therapist; Registered Nurse; Respiratory Therapist; Social Worker; Surgical Technician. **Benefits:** Daycare Assistance; Dental Insurance; Disability Coverage; Employee Discounts; Life Insurance; Medical Insurance; Pension Plan; Tuition Assistance. **Corporate headquarters location:** This Location. **Operations at this facility include:** Service. **Number of employees at this location:** 2,800.

INDIAN RIVER MEMORIAL HOSPITAL
1000 36th Street, Vera Beach FL 32960-6592. 407/567-4311. **Contact:** Human Resources. **Description:** A 294-bed facility.

INTERTECH
5100 Tice Street, Fort Meyers FL 33905. 941/694-2104. **Contact:** Fred Harrison, Manager of Human Relations. **Description:** A manufacturer of surgical and medical instruments.

JACKSON MEMORIAL HOSPITAL/PHT
1611 Northwest 12th Avenue, PP West-L-301, Miami FL 33136. 305/585-6081. **Fax:** 305/326-9470. **Recorded Jobline:** 305/585-7886. **Contact:** Gorden Hampden, Acting Employment Office Manager. **Description:** A hospital. **Common positions include:** Accountant/Auditor; Adjuster; Budget Analyst; Buyer; Clinical Lab Technician; Computer Programmer; Computer Systems Analyst; Construction and Building Inspector; Credit Manager; Customer Service Representative; Dental Assistant/Dental Hygienist; Dental Lab Technician; Dentist; Dietician/Nutritionist; EEG Technologist; EKG Technician; Electrician; Emergency Medical Technician; Environmental Engineer;

Financial Analyst; Health Services Manager; Human Resources Specialist; Industrial Engineer; Licensed Practical Nurse; Mechanical Engineer; Medical Record Technician; Nuclear Medicine Technologist; Occupational Therapist; Paralegal; Pharmacist; Physical Therapist; Physician; Property and Real Estate Manager; Psychologist; Radiologic Technologist; Recreational Therapist; Registered Nurse; Respiratory Therapist; Social Worker; Software Engineer; Speech-Language Pathologist; Statistician; Surgical Technician; Technical Writer/Editor. **Educational backgrounds include:** Accounting; Chemistry; Computer Science; Finance; Health Care. **Benefits:** Dental Insurance; Disability Coverage; Employee Discounts; Life Insurance; Medical Insurance; Pension Plan; Savings Plan; Tuition Assistance. **Operations at this facility include:** Administration. **Number of employees nationwide:** 10,000.

KENDALL REGIONAL MEDICAL CENTER
11750 Bird Road, Miami FL 33175. 305/223-3000. **Contact:** Human Resources. **Description:** A medical center serving the Kendall-Miami area.

LA AMISTAD RESIDENTIAL TREATMENT CENTER
201 Alpine Drive, Maitland FL 32751. 407/647-0660. **Contact:** Human Resources. **Description:** A 50-bed treatment facility.

LEE MEMORIAL HEALTH SYSTEM
P.O. Box 2218, Fort Meyers FL 33902. 941/334-5107. **Fax:** 941/332-6478. **Recorded Jobline:** 941/433-4636. **Contact:** Human Resource Department. **Description:** Lee Memorial Hospital is the second largest employer in Lee County, with over 3,300 employees, 1,400 volunteers and more than 500 physicians. Founded in 1916, Lee Memorial operates as one hospital with two locations, sharing an administration, publicly-elected Board of Directors and many resources between two campuses. Lee Memorial focuses on making health care the most effective it can be. Focused Care Centers and other innovative projects have received national and international attention as Lee Memorial looks at ways to improve a cumbersome delivery system to benefit patients and staff. Focused Care Centers are much like mini hospitals within the hospital. Services such as radiology, pharmacy, laboratory, admitting, and physical therapy are located on a specially designed unit for patients with similar needs. The staff works on Care Teams and is responsible for a patient from admission through discharge. Charting is done by exception only using a care path guideline, or plan developed for the patient's health care needs. Subsidiaries include Healthpark Medical Center, Healthpark Care Center, and various home health and physician's offices. **Common positions include:** Accountant/Auditor; Adjuster; Attorney; Biomedical Engineer; Broadcast Technician; Budget Analyst; Buyer; Claim Representative; Clerical Supervisor; Computer Programmer; Computer Systems Analyst; Counselor; Customer Service Representative; Dietician/Nutritionist; Editor; Electrical/Electronics Engineer; Electrician; Emergency Medical Technician; Financial Analyst; Food Scientist/Technologist; Health Services Manager; Human Resources Specialist; Human Service Worker; Librarian; Licensed Practical Nurse; Medical Record Technician; Nuclear Medicine Technologist; Occupational Therapist; Pharmacist; Physician; Radio/TV Announcer/Newscaster; Radiologic Technologist; Recreational Therapist; Registered Nurse; Respiratory Therapist; Restaurant/Food Service Manager; Social Worker; Speech-Language Pathologist; Surgical Technician; Technical Writer/Editor. **Educational backgrounds include:** Accounting; Business Administration; Communications; Computer Science; Finance; Health Care; Marketing. **Benefits:** 403B; Credit Union; Daycare Assistance; Dental Insurance; Disability Coverage; Employee Discounts; Life Insurance; Medical Insurance; Tuition Assistance. **Corporate headquarters location:** This Location. **Operations at this facility include:** Administration; Service. **Number of employees at this location:** 2,000. **Number of employees nationwide:** 3,300.

LEESBURG REGIONAL MEDICAL CENTER
600 East Dixie Avenue, Leesburg FL 34748. 352/365-4545. **Contact:** Human Resources. **Description:** A medical center.

LINVATEC CORPORATION
11311 Concept Boulevard, Largo FL 34643. 813/392-6464. **Fax:** 813/399-9900. **Contact:** Linda Abair, Human Resources Administrator. **Description:** Linvatec Corporation manufactures and markets products for the least invasive surgery market. **Common positions include:** Accountant/Auditor; Buyer; Compliance Analyst; Computer Programmer; Customer Service Representative; Designer; Draftsperson; Financial Analyst; Mechanical Engineer; Purchasing Agent and Manager; Quality Control Supervisor. **Educational backgrounds include:** Accounting; Computer Science;

Engineering; Finance; Health Care; Marketing. **Benefits:** 401K; Dental Insurance; Disability Coverage; Employee Discounts; Life Insurance; Medical Insurance; Pension Plan; Tuition Assistance. **Corporate headquarters location:** New York NY. **Parent company:** Bristol-Meyers Squibb. **Operations at this facility include:** Administration; Divisional Headquarters; Manufacturing; Research and Development; Sales; Service.

LUCERNE MEDICAL CENTER
P.O. Box C4996, 818 Main Lane, Orlando FL 32802. 407/649-6111. **Contact:** Human Resources. **Description:** A medical center.

MARTIN MEMORIAL MEDICAL CENTER
300 Hospital Avenue, Stuart FL 34994. 407/287-5200. **Contact:** Human Resources. **Description:** A hospital.

MEMORIAL HOSPITAL OF JACKSONVILLE
3625 University Boulevard South, Jacksonville FL 32216. 904/399-6111. **Recorded Jobline:** 904/399-6072. **Contact:** Human Resources. **Description:** A non-profit 300-bed hospital.

MEMORIAL HOSPITAL OF TAMPA
2901 Swann Avenue, Tampa FL 33609. 813/873-6400. **Fax:** 813/873-6494. **Recorded Jobline:** 813/876-7153. **Contact:** Human Resources, Recruiter. **Description:** Provides hospital and outpatient services. **Common positions include:** Accountant/Auditor; Biomedical Engineer; Clinical Lab Technician; EEG Technologist; EKG Technician; Emergency Medical Technician; Human Resources Specialist; Licensed Practical Nurse; Medical Record Technician; Nuclear Medicine Technologist; Pharmacist; Physical Therapist; Physician; Radiologic Technologist; Registered Nurse; Respiratory Therapist; Social Worker. **Educational backgrounds include:** M.D./Medicine. **Benefits:** 401K; Dental Insurance; Disability Coverage; Employee Discounts; Life Insurance; Medical Insurance; Pension Plan; Savings Plan; Tuition Assistance; Vision Insurance. **Corporate headquarters location:** Dallas TX. **Parent company:** AMI. **Operations at this facility include:** Service. **Number of employees at this location:** 600.

MIAMI HEART INSTITUTE
4701 Meridian Avenue, Miami Beach FL 33140. 305/672-1111x3375. **Fax:** 305/535-3662. **Contact:** Desiree Ramirez, Employment Specialist. **Description:** A full-service, acute care medical center. **Common positions include:** EEG Technologist; EKG Technician; Medical Record Technician; Nuclear Medicine Technologist; Occupational Therapist; Pharmacist; Physical Therapist; Radiologic Technologist; Registered Nurse; Respiratory Therapist; Speech-Language Pathologist. **Educational backgrounds include:** Nursing. **Benefits:** 401K; Dental Insurance; Disability Coverage; Employee Discounts; Life Insurance; Medical Insurance; Pension Plan; Tuition Assistance. **Corporate headquarters location:** Louisville KY. **Other U.S. locations:** Nationwide. **Parent company:** Columbia. **Operations at this facility include:** Administration; Service. **Listed on:** American Stock Exchange; New York Stock Exchange. **Number of employees at this location:** 1,200. **Number of employees nationwide:** 170,000.

MIAMI JEWISH HOME & HOSPITAL
5200 NE 2nd Avenue, Miami FL 33137. 305/751-8626. **Contact:** Human Resources. **Description:** A hospital which also operates a nursing home for senior citizens.

NAPLES COMMUNITY HOSPITAL
P.O. Box 413029, Naples FL 33940. 941/436-5000. **Contact:** Human Resources. **Description:** A hospital.

NORTH BROWARD MEDICAL CENTER
201 East Sample Road, Pompano Beach FL 33064. 954/941-8300. **Contact:** Human Resources. **Description:** A hospital.

ORANGE PARK MEDICAL CENTER
P.O. Box 2000, Orange Park FL 32073. 904/276-8500. **Recorded Jobline:** 904/276-8562. **Contact:** Human Resources. **Description:** A non-profit 200-bed hospital.

ORLANDO REGIONAL MEDICAL CENTER
1414 Kuhl Avenue, Orlando FL 32806-2008. 407/841-5111. **Contact:** Human Resources. **Description:** A hospital.

OSCEOLA REGIONAL HOSPITAL
P.O. Box 422589, 700 West Oak Street, Kissimmee FL 34741. 407/846-2266.
Contact: Human Resources. **Description:** Formerly Humana Hospital, Osceola Regional Hospital is a part of the Columbia Healthcare System. Osceola serves Kissimmee and other areas surrounding Orlando.

PALMS OF PASADENA HOSPITAL
1501 Pasadena Avenue South, St. Petersburg FL 33707. 813/381-1000. **Contact:** Human Resources. **Description:** A 310-bed facility.

PAN AMERICAN HOSPITAL
5959 NW 7th Street, Miami FL 33126. 305/264-1000. **Contact:** Human Resources. **Description:** A hospital.

PARKWAY REGIONAL MEDICAL CENTER
160 NW 170th Street, North Miami Beach FL 33169. 305/651-1100. **Recorded Jobline:** 305/651-1100; ask for jobline extension. **Contact:** Human Resources. **Description:** A non-profit 300-bed hospital.

PHARMACY MANAGEMENT SERVICES
3611 Queen Palm Drive, Tampa FL 33619. 813/626-7788. **Contact:** Human Resources. **Description:** Pharmacy Management Services is an independent national provider of medical products and cost-containment services to workers' compensation payers and claimants. **Number of employees at this location:** 985.

MORTON PLANT HOSPITAL
323 Jeffory Street, Clearwater FL 34617. 813/462-7000. **Contact:** Human Resources. **Description:** A hospital.

PLANTATION GENERAL HOSPITAL
401 Northwest 42nd Avenue, Plantation FL 33317. 954/587-5010. **Contact:** Human Resources. **Description:** A hospital.

PSYCHIATRIC CARE CENTER OF WINTER PARK MEMORIAL
1600 Dodd Road, Winter Park FL 32792-9409. 407/677-6842. **Contact:** Human Resources. **Description:** A facility specializing in psychiatrics which operates as a division of a hospital.

ROTECH MEDICAL
4506 L.B. McLeod Road, Suite F, Orlando FL 32811-5665. 407/841-2115. **Contact:** Human Resources. **Description:** Rotech Medical markets, provides, and delivers outpatient health care products and services to patients in the physician's office and at the patient's home. Services and products involve respiratory therapy equipment, convalescent medical equipment, prelabeled and prepackaged pharmaceuticals, and home infusion therapy products. **Number of employees at this location:** 350.

SACRED HEART HOSPITAL
5151 North 9th Avenue, Pensacola FL 32504. 904/474-7175. **Fax:** 904/474-6731. **Recorded Jobline:** 904/474-7170. **Contact:** Lee Ann Mowery, Employment Coordinator. **Description:** A member of the Daughters of Charity national health system. The Sacred Heart Hospital is a 342-bed acute care facility. The hospital offers services in the following areas: Cancer, cardiology, cardiovascular surgery, emergency, gastroenterology, laser surgery, neonatology, neurology, OB/GYN, oncology, opthalmology, orthopedics, otolaryngology, otology, pediatrics, and plastic surgery. It also operates a skilled nursing facility, medical residence programs, and a wellness, health and education center. **Common positions include:** Accountant/Auditor; Buyer; Clinical Lab Technician; Computer Programmer; EEG Technologist; EKG Technician; Emergency Medical Technician; Human Resources Specialist; Licensed Practical Nurse; Medical Record Technician; Nuclear Medicine Technologist; Occupational Therapist; Pharmacist; Physical Therapist; Radiologic Technologist; Registered Nurse; Respiratory Therapist; Social Worker; Speech-Language Pathologist. **Educational backgrounds include:** Accounting; Business Administration; Computer Science; Health Care. **Benefits:** Dental Insurance; Disability Coverage; Employee Discounts; Life Insurance; Medical Insurance; Pension Plan; Savings Plan; Tuition Assistance. **Corporate headquarters location:** St. Louis MO. **Number of employees at this location:** 2,500.

ST. JOSEPH'S HOSPITAL
3001 West Dr. Martin Luther King Boulevard, Tampa FL 33607. 813/870-4000. **Contact:** Personnel Department. **Description:** A hospital.

ST. JOSEPH'S WOMEN'S HOSPITAL
3030 Dr. Martin Luther King Boulevard, Tampa FL 33607. 813/879-4730. **Contact:** Human Resources. **Description:** A 234-bed facility specializing in women's health.

ST. LUKE'S HOSPITAL
4201 Belfort Road, Jacksonville FL 32216. 904/963-3700. **Contact:** Human Resources. **Description:** A 289-bed facility.

ST. VINCENT'S HEALTH SYSTEMS
1800 Barrs Street, P.O. Box 2982, Jacksonville FL 32203-9554. 904/387-7307. **Fax:** 904/981-2951. **Recorded Jobline:** 904/387-7363. **Contact:** Human Resources Department. **Description:** St. Vincent's Health Systems consists of several health care facilities in the Jacksonville area, including the St. Vincent Medical Center and the St. Catherine Laboure Manor nursing home. St. Vincent Medical Center is a 711-bed hospital which provides the following services and facilities: acute care, AIDS, behavioral medicine, a Cancer Center, cardiology, chemical dependency treatment, emergency services, geriatrics, gastroenterology, laser surgery, neonatology, neurosurgery, OB/GYN, occupational health, oncology, opthalmology, orthopedics, otolaryngology, otology, pediatrics, plastic surgery, psychiatric, substance abuse, and women's and children's services. St. Vincent's Health Systems is a member of the Daughters of Charity national health system, which includes Mercy Hospital in Miami, and Sacred Heart Hospital and the Haven of Our Lady of Peace nursing home in Pensacola. **Common positions include:** EKG Technician; Emergency Medical Technician; Licensed Practical Nurse; Medical Record Technician; Occupational Therapist; Pharmacist; Physical Therapist; Registered Nurse; Respiratory Therapist; Speech-Language Pathologist; Surgical Technician. **Educational backgrounds include:** Health Care. **Benefits:** 403B; Dental Insurance; Disability Coverage; Employee Discounts; Life Insurance; Medical Insurance; Tuition Assistance. **Corporate headquarters location:** St. Louis MO. **Number of employees at this location:** 4,000.

SCIENTIFIC INSTRUMENTS, INC.
4400 West Tiffany Drive, West Palm Beach FL 33407. 407/881-8500. **Contact:** Personnel Department. **Description:** Manufactures cryogenic instruments.

SHERWOOD MEDICAL COMPANY
P.O. Box 2078, Deland FL 32721-2078. 904/734-3685. **Contact:** Industrial Relations Manager. **Description:** A manufacturer of disposable hypodermic needles and syringes. **Common positions include:** Biological Scientist/Biochemist; Chemist; Computer Programmer; Draftsperson; Electrical/Electronics Engineer; Industrial Engineer; Industrial Production Manager; Mechanical Engineer; Metallurgical Engineer; Purchasing Agent and Manager; Technical Writer/Editor. **Educational backgrounds include:** Chemistry; Computer Science; Engineering. **Benefits:** Dental Insurance; Disability Coverage; Employee Discounts; Life Insurance; Medical Insurance; Pension Plan; Savings Plan; Tuition Assistance. **Corporate headquarters location:** St. Louis MO. **Parent company:** AHPC. **Operations at this facility include:** Manufacturing. **Listed on:** New York Stock Exchange.

SILOR OPTICAL MANUFACTURING DIVISION
4900 Park Street North, St. Petersburg FL 33709. 813/541-5733. **Contact:** Personnel Director. **Description:** Manufacturers of optical lenses for eye glasses.

SMITH DENTAL PROSTHETICS
2131 Art Museum Drive, Jacksonville FL 32207. 904/398-6844. **Contact:** Human Resources. **Description:** National Dentex Corporation, the parent company of Smith Dental Prosthetics, is one of the largest operators of dental laboratories in the United States. National Dentex serves an active customer base of approximately 6,200 dentists through its 20 full-service and three branch dental laboratories located in 18 states. These dental laboratories provide a full range of custom-made dental prosthetic appliances, divided into three main groups: restorative products (crowns and bridges); reconstructive products (partial and full dentures); and cosmetic products (porcelain veneers and ceramic crowns). Each lab is operated as a stand-alone facility under the direction of a local manager. All sales and marketing is done through each lab's own direct sales force. **Benefits:** 401K; Incentive Plan; Stock Option. **Corporate**

headquarters location: Framingham MA. **Parent company:** National Dentex Corporation. **Listed on:** NASDAQ. **Number of employees nationwide:** 841.

SOUTH MIAMI HOSPITAL
6200 Southwest 73rd Street, Miami FL 33143. 305/661-4611. **Contact:** Human Resources. **Description:** A 500-bed facility.

SOUTH SHORE HOSPITAL & MEDICAL CENTER
630 Alton Road, Miami Beach FL 33139. 305/672-2100. **Contact:** Human Resources. **Description:** A medical center.

SOUTHERN WINDS HOSPITAL
4225 West 20th Avenue, Hialeah FL 33012. 305/558-9700. **Contact:** Human Resources. **Description:** A hospital serving Hialeah and other Miami areas.

TAMPA GENERAL
P.O. Box 1289, Tampa FL 33601. 813/251-7551. **Fax:** 813/253-4017. **Recorded Jobline:** 813/253-4100. **Contact:** Pamela D. Stone, Recruiter. **Description:** A medical facility providing hospital and ambulatory services. **Common positions include:** Accountant/Auditor; Budget Analyst; Clinical Lab Technician; EEG Technologist; EKG Technician; Electrician; Financial Analyst; Food Scientist/Technologist; Human Resources Specialist; Industrial Engineer; Licensed Practical Nurse; Occupational Therapist; Registered Nurse; Respiratory Therapist; Social Worker; Speech-Language Pathologist; Surgical Technician. **Educational backgrounds include:** Health Care. **Benefits:** Dental Insurance; Disability Coverage; Life Insurance; Medical Insurance; Tuition Assistance. **Special Programs:** Internships. **Operations at this facility include:** Administration. **Number of employees at this location:** 3,500.

UNITED STATES AIR FORCE REGIONAL HOSPITAL
96 MEDICAL GROUP
307 Boatner Drive, Suite 114, Eglin Air Force Base FL 32542-1282. 904/882-7242. **Contact:** Human Resources. **Description:** A hospital.

UNITED STATES DEPARTMENT OF VETERANS AFFAIRS
MEDICAL CENTER
Building 22, Room 326, 10000 Bay Pines Boulevard, Bay Pines FL 33504. 813/398-6661. **Recorded Jobline:** 813/398-9493. **Contact:** Human Resources. **Description:** A 1,000-bed U.S. veterans' hospital.

UNITED STATES DEPARTMENT OF VETERANS AFFAIRS
MEDICAL CENTER
Human Resources Management Office (O5C3), 1201 Northwest 16th Street, Miami FL 33125. 305/324-3155. **Fax:** 305/324-3374. **Contact:** Chief, Recruitment and Placement Section. **Description:** The Miami VA Medical Center is a complex tertiary care facility operating 671 acute beds and an attached 241-bed nursing home care unit. The Medical Center offers an active research program and is affiliated with several health care educational institutions offering residency and training programs in most direct and allied health care specialties. Mobility is available between any of the 172 U.S. locations. **NOTE:** Faxed applications will not be accepted. **Common positions include:** Dental Assistant/Dental Hygienist; Dietician/Nutritionist; EKG Technician; Licensed Practical Nurse; Medical Record Technician; Medical Technologist; Occupational Therapist; Pharmacist; Physical Therapist; Physician; Psychologist; Radiologic Technologist; Recreational Therapist; Registered Nurse; Respiratory Therapist; Social Worker; Speech-Language Pathologist; Structural Engineer. **Educational backgrounds include:** Health Care. **Benefits:** 401K; Dental Insurance; Disability Coverage; Employee Discounts; Life Insurance; Medical Insurance; Pension Plan; Savings Plan; Tuition Assistance. **Corporate headquarters location:** Washington DC. **Other U.S. locations:** Nationwide. **Operations at this facility include:** Administration; Research and Development; Service. **Number of employees at this location:** 2,700.

UNIVERSITY COMMUNITY HOSPITAL
3100 East Fletcher Avenue, Tampa FL 33613. 813/972-7290. **Contact:** Kathy Meloy, Employment Manager. **Description:** A 400-bed, full-service, acute care hospital. **Common positions include:** Accountant/Auditor; Administrator; Biomedical Engineer; Buyer; Claim Representative; Computer Programmer; Credit Manager; Customer Service Representative; Electrical/Electronics Engineer; Industrial Engineer; Purchasing Agent and Manager; Systems Analyst. **Educational backgrounds include:** Accounting;

Biology; Business Administration; Chemistry; Computer Science; Finance. **Benefits:** Daycare Assistance; Dental Insurance; Employee Discounts; Life Insurance; Medical Insurance; Pension Plan; Tuition Assistance. **Operations at this facility include:** Administration; Service.

UNIVERSITY HOSPITAL
7201 North University Drive, Tamarac FL 33321. 954/721-2200. **Contact:** Human Resources. **Description:** A hospital serving Tamarac, Margate, Coral Springs, Lauderdale Lakes, and other surrounding cities.

VENICE HOSPITAL
P.O. Box 8998, 540 The Rialato, Venice FL 34285. 813/485-7711. **Contact:** Human Resources. **Description:** A hospital serving the Venice and Sarasota areas.

VICTORIA HOSPITAL
1400 NW 12th Avenue, Miami FL 33136. 305/545-8050. **Contact:** Human Resources. **Description:** A hospital.

VISION EASE
BMC INDUSTRIES
3301 South West 9th Avenue, Fort Lauderdale FL 33315. 954/525-1351. **Contact:** Personnel Director. **Description:** A producer of ophthalmic goods.

VISTAKON INC.
P.O. Box 10157, Jacksonville FL 32247-0157. 904/443-1000. **Contact:** Human Resources. **Description:** A manufacturer of contact lenses. **Parent company:** Johnson & Johnson Corporation.

WESTSIDE REGIONAL MEDICAL CENTER
8201 West Broward Boulevard, Plantation FL 33324. 954/473-6600. **Contact:** Human Resources. **Description:** A hospital.

WINDMERE CORPORATION
5980 Miami Lake Drive, Miami Lake FL 33014. 305/362-2611. **Contact:** Personnel. **Description:** Windmere produces and sells health care products.

XOMED-TREACE
6743 Southpoint Drive North, Jacksonville FL 32216. 904/296-9600. **Contact:** Human Resources Department. **Description:** A manufacturer of medical devices and products for ear, nose, and throat surgery. **Common positions include:** Accountant/Auditor; Biomedical Engineer; Buyer; Customer Service Representative; Draftsperson; Electrical/Electronics Engineer; Electrician; Financial Manager; Machinist; Manufacturer's/Wholesaler's Sales Rep.; Marketing Research Analyst; Mechanical Engineer; Purchasing Agent and Manager; Quality Control Supervisor; Software Engineer; Tool and Die Maker; Typist/Word Processor. **Educational backgrounds include:** Accounting; Business Administration; Communications; Computer Science; Engineering; Finance; Marketing. **Benefits:** Dental Insurance; Disability Coverage; Life Insurance; Medical Insurance; Pension Plan; Profit Sharing; Savings Plan; Tuition Assistance. **Corporate headquarters location:** This Location. **Operations at this facility include:** Divisional Headquarters; Manufacturing; Research and Development.

Note: Because addresses and telephone numbers of smaller companies change rapidly, we recommend you call each company to verify the information below before inquiring about job opportunities. Mass mailings are not recommended.

Additional employers with over 250 employees:

HOSPITALS AND MEDICAL CENTERS

Charter Hospital Orlando South
206 Park Pl Dr, Kissimmee FL 34741-2356. 407/846-0444.

Dade City Hospital
1550 Ft King Hwy, Dade City FL 33525. 904/521-1100.

Englewood Community Hospital
700 Medical Blvd, Englewood FL 34223-3964. 813/475-6571.

Halifax Medical Center
P.O. Box 2830, Daytona Beach FL 32120-2830. 904/254-4000.

Hamilton County Memorial Hospital
P.O. Box 1300, Jasper FL 32052. 904/792-2101.

HCA New Port Richey Hospital
P.O. Box 996, New Port Richey FL 34656-0996. 813/848-1733.

North Broward Hospital
203 SE 17th St, Ft Lauderdale FL 33316-2549. 954/355-5100.

Palm Beaches Medical Center
2201 45th St, West Palm Beach FL 33407-2047. 407/842-6141.

Savannas Hospital
2550 SE Walton Rd, Port St Lucie FL 34952-7197. 407/335-0400.

Shriners Hospital
P.O. Box 31356, Tampa FL 33631-3356. 813/281-0300.

✦ **Madison County Memorial Hospital**
201 E Marion St, Madison FL 32340-2561. 904/973-2271.

Midflorida Health Center
P.O. Box 67, Haines City FL 33845-0067. 813/422-4971.

Morrow Memorial Hospital
P.O. Box 277, Auburndale FL 33823-0277. 813/967-8511.

Brooksville Regional Hospital
P.O. Box 37, Brooksville FL 34605-0037. 352/796-5111.

Everglades Memorial Hospital
200 S Barfield Hwy, Pahokee FL 33476-1897. 407/924-5200.

Nassau General Hospital
1700 E Lime St, Fernandina FL 32034-3020. 904/261-3627.

Golden Glades Regional Medical Center
17300 NW 7th Ave, Miami FL 33169-5407. 305/652-4200.

Imperial Point Medical Center
6401 N Federal Hwy, Ft Lauderdale FL 33308-1405. 954/776-8500.

Jackson Hospital
P.O. Box 1608, Marianna FL 32447-5608. 904/526-2200.

Metropolitan General Hospital
P.O. Box 30, Pinellas Park FL 34664-0030. 813/546-9871.

North Okaloosa Medical Center
151 Redstone Ave, Crestview FL 32536-7304. 904/682-9731.

Brandon Hospital
119 Oakfield Dr, Brandon FL 33511-5779. 813/681-5551.

Coral Gables Hospital
3100 S Douglas Rd, Miami FL 33134-6923. 305/445-8461.

Fort Walton Beach Medical Center
1000 Mar Walt Dr, Ft Walton Beach FL 32547-6708. 904/862-1111.

Munroe Regional Medical Center
P.O. Box 6000, Ocala FL 34478-6000. 352/351-7200.

Pompano Beach Medical Center
600 SW 3rd St, Pompano Beach FL 33060-6931. 954/782-2000.

St. Petersburg General Hospital
P.O. Box 13096, St Petersburg FL 33733-3096. 813/384-1414.

Northside Hospital
6000 49th St N, St Petersburg FL 33709-2114. 813/521-4411.

Charter Hospital Of Pasco
21808 State Road 54, Lutz FL 33549-6938. 813/948-2441.

Pulmonary Rehabilitation Tampa
2901 W Swann Ave, Tampa FL 33609-4056. 813/879-6351.

BRT Cancer Treatment Center
266 W Hillsboro Blvd, Deerfield Beach FL 33441-3322. 954/481-8577.

Cancer Center At Wellington Regional
10141 Forest Hill Blvd, West Palm Beach FL 33414-6103. 407/793-6500.

Comprehensive Cancer Center At JFK
170 John F Kennedy Dr, Lake Worth FL 33462-6671. 407/642-3900.

South FL Comprehensive Cancer Centers
160 NW 170th St, Miami FL 33169. 305/654-5033.

South FL Comprehensive Cancer Centers
11750 Bird Rd, Miami FL 33175-3599. 305/227-5582.

AG Holley State Hospital
P.O. Box 3084, Lake Worth FL 33165-3084.

Naval Hospital
2080 Child St, Jacksonville FL 32214-5005. 904/777-7300.

Children's Hospital At Sacred Heart
5151 N 9th Ave, Pensacola FL 32504-8721. 904/474-7651.

Wolfson Children's Hospital
800 Prudential Dr, Jacksonville FL 32207-8203. 904/858-5000.

East Pasco Medical Center
7050 Gall Blvd, Zephyrhills FL 33541-1399. 813/788-0411.

Jupiter Medical Center
1210 S Old Dixie Hwy, Jupiter FL 33458-7299. 407/747-2234.

Mercy Hospital
3663 S Miami Ave, Miami FL 33133-4237. 305/854-4400.

North Ridge Medical Center
5757 N Dixie Hwy, Ft Lauderdale FL 33334-4135. 954/776-6000.

Polk General Hospital
P.O. Box 816, Bartow FL 33830-0816. 813/533-1111.

Sebastian Hospital
P.O. Box 780838, Sebastian FL 32978-0838. 407/589-3186.

Boca Raton Community Hospital
800 Meadows Rd, Boca Raton FL 33486-2368. 407/395-7100.

Highlands Regional Medical Center
P.O. Box 2066, Sebring FL 33871-2066. 813/385-6101.

Manatee Memorial Hospital
206 2nd St E, Bradenton FL 34208-1000. 813/746-5111.

Mease Hospital Dunedin
P.O. Box 760, Dunedin FL 34697-0760. 813/733-1111.

Palms West Hospital
13001 Southern Blvd,
Loxahatchee FL 33470-
9277. 407/798-3300.

Pembroke Pines Hospital
2301 University Dr,
Hollywood FL 33024.
954/962-9650.

South Seminole Community Hospital
P.O. Box 521607, Longwood
FL 32752-1607. 407/767-
1200.

West Boca Medical Center
21644 State Road 7, Boca
Raton FL 33428-1899.
407/488-8105.

Doctors Hospital Of Sarasota
2750 Bahia Vista St,
Sarasota FL 34239-2677.
813/366-1411.

HOME HEALTH CARE SERVICES

Hospital Staffing Services
6245 N Federal Hwy 500, Ft
Lauderdale FL 33308-1915.
954/771-0500.

Interim Services
2050 Spectrum Blvd, Ft
Lauderdale FL 33309-3008.
954/938-7600.

SPECIALTY OUTPATIENT FACILITIES

Broward General Medical Center
1600 S Andrews Ave, Ft
Lauderdale FL 33316-2510.
954/355-4400.

Cape Coral Hospital
P.O. Box 150010, Cape
Coral FL 33915-0010.
813/574-2323.

Cedars Medical Center
1400 NW 12th Ave, Miami
FL 33136-1087. 305/325-
5511.

Delray Community Hospital
5352 Linton Blvd, Delray
Beach FL 33484-6580.
407/498-4440.

Fish Memorial Hospital
401 Palmetto St, New
Smyrna FL 32168-7322.
904/427-3401.

Holy Cross Hospital
P.O. Box 23460, Ft
Lauderdale FL 33307-3460.
954/771-8000.

Lakeland Regional Medical Center
P.O. Box 95448, Lakeland FL
33804-5448. 813/687-
1100.

Santa Rosa Medical Center
P.O. Box 648, Milton FL
32572-0648. 904/626-
7762.

Winter Haven Hospital
200 Avenue F NE, Winter
Haven FL 33881. 813/297-
1899.

Citrus Memorial Hospital
502 W Highland Blvd,
Inverness FL 34452-4754.
352/344-6583.

Doctors Hospital Of Hollywood
P.O. Box 229105,
Hollywood FL 33022-9105.
954/920-9000.

East Pointe Hospital
1500 Lee Blvd, Lehigh Acres
FL 33936-4897. 813/369-
2101.

Flagler Hospital
400 Health Park Blvd, St
Augustine FL 32086-5779.
904/829-5155.

Good Samaritan Medical Center
P.O. Box 3166, West Palm
Beach FL 33402-3166.
407/655-5511.

Sunrise Rehabilitation Hospital
4399 N Nob Hill Rd, Ft
Lauderdale FL 33351-5813.
954/749-0300.

Retreat Hospital
555 SW 148th Ave, Ft
Lauderdale FL 33325-3010.
954/370-0200.

St. Mary's Hospital
P.O. Box 24620, West Palm
Beach FL 33416-4620.
407/844-6300.

Aventura Hospital and Medical Center
20900 Biscayne Blvd, Miami

FL 33180-1407. 305/932-
0250.

Bay Medical Center
P.O. Box 2515, Panama City
FL 32402-2515. 904/769-
1511.

Sarasota Memorial Hospital
1700 S Tamiami Trl,
Sarasota FL 34239-3555.
813/955-1111.

University Medical Center
655 W 8th St, Jacksonville
FL 32209-6595. 904/549-
5000.

HEALTH AND ALLIED SERVICES

Florida Medical Center Hospital
5000 W Oakland Park Blvd,
Ft Lauderdale FL 33313-
1585. 954/735-6000.

Parrish Medical Center
951 N Washington Ave,
Titusville FL 32796-2111.
407/268-6100.

South Bay Hospital
4016 State Road 674, Sun
City Center FL 33573-5298.
813/634-3301.

SOCIAL SERVICES AT HOSPITALS

Bon Secours Hospital Villa Maria
1050 NE 125th St, Miami FL
33161-5881. 305/891-
8850.

SMH Homestead Hospital
160 NW 13th St, Homestead
FL 33030. 305/248-3232.

University of Miami Hospital & Clinic
1475 NW 12th Ave, Miami
FL 33136-1002. 305/548-
4382.

Clearwater Community Hospital
1521 Druid Rd E, Clearwater
FL 34616-6129. 813/447-
4571.

Melbourne Rehabilitation Medicine
101 E Florida Ave,
Melbourne FL 32901-8301.
407/951-8137.

Additional employers with under 250 employees:

MEDICAL EQUIPMENT

American Hydro Surgical
430 Commerce Dr, Suite 50-
E, Delray Beach FL 33445-
4655. 407/278-5664.

Cuda Products Corp.
6000 Powers Ave,
Jacksonville FL 32217-2212.
904/737-7611.

Florida Medical Industries
P.O. Box 493000, Leesburg

FL 34749-3000. 352/787-
1312.

Innivo Research
12601 Research Pkwy,
Orlando FL 32826-3200.
407/275-3220.

Mercury Medical
11300 49th St N #A,
Clearwater FL 34622-4807.
813/573-0088.

Enviro Med International
2441 E Meadow Blvd,
Tampa FL 33619-3061.
813/623-2702.

**National Equipment
Manufacturing Corp.**
4655 118th Ave N,
Clearwater FL 34622-4408.
813/573-5000.

NDL Products
2313 NW 30th Place,
Pompano Beach FL 33069-
0701. 954/979-4343.

Professional Products
101 Hugh Adams Rd,
Defuniak Springs FL 32433-
3406. 904/892-5731.

Omnia
P.O. Box 1808, Eaton Park
FL 33840-1808. 941/665-
5493.

Advanced Biosystems
1885 NE 149th St, Miami FL
33181-1148. 305/949-
7755.

Omni Technologies
880 Jupiter Park Dr, Jupiter
FL 33458-6001. 407/575-
5107.

Magni-Tech
1500 NW 66th Ave,
Pembroke Pines FL 33024.
954/477-4612.

Milroy Optical
5067 Savarese Circle,
Tampa FL 33634-2404.
813/889-0858.

Storz Ophthalmics
21 N Park Place Blvd,
Clearwater FL 34619-3917.
813/724-6600.

**DOCTORS' OFFICES AND
CLINICS**

Diagnostic Clinic
1551 W Bay Dr, Largo FL
34640-2298. 813/581-
8767.

Health Options
3750 NW 87th Ave, Suite
300, Miami FL 33178-2430.
305/591-9955.

Quincy Womens Center
Hwy 90 E, Quincy FL
32351. 904/875-1100.

Jonathan P Nagy MD
1465 S Fort Harrison Ave,
Suite 2, Clearwater FL
34616-2504. 813/443-
4502.

Robert W Nickeson MD
3131 N McMullen Booth Rd,
Clearwater FL 34621-2021.
813/726-8871.

**DENTISTS' OFFICES AND
CLINICS**

**Princeton Dental
Management Corp.**
2739 US Highway 19,
Holiday FL 34691-2708.
813/942-3600.

**South Florida Orthodontic
Specialists**
10925 N Dale Mabry Hwy,
Tampa FL 33618-4112.
813/960-8400.

The Dental Team
5210 Linton Blvd, Delray
Beach FL 33484-6516.
407/495-2099.

**OFFICES AND CLINICS OF
HEALTH PRACTITIONERS**

**Clinicare Spinal Health
Centers SW**
4350 Fowler St, Fort Myers
FL 33901-2616. 941/275-
7400.

Center For Sight
341 Miami Ave W, Venice FL
34285-2306. 941/488-
4917.

Florida Eye Clinic
493 S Chickasaw Trail,
Orlando FL 32825-7803.
407/281-0866.

Vision 21
30715 US Highway 19 N,
Palm Harbor FL 34684-4400.
813/785-8645.

**Professional Health Care
Service**
3450 W Busch Blvd, Tampa
FL 33618-4400. 813/932-
8182.

Progressive Therapies
5626 Gulf Dr, New Port
Richey FL 34652-4020.
813/847-1507.

Rehab Works Of Florida
575 Lamar Ave, Brooksville
FL 34601-3228. 352/799-
3377.

Therapists Unlimited
500 W Cypress Creek Rd, Ft
Lauderdale FL 33309-6141.
954/492-1116.

VNA Respite Care
604 Courtland St, Orlando FL
32804-1361. 407/644-
2433.

**Clark & Daughtrey Medical
Group**
2625 S Florida Ave, Lakeland

FL 33803-3860. 941/284-
5147.

**NURSING AND PERSONAL
CARE FACILITIES**

Abbey Delray South
1717 Homewood Blvd,
Delray Beach FL 33445-
6876. 407/272-9600.

Alhambra Nursing Home
7501 38th Ave N, St
Petersburg FL 33710-1299.
813/345-9307.

**Alliance Center For Health
Care**
151 W Winnemissett Ave,
Deland FL 32720-6896.
904/734-6401.

Alpine Nursing Center
3456 21st Ave S, St
Petersburg FL 33711-3200.
813/327-1988.

Amelia Island Care Center
2700 Atlantic Ave,
Fernandina FL 32034-2206.
904/261-5518.

Anderson Health Care Center
8401 NW 27th Ave, Miami
FL 33147-4158. 305/691-
8052.

**Apalachicola Health Care
Center**
150 10th St, Apalachicola FL
32320. 904/653-8844.

Arbors At Tallahassee
1650 Phillips Rd, Tallahassee
FL 32308-5304. 904/942-
9868.

**Aristocrat Naples Nurse
Rehab Center**
10949 Parnu St, Naples FL
33942-1405. 941/592-
5501.

**Barrington Terrace Nursing
Home**
215 Annie St, Orlando FL
32806-1289. 407/841-
4371.

**Bay Heritage Nurse &
Convalescent Center**
115 Hart St, Niceville FL
32578. 904/678-6667.

Bay To Bay Nursing Center
3405 W Bay To Bay Blvd,
Tampa FL 33629-7042.
813/839-5325.

**Buckingham Smith Memorial
Home**
169 M L King Ave, St
Augustine FL 32084-5139.
904/824-3638.

**Cambridge Convalescent
Center**
9709 N Nebraska Ave,

Tampa FL 33612-8097.
813/935-2101.

Casa Marti Riverside
2730 N Ridgewood Ave,
Tampa FL 33602-1033.
813/223-1303.

Citrus Health & Rehab Center
701 Medical Ct E, Inverness
FL 34452-4612. 352/860-
0200.

**College Harbor Nursing
Center**
4600 54th Ave S, St
Petersburg FL 33711-4664.
813/866-3124.

Concordia Manor
321 13th Ave N, St
Petersburg FL 33701-1199.
813/822-3030.

**Conway Lakes Nursing
Center**
5201 Curry Ford Rd, Orlando
FL 32812-8741. 407/384-
8838.

**Coral Gables Convalescent
Center**
7060 SW 8th St, Miami FL
33144-4650. 305/261-
1363.

Crest Manor Nursing Center
504 3rd Ave S, Lake Worth
FL 33460-4599. 407/585-
4695.

Dania Nursing Home
440 Phippen Rd, Dania FL
33004-4998. 954/927-
0508.

**Daytona Manor Nursing
Home**
650 Reed Canal Rd, Daytona
Beach FL 32119-3299.
904/767-4831.

Eason Nursing Home
1711 6th Ave S, Lake Worth
FL 33460-4398. 407/582-
1472.

Eastbrook Health Care Center
1445 Howell Ave,
Brooksville FL 34601-1599.
352/799-1451.

Finnish American Rest Home
1800 South Dr, Lake Worth
FL 33461-6133. 407/588-
4333.

**Floridean Nurse & Rehab
Center**
47 NW 32nd Place, Miami FL
33125-4914. 305/649-
2911.

**Forest Park Convalescent
Center**
1702 W Oak Ave, Plant City
FL 33567-4294. 813/752-
4129.

Golfcrest Nursing Home
600 N 17th Ave, Hollywood
FL 33020-4606. 954/927-
2531.

Golfview Nursing Home
3636 10th Ave N, St
Petersburg FL 33713-6599.
813/323-3611.

**Good Samaritan Nursing
Home**
3127 57th Ave N, St
Petersburg FL 33714-1398.
813/525-3017.

**Good Shepherd Hospice Mid
Florida**
1201 First St S, Winter
Haven FL 33880-3904.
941/297-1880.

**Greenbriar Rehab & Nurse
Center**
210 21st Ave W, Bradenton
FL 34205-8336. 941/747-
3786.

Gulf Coast Village
1333 Santa Barbara Blvd,
Cape Coral FL 33991.
941/772-1333.

**Harbor Beach Convalescent
Hospital**
1615 Miami Rd, Ft
Lauderdale FL 33316-2933.
954/523-5673.

Harbour's Edge
401 E Linton Blvd, Delray
Beach FL 33483-5093.
407/272-7979.

Hardee Manor Care Center
401 Orange Place, Wauchula
FL 33873-3417. 941/773-
3231.

Haven Of Our Lady Of Peace
5203 N 9th Ave, Pensacola
FL 32504-8779. 904/477-
0531.

Healthpark Care Center
16131 Roserush Ct, Fort
Myers FL 33908-3634.
941/433-4647.

**Heartland Health Care &
Rehab**
5401 Sawyer Rd, Sarasota
FL 34233-2444. 941/925-
3427.

Heartland Of Lauderhill
2599 NW 55th Ave, Ft
Lauderdale FL 33313-2443.
954/485-8873.

Heritage Healthcare Center
777 9th St N, Naples FL
33940. 941/261-8126.

Hillcrest Nursing Home
1281 W Stratford Rd, Avon
Park FL 33825-8091.
941/453-6674.

Hilliard Manor
3rd St, Hilliard FL 32046.
904/845-7165.

Holiday Care Center
1031 S Beach St, Daytona
Beach FL 32114-6205.
904/255-2453.

**Heritage Health Care Center
Baker County**
755 S 5th St, MacClenny FL
32063-2685. 904/259-
4873.

**Jackson Heights Nursing
Home**
1404 NW 22nd St, Miami FL
33142-7786. 305/325-
1050.

JH Floyd Sunshine Manor
1755 18th St, Sarasota FL
34234-8603. 941/955-
4915.

Lake Eustis Care Center
411 W Woodward Ave,
Eustis FL 32726-4599.
904/357-3565.

**Lake Forest Health Care
Center**
1771 Edgewood Ave W,
Jacksonville FL 32208-3224.
904/766-7436.

Lakeshore Nursing Home
100 N Lake St, Crescent City
FL 32112-2695. 904/698-
2222.

Lakeside Health Center
2501 N Australian Ave,
West Palm Beach FL 33407-
5696. 407/655-7780.

**Lelah G. Warner Nursing
Home**
3409 W 19th St, Panama
City FL 32405-1511.
904/785-0239.

Lely Palms Of Naples
1000 Lely Palms Dr, Naples
FL 33962-8916. 941/775-
7661.

Lisenby Skilled Care Facility
1400 W 11th St, Panama
City FL 32401-1810.
904/747-3694.

Madison Nursing Center
W Hwy 90, Madison FL
32340. 904/973-4880.

Magnolia Manor
3339 US Highway 17 S,
Green Cove Springs FL
32043-9378. 904/284-
3048.

Manor At Bluewater Bay
1500 White Point Rd,
Niceville FL 32578-4249.
904/897-5592.

Mary Lee Depugh Nursing Home
550 W Morse Blvd, Winter Park FL 32789-4206. 407/644-6634.

Meadowbrook Manor Of Labelle
250 Broward Ave, Labelle FL 33935-4903. 941/675-1440.

Memorial Manor
777 S Douglas Rd, Hollywood FL 33025-1353. 954/431-1100.

Miracle Hill Nurse & Convalescent
1329 Abraham St, Tallahassee FL 32304-1998. 904/224-8486.

National Health Care Center
435 42nd Ave S, St Petersburg FL 33705-4504. 813/822-1871.

North Horizon Health Care Center
1301 16th St N, St Petersburg FL 33705-1034. 813/898-5119.

Oak Cove Nursing Unit
210 S Osceola Ave, Clearwater FL 34616. 813/441-3763.

Oaks Of Kissimmee
320 Mitchell St, Kissimmee FL 34741-4414. 407/847-7200.

Oakview Regional Care Center
300 NW First Ave, Williston FL 32696. 904/528-3561.

Orchard Ridge Nursing Home
700 Trouble Creek Rd E, New Port Richey FL 34653. 813/447-0567.

Ormond In Pines Healthcare Center
103 Clyde Morris Blvd, Ormond Beach FL 32174-5982. 904/673-0450.

Palm Garden
1120 Cypress Gardens Blvd, Winter Haven FL 33884-1915. 941/293-3100.

Palm Garden Of Lake City
920 McFarlane Ave, Lake City FL 32025-5602. 904/758-4777.

Palm Garden Orlando
654 N Econlockhatchee Trail, Orlando FL 32825-6402. 407/273-6158.

Pine Lake Nursing Home
E Hwy 90, Greenville FL 32331. 904/948-4761.

Pinehurst Convalescent Center
2401 NE 2nd St, Pompano Beach FL 33062-4897. 954/943-5100.

Pines Nursing Home
301 NE 141st St, Miami FL 33161-2899. 305/893-1102.

Plaza Nursing & Rehab Center
14601 NE 16th Ave, Miami FL 33161-2614. 305/945-7631.

Putnam Memorial Nursing Home
501 S Palm Ave, Palatka FL 32177-4187. 904/328-1472.

Regency Health Care Center
200 Meridian Dr, St Augustine FL 32086-7282. 904/797-7583.

Regency Oaks
2770 Regency Oaks Blvd, Clearwater FL 34619-1514. 813/791-3381.

Renaissance Health Care
900 Imperial Golf Course Blvd, Naples FL 33942-1085. 941/591-4800.

Richey Manor Rehab & Specialty Care
6020 Indiana Ave, New Port Richey FL 34653-3298. 813/849-7555.

Riverside Care Center
899 NW 4th St, Miami FL 33128-1358. 305/326-1236.

Royal Oak Nursing Center
37300 Royal Oak Ln, Dade City FL 33525-5295. 904/567-3122.

Royal Palm Convalescent Center
2180 10th Ave, Vero Beach FL 32960-5398. 407/567-5166.

Sandy Ridge Care Center
101 Glover Ln, Milton FL 32570-4192. 904/626-9225.

Silvercrest Manor
103 Ruby Ln, Crestview FL 32539-7341. 904/682-1903.

Spanish Garden Nursing Center
1061 Virginia St, Dunedin FL 34698-7399. 813/733-2619.

St Anne's Nursing Center
11855 SW 186th St, Miami FL 33177-3270. 305/252-4000.

Sunbelt Living Center
305 E Oak St, Apopka FL 32703-4373. 407/880-2266.

Sunbelt Living Center
250 S Chickasaw Trail, Orlando FL 32825-3503. 407/380-3466.

Suncoast Nursing Home Ltd.
2000 17th Ave S, St Petersburg FL 33712-2797. 813/821-3544.

Sunnyside Village Health Care Center
5201 Bahia Vista St, Sarasota FL 34232-2615. 941/371-2729.

Surrey Place Convalescent Center
5525 21st Ave W, Bradenton FL 34209-5601. 941/795-0448.

Surrey Place Convalescent Center
Hwy 90 & Corner Of Lee, Live Oak FL 32060. 904/364-5961.

Suwanee Health Care Center
1620 Helvenston St SE, Live Oak FL 32060-9593. 904/364-9929.

Suwannee Valley Nursing Center
427 NW 15th Ave, Jasper FL 32052-9643. 904/792-1868.

The Ambrosia Home
1709 N Taliaferro Ave, Tampa FL 33602-2597. 813/223-4623.

Tyrone Medical Inn
1100 66th St N, St Petersburg FL 33710-6294. 813/345-9331.

Unicare Health Facilities
2201 NE 170th St, N Miami Beach FL 33160-3705. 305/945-1401.

University Healthcare & Rehab Center W
545 W Euclid Ave, Deland FL 32720-6771. 904/734-9085.

Victoria Martin Nursing Home
555 31st St S, St Petersburg FL 33712-1498. 813/327-0995.

Whitehall Boca Raton
7300 S Del Prado Circle, Boca Raton FL 33433-3386. 407/392-3000.

Whitehall Nursing Home
5601 31st St S, St
Petersburg FL 33712-4605.
813/867-6955.

Brynwood Center
P.O. Box 21, Monticello FL
32345-0021. 904/997-
1800.

Jefferson Nursing Center
P.O. Box 500, Monticello FL
32345-0500. 904/997-
2313.

**La Posada Convalescent
Center**
5271 SW 8th St, Miami FL
33134-2374. 305/443-
5423.

Moorings Park
120 Moorings Park Dr,
Naples FL 33942-2188.
941/261-1616.

Plymouth Harbor
700 John Ringling Blvd,
Sarasota FL 34236-1541.
941/365-2600.

**Surrey Place Convalescent
Center**
2730 W Marc Knighton Ct,
Lecanto FL 34461-8334.
904/746-9500.

Westminister Asbury Manor
1700 21st Ave W,
Bradenton FL 34205.
941/748-4161.

Convalescent Center
300 15th St, West Palm
Beach FL 33401-2799.
407/832-6409.

**HOSPITALS AND MEDICAL
CENTERS**

Palms West Hospital
13001 Southern Blvd,
Loxahatchee FL 33470-
9277. 407/798-3300.

Walton Regional Hospital
21 College Ave, Defuniak
Springs FL 32433-2842.
904/892-5171.

Ed Fraser Memorial Hospital
159 N 3rd St, MacClenny FL
32063-2103. 904/259-
3151.

South Bay Hospital
4016 State Road 674, Sun
City Center FL 33573-5298.
813/634-3301.

AG Holley State Hospital
P.O. Box 3084, Lantana FL
33465. 407/582-5666.

American Hospital Systems
6784 Daughtry Blvd S,
Jacksonville FL 32210-6934.
904/771-9592.

Bradford Hospital
P.O. Box 1210, Starke FL
32091-1210. 904/964-
6000.

Calhoun-Liberty Hospital
424 Burns Ave, Blountstown
FL 32424-1004. 904/674-
5411.

**Campbellton Graceville
Hospital**
5429 College Dr, Graceville
FL 32440-1897. 904/263-
4431.

CPC Palm Bay Hospital
4400 Dixie Hwy NE, Palm
Bay FL 32905-4334.
407/729-0500.

Delray Community Hospital
5352 Linton Blvd, Delray
Beach FL 33484-6514.
407/395-3472.

Doctors' Memorial Hospital
P.O. Box 188, Bonifay FL
32425-0188. 904/547-
1120.

Emerald Coast Hospital
P.O. Box 610, Apalachicola
FL 32329-0610. 904/653-
8853.

Florida Hospital Apopka
201 N Park Ave, Apopka FL
32703-4147. 407/889-
1000.

Gulf Pines Hospital
P.O. Box 70, Port St Joe FL
32456-0070. 904/227-
1121.

**Hamilton County Memorial
Hospital**
P.O. Box 1300, Jasper FL
32052-1300. 904/792-
2101.

Harbor Oaks Hospital
1015 Mar Walt Dr, Ft Walton
Beach FL 32547-6738.
904/863-4160.

Medfield Hospital
12891 Seminole Blvd, Largo
FL 34648-2300. 813/587-
6000.

Midflorida Health Center
P.O. Box 67, Haines City FL
33845-0067. 941/422-
4971.

Savannas Hospital
2550 SE Walton Rd, Port St
Lucie FL 34952-7197.
407/335-0400.

St Johns River Hospital
6300 Beach Blvd,
Jacksonville FL 32216-2782.
904/724-9202.

United Medical Corporation
P.O. Box 1100, Windermere

FL 34786-1100. 407/876-
2200.

University Pavilion Hospital
7425 N University Dr,
Tamarac FL 33321-2955.
954/722-9933.

**Vencor Hospital Fort
Lauderdale**
1516 E Las Olas Blvd, Ft
Lauderdale FL 33301-2346.
954/764-8900.

Vencor Hospital-Coral Gables
5190 SW 8th St, Coral
Gables FL 33134-2495.
305/445-1364.

Vencor Hospital-Tampa
4555 S Manhattan Ave,
Tampa FL 33611-2305.
813/839-6341.

Morningside
9220 102nd Ave, Largo FL
34647-1032. 813/398-
3808.

**HOME HEALTH CARE
SERVICES**

**First Florida Home Health St
Augustine**
4475 US Highway 1 S, St
Augustine FL 32086-7284.
904/794-5640.

ABC Home Health Services
501 E Olympia Ave, Punta
Gorda FL 33950-3837.
941/575-0026.

ABC Home Health Services
13035 Tamiami Trail, North
Port FL 34287-2120.
941/423-2556.

ABC Home Health Services
9238 US Highway 19, Port
Richey FL 34668-4853.
813/844-3377.

ABC Home Health Services
1160 S McCall Rd,
Englewood FL 34223-4230.
941/475-2995.

ABC Home Health Services
6635 W Commercial Blvd,
Tamarac FL 33319-2141.
954/721-2900.

**Able Care Home Health
Agency**
1401 Tamiami Trail, Punta
Gorda FL 33950-5907.
941/639-8877.

American Home Patient
3003 NW 53rd Ave,
Gainesville FL 32653-1845.
352/376-3848.

American Home Patient
412 W 15th St, Panama City
FL 32401-2270. 904/769-
7631.

Associated Home Health Care
220 Congress Park Dr, Suite 125, Delray Beach FL 33445-4605. 407/272-9494.

Central Health Services
2650 Bahia Vista St, Sarasota FL 34239-2635. 941/366-0149.

Columbia Home Healthcare
129 S Park Ave, Titusville FL 32796-3377. 407/383-3477.

Community Home Health
3250 N Andrews Avenue Ext, Pompano Beach FL 33064-2125. 954/973-9400.

First American Home Care
1505 Bill Beck Blvd, Kissimmee FL 34744-9524. 407/931-3522.

First American Home Care
4235 Mariner Blvd, Spring Hill FL 34609-2400. 352/688-0945.

Hospicare Home Health Agency
5300 East Ave, West Palm Beach FL 33407-2362. 407/844-0405.

Interim Health Care
670 N Orlando Ave, Suite 1003, Maitland FL 32751-4465. 407/740-5284.

Interim Health Care
967 S Federal Hwy, Stuart FL 34994-3702. 407/283-7065.

Interim Healthcare
150 Southpark Blvd, Suite 206, St Augustine FL 32086-5179. 904/824-6123.

Kimberly Olsten Quality Care
579 S Indiana Ave, Englewood FL 34223-3757. 941/474-3115.

Kimberly Olsten Quality Care
3655 Cortez Rd W, Bradenton FL 34210-3147. 941/751-6334.

NMC Homecare
976 Florida Central Pkwy, Suite 13, Longwood FL 32750-7504. 407/339-8648.

Nurses House Call
3975 20th St, Vero Beach FL 32960-2493. 407/562-0215.

Orlando Home Care
7575 Dr Phillips Blvd,
Orlando FL 32819-7216. 407/363-9062.

Paragon Homecare
96 Willard St, Cocoa FL 32922-7991. 407/639-0022.

Paragon Homecare
1485 S Semoran Blvd, Suite 1441, Winter Park FL 32792-5508. 407/679-2522.

Paragon Homecare
5200 16th St N, St Petersburg FL 33703-2612. 813/528-8830.

Pharmathera
826 Creighton Rd, Suite A102, Pensacola FL 32504-7076. 904/484-2844.

PPI Nursing Network
2020 NE 48th Ct, Ft Lauderdale FL 33308-4522. 954/938-0805.

Pro Care International Private Care
70 S Congress Ave, Delray Beach FL 33445-4649. 407/243-6411.

Procare Home Health
2206 W Atlantic Ave, Suite 201, Delray Beach FL 33445-4637. 407/272-0003.

Rescare Home Health
6677 13th Ave N, Suite 3-B, St Petersburg FL 33710-5401. 813/384-4441.

Rescare Home Health
19321A US Highway 19 N, Clearwater FL 34624-3102. 813/535-8188.

Rescare Home Health
3665 Bee Ridge Rd, Sarasota FL 34233-1058. 941/921-2108.

RN Home Healthcare
2151 45th St, Suite 209, West Palm Beach FL 33407-2009. 407/460-1500.

Sebastian Home Care
1627 US Highway 1, Sebastian FL 32958-3875. 407/589-5888.

Tri County Home Health Agency
1233 Miccosukee Rd, Tallahassee FL 32308-5007. 904/656-7454.

Visiting Nursing Association
102 Park Place Blvd, Suite B1, Kissimmee FL 34741-2358. 407/846-3547.

Visiting Nursing Association
734 N 3rd St, Suite 416,
Leesburg FL 34748-4437. 352/365-1392.

Visiting Nursing Association
421 W Church St, Jacksonville FL 32202-4173. 904/824-5751.

Vita Health Care At Home
1825 SE Tiffany Ave, Port St Lucie FL 34952-7522. 407/337-3555.

Visiting Nurse Association
1333 Gateway Dr, Suite 1014, Melbourne FL 32901-2623. 407/676-3232.

KIDNEY DIALYSIS CENTERS

American Outpatient Service Corp.
150 S Pine Island Rd, Plantation FL 33324-2669. 954/474-7701.

Renal Care Center Okeechobee
933 SE First St, Belle Glade FL 33430-4305. 407/996-0602.

SPECIALTY OUTPATIENT FACILITIES

Mental Health Center
P.O. Box 9010, Jacksonville FL 32208-0010. 904/695-9145.

Grove Counseling Center
919 S Persimmon Ave, Sanford FL 32771-2319. 407/330-9383.

Project III Of Central Florida
5600 Clarcona Ocoee Rd, Orlando FL 32810-3213. 407/578-6900.

Act Corporation
803 S Woodland Blvd, Deland FL 32720-6898. 904/822-6274.

HEALTH AND ALLIED SERVICES

American Biodyne
1059 Maitland Center Commons B, Maitland FL 32751-7434. 407/875-1677.

Community Home Health
4175 S Congress Ave, Suite 5, Lake Worth FL 33461-4703. 407/641-3141.

Health Force
4602 N Armenia Ave, Suite D2, Tampa FL 33603-2624. 813/879-4009.

Hospice Of Central Florida
2200 Bronson Memorial Highway, Kissimmee FL 34744. 407/846-8582.

National Home Respiratory Care
14529 Larkspur Ln, West Palm Beach FL 33414-8208. 407/795-2066.

TGC Home Health Agency Polycare
2121 SE Lakeview Dr, Sebring FL 33870-4947. 941/385-1400.

Brevard County Blood Bank
2500 Garden St, Titusville FL 32796-2548. 407/267-6712.

Treasure Coast Blood Bank
2316 Nebraska Ave, Fort Pierce FL 34950-4824. 407/466-1152.

Healthmark
25 W Cedar St, Pensacola FL 32501-5945. 904/433-0136.

RESIDENTIAL CARE

Amelia Island Care Center
2700 Atlantic Blvd, Jacksonville FL 32207-3702. 904/354-3325.

Woodhouse
1001 NE 3rd Ave, Pompano Beach FL 33060-5776. 954/786-0344.

Bay Village Of Sarasota
8400 Vamo Rd, Sarasota FL 34231-7811. 941/966-5611.

Brentwood In The Meadow
1900 W Alpha Ct, Lecanto FL 34461-9198. 904/746-4110.

Catalina Gardens
85 Bulldog Blvd, Melbourne FL 32901. 407/984-7966.

Lake Seminole Square Retirement Community
8333 Seminole Blvd, Seminole FL 34642. 813/391-0500.

Lakeview Terrace Retirement Community
331 Raintree Dr, Altoona FL 32702. 904/669-2133.

Mayflower Retirement Community
1620 Mayflower Ct, Winter Park FL 32792-2500. 407/672-1620.

Oak Bluffs Retirement Center
420 Bay Ave, Clearwater FL 34616. 813/445-4700.

Pinehill Village
5905 Pine Hill Rd, Port Richey FL 34668-6693. 813/845-0527.

Presbyterian Retirement Community
50 W Lucerne Circle, Orlando FL 32801-3743. 407/839-5050.

Prosperity Oaks
11381 Prosperity Farms Rd, Palm Beach Gardens FL 33410-3403. 407/694-9709.

Senior Center Of Manatee Glens
2350 57th Ave E, Bradenton FL 34203-4916. 941/751-7680.

Village At Manor Park
5501 Swift Rd, Sarasota FL 34231-6209. 941/922-8778.

Village On The Isle
920 Tamiami Trail S, Venice FL 34285-3652. 941/484-9753.

Westwood Retirement Community
1001 Mar Walt Dr, Ft Walton Beach FL 32547. 904/863-5174.

Willowwood
2855 W Commercial Blvd, Ft Lauderdale FL 33309-2973. 954/739-4200.

For more information on career opportunities in the health care industry:

Associations

AMERICAN ACADEMY OF FAMILY PHYSICIANS
8880 Ward Parkway, Kansas City MO 64114. 816/333-9700. Promotes continuing education for family physicians.

AMERICAN ACADEMY OF PHYSICIAN ASSISTANTS
950 North Washington Street, Alexandria VA 22314. 703/836-2272. Promotes the use of physician assistants.

AMERICAN ASSOCIATION FOR CLINICAL CHEMISTRY
2101 Lovely Street NW, Suite 202, Washington, DC 20037-1526. 202/857-0717. A non-profit association for clinical, chemical, medical, and technical doctors.

AMERICAN ASSOCIATION OF COLLEGES OF OSTEOPATHIC MEDICINE
6110 Executive Boulevard, Suite 405, Rockville MD 20852. 301/468-2037. Provides applications processing services for colleges of osteopathic medicine.

AMERICAN ASSOCIATION OF COLLEGES OF PODIATRIC MEDICINE
1350 Piccard Drive, Suite 322, Rockville MD 20850. 301/990-7400. Provides applications processing services for colleges of podiatric medicine.

AMERICAN ASSOCIATION OF DENTAL SCHOOLS
1625 Massachusetts Avenue NW, Washington DC 20036. 202/667-9433.

AMERICAN ASSOCIATION OF MEDICAL ASSISTANTS
20 North Wacker Drive, Suite 1575, Chicago IL 60606. 312/899-1500.

AMERICAN ASSOCIATION OF NURSE ANESTHETISTS
222 South Prospect Avenue, Park Ridge IL 60068-4001. 708/692-7050.

AMERICAN ASSOCIATION FOR RESPIRATORY CARE
11030 Ables Lane, Dallas TX 75229-4593. 214/243-2272. Promotes the art and science of respiratory care, while focusing on the needs of the patients.

AMERICAN CHIROPRACTIC ASSOCIATION
1701 Clarendon Boulevard, Arlington VA 22209. 703/276-8800.

AMERICAN COLLEGE OF HEALTHCARE ADMINISTRATORS
325 South Patrick Street, Alexandria VA 22314. 703/549-5822.

AMERICAN COLLEGE OF HEALTHCARE EXECUTIVES
One North Franklin, Suite 1700, Chicago IL 60606. 312/424-2800.

AMERICAN DENTAL ASSOCIATION
211 East Chicago Avenue, Chicago IL
60611. 312/440-2500.

**AMERICAN DENTAL HYGIENISTS
ASSOCIATION**
Division of Professional Development, 444
North Michigan Avenue, Suite 3400,
Chicago IL 60611. 312/440-8900.

AMERICAN DIETETIC ASSOCIATION
216 West Jackson Boulevard, Chicago IL
60606-6995. 312/899-0040 or 800/877-
1600. Promotes optimal nutrition to
improve public health and well-being.

**AMERICAN HEALTH INFORMATION
MANAGEMENT ASSOCIATION**
919 North Michigan Avenue, Suite 1400,
Chicago IL 60611. 312/787-2672.

AMERICAN MEDICAL ASSOCIATION
515 North State Street, Chicago IL 60610.
312/464-5000. An organization for medical
doctors.

AMERICAN MEDICAL TECHNOLOGISTS
710 Higgins Road, Park Ridge IL 60068.
708/823-5169.

AMERICAN NURSES ASSOCIATION
600 Maryland Avenue SW, Suite 100W,
Washington DC 20024-2571. 202/554-
4444.

**AMERICAN OCCUPATIONAL THERAPY
ASSOCIATION**
4720 Montgomery Lane, Bethesda MD
20824-1220. 301/652-2682. 800/377-
8555. Fax: 301/652-7711.

AMERICAN OPTOMETRIC ASSOCIATION
243 North Lindbergh Boulevard, St. Louis
MO 63141. 314/991-4100. Offers
publications, discounts, and insurance
programs for members.

**AMERICAN PHYSICAL THERAPY
ASSOCIATION**
1111 North Fairfax Street, Alexandria VA
22314. 703/684-2782. Small fee required
for information.

**AMERICAN VETERINARY MEDICAL
ASSOCIATION**
1931 North Meacham Road, Suite 100,
Schaumburg IL 60173. 708/925-8070.

Provides a forum for the discussion of
issues of importance to the veterinary
profession, and for the development of
official positions.

NATIONAL MEDICAL ASSOCIATION
1012 Tenth Street NW, Washington DC
20001. 202/347-1895.

Directories

**ENCYCLOPEDIA OF MEDICAL
ORGANIZATIONS AND AGENCIES**
Gale Research Inc., 835 Penobscot Building,
Detroit MI 48226. 313/961-2242.

**HEALTH ORGANIZATIONS OF THE UNITED
STATES, CANADA, AND THE WORLD**
Gale Research Inc., 835 Penobscot Building,
Detroit MI 48226. 313/961-2242.

**MEDICAL AND HEALTH INFORMATION
DIRECTORY**
Gale Research Inc., 835 Penobscot Building,
Detroit MI 48226. 313/961-2242.

Magazines

AMERICAN MEDICAL NEWS
American Medical Association, 515 North
State Street, Chicago IL 60605. 312/464-
5000.

CHANGING MEDICAL MARKETS
Theta Corporation, Theta Building,
Middlefield CT 06455. 203/349-1054.

HEALTH CARE EXECUTIVE
American College of Health Care
Executives, One North Franklin, Suite 1700,
Chicago IL 60606. 312/424-2800.

MODERN HEALTHCARE
Crain Communications, 740 North Rush
Street, Chicago IL 60611. 312/649-5374.

NURSEFAX
Springhouse Corporation, 1111 Bethlehem
Pike, P.O. Box 908, Springhouse PA
19477. This is a jobline service designed to
be used in conjunction with *Nursing*
magazine.

HOTELS AND RESTAURANTS

 *Job opportunities in the restaurant industry are plentiful. A number of trends will boost job growth, including population growth, rising incomes, and more dual-income families. Some demand will be met through labor saving innovations like salad bars, untended meal stations, automated beverage stations, and central kitchens that serve a number of establishments in the same restaurant chain. In the fast-food sector, use of labor-saving technology is essential to remain competitive. Since most time consuming transaction at drive-in windows is making change, some restaurants are experimenting with debit and credit cards to reduce transaction time. However, despite labor-saving innovations, the increased demand for services will increase the need for workers.*

Jobs in hotels, motels and other lodging places will be plentiful throughout the next decade. Driving the growth will be many of the same trends affecting the restaurant industry, as well as low-cost airfares and foreign tourism in the U.S. Another hot trend: legalized gambling. The hotel and motel industry invests heavily in the gaming industry, and that has further fueled job growth. This growth will continue as hotels increasingly attract families by offering relatively inexpensive casino vacation packages.

The greatest growth is in all-suite properties and budget motels. Since they don't have restaurants, dining rooms, lounges, or kitchens, these properties offer few jobs for food and beverage workers, but jobs should be available for managers and assistant managers. The trend toward chain-affiliated lodging places should provide managers with opportunities for advancement into general manager positions and corporate administrative jobs.

BSM MARINA INC.
5000 Burnt Store Road, Punta Gorda FL 33955. 941/639-4151. **Contact:** Personnel Director. **Description:** A resort operation.

BENIHANA OF TOKYO, INC.
8685 Northwest 53rd Terrace, Suite 201, Miami FL 33166. 305/593-0770x217. **Fax:** 305/592-6371. **Contact:** Ana Ramos, Director of Human Resources. **Description:** Benihana Corporation owns and operates 20 Japanese steakhouses and an additional three are operated by licensees. The number of guests served at these locations reached nearly 1.75 million during 1994. In the next few years, Benihana Corporation plans to expand their chain to locate additional restaurants in California and Texas, while also expecting to introduce smaller restaurants designed specifically for malls and shopping centers. **Common positions include:** Accountant/Auditor; Data Entry Clerk; Purchasing Agent and Manager; Restaurant/Food Service Manager. **Educational backgrounds include:** Accounting; Business Administration; Liberal Arts. **Benefits:** Dental Insurance; Life Insurance; Medical Insurance. **Corporate headquarters location:** This Location. **Other U.S. locations:** CA; CO; GA; IL; NJ; NY; OH; OR; TX. **Operations at this facility include:** Regional Headquarters. **Number of employees nationwide:** 1,650.

BONAVENTURE RESORT & SPA
250 Racquet Club Road, Fort Lauderdale FL 33326. 954/389-3300. **Recorded Jobline:** 954/389-0185. **Contact:** Human Resources. **Description:** A 500-room hotel.

BUENA VISTA PALACE HOTEL
P.O. Box 22206, Lake Buena Vista FL 32830. 407/827-3250. **Recorded Jobline:** 407/827-3255. **Contact:** Nancy McDonald, Employment Manager. **Description:** A hotel. **Common positions include:** Food and Beverage Service Worker; Hotel/Motel Clerk; Human Resources Specialist; Purchasing Agent and Manager; Services Sales Representative. **Educational backgrounds include:** Accounting; Business Administration. **Benefits:** 401K; Dental Insurance; Employee Discounts; Life Insurance; Medical Insurance; Savings Plan; Tuition Assistance. **Operations at this facility include:** Service.

CATERAIR INTERNATIONAL CORPORATION
3500 North West 24th Street, Miami FL 33142. 305/635-9516. **Contact:** Emily Sugg, Regional Human Resource Director. **Description:** Caterair prepares and delivers food for airlines. **Common positions include:** Buyer; Computer Programmer; Management Trainee; Operations/Production Manager.

CHECKERS DRIVE-IN RESTAURANTS, INC.
Barnett Bank Building, 600 Cleveland Street, 8th Floor, Clearwater FL 34615. 813/441-3500. **Fax:** 813/443-7047. **Contact:** Anthony L. Austin, Vice President/Human Resources. **Description:** Checkers Drive-In Restaurants, Inc. develops, owns, operates and franchises quick-service double drive-thru restaurants under the Checkers name. As of January 1995, the company had an ownership interest in 261 company-operated restaurants, 235 restaurants operated by franchisees, and plans to develop between 40 and 70 new restaurants and franchises. The restaurants are designed to provide fast and efficient automobile-oriented service, incorporating a 1950's diner and art deco theme with a highly visible, distinctive, and uniform look intended to appeal to customers of all ages. Checkers offers an intensive technical and operational management training. **Common positions include:** Restaurant/Food Service Manager. **Benefits:** 401K; Bonus Award/Plan; Dental Insurance; Disability Coverage; Employee Discounts; Life Insurance; Medical Insurance; Stock Option. **Corporate headquarters location:** This Location. **Listed on:** NASDAQ. **Number of employees at this location:** 150. **Number of employees nationwide:** 12,000.

CROWN ROYAL HOTEL
1601 Biscayne Boulevard, Miami FL 33132. 305/374-0000. **Recorded Jobline:** 305/374-8065. **Contact:** Human Resources. **Description:** A 550-room hotel.

DAVGAR RESTAURANTS, INC.
CENTRAL FLORIDA RESTAURANT GROUP
601 North New York Avenue, Winter Park FL 32789. 407/647-4300. **Fax:** 407/647-5306. **Contact:** Joe Hayes, Vice President of Human Resources. **Description:** A restaurant management company. Restaurants operated by Davgar include Burger King, Pebble, and Miami Subs. **NOTE:** College education is not a requirement. **Common positions include:** Management Trainee. **Educational backgrounds include:** Accounting; Business Administration; Communications; Liberal Arts. **Benefits:** 401K; Dental Insurance; Disability Coverage; Life Insurance; Medical Insurance; Tuition Assistance. **Corporate headquarters location:** This Location. **Listed on:** Privately held.

DORAL OCEAN BEACH RESORT
4833 Collins Avenue, Miami Beach FL 33140. 305/532-3600. **Recorded Jobline:** 305/535-2055. **Contact:** Human Resources. **Description:** A 420-room hotel.

DORAL RESORT AND COUNTRY CLUB
4400 NW 87th Avenue, Miami FL 33178. 305/592-2000. **Recorded Jobline:** 305/591-6424. **Contact:** Human Resources. **Description:** A 650-room resort hotel.

ERICKSON MANAGEMENT COMPANY INC.
1860 Boy Scout Drive, Suite 201, Fort Meyers FL 33907. **Contact:** Human Resources. **Description:** A Perkins restaurant franchisee. **Common positions include:** Management Trainee; Restaurant/Food Service Manager. **Benefits:** Dental Insurance; Employee Discounts; Life Insurance; Medical Insurance; Savings Plan. **Corporate headquarters location:** This Location. **Other U.S. locations:** Cape Coral FL; Murdock FL; Naples FL. **Number of employees nationwide:** 230.

FAMILY STEAK HOUSES OF FLORIDA, INC.
2113 Florida Boulevard, Neptune Beach FL 32266. 904/249-4197. **Contact:** Chet Enten, Director of Human Resources. **Description:** Operates a chain of family restaurants. **Number of employees nationwide:** 1,550.

FAMOUS AMOS RESTAURANTS, INC.
2765 Clydo Road, Jacksonville FL 32207. 904/731-3396. **Contact:** Kenny Rigdon, Operations Manager. **Description:** Corporate office for a chain of 10 restaurants.

FONTAINEBLEAU HILTON RESORT
4441 Collins Avenue, Miami Beach FL 33140. 305/538-2000. **Recorded Jobline:** 305/538-2000, x3723. **Contact:** Human Resources. **Description:** A 1,200-room hotel.

GOLF HOSTS INC.
36750 U.S. Highway 19 North, Palm Harbor FL 34688. 813/942-2000. **Contact:** Human Resources. **Description:** A parent company whose subsidiaries are golf resorts.

GRENELEFE RESORT
3200 State Road 546, Haines City FL 33844-9732. 941/422-7511. **Recorded Jobline:** 941/421-5027. **Contact:** Human Resources. **Description:** A 950-room hotel, which operates a golf course and tennis courts.

H.I. DEVELOPMENT, INC.
111 West Fortune Street, Tampa FL 33602. 813/229-6686. **Contact:** Personnel. **Description:** A hotel-industry management and consulting firm. **Common positions include:** Accountant/Auditor; Administrative Worker/Clerk; Advertising Clerk; General Manager; Hotel Manager/Assistant Manager; Human Resources Specialist; Marketing Specialist. **Educational backgrounds include:** Accounting. **Benefits:** Employee Discounts; Life Insurance; Medical Insurance. **Special Programs:** Training Programs. **Corporate headquarters location:** This Location. **Operations at this facility include:** Regional Headquarters.

HYATT ORLANDO NEIGHBOR TO WALT DISNEY
6375 West Irlo Bronson Memorial Highway, Kissimmee FL 34747. 407/396-1234. **Recorded Jobline:** 407/396-5001. **Contact:** Human Resources. **Description:** A 924-room hotel.

HYATT REGENCY GRAND CYPRESS
One Grand Cypress Boulevard, Orlando FL 32836. 407/239-1234. **Recorded Jobline:** 407/239-3899. **Contact:** Director of Personnel. **Description:** A resort hotel.

HYATT REGENCY ORLANDO INTERNATIONAL AIRPORT
9300 Airport Boulevard, Orlando FL 32827. 407/825-1310. **Fax:** 407/825-1341. **Recorded Jobline:** 407/825-1342. **Contact:** Michelle Anderson, Employment Manager. **Description:** A 446-room hotel. **Common positions include:** Accountant/Auditor; Credit Manager; Electrician; General Manager; Hotel Manager/Assistant Manager; Purchasing Agent and Manager; Restaurant/Food Service Manager. **Educational backgrounds include:** Accounting; Business Administration; Marketing. **Benefits:** 401K; Daycare Assistance; Dental Insurance; Disability Coverage; Employee Discounts; Life Insurance; Medical Insurance; Pension Plan; Tuition Assistance. **Corporate headquarters location:** Chicago IL. **Other U.S. locations:** Nationwide. **Operations at this facility include:** Service. **Listed on:** Privately held. **Number of employees at this location:** 400. **Number of employees nationwide:** 40,000.

HYATT REGENCY PIER SIXTY-SIX
2301 SE 17th Street Causeway, Fort Lauderdale FL 33316. 954/728-3580. **Fax:** 954/728-3509. **Recorded Jobline:** 954/728-3583. **Contact:** Human Resources. **Description:** A 388-room, full-service, four-star resort on 22 acres, with a 142-slip marina. **Common positions include:** Accountant/Auditor; Customer Service Representative; General Manager; Hotel Manager/Assistant Manager; Human Resources Specialist; Restaurant/Food Service Manager. **Educational backgrounds include:** Business Administration; Hospitality/Restaurant; Hotel Administration. **Benefits:** 401K; Dental Insurance; Disability Coverage; Employee Discounts; Life Insurance; Medical Insurance; Pension Plan; Tuition Assistance. **Special Programs:** Internships. **Parent company:** Rahn Properties. **Operations at this facility include:** Administration; Divisional Headquarters; Sales. **Listed on:** Privately held. **Number of employees at this location:** 500.

HYATT REGENCY TAMPA AT TAMPA CITY CENTER
2 Tampa City Center, 211 North Tampa Street, Tampa FL 33602. 813/225-1234.
Recorded Jobline: 813/225-1234; ask for the job hotline extension. **Contact:** Human
Resources. **Description:** A 517-room hotel.

HYATT REGENCY WESTSHORE AT TAMPA INTERNATIONAL
6200 Courtney Campbell Causeway, Tampa FL 33607. 813/874-1234. **Recorded
Jobline:** 813/287-0666. **Contact:** Human Resources. **Description:** A 445-room hotel.

INTERNATIONAL HOUSE OF PANCAKES
FMS MANAGEMENT SYSTEMS, INC.
2655 North East 189th Street, North Miami Beach FL 33180. 305/931-5454.
Contact: Employment. **Description:** Franchises and operates restaurants.

LANGFORD RESORT HOTEL
P.O. Box 970, Winter Park FL 32790. 407/644-3400. **Contact:** Pam Langford,
Personnel Director. **Description:** A resort hotel.

MARRIOTT AT SAWGRASS
1000 TPC Boulevard, Ponte Vedra Beach FL 32082. 904/285-7777. **Recorded
Jobline:** 904/285-7777x6738. **Contact:** Human Resources. **Description:** A 550-room
hotel.

MARRIOTT BISCAYNE
1633 North Bayshore Drive, Miami FL 33132. 305/374-3900. **Contact:** Human
Resources. **Description:** A 605-room hotel.

MARRIOTT ORLANDO
8001 International Drive, Orlando FL 32819. 407/351-2420. **Fax:** 407/352-2054.
Recorded Jobline: 407/351-2420x7722. **Contact:** Sandra Armistad, Human
Resources. **Description:** A 1,076-room hotel, operating as a part of Marriott Hotels,
Resorts, and Suites. Marriott International has nearly 3,800 units, with operations and
franchises in 50 states and 22 countries. The company operates lodging facilities and
is the franchiser under four separate brand names, each serving a part of the lodging
market: Marriott Hotels, Resorts, and Suites (full-service), Courtyard Hotels (moderate
price), Residence Inn (extended stay), and Fairfield Inn (economy). The company also
develops and operates Marriott Ownership Resorts (vacation timesharing). The full-
service Marriott hotel system includes 251 Mariott Hotels, Resorts, and Suites located
in 39 states and 18 foreign countries with a total of 103,985 guest rooms. **Common
positions include:** Accountant/Auditor; Credit Manager; Electrical/Electronics Engineer;
Human Resources Specialist; Restaurant/Food Service Manager. **Educational
backgrounds include:** Accounting; Business Administration; Engineering; Finance;
Hospitality/Restaurant; Hotel Administration. **Benefits:** 401K; Dental Insurance;
Disability Coverage; Employee Discounts; Life Insurance; Medical Insurance; Savings
Plan; Tuition Assistance. **Corporate headquarters location:** Pittsburgh PA. **Other U.S.
locations:** Nationwide. **Parent company:** Interstate Hotels. **Operations at this facility
include:** Administration; Sales. **Listed on:** Privately held. **Number of employees at this
location:** 550. **Number of employees worldwide:** 170,000.

MARRIOTT ORLANDO AIRPORT
7499 Augusta National Drive, Orlando FL 32802. 407/851-9000. **Recorded Jobline:**
407/851-9000x5201. **Contact:** Human Resources. **Description:** A 484-room hotel
operating as part of Marriott International.

MARRIOTT'S ORLANDO WORLD CENTER
8701 World Center Drive, Orlando FL 32821. 407/239-4200. **Recorded Jobline:**
407/238-8822. **Contact:** Human Resources. **Description:** A 1,503-room hotel.

OUTBACK STEAKHOUSE, INC.
550 North Reo Street, Suite 204, Tampa FL 33609. 813/282-1225. **Contact:** Human
Resources. **Description:** The company operates over 125 Outback Steakhouse
Restaurants, which are dinner-only establishments featuring moderately-priced foods
and a casual atmosphere suggestive of the Australian Outback. The menu features
steaks, prime rib, barbecue ribs, pork chops, chicken, seafood and pasta. **Number of
employees nationwide:** 8,800.

PEABODY ORLANDO
9801 International Drive, Orlando FL 32819. 407/352-4000. **Recorded Jobline:** 407/352-6481. **Contact:** Human Resources. **Description:** An 891-room hotel.

REGISTRY RESORT
475 Seagate Drive, Naples FL 33940. 941/597-3232. **Recorded Jobline:** 941/597-4646. **Contact:** Human Resources. **Description:** A 474-room hotel.

RENAISSANCE HOTELS INTERNATIONAL, INC.
2655 LeJune Road, Suite 800, Coral Gables FL 33134. 305/460-1900. **Fax:** 305/460-4200. **Contact:** Human Resources Coordinator. **Description:** An international hotel company. **Common positions include:** Accountant/Auditor; Credit Manager; General Manager; Hotel Manager/Assistant Manager; Human Resources Specialist; Management Trainee; Mechanical Engineer; Purchasing Agent and Manager. **Educational backgrounds include:** Accounting; Business Administration; Communications; Finance; Liberal Arts; Marketing. **Benefits:** 401K; Dental Insurance; Disability Coverage; Employee Discounts; Life Insurance; Medical Insurance; Tuition Assistance. **Corporate headquarters location:** Hong Kong. **Parent company:** New World Development Company. **Operations at this facility include:** Regional Headquarters.

RESTAURANT ADMINISTRATION SERVICES
2699 Lee Road, #200, Winter Park FL 32789. 407/645-4811. **Fax:** 407/629-0641. **Contact:** Dale Lucas, Director of Personnel and Training. **Description:** Operates quick-service restaurants. **Common positions include:** Management Trainee; Restaurant/Food Service Manager. **Educational backgrounds include:** Business Administration. **Benefits:** Dental Insurance; Disability Coverage; Employee Discounts; IRA; Life Insurance; Medical Insurance; Tuition Assistance. **Corporate headquarters location:** This Location. **Listed on:** Privately held. **Number of employees at this location:** 1,200.

RESTAURANT MANAGEMENT SERVICES
POPEYE'S DIVISION
906 Lee Road, Orlando FL 32810. 407/628-0393. **Fax:** 407/628-8311. **Contact:** Personnel Department. **Description:** The largest Popeye's franchise, with over 60 locations in central and northern Florida. **Common positions include:** General Manager; Management Trainee; Restaurant/Food Service Manager. **Benefits:** 401K; Dental Insurance; Life Insurance; Medical Insurance; Tuition Assistance. **Corporate headquarters location:** Macon GA. **Operations at this facility include:** Divisional Headquarters. **Listed on:** Privately held. **Number of employees nationwide:** 2,500.

SERVICO, INC.
1601 Belvedere Road, West Palm Beach FL 33406. 407/689-9970. **Contact:** Personnel Department. **Description:** Servico, Inc. owns or manages 39 hotels located in 16 states and Puerto Rico. These hotels are primarily full-service, providing food and beverage service as well as lodging and meeting facilities. Virtually all of the company's hotels are affiliated with nationally recognized hospitality franchises, including Holiday Inn, Omni, Hilton, Embassy Suites, Radisson, Howard Johnson, Ramada, Days Inn, Comfort Inn, Royce, and Westin.

SHERATON BAL HARBOUR RESORT
9701 Collins Avenue, Bal Harbour FL 33154. 305/865-7511. **Recorded Jobline:** 305/865-7511x3275. **Contact:** Human Resources. **Description:** A 650-room hotel.

SOUTHERN INDUSTRIAL CORPORATION
9009 Regency Square Boulevard, Jacksonville FL 32211. 904/725-4122. **Fax:** 904/723-3498. **Contact:** Jimmy Harms, Director of Franchise Operations. **Description:** A franchiser of Burger King restaurants in Duval, Clay, and St. Johns Counties. **Common positions include:** General Manager; Management Trainee; Restaurant/Food Service Manager.

SUN INTERNATIONAL, INC.
915 North East 125th Street, North Miami FL 33161. 305/891-2500. **Contact:** Human Resources Manager. **Description:** Owners and operators of casinos, resorts, and hotel facilities. **Common positions include:** Accountant/Auditor; Administrative Services Manager; Computer Programmer; Computer Systems Analyst; Customer Service Representative; Hotel Manager/Assistant Manager; Human Service Worker; Management Trainee. **Benefits:** 401K; Dental Insurance; Disability Coverage; Employee Discounts; Medical Insurance; Pension Plan; Tuition Assistance. **Corporate**

headquarters location: Africa. **Number of employees at this location:** 200. **Number of employees nationwide:** 15,000.

TPI ENTERPRISES INC.
3950 RCA Boulevard, Suite 5001, Palm Beach Gardens FL 33401. 407/691-8800. **Contact:** Human Resources. **Description:** A franchiser of restaurants.

WALT DISNEY WORLD DOLPHIN
1500 EPCOT Resorts Boulevard, Lake Buena Vista FL 32830. 407/934-4000. **Recorded Jobline:** 407/934-4200. **Contact:** Human Resources. **Description:** A 1,510-room hotel.

WALT DISNEY WORLD SWAN
1200 EPCOT Resorts Boulevard, Lake Buena Vista FL 32830. 407/934-3000. **Recorded Jobline:** 407/934-1660. **Contact:** Human Resources. **Description:** A 758-room hotel.

Note: Because addresses and telephone numbers of smaller companies change rapidly, we recommend you call each company to verify the information below before inquiring about job opportunities. Mass mailings are not recommended.

Additional employers with over 250 employees:

EATING PLACES

Bayport Restaurant Group
4000 Hollywood Blvd, Hollywood FL 33021-6747. 954/967-6700.

Char-Hut Of America
4800 SW 64th Ave, Ft Lauderdale FL 33314-4438. 954/581-9404.

Coffee Kettle
16900 Front Beach Rd,
Panama City FL 32413-2345. 904/234-5628.

Dow Sherwood Corp.
6304 Benjamin Rd Ste 503, Tampa FL 33634-5128. 813/885-5434.

Great Lakes Restaurants Florida
15600 SW 288th St, Homestead FL 33033-1200. 305/247-0325.

Homestyle Buffet
801 W Bay Dr Ste 704, Largo FL 34640-3266. 813/785-1370.

Phaedra Restaurant Corporation
12381 S Cleveland Ave, Suite 500, Fort Myers FL 33907-3854. 813/275-3399.

Additional employers with under 250 employees:

EATING PLACES

Amigos Original Tex-Mex
255 E Granada Blvd, Ormond Beach FL 32176-6632. 904/677-5159.

An Old Family Recipe Cafe
1500 Lucerne Ave, Lake Worth FL 33460-3654. 407/547-7577.

Angel's Diner & Bakery
611 Dog Track Rd, Longwood FL 32750-6549. 407/339-7657.

Angel's Diner & Bakery
1345 Lee Rd, Orlando FL 32810-5852. 407/291-4832.

Applebee's
5550 Fruitville Rd, Sarasota FL 34232-6405. 941/379-2260.

Arby's Roast Beef Restaurant
801 Lee Rd, Orlando FL 32810-5518. 407/628-3232.

Arby's Roast Beef Restaurant
16005 US Highway 441, Eustis FL 32726-6505. 904/589-7433.

Arby's Roast Beef Restaurant
1920 Gulf To Bay Blvd, Clearwater FL 34625-3537. 813/446-1694.

Arby's Roast Beef Restaurant
1305 Tuskawilla Rd, Winter Springs FL 32708-5064. 407/695-8700.

Arby's Roast Beef Restaurant
219 W Vine St, Kissimmee FL 34741-4431. 407/846-9129.

Baja Beach Club
3200 N Federal Hwy, Suite 201, Ft Lauderdale FL 33306-1064. 954/561-2432.

Banana Boat Restaurant & Lounge
739 E Ocean Ave, Boynton
Beach FL 33435-5199. 407/732-9400.

Bern's Steak House
1208 S Howard Ave, Tampa FL 33606-3197. 813/251-2421.

Bo's Restaurant
1427 N Cove Blvd, Panama City FL 32401-3375. 904/913-9787.

Bob Evans Restaurant
9115 US Highway 19, Port Richey FL 34668-4852. 813/848-7599.

Boca Smokehouse
9774 Glades Rd #8, Boca Raton FL 33434-3915. 407/488-3805.

Bono's Pit Bar-B-Q & Catering
110 Lane Ave S, Jacksonville FL 32254-3524. 904/783-1404.

Boston Market
12705 N Dale Mabry Hwy,
Tampa FL 33618-2801.
813/960-8116.

Boston Market
2301 N Federal Hwy, Ft
Lauderdale FL 33305-2538.
954/561-5310.

Boston Market
7555 W Waters Ave, Tampa
FL 33615-1511. 813/886-
4422.

Boston Market
16215 N Dale Mabry Hwy,
Carrollwood FL 33618-1338.
813/962-2621.

Bud's Chicken & Seafood
4661 Okeechobee Blvd,
West Palm Beach FL 33417-
4623. 407/478-0044.

Bud's Chicken & Seafood
509 E Boynton Beach Blvd,
Boynton Beach FL 33435-
4103. 407/732-3618.

Burger King
3444 US Highway 19,
Holiday FL 34691-1850.
813/848-4923.

Burger King
10142 Phillips Hwy,
Jacksonville FL 32256-1328.
904/268-7017.

Burger King
360 W Tharpe St,
Tallahassee FL 32303-5557.
904/385-8020.

Burger King
5598 W Colonial Dr, Orlando
FL 32808-7656. 407/293-
4362.

Burger King
397 E Main St, Pahokee FL
33476-1809. 407/924-
9331.

Burger King
15298 N Dale Mabry Hwy,
Tampa FL 33618-1809.
813/960-2758.

Burger King
6502 E State Road 64,
Bradenton FL 34208-6259.
941/747-7891.

Burger King
9018 S US Highway 1, Port
St Lucie FL 34952-3408.
407/337-0701.

Burger King
2902 E Fletcher Ave, Tampa
FL 33612-9408. 813/971-
8348.

Burger King
11 S Washington Ave,

Titusville FL 32796-2835.
407/267-3056.

California Smoothie
3302 Dr Martin Luther King
Jr., Tampa FL 33607.
813/873-8375.

Capt. Crab's Take-Away
2431 W Sunrise Blvd, Ft
Lauderdale FL 33311-5715.
954/581-2722.

**Captain D's Seafood
Restaurant**
471 W State Road 50,
Winter Garden FL 34787.
407/877-8272.

**Captain D's Seafood
Restaurant**
750 S US Highway 17 & 92,
Longwood FL 32750-5710.
407/339-9678.

**Cha Cha Coconuts St
Petersburg**
800 2nd Ave NE, St
Petersburg FL 33701-3503.
813/822-6655.

**Cha Cha Coconuts Tropical
Bar**
417 Saint Armands Circle,
Sarasota FL 34236-1408.
941/388-3300.

Char-Hut Of Davie
4400 S University Dr, Davie
FL 33328-3008. 954/475-
4823.

Charley's Steak House
6107 S Orange Blossom
Trail, Orlando FL 32809-
4609. 407/851-7130.

Chefs Of France
Epcot Center France Pavilion,
Orlando FL 32830. 407/827-
8709.

Chick-Fil-A
Orange Park Mall, Orange
Park FL 32073. 904/269-
2210.

Chili's Grill & Bar
13050 N Dale Mabry Hwy,
Tampa FL 33618-2808.
813/963-3882.

Chili's Grill & Bar
4131 S Tamiami Trail,
Sarasota FL 34231-3635.
941/922-7601.

Chili's Grill & Bar
3715 Desoto Junction,
Bradenton FL 34205.
941/747-1893.

Chili's Grill & Bar
4781 Bayou Blvd, Pensacola
FL 32503-2607. 904/476-
7881.

China Coast Restaurant
3552 E Colonial Dr, Orlando
FL 32803-5116. 407/898-
6624.

Church's Fried Chicken
3351 W Broward Blvd, Ft
Lauderdale FL 33312-1114.
954/584-7865.

Church's Fried Chicken
4250 Moncrief Rd,
Jacksonville FL 32209-3938.
904/764-6562.

Clock Restaurant
4991 N University Dr, Ft
Lauderdale FL 33351-4508.
954/749-6231.

Clock Restaurant
910 W Vine St, Kissimmee
FL 34741-4165. 407/846-
7366.

Clock Restaurant
1121 E Oak St, Arcadia FL
33821-8904. 941/494-
4404.

Clock Restaurant
4444 4th St N, St
Petersburg FL 33703-4729.
813/522-7981.

Clock Restaurant
301 Tamiami Trail S, Venice
FL 34285-2423. 941/488-
2488.

Country Kitchen
7437 International Dr,
Orlando FL 32819-8248.
407/345-9366.

**Crab House Seafood
Restaurant**
8291 International Dr,
Orlando FL 32819-9326.
407/352-6140.

**Damon's
The Place For Ribs**
18409 US Highway 19 N,
Clearwater FL 34624-1740.
813/530-7677.

Deli Den
2889 Stirling Rd, Hollywood
FL 33020. 954/961-4070.

Denny's
2277 S Byron Butler Pkwy,
Perry FL 32347-6103.
904/584-7778.

Denny's
1311 W Palmetto Park Rd,
Boca Raton FL 33486-3312.
407/368-3212.

Di Pasqua Enterprises
167 Lookout Place, Maitland
FL 32751-8420. 407/644-
8578.

Dine In/Carryout
2199 S Woodland Blvd,
Deland FL 32720-7912.
904/736-7666.

East Side Mario's
2639 N Monroe St,
Tallahassee FL 32303-4073.
904/385-0170.

El Caribe
5709 N Armenia Ave, Tampa
FL 33603-1019. 813/870-
1066.

Fazoli's Italian Food Fast
1316 S Babcock St,
Melbourne FL 32901-3067.
407/722-2780.

Fazoli's Italian Food Fast
3922 E Colonial Dr, Orlando
FL 32803-5210. 407/894-
7006.

Flanigan's Guppy's
45 S Federal Hwy, Boca
Raton FL 33432-4804.
407/395-4324.

Friendly's Restaurant
1810 W International
Speedway, Daytona Beach
FL 32114-1216. 904/238-
0657.

Fuddruckers Restaurants
1801 N University Dr, Ft
Lauderdale FL 33322-4105.
954/476-8111.

Goodfellas
15363 Amberly Dr, Tampa
FL 33647-2144. 813/972-
2826.

Gumby's Pizza
5651 E Fowler Ave, Tampa
FL 33617-2307. 813/977-
2000.

Ham N Egg Inc.
Florida Division
4405 El Mar Dr, Ft
Lauderdale FL 33308-3605.
954/776-2549.

Hamilton's Seafood
Restaurant
5711 N Lagoon Dr, Panama
City Beach FL 32408-3704.
904/234-1255.

Hardee's
5026 Old US Hwy 301,
Bradenton FL 34203.
941/753-4125.

Hardee's
206 6th St, Port St Joe FL
32456. 904/229-8200.

Hardee's
9612 San Jose Blvd,
Jacksonville FL 32257-5434.
904/268-5244.

Hardee's
300 S Highway 17-92,

Longwood FL 32750.
407/331-4145.

Harvey's Sandwich & Salad
Shop
1214 US Highway 19,
Holiday FL 34691-5639.
813/942-3636.

Holiday House Restaurant
615 E 3rd Ave, New Smyrna
FL 32169-3133. 904/428-
5954.

Holiday House Restaurant
2203 Aloma Ave, Winter
Park FL 32792-3303.
407/671-6181.

Hops Grill & Bar
18825 US Highway 19 N,
Clearwater FL 34624-3122.
813/531-5300.

Hot Dogs & More
801 N Congress Ave,
Boynton Beach FL 33426-
3315. 407/732-6273.

Houston's Restaurant
1451 N Federal Hwy, Ft
Lauderdale FL 33304-1472.
954/563-2226.

JC's Restaurant & Lounge
St Petersburg-Clearwater
Inter, Clearwater FL 34620.
813/531-1611.

Jerry's Family Restaurant
3500 SE Federal Hwy, Stuart
FL 34997-4916. 407/288-
7286.

Jerry's Restaurant & Catering
Service
1 Air Terminal Pkwy,
Melbourne FL 32901-1856.
407/727-3676.

Julie's
2901 N Monroe St,
Tallahassee FL 32303-3636.
904/386-7181.

Kenny Rogers Roasters Of
Florida
1899 N Congress Ave,
Boynton Beach FL 33426-
8203. 407/369-5033.

Kenny Rogers Roasters
9380 N 56th St, Tampa FL
33617-5504. 813/980-
0435.

KFC
5080 N 9th Ave, Pensacola
FL 32504-8720. 904/484-
6411.

KFC
667 Royal Palm Beach Blvd,
Royal Palm Beach FL 33411-
7635. 407/798-8803.

KFC
13200 US Highway 19, Port

Richey FL 34667-1656.
813/868-6179.

KFC
2525 S Military Trail, West
Palm Beach FL 33415-7547.
407/433-9150.

L&N Seafood
3101 PGA Blvd, Palm Beach
Gardens FL 33410.
407/627-0582.

Lawton's Restaurant & Pub
207 Dunlawton Ave,
Daytona Beach FL 32127-
4407. 904/760-4456.

Leverock's Seafood House
565 150th Ave, Madeira
Beach FL 33708-2061.
813/393-0459.

Little Caesar's Pizza
3444 S Westshore Blvd,
Tampa FL 33629-8221.
813/831-6510.

Little Tomoka Yacht Club
State Rd 40, Ormond Beach
FL 32174. 904/672-4695.

Long John Silvers Seafood
10880 W Colonial Dr, Ocoee
FL 34761-2981. 407/656-
5533.

Longhorn Steaks
951 Sand Lake Rd, Orlando
FL 32809-7711. 407/858-
1120.

Luby's Cafeteria
7770 66th St, Pinellas Park
FL 34665-3115. 813/544-
2600.

Lucky Snapper Grill & Bar
76 Highway 98 E, Destin FL
32541-2310. 904/654-
0900.

Manchu Wok Restaurant
8001 S Orange Blossom
Trail, Orlando FL 32809-
7654. 407/859-8197.

Margaritaville Cafe
2755 Ulmerton Rd,
Clearwater FL 34622-3303.
813/571-1121.

Mash Hoagies
2068 N Courtenay Pkwy,
Merritt Is FL 32953-4285.
407/459-1884.

Max's Grille
404 Plaza Real, Boca Raton
FL 33432-3939. 407/391-
7177.

Maxaluna Ristorante
5050 Town Center Circle,
Boca Raton FL 33486-1011.
407/391-7177.

McDonald's Restaurant
1846 State Road 44, New
Smyrna FL 32168-8343.
904/423-3444.

McDonald's Restaurant
3671 S Congress Ave, Lake
Worth FL 33461-3755.
407/968-5286.

McDonald's Restaurant
201 NW 13th St, Gainesville
FL 32601-5125. 352/378-
7910.

McDonald's Restaurant
799 E Highway 50, Clermont
FL 34711-3187. 904/394-
3174.

McDonald's Restaurant
815 E Cervantes St,
Pensacola FL 32501-3211.
904/438-1384.

McDonald's Restaurant
6708 Manatee Ave W,
Bradenton FL 34209-2249.
941/794-6227.

McDonald's Restaurant
1000 Plaza Dr, Kissimmee FL
34743-4069. 407/348-
8644.

McDonald's Restaurant
5401 Altamira Dr, Orlando
FL 32819-9430. 407/345-
9477.

Miami Subs
1915 E Fowler Ave, Tampa
FL 33612-5501. 813/971-
0995.

Miami Subs
4999 S State Road 7, Davie
FL 33314-5648. 954/583-
9990.

Miami Subs
618 E Vine St, Kissimmee FL
34744-4291. 407/846-
8847.

Morrison's
3831 W Irlo Bronson
Memorial Hwy, Kissimmee FL
34741. 407/846-6011.

Morrison's
Gulf View Square Mall, Port
Richey FL 34668. 813/848-
4338.

Murray's Palm Beach Diner
2880 S Ocean Blvd, Lantana
FL 33462-6213. 407/582-
9661.

Murray's Wings & Ribs
200 Semoran Blvd,
Casselberry FL 32707-4964.
407/339-1212.

Naco's Tacos
3101 PGA Blvd, Palm Beach
Gardens FL 33410.
407/775-0464.

Newbern Enterprises
1800 Huntington Ln,
Rockledge FL 32955-3156.
407/631-5203.

O'Charley's
1795 W New Haven Ave, W
Melbourne FL 32904-3909.
407/951-2171.

**Olive Garden Italian
Restaurant**
4900 S Tamiami Trail,
Sarasota FL 34231-4354.
941/923-3136.

**Olive Garden Italian
Restaurant**
1555 Sand Lake Rd, Orlando
FL 32809-7080. 407/851-
0344.

**Olive Garden Italian
Restaurant**
1490 Semoran Blvd,
Casselberry FL 32707-6509.
407/678-6577.

**Olive Garden Italian
Restaurant**
29461 US Highway 19 N,
Clearwater FL 34621-2132.
813/787-3988.

**Olive Garden Italian
Restaurant**
2508 W New Haven Ave, W
Melbourne FL 32904-3702.
407/722-2204.

Original Pancake House
1101 N Federal Hwy, Ft
Lauderdale FL 33304-1444.
954/564-8881.

Pacino's Italian Ristorante
5795 W Irlo Bronson
Memorial Hwy 19,
Kissimmee FL 34746-4748.
407/396-8022.

Parker's Bar-B-Q
3192 Shoal Line Blvd, Spring
Hill FL 34607-3433.
352/596-7826.

Patrick's Restaurant
1442 Main St, Sarasota FL
34236-5715. 941/952-
1170.

Perkins
6023 14th St W, Bradenton
FL 34207-4105. 941/755-
2658.

Perkins
3419 W Vine St, Kissimmee
FL 34741-4630. 407/847-
3577.

Piccadilly Cafeteria
Desoto Square Mall,
Bradenton FL 34205.
941/747-6777.

Piccolo Mondo Ristorante
3131 Clark Rd, Sarasota FL

34231-7320. 941/925-
0226.

Pizza Hut
345 W Lake Mary Blvd,
Sanford FL 32773-5924.
407/324-4900.

Pizza Hut
2934 N State Road 7, Ft
Lauderdale FL 33313-1939.
954/484-1330.

Pizza Hut
239 W Hibiscus Blvd,
Melbourne FL 32901-3044.
407/724-9100.

Pizza Hut
5628 Hansel Ave, Orlando FL
32809-4216. 407/856-
6212.

Pizza Hut
868 Jupiter Blvd NW, Palm
Bay FL 32907-9338.
407/768-6767.

Pizza Hut
3214 Lake Washington Rd,
Melbourne FL 32934-7620.
407/253-0700.

Pizza Hut
2015 State Road 434 W,
Longwood FL 32779-4981.
407/862-1028.

Pizza Hut
12036 Anderson Rd, Tampa
FL 33625-5682. 813/265-
4222.

Pizza Hut
10694 N 56th St, Tampa FL
33617-3641. 813/980-
0333.

Pizza Hut
1403 N Woodland Blvd,
Deland FL 32720-2212.
904/734-0516.

Pizza Hut
38553 US Highway 19 N,
Palm Harbor FL 34684-1033.
813/934-3366.

Pizza Hut
2490 Enterprise Rd, Orange
City FL 32763-7902.
904/775-4077.

Pizza Hut
5439 N Orange Blossom
Trail, Orlando FL 32810-
1012. 407/295-8622.

Pizza Hut
500 Barton Blvd, Rockledge
FL 32955-3172. 407/632-
9911.

Plaza Cafe
4900 Linton Blvd, Delray
Beach FL 33445-6688.
407/499-5311.

Po' Folks
1538 S Washington Ave,
Titusville FL 32780-4713.
407/264-9488.

Pollo Tropical
489 W State Road 436,
Altamonte Springs FL
32714-4103. 407/865-
6750.

Ponderosa Steakhouse
6362 International Dr,
Orlando FL 32819-8214.
407/352-9343.

Prime Time Steak & Spirits
5855 Placida Rd, Englewood
FL 34224-9531. 941/697-
7799.

Rally's Hamburgers
7504 Atlantic Blvd,
Jacksonville FL 32211-8714.
904/720-5487.

Ruby Tuesday Restaurant
Governor's Square Mall,
Tallahassee FL 32301.
904/656-1309.

Ryan's Steak House
1008 Edgewood Ave N,
Jacksonville FL 32254-2324.
904/783-6600.

Sapori Restaurant
2617 E Sunrise Blvd, Ft
Lauderdale FL 33304-3205.
954/565-7447.

SbarroThe Italian Eatery
6901 22nd Ave N, St
Petersburg FL 33710.
813/347-6570.

Sbarro The Italian Eatery
2414 E Sunrise Blvd, Ft
Lauderdale FL 33304-3102.
954/564-3577.

Shells Restaurant
17855 Gulf Blvd, St
Petersburg FL 33708-1133.
813/393-8990.

Shells Restaurant
14380 N Dale Mabry Hwy,
Tampa FL 33618-2018.
813/968-6686.

Shells Restaurant
7253 S Tamiami Trail,
Sarasota FL 34231-5555.
941/924-2568.

Shells Restaurant
1490 W New Haven Ave,
Melbourne FL 32904-3904.
407/722-1122.

Silver Spoon Cafe
4125 Cleveland Ave, Fort
Myers FL 33901-9000.
941/278-9910.

**Sizzler Steak Seafood &
Salad**
9800 Highway A1A Alt,

Palm Beach Gardens FL
33410. 407/626-9200.

Sneaky Pete's
677 75th Ave, St Petersburg
FL 33706-1835. 813/367-
5986.

Sonny's Bar-B-Q
3506 S Orlando Dr, Sanford
FL 32773-5610. 407/321-
9295.

Sonny's Bar-B-Q
4600 Recker Hwy, Winter
Haven FL 33880-1249.
941/293-4744.

Sonny's Bar-B-Q
4834 Palm Beach Blvd, Fort
Myers FL 33905-3233.
941/694-7117.

Sonny's Bar-B-Q
3805 Northdale Blvd, Tampa
FL 33624-1841. 813/960-
3595.

**Southern Restaurants
Management**
15830 N Dale Mabry Hwy,
Tampa FL 33618-1645.
813/960-5665.

Stacey's Buffet
10421 US Highway 19, Port
Richey FL 34668-3133.
813/868-9573.

**Strawberry Hut Sandwich &
Yogurt**
1505 N Wheeler St, Plant
City FL 33566-2359.
813/752-3779.

Sub-Conscious or Not
1303 N Washington Blvd,
Sarasota FL 34236-2720.
941/954-4281.

Subway Sandwich Shop
6041 26th St W, Bradenton
FL 34207-4402. 941/758-
5545.

Subway Sandwich Shop
455 Dr Martin Luther King
Jr. B, Tampa FL 33603.
813/685-4040.

Subway Sandwich Shop
5260 Bronson Memorial
Highway, Kissimmee FL
34746-5349. 407/396-
1200.

Subway Sandwich Shop
5628 Pershing Ave, Orlando
FL 32822-3840. 407/380-
0988.

Subway Sandwich Shop
2004 66th St N, St
Petersburg FL 33710-4710.
813/343-7292.

Subway Sandwich Shop
11608 US Highway 1,

Sebastian FL 32958-8424.
407/388-2011.

**Sunny Italy Restaurant &
Pizza**
9908 Southern Blvd, Royal
Palm Beach FL 33411-3509.
407/791-9550.

Swiss Chalet Chicken & Ribs
601 E Commercial Blvd,
Oakland Park FL 33334-
3239. 954/776-1630.

Taco Bell
5410 Manatee Ave W,
Bradenton FL 34209-3745.
941/746-6890.

Taco Bell
690 S Orlando Ave, Winter
Park FL 32789-4843.
407/647-6668.

Taco Bell
555 NE US Highway 19,
Crystal River FL 34429-
4238. 904/795-4107.

Taco Bell
11893 E Colonial Dr, Orlando
FL 32826-4731. 407/382-
6681.

Taco Bell
1901 S McCall Rd,
Englewood FL 34223-4933.
941/473-1090.

Taco Bell
3550 Ulmerton Rd,
Clearwater FL 34622-4202.
813/572-6807.

Taco Bell
2038 N Dale Mabry Hwy,
Tampa FL 33607-2543.
813/875-2780.

Talk 'N Turkey
2414 E Sunrise Blvd, Ft
Lauderdale FL 33304-3102.
954/565-5070.

Talk Of The Town Restaurant
1260 Central Florida Pkwy,
Orlando FL 32837-9259.
407/851-8400.

Texas Roadhouse
7321 S Tamiami Trail,
Sarasota FL 34231-7003.
941/925-7984.

The Eatery: Soup To Nuts
9409 US Highway 19, Suite
665, Port Richey FL 34668-
4637. 813/845-3399.

The Krystal Company
101 Ridgewood Ave, Holly
Hill FL 32117-5027.
904/252-2665.

The Ocala Ale House
305 SE 17th St, Ocala FL
34471. 352/620-8989.

The Palm Court Grille
1711 N University Dr, Ft
Lauderdale FL 33322-4108.
954/472-5636.

Time Square Pizza Parlor
2304 E Oakland Park Blvd, Ft
Lauderdale FL 33306-1101.
954/566-7772.

**Townsend's Fish House &
Tavern**
35 W Michigan St, Orlando
FL 32806-4416. 407/422-
5560.

Travel Plazas By Marriott
283 N North Lake Blvd, Suite
160, Altamonte Springs FL
32701-3437. 407/331-
0336.

Trolley Station Restaurant
1940 Stickney Point Rd,
Sarasota FL 34231-8859.
941/923-2721.

Vie De France Cafe & Bakery
2414 E Sunrise Blvd, Ft
Lauderdale FL 33304-3102.
954/565-7544.

**Village Inn Restaurant &
Bakery**
6275 Westwood Blvd,
Orlando FL 32821-8016.
407/352-1997.

Vito's Subs & Ice Cream
3318 Edgewater Dr, Orlando
FL 32804-3742. 407/422-
2621.

Waffle House
4352 S Orange Blossom
Trail, Orlando FL 32839-
1212. 407/843-3070.

Waffle House
7954 NE 8th Way, Wildwood
FL 34785-8458. 904/748-
5944.

Waffle House
6531 Dudley Dr, Naples FL
33999-3826. 941/262-
7775.

Waffle House
2037 Bronson Memorial
Highway, Kissimmee FL
34744-4416. 407/931-
1559.

Waffle House
2580 Davie Rd, Ft
Lauderdale FL 33317-7425.
954/792-8150.

Wendy's
850 E Highway 50, Clermont
FL 34711-3213. 904/394-
7700.

Wendy's
2015 N Wickham Rd,
Melbourne FL 32935-8107.
407/254-3251.

Wendy's
3437 Commercial Way,
Spring Hill FL 34606-2622.
352/686-0213.

Wendy's
3300 W Commercial Blvd, Ft
Lauderdale FL 33309-3419.
954/970-7148.

Wendy's
7085 Okeechobee Rd, Fort
Pierce FL 34945-2605.
407/466-7840.

Wendy's
8770 Ulmerton Rd, Largo FL
34641-3874. 813/530-
7204.

Woody's Bar B Q
4291 Roosevelt Blvd,
Jacksonville FL 32210-2061.
904/384-3442.

CJ's Sandwich Shops
3101 Dr Martin Luther King
Jr., Tampa FL 33607.
813/872-5515.

Domino's Pizza
3817 Northdale Blvd, Tampa
FL 33624-1841. 813/960-
1888.

Hungry Howie's Pizza & Subs
1427 S Bumby Ave, Orlando
FL 32806-2437. 407/894-
1322.

Hungry Howie's Pizza & Subs
1119 E Vine St, Kissimmee
FL 34744-3543. 407/846-
9292.

Little Caesar's Pizza
1052 Dixon Blvd, Cocoa FL
32922-6809. 407/631-
7400.

Little Caesar's Pizza
Luria Plaza, Vero Beach FL
32960. 407/770-0404.

Little Caesar's Pizza
2564 Enterprise Rd, Orange
City FL 32763-7904.
904/775-5353.

Papa Joe's Of Ponce Inlet
33 Inlet Harbor Rd, Daytona
Beach FL 32127-7228.
904/760-2200.

Papa John's Pizza
434 E Merritt Island Cswy,
Merritt Is FL 32952-3503.
407/453-8080.

Pizza Hut
3521 N Monroe St,
Tallahassee FL 32303-2746.
904/562-2500.

Incredibly Edible & More
726 Glen Eagle Dr, Winter
Springs FL 32708-5914.
407/539-4552.

DRINKING PLACES

Gilbert's Lounge
555 NE Ocean Blvd, Stuart
FL 34996-1620. 407/225-
3700.

JD Penguin's Night Club
5440 Beach Blvd,
Jacksonville FL 32207-5159.
904/396-3679.

HOTELS AND MOTELS

Beach Retirement Hotel
8008 Blind Pass Rd, St
Petersburg FL 33706-1617.
813/367-7651.

Charter One Hotels
400 N Tamiami Trail,
Sarasota FL 34236-4822.
941/923-2662.

Cypress Pointe Resort
8651 Treasure Cay Ln,
Orlando FL 32836-6437.
407/238-2300.

Gasparilla Inn
P.O. Box 1088, Boca Grande
FL 33921-1088. 941/964-
2201.

Great Outdoors Resort
4505 W Cheney Hwy,
Titusville FL 32780.
407/269-5004.

Holiday Inn
233 Ben Franklin Dr,
Sarasota FL 34236-1205.
941/388-3941.

Holiday Inn Oceanside
3384 Ocean Dr, Vero Beach
FL 32963-1696. 407/231-
2300.

Howard Johnson
6545 Ramona Blvd,
Jacksonville FL 32205-4445.
904/781-1940.

Knights Inn
2728 Graves Rd, Tallahassee
FL 32303-2829. 904/562-
4700.

Marco Polo Resort Hotel
19201 Collins Ave, Miami FL
33160-2202. 305/932-
2233.

**Palm Beaches Park Inn
International**
Lake Ave #1, Lake Worth FL
33460-3970. 407/582-
3301.

**Radisson Sandpiper Beach
Resort**
6000 Gulf Blvd, St
Petersburg Beach FL 33706-
3712. 813/360-5551.

Radisson Suite Resort
600 S Collier Blvd, Marco

Island FL 33937-5697.
941/394-4100.

Sundial Beach & Tennis Resort
1451 Middle Gulf Dr, Sanibel
FL 33957-6521. 941/472-4151.

Driftwood Resort
3150 Ocean Dr, Vero Beach
FL 32963-1954. 407/231-0550.

Econolodge Maingate Central
4985 Bronson Memorial
Highway, Kissimmee FL
34746-5336. 407/396-4343.

Economy Inns Of America
5367 Bronson Memorial
Highway, Kissimmee FL
34746-4711. 407/396-4020.

Hampton Inn Orange Park
6135 Youngerman Circle,
Jacksonville FL 32244-6607.
904/777-5313.

Hampton Inn-Tampa
4817 W Laurel St, Tampa FL
33607-4507. 813/287-0778.

Holiday Inn
W US Hwy 90 & I-75, Lake
City FL 32055. 904/752-3901.

Holiday Inn
15208 Gulf Blvd, Madeira
Beach FL 33708-1815.
813/392-2275.

Holiday Inn Express International
6323 International Dr,
Orlando FL 32819-8213.
407/351-4430.

Howard Johnson
7150 Okeechobee Rd, Fort
Pierce FL 34945-2698.
407/464-4500.

Motel 6
8285 Dix Ellis Trail,
Jacksonville FL 32256-8277.
904/731-8400.

Ramada Airport Hotel & Conference Center
5303 W Kennedy Blvd,
Tampa FL 33609-2414.
813/877-0534.

Sheraton Yankee Clipper Beach
1140 Seabreeze Blvd, Ft
Lauderdale FL 33316-2426.
954/524-5551.

Shoney's Inn
4156 W Vine St, Kissimmee
FL 34741-4502. 407/870-7374.

Courtyard By Marriott
3131 Executive Dr,
Clearwater FL 34622.
813/572-8484.

Doubletree Club Hotel
4700 Salisbury Rd,
Jacksonville FL 32256-6101.
904/281-9700.

Holiday Inn Tampa Busch Gardens
2701 E Fowler Ave, Tampa
FL 33612-6274. 813/971-4710.

Mark Adams Caribbean Gulf Resort
430 Gulfview Blvd,
Clearwater FL 34630.
813/443-5714.

Omni Jacksonville Hotel
245 Water St, Jacksonville

FL 32202-4403. 904/355-6664.

Raleigh Hotel
1775 Collins Ave, Miami
Beach FL 33139-2091.
305/534-6300.

The Breakers Of Ft Lauderdale
941 NE 19th Ave, Ft
Lauderdale FL 33304-3059.
954/522-8315.

Travelodge Hotel
2000 Hotel Plaza Boulevard,
Lake Buena Vista FL 32830.
407/828-2424.

Viscount Hotel
Preview Dr, Lake Buena Vista
FL 32830. 407/396-0666.

Wellesley Inn
100 SW 12th Ave, Deerfield
Beach FL 33442-3198.
954/428-0661.

Wellesley Inn Plantation
7901 SW 6th St, Plantation
FL 33324-3207. 954/473-8257.

Deerfield Beach Hilton
100 Fairway Dr, Deerfield
Beach FL 33441-1894.
954/427-7700.

Howard Johnson Maingate West
7600 W Irlo Bronson
Memorial H, Kissimmee FL
34747-1726. 407/396-2500.

Buena Vista Palace At Walt Disney
1900 Buena Vista Dr,
Orlando FL 32830. 407/827-2727.

For more information on career opportunities in hotels and restaurants:

Associations

AMERICAN HOTEL AND MOTEL ASSOCIATION
1201 New York Avenue NW, Suite 600,
Washington DC 20005-3931. 202/289-3100. Provides lobbying services and
educational programs, maintains and
disseminates industry data, and produces a
variety of publications.

THE EDUCATIONAL FOUNDATION OF THE NATIONAL RESTAURANT ASSOCIATION
250 South Wacker Drive, 14th Floor,
Chicago IL 60606. 312/715-1010. Offers
educational products, including textbooks,
manuals, instruction guides, manager and
employee training programs, videos, and
certification programs.

NATIONAL RESTAURANT ASSOCIATION
1200 17th Street NW, Washington DC
20036. 202/331-5900. Provides a number

of services, including government lobbying,
communications, research and information,
and the Educational Foundation (see
separate address).

Directories

DIRECTORY OF CHAIN RESTAURANT OPERATORS
Business Guides, Inc., Lebhar-Friedman,
Inc., 3922 Coconut Palm Drive, Tampa FL
33619-8321. 813/664-6700.

DIRECTORY OF HIGH-VOLUME INDEPENDENT RESTAURANTS
Lebhar-Friedman, Inc., 3922 Coconut Palm
Drive, Tampa FL 33619-8321. 813/664-6700.

Magazines

CORNELL HOTEL AND RESTAURANT ADMINISTRATION QUARTERLY
Cornell University School of Hotel Administration, Statler Hall, Ithaca NY 14853-6902. 607/255-9393.

HOTEL AND MOTEL MANAGEMENT
120 West 2nd Street, Duluth MN 55802. 218.

INNKEEPING WORLD
Box 84108, Seattle WA 98124. 206/362-7125.

NATION'S RESTAURANT NEWS
Lebhar-Friedman, Inc., 3922 Coconut Palm Drive, Tampa, FL 33619. 813/664-6700.

INSURANCE

What's the job picture in insurance? That depends upon which industry segment you're looking at. Health insurers, who avoided any Washington-based reforms in 1994, are reaping record profits, while property and casualty insurers are still trying to climb out from under the rocks that Mother Nature tossed their way. The California earthquake, snowstorms in the Northeast, floods in both the South and the West -- and especially a growing number of environmental claims made 1994 the property-casualty industry's second worst year in history. While property insurers still have huge cash reserves, many are now paying for cleanups of environmental sites, thanks to liability policies sold back in the '60s and '70s. Analysts expect that some of the burden on the property-casualty industry will be eased by higher premiums.

The life insurance segment is also under a dark cloud. The reputation of the entire industry suffered when Metropolitan Life Insurance agents illegally sold policies as retirement plans. According to Business Week, *the scandal was partly responsible for a four percent industry-wide decline in life insurance sales in 1994.*

The picture in health insurance is much brighter. By moving more and more consumers into managed care, insurers are benefiting from the economies of scale. Many of the biggest players in the insurance industry have moved into managed care -- Metropolitan Life and Travelers Corporation, for example, combined health insurance operations into Metra Health in order to compete with leaders like CIGNA, Aetna, and Prudential.

AETNA LIFE & CASUALTY INSURANCE COMPANY
P.O. Box 31967, Tampa FL 33631. 813/287-7700. **Fax:** 813/289-2545. **Contact:** Rita Blanken, Training Consultant. **Description:** Provides a wide range of insurance services.

AMERICAN BANKERS INSURANCE GROUP
11222 Quail Roost Drive, Miami FL 33157. 305/253-2244. **Contact:** Human Resources. **Description:** American Bankers Insurance Group is a specialty insurance holding company. Through its major subsidiaries, the company markets credit life, credit property, unemployment, accident, health, and homeowners insurance. **Number of employees at this location:** 2,058.

AMERICAN HERITAGE LIFE INSURANCE COMPANY
1776 American Heritage Life Drive, Jacksonville FL 32224. 904/992-1776. **Contact:** Director of Personnel. **Description:** Offers a broad range of insurance services.

FRANK ANDERSON & ASSOCIATES
P.O. Box 5550, Jacksonville FL 32247. 904/725-0985. **Contact:** Human Resources. **Description:** An insurance agency.

BLUE CROSS/BLUE SHIELD OF FLORIDA, INC.
P.O. Box 44088, Jacksonville FL 32231-4088. 904/791-6111. **Contact:** Bob Croteau, Manager/Employment. **Description:** A large health insurance company with regional and district offices throughout the state. **Common positions include:** Accountant/Auditor; Attorney; Claim Representative; Customer Service Representative; Department Manager; Financial Analyst; Industrial Engineer; Services Sales Representative; Systems Analyst. **Educational backgrounds include:** Accounting;

Business Administration; Computer Science; Finance; Insurance; Marketing. **Benefits:** 401K; Dental Insurance; Disability Coverage; Life Insurance; Medical Insurance; Tuition Assistance. **Special Programs:** Internships; Training Programs. **Corporate headquarters location:** This Location.

CAROLINA CASUALTY INSURANCE COMPANY
P.O. Box 2575, Jacksonville FL 32203. 904/363-0900. **Contact:** Ms. Pat Johnson, Human Resources Manager. **Description:** A primary insurance company.

COLONIAL PENN INSURANCE COMPANY
4002 Eisenhower Boulevard, Tampa FL 33634. 813/886-4444. **Contact:** Personnel Department. **Description:** An insurance companies. **Operations at this facility include:** Southeast regional headquarters.

CRAWFORD & COMPANY
P.O. Box 48370, Jacksonville FL 32247-8370. 904/398-0551. **Contact:** Branch Manager. **Description:** A branch office of a regional insurance adjuster. **Corporate headquarters location:** Atlanta GA.

CUSTARD INSURANCE ADJUSTERS, INC.
4161 Carmichael Avenue, Suite 203, Jacksonville FL 32207. 904/399-4458. **Contact:** Office Manager. **Description:** Branch office of an insurance adjustment company. **Corporate headquarters location:** Fort Wayne IN.

DEPENDABLE INSURANCE
7800 Belfort Parkway, Suite 100, Jacksonville FL 32256. 904/279-2600. **Contact:** Personnel. **Description:** An insurance and real estate company. **Number of employees at this location:** 173.

ELLIOTT CLAIMS SERVICE, INC.
P.O. Box 24727, Jacksonville FL 32241-4727. 904/268-5201. **Contact:** Craig H. Miles, Manager. **Description:** An insurance adjusting firm. **Common positions include:** Claim Representative. **Educational backgrounds include:** Insurance. **Benefits:** Life Insurance; Medical Insurance. **Corporate headquarters location:** Daytona Beach FL. **Operations at this facility include:** Service.

FEDERAL HOME LIFE INSURANCE COMPANY
Human Resources Department, 6277 Sea Harbor Drive, Orlando FL 32887. 407/345-2600. **Contact:** Amy Baragar, Human Resources. **Description:** A life insurance company. **Parent company:** Harcourt General Insurance.

GAY & TAYLOR, INC.
4492 Southside Boulevard, Suite 205, Jacksonville FL 32216. 904/645-1777. **Contact:** Branch Manager. **Description:** An insurance adjuster. **Corporate headquarters location:** Winston-Salem NC.

HEALTH PLAN SERVICES
3501 Frontage Road, Tampa FL 33607. 813/289-1000. **Contact:** Personnel Director. **Description:** A third-party administrator and marketer of small group life and health insurance.

INDEPENDENT PROPERTY AND CASUALTY INSURANCE COMPANY
One Independent Drive, Jacksonville FL 32276. 904/358-5150. **Contact:** Personnel. **Description:** A property and casualty insurance company. **Common positions include:** Claim Representative. **Benefits:** Dental Insurance; Disability Coverage; Employee Discounts; Life Insurance; Medical Insurance; Pension Plan; Profit Sharing; Savings Plan; Tuition Assistance. **Special Programs:** Training Programs. **Corporate headquarters location:** This Location. **Operations at this facility include:** Administration; Sales; Service.

LANG BROKERAGE
3550 Spring Park Road, Jacksonville FL 32207. 904/398-2199. **Contact:** Human Resources. **Description:** An insurance brokerage agency.

METROPOLITAN LIFE INSURANCE COMPANY
P.O. Box 30074, Tampa FL 33630-3074. 813/870-8000. **Contact:** Personnel Department. **Description:** Southeast regional headquarters for Metropolitan Life

Insurance, a national insurance and financial services company. **NOTE:** Positions are available in the Metropolitan Executive Training Program for MBA's and JDs.

NATIONAL COUNCIL ON COMPENSATION INSURANCE
750 Park of Commerce Drive, Boca Raton FL 33487. 407/997-1000. **Contact:** Rick Webb, Manager of Employment. **Description:** Establishes rates for workers' compensation. **Number of employees nationwide:** 1,300.

PHYSICIAN CORPORATION OF AMERICA (PCA)
P.O. Box 527500, 5835 Blue Lagoon Drive, Miami FL 33152-7500. 305/267-6633. **Fax:** 305/266-6051. **Contact:** Human Resources. **Description:** A managed health care company that provides comprehensive health care services through its health maintenance organizations, and administrative and management services through its workers compensation third-party administration companies. The company's 650,000 members include commercial groups and individuals as well as beneficiaries of government programs. **Corporate headquarters location:** This Location. **Other locations:** Nationwide; Caribbean. **Subsidiaries include:** PCA Health Plans of Texas, Inc.; PCA Health Plans of Florida, Inc.; PCA Heath Plans of Georgia, Inc.; PCA Health Plans of Alabama Inc.; HealthPlus, Inc.; Century Medical Centers, Inc.; PCA Solutions, Inc.; and PCA Property and Casualty, Inc. **Listed on:** NASDAQ. **Number of employees nationwide:** 1,900.

POE & BROWN INC.
P.O. Box 1348, 702 North Franklin Street, Tampa FL 33602. 813/222-4100. **Recorded Jobline:** 813/222-4268. **Contact:** Human Resources. **Description:** An independent insurance agency organization that provides a variety of insurance products and services to corporate, institutional, professional, and individual clients. Products and services offered fall into four major categories: National Programs, which specialize in liability and property insurance programs; Retail Operations, which provide property, casualty, life and health insurance; Brokerage Operations, which provide property and casualty products; and Service Operations, which provide claims administration. **Common positions include:** Insurance Agent/Broker. **Educational backgrounds include:** Business Administration; Insurance; Marketing. **Benefits:** 401K; Dental Insurance; Disability Coverage; Employee Discounts; Life Insurance; Medical Insurance; Profit Sharing; Stock Option; Tuition Assistance. **Corporate headquarters location:** Daytona FL. **Other U.S. locations:** AZ; CA; CO; CT; FL; GA; NC; NJ; TX. **Operations at this facility include:** Administration; Divisional Headquarters; Sales; Service. **Number of employees at this location:** 250. **Number of employees nationwide:** 1,000.

PROGRESSIVE INSURANCE
3802 Coconut Palm Drive, Tampa FL 33619. 813/623-1781. **Contact:** Kevin Maher, Human Resources Manager. **Description:** An insurance company. **Common positions include:** Accountant/Auditor; Actuary; Administrator; Attorney; Branch Manager; Claim Representative; Computer Programmer; Customer Service Representative; Department Manager; General Manager; Human Resources Specialist; Management Trainee; Marketing Specialist; Operations/Production Manager; Purchasing Agent and Manager; Quality Control Supervisor; Services Sales Representative; Underwriter/Assistant Underwriter. **Educational backgrounds include:** Accounting; Business Administration; Communications; Computer Science; Economics; Finance; Liberal Arts; Marketing; Mathematics. **Benefits:** Dental Insurance; Disability Coverage; Employee Discounts; Life Insurance; Medical Insurance; Savings Plan. **Corporate headquarters location:** Cleveland OH. **Operations at this facility include:** Administration; Divisional Headquarters; Regional Headquarters; Sales; Service. **Listed on:** New York Stock Exchange. **Number of employees nationwide:** 6,700.

PRUDENTIAL INSURANCE COMPANY OF AMERICA
GREATER SOUTHERN OPERATIONS
841 Prudential Drive, 2nd Floor, Plaza One, Jacksonville FL 32207. 904/391-3711. **Contact:** Employment Office. **Description:** Regional administrative operation of the well-known financial services company. **Common positions include:** Accountant/Auditor; Computer Programmer; Management Trainee; Systems Analyst; Underwriter/Assistant Underwriter. **Educational backgrounds include:** Accounting; Business Administration; Communications; Computer Science; Finance; Liberal Arts; Mathematics. **Benefits:** Dental Insurance; Disability Coverage; Employee Discounts; Life Insurance; Medical Insurance; Pension Plan; Savings Plan; Tuition Assistance.

RAMSEY-HMO
75 Valencia Avenue, Coral Gables FL 33134. 305/447-3200. **Contact:** Human Resources. **Description:** Ramsey-HMO operates an HMO providing services in the Miami and Fort Lauderdale areas of South Florida. **Number of employees nationwide:** 1,250.

Note: Because addresses and telephone numbers of smaller companies change rapidly, we recommend you call each company to verify the information below before inquiring about job opportunities. Mass mailings are not recommended.

Additional employers with over 250 employees:

INSURANCE COMPANIES

American Fidelity Life Insurance Company
4060 Barrancas Ave, Pensacola FL 32507-3491. 904/456-7401.

Capital Assurance Co.
P.O. Box 149061, Coral Gables FL 33114-9061. 305/461-7400.

General Insurance Co.
1001 S Bayshore Dr, Suite 2610, Miami FL 33131-4940. 305/674-4000.

United Automobile Insurance
P.O. Box 639000, Miami FL 33163-9000. 305/932-7096.

Yel Co Insurance
3757 NW 36th Street, Miami FL 33142-4915. 305/662-3775.

INSURANCE AGENTS, BROKERS, AND SERVICES

Old Stone Credit Corp.
1801 Art Museum Dr, Room 100, Jacksonville FL 32207-2569. 904/398-7581.

Additional employers with under 250 employees:

INSURANCE COMPANIES

American Merchants Life Insurance Company
301 W Bay St, Suite 2315, Jacksonville FL 32202-5122. 904/358-8700.

Gemco National
7200 W Camino Real, Boca Raton FL 33433-5537. 407/391-5043.

Great Florida Life Insurance Company
815 NW 57th Ave, Suite 423, Miami FL 33126-2042. 305/573-6500.

Guarantee Security Life Insurance
7800 Belfort Pkwy, Suite 265, Jacksonville FL 32256-6920. 904/281-1180.

Life General Security Insurance Company
4950 SW 72nd Ave, Suite 201, Miami FL 33155-5531. 305/667-8441.

Professional Insurance Corporation
135 Riverside Ave Fl 5, Jacksonville FL 32202-4920. 904/354-7171.

Western Pacific Life Insurance Company
P.O. Box 550640, Jacksonville FL 32255-0640. 904/296-2900.

Cigna Dental Management Systems
1525 NW 167th St, Suite 250, Miami FL 33169-5131. 305/621-1100.

Orkin & Associates
3511 W Commercial Blvd, Ft Lauderdale FL 33309-3322. 954/484-6611.

Cypress Insurance Co.
P.O. Box 525100, Miami FL 33152. 305/591-2525.

Commercial Risk Management
P.O. Box 18366, Tampa FL 33679-8366. 813/289-3900.

First American Title Co. Of Florida
2802 W Waters Ave, Tampa FL 33614-1853. 813/933-7871.

INSURANCE AGENTS, BROKERS, AND SERVICES

Martyn G. Belben & Associates
2725 NE 21st St, Ft Lauderdale FL 33305-3614. 954/523-7474.

Acordia Benefits Of Florida
6440 Southpoint Pkwy, Jacksonville FL 32216-0944. 904/390-7700.

Alexander & Alexander
7000 SW 97th Ave, Suite 200, Miami FL 33173-1411. 305/279-7870.

Arthur J Gallagher & Co.
8355 NW 53rd St, Miami FL 33166-4666. 305/592-6080.

Gallagher Bassett Services
1311 Executive Center Dr, Suite 2, Tallahassee FL 32301-5027. 904/656-3003.

Hull and Co.
2150 S Andrews Ave, Ft Lauderdale FL 33316-3432. 954/527-4855.

Liberty Mutual Insurance Group
6363 NW 6th Way, Suite 500, Ft Lauderdale FL 33309-6119. 954/771-4010.

Old Dominion Insurance Company
9428 Baymeadows Rd, Suite 400, Jacksonville FL 32256-7971. 904/739-0873.

Southern Underwriters
8600 NW 36th St Fl 8, Miami FL 33166-6648. 305/599-7449.

Blackburn & Company
3321 Henderson Blvd, Tampa FL 33609-2913. 813/876-8776.

ABI Insurance Group
311 Park Place Blvd, Suite 400, Clearwater FL 34619-3923. 813/796-6666.

For more information on career opportunities in insurance:

Associations

ALLIANCE OF AMERICAN INSURERS
1501 Woodfield Road, Suite 400 West,
Schaumburg IL 60173-4980. 708/330-
8500.

HEALTH INSURANCE ASSOCIATION OF AMERICA
555 13th Street North, Suite 600E,
Washington DC 20004. 202/824-1600.

INSURANCE INFORMATION INSTITUTE
110 William Street, 24th Floor, New York
NY 10038. 212/669-9200. Provides
informational products on property/casualty
insurance.

SOCIETY OF ACTUARIES
475 North Martingale Road, Suite 800,
Schaumburg IL 60173-2226. 708/706-
3500.

Directories

INSURANCE ALMANAC
Underwriter Printing and Publishing
Company, 50 East Palisade Avenue,
Englewood NJ 07631. 201/569-8808.
Hardcover annual, 639 pages, $115.
Available at libraries.

INSURANCE MARKET PLACE
Rough Notes Company, Inc., P.O. Box 564,
Indianapolis IN 46206. 317/634-1541.

INSURANCE PHONE BOOK AND DIRECTORY
Reed Reference Publishing, 121 Chanlon
Road, New Providence NJ 07974.
800/521-8110. $89.95, new editions
available every other year. Might also be
available at libraries.

NATIONAL DIRECTORY OF HEALTH MAINTENANCE ORGANIZATIONS
Group Health Association of America, 1129
20th Street NW, Suite 600, Washington DC
20036. 202/778-3200.

Magazines

BEST'S REVIEW
A.M. Best Company, A.M. Best Road,
Oldwick NJ 08858-9988. 908/439-2200.
Monthly.

INSURANCE JOURNAL
Wells Publishing, 9191 Towne Centre Drive,
Suite 550, San Diego, CA 92122-1231
619/455-7717. A biweekly magazine
covering the insurance industry.
Subscription: $78 per year, $3 for a single
issue.

INSURANCE TIMES
M & S Communications, 20 Park Plaza,
Suite 1101, Boston MA 02116. 617/292-
7117. A regional biweekly insurance
newspaper for insurance professionals.

LEGAL SERVICES

The number of people working in the legal services field has exploded since the early '70s. According to a 1969 survey by the Bureau of Labor Statistics (BLS) there were 387,000 workers in legal services. By 1994, that number had risen to 1.2 million. The glut of lawyers has led to tremendous competition in the legal profession. Law firms are laying off associates and firing unproductive partners. Graduates of prestigious law schools face tough competition for jobs, although for the top graduates, the offers will be there. According to Jon Sargent, an economist for the Office of Economic Growth at the BLS, some jobseekers looking to break into this industry may need to look outside the mainstream legal services industry: non-profit companies, government positions, or law firms in smaller communities.

Paralegals have carved out a niche for themselves and continue to be the fastest growing profession in legal services. "Paralegals have become a cost-effective way to provide legal services in many cases," says Sargent, referring to the realization by many employers that paralegals can do many of the same jobs as associates at a much lower cost.

CARLTON, FIELDS, WARD, EMMANUEL, SMITH & CUTLER
P.O. Box 3239, Tampa FL 33601. 813/223-7000, x111. **Contact:** Anastasia C. Hiotis, Director of Human Resources. **Description:** A firm specializing in real estate, construction, and various other fields of law. **Common positions include:** Accountant/Auditor; Attorney; Paralegal; Secretary. **Benefits:** Credit Union; Dental Insurance; Disability Coverage; Life Insurance; Medical Insurance; Pension Plan; Profit Sharing. **Corporate headquarters location:** This Location. **Operations at this facility include:** Administration; Service. **Number of employees at this location:** 420.

FLORIDA STATE ATTORNEY
1350 NW 12th Avenue, Miami FL 33136. 305/547-0540. **Recorded Jobline:** 305/547-0533. **Contact:** Human Resources. **Description:** The Florida State Attorney investigates and prosecutes legal cases.

FOLEY & LARDNER
200 Laura Street, P.O. Box 240, Jacksonville FL 32201-0240. 904/359-2000. **Contact:** Personnel Director. **Description:** A law firm specializing in real estate, tax, corporate, securities, and litigation.

FOWLER, WHITE, GILLEN, BAGGS, VILLAREAL, BANKER
P.O. Box 1438, Tampa FL 33601. 813/228-7411. **Contact:** Beth Miller, Personnel Director. **Description:** A business law firm.

GREENBERG TRAURIG & HOFFMAN
1221 Brickell Avenue, 21st Floor, Miami FL 33131. 305/579-0500. **Fax:** 305/579-0717. **Contact:** Human Resources. **Description:** A law firm.

MAHONEY, ADAMS, AND CRISER, P.A.
P.O. Box 4099, Jacksonville FL 32201. 904/354-1100. **Contact:** Barbara Galinac, Human Resources Manager. **Description:** A law firm.

MARKS, GRAY, CONROY & GIBBS
P.O. Box 447, Jacksonville FL 32201. 904/398-0900. **Contact:** Nancy Fredman, Office Administration. **Description:** A law firm. **Common positions include:** Attorney; Paralegal; Secretary. **Educational backgrounds include:** Juris Doctorate. **Benefits:**

Dental Insurance; Disability Coverage; Life Insurance; Medical Insurance; Profit Sharing. **Corporate headquarters location:** This Location.

OSBORNE & McNATT
225 Water Street, Suite 1400, Jacksonville FL 32202. 904/354-0624. **Contact:** Michael Obringer, Partner. **Description:** A law firm.

Note: Because addresses and telephone numbers of smaller companies change rapidly, we recommend you call each company to verify the information below before inquiring about job opportunities. Mass mailings are not recommended.

Additional employers with under 250 employees:

LEGAL SERVICES

Annis Mitchell Cockey Edwards Roehn
P.O. Box 3433, Tampa FL 33601-3433. 813/229-3321.

Cobb Cole & Bell
150 Magnolia Ave, Daytona Beach FL 32114-4304. 904/255-8171.

Haynesworth Baldwin Et Al
P.O. Box 40593, Jacksonville FL 32203-0593. 904/353-9691.

Rumberger Kirk & Caldwell
P.O. Box 1873, Orlando FL 32802-1873. 407/425-1802.

Shutts & Bowen
201 S Biscayne Blvd, Miami FL 33131-4332. 305/358-6300.

Maguire Voorhis & Wells PA
P.O. Box 633, Orlando FL 32802-0633. 407/244-1100.

Becker & Poliakoff PA
P.O. Box 9057, Ft Lauderdale FL 33310-9057. 954/987-7550.

Baumer Bradford & Walters PA
50 N Laura St, Suite 2200, Jacksonville FL 32202-3625. 904/358-2222.

Icard Merrill Cullis Et Al PA
2033 Main St, Suite 600, Sarasota FL 34237-6091. 941/366-8100.

MacFarlane Ferguson
P.O. Box 1531, Tampa FL 33601-1531. 813/273-4200.

Stearns Weaver Miller Et Al PA
150 W Flagler St Ph 2200, Miami FL 33130-1558. 305/789-3200.

Stephens Lynn Klein Et Al PA
9130 S Dadeland Blvd, Miami FL 33156-7818. 305/670-3700.

Walton Lantaff Schroeder
2 S Biscayne Blvd, Miami FL 33131-1806. 305/379-6411.

Wicker Smith Tutan Et Al PA
2900 SW 28th Terrace, Miami FL 33133-3766. 305/448-3939.

Cobb Cole & Bell
255 S Orange Ave, Orlando FL 32801-3445. 407/872-2200.

Gunster Yoakley & Stewart PA
P.O. Box 4587, West Palm Beach FL 33402-4587. 407/655-1980.

Henderson Franklin Et Al PA
P.O. Box 280, Fort Myers FL 33902-0280. 941/334-4121.

Rogers Towers Bailey Et Al PA
1301 Riverplace Blvd, Suite 1500, Jacksonville FL 32207-1811. 904/398-3911.

Messer Vickers Caparello
215 S Monroe St, Suite 701, Tallahassee FL 32301-1858. 904/222-0720.

Lowndes Drosdick Doster Et Al
P.O. Box 2809, Orlando FL 32802-2809. 407/843-4600.

Smith Hulsey & Busey
P.O. Box 53315, Jacksonville FL 32201-3315. 904/359-7700.

Holland & Knight
701 Brickell Ave, Suite 3000, Miami FL 33131-2847. 305/374-8500.

Leavitt Wilson & Small PA
111 N Orange Ave, Orlando FL 32801-2316. 407/843-4321.

Squire Sanders & Dempsey
201 S Biscayne Blvd, Miami FL 33131-4332. 305/577-8700.

For more information on career opportunities in legal services:

Associations

AMERICAN BAR ASSOCIATION
750 North Lake Shore Drive, Chicago IL 60611. 312/988-5000. A non-profit organization.

FEDERAL BAR ASSOCIATION
1815 H. Street NW, Suite 408, Washington DC 20006-3697. 202/638-0252.

NATIONAL ASSOCIATION OF LEGAL ASSISTANTS
1516 South Boston, Suite 200, Tulsa OK 74119-4013. 918/587-6828. An educational association. Offers the National Voluntary Association Exam. Memberships are available.

NATIONAL FEDERATION OF PARALEGAL ASSOCIATIONS
P.O. Box 33108, Kansas City MO 64114-0108. 816/941-4000. Offers magazines, seminars, and internet job listings.

MANUFACTURING AND WHOLESALING: MISCELLANEOUS CONSUMER

The consumer goods manufacturing industry is more than just one industry. To generally forecast about the entire range of companies that make products for consumers is risky, since so much can differ from one segment to the next. In fact, many consumer manufacturers are listed under more specific categories in this book.

With that said, some general statements can be made about the outlook for this gigantic field. Over the long term, many analysts are optimistic. An improved economy, as well as an aging baby boom generation with growing disposable income, should provide stimulus for increases in personal durables. Continued growth in international trade should also point to a favorable long-term outlook for household consumer durables.

U.S. exports of household durables should also expand as trade barriers drop. The North American Free Trade Agreement (NAFTA), passed in early 1994, will give U.S. manufacturers even greater access to what is already the second-largest export market for U.S. household durables. Other trade agreements may follow with several Latin American countries. Potential markets in Eastern Europe and independent states of the former Soviet Union may also open.

BARACUDA INTERNATIONAL
3420 Northwest 53rd Street, Fort Lauderdale FL 33309. 954/735-9700. **Contact:** Personnel Department. **Description:** A manufacturer of automatic swimming pool vacuums.

BEAR ARCHERY, INC.
4600 South West 41st Boulevard, Gainesville FL 32608-4999. 352/376-2327. **Contact:** Ed Ward, Controller. **Description:** A manufacturer of archery equipment.

BRIGGS INDUSTRIES
4350 West Cypress Street, Suite 800, Tampa FL 33607. 813/878-0178. **Contact:** Henny Collins, Personnel Director. **Description:** Corporate office for a manufacturer of plumbingware such as bathtubs and sinks.

CAIN AND BULTMAN, INC.
P.O. Box 2815, Jacksonville FL 32203. 904/356-4812. **Contact:** Kathy Whitten, Personnel. **Description:** A wholesale distributor of carpets, vinyl floor coverings, and related materials.

CATALINA YACHT
MORGAN DIVISION
7200 Bryan Dairy Road, Largo FL 34647. 813/544-6681. **Contact:** Sandra Kuusela, Personnel Director. **Description:** A yacht manufacturer.

EVEREADY ENERGIZER POWER SYSTEMS
P.O. Box 147114, Dept. E06, Gainesville FL 32614-7114. 352/462-4719. **Contact:** Ms. Gerry Bryant, Manager of Human Resources. **Description:** A manufacturer of rechargeable batteries (Ni-cd, NiH2). **Common positions include:** Chemical Engineer; Electrical/Electronics Engineer; Mechanical Engineer; Metallurgical Engineer.

Educational backgrounds include: Chemistry; Engineering. **Benefits:** 401K; Dental Insurance; Disability Coverage; Life Insurance; Medical Insurance; Tuition Assistance. **Special Programs:** Internships; Training Programs. **Corporate headquarters location:** This Location. **Operations at this facility include:** Administration; Manufacturing; Research and Development. **Number of employees at this location:** 1,300.

FLORIDA FURNITURE INDUSTRIES
P.O. Box 610, Palatka FL 32178. 904/328-3444. **Contact:** Mr. Tora Syrdahl, Personnel Director. **Description:** A furniture manufacturer.

GALE GROUP
3000 West Orange Avenue, Apopka FL 32703. 407/889-5533. **Contact:** Personnel. **Description:** A manufacturer of plastic lawn and garden items. **Number of employees at this location:** 395.

GOLDEN BEAR INTERNATIONAL, INC.
11780 U.S. Highway One, North Palm Beach FL 33408. 407/626-3900. **Contact:** Maureen Molloy, Personnel Administrator. **Description:** A sporting goods, real estate, and apparel company owned by professional golfer Jack Nicklaus. **Common positions include:** Accountant/Auditor; Administrator; Architect; Civil Engineer; Marketing Specialist. **Educational backgrounds include:** Accounting; Art/Design; Business Administration; Finance; Marketing. **Benefits:** Dental Insurance; Disability Coverage; Life Insurance; Medical Insurance; Profit Sharing. **Operations at this facility include:** Service.

LOREN INDUSTRIES, INC.
2801 Greene Street, Hollywood FL 33020. 954/920-6622. **Contact:** Personnel. **Description:** A manufacturer of jewelry. **Number of employees at this location:** 185.

REGAL GROUP
12800 North West 38th Avenue, Miami FL 33054. 305/688-8100. **Contact:** Personnel Director. **Description:** A manufacturer of notions, including zippers.

REGAL WOOD PRODUCTS
8600 Northwest South River Drive, Miami FL 33166. 305/885-0111. **Contact:** Office Manager of Personnel. **Description:** A manufacturer of kitchen cabinets.

REVLON PRODUCTS
P.O. Box 37557, Jacksonville FL 32236. 904/693-1200. **Fax:** 904/693-1259. **Contact:** Jim House, Human Resources Manager. **Description:** The regional hair products division of the cosmetics and personal care products company. **Common positions include:** Accountant/Auditor; Blue-Collar Worker Supervisor; Buyer; Cashier; Chemical Engineer; Chemist; Clerical Supervisor; Computer Operator; Computer Programmer; Computer Systems Analyst; Credit Clerk and Authorizer; Credit Manager; Dispatcher; Electrical/Electronics Engineer; Electrician; Human Resources Specialist; Industrial Engineer; Machinist; Mechanical Engineer; Order Clerk; Payroll Clerk; Secretary. **Educational backgrounds include:** Business Administration; Chemistry; Engineering. **Benefits:** Dental Insurance; Disability Coverage; Employee Discounts; Life Insurance; Medical Insurance; Pension Plan; Savings Plan; Tuition Assistance. **Other U.S. locations:** NY. **Operations at this facility include:** Administration; Manufacturing; Research and Development. **Number of employees at this location:** 550.

SUNBEAM-OSTER
200 East Las Olas Boulevard, Fort Lauderdale FL 33301. 954/767-2100. **Contact:** Human Resources. **Description:** A designer, manufacturer, and marketer of consumer products. The company is divided into four business groups: Outdoor Products, Household Products, Specialty Products, and International. Outdoor Products include propane, natural gas, electric, and charcoal barbecue grills; aluminum lawn and patio furniture and related accessories; and wrought iron and wood furniture. The company is estimated to have a 50 percent market share in grills and aluminum furniture. Household Products include electric and conventional blankets, comforters, and heated throws, heating pads, bath scales, health-monitoring systems, vaporizers, humidifiers, irons, steamers, and dental and hair care products. Small kitchen appliances include stand mixers, hand mixers, blenders, food processors, juice extractors, toasters, can openers, waffle makers, and other culinary accessories. Sunbeam also produces barber and beauty products, personal care products, and pet and large animal products, as well as clocks, timers, thermometers, and weather instruments. The company operates in over 60 countries through its international unit, primarily throughout Latin

America and Canada, with manufacturing facilities in Mexico and Venezuela. International sales consist primarily of small appliances. **Corporate headquarters location:** This Location. **Listed on:** New York Stock Exchange.

TUPPERWARE WORLD HEADQUARTERS

P.O. Box 2353, Orlando FL 32802. 407/826-5050. **Fax:** 407/826-8829. **Recorded Jobline:** 407/826-4496. **Contact:** Ginnette Colon, Associate Relations Assistant. **Description:** Tupperware manufactures plastic food-storage and serving containers. The world headquarters is located near Kissimmee, FL. **Common positions include:** Accountant/Auditor; Adjuster; Administrative Assistant; Attorney; Budget Analyst; Buyer; Customer Service Representative; Designer; Draftsperson; Economist/Market Research Analyst; Editor; Electrician; Environmental Engineer; Financial Analyst; Human Resources Specialist; Purchasing Agent and Manager; Travel Agent; Underwriter/Assistant Underwriter. **Educational backgrounds include:** Accounting; Art/Design; Business Administration; Communications; Computer Science; Finance; Marketing; Mathematics. **Benefits:** 401K; Dental Insurance; Disability Coverage; Employee Discounts; Life Insurance; Medical Insurance; Pension Plan; Savings Plan; Tuition Assistance. **Corporate headquarters location:** This Location. **Parent company:** Premark. **Operations at this facility include:** Administration; Divisional Headquarters; Research and Development. **Number of employees at this location:** 450.

TRAVELPRO LUGGAGE

501 Fairway, Deerfield Beach FL 33441. 954/426-5996. **Contact:** Human Resources. **Description:** Travelpro Luggage is an *Inc.* 500 manufacturer and distributor of luggage.

TROPITONE FURNITURE COMPANY

1401 Commerce Blvd, Sarasota FL 34243-5054. 813/355-2715. **Contact:** Human Resources. **Description:** A furniture manufacturer.

WINSLOEW FURNITURE, INC.

2665 South Bayshore Drive, Suite #800, Miami FL 33133-5462. 305/858-2200. **Fax:** 305/285-0102. **Contact:** Human Resources. **Description:** WinsLoew Furniture is the result of the late 1994 merger of Winston Furniture Company in Haleyville, Alabama, and Loewstein Furniture Group, Inc. in Pompano Beach, Florida. Winston Furniture previously designed, manufactured, and distributed indoor and outdoor furniture under the names Winston, Lyon Shaw, and Winston International. Loewstein Furniture Group previously designed, manufactured, and distributed furniture products for commercial and residential use, specifically contract seating and ready-to-assemble furniture segments. WinsLoew Furniture incorporates both businesses, designing, manufacturing, and distributing aluminum and wrought iron casual furniture for indoor and outdoor use, contract seating for the hospitality and office furniture markets, and ready-to-assemble furniture including futons and spindle and flat-line goods. **Corporate headquarters location:** This Location.

Note: Because addresses and telephone numbers of smaller companies change rapidly, we recommend you call each company to verify the information below before inquiring about job opportunities. Mass mailings are not recommended.

Additional employers with under 250 employees:

WOOD KITCHEN CABINETS

Innovative Design In Cabinetry
4100 N Powerline Rd, Pompano Beach FL 33073-3083. 954/972-7332.

Modernage Kitchens
100 Modern Age Blvd, Holly Hill FL 32117-4394. 904/253-7666.

Precision Panel Products
12440 73rd Ct, Largo FL 34643-3046. 813/539-7119.

Triangle Pacific Corp.
3820 Maine Ave, Lakeland FL 33801-9757. 407/628-3030.

HOUSEHOLD FURNITURE

Casualine
1065 E Story Rd, Winter Garden FL 34787-3732. 407/656-9722.

Higdon Furniture Co.
130 N Virginia St, Quincy FL 32351-1951. 904/627-7564.

Mactavish Furniture Industries
1703 Florida Ave, Quincy FL 32351-2835. 904/627-7561.

Carlton Manufacturing
1101 SW 37th Ave, Ocala FL 34474-2813. 352/237-1286.

Kanes Masterbuilt Furniture Company
5851 NW 35th Ave, Miami FL 33142-2001. 305/633-0542.

Maven Furniture Industries
P.O. Box 300, Eaton Park FL
33840-0300. 941/665-
5780.

Lineal Group Inc. Halcyon Division
6142 15th St E, Bradenton
FL 34203-7754. 941/758-
3891.

Capris Furniture Industries
1401 NW 27th Ave, Ocala
FL 34475-4723. 352/629-
8889.

New Tradewinds
16301 NW 15th Ave, Miami
FL 33169-5615. 305/624-
4411.

Tropitone Furniture Co.
1401 Commerce Blvd,
Sarasota FL 34243-5054.
941/355-2715.

MISC. FURNITURE AND FIXTURES

Hunter Douglas Fabrication Co.
2392 31st St S, St
Petersburg FL 33712-3348.
813/327-6434.

Vista Products
1788 Barber Rd, Sarasota FL
34240-9394. 941/378-
3844.

Comfortex Corporation
295 North Dr, Suite C,
Melbourne FL 32934-9261.
407/253-1422.

Mactavish Furniture Industries
5214 Vanguard St, Orlando
FL 32819-8527. 407/345-
8810.

COSMETICS AND RELATED PRODUCTS

Hawaiian Tropics
US Hwy 1, Ormond Beach FL
32174. 904/677-9559.

SMALL ARMS

Navegar
12405 SW 130th St, Miami

FL 33186-6209. 305/232-
1821.

POWER-DRIVEN HAND TOOLS

Daniels Manufacturing Corp.
526 Thorpe Rd, Orlando FL
32024-0133. 407/855-
6161.

HOUSEHOLD APPLIANCES

Warren Manufacturing Company
2050 W 73rd St, Hialeah FL
33016-1816. 305/556-
6933.

JEWELRY, SILVERWARE, AND PLATED WARE

William Schneider
16400 NW 15th Ave, Miami
FL 33169-5676. 305/625-
5171.

MUSICAL INSTRUMENTS

Stannard Company
611 Commerce Dr, Largo FL
34640-1834. 813/587-
0900.

TOYS AND SPORTING GOODS

The Penna Golf Co.
7830 W Industrial Way,
Suite 7, West Palm Beach FL
33404-3332. 407/881-
7916.

WHOLESALE FURNITURE AND HOME FURNISHINGS

Farmer's Furniture Company
2030 S Jefferson St, Perry
FL 32347-5619. 904/584-
8144.

Kalin Enterprises
P.O. Box 45900, Sarasota FL
34277-4900. 941/924-
1271.

Decora Office Furniture
7565 Currency Dr, Orlando
FL 32809-6982. 407/851-
6766.

Global Wholesalers
5147 W Rio Vista Ave,
Tampa FL 33634-5343.
813/888-8466.

The Knoll Group
1251 Ravida Woods Dr,
Apopka FL 32703-7479.
407/884-1873.

Cooper Distributors
2700 Hazelhurst Ave,
Orlando FL 32804-2796.
407/299-7230.

Shaw Industries
2900 Titan Row, Orlando FL
32809-5691. 407/855-
4615.

SPORTING AND RECREATIONAL GOODS AND SUPPLIES WHOLESALE

BLN
2394 Saint Johns Bluff Rd S,
Jacksonville FL 32246-2310.
904/642-9400.

Gorman Company
5757 McIntosh Rd, Sarasota
FL 34233-3457. 941/921-
7971.

Flow Tronex International
3808 Gunn Hwy, Tampa FL
33624-4720. 813/968-
9695.

PAPER AND OFFICE SUPPLIES WHOLESALE

Simplex Products
2315 Beach Blvd, Suite 304,
Jacksonville Beach FL
32250-4055. 904/249-
1601.

McBee Systems
3830 Crown Point Rd, Suite
B, Jacksonville FL 32257-
8974. 904/268-2100.

Wilmer Service Line
16710 Beauclaire Ct,
Tavares FL 32778-9790.
352/343-2577.

Double Envelope Corp.
4879 Holly Dr, Palm Beach
Gardens FL 33418-4507.
407/626-5504.

For more information on career opportunities in consumer manufacturing and wholesaling:

Associations

ASSOCIATION FOR MANUFACTURING TECHNOLOGY
7901 Westpark Drive, McLean VA 22102.
703/893-2900. Offers research services.

ASSOCIATION OF HOME APPLIANCE MANUFACTURERS
20 North Wacker Drive, Chicago IL 60606.
312/984-5800.

NATIONAL ASSOCIATION OF MANUFACTURERS
1331 Pennsylvania Avenue NW, Suite
1500, Washington DC 20004. 202/637-
3000. A lobbying association for
manufacturers.

NATIONAL HOUSEWARES MANUFACTURERS ASSOCIATION
6400 Schafer Court, Suite 650, Rosemont

IL 60018. 708/292-4200. Offers shipping discounts and other services.

SOCIETY OF MANUFACTURING ENGINEERS
P.O. Box 930, One SME Drive, Dearborn MI 48121. 313/271-1500. Offers educational events and educational materials on manufacturing.

Directories

APPLIANCE MANUFACTURER ANNUAL DIRECTORY
Appliance Manufacturer, 5900 Harper Road, Suite 105, Solon OH 44139. 216/349-3060. $25.00.

HOUSEHOLD AND PERSONAL PRODUCTS INDUSTRY BUYERS GUIDE
Rodman Publishing Group, 17 South Franklin Turnpike, Ramsey NJ 07446. 201/825-2552. $12.00.

Magazines

APPLIANCE
1110 Jorie Boulevard, Oak Brook IL 60522-9019. 708/990-3484. Monthly. $70.00 for a one-year subscription.

COSMETICS INSIDERS REPORT
Advanstar Communications, 7500 Old Oak Boulevard, Cleveland OH 44130. 216/243-8100. $189.00. Monthly. Features timely articles on cosmetics marketing and research.

MANUFACTURING AND WHOLESALING: MISCELLANEOUS INDUSTRIAL

Factories have been operating at their highest rate of capacity in more than five years. After an unparalleled year for growth, machine manufacturers expect another good year. With money to spend, manufacturers should be adding more equipment to increase production and efficiency. Export markets are expected to pick up the demand where the domestic market leaves off. With increased product demand, the demand for engineers should also increase.

The employment of the wholesale trade is closely tied to the growth of the economy. However, industry trends will change the composition and nature of much of the wholesale trade employment. Consolidation of the industry into fewer firms and the spread of new technology should slow growth in some occupations, but many new jobs will be created in others as firms provide a growing array of support services. In addition, these trends will change the role of many other workers.

Heightened competition and pressure to lower operating costs should continue to force distributors to merge with or acquire other firms. The resulting consolidation of wholesale trade among fewer, larger firms will reduce the demands for some workers as merged companies eliminate duplicated staff. Consolidation and greater competition among wholesale trade firms, however, will lead more firms to expand customer service, increasing demands for related workers. Clerks or sales workers will advance to many of these new customer service or marketing jobs, and new workers may be needed for financial, logistical, technical, or advertising positions.

AQUAFILTER CORPORATION
P.O. Box 5378, Fort Lauderdale FL 33310. 954/491-2200. **Contact:** Personnel Department. **Description:** A manufacturer of cigarette filters.

BAIRNCO CORPORATION
2251 Lucien Way, Suite 300, Maitland FL 32751. 407/875-2222. **Contact:** Barry Steinhart, Vice President of Administration. **Description:** A holding company operating through three subsidiaries: Shielding Systems Corporation, a manufacturer of products such as electromagnetic shielding and secure communications; Kasco Corporations, a manufacturer and servicer of equipment for the supermarket industry; and Arlon Inc., a manufacturer of coated and laminated materials for industrial and commercial use. Markets include civilian and military communications, radar and computer systems, electronic testing, and other industrial, scientific, automotive, and military applications. **NOTE:** Hiring is done primarily through operating divisions. **Common positions include:** Accountant/Auditor; Chemist; Computer Programmer; Electrical/Electronics Engineer; Financial Analyst; General Manager; Human Resources Specialist; Industrial Engineer; Mechanical Engineer; Operations/Production Manager; Supervisor. **Educational backgrounds include:** Accounting; Business Administration; Chemistry; Computer Science; Engineering; Finance; Marketing. **Benefits:** 401K; Life Insurance; Medical Insurance; Pension Plan; Tuition Assistance. **Corporate headquarters location:** This

Location. **Operations at this facility include:** Administration. **Listed on:** New York Stock Exchange. **Number of employees nationwide:** 900.

CONAX FLORIDA CORPORATION
2801 75th Street North, St. Petersburg FL 33710. 813/345-8000. **Fax:** 813/345-4217. **Contact:** Anita Stelljes, Personnel Administrator. **Description:** Manufactures temperature sensing devices, explosive actuated devices, and electrical penetrations. **Common positions include:** Electrical/Electronics Engineer; Mechanical Engineer. **Educational backgrounds include:** Engineering. **Benefits:** 401K; Dental Insurance; Disability Coverage; Life Insurance; Medical Insurance; Tuition Assistance. **Corporate headquarters location:** This Location. **Listed on:** Privately held. **Number of employees at this location:** 125.

CROWN CORK & SEAL
P.O. Box 770369, Wintergarden FL 34777-0639. 407/654-0225. **Contact:** Betty Allen, Manager of Employee Relations. **Description:** Manufactures containers.

EDWARD DON & COMPANY
2200 South West 45th Street, Fort Lauderdale FL 33312. 954/983-3000x308. **Contact:** Human Resources. **Description:** Distributes furniture and equipment to restaurants, hotels, and schools. **Common positions include:** Buyer; Customer Service Representative; Sales Representative. **Educational backgrounds include:** Business Administration. **Benefits:** 401K; Dental Insurance; Disability Coverage; Employee Discounts; Life Insurance; Medical Insurance; Profit Sharing; Tuition Assistance. **Operations at this facility include:** Administration; Divisional Headquarters; Sales. **Listed on:** Privately held. **Number of employees at this location:** 270. **Number of employees nationwide:** 1,100.

EVA-TONE
4801 Ulmerton Road, Clearwater FL 34622. 813/572-7000. **Fax:** 813/571-3124. **Recorded Jobline:** 813/572-7076x799. **Contact:** Chris Guella, Human Resources Generalist. **Description:** Eva-tone is a manufacturer of audio materials, CDs, CD-ROMs, cassettes, and soundsheets. The company also provides commercial printing, mailing, and packaging services. **Common positions include:** Factory Worker; Production Worker. **Educational backgrounds include:** Manufacturing Management. **Benefits:** 401K; Dental Insurance; Disability Coverage; Life Insurance; Medical Insurance; Profit Sharing; Tuition Assistance. **Corporate headquarters location:** This Location. **Operations at this facility include:** Administration; Manufacturing; Research and Development; Sales. **Listed on:** Privately held. **Number of employees at this location:** 360.

FMC
FOOD PROCESSING SYSTEMS DIVISION
P.O. Box 1708, Lakeland FL 33802. 941/683-5411. **Contact:** Human Resources. **Description:** A manufacturer of citrus fruit processing machinery. The parent company, FMC Corporation, is a producer of chemicals and machinery for industry, agriculture and government. FMC participates on a worldwide basis in selected segments of five broad markets: Performance Chemicals; Industrial Chemicals; Machinery and Equipment; Defense Systems; and Precious Metals.

GENCOR INDUSTRIES INC.
5201 North Orange Blossom Trail, Orlando FL 32810. 407/290-6000. **Contact:** Personnel Department. **Description:** Manufactures combustion systems and related electronic heat process controls.

HUGHES SUPPLY INC.
P.O. Box 2273, Orlando FL 32802-2273. 407/841-4755. **Contact:** Human Resources. **Description:** A wholesale distributor of industrial machinery.

IDAB, INC.
3200 West 84th Street, Hialeah FL 33016. 305/823-4000. **Contact:** Sandra Cook, Administrative Assistant. **Description:** Manufacturer of materials handling equipment and robotics.

INTER-AMERICAN TRANSPORT EQUIPMENT
3690 North West 62nd Street, Miami FL 33147. 305/633-0351. **Contact:** Antonio Vera, Director of Personnel. **Description:** Exporters of heavy industrial equipment.

IRVINGTON-MOORE
P.O. Box 40666, Jacksonville FL 32203. 904/354-2301. **Contact:** Norm Caudle, Personnel Manager. **Description:** A manufacturer of wood drying kilns. **Common positions include:** Customer Service Representative; Draftsperson; Manufacturer's/Wholesaler's Sales Rep.; Mechanical Engineer. **Educational backgrounds include:** Engineering; Marketing. **Benefits:** Disability Coverage; Life Insurance; Medical Insurance; Pension Plan; Savings Plan; Tuition Assistance. **Operations at this facility include:** Divisional Headquarters.

JENSEN CORPORATION
2775 North West 63rd Court, Fort Lauderdale FL 33309. 954/974-6300. **Contact:** Jean Hauck-Watson, Personnel Coordinator. **Description:** Manufactures commercial laundry equipment (folders, feeders, and finishing equipment).

KAYDON CORPORATION
19345 U.S. Highway 19 North, Suite 500, Clearwater FL 34624. 813/531-1101. **Contact:** Human Resources. **Description:** Manufactures custom-engineered products, including rings, seals, bearings, and filter systems. **Corporate headquarters location:** This Location.

KELLER INDUSTRIES, INC.
3499 NW 53rd Street, Fort Lauderdale FL 33309. 954/777-2060. **Contact:** Human Resources. **Description:** A manufacturer of windows, glass, and aluminum furniture.

LINDER INDUSTRIAL MACHINERY
P.O. Box 3699, Plant City FL 33564. 813/754-2727. **Contact:** Roxanne Dancy, Human Resource Coordinator. **Description:** Distributor of construction and mining equipment.

MARTIN ELECTRONICS, INC.
Route One, Box 700, Perry FL 32347. 904/584-2634. **Contact:** Miss Ann Nola, Director of Personnel. **Description:** Martin Electronics, Inc. manufactures pyrotechnic and explosive devices for ordnance applications. **Common positions include:** Blue-Collar Worker Supervisor; Chemical Engineer; Electrician; Environmental Engineer; Production Worker; Purchasing Agent and Manager; Quality Control Supervisor. **Educational backgrounds include:** Engineering. **Benefits:** 401K; Disability Coverage; Employee Discounts; Life Insurance; Medical Insurance; Tuition Assistance. **Corporate headquarters location:** This Location. **Operations at this facility include:** Administration; Manufacturing. **Number of employees at this location:** 300.

OLIN ORDNANCE DEFENSE
10101 9th Street North, St. Petersburg FL 33716. 813/578-8100. **Contact:** Personnel Director. **Description:** A defense contractor, manufacturing ordnance products.

PALL AEROPOWER
10540 Ridge Road, New Port Richey FL 34654. 813/849-9999. **Fax:** 813/848-5719. **Contact:** Joseph J. DelGobbo, Manager, Human Resources. **Description:** Pall Aeropower manufactures filtration products for helicopters and Army tanks. **Common positions include:** Aerospace Engineer; Aircraft Mechanic/Engine Specialist; Buyer; Chemist; Cost Estimator; Designer; Electrician; Human Resources Specialist; Industrial Engineer; Mechanical Engineer; Operations/Production Manager; Purchasing Agent and Manager; Quality Control Supervisor. **Educational backgrounds include:** Engineering; Finance. **Benefits:** 401K; Dental Insurance; Disability Coverage; Employee Discounts; Life Insurance; Medical Insurance; Pension Plan; Profit Sharing; Savings Plan; Tuition Assistance. **Corporate headquarters location:** East Hills NY. **Parent company:** Pall Corporation. **Operations at this facility include:** Manufacturing. **Number of employees at this location:** 235. **Number of employees nationwide:** 6,500.

PARKSON CORPORATION
2727 Northwest 62nd Street, Fort Lauderdale FL 33309. 954/974-6610. **Contact:** Fran Rudman, Personnel Coordinator. **Description:** Manufactures water and wastewater treatment equipment.

PHOTO ELECTRONICS CORPORATION
1100 Fairfield Drive, West Palm Beach FL 33407. 407/848-7211. **Fax:** 407/881-0740. **Contact:** Melissa Bittner, Personnel Representative. **Description:** Photo Electronics Corporation is a manufacturing company specializing in photo analyzing equipment used in professional color labs. **Common positions include:**

Accountant/Auditor; Computer Programmer; Electrical/Electronics Engineer; Electronics Technician; Genetic Engineer; Human Resources Specialist; Machinist; Manufacturer's/Wholesaler's Sales Rep.; Purchasing Agent and Manager. **Educational backgrounds include:** Accounting; Business Administration; Computer Science; Engineering. **Benefits:** 401K; Dental Insurance; Disability Coverage; Employee Discounts; Life Insurance; Medical Insurance; Savings Plan; Tuition Assistance. **Corporate headquarters location:** This Location. **Operations at this facility include:** Administration; Manufacturing; Research and Development; Sales; Service. **Listed on:** Privately held. **Number of employees at this location:** 15.

PRECISION METERS, INC.
11100 Astronaut Boulevard, Orlando FL 32837. 407/851-4470. **Contact:** Ralph Celeiro, Personnel. **Description:** A manufacturer of water meters. **Common positions include:** Accountant/Auditor; Administrative Services Manager; Budget Analyst; Credit Manager; Materials Engineer; Mechanical Engineer; Metallurgical Engineer; Purchasing Agent and Manager; Structural Engineer. **Educational backgrounds include:** Accounting; Business Administration; Computer Science; Engineering; Finance. **Operations at this facility include:** Administration; Manufacturing; Research and Development; Sales; Service. **Number of employees at this location:** 60.

Q.M.S. INC.
555 Winderley Place, Suite 114, Maitland FL 32751. 407/660-1244. **Contact:** Human Resources. **Description:** The sales office for a laser printer manufacturer.

STAINLESS INCORPORATED
One Stainless Plaza, Deerfield Beach FL 33441. 954/421-4290. **Contact:** Lori Mollnow, Manager, Human Resources. **Description:** A manufacturer and distributor of commercial restaurant equipment. **Common positions include:** Accountant/Auditor; Administrator; Architectural Engineer; Blue-Collar Worker Supervisor; Buyer; Computer Programmer; Credit Manager; Customer Service Representative; Department Manager; Draftsperson; Human Resources Specialist; Manufacturer's/Wholesaler's Sales Rep.; Operations/Production Manager; Quality Control Supervisor; Transportation/Traffic Specialist. **Educational backgrounds include:** Accounting; Business Administration; Liberal Arts. **Benefits:** Dental Insurance; Disability Coverage; Employee Discounts; Life Insurance; Medical Insurance; Pension Plan; Profit Sharing; Tuition Assistance. **Corporate headquarters location:** This Location. **Operations at this facility include:** Administration; Manufacturing; Sales. **Number of employees at this location:** 150.

UNIWELD PRODUCTS, INC.
2850 Ravenswood Road, Fort Lauderdale FL 33312. 954/584-2000. **Contact:** Amy Lumford, Personnel. **Description:** A manufacturer of gas welding and cutting equipment and pressure gauges. **Common positions include:** Accountant/Auditor; Buyer; Commercial Artist; Credit Manager; Customer Service Representative; Draftsperson; Human Resources Specialist; Industrial Engineer; Manufacturer's/Wholesaler's Sales Rep.; Mechanical Engineer; Purchasing Agent and Manager; Quality Control Supervisor. **Educational backgrounds include:** Accounting; Business Administration; Computer Science; Engineering. **Benefits:** Credit Union; Dental Insurance; Employee Discounts; Life Insurance; Medical Insurance; Tuition Assistance. **Corporate headquarters location:** This Location. **Operations at this facility include:** Administration; Manufacturing; Research and Development; Sales; Service.

WESTINGHOUSE ELECTRIC CORPORATION
ENERGY CENTER
4400 Alafaya Trail, Orlando FL 32826-2399. 407/281-2000. **Contact:** Human Resources Department. **Description:** A manufacturer of steam turbine generators.

Note: Because addresses and telephone numbers of smaller companies change rapidly, we recommend you call each company to verify the information below before inquiring about job opportunities. Mass mailings are not recommended.

Additional employers with over 250 employees:

METAL HARDWARE
Ideal
3200 Parker Dr, St
Augustine FL 32095-0891.
904/829-1000.

Perko
16490 NW 13th Ave, Miami FL 33169-5707. 305/621-7525.

FOOD PRODUCTS MACHINERY

VHC Ltd.
777 S Flagler Dr, West Palm Beach FL 33401. 407/659-7770.

SPECIAL INDUSTRIAL MACHINERY

Anchor Coupling Co.
135 W Bay St Ste 500, Jacksonville FL 32202-3840. 904/353-6336.

FANS, BLOWERS, AND AIR PURIFICATION EQUIPMENT

Mectron Industries
6301 49th St, Pinellas Park FL 34665-5721. 813/522-3111.

Precisionaire
P.O. Box 2728, Bartow FL 33830-2728. 813/533-8300.

MISC. INDUSTRIAL MACHINERY AND EQUIPMENT

Pneumatic Products Corp.
4647 SW 40th Ave, Ocala FL 34474-5730. 352/237-1220.

COMMERCIAL LAUNDRY, DRY-CLEANING, AND PRESSING MACHINES

Unimac Co.
Industrial Park, Marianna FL 32446. 904/526-3405.

MOTORS AND GENERATORS

Mercury Marine
1000 Robinson Ave, Saint Cloud FL 34769-4026. 407/892-2121.

MEASURING AND CONTROLLING EQUIPMENT

TIF Instruments
9101 NW 7th Ave, Miami FL 33150 305/757-8811.

United Technologies Optical
P.O. Box 109660, West Palm Beach FL 33410-9660. 407/775-4000.

Ametek US Gauge
P.O. Box 1959, Bartow FL 33830. 813/534-1504.

Additional employers with under 250 employees:

PACKAGING PAPER AND PLASTICS FILM

Malnove Inc. Of Florida
4115 University Boulevard Ct, Jacksonville FL 32217-2223. 904/733-4770.

GASKETS, PACKING, AND SEALING DEVICES

Eagle-Picher Industries
10825 County Road 44, Leesburg FL 34788-2616. 352/787-3015.

METAL HARDWARE

JD Industries
227 Harrison Ave, Panama City FL 32401-2727. 904/784-3900.

MISC. PIPE FITTINGS AND/OR -VALVES

Hoerbiger Corp. Of America
P.O. Box 8888, Ft Lauderdale FL 33310-8888. 954/974-5700.

Stanzdyne
2919 Commonwealth Blvd, Tallahassee FL 32303-3156. 904/575-8181.

Halkey Roberts Corp.
11600 9th St N, St Petersburg FL 33716-2397. 813/577-1300.

Hoerbiger Corp. Of America
1381 SW 30th Ave, Pompano Beach FL 33069-4824. 954/974-5700.

Parker-Hannifin Corp.
777 Bennett Dr, Longwood FL 32750-6365. 407/767-2922.

Shaw Aero Devices
12291 Towne Lake Dr, Fort Myers FL 33913-8012. 941/768-5644.

FABRICATED PIPE AND PIPE FITTINGS

Wellstream Corp.
1700 C Ave, Panama City FL 32401-1057. 904/769-9471.

FARM MACHINERY AND EQUIPMENT

LESCO
413 Big Bnd, Sebring FL 33870-7535. 941/655-2424.

ELEVATORS AND MOVING STAIRWAYS

EMAC
Hwy 20 W, Blountstown FL 32424. 904/674-5989.

Mowrey Elevator Co.
3300 SW 50th Ave, Ft Lauderdale FL 33314-2105. 954/581-8900.

Miami Elevator Co.
6942 Phillips Parkway Dr S, Jacksonville FL 32256-1566. 904/260-4656.

Montgomery Elevator Company
1304 N Clearview Ave #A, Tampa FL 33607-4912. 813/879-5200.

CONVEYORS AND CONVEYING EQUIPMENT

BCE Technologies
620 S Ware Blvd, Tampa FL 33619. 813/621-8128.

Merrick Industries
10 Arthur Dr, Lynn Haven FL 32444-1685. 904/265-3611.

METAL CUTTING OR FORMING TOOLS

Michigan Drill Corp.
8405 NW 66th St, Miami FL 33166-2630. 305/592-7777.

Quality Products
3820 Northdale Blvd, Tampa FL 33624-1863. 813/963-1300.

INDUSTRIAL PATTERNS

BWI Inex Vision Systems
13327 US Highway 19 N, Clearwater FL 34624-7225. 813/535-5502.

PRINTING MACHINERY AND EQUIPMENT

Anchor/Lith Kemko
50 Industrial Loop N, Orange Park FL 32073-2849. 904/264-3500.

FOOD PRODUCTS MACHINERY

Acme
P.O. Box 1935, Sanford FL 32772-1935. 407/322-6294.

Bangold
4223 E Riverhills Dr, Tampa FL 33617-7406. 813/989-8821.

Nylonge Corp.
P.O. Box 10520, Naples FL 33941-0520. 941/434-0424.

SPECIAL INDUSTRIAL MACHINERY

ABC Packaging Machine Corporation
811 Live Oak St, Tarpon Springs FL 34689-4137. 813/937-5144.

Curt G. Joa
1500 High Ridge Rd, Boynton Beach FL 33426-8724. 407/732-7177.

Datamax Corporation
4501 Parkway Commerce Blvd, Orlando FL 32808-1089. 407/578-8007.

ITW Mima
1081 Holland Dr, Boca Raton FL 33487-2702. 407/241-8222.

Klockner-Bartelt
5501 N Washington Blvd, Sarasota FL 34243-2249. 941/359-4000.

Perry Technologies
100 E 17th St, Riviera Beach FL 33404-5664. 407/842-5261.

FANS, BLOWERS, AND AIR PURIFICATION EQUIPMENT

American Coolair Corp.
P.O. Box 2300, Jacksonville FL 32203-2300. 904/389-3646.

Flair Corporation
4647 SW 40th Ave, Ocala FL 34474-5730. 352/237-1220.

PACKAGING MACHINERY

Aidlin Automation Corp.
P.O. Box 13125, Sarasota FL 34278-3125. 941/756-0641.

MISC. INDUSTRIAL MACHINERY AND EQUIPMENT

Beloit Corporation
6620 Southpoint Dr S, Suite 500, Jacksonville FL 32216-0912. 904/296-0035.

Memtec America Corp.
1750 Memtec Dr, Deland FL 32724-2045. 904/822-8000.

Pall Industrial Hydraulics Company
4245 Evans Ave, Fort Myers FL 33901-9311. 941/936-8700.

Technetics Corp.
1600 Industrial Dr, Deland FL 32724-2095. 904/736-7373.

AIR-CONDITIONING, HEATING, AND REFRIGERATION EQUIPMENT

Addison Products Co.
P.O. Box 607715, Orlando FL 32860-7715. 407/292-4400.

FHP Manufacturing A Harrow Company
601 NW 65th Ct, Ft Lauderdale FL 33309-6109. 954/776-5471.

SERVICE INDUSTRY MACHINERY

Precision Industries
1135 NW 159th Dr, Miami FL 33169-5807. 305/887-1717.

Vac-Con
969 Hall Park Dr, Green Cove Springs FL 32043. 904/284-4200.

INDUSTRIAL AND COMMERCIAL MACHINERY AND EQUIPMENT

Belfab Division
P.O. Box 9370, Daytona Beach FL 32120-9370. 904/253-0628.

Precision Machining
3820 Hopkins St, Pensacola FL 32505-5223. 904/434-5331.

TJS Tool & Mold
1555 17th St W, Palmetto FL 34221-6123. 941/722-4838.

MEASURING AND CONTROLLING EQUIPMENT

Lambda Novatronics
P.O. Box 878, Pompano Beach FL 33061-0878. 954/942-5200.

Ametek
8600 Somerset Dr, Largo FL 34643-2713. 813/536-7831.

Glendale Protectivech
5300 Region Ct, Lakeland FL 33801-3121. 941/687-0431.

Teleflex
1816 57th St, Sarasota FL 34243-2229. 941/355-7721.

OFFICE EQUIPMENT WHOLESALE

Copytronics
2461 Rolac Rd, Jacksonville FL 32207-7916. 904/731-5100.

Copytronics
26 Oleander St, Cocoa FL 32922-7959. 407/631-8933.

Konica Business Systems
3201 W Commercial Blvd, Suite 110, Ft Lauderdale FL 33309-3452. 954/945-1229.

Lanier Worldwide
5625 W Waters Ave, Tampa FL 33634-1226. 813/935-3103.

Lanier Worldwide
10251 Metro Pkwy, Fort Myers FL 33912-1010. 941/939-1033.

EGP
2810 Scherer Dr N, Suite 120, St Petersburg FL 33716-1018. 813/573-0020.

Xerox Corporation
800 S Douglas Rd Fl 8, Coral Gables FL 33134-3125. 305/447-6000.

Electronic Merchant Systems
4902 Eisenhower Blvd, Suite 380, Tampa FL 33634-6344. 813/847-1405.

COMMERCIAL EQUIPMENT WHOLESALE

Ampco Products
7795 NW 20th Ct, Ft Lauderdale FL 33322-3903. 954/565-1835.

Kasco Atlantic Service Company
677 NE 42nd St, Oakland Park FL 33334-3140. 954/561-8595.

Cambro Manufacturing Co.
3015 Hartley Rd, Suite 13C, Jacksonville FL 32257-6258. 904/268-8879.

Superior Products
2301 Premier Row, Orlando FL 32809-5602. 407/859-7300.

Federal APD
773 S Kirkman Rd, Orlando FL 32811-2046. 407/299-0731.

REFRIGERATION EQUIPMENT WHOLESALE

United Refrigeration
455 N Westmoreland Dr, Orlando FL 32805-1447. 407/649-3300.

Carrier Transicold Of Florida
5635 E Powhatan Ave, Tampa FL 33610-2025. 813/626-5101.

INDUSTRIAL MACHINERY AND EQUIPMENT WHOLESALE

Senco Of Florida
1403 W Boynton Beach Blvd, Boynton Beach FL 33426-3411. 407/734-8171.

Florida Detroit Diesel Allison
P.O. Box 16595, Jacksonville FL 32245-6595. 904/737-7330.

Nestor Sales Co.
7337 Bryan Dairy Rd, Largo FL 34647-1507. 813/535-6411.

Demaco Division Howden Food Equipment
7825 Ellis Rd, W Melbourne FL 32904-1107. 407/768-0333.

Florida Lift Systems
7685 Currency Dr, Orlando FL 32809-6984. 407/292-6005.

Badger Meter
13910 N Dale Mabry Hwy, Tampa FL 33618-2440. 813/265-4600.

Peabody Floway
300 Lake Marie Blvd, Winter Haven FL 33884-1436. 941/324-8555.

Southeastern Municipal Supply
2001 University Pkwy, Sarasota FL 34243-2820. 941/355-5288.

The Pitman Company
5902 Johns Rd, Tampa FL 33634-4422. 813/822-5080.

Bitec
8123 Ridge Rd, Port Richey

FL 34668-7057. 813/849-9353.

Grainger
4180 L B McLeod Rd, Orlando FL 32811-5695. 407/843-3220.

Grainger
8450 Phillips Hwy, Jacksonville FL 32256-8206. 904/636-8896.

Jenkins Industrial Products
3820 7th Ave N, Tampa FL 33605. 813/247-2310.

Juno Industries
4355 Drane Field Rd, Lakeland FL 33811-1212. 941/646-1493.

Miller Bearings
1 SW Moreland Dr, Orlando FL 32805. 407/425-9078.

Process Solutions
3630 Consumer St, Riviera Beach FL 33404-1717. 407/840-0050.

Dixon Valve & Coupling Company
4946 Distribution Dr, Tampa FL 33605-5926. 813/247-3500.

Bell Fasteners Tampa
4721 Transport Dr, Tampa FL 33605-5940. 813/247-1694.

Dixie Bearings
626 N 13th St, Tampa FL 33602-3108. 813/228-7702.

Morgan Matroc
100 Rialto Place, Suite 726, Melbourne FL 32901-3071. 407/728-7049.

Ryko Manufacturing Co.
976 Florida Central Pkwy,

Longwood FL 32750-7504. 407/260-5999.

Stokes Vacuum
5840 S Semoran Blvd, Orlando FL 32822-4812. 407/658-2078.

Southland Supplies
4924 Distribution Dr, Tampa FL 33605-5926. 813/247-4600.

York Distributors
3001 NW 60th St, Ft Lauderdale FL 33309-2254. 954/977-0359.

SCRAP AND WASTE MATERIALS WHOLESALE

David J. Joseph Co.
4201 Maritime Blvd, Tampa FL 33605-6862. 813/247-6303.

COMMERCIAL FURNITURE AND FIXTURES

Jansko
4101 Ravenswood Rd, Ft Lauderdale FL 33312-5373. 954/797-5044.

Amertec-Granada
7007 N Waterway Dr, Miami FL 33155-2808. 305/266-6200.

Ampco Products
7795 W 20th Ave, Hialeah FL 33014-3227. 305/821-5700.

Edron Fixture Corp.
3595 NW 125th St, Miami FL 33167-2413. 305/687-9100.

Associated Rack Corporation
7150 20th St, Suite C, Vero Beach FL 32966-8805. 407/567-2262.

For more information on career opportunities in industrial manufacturing and wholesaling:

Associations

APPLIANCE PARTS DISTRIBUTORS ASSOCIATION
228 East Baltimore Street, Detroit MI 48202. 313/875-8455. A wholesale distributor of parts.

ASSOCIATION FOR MANUFACTURING TECHNOLOGY
7901 Westpark Drive, McLean VA 22102. 703/893-2900. A trade association.

INSTITUTE OF INDUSTRIAL ENGINEERS
25 Technology Park, Norcross GA 30092. 404/449-0460. A non-profit organization with 27,000 members. Conducts seminars and offers reduced rates on its books and publications.

NATIONAL ASSOCIATION OF MANUFACTURERS
1331 Pennsylvania Avenue NW, Suite 1500, Washington DC 20004. 202/637-3000. A lobbying association.

NATIONAL SCREW MACHINE PRODUCTS ASSOCIATION
6700 West Snowville Road, Brecksville OH 44141. 216/526-0300. Provides resource information.

NATIONAL TOOLING AND MACHINING ASSOCIATION
9300 Livingston Road, Fort Washington MD 20744. 301/248-1250. Reports on wages and operating expenses. Produces monthly newsletters. Offers legal advice.

SOCIETY OF MANUFACTURING ENGINEERS
P.O. Box 930, One SME Drive, Dearborn MI 48121. 313/271-1500. Offers educational events and educational materials on manufacturing.

Directories

DIRECTORY OF TEXAS MANUFACTURERS
University of Texas at Austin, Bureau of Business Research, Box 7459, Austin TX 78713. 512/471-1616.

TEXAS MANUFACTURERS REGISTER
Manufacturer's News, Inc., 1633 Central Street, Evanston IL 60201. 708/864-7000.

Special Programs

BUREAU OF APPRENTICESHIP AND TRAINING
U.S. Department of Labor, 200 Constitution Avenue NW, Washington, DC 20210. 202/219-6540.

MINING/GAS/PETROLEUM/ENERGY RELATED

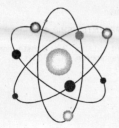

The energy industry is poised for a potentially huge growth cycle. While 10 years of layoffs and restructuring have tempered this optimism, a huge demand abroad is causing U.S. oil companies to turn their attention overseas. However, if the Iraqi oil embargo is lifted, foreign demand will be softer.

Even so, jobseekers can't expect increased production to lead to much employment growth. Layoffs are expected to continue, but advanced technologies used by the energy industry continue to crop up, and jobseekers with engineering backgrounds should watch for energy-related high-tech jobs.

In mining, earnings are much higher than average, but technological innovations, international competition, and environmental regulation will reduce employment. Best bets in the mining industry right now are for scientific technicians, professional specialty workers (such as geologists), and truck drivers.

AGRICO IMC COMPANY
P.O. Box 2000, Mulberry FL 33860. **Contact:** Human Resources Manager. **Description:** Engaged in the production of phosphate rock and related surface mining activities.

OCCIDENTAL CHEMICAL CORPORATION
P.O. Box 300, White Springs FL 32096. 904/397-8101. **Contact:** Human Resources. **Description:** A miner of phosphate. **Other U.S. locations:** Nationwide.

PETROLANE
705 South Chrome, Homestead FL 33030. 305/247-2421. **Contact:** Director of Human Resources. **Description:** Petrolane markets LP-gas (propane). **Common positions include:** Accountant/Auditor; Computer Programmer; Credit Manager; Department Manager; Financial Analyst; Human Resources Specialist; Management Trainee; Marketing Specialist; Purchasing Agent and Manager; Systems Analyst; Technical Writer/Editor. **Educational backgrounds include:** Accounting; Business Administration; Computer Science; Finance. **Benefits:** Dental Insurance; Disability Coverage; Employee Discounts; Life Insurance; Medical Insurance; Pension Plan; Profit Sharing; Savings Plan. **Corporate headquarters location:** White Plains NY.

SEMINOLE ELECTRIC COOPERATIVE INC.
P.O. Box 272000, Tampa FL 33688. 813/963-0994. **Contact:** Human Resources. **Description:** Owns power plants that provide electricity to utility companies, who then provide power to residences.

U.S. AGRI-CHEMICALS CORPORATION
3225 State Road, 630 West, Fort Meade FL 33841. 941/285-7123. **Contact:** Irene Dobson, Manager of Employee Relations. **Description:** A phosphate mining company producing granular fertilizer products the wholesale domestic and international markets. **Common positions include:** Accountant/Auditor; Buyer; Chemist; Civil Engineer; Electrical/Electronics Engineer; Geologist/Geophysicist; Human Resources Specialist; Mechanical Engineer; Metallurgical Engineer; Mining Engineer; Operations/Production Manager; Public Relations Specialist; Purchasing Agent and Manager; Quality Control Supervisor; Systems Analyst; Transportation/Traffic Specialist. **Educational backgrounds include:** Accounting; Business Administration; Chemistry; Engineering; Geology. **Benefits:** 401K; Dental Insurance; Disability Coverage; Employee Discounts; Life Insurance; Medical Insurance; Pension Plan; Tuition Assistance; Vision Insurance. **Special Programs:** Training Programs. **Corporate**

headquarters location: This Location. **Parent company:** Sinochem. **Operations at this facility include:** Administration; Manufacturing; Regional Headquarters; Sales.

Note: Because addresses and telephone numbers of smaller companies change rapidly, we recommend you call each company to verify the information below before inquiring about job opportunities. Mass mailings are not recommended.

Additional employers with under 250 employees:

PETROLEUM AND PETROLEUM PRODUCTS WHOLESALE

Coastal Unilube
2501 Industrial St, Leesburg FL 34748-3652. 352/787-3041.

D&H Oil Company
141 N John Sims Pkwy,

Valparaiso FL 32580-1005. 904/678-2510.

PETROLEUM REFINING

Exxon Co. USA
Oil Plant Rd, Jay FL 32565. 904/675-6892.

Star Enterprises
555 Winderley Place,

Maitland FL 32751-7225. 407/875-7600.

MINING MACHINERY AND EQUIPMENT

Driltech
Driltech Dr & Hwy 235, Alachua FL 32615. 352/462-4100.

For more information on career opportunities in the mining, gas, petroleum and energy industries:

Associations

AMERICAN ASSOCIATION OF PETROLEUM GEOLOGISTS
P.O. Box 979, Tulsa OK 7410-0979. 918/584-2555. International headquarters for petroleum geologists.

AMERICAN GEOLOGICAL INSTITUTE
4220 King Street, Alexandria VA 22302-1507. 703/379-2480. Scholarships available. Publishes monthly *Geotimes*. Offers job listings.

AMERICAN NUCLEAR SOCIETY
555 North Kensington Avenue, La Grange Park IL 60525. 708/352-6611. Offers educational services.

AMERICAN PETROLEUM INSTITUTE
1220 L Street NW, Suite 900, Washington DC 20005. 202/682-8000. A trade association.

GEOLOGICAL SOCIETY OF AMERICA
3300 Penrose Place, P.O. Box 9140, Boulder CO 80301. 303/447-2020. Membership of over 17,000. Offers sales items and publications. Also conducts society meetings.

SOCIETY OF EXPLORATION GEOPHYSICISTS
P.O. Box 702740, Tulsa OK 74170-2740. 918/493-3516. A membership association. Offers publications.

Directories

BROWN'S DIRECTORY OF NORTH AMERICAN AND INTERNATIONAL GAS COMPANIES
Advanstar Communications, 7500 Old Oak Boulevard, Cleveland OH 44130. 800/225-4569.

NATIONAL PETROLEUM NEWS FACT BOOK
Hunter Publishing Company, 25 NW Point Boulevard, Suite 800, Elk Grove Village, IL 60007. 708/427-9512.

OIL AND GAS DIRECTORY
Geophysical Directory, Inc., P.O. Box 130508, Houston TX 77219. 713/529-8789.

Magazines

AMERICAN GAS MONTHLY
1515 Wilson Boulevard, Arlington VA 22209. 703/841-8686.

GAS INDUSTRIES
Gas Industries News, Inc., 6300 North River Road, Suite 505, Rosemont IL 60018. 312/693-3682.

NATIONAL PETROLEUM NEWS
Hunter Publishing Company, 25 NW Point Boulevard, Elk Grove IL 60007. 708/296-0770.

OIL AND GAS JOURNAL
PennWell Publishing Company, 1421 South Sheridan Road, P.O. Box 1260. Tulsa OK 74101. 918/835-3161.

PAPER AND WOOD PRODUCTS

Midway through the year, 1995 was shaping up to be a great year for the paper industry. As of April 1995, paper prices were up 63 percent from the previous August. And continuing price increases and growing demand should allow paper companies to prosper in the next few years. Expansion and new facilities for many companies are expected, but only after debt from the last five years is paid off and restructuring occurs. In the next several years, mergers and the sale of family-owned companies (which are prevalent in this industry) may occur as some of the largest firms have already sold portions of their companies in order to focus on fewer markets. Environmental concerns voiced by the public should give the paper packaging segment an advantage over plastics, as companies move to become "green." The industry hopes to recycle at least half of the paper they make by the turn of the century.

Although the forestry sector is struggling with increasing costs and a decreasing supply of timber and wood adhesives, the outlook for college students enrolled in forest products programs is promising -- available positions exceed the number of jobseekers entering this industry. Especially promising for these students: jobs with the U.S. Forestry Service.

CHAMPION INTERNATIONAL CORPORATION
Seed Plant, Lee FL 32059. 904/971-5674. **Contact:** Human Resources. **Description:** A producer of paper and forest products. The company has the capacity to produce 6.2 million tons of paper, board, and market pulp a year, and owns or controls 5.1 million acres of timberland. Champion has five major business units: Printing and Writing Papers; Publication Papers; Newsprint and Kraft; Forest Products; and Marketing, which includes nationwide papers, *Champion Export*, and *Pulp Sales*. The company also has two major foreign subsidiaries: Weldwood of Canada and Champion Papel e Celulose, Brazil. **Corporate headquarters location:** Stamford CT. **Other U.S. locations:** Roanoke Rapid NC; Waynesville NC; Canton NC; Hamilton OH; Houston TX.

COASTAL LUMBER COMPANY
FLORIDA DIVISION
P.O. Box 1128, Havana FL 32333. 904/539-6432. **Contact:** Steve Hoffman, Human Resources Manager. **Description:** A lumber company. **Common positions include:** Accountant/Auditor; Blue-Collar Worker Supervisor; Forester/Conservation Scientist; General Manager; Operations/Production Manager; Production Manager; Supervisor. **Educational backgrounds include:** Accounting; Business Administration. **Benefits:** Dental Insurance; Disability Coverage; Life Insurance; Medical Insurance; Savings Plan. **Corporate headquarters location:** Weldon NC. **Operations at this facility include:** Manufacturing.

CONSTANTINE'S WOOD CENTER OF FLORIDA
1040 East Oakland Park Boulevard, Fort Lauderdale FL 33334. 954/561-1716. **Contact:** Human Resources. **Description:** A forest products company.

CONTAINER CORPORATION OF AMERICA
MILL DIVISION
P.O. Box 2000, Fernandina Beach FL 32035. 904/261-5551. **Contact:** Lance Hausc, Employee Relations Manager. **Description:** Manufacturers of kraft paper and containers.

FLORIDA PLYWOOD, INC.

P.O. Box 458, Highway 221 North, Greenville FL 32331. 904/948-2211. **Contact:** Arthur Maultsby, Personnel Manager. **Description:** A processor of lumber. **Common positions include:** Accountant/Auditor; Blue-Collar Worker Supervisor; Electrical/Electronics Engineer; General Manager; Machine Operator; Mechanical Engineer; Purchasing Agent and Manager. **Educational backgrounds include:** Accounting; Engineering. **Benefits:** Life Insurance; Medical Insurance; Profit Sharing. **Corporate headquarters location:** Whiteville NC. **Operations at this facility include:** Manufacturing; Sales.

GEORGIA PACIFIC CORPORATION

P.O. Box 919, Palatka FL 32178. 904/325-2001. **Contact:** Human Resources. **Description:** Makes pulp and paper as part of the national paper manufacturing company. **Other U.S. locations:** Nationwide.

GREAT SOUTH TIMBER INC.

P.O. Box 2249, Lake City FL 32056. 904/755-3046. **Contact:** Human Resources. **Description:** A timber broker.

GULF STREAM LUMBER COMPANY

P.O. Box 160, Boynton Beach FL 33425. 407/732-9763. **Contact:** Barbara Yodlowski, Personnel Director. **Description:** Produces retail lumber, trusses, and doors.

JEFFERSON SMURFIT CORPORATION

P.O. Box 150, Jacksonville FL 32201. 904/353-3611. **Contact:** Steven A. Zimmerman, Human Resources Manager. **Description:** A manufacturer of kraft linerboard. **Common positions include:** Accountant/Auditor; Blue-Collar Worker Supervisor; Buyer; Chemical Engineer; Chemist; Clerical Supervisor; Electrical/Electronics Engineer; Electrician; General Manager; Human Resources Specialist; Industrial Production Manager; Licensed Practical Nurse; Management Trainee; Mechanical Engineer; Operations/Production Manager; Purchasing Agent and Manager; Quality Control Supervisor; Registered Nurse; Transportation/Traffic Specialist. **Educational backgrounds include:** Engineering. **Benefits:** 401K; Dental Insurance; Disability Coverage; Life Insurance; Medical Insurance; Pension Plan; Tuition Assistance. **Corporate headquarters location:** St. Louis MO. **Operations at this facility include:** Administration; Manufacturing. **Listed on:** NASDAQ. **Number of employees at this location:** 300.

MAC PAPERS INC.

P.O. Box 5369, Jacksonville FL 32207. 904/396-5312. **Contact:** Human Resources. **Description:** A wholesale distributor of paper to the printing industry.

ROBBINS MANUFACTURING COMPANY

P.O. Box 17939, Tampa FL 33682. 813/971-3030. **Fax:** 813/971-3980. **Contact:** Human Resources. **Description:** A lumber mill. **Common positions include:** Blue-Collar Worker Supervisor; Branch Manager; Buyer; Clerical Supervisor; Computer Programmer; Computer Systems Analyst; Credit Manager; Customer Service Representative; Draftsperson; Human Resources Specialist; Manufacturer's/Wholesaler's Sales Rep.; Mechanical Engineer; Operations/Production Manager; Software Engineer; Wholesale and Retail Buyer. **Benefits:** 401K; Medical Insurance; Profit Sharing. **Corporate headquarters location:** This Location. **Other U.S. locations:** CA; NC; TX; WA. **Listed on:** Privately held. **Number of employees at this location:** 250. **Number of employees nationwide:** 400.

ST. JOE PAPER COMPANY

P.O. Box 1380, Jacksonville FL 32201. 904/396-6600. **Contact:** Mr. C. Masse Petty, Treasurer. **Description:** Engaged in the production of corrugated and solid fiber containers, including the cultivation and harvesting of pulpwood and the manufacture of linerboard. St. Joe Paper Company is engaged in five principal lines of business including Forest Products, Transportation, Sugar, Communications, and Real Estate. **Benefits:** Pension Plan; Retirement Plan. **Listed on:** New York Stock Exchange.

STONE CONTAINER CORPORATION

P.O. Box 47, Yulee FL 32097. 904/225-5121. **Contact:** Diane Griffin, Personnel Manager. **Description:** Stone Container Corporation is a multinational paper and packaging company with annual sales of approximately $5 million. Its primary businesses are paperboard and paper packaging, and white paper and pulp operations. The paperboard and paper packaging business is composed primarily of facilities which produce and sell containerboard and corrugated containers for manufacturers of consumable and durable goods and other manufacturers of corrugated containers; boxboard, folding cartons, and other products for manufacturers of consumable goods, especially food, beverage, and tobacco products, and for other box manufacturers; and kraft paper and bags and sacks for supermarket chains and other retailers of consumable products, as well as for the food, agricultural, chemical, and cement industries. White paper and pulp operations produce and sell newsprint for newspaper publishers and commercial printers; uncoated groundwood paper for producers of advertising materials, magazines, directories, and computer papers; and market pulp for manufacturers of paper products, including fine papers, photographic papers, tissue, and newsprint. Other operations consist primarily of wood products operations which produce and sell lumber, plywood, and veneer for the construction and furniture industries. Including its subsidiaries and affiliates, Stone Container maintains nearly 200 manufacturing facilities and sales offices in North America, Latin America, Europe, and the Far East. **Common positions include:** Accountant/Auditor; Blue-Collar Worker Supervisor; Commercial Artist; General Manager; Operations/Production Manager; Purchasing Agent and Manager. **Educational backgrounds include:** Accounting; Art/Design; Business Administration; Engineering; Mathematics. **Benefits:** Daycare Assistance; Dental Insurance; Disability Coverage; Life Insurance; Medical Insurance; Pension Plan; Savings Plan; Tuition Assistance. **Special Programs:** Training Programs. **Corporate headquarters location:** Chicago IL. **Operations at this facility include:** Manufacturing. **Listed on:** American Stock Exchange.

Note: Because addresses and telephone numbers of smaller companies change rapidly, we recommend you call each company to verify the information below before inquiring about job opportunities. Mass mailings are not recommended.

Additional employers with over 250 employees:

MILLWORK, PLYWOOD, AND STRUCTURAL MEMBERS

Georgia Pacific Corp.
P.O. Box 370, Hawthorne FL 32640-0370. 352/481-4311.

PAPER MILLS

ITT Rayonier
P.O. Box 2002, Fernandina FL 32035-1309. 904/261-3611.

Volusia Timber Corp.
2490 Jewett Ln, Sanford FL 32771-1692. 407/330-2252.

Walton Timber Resources
Hwy 90 W, Monticello FL 32344. 904/997-2005.

International Paper
621 NW 53rd St, Boca Raton FL 33487-8220. 407/995-0077.

Mead Paper
10014 N Dale Mabry Hwy, Tampa FL 33618-4410. 813/968-2922.

Paper Systems
233 SW 57th Ave, Ocala FL 34474-9346. 352/873-3200.

Stone Container Corp.
P.O. Box 105, Cantonment FL 32533. 904/968-1116.

PAPER BAGS

Central States Diversified
1400 Reid St, Palatka FL 32177-3297. 904/325-5311.

DIE-CUT PAPER AND PAPER PRODUCTS

Seminole Kraft Corp.
P.O. Box 26998, Jacksonville FL 32226-6998. 904/751-6400.

CONVERTED PAPER AND PAPERBOARD PRODUCTS

Consolidated Packaging
4190 Belfort Rd, Suite 222, Jacksonville FL 32216-1459. 904/296-8638.

Additional employers with under 250 employees:

WOOD MILLS

Gilman Building Products
6640 State Rd, Jacksonville FL 32234. 904/289-7261.

Louisiana-Pacific Corp.
8731 Steelfield Rd, Panama City Beach FL 32413-9427. 904/234-2777.

Louisiana-Pacific Corp.
Hwy 90 W, Crestview FL 32536. 904/537-5331.

Suwannee Lumber Manufacturing Co.
Hwys 19 & 351-A, Cross City FL 32628. 352/498-3363.

Wayne-Dalton Corp.
3395 Addison Dr, Pensacola FL 32514-7066. 904/474-9890.

PAPER MILLS

Paveca International
7850 SW 146th St, Miami

FL 33158-2014. 305/819-4201.

Scott Paper Company
8356 SW 58th St, Miami FL 33143-1504. 305/598-4838.

Scott Paper Company Commercial Products
3316 Deer Creek Alba Circle, Deerfield Beach FL 33442. 954/421-4003.

Simplex Products
1302 Eastport Rd,
Jacksonville FL 32218-2299.
904/757-7300.

Strathmore Paper Co.
13811 Old Dixie Hwy,
Hudson FL 34667-1585.
813/862-0269.

MILLWORK, PLYWOOD, AND STRUCTURAL MEMBERS

Addison Corporation
1101 Snively Ave, Eloise FL
33880-5554. 941/324-
6161.

Cox Lumber Company
320 Enterprise St, Ocoee FL
34761-3002. 407/656-
8424.

Forest Products Supply
5330 Pinkney Ave, Sarasota
FL 34233-2420. 941/922-
0731.

Gulf Port Industries
6222 Adamo Dr, Tampa FL
33619. 813/621-5821.

Premdor USA
5110 W Clifton St, Tampa
FL 33634-8012. 813/884-
3456.

Cox Lumber Company
3300 Fairfield Ave S, St
Petersburg FL 33712-1899.
813/327-4503.

Fort Myers Lumber & Supply
3530 Metro Pkwy, Fort
Myers FL 33916-7603.
941/332-1753.

H.J. Granger & Sons Inc.
1180 Lane Ave S,
Jacksonville FL 32205-6234.
904/781-4116.

Naples Lumber & Supply Co.
3828 Radio Rd, Naples FL
33942. 941/643-7000.

Pine Island Lumber
1118 Pondella Rd, Fort
Myers FL 33903-5199.
941/574-6600.

Southern Building Products
4922 Dyer Blvd, West Palm
Beach FL 33407-1016.
407/848-6646.

W-D Lumber & Truss
12019 State Road 54,
Odessa FL 33556-3434.
813/920-6653.

WOOD BOXES AND SHOOK

Bufkor
2600 118th Ave N, St
Petersburg FL 33716-1921.
813/572-9991.

WOOD PALLETS AND SKIDS

Ridge Pallets
1470 US Highway 17 S,
Bartow FL 33830-6627.
941/533-1147.

WOOD PRODUCTS

Goldbond Building Products
6110 W Commerce St,
Tampa FL 33616-1938.
813/839-2111.

Corbitt Manufacturing Co.
RR 8 Box 20, Lake City FL
32055-9032. 904/397-
2676.

PAPERBOARD CONTAINERS AND BOXES

Gaylord Container Corp.
8700 Adamo Dr, Tampa FL
33619. 813/621-3591.

Inland Container Corp.
10 E Lancaster Rd, Orlando
FL 32809-6625. 407/855-
2121.

International Paper Co.
525 Recker Hwy, Auburndale
FL 33823-4072. 941/967-
4151.

Jefferson Smurfit Container
8209 County Road 131,
Wildwood FL 34785-7716.
904/748-2900.

Micon Packaging Products
301 Commerce Blvd,
Oldsmar FL 34677-2806.
813/855-4651.

Packaging Corp. Of America
659 Eastport Rd,
Jacksonville FL 32218-3913.
904/757-8140.

Packaging Corp. Of America
2155 42nd St NW, Winter
Haven FL 33881-1947.
941/967-0641.

Tropical Paper Box Co.
7000 NW 25th St, Miami FL
33122. 305/592-5520.

Union Camp Corp.
2808 New Tampa Hwy,
Lakeland FL 33801-3465.
941/682-0123.

Weyerhaeuser Containerboard
6706 N 53rd St, Tampa FL
33610-1906. 813/621-
3011.

International Paper Co.
P.O. Box P, Plant City FL
33564-9011. 813/757-
3204.

Rex Packaging
136 Eastport Rd,
Jacksonville FL 32218-3906.
904/757-5210.

PAPER PRODUCTS

Atlantic Envelope Co.
240 NE 72nd St, Miami FL
33138-5393. 305/751-
2528.

Walter Papers
5406 W 1st St, Jacksonville
FL 32254-1648. 904/783-
1550.

LUMBER AND WOOD WHOLESALE

A&M Supply
6701 90th Ave, Pinellas Park
FL 34666-4596. 813/541-
6631.

Dyke Industries
2349 Silver Star Rd, Orlando
FL 32804-3309. 407/298-
7636.

Pleasants Contract Hardware
231 E Palmer Ave,
Tallahassee FL 32301-5533.
904/222-7141.

Furman Lumber
301 Mary Jess Rd, Orlando
FL 32839-2900. 407/851-
0107.

McEwen Lumber Co.
2620 N 36th St, Tampa FL
33605-3114. 813/248-
4111.

Cox Lumber Co.
1451 Cattlemen Rd,
Sarasota FL 34232-6288.
941/377-0110.

INDUSTRIAL PAPER AND RELATED PRODUCTS WHOLESALE

Zellerbach Company
9105 Sabal Industrial Blvd,
Tampa FL 33619-1347.
813/622-6100.

For more information on career opportunities in the paper and wood products industries:

Associations

AMERICAN FOREST AND PAPER ASSOCIATION
1111 19th Street NW, Suite 700, Washington DC 20036. 202/463-2700. A lobbying group that conducts informational gatherings.

AMERICAN FOREST AND PAPER ASSOCIATION
260 Madison Avenue, New York NY 10016. 212/340-0600. Headquartered in Washington DC. A lobbying group that conducts informational gatherings.

FOREST PRODUCTS SOCIETY
2801 Marshall Court, Madison WI 53705-2295. 608/231-1361. An international, nonprofit, educational association that provides an information network for all segments of the forest products industry. Offers employment referral service.

NATIONAL PAPER TRADE ASSOCIATION
111 Great Neck Road, Great Neck NY 11021. 516/829-3070. Offers management services to wholesalers. Offers books and seminars; and research services.

PAPERBOARD PACKAGING COUNCIL
888 17th Street NW, Suite 900, Washington DC 20006. 202/289-4100. Offers statistical and lobbying services.

TECHNICAL ASSOCIATION OF THE PULP AND PAPER INDUSTRY
P.O. Box 105113, Atlanta GA 30348.

404/446-1400. Non-profit. Offers conferences and education.

Directories

DIRECTORY OF THE FOREST PRODUCTS INDUSTRY
Miller Freeman Publications, Inc., 600 Harrison Street, San Francisco CA 94107. 415/905-2200.

LOCKWOOD-POST'S DIRECTORY OF THE PAPER AND ALLIED TRADES
Miller Freeman Publications, Inc., 600 Harrison Street, San Francisco CA 94107. 415/905-2200.

POST'S PULP AND PAPER DIRECTORY
Miller Freeman Publications, Inc., 600 Harrison Street, San Francisco CA 94107. 415/905-2200.

Magazines

PAPERBOARD PACKAGING
Advanstar Communications, 131 West First Street, Duluth MN 55802. 218/723-9200.

PULP AND PAPER WEEK
Miller Freeman Publications, Inc., 600 Harrison Street, San Francisco CA 94107. 415/905-2200.

WOOD TECHNOLOGIES
Miller Freeman Publications, Inc., 600 Harrison Street, San Francisco CA 94107. 415/905-2200.

PRINTING AND PUBLISHING

The big news in publishing is the paper shortage. As of April 1995, paper prices were up 63 percent from the previous August. The cost of paper accounts for 30 to 40 percent of the manufacturing costs of a book, which in turn represent about one-third of the total book cost. Fortunately, rising costs are not expected to result in job losses, but instead will be compensated for through tighter design, lower paper grades, and increased book prices. The paper pinch is also affecting the magazine and newspaper industries. Newsprint prices rose more than 30 percent from early 1994 to early 1995, and magazines are growing noticeably shorter. One good sign for newspapers and magazines: as the economy improves, companies will increase their print advertising budgets.

Another way some publishers are balancing their books against the paper crunch is by looking to electronic media, a competitive and rapidly expanding medium. Many book publishers are offering CD-ROM versions of popular books, especially educational, reference, and children's books. Also, books on tape are growing in popularity. Magazines and newspapers also are jumping on the electronic bandwagon -- many periodicals and newspapers are now available online.

Book printing and distribution is also evolving. Traditionally, long print runs were necessary to keep costs down. But thanks to new digital presses that don't use plates, books can now be printed and distributed in small batches according to demand. Instead of printing and then distributing, publishers can now distribute and then print. Publishers will be able to use many small presses across the country, instead of one or two strategically placed large presses. The result: increased demand for computer-savvy printing professionals and dramatic cuts in shipping and warehousing.

ACROPOLIS BOOKS LTD.
415 Wood Duck Drive, Sarasota FL 34236. 941/953-5214. **Contact:** Personnel Department. **Description:** A book publishing company.

ADD INC.
1564 Kingsley, Orange Park FL 32073. 904/264-3200. **Fax:** 904/278-9118. **Contact:** Regina Hodges, General Manager. **Description:** A publishing company.

AVANTI PRESS
13449 North West 42nd Avenue, Miami FL 33054. 305/685-7381. **Contact:** Ana Romero, Director of Personnel. **Description:** Avanti Press is a commercial printer.

BETTER BUSINESS FORMS
P.O. Box 250, Pinellas Park FL 34664. 813/545-7251. **Fax:** 813/545-2605. **Contact:** Patricia Rojas, Personnel Manager. **Description:** A printer of a wide variety of business forms. **Common positions include:** Accountant/Auditor; Administrative Services Manager; Clerical Supervisor; Computer Programmer; Computer Systems Analyst; Credit Manager; Customer Service Representative; General Manager; Human Resources Specialist. **Educational backgrounds include:** Accounting; Computer Science; Finance. **Benefits:** 401K; Dental Insurance; Disability Coverage; Employee Discounts; Life Insurance; Medical Insurance; Pension Plan; Profit Sharing; Savings

Plan. **Corporate headquarters location:** This Location. **Parent company:** Wesley Business forms. **Number of employees at this location:** 430.

BOCA RATON NEWS
33 Southeast 3rd Street, Boca Raton FL 33432. 407/395-8300. **Contact:** Human Resources. **Description:** A newspaper publisher.

THE BRADENTON HERALD
P.O. Box 921, Bradenton FL 34206. 941/748-0411. **Contact:** Barbara Cashion, Human Resources Director. **Description:** Publisher of a daily newspaper. **Common positions include:** Accountant/Auditor; Advertising Clerk; Commercial Artist; Computer Programmer; Credit Manager; Customer Service Representative; Editor; Operations/Production Manager; Photographer/Camera Operator; Reporter; Services Sales Representative. **Educational backgrounds include:** Accounting; Business Administration; Communications; Finance; Liberal Arts; Marketing. **Benefits:** Dental Insurance; Disability Coverage; Employee Discounts; Life Insurance; Medical Insurance; Pension Plan; Savings Plan; Tuition Assistance. **Corporate headquarters location:** Miami FL. **Parent company:** Knight Ridder, Inc. **Listed on:** New York Stock Exchange.

THE BRANDON NEWS SHOPPER
3901 Coconut Palm Drive, Suite 111, Tampa FL 33619. 813/654-9333. **Contact:** Human Resources. **Description:** A newspaper publisher.

BREEZE NEWSPAPERS
2510 Del Prado Boulevard, Cape Coral FL 33904. 941/574-1110. **Fax:** 941/574-3403. **Contact:** Scott Blonde, Account Manager. **Description:** A newspaper publisher. **Common positions include:** Accountant/Auditor; Advertising Clerk; Public Relations Specialist; Reporter; Services Sales Representative. **Educational backgrounds include:** Accounting; Communications. **Benefits:** 401K; Life Insurance; Medical Insurance. **Corporate headquarters location:** Wheeling WV. **Operations at this facility include:** Sales. **Number of employees at this location:** 200.

CAPE PUBLICATIONS, INC.
P.O. Box 419000, Melbourne FL 32941-9000. 407/242-3753. **Contact:** Human Resources Department. **Description:** A newspaper publishing company. **Common positions include:** Advertising Clerk; Credit Clerk and Authorizer; Customer Service Representative; Editor; Reporter; Services Sales Representative. **Educational backgrounds include:** Accounting; Art/Design; Business Administration; Communications; Computer Science; Finance; Journalism; Liberal Arts; Marketing. **Benefits:** 401K; Dental Insurance; Employee Discounts; Life Insurance; Medical Insurance; Pension Plan; Tuition Assistance. **Special Programs:** Internships. **Corporate headquarters location:** Arlington VA. **Parent company:** Gannett Company, Inc. **Operations at this facility include:** Divisional Headquarters; Manufacturing; Sales. **Listed on:** New York Stock Exchange. **Number of employees at this location:** 590.

CENTRAL FLORIDA PRESS, L.C.
4560 L.B. McLeod Road, Orlando FL 32811. 407/843-5811. **Contact:** Human Resources. **Description:** Engaged in promotional and other printing services. The parent company, Cadmus Communications Corporation, is a graphic communications company offering specialized products and services in three broad areas: printing, marketing, and publishing. Cadmus is one of the largest graphic communications companies in North America. Product lines include annual reports, catalogs, direct marketing financial printing, point-of-sale marketing, promotional printing, publishing, research journals, specialty magazines, and specialty packaging. **Other subsidiaries of Cadmus Communications Corporation include:** American Graphics, Inc. (Atlanta, GA); Cadmus Color Center, Inc. (Richmond, VA); Cadmus Direct Marketing, Inc. (Charlotte, VA); Cadmus Interactive (Tucker, GA); Cadmus Journal Services (Linthicum, MD, Eaton, MD, and Richmond, VA); Expert Brown (Richmond, VA); Garamond, Inc. (Baltimore, MD); Graphtech Corporation (Charlotte, NC); Marblehead Communications, Inc. (Boston, MA); Three Score, Inc. (Tucker, GA); Tuff Stuff Publications, Inc. (Washburn Graphics, Inc. (Charlotte, NC); The William Byrd Press (Richmond, VA).

CLAY TODAY
1564 Kingsley, Orange Park FL 32073. 904/264-3200. **Contact:** Personnel. **Description:** A newspaper publisher.

THE COURIER
THE PLANT CITY SHOPPER
102 South Evers Street, Plant City FL 33566. 813/752-3113. **Contact:** Personnel. **Description:** A newspaper publisher.

DAILY BUSINESS REVIEW
P.O. Box 010589, Miami FL 33101. 305/377-3721. **Contact:** Jackie Pietro, Director of Personnel. **Description:** A business periodical publisher.

DAILY NEWS
P.O. Drawer 2949, Ft. Walton Beach FL 32549. 904/863-1111. **Contact:** Personnel. **Description:** A newspaper publisher.

DAILY NEWS
P.O. Box 777, Palatka FL 32178. 904/328-2721. **Fax:** 904/325-0663. **Contact:** Joyce Guthrie, Business Office Manager. **Description:** A newspaper publisher. **Common positions include:** Accountant/Auditor; Advertising Clerk; Editor; Reporter. **Educational backgrounds include:** Accounting; Business Administration; Communications; Finance. **Benefits:** 401K; Dental Insurance; Disability Coverage; Employee Discounts; Life Insurance; Medical Insurance; Pension Plan; Savings Plan; Tuition Assistance. **Corporate headquarters location:** Atlanta GA. **Parent company:** New York Times. **Operations at this facility include:** Administration; Sales. **Number of employees at this location:** 50.

EDITORIAL AMERICA
6355 North West 36th Street, Virginia Gardens FL 33166. 305/871-6400. **Contact:** Alfredo Castro, Personnel Director. **Description:** Produces a Spanish language publication.

ENQUIRER/STAR GROUP, INC.
600 South East Coast Avenue, Lantana FL 33462. 407/586-1111. **Contact:** Susan Napolitano, Personnel Director. **Description:** Enquirer/Star Group, Inc., a corporation organized in June 1990, operates through its subsidiaries as a publisher in the field of personality journalism. Enquirer/Star, Inc., a wholly-owned subsidiary, conducts all of the company's publishing operations and owns substantially all of the company's assets including the capital stock of its subsidiaries. Enquirer/Star, Inc. publishes the *National Enquirer, Star, Weekly World News* and *Soap Opera Magazine*, with a current aggregate weekly circulation of approximately 7 million copies. In April 1994, the company launched its publication, *Country Weekly*. The company's subsidiary, Distributions Services, Inc., arranges for the placement of its periodicals in approximately 180,000 locations in North America. **Common positions include:** Computer Programmer; Editor; Layout Specialist; Reporter; Systems Analyst. **Educational backgrounds include:** Communications; Computer Science; Journalism; Liberal Arts. **Benefits:** Accident Insurance; Dental Insurance; Disability Coverage; Employee Discounts; Fitness Program; Life Insurance; Medical Insurance; Profit Sharing; Savings Plan; Tuition Assistance. **Operations at this facility include:** Administration; Research and Development; Service. **Corporate headquarters location:** This Location. **Listed on:** New York Stock Exchange.

FINANCIAL NEWS AND DAILY RECORD
P.O. Box 1769, Jacksonville FL 32201. 904/356-2466. **Contact:** James F. Bailey, Jr., Publisher. **Description:** A daily business and legal newspaper publisher. **Common positions include:** Advertising Clerk; Editor; Reporter; Services Sales Representative. **Benefits:** Life Insurance; Medical Insurance. **Corporate headquarters location:** This Location.

FLORIDA SENTINEL BULLETIN
P.O. Box 3363, Tampa FL 33601. 813/248-1921. **Contact:** Sybil K. Wells, General Manager. **Description:** A newspaper publisher.

FLORIDA STAR NEWSPAPER
P.O. Box 40629, Jacksonville FL 32203. 904/766-8834. **Contact:** Personnel. **Description:** A newspaper publisher.

THE FLORIDA TIMES-UNION
FLORIDA PUBLISHING COMPANY
P.O. Box 1949, Jacksonville FL 32231. 904/359-4600. **Fax:** 904/359-4650. **Recorded Jobline:** 904/359-4588. **Contact:** Sherwin Pulmano, Employment Manager.

Description: The *Florida Times-Union*, the only daily newspaper in Jacksonville, Florida, is published by the Florida Publishing Company of Morris Communications Corporation. Florida Publishing Company also provides other products and services in northeast Florida and southeast Georgia. **Common positions include:** Advertising Clerk; Blue-Collar Worker Supervisor; Branch Manager; Commercial Artist; Customer Service Representative; Editor; Reporter; Services Sales Representative. **Educational backgrounds include:** Advertising; Art/Design; Communications; Journalism; Marketing. **Benefits:** Dental Insurance; Disability Coverage; Employee Discounts; Life Insurance; Medical Insurance; Profit Sharing; Savings Plan. **Special Programs:** Internships. **Corporate headquarters location:** Augusta GA. **Parent company:** Morris Communications Corporation. **Operations at this facility include:** Administration; Manufacturing; Research and Development; Sales; Service. **Listed on:** Privately held. **Number of employees at this location:** 1,200.

FORT PIERCE TRIBUNE
P.O. Box 69, Ft. Pierce FL 34954. 407/461-2050. **Contact:** Personnel. **Description:** A newspaper publisher.

GTE DIRECTORIES
10200 9th Street North, St. Petersburg FL 33716. 813/576-1990. **Contact:** Human Resources. **Description:** The company is responsible for printing GTE catalogs.

GAINESVILLE SUN
P.O. Box 147147, Gainesville FL 32614. 352/374-5000. **Contact:** Personnel. **Description:** A newspaper publisher.

GRAPHLINE COMPANY
5701 North West 94th Avenue, Tamarac FL 33321-4399. 954/724-2212. **Fax:** 954/724-2268. **Contact:** Mr. Pat Yonker, Director of Human Resources. **Description:** A distributor of graphic arts products through a dealer channel. Products and services include supplies, equipment, and the service of traditional and prepress products. **Common positions include:** Accountant/Auditor; Advertising Clerk; Buyer; Computer Programmer; Credit Clerk and Authorizer; Customer Service Representative; Financial Manager; Management Trainee; Payroll Clerk; Receptionist; Secretary; Services Sales Representative; Stock Clerk. **Educational backgrounds include:** Accounting; Business Administration; Marketing. **Benefits:** 401K; Dental Insurance; Disability Coverage; Life Insurance; Medical Insurance; Profit Sharing. **Corporate headquarters location:** This Location. **Operations at this facility include:** Administration; Sales; Service. **Number of employees at this location:** 85. **Number of employees nationwide:** 125.

HARCOURT BRACE AND COMPANY
Human Resources Department, Orlando FL 32887. 407/345-3150. **Recorded Jobline:** 407/345-3060. **Contact:** Human Resources Manager. **Description:** The company's publishing operations are divided into Elementary and Secondary Education, and University and Professional Education. The Elementary and Secondary Education division publishes textbooks and other instructional materials, publishes and scores achievement and aptitude tests, and manufactures and markets school and office supplies and equipment. The University and Professional Education division publishes textbooks and other instructional materials for higher education, scientific and medical books and journals, and general fiction and nonfiction; publishes books and conducts courses and seminars for law, accounting, and business; and provides outplacement counseling services. **Benefits:** Dental Insurance; Disability Coverage; Employee Housing; Life Insurance; Medical Insurance; Pension Plan; Profit Sharing; Savings Plan; Stock Option; Tuition Assistance. **Listed on:** New York Stock Exchange. **Number of employees at this location:** 1,500.

THE HIGHLANDER
P.O. Box 1440, Winter Haven FL 33881. 941/676-2571. **Contact:** Personnel. **Description:** A newspaper publisher.

JACKSON COUNTY FLORIDIAN
P.O. Box 520, Marianna FL 32447. 904/526-3614. **Contact:** Personnel. **Description:** A newspaper publisher.

JACKSONVILLE BUSINESS JOURNAL
1200 Riverplace Boulevard, Suite 201, Jacksonville FL 32207. 904/396-3502. **Contact:** Personnel. **Description:** A business newspaper publisher.

KEY WEST CITIZEN
P.O. Box 1800, Key West FL 33041. 305/294-6641. **Contact:** Personnel. **Description:** A newspaper publisher.

KNIGHT-RIDDER, INC.
One Herald Plaza, Miami FL 33132. 305/376-3800. **Contact:** Human Resources. **Description:** Knight-Ridder, a newspaper publishing company, owns 28 dailies in 15 states, and three nondailies in suburban areas. The company also produces niche publications such as *Myrtle Beach's Golf*, *CubaNews* newsletter in Miami and *Northland Outdoors* in Grand Forks. The larger papers include the *Miami Herald*, *Philadelphia Inquirer*, *Philadelphia Daily News*, *Detroit Free Press*, and *San Jose Mercury News*. Knight-Ridder also has interests in the information distribution market through Business Information Services with subsidiaries Knight-Ridder Information, Inc., Knight-Ridder Financial, and Technimetrics. Dialog online information retrieval serves the business, scientific, technology, medical, education, and medical communities in more than 100 countries. Knight-Ridder Financial provides real-time financial news and pricing information through primary products MoneyCenter, Digital Datafeed, ProfitCenter, and TradeCenter. Knight-Ridder also has interests in cable television; TKR Cable, a 50-50 joint venture with Liberty Media Corporation, serves 344,000 basic subscribers in New Jersey and New York and manages Kentucky systems with 277,000 subscribers. Through TKR Cable Partners, Knight-Ridder owns a 15 percent share of TCI/TKR L.P. cable systems with 867,000 subscribers in five states. Other interests include partial ownership of the Seattle Times Company, two paper mills, a newspaper advertising sales company, and SCI Holdings. **Corporate headquarters location:** This Location. **Listed on:** New York Stock Exchange.

LAKE CITY REPORTER
P.O. Box 1709, Lake City FL 32056. 904/752-1293. **Contact:** Human Resources. **Description:** A newspaper publisher.

THE LEDGER
P.O. Box 408, Lakeland FL 33802. 941/687-7000. **Contact:** Personnel. **Description:** A newspaper publisher.

THE MIAMI HERALD PUBLISHING COMPANY
EL NUEVO HERALD
One Herald Plaza, Miami FL 33132. 305/376-3525. **Fax:** 305/995-8021. **Recorded Jobline:** 305/376-2880. **Contact:** Clive Bridges, Employment Manager. **Description:** A regional daily newspaper publisher. **Common positions include:** Accountant/Auditor; Advertising Clerk; Budget Analyst; Customer Service Representative; Financial Analyst; Reporter; Services Sales Representative. **Educational backgrounds include:** Accounting; Business Administration; Communications; Finance; Liberal Arts; Marketing. **Benefits:** 401K; Daycare Assistance; Dental Insurance; Disability Coverage; Employee Discounts; Life Insurance; Medical Insurance; Pension Plan; Savings Plan; Tuition Assistance. **Special Programs:** Internships. **Corporate headquarters location:** This Location. **Parent company:** Knight-Ridder, Inc. **Operations at this facility include:** Administration; Sales. **Listed on:** New York Stock Exchange. **Number of employees at this location:** 2,500.

MIAMI TIMES
900 North West 54th Street, Miami FL 33127. 305/757-1147. **Contact:** Jackie Dean, Office Manager. **Description:** A newspaper publisher. **Common positions include:** Advertising Clerk; Clerical Supervisor; Customer Service Representative; Editor; General Manager; Manufacturer's/Wholesaler's Sales Rep.; Reporter; Services Sales Representative. **Educational backgrounds include:** Business Administration; Communications; Liberal Arts; Marketing. **Benefits:** Dental Insurance; Life Insurance; Medical Insurance. **Special Programs:** Internships. **Corporate headquarters location:** This Location. **Number of employees at this location:** 20.

MIAMI TODAY
P.O. Box 1368, Miami FL 33101. 305/358-2663. **Contact:** Michael Lewis, Publisher. **Description:** The publisher of a weekly newspaper serving the business community. **Common positions include:** Accountant/Auditor; Advertising Clerk; Advertising Sales; Department Manager; Editor; Management Trainee; Reporter. **Educational backgrounds include:** Business Administration; Communications; Liberal Arts; Marketing. **Benefits:** Life Insurance; Medical Insurance. **Special Programs:** Internships; Training Programs. **Corporate headquarters location:** This Location. **Operations at this facility include:** Administration; Sales.

THE NAPLES DAILY NEWS
P.O. Box 7009, Naples FL 33940. 941/262-3161. **Contact:** Corbin Wyant, Publisher.
Description: A newspaper publisher.

NEWS HERALD
P.O. Box 1940, Panama City FL 32402. **Contact:** Personnel. **Description:** A newspaper
publisher.

NEWS-JOURNAL CORPORATION
901 Sixth Street, Daytona Beach FL 32117-8099. 904/252-1511. **Contact:** Human
Resources. **Description:** The publisher of a daily newspaper, the *News-Journal,* with a
circulation of over 100,000.

NEWS PRESS
2442 Dr. Martin Luther King Jr. Boulevard, Fort Meyers FL 33901. 941/335-0421.
Fax: 941/335-0297. **Contact:** Michel Harris, Recruitment and Development Specialist.
Description: A newspaper. **Common positions include:** Accountant/Auditor;
Advertising Clerk; Computer Programmer; Computer Systems Analyst; Credit Manager;
Customer Service Representative; Editor; Electrical/Electronics Engineer; Human
Resources Specialist; Librarian; Purchasing Agent and Manager; Quality Control
Supervisor. **Educational backgrounds include:** Accounting; Art/Design; Business
Administration; Communications; Computer Science; Economics; Finance; Marketing.
Benefits: 401K; Dental Insurance; Disability Coverage; Employee Discounts; Life
Insurance; Medical Insurance; Pension Plan; Tuition Assistance. **Special Programs:**
Internships. **Corporate headquarters location:** Arlington VA. **Parent company:** Gannett
Company, Inc. **Listed on:** Privately held. **Number of employees at this location:** 650.
Number of employees nationwide: 38,000.

OCALA STAR BANNER
P.O. Box 490, Ocala FL 34478. 352/867-4010. **Contact:** Personnel. **Description:** A
newspaper publisher.

ORLANDO BUSINESS JOURNAL
315 East Robinson Street, Suite 250, Orlando FL 32801-4323. 407/649-8470.
Contact: Kent Hoover, Editor. **Description:** A business publication. **Common positions
include:** Accountant/Auditor; Advertising Account Executive; Commercial Artist;
Customer Service Representative; Department Manager; Editor;
Manufacturer's/Wholesaler's Sales Rep.; Operations/Production Manager; Reporter.
Educational backgrounds include: Accounting; Art/Design; Communications;
Economics; Finance; Journalism; Marketing. **Benefits:** 401K; Disability Coverage; Life
Insurance; Medical Insurance; Profit Sharing; Tuition Assistance. **Corporate
headquarters location:** This Location. **Operations at this facility include:**
Administration; Sales; Service.

ORLANDO SENTINEL
633 North Orange Avenue, Orlando FL 32801. 407/420-5373. **Contact:** Employment
Center. **Description:** A newspaper publisher. **Common positions include:** Advertising
Clerk; Blue-Collar Worker Supervisor; Buyer; Commercial Artist; Computer
Programmer; Credit Manager; Customer Service Representative; Department Manager;
Editor; Financial Analyst; General Manager; Manufacturer's/Wholesaler's Sales Rep.;
Marketing Specialist; Public Relations Specialist; Purchasing Agent and Manager;
Quality Control Supervisor; Reporter; Systems Analyst; Technical Writer/Editor.
Educational backgrounds include: Accounting; Art/Design; Business Administration;
Communications; Computer Science; Finance; Liberal Arts; Marketing. **Benefits:** Dental
Insurance; Disability Coverage; Employee Discounts; Life Insurance; Medical Insurance;
Pension Plan; Savings Plan; Tuition Assistance. **Corporate headquarters location:**
Chicago IL. **Parent company:** Tribune Company. **Number of employees at this location:**
1,425.

ORLANDO TIMES
4403 Vineland Road, Suite B5, Orlando FL 32811. 407/841-3052. **Contact:** Lottie
Collins, General Manager. **Description:** A newspaper publisher.

PALM BEACH NEWSPAPERS, INC.
P.O. Box 24700, West Palm Beach FL 33416-4700. 407/820-4190. **Fax:** 407/820-
4192. **Recorded Jobline:** 407/820-4511x1090. **Contact:** Human Resources.
Description: A newspaper and shopper publisher. Publications include *The Palm Beach*

Post, Palm Beach Daily News, and *The Florida Pennysaver.* **Common positions include:** Accountant/Auditor; Advertising Clerk; Blue-Collar Worker Supervisor; Clerical Supervisor; Commercial Artist; Computer Programmer; Computer Systems Analyst; Editor; Electrician; Librarian; Library Technician; Management Trainee; Manufacturer's/Wholesaler's Sales Rep.; Marketing Specialist; Public Relations Specialist; Reporter. **Educational backgrounds include:** Accounting; Art/Design; Business Administration; Communications; Computer Science; Liberal Arts. **Benefits:** Dental Insurance; Disability Coverage; Employee Discounts; Life Insurance; Medical Insurance; Pension Plan; Savings Plan; Tuition Assistance. **Special Programs:** Internships; Training Programs. **Corporate headquarters location:** Atlanta GA. **Parent company:** Cox Enterprises, Inc. **Operations at this facility include:** Administration; Manufacturing; Sales. **Listed on:** Privately held. **Number of employees at this location:** 1,300. **Number of employees nationwide:** 22,000.

PENSACOLA NEWS JOURNAL, INC.
P.O. Box 12710, Pensacola FL 32574-2710. 904/435-8500. **Contact:** Jim Barnett, Personnel Director. **Description:** A newspaper publishing company.

THE PRINTING HOUSE, INC.
P.O. Box 310, Quincy FL 32353. 904/875-1500. **Contact:** Ray Conners, Human Resources Supervisor. **Description:** A commercial printing company. **NOTE:** Please send resumes to 1600 Capital Circle SW, Tallassee, AL 32310.

ROSE PRINTING COMPANY, INC.
P.O. Box 5078, Tallahassee FL 32314. 904/576-4151. **Contact:** Personnel. **Description:** A printing company.

ST. AUGUSTINE RECORD
P.O. Box 1630, St. Augustine FL 32085. 904/829-6562. **Contact:** Personnel. **Description:** A newspaper publisher.

SANFORD EVENING HERALD
P.O. Box 1667, Sanford FL 32772-1667. 407/322-2611. **Contact:** Personnel Director. **Description:** A newspaper publisher.

SENTINEL COMMUNICATIONS COMPANY
633 North Orange Avenue, Orlando FL 32801. 407/420-5000. **Contact:** Employment Center. **Description:** A newspaper publisher and printer.

SOUTH FLORIDA BUSINESS JOURNAL
1050 Lee Wagener Boulevard, Suite 302, Fort Lauderdale FL 33315. 954/359-2100. **Fax:** 954/359-2135. **Contact:** Giselle Auffant, Business Manager. **Description:** A publisher of a weekly business newspaper. **Common positions include:** Advertising Clerk; Customer Service Representative; Services Sales Representative. **Educational backgrounds include:** Art/Design; Business Administration; Communications; Liberal Arts; Marketing. **Benefits:** 401K; Dental Insurance; Disability Coverage; Life Insurance; Medical Insurance. **Corporate headquarters location:** Charlotte NC. **Operations at this facility include:** Administration; Research and Development; Sales. **Listed on:** NASDAQ. **Number of employees at this location:** 30.

SOUTH FLORIDA MAGAZINE
P.O. Box 019068, Suite 500, Miami FL 33101. 305/445-4500. **Fax:** 305/445-4600. **Contact:** Clara Cummings, Assistant to the Publisher. **Description:** The publisher of *South Florida Region Magazine.* **Common positions include:** Editor; Services Sales Representative; Technical Writer/Editor. **Educational backgrounds include:** Art/Design; Business Administration; Communications; Marketing. **Benefits:** 401K; Dental Insurance; Disability Coverage; Life Insurance; Medical Insurance. **Special Programs:** Internships. **Corporate headquarters location:** Morristown NJ. **Operations at this facility include:** Administration; Manufacturing; Sales. **Number of employees at this location:** 17.

THE STUART NEWS
1939 South Federal Highway, Stuart FL 34994. 407/464-8414. **Contact:** Personnel. **Description:** A newspaper publisher.

THE SUN SENTINEL
200 East Las Olas Boulevard, Fort Lauderdale FL 33301-2293. 954/356-4000. **Contact:** Human Resources. **Description:** A newspaper publisher.

T.S. PUBLICATIONS
P.O. Box 811, Bradenton FL 34208. 941/748-4140. **Contact:** Sandy Stern, Personnel Director. **Description:** The company publishes the *Florida Sun*, a weekly magazine.

THE TALLAHASSEE DEMOCRAT
277 North Magnolia Drive, Tallahassee FL 32302. 904/599-2128. **Contact:** Cordelia Leon, Employment Services Administrator. **Description:** A newspaper publisher. **Common positions include:** Accountant/Auditor; Advertising Clerk; Cashier; Computer Operator; Computer Programmer; Computer Systems Analyst; Credit Manager; Customer Service Representative; Dispatcher; Editor; Education Administrator; Employment Interviewer; Graphic Artist; Librarian; Payroll Clerk; Photographer/Camera Operator; Receptionist; Reporter; Secretary; Services Sales Representative; Systems Analyst; Truck Driver. **Educational backgrounds include:** Art/Design; Marketing. **Benefits:** Dental Insurance; Disability Coverage; Employee Discounts; Life Insurance; Medical Insurance; Pension Plan; Savings Plan. **Corporate headquarters location:** Miami FL. **Operations at this facility include:** Manufacturing. **Number of employees at this location:** 311.

TAMPA TRIBUNE
P.O. Box 191, Tampa FL 33601. **Contact:** Employment. **Description:** A newspaper publisher.

TIME CUSTOMER SERVICE, INC.
1 North Dale Mabry Highway, Tampa FL 33609. 813/878-6100. **Fax:** 813/878-6208. **Contact:** Vicki Zarcone, Recruiter. **Description:** The divisional headquarters of the magazine subscription service. **Common positions include:** Buyer; Computer Programmer; Computer Systems Analyst; Customer Service Representative; Financial Analyst; Human Resources Specialist; Librarian; Software Engineer. **Educational backgrounds include:** Computer Science; Engineering; Finance. **Benefits:** 401K; Dental Insurance; Disability Coverage; Life Insurance; Medical Insurance; Pension Plan; Profit Sharing; Tuition Assistance. **Corporate headquarters location:** This Location. **Operations at this facility include:** Administration.

TIMES PUBLISHING COMPANY, INC.
P.O. Box 1121, St. Petersburg FL 33731. 813/893-8426. **Fax:** 813/893-8426. **Recorded Jobline:** 813/893-8404. **Contact:** Cindy Durning, Director of Human Services. **Description:** The publisher of the newspaper, *St. Petersburg Times*. **Common positions include:** Accountant/Auditor; Administrative Services Manager; Advertising Clerk; Blue-Collar Worker Supervisor; Budget Analyst; Buyer; Clerical Supervisor; Computer Programmer; Computer Systems Analyst; Counselor; Credit Manager; Customer Service Manager; Editor; Electrical/Electronics Engineer; Electrician; Human Service Worker; Librarian; Library Technician; Management Analyst/Consultant; Management Trainee; Manufacturer's/Wholesaler's Sales Rep.; Operations/Production Manager; Quality Control Supervisor; Reporter; Securities Sales Rep.; Services Sales Representative; Software Engineer; Technical Writer/Editor; Transportation/Traffic Specialist; Wholesale and Retail Buyer. **Educational backgrounds include:** Accounting; Business Administration; Communications; Computer Science; Finance; Liberal Arts; Marketing. **Benefits:** 401K; Dental Insurance; Disability Coverage; Life Insurance; Medical Insurance; Pension Plan; Profit Sharing; Savings Plan; Tuition Assistance. **Corporate headquarters location:** This Location. **Operations at this facility include:** Administration; Divisional Headquarters; Manufacturing; Sales; Service.

TRADER PUBLISHING COMPANY
P.O. Box 19003, Clearwater FL 34618. 813/530-5656. **Contact:** Debbie Moyer, Human Resources Manager. **Description:** A magazine publisher with 72 offices throughout the United States. **Corporate headquarters location:** Norfolk VA. **Number of employees nationwide:** 3,000.

USA TODAY
10315 U.S.A. Today Way, Miramar FL 33025. 954/435-6222. **Contact:** Christine Surdyk, Personnel. **Description:** Regional office of the national newspaper.

WARNER BROTHERS PUBLICATIONS
15800 North West 48th Avenue, Miami FL 33014. 305/620-1500. **Contact:** Manager, Human Resources. **Description:** A printer and publisher of sheet music. **Common positions include:** Accountant/Auditor; Credit Manager; Customer Service Representative; Department Manager; Editor; Musician/Musical Arranger;

Operations/Production Manager; Services Sales Representative. **Educational backgrounds include:** Accounting; Art/Design; Business Administration; Computer Science; Finance; Liberal Arts; Marketing; Music. **Benefits:** Dental Insurance; Disability Coverage; Employee Discounts; Life Insurance; Medical Insurance; Pension Plan; Savings Plan; Tuition Assistance. **Special Programs:** Internships. **Corporate headquarters location:** This Location. **Operations at this facility include:** Administration; Manufacturing; Sales; Service.

A.D. WEISS LITHOGRAPH COMPANY, INC.
2025 McKinley Street, Hollywood FL 33020. 954/920-7300. **Contact:** Personnel Administrator. **Description:** A lithography company.

Note: Because addresses and telephone numbers of smaller companies change rapidly, we recommend you call each company to verify the information below before inquiring about job opportunities. Mass mailings are not recommended.

Additional employers with under 250 employees:

NEWSPAPERS: PUBLISHING AND/OR PRINTING

Campus Communications
P.O. Box 14257, Gainesville FL 32604-2257. 352/376-4446.

Citrus Publishing
1624 N Meadowcrest Blvd, Crystal River FL 34429-5760. 904/563-6363.

Diario Las Americas
2900 NW 39th St, Miami FL 33142-5193. 305/633-3341.

Jupiter Courier
800 W Indiantown Rd, Jupiter FL 33458-7501. 407/746-5111.

Leesburg Daily Commercial
212 E Main St, Leesburg FL 34748-5227. 352/365-8200.

Manatee AM Tribune
905 6th Ave W, Bradenton FL 34205-7701. 941/746-2178.

Northwest Florida Daily News
200 Racetrack Rd NW, Ft Walton Beach FL 32547-1645. 904/863-1111.

Sarasota Herald Tribune
1800 University Pkwy, Sarasota FL 34243-2298. 941/957-5110.

South Fl Newspaper Network
601 Fairway Dr, Deerfield Beach FL 33441-1867. 954/698-6397.

Sunbelt Newspaper Co.
6214 US Highway 19, New Port Richey FL 34652-2528. 813/849-7500.

The Lake Sentinel
720 W Burleigh Blvd, Tavares FL 32778-2302. 352/742-5900.

The Miami Laker
6843 Main St, Hialeah FL 33014-2048. 305/821-1130.

Vero Beach Press Journal
1801 US Highway 1, Vero Beach FL 32960-5415. 407/562-2315.

Worrell Enterprises
1450 S Dixie Hwy, Boca Raton FL 33432-7315. 407/338-3298.

PERIODICALS: PUBLISHING AND/OR PRINTING

Tampa Bay Publications
2531 Landmark Dr, Clearwater FL 34621-3911. 813/791-4800.

The Flyer Publishing Company
201 Kelsey Ln, Tampa FL 33619-4312. 813/622-7571.

American Press
1061 Maitland Center Commons, Suite 1, Maitland FL 32751-7435. 407/660-4577.

BOOKS: PUBLISHING AND/OR PRINTING

Commerce Clearing House
10100 9th St N, St Petersburg FL 33716-3898. 813/577-1119.

Realtron Publishing
750 SW 12th Ave, Pompano Beach FL 33069-4528. 954/946-6432.

COMMERCIAL PRINTING

Catalogs America
111 2nd St N, Suite 907, St Petersburg FL 33701-3311. 813/821-8843.

Graphic Productions Corporation
5600 NW 32nd Ave, Miami FL 33142-2113. 305/635-4895.

Rex Three
15431 SW 14th St, Ft Lauderdale FL 33326-1937. 954/945-8856.

SS Designs
5558 Commercial Blvd, Winter Haven FL 33880-1008. 941/965-2576.

Carlson Color Graphics
3310 SW 7th St, Ocala FL 34474-1962. 352/732-7787.

Colonial Press International
3690 NW 50th St, Miami FL 33142-3934. 305/633-1581.

Deluxe Check Printers Corporation
6531 NW 18th Ct, Ft Lauderdale FL 33313-4577. 954/581-0500.

Graphic Dynamics
2901 Gateway Dr, Pompano Beach FL 33069-4326. 954/979-6212.

Haff-Daugherty Graphics
950 SE 8th St, Hialeah FL 33010-5740. 305/885-8707.

Hillsboro Printing Co.
2442 W Mississippi Ave, Tampa FL 33629-6110. 813/251-2401.

John H Harland Co.
3550 Saint Johns Bluff Rd S,
Jacksonville FL 32224-2614.
904/641-5566.

Media Printing Corporation
8050 NW 74th Ave, Miami
FL 00166 7542. 305/888-
1300.

Modern Graphic Arts
1527 102nd Ave N, St
Petersburg FL 33716-5049.
813/579-1527.

Moran Printing Co.
9125 Bachman Rd, Orlando
FL 32824-8020. 407/859-
2030.

News Time Printing
1122 S Congress Ave, West
Palm Beach FL 33406-5115.
407/967-7355.

SIRS
1100 Holland Dr, Boca Raton
FL 33487-2701. 407/994-
0079.

St Petersburg Printing Co.
118 18th St S, St Petersburg
FL 33712-1334. 813/822-
8400.

Sun N Fun Printing Co.
4820 122nd Ave N,
Clearwater FL 34622-4489.
813/573-0370.

Taylor Corporation
112 Commerce Dr, Madison
FL 32340-3213. 904/973-
2290.

Graphics 3
1400 W Indiantown Rd,
Jupiter FL 33458-3910.
407/746-6746.

**BLANK BOOKS AND
BOOKBINDING**

Harland Company
14100 NW 4th St, Ft
Lauderdale FL 33325-6208.
954/846-0211.

PRINTING TRADE SERVICES

Colortronics Co.
1405 Poinsettia Dr, Delray
Beach FL 33444-1249.
407/265-1882.

Graphics Illustrated
1500 Australian Ave, Riviera
Beach FL 33404-5304.
407/848-8989.

**PHOTOGRAPHIC
EQUIPMENT AND SUPPLIES**

Cues
3501 Vineland Rd, Orlando
FL 32811-6484. 407/849-
0190.

**BOOKS, PERIODICALS, AND
NEWSPAPERS WHOLESALE**

**FEC News Distributing
Company**
2201 4th Ave N, Lake Worth
FL 33461-3835. 407/547-
3000.

ETD Gulf Coast Division
2001 Limbus Ave, Sarasota
FL 34243 941/755-4145.

Speedimpex USA
805 Parkway Plaza Blvd,
Kissimmee FL 34744-1450.
407/933-5339.

**COMMERCIAL ART AND
GRAPHIC DESIGN**

Avionics Research Corp.
706 E Colonial Dr, Orlando
FL 32803-4685. 407/841-
1070.

NEWS SYNDICATES

Florida Freedom Newspapers
336 E College Ave, Suite
206, Tallahassee FL 32301-
1559. 904/222-4344.

**PHOTO FINISHING
LABORATORIES**

Qualex
1200 S Dixie Hwy, Miami FL
33146-2902. 305/947-
6932.

CPI One Hour Photo Finish
10300 Southside Blvd,
Jacksonville FL 32256-0770.
904/363-3284.

Wolf Camera & Video
515 E Altamonte Dr,
Altamonte Springs FL
32701. 407/339-6190.

Wolf Camera & Video
5401 W Oak Ridge Rd, Suite
58, Orlando FL 32819-9414.
407/351-1461.

For more information on career opportunities in printing and publishing:

Associations

AMERICAN BOOKSELLERS ASSOCIATION
828 South Broadway, Tarrytown NY
10591. 914/591-2665.

AMERICAN INSTITUTE OF GRAPHIC ARTS
919 3rd Avenue, 22nd Floor, New York NY
10003-3004. 212/807-1990. A 36-
chapter, nationwide organization sponsoring
programs and events for graphic designers
and related professionals.

**AMERICAN SOCIETY OF NEWSPAPER
EDITORS**
P.O. Box 4090, Reston VA 22090-1700.
703/648-1144.

ASSOCIATION OF GRAPHIC ARTS
330 7th Avenue, 9th Floor, New York NY
10001-5010. 212/279-2100. Offers
educational classes and seminars.

BINDING INDUSTRIES OF AMERICA
70 East Lake Street, Suite 300, Chicago IL
60601. 312/372-7606. Offers credit
collection, government affairs, and
educational services.

THE DOW JONES NEWSPAPER FUND
P.O. Box 300, Princeton NJ 08543-0300.
609/520-4000. Publishes *The Wall Street
Journal*.

GRAPHIC ARTISTS GUILD
11 West 20th Street, 8th Floor, New York
NY 10011. 212/463-7730. A union for
artists.

**INTERNATIONAL GRAPHIC ARTS
EDUCATION ASSOCIATION**
4615 Forbes Avenue, Pittsburgh PA 15213.
412/682-5170.

MAGAZINE PUBLISHERS ASSOCIATION
919 Third Avenue, 22nd Floor, New York
NY 10022. 212/752-0055. A membership
association.

**NATIONAL ASSOCIATION OF PRINTERS
AND LITHOGRAPHERS**
780 Pallisade Avenue, Teaneck NJ 07666.
201/342-0700. Membership. Offers
consulting services and a publication.

NATIONAL NEWSPAPER ASSOCIATION
1525 Wilson Boulevard, Arlington VA
22209. 703/907-7900.

NATIONAL PRESS CLUB
529 14th St. NW, 13th Floor, Washington
DC 20045. 202/662-7500. Offers a private
club/meeting hall, private restaurants, and
private health clubs.

NEWSPAPER ASSOCIATION OF AMERICA
Newspaper Center, 11600 Sunrise Valley
Drive, Reston VA 22091. 703/648-1000.
The technology department publishes
marketing research.

THE NEWSPAPER GUILD
Research and Information Department,
8611 2nd Avenue, Silver Spring MD
20910. 301/585-2990. A trade union.

PRINTING INDUSTRIES OF AMERICA
100 Dangerfield Road, Alexandria VA
22314. 703/519-8100. Members are
offered publications, insurance, and political
action.

**TECHNICAL ASSOCIATION OF THE
GRAPHIC ARTS**
68 Lomb memorial Drive, Rochester NY
14623. 716/475-7470. Conducts an
annual conference and offers newsletters.

WRITERS GUILD OF AMERICA WEST
8955 Beverly Boulevard, West Hollywood
CA 90048. 310/550-1000. A membership
association which registers scripts.

Directories

**EDITOR & PUBLISHER INTERNATIONAL
YEARBOOK**
Editor & Publisher Company Inc., 11 West
19th Street, New York NY 10011.
212/675-4380. $100.00. Offers
newspapers to editors in both the United
States and foreign countries.

GRAPHIC ARTS BLUE BOOK
A.F. Lewis & Company, 245 Fifth Avenue,
New York NY 10016. 212/679-0770.
$80.00. Manufacturers and dealers.

**JOURNALISM CAREER AND SCHOLARSHIP
GUIDE**
The Dow Jones Newspaper Fund, P.O. Box
300, Princeton NJ 08543-0300. 609/520-
4000.

Magazines

AIGA JOURNAL
American Institute of Graphic Arts, 164
Third Avenue, New York NY 10010.
212/752-0813. $21.50. A 56-page
quarterly magazine dealing with
contemporary issues.

EDITOR AND PUBLISHER
Editor & Publisher Company Inc., 164 Third
Avenue, New York NY 10010. 212/807-
1990.

GRAPHIC ARTS MONTHLY
249 West 49th Street, New York NY
10011. 212/463-6836.

GRAPHIS
141 Lexington Avenue, New York NY
10016. 212/532-9387. $89.00. Magazine
covers portfolios, articles, designers,
advertising, and photos.

PRINT
104 Fifth Avenue, 19th Floor New York NY
10011. 212/463-0600. Offers a graphic
design magazine. $55.00 for subscription.

PUBLISHER'S WEEKLY
249 West 17th Street, New York NY
10011. Weekly publication for book
publishers and sellers.

Special Book and Magazine Programs

**THE NEW YORK UNIVERSITY SUMMER
PUBLISHING PROGRAM**
48 Cooper Square, Room 108, New York
NY 10003. 212/998-7219.

THE RADCLIFFE PUBLISHING COURSE
77 Brattle Street, Cambridge MA 02138.
617/495-8678.

RICE UNIVERSITY PUBLISHING PROGRAM
Office of Continuing Studies, P.O. Box
1892, Houston TX 77251-1892. 713/520-
6022.

**UNIVERSITY OF DENVER PUBLISHING
INSTITUTE**
2075 South University Boulevard, #D-114,
Denver CO 80208. 303/871-4868.

REAL ESTATE

 *Rising interest rates have already begun causing housing starts to drop and sales of existing single-family homes to moderately decline. However, solid opportunities for jobseekers are available for those looking to enter the real estate field. Occupancy will go up in the office sector as little new office properties are being built. Apartment construction, on the other hand, is on the rise. Commercial property sales will help keep up employment opportunities for real estate agents, brokers, and appraisers. The number of job openings in these occupations is expected to match the number of openings for most other careers nationwide. Most of these openings, however, will be replacement positions, as agents return or leave the field, rather than new positions being created.*

Property and real estate managers will have even greater luck finding employment, as more openings appear for these positions than other occupations. The people with the most qualified backgrounds for these positions will be those with college degrees in business administration and other related studies.

ATLANTIC GULF COMMUNITIES CORPORATION
2601 South Bayshore Drive, Miami FL 33133. 305/859-4000. **Contact:** Human Resources. **Description:** Engaged in real estate and land developing.

AVATAR HOLDINGS INC.
255 Alhambra Circle, Coral Gables FL 33134. 305/442-7000. **Contact:** Human Resources. **Description:** A real estate company.

COLDWELL BANKER
423 Saint Armands Circle, Sarasota FL 34236-1483. 941/388-3966. **Contact:** Human Resources. **Description:** Coldwell Banker is one of the three largest residential real estate companies in the United States and Canada in terms of total home sales transactions. Coldwell Banker also is a leader in meeting corporate America's specialized relocation needs on a worldwide basis. In the late 1970s, the company purchased a 51 percent interest in Executrans, Inc., a corporate relocation management company, from Allstate. That company became Coldwell Banker Relocation Services. Coldwell Banker was acquired by Sears, Roebuck & Co. in late 1981. At the same time, the company launched Coldwell Banker Residential Affiliates, Inc. aimed at franchising select brokers who served small- to medium-sized markets. In October 1993, The Fremont Group, together with Coldwell Banker senior management, purchased the company from Sears, Roebuck & Co. **Corporate headquarters location:** Mission Viejo CA. **Other U.S. locations:** Dallas TX. **Listed on:** American Stock Exchange; New York Stock Exchange.

COLDWELL BANKER
3322 Bee Ridge Road, Sarasota FL 34239. 941/927-3990. **Contact:** Human Resources. **Description:** Coldwell Banker is one of the three largest residential real estate companies in the United States and Canada in terms of total home sales transactions. Coldwell Banker also is a leader in meeting corporate America's specialized relocation needs on a worldwide basis. In the late 1970s, The company purchased a 51 percent interest in Executrans, Inc., a corporate relocation management company, from Allstate. That company became Coldwell Banker Relocation Services. Coldwell Banker was acquired by Sears, Roebuck & Co. in late 1981. At the same time, the company launched Coldwell Banker Residential Affiliates, Inc. aimed at franchising select brokers who served small- to medium-sized markets. In October 1993, The Fremont Group, together with Coldwell Banker senior management, purchased the company from Sears, Roebuck & Co. **Corporate**

headquarters location: Mission Viejo CA. **Listed on:** American Stock Exchange; New York Stock Exchange.

DELTONA CORPORATION
3250 South West 3rd Avenue, Miami FL 33129-2700. 305/854-1111. **Contact:** Personnel Department. **Description:** A real estate company.

DISNEY DEVELOPMENT COMPANY
Westwood Center, 6649 Westwood Boulevard, Suite 300, Orlando FL 32821. 407/827-1900. **Fax:** 407/827-7999. **Contact:** Professional Staffing. **Description:** Plans, develops, and operates real estate and new business opportunities with Disney's entertainment mission. **Parent company:** Walt Disney Company.

DIVI TIMESHARE DIVISION
9737 NW 41st Street, Suite 176, Miami FL 33138. 305/633-3484. **Contact:** Human Resources. **Description:** As a division of Divi Hotels Inc., this location sells timeshares in Florida. The Divi Hotel is located in Chapel Hill, NC. **Parent company:** Divi Hotels Inc.

FLORIDA DESIGN COMMUNITY
P.O. Box 5698, Sun City Center FL 33571. 813/634-3311. **Contact:** Karen Crenna, Vice President/Human Resources. **Description:** A community developer and manager. **Common positions include:** Accountant/Auditor; Advertising Clerk; Blue-Collar Worker Supervisor; Computer Programmer; Construction Contractor and Manager; Credit Manager; Customer Service Representative; Draftsperson; Hotel Manager/Assistant Manager; Marketing Specialist. **Educational backgrounds include:** Accounting; Business Administration; Finance; Marketing. **Benefits:** Dental Insurance; Disability Coverage; Employee Discounts; Life Insurance; Medical Insurance; Pension Plan; Profit Sharing; Savings Plan; Tuition Assistance. **Corporate headquarters location:** This Location. **Operations at this facility include:** Resort/Support Functions.

HOLLYWOOD, INC.
200 South Park Road, Suite 200, Hollywood FL 33021. 954/981-1000. **Contact:** Personnel. **Description:** A real estate developer.

KILLEARN PROPERTIES
CAPITAL FIRST, INC.
7118 Beech Ridge Trail, Tallahassee FL 32312. 904/893-2111. **Contact:** Personnel. **Description:** Develops and sells home sites in Leon County. **Number of employees at this location:** 138.

J.I. KISLAK MORTGAGE CORPORATION
7900 Miami Lakes Drive West, Miami Lakes FL 33016. 305/364-4116. **Contact:** Human Resources. **Description:** A mortgage banking and real estate firm. **Common positions include:** Accountant/Auditor; Bank Officer/Manager; Branch Manager; Claim Representative; Computer Programmer; Customer Service Representative; Department Manager; Financial Analyst; Human Resources Specialist; Industrial Agent/Broker; Loan Officer; Marketing Specialist; Systems Analyst; Underwriter/Assistant Underwriter. **Educational backgrounds include:** Accounting; Business Administration; Computer Science; Finance; Marketing. **Benefits:** Dental Insurance; Disability Coverage; Employee Discounts; Life Insurance; Medical Insurance; Pension Plan; Profit Sharing; Tuition Assistance. **Corporate headquarters location:** This Location.

LEHIGH CORPORATION
201 East Joel Boulevard, Lehigh Acres FL 33936. 941/368-1900. **Contact:** Angela Pietrangelo, Personnel Director. **Description:** A land sales company.

LENNAR CORPORATION
700 Northwest 107th Avenue, Miami FL 33172. 305/559-4000. **Contact:** Carol Burgin, Personnel Director. **Description:** Lennar Corporation is a full-service real estate company that builds and sells homes, develops and manages commercial and residential properties, and provides real estate-related financial services. The Homebuilding division constructs and sells single-family attached and detached and multifamily homes. These activities also include the purchase, development, and sale of residential land. The company is one of the nation's largest home builders with operations in Florida, Arizona, and Texas. The Investment Division is involved in the development, management, and leasing, as well as the acquisition and sale, of commercial and residential properties and land. During the past three years, this

division became a participant and manager in six partnerships which acquired portfolios of commercial mortgage loans and real estate. Financial services activities are conducted primarily through Lennar Financial Services, Inc. and five principal subsidiaries. These subsidiaries perform mortgage servicing activities, and arrange mortgage financing, title insurance, and closing services for a wide variety of borrowers and homebuyers. This division also invests in rated portions of commercial real estate mortgage-backed securities for which Lennar's Investment Division is the special servicer, and an investor in the unrated portion of those securities. **Operations at this facility include:** Service. **Listed on:** New York Stock Exchange. **Number of employees nationwide:** 1,326.

PATTEN CORPORATION

5295 Town Center Road, Suite 400, Boca Raton FL 33433. 407/361-2700. **Fax:** 407/361-2800. **Contact:** Director of Human Resources. **Description:** A national real estate company specializing in rural land acquisitions and sales. The company also does business as a mortgage company. **Common positions include:** Accountant/Auditor; Advertising Clerk; Computer Programmer; Computer Systems Analyst; Human Resources Specialist. **Educational backgrounds include:** Accounting; Business Administration; Computer Science; Finance; Marketing. **Benefits:** 401K; Dental Insurance; Disability Coverage; Employee Discounts; Life Insurance; Medical Insurance; Tuition Assistance. **Corporate headquarters location:** This Location. **Other U.S. locations:** Nationwide. **Operations at this facility include:** Administration. **Listed on:** New York Stock Exchange; Pacific Exchange. **Number of employees at this location:** 70. **Number of employees nationwide:** 400.

TRW REDI PROPERTY DATA

1700 North West 66th Avenue, Fort Lauderdale FL 33313. 954/792-2000. **Fax:** 954/321-7474. **Contact:** Human Resources. **Description:** A national provider of information services to the real estate industry. **Common positions include:** Accountant/Auditor; Adjuster; Assistant Manager; Bindery Worker; Blue-Collar Worker Supervisor; Computer Operator; Computer Programmer; Computer Systems Analyst; Construction and Building Inspector; Construction Trade Worker; Customer Service Representative; Department Manager; Draftsperson; Electrical/Electronics Engineer; Electrician; General Manager; Graphic Artist; Human Resources Specialist; Industrial Engineer; Machinist; Marketing Research Analyst; Marketing Specialist; Marketing/Advertising/PR Manager; Mechanical Engineer; Operations/Production Manager; Printing Press Operator; Receptionist; Services Sales Representative; Software Engineer; Stock Clerk; Surveyor; Systems Analyst; Truck Driver; Typist/Word Processor. **Educational backgrounds include:** Accounting; Business Administration; Communications; Computer Science; Economics; Finance; Liberal Arts; Marketing. **Benefits:** Credit Union; Dental Insurance; Disability Coverage; Employee Discounts; Life Insurance; Medical Insurance; Profit Sharing; Savings Plan; Tuition Assistance. **Parent company:** TRW & Elsevier Information Service. **Operations at this facility include:** Administration; Manufacturing; Regional Headquarters; Research and Development; Sales; Service. **Number of employees at this location:** 320. **Number of employees nationwide:** 1,200.

Note: Because addresses and telephone numbers of smaller companies change rapidly, we recommend you call each company to verify the information below before inquiring about job opportunities. Mass mailings are not recommended.

Additional employers with under 250 employees:

REAL ESTATE OPERATORS

Record Press Building
154 Cordova St, St Augustine FL 32084-5020. 904/829-6586.

Goodman Segar Hogan Hoffler
2400 Maitland Center Pkwy, Suite 10, Maitland FL 32751-4127. 407/660-2098.

Plaza Office Suites
431 E Central Blvd, Orlando FL 32801-1911. 407/849-6330.

Plaza Tower
111 2nd Ave NE, St Petersburg FL 33701-3434. 813/821-4989.

Sarasota City Center
1819 Main St, Sarasota FL 34236-5951. 941/365-1819.

Tampa Commons Office Building
1 N Dale Mabry Hwy, Tampa FL 33609-2764. 813/872-6005.

Cedar Hills Shopping Center
3728 Blanding Blvd, Jacksonville FL 32210-5243. 904/778-8389.

Church Street Market
55 W Church St, Orlando FL

32801-3326. 407/872-3500.

McNeil Real Estate Management
2200 McGregor Blvd, Fort Myers FL 33901-3312. 941/337-3677.

The Great American Bazaar
7551 Canada Ave, Orlando FL 32819-8274. 407/345-8080.

Volusia Mall Management Office
1700 W International Speedway, Daytona Beach FL 32114. 904/253-6783.

Carlton Arms Apartments Of Winter Park
300 Jamestown Dr, Winter Park FL 32792-3643. 407/671-3500.

Cedar Trace Apartments
2200 Cedar Trace Circle, Tampa FL 33613-2558. 813/972-2924.

Palmway Village Apartments
411 77th Ave N, St Petersburg FL 33702-4315. 813/577-5565.

Parker's Landing
5365 Harborside Dr, Tampa FL 33615-3675. 813/855-4834.

Riverchase Apartments
6900 Aruba Ave, Tampa FL 33637-5696. 813/989-2052.

Riverside Terrace
5001 E Sligh Ave, Tampa FL 33617-8447. 813/626-1475.

Amberwood Apartments Ltd.
3001 McFarlane Ave, Lake City FL 32025-6583. 904/752-8848.

Azalea Hills Apartments
420 N Mill St, Leesburg FL 34748-7130. 352/787-5517.

Blue Tree Ridge
12021 Terrace Ridge Dr, Orlando FL 32836-6418. 407/239-6662.

Boca East Apartments
300 W Royal Palm Rd, Boca Raton FL 33432. 407/392-7535.

Bridge Tower Apartment Homes
2540 Roy Hanna Dr S, St Petersburg FL 33712-5664. 813/866-2488.

Calibre Bend Apartments
3924 Calibre Bend Ln,

Winter Park FL 32792-8605. 407/679-9100.

Cedar Creek Apartments
2450 Hartwell Ave, Sanford FL 32771-4169. 407/324-4334.

Chase Crossing Apartments
250 Belle Chase Circle, Tampa FL 33634-6261. 813/886-6461.

Colony Apartments
6050 34th St W, Bradenton FL 34210. 941/753-6850.

Copper Terrace Apartments
1801 S Kirkman Rd, Orlando FL 32811-2328. 407/293-3355.

Country Club Village Apartments
1601 NW 13th St, Boca Raton FL 33486-1102. 407/368-7007.

Crossroads Apartments
4381 Crossroads Ct, Orlando FL 32811-5677. 407/843-8436.

Cypress Greens Apartments
4860 Cypress Woods Dr, Orlando FL 32811-3730. 407/843-4663.

Cypress Pointe Apartments
5119 E Fletcher Ave, Tampa FL 33617-1140. 813/989-1610.

Dover Village Apartments
5762 Folkstone Ln, Orlando FL 32822-9432. 407/282-6190.

Dovetail Villas
5916 Mausser Dr, Orlando FL 32822-4279. 407/275-3790.

Eastlake Apartments
248 E Collins St, Umatilla FL 32784-7418. 352/669-6777.

Egret Landing Audubon Village Apartments
5830 Memorial Hwy, Tampa FL 33615. 813/886-5568.

Fisherman's Landing Apartments
8900 Fishermans Pointe Dr, Tampa FL 33637-1864. 813/989-0586.

Forest Hills Apartments
2404 SE 5th Circle, Ocala FL 34471-5972. 352/732-2254.

Fredericksburg Apartments
13142 N 22nd St, Tampa FL 33612. 813/971-4413.

Freedom Village
1167 Turner St, Clearwater FL 34616. 813/443-6799.

Glen Nova Apartments
1000 S Nova Rd, Daytona Beach FL 32114-7325. 904/258-5064.

Greenhouse Apartments
5510 N Himes Ave, Tampa FL 33614-5728. 813/879-1251.

Harbor Town Of Jacaranda
8101 NW 14th St, Ft Lauderdale FL 33322-4653. 954/472-5466.

Hideaway Bay Club
3815 Hideaway Bay Blvd, Kissimmee FL 34741-2511. 407/847-8863.

Highland Apartments
100 Joey Dr, Green Cove Springs FL 32043-3908. 904/284-7256.

Hollowbrook Apartments
5465 Curry Ford Rd, Orlando FL 32812-8548. 407/275-9476.

La Plaza Apartments
497 N Wymore Rd, Winter Park FL 32789-2824. 407/869-0887.

Lake Conway Woods Apartments
4830 S Conway Rd, Orlando FL 32812-1297. 407/851-9510.

Lakes Of Northdale
16297 Northdale Oaks Dr, Tampa FL 33624-1300. 813/969-3333.

Landings Apartments
2803 W Sligh Ave, Tampa FL 33614-4248. 813/933-2449.

Lindru Garden Apartments
711 S Lincoln Ave, Clearwater FL 34616. 813/446-6676.

Longwood Villas Apartments
1000 Douglas Ave, Altamonte Springs FL 32714-2011. 407/862-8891.

Lookout Pointe
6301 S Westshore Blvd, Tampa FL 33616. 813/831-2538.

Normandy Park Apartments
11110 N 56th St, Tampa FL 33617-2902. 813/988-5877.

North Grove Manor
713 N Grove Ln, Seffner FL

33584-4577. 813/681-3089.

Oakmeade Apartments
1831 13th Ave E, Bradenton
FL 34208. 941/746-3855.

Omega Apartments
2811 Gamma Dr, Orlando FL
32810-3755. 407/295-4786.

Orlando Cloisters
757 S Orange Ave, Orlando
FL 32801-3755. 407/423-1928.

Palm Breeze Apartments
8014 Tommy Ct, Tampa FL
33619-4833. 813/626-4455.

Palm Cove Apartments
1805 Palm Cove Blvd, Delray
Beach FL 33445-6750.
407/243-6455.

Palm Side Apartments
210 Interchange Dr NE, Palm
Bay FL 32907-5530.
407/984-0215.

Parkway North
8049 Stillwater Ct, Fort
Myers FL 33903-4378.
941/997-3090.

Perry Apartments
2273 S Byron Butler Pkwy,
Perry FL 32347. 904/584-6444.

**Pines At Springdale
Apartments**
2500 Springdale Blvd, Lake
Worth FL 33461-6388.
407/967-2233.

Post Bay Apartments
11901 4th St N, St
Petersburg FL 33716-1700.
813/577-1822.

Post Lake Apartments
700 Post Lake Place, Apopka
FL 32703-6124. 407/682-1050.

Prince Manor Apartments
13016 Leeds Ct, Tampa FL
33612-9205. 813/971-8750.

Quails Bluff
550 Burns Ave, Lake Wales
FL 33853. 941/676-7917.

Ridgeview Apartments
6321 113th St, Seminole FL
34642. 813/397-5551.

Sabal Park Apartments
302 Sabal Park Place,
Longwood FL 32779-6087.
407/682-4501.

San Marco Club Apartments
3997 Rosewood Way,

Orlando FL 32808-1063.
407/291-1891.

Sandlake Apartments
13715 N 12th St, Tampa FL
33613-4270. 813/972-0240.

Siesta Royale Apartments
6334 Midnight Pass Rd,
Sarasota FL 34242-2498.
941/349-4014.

Siesta Sun Apartments
6424 Midnight Pass Rd,
Sarasota FL 34242-3428.
941/349-8233.

South Ridge Apartments
440 W Oak Ridge Rd,
Orlando FL 32809-4041.
407/851-8970.

Southern Pointe Apartments
1 Block North Of Broward
Mall, Ft Lauderdale FL
33322. 954/472-4733.

Spring Harbor
1495 Spring Harbor Dr,
Delray Beach FL 33445.
407/276-7446.

Sunrise Apartments
3805 S Hopkins Ave Apt 12,
Titusville FL 32780-5755.
407/267-6954.

Suntree Apartments Ltd.
1769 Shadetree Way, West
Palm Beach FL 33406-6567.
407/439-6812.

Tampa Park Apartments
1417 Tampa Park Plaza St,
Tampa FL 33605-4821.
813/229-1845.

Tanglewood Apartments
13783 Tournament Dr, Palm
Beach Gardens FL 33410-1290. 407/622-1777.

The Lakes At Rosemont
4901 Bottlebrush Ln,
Orlando FL 32808-1778.
407/297-6111.

The Pines At Monterey
4401 S Kirkman Rd, Orlando
FL 32811-2835. 407/297-1500.

The Regent Apartments
4131 E Busch Blvd, Tampa
FL 33617-5935. 813/989-0572.

**Timberwalk Apartment
Community**
10263 Whispering Forest Dr,
Jacksonville FL 32257.
904/260-0807.

Viridan Lakes Apartments
3701 Winkler Ext, Fort
Myers FL 33916-7703.
941/939-5969.

**Westminster Apartment
Homes**
7350 Blanding Blvd,
Jacksonville FL 32244.
904/778-1791.

Whalers Cove Apartments
2301 S Congress Ave,
Boynton Beach FL 33426.
407/369-3145.

**Wildwood Commons
Apartments**
1000 Lee St, Wildwood FL
34785-3128. 904/748-0047.

Windover West Melbourne
2264 Crippen Ct, W
Melbourne FL 32904-5000.
407/768-2035.

Winter Park Villas
657 Saint Johns Ct, Winter
Park FL 32792-4917.
407/657-4949.

Woods Edge Apartments
4070 Woods Edge Circle,
West Palm Beach FL 33410-6429. 407/842-3333.

Arrowood
3500 Fell Rd, Melbourne FL
32904-7502. 407/725-3500.

Floridana Homeowners
304 52nd Avenue Terrace
W, Bradenton FL 34207-2952. 941/755-5666.

Genesis Communities
7003 Date Palm Ln, Ellenton
FL 34222-4317. 941/722-1730.

**Hawaiian Village Mobile
Home Park**
104 63rd Ave W, Bradenton
FL 34207-4901. 941/755-6103.

Holiday Ranch Mobile Home
4300 E Bay Dr, Clearwater
FL 34624-6892. 813/531-7939.

Kings Manor Estates
1399 Belcher Rd S, Largo FL
34641. 813/531-3409.

**Kissimmee Gardens Mobile
Home Community**
2552 Tohope Blvd,
Kissimmee FL 34741-1618.
407/846-4200.

Lake Worth Village
5160 Lake Worth Rd, Lake
Worth FL 33463-3351.
407/965-4129.

San Souci Lakes
3000 N Tamiami Trail, Fort
Myers FL 33903-2293.
941/995-5455.

Sea Breeze Mobile Homeowners
10885 SE Federal Hwy, Hobe Sound FL 33455-5004. 407/546-2300.

Swiss Village
366 Alpine Dr S, Winter Haven FL 33881-9507. 941/293-4199.

Westwind I & II Mobile Home Parks
3301 Alt 19, Dunedin FL 34698. 813/784-4380.

Windmill Village South
3000 N Tuttle Ave, Sarasota FL 34234-6400. 941/355-7667.

REAL ESTATE AGENTS AND MANAGERS

Berkley Group
3015 N Ocean Blvd, Suite 121, Ft Lauderdale FL 33308-7300. 954/563-2444.

CMT Holding
1988 Gulf To Bay Blvd, Clearwater FL 34625-3541. 813/442-4111.

Galaxy Group Management
2345 Sand Lake Rd, Orlando FL 32809-9120. 407/856-7190.

Ballenisles Realty Commercial Property
3910 RCA Blvd, Palm Beach Gardens FL 33410-4213. 407/625-4488.

Clayton Williams & Sherwood
2500 Maitland Center Pkwy, Suite 10, Maitland FL 32751-7224. 407/660-0050.

Codina Klein Realty
2 Alhambra Plaza Ph, Coral Gables FL 33134-5202. 305/520-2300.

Coldwell Banker
3011 Yamato Rd, Suite A6, Boca Raton FL 33434-5352. 407/997-7300.

Coldwell Banker
15500 New Barn Rd, Hialeah FL 33014-2177. 305/556-7880.

Cushman & Wakefield Of Florida
1 Tampa City Center, Suite 1900, Tampa FL 33602-5813. 813/223-6300.

Florida Home Finders
5240 Babcock St NE, Palm Bay FL 32905-4692. 407/724-9500.

Gimelstob Realty Inc. Better Homes
1 S Ocean Blvd, Boca Raton FL 33432-5142. 407/395-2233.

Keyes Company
1 SE 3rd Ave, Miami FL 33131-1704. 305/371-3592.

Ponte Vedra Club Realty
280 Ponte Vedra Blvd, Ponte Vedra FL 32082-1821. 904/285-6927.

Prudential Florida Realty Residential Sales
3100 E Commercial Blvd, Ft Lauderdale FL 33308-4327. 954/771-2600.

Realtymasters
915 W Sunrise Blvd, Ft Lauderdale FL 33311-7130. 954/523-0943.

Rowe Realty
220 King St, Cocoa FL 32922-7940. 407/632-2600.

Southeastern Property Management
6220 Manatee Ave W, Bradenton FL 34209-2376. 941/795-2524.

Keyes Company
703 E 3rd Ave, New Smyrna FL 32169-3101. 904/428-5723.

Vernon Mount Realty Co.
5379 Ocean Blvd, Sarasota FL 34242-3327. 941/346-1161.

VIP Realty Group
13061 McGregor Blvd, Fort Myers FL 33919-5936. 941/481-6111.

Watson Realty Associates
3951 Baymeadows Rd, Jacksonville FL 32217-4636. 904/737-2290.

Bay Tec Center Leasing
2830 Scherer Dr N, St Petersburg FL 33716-1020. 813/572-5075.

Buschwood III
3350 W Busch Blvd, Tampa FL 33618-4300. 813/933-2566.

Crossroads Hospitality Company
4405 Vineland Rd, Orlando FL 32811-7363. 407/648-7411.

First Property Management
5729 Hoover Blvd, Suite 212, Tampa FL 33634-5302. 813/886-6600.

First Property Management
1 N Dale Mabry Hwy, Suite 1000, Tampa FL 33609-2759. 813/461-5759.

George W Lackey Co.
601 Bayshore Blvd, Tampa FL 33606-2747. 813/254-5959.

Insignia Management Group
5405 Cypress Center Dr, Tampa FL 33609-1052. 813/289-7586.

Landex Corporation
1100 Homestead Rd N, Lehigh Acres FL 33936-6002. 941/369-5848.

McCoy Realty Group
6301 NW 5th Way, Ft Lauderdale FL 33309-6139. 954/493-8222.

Stiles Property Management
901 Northpoint Pkwy, Suite 302, West Palm Beach FL 33407-1953. 407/689-6835.

Timber Lake Plaza
8608 Griffin Rd, Cooper City FL 33328-3719. 954/434-9886.

Beachplace Association
1109 Gulf Of Mexico Dr, Longboat Key FL 34228-3603. 941/383-4076.

Central Park Apartments
1910 Wood St, Sarasota FL 34236-7810. 941/953-4433.

Hawaiian Gardens Phase II
5101 W Oakland Park Blvd, Ft Lauderdale FL 33313-1504. 954/731-9722.

High Point Of Delray
1221 Club Dr W, Delray Beach FL 33445-2825. 407/496-4628.

Midnight Cove Condominium
6032 Midnight Cove Rd, Sarasota FL 34242. 941/349-3004.

Ocean Park Jupiter Condo Association
300 Alternate A 1 A, Jupiter FL 33477. 407/744-0668.

The Pointe
9390 Midnight Pass Rd, Sarasota FL 34242-2924. 941/349-6446.

University Oakwoods
1250 E 113th Ave, Tampa FL 33612. 813/977-3401.

Homeport Realty
Homeport Bldg, Hobe Sound FL 33455. 407/546-4663.

Prudential Florida Realty
3685 Bee Ridge Rd, Sarasota
FL 34233-1002. 941/923-
1602.

Real Estate Ex Services
3550 W Busch Blvd, Suite
190, Tampa FL 33618-
4435. 813/933-4966.

Warren Hunnicutt Jr.
696 First Ave N Fl 2, St
Petersburg FL 33701-3610.
813/821-6515.

**LAND SUBDIVIDERS AND
DEVELOPERS**

**Allen Morris Oncor
International**
300 NE 3rd Ave, Ft
Lauderdale FL 33301-1173.
954/765-1000.

**Allen Morris Oncor
International**
1800 Eller Dr, Ft Lauderdale
FL 33316-4200. 954/523-
2020.

Bonita Bay Properties
3451 Bonita Bay Blvd, Suite
202, Bonita Springs FL
33923-4354. 941/495-
1000.

Coastal Real Estate
5647 Park Blvd, Pinellas Park
FL 34665-3330. 813/544-
7558.

Consolidated-Tomoka Land
149 C S Ridgewood Ave
Box, Daytona Beach FL
32120. 904/255-7558.

Corporex
3902 Corporex Park Dr,
Suite 550, Tampa FL 33619-
1132. 813/622-8000.

Epoch Management
20 N Orange Ave, Suite
1600, Orlando FL 32801-
4624. 407/425-2552.

Fill Site Development Co.
12232 N 56th St, Tampa FL
33617. 813/989-9197.

First Florida Equities
7740 SW 104th St, Suite
200, Miami FL 33156-3149.
305/666-5588.

Fletcher Land Corporation
4400 Marsh Landing Blvd,
Ponte Vedra FL 32082-
1275. 904/285-6921.

**Grand Bay Commercial
Properties**
8019 N Himes Ave, Tampa
FL 33614-2712. 813/930-
0259.

Levitt Corporation
410-7777 Glades Rd, Boca
Raton FL 33434. 407/482-
5100.

Lincoln Property Co.
4830 W Kennedy Blvd, Suite
100, Tampa FL 33609-
2517. 813/286-4001.

M&H Developers
3923 Lake Worth Rd, Lake
Worth FL 33461-4039.
407/439-2830.

Oaks Club
1507 N Tamiami Trail,
Osprey FL 34229-8822.
941/966-3025.

Polo's South
2109 Polo Club Dr,
Kissimmee FL 34741-2618.
407/238-1433.

Port Saint Lucie
9801 S Federal Hwy, Port St
Lucie FL 34952. 407/335-
5640.

Prince Bush Investments
227 W New England Ave,
Winter Park FL 32789-4260.
407/629-4776.

Quail Hollow Companies
907 Augusta National Blvd,
Winter Springs FL 32708-
4223. 407/365-3214.

RAL Business Park
1705 Industrial Ave,
Edgewater FL 32132-3560.
904/423-4056.

Riverview Development
2411 Landings Circle,
Bradenton FL 34209-9675.
941/794-6727.

Shadow Lakes
780 W Lumsden Rd, Brandon

FL 33511-8804. 813/681-
4252.

Stiles Property Management
13790 NW 4th St, Ft
Lauderdale FL 33325-6216.
954/846-0883.

The Krauss Schwartz Co.
5215 W Laurel St, Tampa FL
33607-1728. 813/888-
5599.

Treco Realty Group
1325 San Marco Blvd,
Jacksonville FL 32207-8568.
904/396-1600.

United Resources
2699 S Bayshore Dr, Suite
800 A, Miami FL 33133-
5426. 305/856-3930.

**CEMETERY SUBDIVIDERS
AND DEVELOPERS**

**Brevard Memorial Park Sales
Division**
300 Spring St, Cocoa FL
32927-4833. 407/631-
7311.

Deland Memorial Gardens
600 E Beresford Ave, Deland
FL 32724-7099. 904/734-
6956.

**Deltona Memorial Gardens &
Mausoleum**
1295 Saxon Blvd, Orange
City FL 32763-8464.
904/775-4260.

**Live Oak Park Memorial
Cemetery**
112 E North Ave, Crestview
FL 32536-2334. 904/682-
3813.

Manasota Memorial Park
5350 15th St E, Bradenton
FL 34203-6107. 941/756-
3389.

**Palms Memorial Park &
Mausoleum**
5200 Fruitville Rd, Sarasota
FL 34232-2212. 941/371-
4962.

Gibraltar Mausoleum
218 B E New York Ave,
Deland FL 32724. 904/738-
0470.

For more information on career opportunities in real estate:

Associations

**INSTITUTE OF REAL ESTATE
MANAGEMENT**
430 North Michigan Avenue, P.O. Box
109025, Chicago IL 60610-9025.
312/661-1930. Dedicated to educating and
identifying real estate managers who are
committed to meeting the needs of real
estate owners and investors.

**INTERNATIONAL ASSOCIATION OF
CORPORATE REAL ESTATE EXECUTIVES**
440 Columbia Drive, Suite 100, West Palm
Beach FL 33409. 407/683-8111. An
international association of real estate
brokers.

Magazines

JOURNAL OF PROPERTY MANAGEMENT
Institute of Real Estate Management, 430
North Michigan Avenue, Chicago IL 60610.
312/661-1930.

NATIONAL REAL ESTATE INVESTOR
6151 Powers Ferry Road, Atlanta GA
30339. 404/955-2500.

RETAIL

The '90s have been turbulent times for the retail industry. During the early years of the decade, the industry struggled as the national economy remained mired in recession. Even as late as 1994, the troubled department store sector was still straggling. During that year alone, two of retail's giants, Federated Department Stores and R.H. Macy's merged, while Kmart continued to struggle, and even once-booming companies like The Limited and The Gap hit bumps in the road.

On the other hand, 1994 was actually a great year for retailers. Especially hot: the sale of men's suits and personal computers. While rising interest rates have cut into consumer spending, at press time the industry also appeared to be in for a relatively solid 1996. Clothing prices have fallen, partly due to increased imports and efforts by Sears, Wal-Mart, Kmart and JCPenney to strengthen their apparel businesses. The reason behind this focus on apparel is simple: clothes generate much higher profit margins than hard goods.

Even so, jobseekers can expect the retail industry to be as volatile as ever. New stores will continually open and others will close. Alternative retail outlets, such as mail order companies or home shopping have carved a niche for themselves in the market and have taken away customers who usually shop at the traditional retail stores. And look for mergers, acquisitions and even bankruptcies among the large department stores to continue.

ABC LIQUORS
P.O. Box 593688, Orlando FL 32859. 407/851-0000. **Contact:** Steve Melson, Personnel Director. **Description:** A wine and spirits merchant operating 200 stores statewide.

ANTHONY ABRAHAM CHEVROLET
4181 SW 8th Street, Miami FL 33134. 305/442-1000. **Contact:** Al Alverez, Personnel Manager. **Description:** A new and used car dealership.

AUTOMOTIVE INDUSTRIES INC.
522 Park Street, Jacksonville FL 32204. 904/355-7511. **Contact:** Human Resources. **Description:** An automotive supply store.

B&B CASH GROCERY STORES INC.
HANDY FOOD STORES, INC.
P.O. Box 1808, Tampa FL 33601. 813/621-6411. **Contact:** Kathleen Coatsworth, Director of Human Resources. **Description:** The corporate office of a supermarket and convenience store chain. **Common positions include:** Accountant/Auditor; Advertising Clerk; Blue-Collar Worker Supervisor; Human Resources Specialist; Management Trainee. **Educational backgrounds include:** Food Services. **Benefits:** Dental Insurance; Disability Coverage; Life Insurance; Medical Insurance; Profit Sharing; Savings Plan. **Corporate headquarters location:** This Location. **Operations at this facility include:** Administration; Divisional Headquarters; Regional Headquarters.

W.S. BADCOCK CORPORATION
P.O. Box 497, Mulberry FL 33860. 941/425-4921. **Contact:** Jim Vernon, Director of Personnel. **Description:** The corporate office for a chain of furniture stores.

BEALL'S DEPARTMENT STORES
1806 38th Avenue East, Bradenton FL 34208. 941/747-2355. **Contact:** Chuck Driscoll, Vice President of Stores and Development. **Description:** Sells clothing and linens.

BELK-LINDSEY STORES
3800 U.S. Highway 98 North, Lakeland FL 33809. 941/859-6551. **Contact:** Personnel Department. **Description:** Part of a chain of retail stores, selling a wide range of products including clothing, housewares, and cosmetics. **Corporate headquarters location:** This Location.

BLOCKBUSTER ENTERTAINMENT CORPORATION
One Blockbuster Plaza, Fort Lauderdale FL 33301. 954/832-3000. **Contact:** Scott Milford, Recruiter. **Description:** A video store, part of the nationwide chain. There are approximately 2,000 domestic Blockbuster outlets in the United States. **Number of employees nationwide:** 46,000.

BODY SHOP, INC.
6225 Powers Avenue, Jacksonville FL 32217. 904/737-0811. **Contact:** Payroll Supervisor. **Description:** A women's clothing store.

BURDINE'S
22 East Flagler Street, Miami FL 33131. 305/577-1998. **Contact:** Human Resources Coordinator. **Description:** A department store chain. **Parent company:** Allied Stores Corporation. **Corporate headquarters location:** This location. **Number of employees nationwide:** 17,500.

BURDINE'S
1333 North East 163rd Street, North Miami Beach FL 33162. 305/940-4313. **Fax:** 305/940-4344. **Contact:** Human Resource Manager. **Description:** A department store chain. **Common positions include:** Branch Manager; Buyer; Claim Representative; Credit Manager; Customer Service Representative; Department Manager; General Manager; Human Resources Specialist; Operations/Production Manager. **Educational backgrounds include:** Business Administration. **Benefits:** 401K; Dental Insurance; Disability Coverage; Employee Discounts; Life Insurance; Medical Insurance; Pension Plan; Profit Sharing; Savings Plan; Stock Option. **Special Programs:** Internships; Training Programs. **Corporate headquarters location:** Miami FL. **Parent company:** Allied Stores Corporation. **Operations at this facility include:** Administration; Sales; Service. **Number of employees at this location:** 300. **Number of employees nationwide:** 17,500.

CWC COMPANIES INC.
600 Cleveland St, Clearwater FL 34615-4151. 813/443-0605. **Contact:** Human Resources. **Description:** Operates a regional chain of retail supermarkets.

CAUSEWAY LUMBER COMPANY
P.O. Box 21088, Fort Lauderdale FL 33335. 954/763-1224. **Contact:** Janet Beets, Personnel. **Description:** A lumber yard.

CHAMPS SPORTS
311 Manatee Avenue West, Bradenton FL 34205. 941/741-7158. **Fax:** 941/741-7524. **Contact:** Penny Campell, Human Resources Administrator. **Description:** A specialty and sporting goods retailer. Products include hardgoods, apparel, footwear, and accessories. **Common positions include:** Advertising Clerk; Buyer; Clerical Supervisor; Computer Programmer; Computer Systems Analyst; Customer Service Representative; General Manager; Human Resources Specialist; Management Trainee; Merchandiser; Operations Research Analyst; Purchasing Agent and Manager; Services Sales Representative. **Educational backgrounds include:** Business Administration; Communications; Liberal Arts; Marketing. **Benefits:** Dental Insurance; Disability Coverage; Employee Discounts; Life Insurance; Medical Insurance; Tuition Assistance. **Special Programs:** Internships. **Corporate headquarters location:** This Location. **Other U.S. locations:** Virgin Islands; Puerto Rico; Hawaii. **Parent company:** Woolworth Corporation. **Listed on:** New York Stock Exchange. **Number of employees at this location:** 115.

CLAIRE'S STORES INC.
Three South West 129th Avenue, Hollywood FL 33027. 954/433-3900. **Fax:** 954/433-3999. **Contact:** Tina Perkins, Executive Director of Human Resources.

Description: A specialty store offering women's accessories. **Number of employees at this location:** 5,200.

DEVON CAPITAL CORPORATION
1451 West Cypress Creek Road, Fort Lauderdale FL 33309. 954/928-2812. **Contact:** Personnel Department. **Description:** Operates a chain of retail jewelry stores.

DILLARDS DEPARTMENT STORES, INC.
500 North Orlando Avenue, Winter Park FL 32789. 407/644-8511. **Contact:** Personnel. **Description:** A department store chain. This location serves as one of the retail locations of Dillards and houses the regional offices (although the main Florida offices are located in St. Petersburg). **Corporate headquarters location:** Little Rock AR. **Listed on:** New York Stock Exchange.

DILLARDS DEPARTMENT STORES, INC.
Regency Square, 9501 Arlington Expressway, St. Petersburg FL 33710. 813/721-9166. **Contact:** Division Office Manager. **Description:** Florida divisional headquarters of a department store chain. **Common positions include:** Customer Service Representative; Retail Sales Worker; Sales Manager; Services Sales Representative. **Benefits:** Dental Insurance; Employee Discounts; Life Insurance; Medical Insurance; Pension Plan; Savings Plan. **Special Programs:** Training Programs. **Corporate headquarters location:** Little Rock AR. **Operations at this facility include:** Sales. **Listed on:** New York Stock Exchange.

DISCOUNT AUTO PARTS, INC.
4900 Frontage Road South, Lakeland FL 33801. 941/687-9226. **Contact:** Butch Vinson, Director of Training/Team Development. **Description:** Discount Auto Parts, which was founded in 1971 with an 800 square foot store in Winter Park, Florida, is a specialty retailer of automotive replacement parts, maintenance items, and accessories for the do-it-yourself customer. As of July 1994, the company operated a chain of over 200 stores located in Florida, Georgia, and Alabama and in 1995, Discount Auto Parts expected the opening of 35 to 40 new stores. **NOTE:** The company uses extensive formal employee training programs focusing on automotive parts knowledge, selling skills, store operational procedures and personal development, and encourages promotion from within. **Corporate headquarters location:** This Location. **Listed on:** New York Stock Exchange. **Number of employees nationwide:** 2,172.

ECKERD CORPORATION
P.O. Box 4689, Clearwater FL 34618. 813/399-6000. **Recorded Jobline:** 813/399-6443. **Contact:** Luisa Hollingsworth, Human Resources. **Description:** Eckerd Corporation is one of the largest drug store chains in the United States with approximately 1690 stores in Florida, Texas, and 13 sunbelt states. The stores feature some general merchandise, prescription and over-the-counter drugs, and photo development services. Eckerd operates 398 Eckerd Express photo centers which offer overnight service and plans to add 240 new centers by 1997. Non-pharmacy merchandise at Eckerd stores includes health and beauty aids, greeting cards, and other convenience products. Stores also offer a line of Eckerd-brand products. The Eckerd Vision Group operates 47 optical superstores and 30 optical centers with one-hour service. Insta-Care Pharmacy Service centers provide prescription drugs and offer patient record and consulting services to health care institutions. **Common positions include:** Accountant/Auditor; Attorney; Buyer; Human Resources Specialist; Operations/Production Manager; Paralegal; Pharmacist; Transportation/Traffic Specialist. **Educational backgrounds include:** Accounting; Business Administration; Communications; Finance; Marketing. **Benefits:** 401K; Dental Insurance; Disability Coverage; Employee Discounts; Life Insurance; Medical Insurance; Pension Plan; Profit Sharing; Savings Plan. **Special Programs:** Internships. **Corporate headquarters location:** This Location. **Operations at this facility include:** Administration; Research and Development. **Listed on:** New York Stock Exchange. **Number of employees at this location:** 1,000. **Number of employees nationwide:** 40,000.

ECKERD CORPORATION
8333 Bryan Dairy Road, Largo FL 34647. 813/399-6000. **Contact:** Human Resources. **Description:** Eckerd Corporation is one of the largest drug store chains in the United States with approximately 1690 stores in Florida, Texas, and 13 sunbelt states. The stores feature some general merchandise, prescription and over-the-counter drugs, and photo development services. Eckerd operates 398 Eckerd Express photo centers which offer overnight service and plans to add 240 new centers by 1997. Non-pharmacy merchandise at Eckerd stores includes health and beauty aids, greeting cards, and

other convenience products. Stores also offer a line of Eckerd-brand products. The Eckerd Vision Group operates 47 optical superstores and 30 optical centers with one-hour service. Insta-Care Pharmacy Service centers provide prescription drugs and offer patient record and consulting services to health care institutions. **Corporate headquarters location:** Clearwater FL. **Listed on:** New York Stock Exchange.

ECKERD CORPORATION
8201 Chancellor Drive, Orlando FL 32809. 407/858-4000. **Contact:** Ron Tarpley, Human Resources Director. **Description:** A regional office of the drug store chain. Eckerd Corporation is one of the largest drug store chains in the United States with approximately 1690 stores in Florida, Texas, and 13 sunbelt states. The stores feature some general merchandise, prescription and over-the-counter drugs, and photo development services. Eckerd operates 398 Eckerd Express photo centers which offer overnight service and plans to add 240 new centers by 1997. Non-pharmacy merchandise at Eckerd stores includes health and beauty aids, greeting cards, and other convenience products. Stores also offer a line of Eckerd-brand products. The Eckerd Vision Group operates 47 optical superstores and 30 optical centers with one-hour service. Insta-Care Pharmacy Service centers provide prescription drugs and offer patient record and consulting services to health care institutions. **Common positions include:** Assistant Manager; Department Manager; Management Trainee. **Educational backgrounds include:** Business Administration; Liberal Arts. **Benefits:** 401K; Dental Insurance; Disability Coverage; Employee Discounts; Life Insurance; Medical Insurance; Pension Plan; Profit Sharing. **Corporate headquarters location:** Clearwater FL. **Operations at this facility include:** Divisional Headquarters. **Listed on:** New York Stock Exchange.

ELI WHITNEY
P.O. Box 1510, Ocala FL 34478. 352/245-5151. **Contact:** Don Cochran, Personnel Manager. **Description:** Offices for a chain of grocery stores. **Common positions include:** Advertising Clerk; Buyer; Computer Programmer; Services Sales Representative; Systems Analyst. **Educational backgrounds include:** Computer Science; Marketing. **Benefits:** Credit Union; Dental Insurance; Disability Coverage; Employee Discounts; Life Insurance; Medical Insurance; Profit Sharing; Savings Plan; Tuition Assistance. **Corporate headquarters location:** This Location.

FARM STORES
5800 North West 74th Avenue, Miami FL 33166. 305/592-3100. **Contact:** Barbara Ward, Personnel Director. **Description:** Corporate office for a regional chain of convenience stores.

FERMAN MOTOR CAR COMPANY
9751 Adamo Drive, Tampa FL 33619. 813/623-2411. **Contact:** Personnel Department. **Description:** A dealer of new and used automobiles.

GOLD COAST AUTO-MALL
21111 South Dixie Highway, Miami FL 33189. 305/238-0000. **Contact:** Marc Davis, General Manager. **Description:** Automobile dealership. **Common positions include:** Accountant/Auditor; Automotive Mechanic/Body Repairer. **Educational backgrounds include:** Accounting; Business Administration; Marketing. **Benefits:** 401K; Employee Discounts; Medical Insurance. **Special Programs:** Internships. **Other U.S. locations:** Nationwide. **Parent company:** Potamkin Companies. **Operations at this facility include:** Administration; Sales; Service. **Listed on:** Privately held. **Number of employees at this location:** 114.

HIT OR MISS, INC.
Colonial Promenade, 4632 East Colonial Drive, Orlando FL 32803. 407/898-2540. **Contact:** Regional Manager. **Description:** A chain of women's fashion stores with over 550 stores in 35 states. **Common positions include:** Assistant Buyer; Assistant Store Manager-In-Training; Branch Manager; Buyer; Loss Prevention Specialist; Sales Associate; Store Detective; Store Manager. **Benefits:** Dental Insurance; Disability Coverage; Life Insurance; Medical Insurance; Tuition Assistance. **Special Programs:** Internships; Training Programs. **Corporate headquarters location:** Stoughton MA. **Parent company:** TJX, Inc. **Operations at this facility include:** Sales. **Listed on:** New York Stock Exchange.

HOLIDAY RV SUPERSTORES, INC.
7851 Greenbriar Parkway, Orlando FL 32819. 407/363-9211. **Fax:** 407/363-2065. **Contact:** Paula Oulette, Personnel Director. **Description:** One of the largest retailers of

recreational vehicles in the United States. Holiday RV Superstores operates 10 retail sales and service dealerships. **Common positions include:** Branch Manager; General Manager; Management Trainee; Operations/Production Manager; Purchasing Agent and Manager. **Educational backgrounds include:** Accounting; Business Administration. **Benefits:** 401K; Dental Insurance; Disability Coverage; Employee Discounts; Life Insurance; Medical Insurance; Pension Plan; Profit Sharing; Savings Plan; Tuition Assistance. **Special Programs:** Internships; Training Programs. **Corporate headquarters location:** This Location. **Other U.S. locations:** CA; GA; SC. **Operations at this facility include:** Divisional Headquarters; Sales; Service. **Listed on:** NASDAQ. **Number of employees at this location:** 14. **Number of employees nationwide:** 211.

HOME SHOPPING NETWORK, INC.
P.O. Box 9090, Clearwater FL 34618-9090. 813/572-8585. **Recorded Jobline:** 813/572-8585x6117. **Contact:** Human Resources. **Description:** Home Shopping Network, Inc. is a holding company, the subsidiaries of which conduct the day-to-day operations of the company's various business activities. The company's primary business is electronic retailing conducted by Home Shopping Club, Inc. (HSC), which offers customers jewelry, hardgoods, softgoods, cosmetics, and other items via live on-air television presentations. Home Shopping Network is also engaged in other merchandising facets, distribution, and programming. The company distributes four mail order catalogs, operates three television networks and eight broadcast studios, and has relationships with multiple system cable operators (MSOs). In September 1994, the company acquired Internet Shopping Network (ISN), which delivers online shopping to Internet users. The company's HSN Direct division, which produces and airs infomercials and distributes infomercial products, was also formed in 1994. **Corporate headquarters location:** St. Petersburg FL. **Listed on:** New York Stock Exchange. **Number of employees nationwide:** 5,018.

J.M. FAMILY ENTERPRISES
8019 Bayberry Road, Jacksonville FL 32256. 904/443-6650. **Contact:** Jennifer Cofer, Human Resources Manager. **Description:** An automotive distributor.

JAN-BELL MARKETING, INC.
13801 Northwest 14th Street, Sunrise FL 33323-2845. 954/846-8000. **Fax:** 954/846-2787. **Recorded Jobline:** 800/223-6964x5408. **Contact:** Nadine Rudowitz, Human Resources Recruiter. **Description:** A retailer, merchandiser, and distributor of fine jewelry, watches, sunglasses, fragrances, and collectibles. The company's outlet stores are located nationwide. **Common positions include:** Accountant/Auditor; Blue-Collar Worker Supervisor; Buyer; Computer Programmer; Computer Systems Analyst; Customer Service Representative; Department Manager; Financial Analyst; Graphic Artist; Human Resources Specialist; Order Clerk; Payroll Clerk; Receptionist; Stock Clerk; Wholesale and Retail Buyer. **Educational backgrounds include:** Accounting; Art/Design; Business Administration; Communications; Computer Science; Economics; Finance; Liberal Arts; Marketing; Mathematics. **Benefits:** 401K; Dental Insurance; Disability Coverage; Employee Discounts; Life Insurance; Medical Insurance; Stock Option. **Corporate headquarters location:** This Location. **Operations at this facility include:** Administration; Distribution. **Listed on:** American Stock Exchange. **Number of employees at this location:** 500. **Number of employees nationwide:** 2,500.

JEWELMASTERS, INC.
Phillips Point, 777 South Flagler Drive, Promenade Level, West Palm Beach FL 33401. 407/655-7260. **Contact:** William Tayman, Vice President. **Description:** A retail jewelry store chain. **Corporate headquarters location:** This Location.

KANE FURNITURE
5700 70th Avenue, Pinellas Park FL 34665. 813/545-9555. **Fax:** 813/541-6960. **Contact:** Evelyn Zucchero, Human Resources Director. **Description:** A furniture seller. **Common positions include:** Accountant/Auditor; Administrative Services Manager; Clerical Supervisor; Customer Service Representative; Designer; Management Trainee; Services Sales Representative. **Educational backgrounds include:** Accounting; Business Administration; Communications; Marketing. **Benefits:** Dental Insurance; Disability Coverage; Employee Discounts; Life Insurance; Medical Insurance; Profit Sharing. **Corporate headquarters location:** This Location. **Operations at this facility include:** Administration. **Listed on:** Privately held. **Number of employees at this location:** 250. **Number of employees nationwide:** 750.

KASH N' KARRY FOOD STORES
6422 Harney Road, Tampa FL 33610. 813/621-0200. **Contact:** Recruiter. **Description:** Kash n' Karry operates retail food and liquor stores. **Number of employees nationwide:** 8,400.

LANSON'S STYLES FOR MEN
15675 North West 15th Avenue, Miami FL 33169. 305/621-3191. **Contact:** Jay Kaiser, Personnel Manager. **Description:** A retailer of men's wear.

LEVITZ FURNITURE CORPORATION
6111 Broken Sound Parkway NW, Boca Raton FL 33487. 407/994-6006. **Contact:** Human Resources. **Description:** A national furniture store chain. **Corporate headquarters location:** This Location. **Other U.S. locations:** Phoenix AZ. **Listed on:** New York Stock Exchange. **Number of employees nationwide:** 6,000.

THE LEWIS BEAR COMPANY
P.O. Box 17209, Pensacola FL 32522. 904/438-9651. **Contact:** Tod Ioakim, Director of Personnel. **Description:** A retailing firm handling groceries, beer, drugs, and electrical appliances.

LIL CHAMP FOOD STORES, INC.
P.O. Box 23180, Suite 200, Jacksonville FL 32241. 904/464-7200. **Contact:** Gloria Wilson, Assistant Controller/Office Manager. **Description:** A chain of retail grocery stores.

GUS MACHADO ENTERPRISES
1200 West 49th Street, Hialeah FL 33012. 305/822-3211. **Contact:** Personnel Department. **Description:** An automotive dealer.

MARTINE'S CORPORATION
6565 North W Street, Suite 260, Pensacola FL 32505. 904/484-7395. **Contact:** Personnel Department. **Description:** Operates fast-food establishments, liquor stores, and shopping centers.

THE MASSEY GROUP
2434 Atlantic Boulevard, Jacksonville FL 32207. 904/398-6877. **Contact:** Bob Massey, Jr., Personnel. **Description:** A new and used automobile dealership.

OFFICE DEPOT
2200 Old Germantown Road, Del Ray Beach FL 33445. 407/278-4800. **Contact:** Human Resources. **Description:** Office Depot operates a chain of large-volume office products warehouse stores that sell high-quality, brand name office merchandise primarily to small- and medium-sized businesses. The retail locations also serve the growing home office market. The company carries a full inventory of more than 5,600 products. Its major merchandise categories include general office supplies, office furniture, computer hardware and software, copiers, telephones and fax machines, paper, writing instruments, briefcases, accounting supplies, and back-to-school necessities. Office Depot has over 420 stores, a national network of 24 customer service delivery centers, and 62 sales offices in 32 states and Canada. The company's Business Services Division serves the needs of larger businesses--those with more than 50 employees--by combining its commercial delivery business with that of the eight contract stationers acquired over the last two years. The company has seen substantial increase in sales of computers, printers, and other electronic products as a result of the introduction of Business Machine Specialists in every store. These are specially-trained Associates who are able to answer customer questions on a wide variety of technically sophisticated subjects. **Corporate headquarters location:** This Location. **Other U.S. locations:** AL; AZ; FL; GA; KY; LA; TN; TX; VA; WV. **Listed on:** New York Stock Exchange. **Number of employees nationwide:** 11,030.

PUBLIX SUPERMARKETS, INC.
P.O. Box 2226F, Jacksonville FL 32231-0084. 904/781-8600. **Contact:** Director of Personnel. **Description:** Part of a large regional chain of retail supermarkets with over 425 stores in Florida, Georgia, and South Carolina. The company also produces dairy, delicatessen, and bakery items for sale in its stores through four plants and conducts distribution operations through seven centers in Florida. **Number of employees nationwide:** 82,000.

PUBLIX SUPERMARKETS, INC.
P.O. Box 407, Lakeland FL 33802. 941/688-1188. **Contact:** Employment Office. **Description:** The offices of a large regional chain of retail supermarkets with over 425 stores in Florida, Georgia, and South Carolina. The company also produces dairy, delicatessen, and bakery items for sale in its stores through four plants and conducts distribution operations through seven centers in Florida. **Number of employees nationwide:** 82,000.

PUBLIX SUPERMARKETS, INC.
P.O. Box 699030, Miami FL 33269-9030. 305/652-2411. **Contact:** Don Reynolds, Personnel. **Description:** Part of a large regional chain of retail supermarkets with over 425 stores in Florida, Georgia, and South Carolina. The company also produces dairy, delicatessen, and bakery items for sale in its stores through four plants and conducts distribution operations through seven centers in Florida. **Number of employees nationwide:** 82,000.

RAYBRO CED
1212 North 39th Street, Suite 200, Tampa FL 33605. 813/248-6699. **Contact:** Personnel. **Description:** A retail electrical supply store.

ROBB AND STUCKEY OF NAPLES
P.O. Box 60479, Fort Myers FL 33906. 941/936-0030. **Contact:** Personnel Director. **Description:** Robb and Stuckey operates a chain of furniture stores.

LILLIAN RUBIN AFFILIATES, INC.
15705 North West 13th Avenue, Miami FL 33169. 305/624-4200. **Contact:** John Durham, Director of Operations. **Description:** A retailer of women's clothing.

SEARS, ROEBUCK & COMPANY
9501 Arlington Expressway, Jacksonville FL 32225. 904/727-3255. **Contact:** Agnes Jazwinski, Personnel Director. **Description:** A branch office of the retail store.

SOUND ADVICE, INC.
1901 Tigertail Boulevard, Dania FL 33004. 954/922-4434. **Contact:** Personnel. **Description:** Engaged in retailing and servicing home and automobile audio equipment and video equipment. **Number of employees at this location:** 522.

SPEC'S MUSIC INC.
1666 Northwest 82nd Avenue, Miami FL 33126. 305/592-7288. **Contact:** Human Resources. **Description:** A music and video store.

SUNSHINE-JR. STORES, INC.
P.O. Box 2498, 109 West Fifth Street, Panama City FL 32401. 904/769-1661. **Contact:** Director of Human Resources. **Description:** Sunshine-Jr. Stores, Inc. operates 205 regional convenience stores in Florida, Alabama, Mississippi, Georgia, and Louisiana under the trade name Jr. Food Stores. All stores are self-service, offering gasoline and merchandise, which includes a selection of food staples, convenience foods, snacks, tobacco products, soft drinks, beer, wine, dairy goods, and health and beauty aids. Some Jr. Food Stores also have deli facilities. **Common positions include:** Accountant/Auditor; Buyer; Computer Programmer; Department Manager; District Manager; Food Scientist/Technologist; Human Resources Specialist; Management Trainee; Marketing Specialist. **Educational backgrounds include:** Accounting; Business Administration; Communications; Computer Science; Finance; Liberal Arts; Marketing. **Benefits:** Disability Coverage; Life Insurance; Medical Insurance; Retirement Plan; Savings Plan. **Listed on:** American Stock Exchange. **Number of employees nationwide:** 1,400.

TALLAHASSEE FORD MOTORS
P.O. Box 510, Tallahassee FL 32302. 904/877-1171. **Contact:** Wayne Creel, Personnel Director. **Description:** A new and used automotive dealer.

VOGUE SHOPS INC.
6225 Powers Avenue, Jacksonville FL 32217-2215. 904/737-0811. **Contact:** Human Resources. **Description:** The company offers a variety of products including clothing and specialty soaps and lotions.

WINN-DIXIE STORES, INC.

3015 Coastline Drive, Orlando FL 32808. 407/578-4000. **Contact:** Human Resources Department. **Description:** The main headquarters of the Orlando division of Winn-Dixie, one of the largest supermarket operators in the 13 states of the Sunbelt and one of the largest everyday low-price supermarket chains in the country, with over 1,150 stores. The heaviest concentration of Winn-Dixie stores, which operate under the names Winn-Dixie, Marketplace, and Buddies, is in Florida, North Carolina, Georgia, South Carolina, Alabama, Louisiana, and Texas. The company has placed emphasis on the development of superstores which offer general merchandise and specialized foods as well as the usual foodstuffs. Winn-Dixie also operates 16 warehousing and distribution centers and a host of manufacturing and processing facilities. A subsidiary of the company operates 14 stores in the Bahamas. **Number of employees nationwide:** 112,000.

WINN-DIXIE STORES, INC.

Box 44110, Jacksonville FL 32231-4110. 904/695-7840. **Contact:** Kevin Morbach, Human Resources Department. **Description:** Winn-Dixie is one of the largest supermarket operators in the 13 states of the Sunbelt and one of the largest everyday low-price supermarket chains in the country, with over 1,150 stores. The heaviest concentration of Winn-Dixie stores, which operate under the names Winn-Dixie, Marketplace, and Buddies, is in Florida, North Carolina, Georgia, South Carolina, Alabama, Louisiana, and Texas. The company has placed emphasis on the development of superstores which offer general merchandise and specialized foods as well as the usual foodstuffs. Winn-Dixie also operates 16 warehousing and distribution centers and a host of manufacturing and processing facilities. A subsidiary of the company operates 14 stores in the Bahamas. **Number of employees nationwide:** 112,000.

Note: Because addresses and telephone numbers of smaller companies change rapidly, we recommend you call each company to verify the information below before inquiring about job opportunities. Mass mailings are not recommended.

Additional employers with under 250 employees:

RETAIL LUMBER AND BUILDING MATERIALS

Atlantic Building Materials
540 Gus Hipp Blvd,
Rockledge FL 32955-4803.
407/631-7997.

Boral Bricks-Orlando Center
2175 W 8th St, Sanford FL
32771-1680. 407/321-
0429.

Builders Square
590 W 49th St, Hialeah FL
33012-3605. 305/558-
1724.

Holmes Lumber Co.
6550 Roosevelt Blvd,
Jacksonville FL 32244-4098.
904/772-6100.

Home Depot
1712 N Dale Mabry Hwy,
Tampa FL 33607-2520.
813/879-1000.

Home Depot
6101 W Oakland Park Blvd,
Ft Lauderdale FL 33313-
1211. 954/977-9600.

Home Depot
1951 S State Road 7,
Hollywood FL 33023-6733.
954/961-4330.

Home Depot
6101 NW 31st St, Margate
FL 33063-7015. 954/977-
9600.

Home Depot
3001 N State Road 7, Ft
Lauderdale FL 33313-1900.
954/733-0077.

Home Depot
5309 N Davis Hwy,
Pensacola FL 32503-2005.
904/477-7005.

Home Depot
9021 Southside Blvd,
Jacksonville FL 32256-8417.
904/363-8420.

Kinco Limited
7852 Ellis Rd, W Melbourne
FL 32904-1108. 407/727-
1155.

Lowe's Of Panama City
300 E 23rd St, Panama City
FL 32405-4523. 904/913-
1600.

Raymond Building Supply
1314 N Tamiami Trail, Fort
Myers FL 33903-5337.
941/995-5467.

Seacoast Supply
9410 Eden Ave, Hudson FL
34667-4383. 813/869-
9899.

SPS Home Centers & True Value
657 NE Dixie Hwy, Jensen
Beach FL 34957-6110.
407/334-2700.

Alside Supply Center
3122 Shader Rd, Suite C,
Orlando FL 32808-3951.
407/293-9010.

Ashe Industries
4505 Transport Dr, Tampa
FL 33605-5927. 813/247-
2743.

MKV Millwork
1110 2nd Ave S, Lake Worth
FL 33460-4002. 407/547-
6008.

Tarmac
333 Parkridge Ave, Orange
Park FL 32065-7506.
904/296-3600.

ER Jahna Industries
13308 Emil Jahna Rd,
Clermont FL 34711-9594.
407/656-3440.

ER Jahna Industries
122 E Tillman Ave, Lake
Wales FL 33853-4130.
941/676-9431.

Sunburst Shutters
279 Douglas Ave, Altamonte
Springs FL 32714-3324.
407/862-3100.

Kitchens By Acclaim
3155-A W Hillsborough,
Tampa FL 33614. 813/931-
8808.

Whirlpool Corporation
7600 NW 6th Ave, Boca
Raton FL 33487-1319.
407/998-3550.

USA Roofing & Fence Supply
2751 Avenue Of The
Americas, Englewood FL
34224-8235. 941/475-
6707.

Bradco Supply Corp.
9960 S Orange Ave, Orlando
FL 32824-8465. 407/855-
5544.

Gulfside Supply
1565 Northgate Blvd,
Sarasota FL 34234-4760.
941/355-7161.

Gulfside Supply
2649 Rosselle St,
Jacksonville FL 32204-3019.
904/387-0441.

Gulfside Supply
3208 W Tharpe St #A,
Tallahassee FL 32303-1134.
904/574-7650.

Prudential Building Materials
4241 SW 70th Terrace, Ft
Lauderdale FL 33314-3135.
954/523-2002.

**PAINT, GLASS, AND
WALLPAPER STORES**

PPG Industries
4501 Acline Dr E, Tampa FL
33605-5911. 813/247-
3434.

Glidden Paints
6794 Pensacola Blvd,
Pensacola FL 32505-1708.
904/474-0911.

Glidden Paints
445 Park St, Jacksonville FL
32204-2981. 904/353-
4446.

MAB Paints
9421 S Orange Blossom
Trail, Orlando FL 32837-
8320. 407/826-5061.

**Richard's Paint &
Wallcovering**
1500 Palm Bay Rd NE, Palm
Bay FL 32905-3843.
407/984-0323.

HARDWARE STORES

J&J True Value Hardware
1380 Tuskawilla Rd, Winter
Springs FL 32708-5031.
407/699-6700.

Bill's Service & Hardware
350 Business Park Way,
Suite 107, Royal Palm Beach
FL 33411-1712. 407/795-
7721.

**Proctor Ace Hardware &
Garden Center**
525 3rd St N, Jacksonville
Beach FL 32250-7030.
904/249-5622.

Sewell Hardware
201 S Babcock St,
Melbourne FL 32901-1209.
407/725-4340.

Sunshine Hardware
141 9th St S, Naples FL
33940-6260. 941/262-
2940.

Ace Tool Company
5610 NW 12th Ave, Ft
Lauderdale FL 33309-6608.
407/686-4380.

**RETAIL NURSERIES AND
GARDEN SUPPLY STORES**

Pursley Turf Garden Center
9049 59th Avenue Circle E,
Bradenton FL 34202-9665.
941/756-8441.

Century Rain Aid
11475 49th St N,
Clearwater FL 34622-4810.
813/573-9284.

Fields Equipment Company
17215 US Highway 27,
Clermont FL 34711-9273.
904/394-7181.

Lesco Service Center
239 Grove St S, Venice FL
34292-2612. 941/485-
5119.

Lesco Service Center
7920 Congress St, Port
Richey FL 34668-6713.
813/845-3508.

Lesco Service Center
6551 44th St, Pinellas Park
FL 34665-5968. 813/525-
9008.

Lesco Service Center
4507 Clark Rd, Sarasota FL
34233-3421. 941/923-
6159.

Florida Cypress Creations
6344 Toucan Trail, Spring
Hill FL 34607-2639.
352/686-3700.

Lesco Service Center
4643 NW 6th St, Gainesville
FL 32609-1783. 352/371-
8011.

White Rose Crafts & Nursery
1355 SR 436, Casselberry
FL 32707. 407/679-7222.

White Rose Crafts & Nursery
3150 N Hiawassee Rd,
Orlando FL 32818-3334.
407/291-7212.

Skinners Wholesale Nursery
Highway 11, Bunnell FL
32110. 904/437-5529.

MOBILE HOME DEALERS

Luv Homes Of Jacksonville
6021 Blanding Blvd,
Jacksonville FL 32244-2809.
904/772-8031.

Prestige Home Centers
2521 W Tennessee St,
Tallahassee FL 32304-2505.
904/576-5458.

Prestige Home Centers
10910 N Nebraska Ave,
Tampa FL 33612-5725.
813/972-7744.

DEPARTMENT STORES

Sears Roebuck & Co.
5900 Glades Rd, Boca Raton
FL 33431-7203. 407/338-
1119.

JCPenney Co.
7328 SW 48th St, Miami FL
33155-5523. 305/252-
9836.

JCPenney Co.
Boynton Beach Mall, Boynton
Beach FL 33426. 407/736-
8500.

JCPenney Co.
1701 Biscayne Blvd, Miami
FL 33132-1123. 305/377-
0341.

Kmart Stores
7900 SW 104th St, Miami
FL 33156-3632. 305/274-
2983.

Kmart Stores
1777 US Highway 1 S, St
Augustine FL 32086-4238.
904/824-8361.

Kmart Stores
3535 Fruitville Rd, Sarasota
FL 34237-9027. 941/957-
1460.

Kmart Stores
2403 SW 27th Ave, Ocala
FL 34474-4407. 352/237-
2211.

Kmart Stores
900 N Miami Beach Blvd,
Miami FL 33162-3716.
305/944-1681.

Sears Roebuck & Co.
1625 NW 107th Ave, Miami
FL 33172-2707. 305/470-
7850.

Sears Roebuck & Co.
7500 NW 25th St, Miami FL
33122-1713. 305/591-
7900.

Wal-Mart
15885 SW 88th St, Miami
FL 33196-1000. 305/383-
3611.

Wal-Mart
17250 NW 57th Ave,
Hialeah FL 33015-5100.
305/558-6069.

Lord & Taylor
2596 E Sunrise Blvd, Ft
Lauderdale FL 33304-3204.
954/561-8880.

Lord & Taylor
19501 Biscayne Blvd, Miami
FL 33180. 305/932-2777.

Lord & Taylor
301 N University Dr,
Plantation FL 33324-1915.
954/370-2600.

Marshall's
20515 Biscayne Blvd, Miami
FL 33180-1538. 305/937-
2525.

Marshall's
1650 S Federal Hwy, Delray
Beach FL 33483-5030.
407/265-0566.

Marshall's
801 S University Dr,
Plantation FL 33324-3336.
954/476-0505.

Mervyn's
1275 NW 107th Ave, Miami
FL 33172-2728. 305/597-
8800.

Mervyn's
8000 W Broward Blvd, Ft
Lauderdale FL 33388-0024.
954/370-8886.

Mervyn's
700 W 49th St, Hialeah FL
33012-3609. 305/556-
8700.

Saks Fifth Avenue
Galleria Mall, Ft Lauderdale
FL 33304. 954/563-7600.

Target Stores
2000 SW College Rd, Ocala
FL 34474-3020. 352/629-
1333.

Belz Factory Outlet World
5401 W Oak Ridge Rd,
Orlando FL 32819-9416.
407/354-0126.

Bugle Boy Factory Store
250 E Palm Dr, Homestead
FL 33034. 305/242-0086.

Cape Isle Knitters
12801 W Sunrise Blvd, Ft
Lauderdale FL 33323-2997.
954/846-7940.

Fanny Discount
4700 NW 7th St, Miami FL
33126-2252. 305/448-
6388.

Farah Factory Store
250 W Palm Dr #410,
Homestead FL 33034-3424.
305/248-2985.

La Habana Discount
156 NW 57th Ave, Miami FL
33126-4805. 305/264-
2256.

Burdine's Department Stores
1500 Apalachee Pkwy,
Tallahassee FL 32301.
904/878-8126.

Killian Discount
9973 SW 142nd Ave, Miami
FL 33186-6844. 305/387-
7434.

VARIETY STORES

Brookstone Company
Church St Market, Orlando
FL 32801. 407/649-9671.

Dollar General
732 Edgewood Ave N,
Jacksonville FL 32254-3014.
904/384-1824.

FW Woolworth Co.
1801 Palm Beach Lakes
Blvd, West Palm Beach FL
33401-2009. 407/683-
3220.

**MISC. GENERAL
MERCHANDISE STORES**

Luria's
8903 Glades Rd, Boca Raton
FL 33434-4019. 407/479-
1400.

Dollar Tree
1944 US Highway 1 S Rte 4,
St Augustine FL 32086-
4233. 904/824-0505.

Service Merchandise Co.
3750 Bee Ridge Rd, Sarasota
FL 34233-1101. 941/923-
9009.

Sharper Image
55 W Church St, Suite 150,
Orlando FL 32801-3326.
407/843-6130.

Luria's
3717 S Orlando Dr, Sanford
FL 32773-5613. 407/321-
3582.

Luria's
5681 E Fowler Ave, Tampa
FL 33617-2307. 813/988-
3900.

**GROCERY AND
CONVENIENCE STORES**

Dixie Food Station
3425 Thomasville Rd,
Tallahassee FL 32308-3403.
904/893-2972.

E-Z Foods
3104 E Hinson Ave, Haines
City FL 33844-9143.
941/422-4239.

Farm Stores
3138 17th St, Sarasota FL
34234-7902. 941/951-
1591.

First Oriental Market
4205 W Waters Ave, Tampa
FL 33614-1936. 813/882-
4668.

Food Lion
5353 Gunn Hwy, Tampa FL
33624-4103. 813/264-
2692.

Food Lion
819 E Base St, Madison FL
32340-2901. 904/973-
8982.

Gooding's Supermarkets
911 N Woodland Blvd,
Deland FL 32720-2734.
904/736-4599.

Gooding's Supermarkets
5270 Babcock St NE, Suite
28A, Palm Bay FL 32905-
4654. 407/984-4385.

Gooding's Supermarkets
155 S Orlando Ave, Maitland
FL 32751-5601. 407/644-
0852.

Handy Way Food Store
551 S Summit St, Crescent
City FL 32112-3043.
904/698-2830.

Handy Way Food Store
1095 State Road 434 W,
Casselberry FL 32708-2309.
407/695-7063.

Handy Way Food Store
7609 US Highway 441,
Leesburg FL 34788-8246.
352/787-6899.

Handy Way Food Store
Tuskawilla Rd, Casselberry
FL 32707. 407/327-1217.

Handy Way Food Stores
6015 SW Highway 200,
Ocala FL 34476-5557.
352/237-1526.

Hitchcock & Sons
105 N Main St, Alachua FL
32615. 352/462-2284.

**Handy Way Food Stores
South Division**
1721 N Volusia Ave, Orange
City FL 32763-2825.
904/775-1440.

Hometown Food Stores
1201 W SR 50, Clermont FL
34711. 904/394-4442.

Island Food Stores Ltd.
1931 SW 27th Ave, Ocala
FL 34474-2018. 352/237-
7357.

Jiffy Food Store
201 Main St, Daytona Beach
FL 32118-4433. 904/252-
9867.

Kwik King Food Stores
6701 SW Highway 200,
Ocala FL 34476-7057.
352/237-4830.

Kwik King Food Stores
101 NE 16th Ave, Ocala FL
34470-8219. 352/732-
4464.

Lil Champ Food Stores
1297 Simpson Rd,
Kissimmee FL 34744-4603.
407/348-6649.

Lil Champ Food Stores
2691 N Orange Blossom
Trail, Zellwood FL 32798.
407/889-0054.

Lil Champ Food Stores
3013 Washington St,
Zellwood FL 32798.
407/889-3081.

Lil Champ Food Stores
9146 W Halls River Rd,
Homosassa FL 34448-3609.
904/628-2232.

Lil Champ Food Stores
4301 13th St, Saint Cloud
FL 34769-6724. 407/957-
3883.

Lil Champ Food Stores
2200 Fiske Blvd S,
Rockledge FL 32955-3402.
407/633-7383.

New Tropical Supermarket
1895 SW 8th St, Miami FL
33135-3417. 305/541-
4920.

Pic N Payless Supermarkets
2690 W Broward Blvd, Ft
Lauderdale FL 33312-1394.
954/583-8117.

Pic N Pay Supermarkets
130 SW 1st Ave, Dania FL
33004-3632. 954/922-
2274.

Pick Kwik
4229 Park Blvd, Pinellas Park
FL 34665-3646. 813/546-
1279.

Pick Kwik Food Stores
1108 Court St, Clearwater
FL 34616-5749. 813/443-
6240.

Pick Kwik Food Stores
2485 Nebraska Ave, Palm
Harbor FL 34683-3951.
813/785-3466.

Pick Kwik Food Stores
1211 Gulf Blvd, Indian Rocks
Beach FL 34635-2746.
813/595-3547.

Piggly Wiggly
2507 Ferdon Blvd S,
Crestview FL 32536-9436.
904/682-3430.

Publix Super Markets
1667 US Highway 41
Bypass S, Venice FL 34293-
1034. 941/493-4110.

Publix Super Markets
1491 Main St, Dunedin FL
34698-4612. 813/736-
5681.

Publix Super Markets
9846 Glades Rd, Boca Raton
FL 33434-3917. 407/852-
5580.

Publix Super Markets
4701 S University Dr, Davie
FL 33328-3819. 954/434-
6202.

Publix Super Markets
160 Mariner Blvd, Spring Hill
FL 34609-5689. 352/688-
0977.

Publix Super Markets
4771 W Atlantic Ave, Delray
Beach FL 33445-3838.
407/498-0500.

Publix Super Markets
1930 Brandon Brook Rd,
Valrico FL 33594-3024.
813/684-1758.

Publix Super Markets
1337 S Military Trail,
Deerfield Beach FL 33442-
7634. 954/427-5828.

Publix Super Markets
8160 Wiles Rd, Coral Springs
FL 33067. 954/753-3307.

Publix Super Markets
1551 US Highway 1, Vero
Beach FL 32960-5735.
407/567-9064.

Publix Super Markets
101499 Overseas Hwy, Key
Largo FL 33037-4553.
305/451-0808.

Publix Super Markets
2984 S Ridgewood Ave,
Edgewater FL 32141-7527.
904/427-6022.

Publix Super Markets
3740 W Hillsboro Blvd,
Deerfield Beach FL 33442-
9411. 954/481-2266.

Publix Super Markets
5600 W Sample Rd,
Pompano Beach FL 33073-
3423. 954/977-2400.

Publix Super Markets
6900 Daniels Pkwy, Fort
Myers FL 33912-7513.
941/768-2101.

Publix Super Markets
1324 Homestead Rd N,
Lehigh Acres FL 33936-
6016. 941/369-2149.

Publix Super Markets
1719 Apalachee Pkwy,
Tallahassee FL 32301-3009.
904/877-7171.

Publix Super Markets
1795 US Highway 1 S, St
Augustine FL 32086-4238.
904/824-8338.

Publix Super Markets
383 SE 17th St, Ocala FL
34471-4434. 352/368-
2855.

Publix Super Markets
220 N Nova Rd, Ormond
Beach FL 32174-5124.
904/677-0344.

Publix Super Markets
4115 NW 16th Blvd,
Gainesville FL 32605-3505.
352/376-4616.

Publix Super Markets
10019 W Hillsborough Ave,
Tampa FL 33615-3000.
813/886-9300.

Publix Super Markets
4121 W Commercial Blvd,
Tamarac FL 33319-3303.
954/735-0883.

Publix Super Markets
1313 S Dale Mabry Hwy,
Tampa FL 33629-5010.
813/251-8681.

Publix Super Markets
7018 W Waters Ave, Tampa
FL 33634. 813/884-3764.

Publix Super Markets
7230 W Atlantic Blvd,
Margate FL 33063-4214.
954/979-2555.

Publix Super Markets
8450 Lockwood Ridge Rd,
Sarasota FL 34243-2920.
941/351-5856.

Publix Super Markets
871 Vanderbilt Beach Rd,
Naples FL 33963-8710.
941/597-2138.

Publix Super Markets
1500 Placida Rd, Englewood
FL 34223-4955. 941/475-
8823.

Publix Super Markets
540 S Hunt Club Blvd,
Apopka FL 32703-4960.
407/862-5255.

Publix Super Markets
81 Alafaya Woods Blvd,
Oviedo FL 32765-6235.
407/366-8119.

Publix Super Markets
3235 SW Port Saint Lucie
Blvd, Port St Lucie FL
34953-3490. 407/336-
5660.

Publix Super Markets
1420 Highway 41 N,
Inverness FL 34450-2405.
352/344-8990.

Publix Super Markets
3400 N Federal Hwy, Ft
Lauderdale FL 33306-1036.
954/564-9612.

Publix Super Markets
2873 S Orange Ave, Orlando
FL 32806-5403. 407/872-
0395.

Publix Super Markets
5804 Bee Ridge Rd, Sarasota
FL 34233-5051. 941/378-
2111.

Publix Super Markets
4049 13th St, Saint Cloud
FL 34769-6772. 407/957-
1334.

Publix Super Markets
15151 N Dale Mabry Hwy,
Tampa FL 33618-1818.
813/265-3288.

Publix Supermarkets
1980 Osceola Pkwy,
Kissimmee FL 34743-8600.
407/348-8422.

Publix Supermarkets
2724 N Hiawassee Rd,
Orlando FL 32818-3008.
407/298-5013.

Publix Supermarkets
2915 Vineland Rd,

Kissimmee FL 34746-5505.
407/396-7525.

Quick Stop Food Stores
1624 N Washington Blvd,
Sarasota FL 34236-2725.
941/953-3260.

Save-A-Lot Food Stores
1275 1st St S, Winter Haven
FL 33880-3946. 941/294-
8593.

Save-A-Lot Food Stores
2701 S Orlando Dr, Sanford
FL 32773-5311. 407/321-
4901.

Save-A-Lot Food Stores
4225 14th St W, Bradenton
FL 34205-6009. 941/747-
4930.

Save-A-Lot Food Stores
2830 S Bay St, Eustis FL
32726-6537. 904/357-
1999.

Starvin' Marvin Food Store
485 E Main St, Apopka FL
32703-5375. 407/889-
5211.

Starvin' Marvin Food Store
1680 S McCall Rd,
Englewood FL 34223-4848.
941/475-2809.

Starvin' Marvin Food Store
5215 Memphis Rd, Palmetto
FL 34221. 941/729-6288.

Suwannee Swifty Store
1610 S Byron Butler Pkwy,
Perry FL 32347-5433.
904/584-3069.

Suwannee Swifty Store
2002 NW 1st Ave, Ocala FL
34475-9124. 352/867-
1244.

U-Save Supermarket
4407 N Nebraska Ave,
Tampa FL 33603-4146.
813/237-6871.

U-Save Supermarket
328 E Sugarland Hwy,
Clewiston FL 33440-3124.
941/983-6917.

**Vernon Mount Foodway
Supermarket**
9516 Cortez Rd W,
Bradenton FL 34210-1800.
941/794-6455.

Express Lane
1328 Jenks Ave, Panama
City FL 32401-2443.
904/769-8977.

Farm Stores
1695 W Indiantown Rd,
Jupiter FL 33458-4605.
407/744-8059.

Farm Stores
1705 W Hillsborough Ave,
Tampa FL 33603-1130.
813/870-3289.

Farm Stores
5701 N Armenia Ave, Tampa
FL 33603-1019. 813/872-
4498.

Handy Food Store
478 Broad St, Masaryktown
FL 34609-7430. 904/799-
6891.

Happy Store
671 Highway 98 E, Destin
FL 32541-2456. 904/837-
6550.

Hop N Save
1202 W Vine St, Kissimmee
FL 34741-4047. 407/932-
0666.

Joy Food Stores
5315 E Busch Blvd, Tampa
FL 33617-5415. 813/989-
0504.

Majik Market
2835 S Bumby Ave, Orlando
FL 32806-8703. 407/898-
6130.

Mapco Express
834 W Madison St, Starke
FL 32091-3015. 904/964-
8020.

Pick Kwik Food Store
75 Broad St, Masaryktown
FL 34609-7201. 904/799-
0473.

Pick Kwik Food Stores
4307 Calienta St, Spring Hill
FL 34607-3102. 352/596-
6789.

Scotchman Store
18226 Powell Rd, Brooksville
FL 34609-7602. 352/799-
6280.

Sing Food Store
210 E 7th Ave, Tallahassee
FL 32303-5519. 904/681-
3691.

Site Food Mart
4431 53rd Ave E, Bradenton
FL 34203-5549. 941/753-
1275.

Sparky's Of Plant City
101 W Oak St, Wauchula FL
33873-2628. 941/773-
2313.

Step Saver
3414 London Blvd, Cocoa FL
32926. 407/639-6982.

Stop 'N Shop
1070 US Highway 27 N,
Lake Placid FL 33852-9436.
941/699-5720.

Suwannee Swifty
2001 Reid St, Palatka FL
32177-2939. 904/328-
0868.

Food Lion
943 Alt 19, Palm Harbor FL
04682-4348. 813/937-
4909.

IGA Food Villa
1661 Gulf To Bay Blvd,
Clearwater FL 34615-6422.
813/442-5243.

MISC. FOOD STORES

Honeybaked Ham Co.
2924 E Colonial Dr, Orlando
FL 32803-5039. 407/895-
9880.

Colorado Prime Sales
3020 Hartley Rd, Suite 370,
Jacksonville FL 32257-8207.
904/268-3229.

Anna Maria Island Produce
5424 Marina Dr, Bradenton
Beach FL 34217-1763.
941/778-7964.

Oakley Brothers
907 Angle Rd, Fort Pierce FL
34947-1701. 407/567-
4572.

Fannie May Candy Shops
7461 Manatee Ave W,
Bradenton FL 34209-3444.
941/794-1913.

Fanny Farmer Candy Shops
8001 S Orange Blossom
Trail, Orlando FL 32809-
7654. 407/857-5691.

A Healthy Connection
7332 W Waters Ave, Tampa
FL 33634-2222. 813/889-
7262.

Granary Natural Foods
1930 Stickney Point Rd,
Sarasota FL 34231-8849.
941/924-4754.

General Nutrition Center
4961 W Atlantic Ave, Delray
Beach FL 33445-3842.
407/499-8221.

RETAIL BAKERIES

Holsum Bakers
790 E Oakland Park Blvd,
Oakland Park FL 33334-
2748. 954/564-8596.

Merita Thrift Store
2311 28th St N, St
Petersburg FL 33713-4228.
813/321-6364.

Offerdahl's Bagel Gourmet
1164 Weston Rd, Ft
Lauderdale FL 33326-1915.
954/384-6479.

Coastal Cookie Co.
2 Independent Dr, Suite 126,
Jacksonville FL 32202-5016.
904/353-3232.

AUTO DEALERS

Autohaus
744 N Federal Hwy,
Pompano Beach FL 33062-
4303. 954/943-5000.

Bev Smith Ford
1210 Northlake Blvd, Lake
Park FL 33403-2096.
407/845-2900.

Bill Branch Chevrolet
3890 Fowler St, Fort Myers
FL 33901-2602. 941/936-
8561.

Hull Chevrolet
8725 Arlington Expy,
Jacksonville FL 32211-8112.
904/721-1880.

Maher Chevrolet
2901 34th St N, St
Petersburg FL 33713-3636.
813/323-5000.

Massey Cadillac
4241 N John Young Pkwy,
Orlando FL 32804-1919.
407/299-6161.

Palm Automotive Group
1901 Tamiami Trail, Punta
Gorda FL 33950-5917.
941/639-5500.

Paul West Ford
3333 N Main St, Gainesville
FL 32609-2394. 352/376-
5371.

Reeves Import Motorcars
11333 N Florida Ave, Tampa
FL 33612-5665. 813/933-
2811.

Truck & Van Depot
250 S State Road 7,
Plantation FL 33317-3757.
954/584-5566.

Velde Ford
1395 US Highway 1, Vero
Beach FL 32960-5792.
407/569-3400.

Sunshine BMW-Volvo
3141 US Highway 19,
Holiday FL 34691-1843.
813/942-4800.

**Sunshine Chevy Olds Geo
BMW**
43520 US Highway 19 N,
Tarpon Springs FL 34689-
6299. 813/934-5789.

Vista Volkswagen BMW
700 N Federal Hwy, Miami
FL 33146. 305/940-1226.

Fields Cadillac Olds Buick
US Hwy 27 S, Lake Wales FL
33853. 941/676-2503.

**Sullivan Pontiac Cad GMC
Truck**
3230 S Pine Ave, Ocala FL
34471-6618. 352/732-
4700.

Bill Seidle Chevy GEO & Olds
14138 SR 50, Clermont FL
34711. 904/394-6176.

Register Chevrolet & Olds
401 S Broad St, Brooksville
FL 34601-2836. 352/796-
3555.

Boniface Chrysler Dodge
1775 E Merritt Island Cswy,
Merritt Is FL 32952-2662.
407/452-8181.

**Galeana Chrysler Plymouth
Jeep Eagle**
1302 SW Pine Island Rd,
Cape Coral FL 33991-2160.
941/772-3444.

**Sansone Galleria Chrysler
Plymouth**
3701 Northlake Blvd, Lake
Park FL 33403-1629.
407/622-0101.

Al Packer Ford
1530 N Military Trail, West
Palm Beach FL 33409-4792.
407/689-6550.

Cook-Whitehead Ford
730 W 15th St, Panama City
FL 32401-2243. 904/747-
7400.

Ocala Ford Motors
10786 SE US Highway 441,
Belleview FL 34420-3805.
352/245-9181.

Tallahassee Motors
2417 W Tennessee St,
Tallahassee FL 32304-2658.
904/575-4575.

Brandon Honda
9209 Adamo Dr, Tampa FL
33619-2603. 813/664-
1234.

Honda Cars Of Bradenton
5515 14th St W, Bradenton
FL 34207-3602. 941/758-
7997.

Carlisle Hyundai
8390 US Highway 19 N,
Pinellas Park FL 34665-
1709. 813/545-5666.

Stuart Jeep Eagle
2685 S Federal Hwy, Stuart
FL 34994-4534. 407/220-
3600.

Contemporary Cars
810 N Orlando Ave, Winter

Park FL 32789-2922.
407/645-0002.

Norman Brothers Subaru Suzuki
5474 S Orange Blossom Trail, Orlando FL 32839-2706. 407/859-1016.

Arnie Smith Volkswagen
600 W Sunrise Blvd, Ft Lauderdale FL 33311-7236. 954/621-3675.

Saturn Of Fort Myers
4201 Fowler St, Fort Myers FL 33901-2612. 941/939-7474.

Roger Holler Chevrolet GEO
1221 Minnesota Ave, Winter Park FL 32789-4832. 407/628-4747.

Henry Warren Automobiles
20850 NW 2nd Ave, Miami FL 33169-2104. 305/652-9999.

Kendall's Used Car Depot
17120 S Dixie Hwy, Perrine FL 33157-4352. 305/256-6410.

Auto Sales
825A S Yonge St, Ormond Beach FL 32174-7633. 904/677-2955.

OK Used Cars
401 N Dixie Fwy, New Smyrna FL 32168-6705. 904/427-7429.

Fountain Auto Mall
2741 N Orange Blossom Trail, Kissimmee FL 34744-1373. 407/239-0446.

Fountain Motors Wholesale
1406 Sand Lake Rd, Orlando FL 32809-7054. 407/856-0305.

Toyotaland Auto Sales
3190 N Highway 17-92, Sanford FL 32771. 407/322-9695.

CONSUMER SUPPLY STORES

Allied Tire Sales
3320 Maggie Blvd, Suite A, Orlando FL 32811-6607. 407/648-1555.

Technicar
450 Kim Gong Rd, Oldsmar FL 34677. 813/855-0022.

Tire Kingdom
2001 N Congress Ave, Riviera Beach FL 33404-5198. 407/842-4290.

Affordable Auto Repair & Tires
1103 N Washington Blvd,

Sarasota FL 34236-3427. 941/365-1230.

Affordable Auto Repair & Tires
2000 S Bay St, Eustis FL 32726-6355. 904/357-7645.

Auto Air Muffler City
815 E Hillsborough Ave, Tampa FL 33604-7107. 813/238-0451.

Ace Auto Parts
4216 Commercial Way, Spring Hill FL 34606-2325. 352/686-0647.

Ace Auto Parts
5193 73rd Ave, Pinellas Park FL 34665-4352. 813/546-9889.

Action Gator Goodyear Tire Stores
10109 E Colonial Dr, Orlando FL 32817-4330. 407/275-7172.

Allied Discount Tires
1615 S Ridgewood Ave, Daytona Beach FL 32119-2232. 904/756-0055.

Anderson Auto Parts Co.
608 19th Ave W, Bradenton FL 34205-8393. 941/746-4181.

Anderson Auto Parts Co.
2347 17th St, Sarasota FL 34234-1998. 941/955-8107.

Automotive One Parts Stores
2535 S French Ave, Sanford FL 32773-5302. 407/323-7590.

Automotive One Parts Stores
5251 S Highway 17-92, Casselberry FL 32707. 407/831-3323.

Automotive One Parts Stores
704 King St, Cocoa FL 32922-8610. 407/636-3870.

Automotive One Parts Stores
715 N Powers Dr, Orlando FL 32818-6870. 407/293-5393.

Automotive One Parts Stores
736 S Dillard St, Winter Garden FL 34787-3908. 407/877-7118.

Bennett Auto Supply
219 E Indiantown Rd, Jupiter FL 33477-5051. 407/744-2778.

Big A Auto Parts
733 N Magnolia Ave, Ocala FL 34475. 352/732-8680.

Carport Discount Auto Parts
310 W Hwy 90, Crestview FL 32536. 904/689-2481.

Carquest Auto Parts
412 N Duval St, Tallahassee FL 32301-1132. 904/222-8780.

Jessline Enterprises
804 W Baker St, Plant City FL 33566-4428. 813/754-7865.

Lake Shore Radiator & Specialty Auto
5135 Adanson St, Orlando FL 32804-1353. 407/647-5510.

Napa Auto Parts
729 E Sugarland Hwy, Clewiston FL 33440-3214. 941/983-2141.

Napa Auto Parts
5610 US Highway 19, New Port Richey FL 34652-3748. 813/849-2212.

Parts City West
190 Malabar Rd SW, Suite 129, Palm Bay FL 32907-2953. 407/951-8800.

Parts Plus Autostore
6710 N Atlantic Ave, Cape Canaveral FL 32920-3854. 407/799-2330.

Parts Plus Autostore
10821 Satellite Blvd, Orlando FL 32837-8403. 407/857-5855.

Parts Plus Autostore
140 N Banana River Dr, Merritt Is FL 32952-2513. 407/459-1159.

Rose Auto Stores
6136 E Colonial Dr, Orlando FL 32807-3483. 407/658-0182.

Rose Auto Stores
4290 Park Blvd, Pinellas Park FL 34665-3645. 813/544-2176.

Rose Auto Stores
11 W Main St, Apopka FL 32703-5155. 407/886-8822.

Rose Auto Stores
7102 S Military Trail, Lake Worth FL 33463-7812. 407/642-4100.

Rose Auto Stores
2432 S French Ave, Sanford FL 32771. 407/323-1224.

Rose Auto Stores
2791 Davie Blvd, Ft Lauderdale FL 33312-2926. 954/584-2802.

Rose Auto Stores
4125 Gunn Hwy, Tampa FL
33624. 813/960-0001.

Rose Auto Stores
14215 W Colonial Dr, Winter
Garden FL 34787-4208.
407/656-0071.

Steego Auto Parts
4547 Pine Island Rd NW,
Matlacha FL 33909-9780.
941/283-1091.

Western Auto
3842 Sunbeam Rd,
Jacksonville FL 32257-7533.
904/262-0599.

Western Auto
14910 N Dale Mabry Hwy,
Tampa FL 33618-1814.
813/963-0775.

Allied Discount Tires
2201 66th St N, St
Petersburg FL 33710-3921.
813/347-9986.

Discount Auto Parts
3759 S Nova Rd, Port
Orange FL 32119-4233.
904/788-2995.

Discount Auto Parts
1518 Leonid Rd & Dunn Ave,
Jacksonville FL 32218-4799.
904/751-0883.

Belbro Discount Auto Parts
113 W John C Sims Pkwy,
Valparaiso FL 32580.
904/678-9445.

Allied Discount Tires
5825 Beach Blvd,
Jacksonville FL 32207-5164.
904/391-0010.

Allied Discount Tires
9927 Atlantic Blvd,
Jacksonville FL 32225-6507.
904/724-5111.

Allied Discount Tires
13703 N Dale Mabry Hwy,
Tampa FL 33618-2417.
813/963-3616.

Allied Discount Tires
376 Barton Blvd, Rockledge
FL 32955-2708. 407/690-
2245.

Allied Discount Tires
2035 Palm Bay Rd NE, Palm
Bay FL 32905-2916.
407/676-0383.

Allied Discount Tires
18300 US Highway 19 N,
Clearwater FL 34624-1723.
813/530-3656.

Allied Discount Tires
2416 1st St, Bradenton FL
34208-3658. 941/748-
2594.

Don Olson Tire & Auto
Centers
860 Sun Dr, Lake Mary FL
32746-2406. 407/333-
3429.

Norton Tire
755 21st St, Vero Beach FL
32960-5483. 407/567-
1174.

Big 10 Tire Stores
161 N Tyndall Pkwy,
Panama City FL 32404-
6431. 904/769-0261.

Treadco
4111 N John Young Pkwy,
Orlando FL 32804-2699.
407/295-7063.

Tire Kingdom
19571 State Road 7, Boca
Raton FL 33498-4766.
407/477-8210.

Tire Kingdom
5206 Cortez Rd W,
Bradenton FL 34210-2811.
941/792-5958.

Tire Kingdom
1324 N Washington Blvd,
Sarasota FL 34236-2721.
941/365-7098.

Tire Kingdom
7900 49th St N, Clearwater
FL 34622. 813/541-6677.

Tire Kingdom
8650 Seminole Blvd, Largo
FL 34642-3801. 813/391-
9983.

Tire Kingdom
6011 14th St W, Bradenton
FL 34207-4105. 941/753-
4667.

Tire Kingdom
3030 S Congress Ave,
Boynton Beach FL 33426-
9013. 407/737-6500.

Tire Kingdom
3398 34th St N, St
Petersburg FL 33713-2410.
813/527-9555.

Tire Kingdom
7602 W Hillsborough Ave,
Tampa FL 33615-4106.
813/885-1781.

Tire Kingdom
805 State Road 434 W,
Longwood FL 32750-5101.
407/830-5040.

Allied Discount Tires
6000 S Orange Blossom
Trail, Orlando FL 32809-
4608. 407/851-2941.

Allied Discount Tires
4857 Edgewater Dr, Orlando
FL 32804. 407/290-3389.

Allied Discount Tires
3603 S Dale Mabry Hwy,
Tampa FL 33629-8608.
813/870-0701.

Tire Kingdom
750 NE 5th St, Crystal River
FL 34429-4326. 904/795-
9585.

Tire Kingdom
1316 Royal Palm Beach Blvd,
Royal Palm Beach FL 33411-
1604. 407/798-6422.

Tire Kingdom
11350 SE Federal Hwy,
Hobe Sound FL 33455-5207.
407/545-0005.

Tire Kingdom
555 W Indiantown Rd,
Jupiter FL 33458-3540.
407/746-4844.

Tire Kingdom
1633 US Highway 19,
Holiday FL 34691-5602.
813/937-4101.

Tire Kingdom
14777 N Dale Mabry Hwy,
Tampa FL 33618-2025.
813/269-0554.

BOAT DEALERS

E&B Boatgear Discount
Marine
218 Eglin Pkwy NE, Ft
Walton Beach FL 32547-
2857. 904/664-2254.

West Marine
4415 Roosevelt Blvd,
Jacksonville FL 32210-3350.
904/388-7510.

RV DEALERS

Stag-Parkway
3601 Parkway Blvd,
Leesburg FL 34748-9723.
352/728-5077.

MOTORCYCLE DEALERS

Dehart Custom Cycle Design
Group
2187 Siesta Dr, Sarasota FL
34239-5235. 941/365-
1055.

APPAREL AND ACCESSORY
STORES

Dejaiz
3417 E Colonial Dr, Orlando
FL 32803-5157. 407/894-
6917.

Dejaiz
451 E Altamonte Dr,
Altamonte Springs FL
32701-4613. 407/834-
3262.

DJ's Fashion Center For Men
8001 S Orange Blossom
Trail, Orlando FL 32809-
7654. 407/859-6885.

J Riggins
5100 N 9th Ave, Suite
L1105, Pensacola FL 32504-
8765. 904/478-4996.

Levi Outlet By Design
12801 W Sunrise Blvd,
Sunrise FL 33323-2997.
954/846-0581.

Levy-Wolf
Regency Square, Jacksonville
FL 32225. 904/724-4507.

Merry-Go-Round
3302 Dr Martin Luther King
Jr., Tampa FL 33607.
813/879-0923.

S&K Men's Wear
Belz Factory Outlet Mall 11,
Orlando FL 32819. 407/363-
1320.

Structure
1801 Palm Beach Lakes
Blvd, West Palm Beach FL
33401-2009. 407/688-
0021.

Structure
2145 University Square Mall,
Tampa FL 33612-5515.
813/977-5355.

Structure
1610 W Snow Ave, Tampa
FL 33606-2837. 813/251-
2887.

Structure
3501 S Tamiami Trail,
Sarasota FL 34239-6112.
941/366-2001.

Aileen Stores
2791 Peters Rd, Fort Pierce
FL 34945-2620. 407/468-
2059.

Carole Little
5629 Factory Shops Blvd,
Ellenton FL 34222-4112.
941/729-7900.

Catherine's
9782 Atlantic Blvd,
Jacksonville FL 32225-8223.
904/727-9286.

Catherine's
8872 N 56th St, Tampa FL
33617-6206. 813/985-
5504.

Catherine's
1213 Apalachee Pkwy,
Tallahassee FL 32301-4543.
904/878-5197.

Catherine's
2008 66th St N, St

Petersburg FL 33710-4710.
813/341-1717.

Charles Caren
4125 Cleveland Ave, Fort
Myers FL 33901-9000.
941/278-0606.

Clothestime
2056 66th St N, St
Petersburg FL 33710-4710.
813/347-3154.

Colony Shops
3415 Frontage Rd, Tampa FL
33607. 813/287-0077.

County Seat Stores
3302 Dr Martin Luther King
Jr., Tampa FL 33607.
813/876-4776.

Episode
3101 P G A Blvd, Palm
Beach Gardens FL 33410.
407/694-2164.

Express
1700 W New Haven Ave,
Suite 869, Melbourne FL
32904-3919. 407/723-
3257.

Express
2415 N Monroe St,
Tallahassee FL 32303.
904/386-3612.

Fashions Of Orlando
5401 W Oak Ridge Rd,
Orlando FL 32819-9416.
407/345-5622.

First Issue
2400 E Sunrise Blvd, Ft
Lauderdale FL 33304-3102.
954/563-9374.

Frayne Fashions
10601 US Highway 441,
Leesburg FL 34788-7237.
352/360-0362.

Jay Jacobs
451 E Altamonte Dr,
Altamonte Springs FL
32701-4613. 407/830-
8491.

Jay Jacobs
8201 S Tamiami Trail,
Sarasota FL 34238-2966.
941/924-8480.

Jennifer's
7471 Manatee Ave W,
Bradenton FL 34209-3444.
941/792-6695.

Jonathan Logan Outlet
2795 Peters Rd, Fort Pierce
FL 34945-2621. 407/468-
6938.

Jones New York Factory Store
5613 Factory Shops Blvd,

Ellenton FL 34222-4112.
941/729-7276.

Lane Bryant
3302 Tampa Bay Center Unit
200, Tampa FL 33607-
6225. 813/877-2554.

Limited Express
225 Worth Ct N, West Palm
Beach FL 33405-2751.
407/832-4906.

Market Fair
8014 Beach Blvd,
Jacksonville FL 32216-3133.
904/725-8656.

Maurice's
10401 US Highway 441,
Leesburg FL 34788-8786.
352/787-6177.

Mondi International
362B John Ringling Blvd,
Sarasota FL 34236-1321.
941/388-5126.

One Stop Fashions
Sawgrass Mills, Sunrise FL
33323. 954/846-2559.

Patchington
3335 Ocean Dr, Vero Beach
FL 32963-1959. 407/231-
3543.

Patchington
374 Saint Armands Circle,
Sarasota FL 34236-1313.
941/388-2801.

R&Y Fashion and More
4737 S Orange Ave, Orlando
FL 32806-6942. 407/855-
0104.

Rheinauers
P.O. Box 1520, Winter
Haven FL 33882-1520.
941/294-5931.

Scribbles
451 E Altamonte Dr,
Altamonte Springs FL
32701-4613. 407/260-
2640.

Simply 6 Fashions
161 E State Rd 436, Fern
Park FL 32730. 407/339-
3220.

Stuarts
3976 3rd St S, Jacksonville
Beach FL 32250-5847.
904/241-5385.

The Limited
Boca Town Center, Boca
Raton FL 33432. 407/391-
6651.

The Limited
Fashion Square Mall, Orlando
FL 32803. 407/896-3791.

The Limited
Desoto Square Mall,
Bradenton FL 34205.
941/749-1685.

Today's Woman
840 Tyrone Blvd N, St
Petersburg FL 33710-7129.
813/343-0866.

Today's Woman
5139 US Highway 19, New
Port Richey FL 34652-3966.
813/842-4893.

Today's Woman
Edison Mall, Fort Myers FL
33901. 941/939-5191.

Units
6000 Glades Rd, Boca Raton
FL 33431-7204. 407/368-
4157.

Wet Seal
2414 E Sunrise Blvd, Ft
Lauderdale FL 33304-3102.
954/563-4270.

Wet Seal
3302 Dr Martin Luther King
Jr., Tampa FL 33607.
813/876-8808.

Wet Seal
12801 W Sunrise Blvd,
Sunrise FL 33323-2997.
954/846-8606.

Ann Taylor
2149 University Square Mall,
Tampa FL 33612-5515.
813/971-5200.

Afterthoughts
Vero Beach Mall, Vero Beach
FL 32962. 407/770-3221.

Cacique
8201 S Tamiami Trail,
Sarasota FL 34238-2966.
941/924-6898.

Victoria's Secret
2414 E Sunrise Blvd, Ft
Lauderdale FL 33304-3102.
954/564-2165.

Gap Kids
2516 E Sunrise Blvd, Ft
Lauderdale FL 33304-3204.
954/568-1434.

He-Ro Group
5657 Factory Shops Blvd,
Ellenton FL 34222-4112.
941/723-2424.

SBX Dress Barn
12801 W Sunrise Blvd #Z96,
Sunrise FL 33323-2997.
954/846-1013.

Alexander Smith & Company
4 Sawgrass Village Dr, Ponte
Vedra FL 32082-5013.
904/273-0213.

Merle Harmon's Fan Fair
2137 University Square Mall,
Tampa FL 33612-5515.
813/979-0528.

Repp Ltd. Big & Tall Athletic
7939 S Orange Blossom
Trail, Orlando FL 32809-
6903. 407/855-3208.

**Sports Fan Going To The
Game**
3302 Tampa Bay Center
Mall, Tampa FL 33607-
6225. 813/879-1683.

Everything But Water
3419 E Colonial Dr, Orlando
FL 32803-5157. 407/896-
3301.

Swim 'N' Sport
2396 NW 96th Ave, Miami
FL 33172-2323. 305/593-
5071.

Way Cool
201 S Gulfview Blvd,
Clearwater FL 34630-2443.
813/442-7558.

Easyriders
605 Main St, Daytona Beach
FL 32118-4219. 904/238-
1645.

SHOE STORES

Naturalizer Shoes
1700 W New Haven Ave,
Suite 257, Melbourne FL
32904-3919. 407/725-
8425.

Sports A Foot
9802 Baymeadows Rd, Suite
12, Jacksonville FL 32256-
7987. 904/731-3957.

Fayva Shoes
3716 W Oakland Park Blvd,
Ft Lauderdale FL 33311-
1150. 954/733-4251.

Florsheim Shoe Shops
8000 W Broward Blvd, Ft
Lauderdale FL 33388-0024.
954/473-8553.

Florsheim Shoe Shops
Sarasota Square Mall,
Sarasota FL 34238.
941/921-3363.

**Bostonian Hanover Shoe
Outlet**
12801 W Sunrise Blvd,
Sunrise FL 33323-2997.
954/846-8382.

Hanover Shoe Store
1700 W New Haven Ave,
Suite 767, Melbourne FL
32904-3919. 407/724-
5670.

Payless Shoe Source
945 W State Road 436,
Altamonte Springs FL
32714-2918. 407/869-
6890.

Payless Shoe Source
999 E Commercial Blvd,
Oakland Park FL 33334-
3205. 954/101-6396.

Payless Shoe Source
9501 Arlington Expy,
Jacksonville FL 32225.
904/721-1488.

Lady Foot Locker
1500 Apalachee Pkwy,
Tallahassee FL 32301.
904/877-8553.

The Athlete's Foot
3302 Tampa Bay Center Unit
201, Tampa FL 33607-
6225. 813/877-8698.

Easy Spirit Shoe Store
3800 US Highway 98 N,
Suite 638, Lakeland FL
33809-3828. 941/853-
1082.

Red Wing Shoe Store
1133 NW 76th Blvd,
Gainesville FL 32606-6752.
352/332-2912.

Bannister Shoe
Sawgrass Mills Mall, Sunrise
FL 33323. 954/846-0364.

Bannister Shoe
2803 Peters Rd, Fort Pierce
FL 34945-2621. 407/468-
4365.

Bass Shoe Factory Outlet
5700 Okeechobee Blvd,
West Palm Beach FL 33417-
4354. 407/687-8303.

Butler Shoe Corp.
6901 22nd Ave N, St
Petersburg FL 33710.
813/347-0419.

Capezio Factory Direct
12801 W Sunrise Blvd,
Sunrise FL 33323-2997.
954/846-0799.

Cincinnati Shoe Co.
3916 N Dale Mabry Hwy,
Tampa FL 33607. 813/839-
6598.

Dolcis Shoes
801 N Congress Ave,
Boynton Beach FL 33426-
3315. 407/738-0380.

Fashion Footware
1846 Tamiami Trail S, Suite
3, Venice FL 34293-3135.
941/492-9675.

Father & Son Shoe Store
Avenues Mall, Jacksonville
FL 32216. 904/363-1580.

Father & Son Shoe Store
Florida Mall, Orlando FL
32809. 407/851-4623.

Footaction USA
1700 W New Haven Ave,
Suite 935, Melbourne FL
32904-3919. 407/724-
6565.

Footlocker Outlet
3650 W Broward Blvd, Ft
Lauderdale FL 33312-1014.
954/584-0229.

Johnston & Murphy Shop
Towne Center Mall, Boca
Raton FL 33486. 407/392-
9784.

Rack Room Shoes
12801 W Sunrise Blvd,
Sunrise FL 33323-2997.
954/846-0774.

Sas Shoes Store
9965 San Jose Blvd,
Jacksonville FL 32257-5856.
904/268-7823.

Shoe City
3285 Central Ave, St
Petersburg FL 33713-8520.
813/321-8277.

Shoe World
1710 Citrus Blvd, Suite 4,
Leesburg FL 34748-3468.
352/326-5615.

The Shoe Works
1721 N Congress Ave,
Boynton Beach FL 33426-
8205. 407/734-4170.

Unisa Shoe Outlet
Sawgrass Mills, Sunrise FL
33323. 954/846-9279.

FURNITURE STORES

**Badcock Home Furnishing
Centers**
2147 Pembroke Rd,
Hollywood FL 33020-6250.
954/921-2884.

Baers Furniture Co.
1025 Federal Hwy, Dania FL
33004. 954/946-8001.

Big Sandy Showplace
2301 E Main St, Leesburg FL
34748. 352/787-7393.

Clearwater Mattress
4060 Park St N, St
Petersburg FL 33709-4034.
813/343-6899.

Farmers Furniture Co.
2770 US Highway 1 S, St
Augustine FL 32086-6337.
904/797-1582.

Farmers Furniture Co.
657 SE US Highway 19,
Crystal River FL 34429-
4807. 904/795-3733.

Farmers Furniture Co.
2440 S French Ave, Sanford
FL 32771-4276. 407/323-
2132.

Haverty's Fine Furniture
410 S Ware Blvd, Tampa FL
33619-4478. 813/623-
2118.

Heilig-Meyers Furniture
2959 Garden St, Titusville FL
32796-3010. 407/264-
2689.

Heilig-Meyers Furniture
209-211 Reid Ave, Port St
Joe FL 32456. 904/227-
1798.

Kane Furniture Company
2601 E Colonial Dr, Orlando
FL 32803-5022. 407/894-
6666.

New Dawn Futon & Furniture
4984 E Colonial Dr, Orlando
FL 32803-4376. 407/894-
8265.

**Palm Casual Furniture
Products**
11323 Beach Blvd,
Jacksonville FL 32246-3803.
904/641-8308.

Pine Factory
4300 Okeechobee Rd, Fort
Pierce FL 34947-5407.
407/461-0362.

Rhodes Furniture
322 Racetrack Rd, Ft Walton
Beach FL 32547. 904/862-
2184.

Rhodes Furniture
2418 E Colonial Dr, Orlando
FL 32803-5019. 407/898-
0270.

Rhodes Furniture
1318 W 15th St, Panama
City FL 32401-2049.
904/763-1726.

**Roberds Furniture &
Appliance Co.**
116 E Fletcher Ave, Tampa
FL 33612-3407. 813/960-
7704.

Scan Design
5135 N University Dr, Ft
Lauderdale FL 33351-5015.
954/742-4911.

Scan Design Inc. Of Tampa
2905 N Dale Mabry Hwy,
Tampa FL 33607-2414.
813/879-4761.

Sleep-O-Rama
886 S Federal Hwy, Stuart
FL 34994-2939. 407/283-
3141.

The Bombay Company
9501 Arlington Expy,
Jacksonville FL 32225.
904/721-4859.

**Water Bedroom Land
Sleepcenter**
3455 N US 1, Cocoa FL
32926. 407/631-6661.

Beds Beds Beds
4370 N US Hwy 1, Cocoa FL
32927. 407/639-9960.

Mattress Giant Warehouse
1600 NE 12th Terrace, Ft
Lauderdale FL 33305-3131.
954/525-4614.

Waterbed City
524 Northlake Blvd, No Palm
Beach FL 33408-5409.
407/848-2585.

**MISC. HOME FURNISHINGS
STORES**

Beneby's Place
1117 Broadway, Riviera
Beach FL 33404-6924.
407/848-0388.

Color Tile
14306 N Dale Mabry Hwy,
Tampa FL 33618-2052.
813/960-2838.

Color Tile Supermart
1666 N Federal Hwy, Boca
Raton FL 33432-1930.
407/750-7106.

New York Carpet World
S Orange Blossom Trail,
Orlando FL 32837. 407/240-
9881.

New York Carpet World
3770 W New Haven Ave,
Melbourne FL 32904-3532.
407/728-7944.

New York Carpet World
5137 14th St W, Bradenton
FL 34207-2431. 941/755-
8313.

**Sherwin-Williams Home
Builder**
4420 N Hesperides St,
Tampa FL 33614-7619.
813/876-8400.

Farberware
5509 Factory Shops Blvd,
Ellenton FL 34222-4111.
941/722-6835.

Lechters Homestore
1500 Apalachee Pkwy,
Tallahassee FL 32301.
904/877-1311.

Lechters Housewares
Boca Town Center Mall,
Boca Raton FL 33432.
407/750-4017.

Lechters Housewares
Florida Mall, Orlando FL
32809. 407/855-4821.

Lechters Housewares
Orlando Fashion Square,
Orlando FL 32803. 407/895-
0886.

Lechters Housewares
4125 Cleveland Ave, Fort
Myers FL 33901-9000.
941/936-1794.

Lechters Housewares
Sarasota Square Mall,
Sarasota FL 34238.
941/924-4934.

Linen Supermarket
16032 US Highway 19 N,
Clearwater FL 34624-6802.
813/536-8600.

Linen Supermarket
Desoto Center, Bradenton FL
34205. 941/747-5894.

Linen Supermarket
935 N Beneva Rd, Sarasota
FL 34232-1338. 941/957-
0117.

Linen Supermarkets
3908 Britton Plaza, Tampa
FL 33611-1408. 813/831-
0009.

Linen Supermarkets
3904 W Hillsborough Ave,
Tampa FL 33614-5653.
813/870-0804.

Mikasa Factory Store
5661 Factory Shops Blvd,
Ellenton FL 34222-4112.
941/723-2706.

Royal Doulton Direct
5700 Okeechobee Blvd,
West Palm Beach FL 33417-
4354. 407/687-4600.

Rolling Pin Kitchen Emporium
9409 US Highway 19, Suite
641, Port Richey FL 34668-
4636. 813/847-2804.

Salad Master
911 N Main St, Kissimmee
FL 34744-4520. 407/847-
8553.

Galleria Of Lighting
1027 S Dillard St, Winter
Garden FL 34787-3913.
407/877-0422.

**Vertical Blind Manufacturers
Corp.**
1270 N Wickham Rd,
Melbourne FL 32935-8923.
407/255-1300.

Bed Bath & Beyond
12801 W Sunrise Blvd, Suite
615, Ft Lauderdale FL
33323-2965. 954/846-
0020.

Linen Supermarket
3201 N State Road 7, Ft
Lauderdale FL 33319-5614.
954/484-1285.

AG Mauro Co. Of Florida
1105 Sand Pond Rd, Lake
Mary FL 32746-3354.
407/333-0500.

Bath & Body Works
8000 W Broward Blvd, Ft
Lauderdale FL 33388-0024.
954/473-2406.

HOUSEHOLD APPLIANCE STORES

Mariarossi Appliances
7221 N 40th St, Tampa FL
33604-4501. 813/962-
7181.

Sawyer Gas and Appliances
21 Orange Ave S, Green
Cove Springs FL 32043-
3405. 904/284-5813.

Dan's Fan City
1698 10th St SE, Winter
Haven FL 33880-4610.
941/299-2777.

CONSUMER ELECTRONICS STORES

Audio Systems Of Florida
1740 W Fairbanks Ave,
Winter Park FL 32789-4684.
407/644-0447.

Circuit City Superstore
4495 14th St W, Bradenton
FL 34207-1400. 941/758-
2726.

Cruising Tunes
4201 W Colonial Dr, Orlando
FL 32808-8136. 407/290-
6949.

**Osborn Sound &
Communications**
9325 Bay Plaza Blvd #205,
Tampa FL 33619-4405.
813/623-3116.

Rex TV & Appliances
5735 14th St W, Bradenton
FL 34207-4004. 941/755-
1480.

Beyond Electronics
12517 State Road 535,
Orlando FL 32836-6724.
407/827-1265.

Dow Electronics
3305 Bartlett Blvd, Orlando
FL 32811-6401. 407/426-
6822.

Rex TV & Appliance
12905 US Highway 19,
Hudson FL 34667-1746.
813/868-7904.

Rex TV & Stereo
4220 S Washington Ave,
Titusville FL 32780-6642.
407/268-5824.

Rex TV & Stereo
2450 Apalachee Pkwy,
Tallahassee FL 32301-4924.
904/877-0499.

Video Concepts
Gardens Mall, West Palm
Beach FL 33410. 407/775-
5707.

COMPUTER AND SOFTWARE STORES

American Micro Tech
8997 131st Place, Largo FL
34643-1411. 813/581-
3848.

Anixter Brothers
7550 Brokerage Dr, Orlando
FL 32809-5650. 407/240-
1888.

Avnet Computer
541 S Orlando Ave, Suite
203, Maitland FL 32751-
5669. 407/539-1666.

Century Data Systems
3902 Corporex Park Dr,
Suite 600, Tampa FL 33619-
1132. 813/621-4020.

Comp USA
900 Park Centre Blvd, Miami
FL 33169-5367. 954/628-
8503.

**Integrated Computer
Solutions**
7120 NW 72nd Ave, Miami
FL 33166-2932. 954/887-
1733.

MAI Basic Four
4739 NW 45th Ct, Ft
Lauderdale FL 33319-3669.
954/581-2500.

National Data Products
218 E Orange Ave, Lake
Wales FL 33853-3734.
941/676-0087.

Pioneer Technologies
337 S North Lake Blvd, Suite
1000, Altamonte Springs FL
32701-5264. 407/834-
9090.

RCM Data Corp.
1425 Seagrape Circle, Ft
Lauderdale FL 33326-2727.
954/384-4397.

Salcris Systems
5660 W Cypress St, Tampa
FL 33607. 813/287-0302.

Sequent Computer System
1451 NE 62nd St, Ft
Lauderdale FL 33334-5133.
954/938-7040.

Stratus Computer
1200 N Federal Hwy, Boca
Raton FL 33432-2803.
407/392-9239.

The Electronics Boutique
253 N Westshore Blvd,
Tampa FL 33609-1917.
813/286-2807.

Total Tec Systems
10 Central Pkwy, Stuart FL
34994-5901. 407/220-
9929.

General Computer Corp.
13945 Tennyson Dr, Hudson
FL 34667-8519. 813/868-
5008.

**RECORD AND
PRERECORDED TAPE
STORES**

Coconuts District Office
9450 Arlington Expy,
Jacksonville FL 32225-8231.
904/724-0674.

Music 4 Less
5401 W Oak Ridge Rd, Suite
11, Orlando FL 32819-9413.
407/352-7947.

Peaches Music & Video
1500 E Sunrise Blvd, Ft
Lauderdale FL 33304-2327.
954/763-1845.

Peaches Music & Video
2901 E Colonial Dr, Orlando
FL 32803-5037. 407/894-
1700.

Spec's Music
2244 N Congress Ave,
Boynton Beach FL 33426-
8604. 407/364-7460.

Tape World
9501 Arlington Expy,
Jacksonville FL 32225.
904/724-4431.

Saturday Matinee
5100 N 9th Ave, Suite
D407, Pensacola FL 32504-
8768. 904/484-6422.

**Suncoast Motion Picture
Company**
303 US Highway 301 Blvd
W, Bradenton FL 34205-
7955. 941/750-9516.

Spec's Music
4330 44th Ave E, Bradenton
FL 34203. 941/792-4500.

Spec's Music
8025 W Hillsborough Ave,
Tampa FL 33615-4107.
813/885-3343.

Music Express
9409 US Highway 19, Port
Richey FL 34668-4625.
813/841-7748.

Musicland
725 Countryside Mall,
Clearwater FL 34621.
813/796-1498.

Spec's Music
14330 N Dale Mabry Hwy,
Tampa FL 33618-2018.
813/961-1760.

**MUSICAL INSTRUMENT
STORES**

Fletcher Music Center
3100 SW College Rd, Ocala
FL 34474-7446. 352/237-
1331.

DRUG STORES

Joel & Jerry's
7431 114th Ave, Largo FL
34643-5119. 813/545-
5681.

Rite Aid Discount Pharmacies
1931 Knox McRae Dr,
Titusville FL 32780-5360.
407/383-1706.

Rite Aid Discount Pharmacies
Deltona Plaza, Deltona FL
32725. 407/860-1420.

Rite Aid Pharmacies
6755 W Indiantown Rd,
Jupiter FL 33458-3977.
407/743-1736.

Eckerd Drugs
1719 SE Lake Weir Rd,
Ocala FL 34471-5428.
352/629-8745.

Eckerd Drugs
2626 Clint Moore Rd, Boca
Raton FL 33496. 407/994-
2490.

Fedco Drugs
2310 E Sunrise Blvd, Ft
Lauderdale FL 33304-2517.
954/566-8653.

**Florida Retired Persons
Pharmacy**
6500 34th St N, Pinellas
Park FL 34665. 813/522-
0531.

**Pharmacy Corporation Of
America**
2102 Corporate Dr, Boynton
Beach FL 33426-6644.
407/272-4400.

LIQUOR STORES

Bernie Little Distributors
916 NW 12th St, Belle Glade
FL 33430-1702. 407/996-
3864.

ABC Liquors
227 E Altamonte Dr,
Altamonte Springs FL
32701-4326. 407/339-
2141.

ABC Liquors
4477 W Vine St, Kissimmee
FL 34746-5316. 407/396-
0220.

ABC Liquors
6020 N Atlantic Ave, Cape
Canaveral FL 32920-3955.
407/799-0049.

ABC Liquors
5541 Roosevelt Blvd,
Jacksonville FL 32244-2345.
904/389-2605.

ABC Liquors
2885 S Orlando Dr, Sanford
FL 32773-5313. 407/323-
1141.

ABC Liquors
2001 N Dale Mabry Hwy,
Tampa FL 33607-2542.
813/875-6214.

ABC Liquors
3015 W Kennedy Blvd,
Tampa FL 33609-3105.
813/876-5330.

ABC Liquors
2330 E Fletcher Ave, Tampa
FL 33612-9404. 813/971-
2122.

ABC Liquors
4021 W Hillsborough Ave,
Tampa FL 33614-5629.
813/884-7834.

ABC Liquors
7605 SW Highway 200,
Ocala FL 34476-7051.
352/873-3259.

ABC Liquors
13999 W Colonial Dr, Winter
Garden FL 34787-4203.
407/877-8875.

Crown Liquors
910 NW 10th Place, Ft
Lauderdale FL 33311-6199.
954/763-6831.

Delchamp's Liquors
115 Racetrack Rd NW, Ft
Walton Beach FL 32547-
1641. 904/864-3117.

Kash N' Karry Liquor Stores
5201 33rd St E, Bradenton
FL 34203-4329. 941/753-
5774.

Rite Aid Liquors
Boca Green Plaza, Boca
Raton FL 33498. 407/477-
0900.

USED MERCHANDISE STORES

Embassy Boutique
210 Sunset Ave, Palm Beach
FL 33480-3823. 407/832-
8199.

Nearly New Thrift Shop
242 S County Rd, Palm
Beach FL 33480-4252.
407/655-3230.

Parc Resale Stores
551 Central Ave, St
Petersburg FL 33701-3703.
813/821-1057.

Worc Thrift Store
122 Volusia Ave, Daytona
Beach FL 32114. 904/254-
5069.

SPORTING GOODS STORES

Athletic Attic
Sarasota Square Mall,
Sarasota FL 34238.
941/923-3357.

Champs Sports
Sarasota Square Mall,
Sarasota FL 34238.
941/924-1991.

Ron Jon Surf Shop
3850 S Banana River Blvd,
Cocoa Beach FL 32931.
407/799-8888.

Sports Unlimited
2075 Semoran Blvd, Winter
Park FL 32792-2288.
407/679-6100.

Tampa Sports
4545 W Hillsborough Ave,
Tampa FL 33614-5441.
813/886-0591.

The Sports Authority
Sawgrass Mills, Ft
Lauderdale FL 33323.
954/846-9395.

Balimoy-Mulberry
2701 State Road 37 S,
Mulberry FL 33860-8966.
941/425-1745.

Champs Sports
Coastland Center, Naples FL
33940. 941/263-6116.

Good Vibrations
451 E Altamonte Dr,
Altamonte Springs FL
32701-4613. 407/339-
4072.

BOOKSTORES

Book Warehouse
5700 Okeechobee Blvd,
West Palm Beach FL 33417-
4354. 407/478-3568.

Bookstop
8903 Glades Rd, Boca Raton
FL 33434-4019. 407/479-
2114.

Bookstop
303 E Altamonte Dr, Suite
1300, Altamonte Springs FL
32701-4403. 407/339-
6555.

Doubleday Book Shop
1604 W Snow Ave, Tampa
FL 33606-2837. 813/254-
5958.

Bookstop
1135 W New Haven Ave, W
Melbourne FL 32904-4055.
407/722-3662.

STATIONERY AND OFFICE SUPPLY STORES

**Staples The Office
Superstore**
2004 34th St N, St
Petersburg FL 33713-3608.
813/327-2292.

**Staples The Office
Superstore**
3910 W Hillsborough Ave,
Tampa FL 33614-5628.
813/870-6320.

**Staples The Office
Superstore**
6239 Tacoma Dr, Port
Richey FL 34668-4552.
813/841-9942.

Office Max
3001 E Colonial Dr, Orlando
FL 32803-5044. 407/895-
2400.

Tab Products Company
4710 Eisenhower Blvd #B,
Tampa FL 33634-6335.
813/886-6364.

Apex Office Products
2484 Sand Lake Rd, Orlando
FL 32809-7672. 407/856-
4273.

Barnett's Office Supplies
5959 SW 35th Ave, Ft
Lauderdale FL 33312-6347.
954/463-9680.

Office Depot
3251 W Hillsborough Ave,
Tampa FL 33614-5928.
813/877-4233.

Office Depot
8653 Baymeadows Rd,
Jacksonville FL 32256-7423.
904/733-0075.

JEWELRY STORES

Claire's Boutiques
4872 Poseidon Place, Lake
Worth FL 33463-7285.
407/433-4862.

Claire's Boutiques
University Square Mall,
Tampa FL 33612. 813/971-
0827.

Claire's Boutiques
Pinellas Square Mall, Pinellas
Park FL 34665. 813/527-
5197.

Friedman's Jewelers
Altamonte Mall, Altamonte
Springs FL 32701-4613.
407/830-1022.

Friedman's Jewelers
1801 Palm Beach Lakes
Blvd, West Palm Beach FL
33401-2009. 407/683-
9755.

Gold 'N Gifts
1700 Volusia Ave, Daytona
Beach FL 32114. 904/253-
7164.

Gordon's Jewelers
8201 S Tamiami Trail Unit
28, Sarasota FL 34238-
2949. 941/922-8052.

Littman Jewelers
Desoto Square Mall,
Bradenton FL 34205.
941/748-0790.

Lundstrom Jewelers
1750 Tamiami Trail N,
Naples FL 33940-5211.
941/263-4474.

Piercing Pagoda
Orlando Fashion Square,
Orlando FL 32803. 407/896-
7427.

Piercing Pagoda
4300 Okeechobee Rd, Fort
Pierce FL 34947-5407.
407/465-4764.

Piercing Pagoda
Boynton Beach Mall, Boynton
Beach FL 33426. 407/736-
4849.

The Gold Chain Gang
23 Ponce De Leon Ave, St
Augustine FL 32084-4645.
904/794-2375.

Thompson Jewelers
1372 E Vine St, Kissimmee
FL 34744. 407/846-2223.

Whims Outlet
4949 International Dr,
Orlando FL 32819-9400.
407/351-0013.

The Best Of Times
Regency Mall, Jacksonville
FL 32225. 904/721-2662.

Littman Jewelers
Gulfview Square Mall, Port
Richey FL 34668. 813/848-
6086.

HOBBY, TOY, AND GAME SHOPS

Brian Crafts
920 13th St, Saint Cloud FL 34769-4454. 407/892-6232.

Crafts & Stuff
9810 Alt A1A, Palm Beach Gardens FL 33410. 407/694-0750.

Old America Store
1200 N Bermuda Ave, Kissimmee FL 34741-4206. 407/847-7999.

Kay-Bee Toy & Hobbie Shop
6000 Glades Rd, Boca Raton FL 33431-7204. 407/391-1487.

CAMERA AND PHOTOGRAPHIC SUPPLY STORES

Phillips & Jacobs
3800 Commerce Loop, Orlando FL 32808-3818. 407/290-5723.

Ritz Camera
1801 Palm Beach Lakes Blvd, West Palm Beach FL 33401-2009. 407/689-9313.

Ritz Camera
Gulfview Square Mall, Port Richey FL 34668. 813/848-7898.

Ritz Camera
1500 Apalachee Pkwy, Tallahassee FL 32301. 904/878-8694.

GIFT, NOVELTY, AND SOUVENIR SHOPS

Arribas Brothers
P.O. Box 809, Windermere FL 34786-0809. 407/828-4840.

Sandi's Country Corner
375 Piedmont Ct, Bartow FL 33830-4440. 941/533-6601.

The Discount Party Warehouse
13133 N Dale Mabry Hwy, Tampa FL 33618-2405. 813/962-2552.

Exotic Gardens
4651 N Federal Hwy, Boca Raton FL 33431-5133. 407/734-0033.

Card America
130 Clearwater Mall, Clearwater FL 34624-7303. 813/797-7971.

Cracker Barrel Old Country Store
Rte 192 At Scott Rd, Kissimmee FL 34746. 407/396-6521.

East Coast Impex
12444 State Road 535, Orlando FL 32836-6721. 407/239-6222.

Gallery 92
3302 Dr MLK Jr. Blvd W, Tampa FL 33607. 813/876-1093.

Kirkland Governor Square
1500 Apalachee Pkwy, Tallahassee FL 32301. 904/877-9553.

One Stop Discount
5180 W Irlo Bronson Memorial H, Kissimmee FL 34746-5346. 407/396-0676.

Out N Out Gifts
3800 US Highway 98 N, Suite 372, Lakeland FL 33809-3824. 941/853-1646.

Pier 1 Imports
4949 4th St N, St Petersburg FL 33703-3800. 813/528-0017.

Russell's
201 N Franklin St, Tampa FL 33602-5187. 813/223-3305.

Spencer Gifts
8000 W Broward Blvd, Ft Lauderdale FL 33388-0024. 954/370-8507.

The Disney Store
342 Westshore Plaza, Tampa FL 33609. 813/289-0099.

The Paradies Shops
Sarasota-Bradenton Airport, Sarasota FL 34243. 941/359-5371.

Things Remembered
Fashion Square Mall, Orlando FL 32803. 407/894-8500.

Trudy's Hallmark Cards & Gifts
13170 Atlantic Blvd, Suite 41, Jacksonville FL 32225-4150. 904/221-8383.

Welcome Home
12801 W Sunrise Blvd, Sunrise FL 33323-2997. 954/846-1332.

Welcome Home
2735 Peters Rd, Fort Pierce FL 34945-2622. 407/489-6637.

WH Smith Gift Shop
630 Clearwater Park Rd, West Palm Beach FL 33401-6232. 407/832-1811.

WH Smith Gift Shop
9700 International Dr, Orlando FL 32819-8100. 407/354-0330.

The Paper Factory
5549 Factory Shops Blvd, Ellenton FL 34222-4111. 941/722-2481.

Amy's Hallmark Shop
Bardmoor Village Shopping Cent, Largo FL 34647. 813/393-8224.

LUGGAGE AND LEATHER GOODS STORES

Bentley's Luggage & Gifts
Tyrone Square Mall, St Petersburg FL 33710. 813/347-9516.

Bentley's Luggage & Gifts
Gulf View Square Mall, Port Richey FL 34668. 813/842-3747.

SEWING SUPPLIES STORES

Cloth World
544 SE 15th Ave, Boynton Beach FL 33435-6033. 407/734-6324.

Fabric King
801 Dixon Blvd, Cocoa FL 32922-6855. 407/636-4235.

Fabric King
3966 W Hillsborough Ave, Tampa FL 33614-5628. 813/879-3653.

Jo-Ann Fabrics
730 Sand Lake Rd, Orlando FL 32809-7747. 407/850-0636.

Jo-Ann Fabrics
4270 Bee Ridge Rd, Sarasota FL 34233-2563. 941/378-5623.

Piece Good Shop
6621 N Davis Hwy, Pensacola FL 32504-6301. 904/476-0315.

Rag Shop
770 S Military Trail, West Palm Beach FL 33415-3906. 407/689-0411.

Leewards
2010 34th St N, St Petersburg FL 33713-3608. 813/323-4333.

FUEL DEALERS

JA Miles Oil Company
204 State Road 60 E, Plant
City FL 33567-9253.
813/737-3677.

Public Gas Company
8420 NW 52nd St, Miami FL
33166-5314. 305/594-
4510.

Petrolane Gas Service
7224 Highway 90, Milton FL
32583-3044. 904/623-
9021.

Suburban Propane
1351 N US Highway 1,
Titusville FL 32796-2162.
407/267-6411.

OPTICAL GOODS STORES

Lenscrafters
2022 Tampa Bay Center
Mall, Suite, Tampa FL
33607-6227. 813/875-
8474.

Lenscrafters
2508 E Colonial Dr, Orlando
FL 32803-5021. 407/898-
3580.

Eye Centers Of Florida
1441 Tamiami Trail, Punta
Gorda FL 33950-5907.
941/743-2020.

Opti-Mart
4150 Hancock Bridge Pkwy,
Suite 22, Fort Myers FL
33903-4296. 941/656-
5040.

Opti-Mart
4171 Tamiami Trail S,
Venice FL 34293-5111.
941/497-6676.

Opti-Mart
10470 Roosevelt Blvd N, St
Petersburg FL 33716-3820.
813/578-1366.

Opti-World
2526 3rd St S, Jacksonville
Beach FL 32250-6024.
904/247-2374.

Sam's Optical
355 E State Rd 436, Fern
Park FL 32730. 407/260-
1566.

MISC. RETAIL STORES

Smoke & Snuff
Desoto Square Mall,
Bradenton FL 34205.
941/747-9700.

Hearx Ltd.
471 Spencer Dr, West Palm
Beach FL 33409-3675.
407/478-8770.

LM Gunkel
8500 Royal Palm Blvd, Coral
Springs FL 33065-5715.
954/752-9500.

Team Telecom
916 N 7th Ave, Wauchula FL
33873-2015. 941/773-
5777.

Videoconcepts
Sarasota Square Mall,
Sarasota FL 34238.
941/923-3993.

Videoconcepts
133 Clearwater Mall,
Clearwater FL 34624-7303.
813/726-2589.

JE Hanger Inc. Of Florida
305 SW 5th St, Gainesville
FL 32601-6545. 352/372-
8694.

A Rich Sound
1794 N Mills Ave, Orlando
FL 32803-1852. 407/896-
1283.

Beltone Hearing Aid Service
1310 Dunn Ave, Jacksonville
FL 32218-4836. 904/757-
5543.

Lincare
999 Cattlemen Rd Unit B,
Sarasota FL 34232-2849.
941/925-1161.

L'Nard Associates
11236 47th Ave N, St
Petersburg FL 33708.
813/573-1595.

Broedell Plumbing Supply
362 Commerce Way, Suite
108, Longwood FL 32750-
7610. 407/830-6767.

Accessory Place
451 E Altamonte Dr,
Altamonte Springs FL
32701-4613. 407/767-
2565.

PFC Fragrance & Cosmetics
127 Miracle Strip Pkwy SW,
Ft Walton Beach FL 32548-
6614. 904/244-8994.

Roll Shutter & Shade
915 S Dixie Hwy, West Palm
Beach FL 33401-6401.
407/655-5260.

Lagasse Brothers
4719 Distribution Dr, Tampa
FL 33605. 813/247-6669.

Ferguson Enterprises
430 NW Enterprise Dr, Port
St Lucie FL 34986-2201.
407/340-3533.

Gorman Company
1930 W Beaver St,
Jacksonville FL 32209-7564.
904/354-0631.

Gorman Company
4149 Warehouse Ln,
Pensacola FL 32505-4061.
904/434-5669.

Rigorno Sunglass
2414 E Sunrise Blvd, Ft
Lauderdale FL 33304-3102.
954/568-2562.

Sunglass Hut
3302 Tampa Bay Center Unit
107, Tampa FL 33607-
6225. 813/875-4150.

Sunglass Hut
451 E Altamonte Dr,
Altamonte Springs FL
32714-4613. 407/834-
1500.

Sunglass Hut
Southgate Shopping Center,
Sarasota FL 34239.
941/957-1406.

Sunglass Hut Of Florida
2 Independent Dr, Suite 145,
Jacksonville FL 32202-5016.
904/634-4756.

VIDEO TAPE RENTAL

American Video Network
1032 Montgomery Rd,
Altamonte Springs FL
32714-7420. 407/774-
9119.

American Video Network
1355 E Vine St, Kissimmee
FL 34744-3602. 407/931-
0005.

Turtle's Music & Video
9550 Baymeadows Rd,
Jacksonville FL 32256-0710.
904/448-0140.

Video Express
1387 S Babcock St,
Melbourne FL 32901-3068.
407/951-9444.

Video Library
6033 26th St W, Bradenton
FL 34207-4402. 941/755-
0464.

Video Library
7051 Manatee Ave W,
Bradenton FL 34209-2256.
941/795-8988.

For more information on career opportunities in retail:

Associations

INTERNATIONAL ASSOCIATION OF CHAIN STORES
3800 Moor Place, Alexandria VA 22305. 703/549-4525.

INTERNATIONAL COUNCIL OF SHOPPING CENTERS
665 Fifth Avenue, New York NY 10022. 212/421-8181. Offers conventions, research, education, a variety of publications, and awards programs.

NATIONAL AUTOMOTIVE DEALERS ASSOCIATION
8400 Westpark Drive, McLean VA 22102. 703/821-7000.

NATIONAL INDEPENDENT AUTOMOTIVE DEALERS ASSOCIATION
2521 Brown Boulevard, Suite 100, Arlington TX 76006. 817/640-3838.

NATIONAL RETAIL FEDERATION
325 7th Street NW, Suite 1000, Washington DC 20004. 202/783-7971. Provides information services, industry outlooks, and a variety of educational opportunities and publications.

Directories

AUTOMOTIVE NEWS MARKET DATA BOOK
Automotive News, Crain Communication, 1400 Woodbridge Avenue, Detroit MI 48207-3187. 313/446-6000.

STONE, CLAY, GLASS AND CONCRETE PRODUCTS

Growth in stone, clay, glass, concrete and related materials is closely tied to the success of the construction industry. On one hand, analysts believe that the fortunes of the construction industry should remain solid in the short-term, despite the added pressure of higher interest rates and an economy that has begun to cool from its torrid pace of growth in 1994 and early 1995. On the other, the longer-term forecast is for much slower growth, since infrastructure construction is dependent on shrinking local government budgets. All in all, the stone, clay, glass and concrete industry should see revenue growth of about 1 to 2 percent annually.

ALUMA SYSTEMS
6402 East Hanna Avenue, Tampa FL 33610. **Toll free phone:** 800/282-9199. **Contact:** Human Resources. **Description:** A supplier of concrete forming accessories. **Common positions include:** Manufacturer's/Wholesaler's Sales Rep. **Educational backgrounds include:** Business Administration; Construction; Marketing. **Benefits:** Disability Coverage; Life Insurance; Medical Insurance; Profit Sharing; Tuition Assistance. **Operations at this facility include:** Sales.

AMERICAN FLAT GLASS DISTRIBUTORS, INC. (AFGD)
6600 Suemac Place, Jacksonville FL 32254. 904/786-6611. **Fax:** 904/781-9779. **Contact:** Stan Mesnik, Branch Manager. **Description:** Founded in the early 1960's, AFGD specializes in architectural insulated glass units and custom tempering. The company was originally founded as Southern Wholesale Glass, Inc. In 1983, AFG Industries, Inc. purchased Southern Wholesale Glass, Inc. and changed its name to American Flat Glass Distributors. Today, AFGD manufactures a complete line of insulated glass units for commercial and residential applications. Products include clear, tint, and reflective glass; wire glass; and equipment for the handling, storage, and transportation of glass. A customized order entry system allows orders to be processed upon receipt and shipped the following day. There are 19 AFGD locations throughout the United States in metropolitan areas, with the largest facilities at Marietta, Georgia and Opelousas, Louisiana. **Subsidiary:** AFGD Canada. **Common positions include:** Blue-Collar Worker Supervisor; Branch Manager; Clerical Supervisor; Credit Manager; Customer Service Representative; Industrial Engineer; Industrial Production Manager; Management Trainee; Manufacturer's/Wholesaler's Sales Rep.; Mechanical Engineer; Metallurgical Engineer; Operations/Production Manager. **Educational backgrounds include:** Business Administration; Engineering; Finance; Marketing; Sales. **Benefits:** 401K; Disability Coverage; Life Insurance; Medical Insurance; Profit Sharing; Savings Plan; Tuition Assistance. **Corporate headquarters location:** Atlanta GA. **Other U.S. locations:** Nationwide. **Parent company:** AFG Industries. **Operations at this facility include:** Manufacturing; Sales. **Number of employees at this location:** 75. **Number of employees nationwide:** 1,000.

ANCHOR GLASS CONTAINER CORPORATION
One Anchor Plaza, 4343 Anchor Plaza Parkway, Tampa FL 33634. 813/884-0000. **Contact:** Director of Personnel. **Description:** A manufacturer of glass containers. **Common positions include:** Accountant/Auditor; Administrator; Attorney; Buyer; Chemical Engineer; Civil Engineer; Computer Programmer; Credit Manager; Customer Service Representative; Department Manager; Draftsperson; Electrical/Electronics Engineer; Financial Analyst; General Manager; Human Resources Specialist; Industrial Engineer; Management Trainee; Manufacturer's/Wholesaler's Sales Rep.; Mechanical Engineer; Metallurgical Engineer; Purchasing Agent and Manager; Quality Control Supervisor; Systems Analyst; Transportation/Traffic Specialist. **Educational backgrounds include:** Accounting; Business Administration; Communications; Computer Science; Engineering; Finance; Liberal Arts. **Benefits:** Dental Insurance; Disability Coverage; Life Insurance; Medical Insurance; Pension Plan; Savings Plan;

Tuition Assistance. **Corporate headquarters location:** This Location. **Other U.S. locations:** Jacksonville FL. **Operations at this facility include:** Administration. **Listed on:** New York Stock Exchange. **Number of employees nationwide:** 6,900.

ANCHOR GLASS CONTAINER CORPORATION
2121 Huron Street, Jacksonville FL 32254. 904/786-1010. **Contact:** Manager of Personnel Services. **Description:** A manufacturer of glass containers. **Common positions include:** Accountant/Auditor; Customer Service Representative; Department Manager; Electrical/Electronics Engineer; General Manager; Industrial Engineer; Manufacturer's/Wholesaler's Sales Rep.; Mechanical Engineer; Metallurgical Engineer; Operations/Production Manager; Purchasing Agent and Manager; Quality Control Supervisor; Supervisor; Transportation/Traffic Specialist. **Educational backgrounds include:** Accounting; Business Administration; Engineering. **Benefits:** Dental Insurance; Disability Coverage; Life Insurance; Medical Insurance; Pension Plan; Savings Plan; Tuition Assistance. **Corporate headquarters location:** Tampa FL.

APAC-FLORIDA INC.
P.O. Box 2579, Sarasota FL 34230. 941/355-7178. **Contact:** Human Resources. **Description:** A manufacturer of asphalt.

DEVCON INTERNATIONAL CORPORATION
1350 East Newport Center, Deerfield FL 33442. 954/429-1500. **Contact:** Personnel. **Description:** Manufactures heavy construction and concrete products. **Number of employees at this location:** 638.

FLORIDA CRUSHED STONE COMPANY
P.O. Box 490300, Leesburg FL 34749-0300. 352/787-0608. **Contact:** Emmett Crews, Human Resource Manager. **Description:** A minerals-processing and stone-crushing plant.

FLORIDA ROCK INDUSTRIES, INC.
155 East 21st Street, Jacksonville FL 32206. 904/355-1781. **Contact:** Bob Banks, Director of Human Resources. **Description:** A mining, concrete production, and heavy-hauling operation. **Common positions include:** Accountant/Auditor; Administrator; Civil Engineer; Credit Manager; Department Manager; General Manager; Geologist/Geophysicist; Mining Engineer; Systems Analyst. **Educational backgrounds include:** Business Administration; Computer Science; Engineering; Geology. **Benefits:** Dental Insurance; Disability Coverage; Employee Discounts; Life Insurance; Medical Insurance; Profit Sharing; Savings Plan; Tuition Assistance. **Corporate headquarters location:** This Location. **Operations at this facility include:** Administration. **Listed on:** American Stock Exchange.

FLORIDA TILE
P.O. Box 447, Lakeland FL 33802. 941/687-7171. **Contact:** Personnel Director. **Description:** A manufacturer of ceramic wall and floor tiles.

HARDRIVES INC.
2350 South Congress Avenue, Delray Beach FL 33445-7398. 407/278-0456. **Contact:** Osvaldo Vidal, Personnel Director. **Description:** A manufacturer of paving rouxes and related materials. **Common positions include:** Accountant/Auditor. **Benefits:** Medical Insurance; Pension Plan; Profit Sharing. **Number of employees at this location:** 400.

MONIER ROOF TILE INC.
135 Northwest 20th Street, Boca Raton FL 33431. 407/485-9940. **Contact:** Human Resources. **Description:** A manufacturer of concrete roof tile.

RMC-EWELL INDUSTRIES, INC.
P.O. Box 3858, Lakeland FL 33802. 941/688-5787. **Contact:** Khakie Maulden, Personnel Manager. **Description:** Produces concrete products, including ready-mix concrete, and concrete pipe. **Common positions include:** Accountant/Auditor; Administrator; Blue-Collar Worker Supervisor; Computer Programmer; Credit Manager; General Manager; Management Trainee; Manufacturer's/Wholesaler's Sales Rep.; Operations/Production Manager; Purchasing Agent and Manager; Quality Control Supervisor; Systems Analyst. **Educational backgrounds include:** Accounting; Business Administration; Communications; Finance. **Benefits:** Dental Insurance; Disability Coverage; Life Insurance; Medical Insurance; Pension Plan; Savings Plan; Tuition Assistance. **Special Programs:** Training Programs. **Parent company:** RMC Industries

Corporation. **Operations at this facility include:** Administration; Manufacturing; Sales; Service. **Number of employees at this location:** 300.

RANGER CONSTRUCTION INDUSTRIES
P.O. Box 15065, West Palm Beach FL 33416. 407/793-9400. **Contact:** Barbara Ritchy, Personnel Director. **Description:** A manufacturer of paving mixes and related materials.

RINKER MATERIALS CORPORATION
1501 Belvedere Road, West Palm Beach FL 33406-4635. 407/833-5555. **Contact:** Tim Dugan, Area Personnel Manager. **Description:** A manufacturer and supplier of assorted concrete, cement, and aggregate products. **Common positions include:** Accountant/Auditor; Attorney; Buyer; Civil Engineer; Computer Programmer; Department Manager; Draftsperson; Electrical/Electronics Engineer; Human Resources Specialist; Industrial Engineer; Management Trainee; Quality Control Supervisor. **Educational backgrounds include:** Accounting; Business Administration; Engineering; Liberal Arts. **Benefits:** Disability Coverage; Employee Discounts; Life Insurance; Medical Insurance; Pension Plan; Profit Sharing; Savings Plan; Tuition Assistance. **Corporate headquarters location:** This Location. **Parent company:** CSR America. **Operations at this facility include:** Administration; Divisional Headquarters; Regional Headquarters.

WATER BONNET MANUFACTURING INC.
350 Anchor Road, Casselberry FL 32707. 407/831-2122. **Contact:** Human Resources. **Description:** A manufacturer of windshields for boats and Caterpillar tractors, as well as canvas tops for boats.

Note: Because addresses and telephone numbers of smaller companies change rapidly, we recommend you call each company to verify the information below before inquiring about job opportunities. Mass mailings are not recommended.

Additional employers with under 250 employees:

CRUSHED AND BROKEN STONE

Florida Crushed Stone Company
11430 Camp Mine Rd, Brooksville FL 34601-8605. 352/796-3522.

SAND AND GRAVEL

Tarmac Florida
11000 NW 121st Way, Miami FL 33178-1009. 305/823-8800.

MISC. MINERALS

Marcona Ocean Industries
30 Skyline Dr, Lake Mary FL 32746-6238. 407/444-0410.

ASPHALT

Atlantic Coast Asphalt Company
5154 Edwards St, Jacksonville FL 32205. 904/786-1020.

Community Asphalt Corp.
14007 NW 186th St, Hialeah FL 33015-6451. 305/432-0804.

Gator Asphalt Co.
P.O. Box 20309, Bradenton FL 34203. 941/355-9306.

Golden Triangle Asphalt Paving
12625 40th St N, Clearwater FL 34622-4237. 813/573-3027.

Halifax Paving
860 Hull Rd, Ormond Beach FL 32174. 904/676-0200.

GAF Building Materials Corp.
5138 Madison Ave, Tampa FL 33619. 813/248-6202.

GLASS AND GLASS PRODUCTS

Seasonshield
355 Center Ct, Venice FL 34292. 941/497-1984.

Glass Container
2222 W Bella Vista St, Lakeland FL 33809-0601. 941/680-4800.

CEMENT

Lafarge Corporation
1111 N Westshore Blvd, Suite 305, Tampa FL 33607-4701. 813/872-7777.

Rinker Materials Corp.
1200 NW 137th Ave, Miami FL 33182-1803. 305/221-7645.

Rinker Portland Cement Corporation
P.O. Box 650679, Miami FL 33265-0679. 305/221-7645.

Southdown Inc. Brooksville
16301 Ponce De Leon Blvd, Brooksville FL 34614-0849. 352/796-7241.

POTTERY PRODUCTS

Gale Group Molding Division
2710 N Bermuda Ave, Kissimmee FL 34741-1266. 407/239-8850.

CONCRETE, GYPSUM, AND PLASTER PRODUCTS

Florida Rock Industries
P.O. Box 277, Estero FL 33928-0277. 941/267-3500.

Pioneer Concrete Tile
1340 SW 34th Ave, Deerfield Beach FL 33442-8141. 954/421-2077.

Sunshine Materials
1422 Railroad Ave, Eustis FL
32726-5480. 904/589-
7771.

Capitol Concrete
700 Palmetto St,
Jacksonville FL 32202-2499.
904/354-8281.

Coreslab Structures
10501 NW 121st Way,
Miami FL 33178-1011.
305/823-8950.

Crom Corporation
250 SW 36th Terrace,
Gainesville FL 32607-2889.
352/372-3436.

Dura-Stress
11325 County Road 44,
Leesburg FL 34788-2615.
352/787-1422.

Ewell Industries
971 Baker Ave, Jacksonville
FL 32209. 904/353-9616.

FECP Corporation
6324 County Road 579,
Seffner FL 33584-3006.
813/621-4641.

Finfrock Industries
2542 Apopka Blvd, Orlando
FL 32860. 407/293-4320.

Florida Rock & Sand
P.O. Box 3004, Florida City
FL 33034. 305/247-3011.

Gate Concrete Co.
402 Heckscher Dr,
Jacksonville FL 32226-2604.
904/757-0860.

Mack Concrete Industries
23902 County Road 561,
Astatula FL 34705-9420.
904/742-2333.

**Southeastern Prestressed
Concrete**
860 Benoist Farms Rd, West
Palm Beach FL 33411-3749.
407/793-1177.

Southern Culvert
4202 Sydney Rd, Plant City
FL 33567-1193. 813/752-
5138.

Taylor Precast
4190 US Highway 17 S,
Green Cove Springs FL
32043-8137. 904/284-
3213.

Florida Rock Industries
5920 W Linebaugh Ave,
Tampa FL 33625-5613.
813/962-3213.

Krehling Industries
1425 Wiggins Pass Rd E,
Naples FL 33963-1371.
941/597-3162.

Schwab Ready Mix
P.O. Box 4727, Fort Myers
FL 33918-4727. 941/574-
4252.

Sunshine Materials
2461 E Gulf To Lake Hwy,
Inverness FL 34453-3232.
352/726-1071.

Tampa Block Plant
9117 Florida Mining Blvd,
Tampa FL 33634-1234.
813/886-1721.

Tarmac Florida
500 N Maitland Ave, Suite
310, Maitland FL 32751-
4463. 407/647-6997.

Thomas Concrete Of Florida
5800 SW 127th Ave, Miami
FL 33183-1475. 305/592-
9797.

CUT STONE AND STONE PRODUCTS

Limerock Industries
Hwy 19 N, Chiefland FL
32626. 904/493-1447.

Rinker Materials Corp.
P.O. Box 5230, Hialeah FL
33014-1230. 305/821-
5661.

Rinker Materials Corp.
4001 Isle Of Capri Rd, Bonita
Springs FL 33923. 941/992-
1400.

Rozzo
17200 Pines Blvd, Pembroke
Pines FL 33029-1505.
954/435-8501.

EARTH AND MINERALS

Floridin Company
1101 N Madison St, Quincy
FL 32351-9646. 904/627-
7688.

MINERAL WOOL

AVL Systems
5540 SW 6th Place, Ocala
FL 34474-9372. 352/854-
1170.

For more information on career opportunities in stone, clay, glass and concrete products:

Associations

THE AMERICAN CERAMIC SOCIETY
735 Ceramic Place, Westerville OH 43081.
614/890-4700. Offers a variety of
publications, meetings, information, and
educational services. Also operates Ceramic
Futures, an employment service with a
resume database.

NATIONAL GLASS ASSOCIATION
8200 Greensboro Drive, Suite 802, McLean
VA 22102. 703/442-4890.

Magazines

GLASS MAGAZINE
National Glass Association, 8200
Greensboro Drive, McLean VA 22102.
703/442-4890.

ROCK PRODUCTS
MacLean Hunter Publishing Company, 29
North Wacker Drive, Chicago IL 60606.
312/726-2805.

TRANSPORTATION

According to Labor Department estimates the number of jobs in the air transportation industry will increase faster than average. Passenger and cargo traffic should increase in response to a rise in population, incomes and business activity. Employment in other air transport activities will also increase as more aircraft are purchased for business, agriculture and recreation. Despite this expected growth, jobseekers should expect strong competition as the number of applicants for airline jobs exceeds the number of jobs available. Not only are airline jobs highly sought after, but the industry has been going through a period of consolidation, and today more and more of the business is concentrated with a handful of the major carriers, such as American, Delta, and USAir.

In the trucking and warehousing industry, the number of jobs created is very closely related to the health of the national economy. Competition in the industry is intense, both among truckers and with the railroads. Trucking companies compete by slashing rates or offering more customized service. Motor carriers must quote rates high enough to cover costs but low enough to remain competitive. Still, job opportunities for truckers are expected to be good. In some areas, companies have had trouble recruiting well-trained drivers. Although some routes have switched to intermodal transportation and recent downturns in the economy have eased some driver shortages, turnover is relatively high. That should ensure a steady supply of jobs.

On the railroads, the use of both freight and passenger rail will climb. And according to the U.S. Commerce Department, increased trade and stronger freight rates should help the performance of U.S. flag liner companies operating in the Asian markets. Domestic use of water transportation should also increase, especially between Alaska and the lower 48 states.

AAA/AMERICAN AUTOMOBILE ASSOCIATION
1000 AAA Drive, Heathrow FL 32746-5063. 407/444-7537. **Fax:** 407/444-7504. **Recorded Jobline:** 407/444-7500. **Contact:** Karen Wall. Human Resources. **Description:** AAA provides travel services, motoring services, insurance, and financial and banking services. **Common positions include:** Accountant/Auditor; Administrative Assistant; Advertising Clerk; Architect; Attorney; Blue-Collar Worker Supervisor; Branch Manager; Budget Analyst; Buyer; Claim Representative; Clerical Supervisor; Computer Programmer; Computer Systems Analyst; Counselor; Credit Manager; Customer Service Representative; Draftsperson; Economist/Market Research Analyst; Editor; Education Administrator; Financial Analyst; General Manager; Human Resources Specialist; Insurance Agent/Broker; Librarian; Library Technician; Management Trainee; Public Relations Specialist; Purchasing Agent and Manager; Restaurant/Food Service Manager; Services Sales Representative; Stationary Engineer; Statistician; Technical Writer/Editor; Travel Agent; Underwriter/Assistant Underwriter. **Educational backgrounds include:** Accounting; Art/Design; Business Administration; Communications; Computer Science; Economics; Finance; Liberal Arts; Marketing. **Benefits:** Disability Coverage; Employee Discounts; Life Insurance; Medical Insurance; Paid Vacation; Pension Plan; Savings Plan; Tuition Assistance. **Corporate headquarters location:** This Location. **Other U.S. locations:** District of Columbia; Virginia; Maryland; New Hampshire; Massachusetts; Louisiana; Mississippi; Texas; Wisconsin; Wyoming;

Oklahoma; Alabama; New Mexico. **Number of employees at this location:** 1,100. **Number of employees nationwide:** 33,000.

ALAMO RENT-A-CAR
P.O. Box 22776, Fort Lauderdale FL 33335. 954/522-0000. **Contact:** Edmiree Hall, Manager, Recruitment and Selection. **Description:** Alamo Rent-a-Car is one of the nation's largest car rental companies. **Common positions include:** Accountant/Auditor; Computer Programmer; Customer Service Representative; Financial Analyst; Secretary. **Educational backgrounds include:** Accounting; Business Administration; Computer Science; Finance; Marketing. **Benefits:** 401K; Dental Insurance; Employee Discounts; Life Insurance; Medical Insurance; Tuition Assistance. **Corporate headquarters location:** This Location. **Operations at this facility include:** Administration. **Listed on:** Privately held.

ALTERMAN TRANSPORT LINES
P.O. Box 425, Opa Locka FL 33054. 305/688-3571. **Contact:** Personnel. **Description:** An interstate trucking company.

ARROW AIR, INC.
P.O. Box 02062, Miami FL 33102-6062. 305/526-0900. **Contact:** Jean Tucker, Manager of Personnel. **Description:** An air cargo carrier service. **Common positions include:** Administrator; Aerospace Engineer; Flight Attendant; Mechanical Engineer; Operations/Production Manager; Pilot.

ATLANTIC MARINE & DRYDOCK CORPORATION
8500 Heckscher Drive, Jacksonville FL 32226. 904/251-3164. **Contact:** Mr. T.J. Welsh, Personnel Manager. **Description:** A ship repair and construction firm.

BERTRAM YACHT, INC.
3663 North West 21st Street, Miami FL 33142. 305/633-8011. **Fax:** 305/635-9953. **Contact:** Ursula Medero, Personnel Administrator. **Description:** A manufacturer of yachts. **Common positions include:** Buyer; Computer Programmer; Computer Systems Analyst; Draftsperson; Electrical/Electronics Engineer; Electrician; Financial Analyst; Human Resources Specialist; Mechanical Engineer; Operations/Production Manager; Quality Control Supervisor; Structural Engineer; Systems Analyst. **Educational backgrounds include:** Accounting; Engineering; Finance; Marketing. **Benefits:** Dental Insurance; Disability Coverage; Life Insurance; Medical Insurance; Pension Plan; Savings Plan; Tuition Assistance. **Corporate headquarters location:** This Location. **Parent company:** Bertram, Inc. **Operations at this facility include:** Divisional Headquarters; Manufacturing. **Number of employees at this location:** 239.

BIRDSALL INC.
821 Avenue E, West Palm Beach FL 33404-7598. 407/881-3956. **Contact:** Human Resources. **Description:** Involved in import services including boat trailer loading.

BLACKBEARD CRUISES
P.O. Box 661091, Miami Springs FL 33266. **Contact:** Human Resources. **Description:** A cruise line that sails to the Bahamas. **Common positions include:** Automotive Mechanic/Body Repairer; Chef/Cook/Kitchen Worker.

CSX CORPORATION
500 Water Street, Jacksonville FL 32202-4423. 904/237-2000. **Contact:** Human Resources. **Description:** An operator of a freight railroad.

CARNIVAL CORPORATION
Carnival Place, 3655 Northwest 87 Avenue, Miami FL 33178-2428. 305/599-2600. **Contact:** Human Resources. **Description:** Carnival Corporation and its subsidiaries operate three separate multinight cruise lines under the names Carnival Cruise Lines, Holland America Line, and Windstar Cruises and a tour business, Holland America Westours. Carnival Cruise Lines operates nine cruise ships serving the Caribbean and Mexican Riviera, Holland America Line operates seven cruise ships serving primarily the Caribbean and Alaska and through the Panama Canal, and Windstar Cruises operates three sail-powered vessels which call on locations inaccessible to larger ships. Holland America Westours markets sight-seeing tours both separately and as a part of Holland America Line cruise/tour packages. During the past few years, Carnival Corporation has seen an increase in revenues as a result of the expansion of its fleet capacity; however, its businesses experience varying degrees of seasonality with greater demand occurring during the periods from late December through April and the

summer months. **Corporate headquarters location:** This Location. **Listed on:** New York Stock Exchange.

CELEBRITY CRUISES
5200 Blue Lagoon Drive, Miami FL 33126. 305/262-6677. **Contact:** Human Resources. **Description:** An ocean cruise line.

COMMODORE CRUISE LINE
800 Douglas Road, Suite 700, Coral Gables FL 33134. 305/529-3000. **Contact:** Human Resources. **Description:** An ocean cruise line.

COSTA CRUISES
80 SW 8th Street, Suite 2700, Miami FL 33130. 305/358-7325. **Contact:** Human Resources. **Description:** An ocean cruise line.

CROWLEY MARITIME CORPORATION
P.O. Box 2110, Jacksonville FL 32203-2110. 904/727-2200. **Contact:** Personnel Manager. **Description:** An ocean freight company.

CUSTOMIZED TRANSPORTATION, INC.
10407 Centurion Parkway North, Suite 400, Jacksonville FL 32256. 904/928-1400. **Contact:** Personnel Department. **Description:** A trucking and contract carrying company.

DOLPHIN CRUISE LINE
P.O. Box 025420, Miami FL 33102-5420. 305/358-5122. **Contact:** Human Resources. **Description:** An ocean cruise line.

DYNAIR TECH OF FLORIDA
P.O. Box 6063, Miami FL 33102-6063. 305/871-6650. **Contact:** Personnel Department. **Description:** A repair station for aircraft.

FLORIDA EAST COAST RAILWAY COMPANY
P.O. Box 1048, St. Augustine FL 32085-1048. 904/829-3421. **Contact:** Gloria S. Taylor, Personnel Administrator. **Description:** A railway transportation company. **Common positions include:** Clerk; Engineer; Human Resources Specialist; Transportation/Traffic Specialist. **Benefits:** Life Insurance; Medical Insurance. **Corporate headquarters location:** This Location. **Operations at this facility include:** Administration. **Number of employees at this location:** 200. **Number of employees nationwide:** 1,480.

GALAPAGOS, INC.
7800 Red Road, Suite 112, South Miami FL 33143. 305/665-0841. **Contact:** Human Resources. **Description:** An ocean cruise line.

LAND SPAN, INC.
1120 West Griffin Road, Lakeland FL 33805. 941/688-1102. **Contact:** Human Resources. **Description:** A company providing irregular-route transport of dry and refrigerated freight. **Common positions include:** Administrator; Computer Programmer; Credit Manager; Customer Service Representative; Department Manager; Human Resources Specialist; Operations/Production Manager; Services Sales Representative; Transportation/Traffic Specialist. **Educational backgrounds include:** Business Administration; Communications; Computer Science; Finance; Marketing; Mathematics. **Benefits:** Dental Insurance; Disability Coverage; Employee Discounts; Life Insurance; Medical Insurance; Pension Plan; Profit Sharing; Savings Plan; Tuition Assistance. **Special Programs:** Training Programs. **Corporate headquarters location:** This Location. **Other U.S. locations:** Norcross GA; Chicago IL; Hagerstown MD; Charlotte NC; El Paso TX; Fort Worth TX. **Parent company:** Watkins Associated Industries, Inc. **Number of employees at this location:** 300.

LUHRS CORPORATION
255 Diesel Road, St. Augustine FL 32086. 904/829-0500. **Fax:** 904/829-0683. **Contact:** Judy Caputo, Personnel Manager. **Description:** A manufacturer of fiberglass boats ranging from 25 feet to 47 feet. **Common positions include:** Automotive Mechanic/Body Repairer; Blue-Collar Worker Supervisor; Buyer; Carpenter; Customer Service Representative; Draftsperson; Electrician; Industrial Engineer; Mechanical Engineer. **Benefits:** 401K; Dental Insurance; Life Insurance; Medical Insurance; Paid Vacation; Prescription Drugs. **Corporate headquarters location:** This Location.

Operations at this facility include: Administration; Manufacturing; Sales; Service.
Number of employees at this location: 375.

McKENZIE TANK LINES, INC.
P.O. Box 1200, Tallahassee FL 32302. 904/576-1221. **Contact:** Sarah Gainey,
Personnel Director. **Description:** An interstate trucking company.

NORTH FLORIDA SHIPYARDS, INC.
P.O. Box 3255, Jacksonville FL 32206. 904/354-3278. **Contact:** Bob McNicholas,
Personnel Director. **Description:** A shipyard.

NORWEGIAN CRUISE LINES
95 Merrick Way, Coral Gables FL 33134. 305/447-9660. **Contact:** Human Resources.
Description: An ocean cruise line.

P-I-E NATIONWIDE, INC.
P.O. Box 44034, Jacksonville FL 32231. 904/731-0580. **Contact:** Vice
President/Human Resources. **Description:** An interstate freight company.

PEARL CRUISE LINES
6301 NW 5th Way, Suite 4000, Fort Lauderdale FL 33309. 954/772-8600. **Contact:**
Human Resources. **Description:** An ocean cruise line. **NOTE:** On-ship hiring done in
Monaco.

PLOOF TRUCK LINES, INC.
P.O. Box 26949, Jacksonville FL 32226-9967. 904/353-8641. **Contact:** Personnel
Director. **Description:** An interstate trucking company.

PREMIER CRUISE LINES
BIG RED BOAT
400 Challenger Road, Cape Canaveral FL 32920. 407/783-5061. **Contact:** Human
Resources. **Description:** An ocean cruise line.

REGAL MARINE INDUSTRIES
2300 Jetport Drive, Orlando FL 32809. 407/851-4360. **Contact:** Scot Socobee,
Director of Human Resources. **Description:** A boat builder.

ROYAL CARIBBEAN
1050 Caribbean Way, Miami FL 33132. 305/539-6000. **Contact:** Personnel Director.
Description: An ocean cruise line that operates nine ships serving in the Caribbean, the
Bahamas, Bermuda, Mexico, Alaska, the Mediterranean, Europe, the Greek Isles,
Panama Canal, Hawaii, Scandinavia/Russia, and the Far East. By 1998, the company
hopes to increase its capacity by purchasing six additional ships. **Corporate
headquarters location:** This Location. **Listed on:** New York Stock Exchange. **Number of
employees nationwide:** 6,900.

RYDER SYSTEM, INC.
P.O. Box 020816, Miami FL 33102-0816. 305/593-3726. **Recorded Jobline:**
305/593-3066. **Contact:** Personnel. **Description:** Ryder System is involved in leasing
trucks, hauling automobiles, providing contract carriage and logistics services, and
providing school bus transportation. Truck leasing operations are conducted in the
United States, Puerto Rico, United Kingdom, Germany, and Poland with over 78,000
vehicles. The company provides maintenance, leasing, and related supplies, and also
maintains over 27,000 nonleased trucks. Ryder System's commercial truck fleet
consists of 33,700 vehicles which operate through 4,650 company locations and
independent dealers. The company also operates 7,140 school buses in 19 states and
manages or operates 88 public transit systems. **Listed on:** New York Stock Exchange.

SEA ESCAPE LTD.
8751 West Broward Boulevard, Suite 410, Plantation FL 33324. 954/379-0000.
Contact: Human Resources. **Description:** An ocean cruise line.

TAMPA SHIPYARD, INC.
P.O. Box 1277, Tampa FL 33601. 813/247-1183. **Contact:** Personnel Department.
Description: A shipyard with construction facilities.

WELLCRAFT MARINE
1651 Whitfield Avenue, Sarasota FL 34243. 941/753-7811. **Contact:** Linda Monoz, Employee Coordinator. **Description:** A manufacturer of boats. **Common positions include:** Accountant/Auditor; Administrator; Blue-Collar Worker Supervisor; Buyer; Computer Programmer; Customer Service Representative; Department Manager; Draftsperson; Electrical/Electronics Engineer; General Manager; Human Resources Specialist; Industrial Engineer; Industrial Production Manager; Manufacturer's/Wholesaler's Sales Rep.; Marketing Specialist; Operations/Production Manager; Purchasing Agent and Manager; Quality Control Supervisor; Systems Analyst. **Educational backgrounds include:** Accounting; Business Administration; Engineering; Finance; Marketing. **Benefits:** Daycare Assistance; Dental Insurance; Disability Coverage; Employee Discounts; Life Insurance; Medical Insurance; Pension Plan; Profit Sharing; Savings Plan; Tuition Assistance. **Corporate headquarters location:** Minneapolis MN. **Parent company:** Genmar. **Operations at this facility include:** Administration; Divisional Headquarters; Manufacturing; Research and Development; Sales; Service.

WINDJAMMER BAREFOOT CRUISES
P.O. Box 120, Miami Beach FL 33119. 305/672-6453. **Contact:** Human Resources. **Description:** A cruise line ship.

Note: Because addresses and telephone numbers of smaller companies change rapidly, we recommend you call each company to verify the information below before inquiring about job opportunities. Mass mailings are not recommended.

Additional employers with over 250 employees:

SHIP/BOAT BUILDING AND REPAIRING

Boston Whaler
4121 US Highway 1,
Edgewater FL 32141-7221.
904/428-0057.

Sea Ray Boats Florida Corp.
P.O. Box 420010, Palm
Coast FL 32142-0010.
904/439-3401.

TRUCKING

Unit Contract Carriers
1301 Gulf Life Dr Ste 1800,
Jacksonville FL 32207-9023.
904/396-2517.

LOCAL AND INTERURBAN PASSENGER TRANSIT

Airocar
1800 NW 23rd Ave, Ft
Lauderdale FL 33311-4540.
954/587-8080.

COURIER SERVICES

General Parcel Service
8923 Western Way Ste 22,
Jacksonville FL 32256-8390.
904/363-0089.

TRANSPORTATION EQUIPMENT

Oshkosh Trailers
P.O. Box 511, Bradenton FL
34206. 813/748-3900.

Additional employers with under 250 employees:

SHIP/BOAT BUILDING AND REPAIRING

International Marine & Industrial Applicators
3226 Talleyrand Ave,
Jacksonville FL 32206-2640.
904/365-1530.

Trident Ship Works Corp.
5201 W Tyson Ave, Tampa
FL 33611-3223. 813/839-5151.

Bayliner Marine Corp.
4755 Capital Circle NW,
Tallahassee FL 32303-7240.
904/562-5905.

Black Fin Yacht Corp.
P.O. Box 22982, Ft
Lauderdale FL 33335-2982.
954/525-6314.

Broward Marine
1601 SW 20th St, Ft
Lauderdale FL 33315-1823.
954/522-1701.

Century Boat Company
6725 Bayline Dr, Panama
City FL 32404-4809.
904/769-0311.

Correct Craft
6100 S Orange Ave, Orlando
FL 32809-5106. 407/855-4141.

DM Industries
2320 NW 147th St, Opa
Locka FL 33054-3190.
305/685-5739.

Hunter Marine Corp.
Rte 441 Box 1030, Alachua
FL 32615. 352/462-3077.

International Ship Repair
1616 Penny St, Tampa FL
33605-6058. 813/248-6496.

Island Packet Yachts
1979 Wild Acres Rd, Largo
FL 34641-3815. 813/535-6431.

Mako Marine
4355 NW 128th St, Opa
Locka FL 33054-5123.
305/685-6591.

Pro-Line Boats
1520 S Suncoast Blvd,
Homosassa FL 34448-1463.
904/795-4111.

Rybovich & Sons Boat Works
4200 Poinsettia Ave, West
Palm Beach FL 33407-4221.
407/844-4331.

Rybovich Spencer
4200 S Dixie Hwy, West
Palm Beach FL 33405-2645.
407/844-1800.

Wellcraft Marine
1315 State Rd 64 W, Avon
Park FL 33825. 941/453-
6616.

RAILROAD
TRANSPORTATION

**Atlanta & St Andrews Bay
Railways**
1 S Everitt Ave #2560,
Panama City FL 32401-
6900. 904/769-6714.

**Florida East Coast Railway
Company**
353 Florida Ave, Fort Pierce
FL 34950-1550. 407/461-
8657.

Railamerica
301 Yamato Rd #2222,
Boca Raton FL 33431-4917.
407/994-6015.

LOCAL AND INTERURBAN
PASSENGER TRANSIT

Ranger Transportation
P.O. Box 19060,
Jacksonville FL 32245-9060.
904/260-3800.

Gray Line Of Orlando
4950 L B McLeod Rd,
Orlando FL 32811-6480.
407/422-0744.

**Pinellas Suncoast
Transportation Authority**
14840 49th St N,
Clearwater FL 34622-2835.
813/530-9911.

**Quality Transportation
Service**
650 NW 27th Ave, Ft
Lauderdale FL 33311-8656.
954/791-2505.

Prestige Taxi Co.
502 N Oregon Ave, Tampa
FL 33606-1215. 813/229-
1888.

Shannon's Chariots
2671 21st Ave SW, Largo FL
34644-1802. 813/586-
6253.

Community Transportation
5514 N Davis Hwy,
Pensacola FL 32503-2009.
904/484-7770.

TRUCKING

AAA Cooper Transportation
8815 Industrial Dr, Tampa FL
33637-6797. 813/899-
1306.

Armellini Express Lines
9433 Tradeport Dr, Orlando
FL 32827-5361. 407/857-
0090.

Averitt Express
11250 Intermodal Way,
Orlando FL 32824-7609.
407/291-2850.

Bulkmatic Transport Co.
200 S Nebraska Ave, Tampa
FL 33602-5532. 813/227-
9444.

**Carolina Freight Carriers
Corporation**
6251 31st St E, Bradenton
FL 34203-5357. 941/756-
9778.

Carroll Fulmer & Co.
5395 L B McLeod Rd,
Orlando FL 32811-2952.
407/299-0900.

**Evergreen Transportation
Company**
300 Highway 95A S,
Cantonment FL 32533-
8623. 904/968-1702.

Florida Rock & Tank Lines
625 S Bluford Ave, Ocoee FL
34761-2752. 407/656-
2772.

Florida Rock & Tank Lines
5714 Buffalo Ave,
Jacksonville FL 32208-5419.
904/356-2456.

Shaw Trucking
P.O. Box 8217, Ft
Lauderdale FL 33310-8217.
954/731-6330.

Southern Freight
1407 N 27th St, Tampa FL
33605-5548. 813/247-
7107.

TNT Dugan
7801 Industrial Ln, Tampa FL
33637-6740. 813/980-
1166.

Wooten Transport Co.
8327 New Kings Rd,
Jacksonville FL 32219-3613.
904/765-3360.

Yellow Freight System
222 Yellow Place, Rockledge
FL 32955-5327. 407/639-
2300.

Lauderback Worldwide
1919 NW 19th St, Ft
Lauderdale FL 33311-3538.
954/761-7872.

Super Transport
951 Broken Sound Pkwy
NW, Suite, Boca Raton FL
33487-3528. 407/241-
0100.

Florida Distribution Centers
5001 L B McLeod Rd,
Orlando FL 32811-6632.
407/297-1004.

Commercial Carrier Corp.
P.O. Box 2046, Brooksville
FL 34605-2046. 352/796-
5145.

**Indian River Transport
Company**
P.O. Box 2119, Winter
Haven FL 33883-2119.
941/324-2430.

Old Dominion Freight Line
5701 Carder Rd, Orlando FL
32810-4742. 407/292-
1925.

**Smalley Transportation
Company**
4224 Henderson Blvd,
Tampa FL 33629-5611.
813/254-0442.

Transport Service Co.
3525 N US 1, Cocoa FL
32926. 407/639-0010.

Shadd's Trucking
State Rd 121 S, Lake Butler
FL 32054. 904/355-7892.

Terry Dicks Trucking Co.
8423 Sunstate St, Tampa FL
33634-1306. 813/889-
7393.

Commercial Carrier Corp.
9126 Bachman Rd, Orlando
FL 32824-8019. 407/851-
4661.

Smart Move Moving Co.
955 Central Ave, St
Petersburg FL 33705-1646.
813/894-3697.

**Steven's Shipping/Terminal
Co.**
1145 E Cass St, Tampa FL
33602-3536. 813/228-
0053.

Metcalf-Mayflower
7331 Presidents Dr, Orlando
FL 32809-5621. 407/851-
0092.

COURIER SERVICES

Per-Doc's Orders Permit
840 County Road 427 S,
Longwood FL 32750-6448.
407/830-1288.

Redwing Carriers
8515 Palm River Rd, Tampa
FL 33619-4315. 813/621-
2046.

WAREHOUSING AND
STORAGE

Davie Self Storage
5370 S University Dr, Davie
FL 33328-5304. 954/741-
4544.

National Distribution Center
7551 Presidents Dr, Orlando
FL 32809-5606. 407/857-
0649.

Aloma-Forsyth Center
3500 Aloma Ave, Winter
Park FL 32792-4007.
407/671-7713.

Center Park Self Storage
114 Datura St, Jupiter FL
33458-5096. 407/575-
0934.

Dade Discount Distributing
7500 NW 69th Ave, Medley
FL 33166-2560. 305/885-
9774.

Private Mini Storage
3182 Curlew Rd, Oldsmar FL
34677-2606. 813/855-
7706.

Private Mini Storage
6118 US Highway 19, New
Port Richey FL 34652-2526.
813/841-0514.

Southern Self Storage
2308 N John Young Pkwy,
Orlando FL 32804-4125.
407/684-3364.

U-Store-It
10300 NW 55th St, Ft
Lauderdale FL 33351-8703.
954/742-9415.

Uncle Bob's Self-Storage
11955 S Orange Blossom
Trail, Orlando FL 32837-
9252. 407/826-0242.

Kangaroom Mini Storage
5717 14th St W, Bradenton
FL 34207-4004. 941/755-
3688.

**Browning Treyz Moving &
Storage Company**
120 SW 5th Ave, Boca
Raton FL 33432-4728.
407/368-5441.

Storage Express
5200 Park St N, St
Petersburg FL 33709-1012.
813/546-1572.

The Extra Closet
2401 Anvil St N, St
Petersburg FL 33710-3907.
813/344-1604.

**WATER TRANSPORTATION
OF FREIGHT**

Hvide Shipping
P.O. Box 13038, Ft
Lauderdale FL 33316-0100.
954/523-2200.

Tecmarine Lines
9900 NW 25th St, Miami FL
33172-2205. 305/597-
7000.

Crowley American Transport
4300 McIntosh Rd, Ft
Lauderdale FL 33335.
954/760-7900.

**Marine Transportation
Service**
3830 Frankford Ave, Panama
City FL 32405-1908.
904/769-1459.

Nedloyd Lines
9620 Dave Rawls Rd,
Jacksonville FL 32226-4022.
904/757-7208.

**Zim American Israeli Shipping
Company**
4080 Woodcock Dr,
Jacksonville FL 32207-2722.
904/399-5693.

**WATER TRANSPORTATION
OF PASSENGERS**

Grundstad Maritime Overseas
2790 N Federal Hwy, Boca
Raton FL 33431-7720.
407/394-7450.

Europa Cruises Corp.
150 153rd Ave, St
Petersburg FL 33708-1856.
813/393-2885.

MARINE CARGO HANDLING

Pomtoc
2020 Port Blvd, Miami FL
33132-2088. 305/373-
6317.

**TOWING AND TUGBOAT
SERVICES**

**Admiral Towing and Barge
Company**
P.O. Box 4905, Pensacola FL
32507-0905. 904/453-
4331.

Bay Transportation Corp.
Hookers Point, Tampa FL
33605. 813/247-3187.

Biscayne Towing & Salvage
1633 N Bayshore Dr, Miami
FL 33132-1215. 305/358-
1486.

**Horton Marine Commercial
Assistance Tow**
108 Cousineau Rd,
Pensacola FL 32507-3712.
904/457-4304.

Moran Towing Of Florida
9485 Regency Square Blvd,
Suite 4, Jacksonville FL
32225-9100. 904/721-
7000.

**MISC. WATER
TRANSPORTATION
SERVICES**

Bay Towing
1305 Shoreline Dr, Tampa FL

33605-6756. 813/247-
1552.

**AIR TRANSPORTATION AND
SERVICES**

Airways International
P.O. Box 1244, Miami
Springs FL 33266. 305/526-
3852.

Lacsa Airlines
1600 S Le Jeune Rd, Suite
100, Miami FL 33134-3875.
305/871-0144.

Amerjet International
498 SW 34th St, Ft
Lauderdale FL 33315-3610.
954/359-0077.

Associated Air Freight
6308 Benjamin Rd, Tampa
FL 33634-5174. 813/888-
6944.

Caicos Caribbean Air Ways
3415 SW 9th Ave, Miami FL
33135. 305/949-6301.

Landair Services
5422 W Crenshaw St,
Tampa FL 33634-3009.
813/882-9701.

Crescent Airways
7501 Pembroke Rd, W
Hollywood FL 33023-2579.
954/987-1900.

Airman's Aero Club
St Petersburg-Clearwater
Inter, Clearwater FL 34622.
813/531-4101.

IBC Airways
3450 NW 62nd St, Miami FL
33147-7536. 305/871-
2334.

Suncoast Helicopters
4111 W Columbus Dr,
Tampa FL 33607-5723.
813/872-6625.

Advance Cargo Services
2461 NW 67th St, Miami FL
33147-7260. 305/871-
0709.

Dispatch Services
Miami International Airport,
Miami FL 33159. 305/526-
5290.

Miami Aircraft Support
2461 NW 66th St, Miami FL
33147-7264. 305/871-
1314.

Narcam Aircraft
5300 NW 36th Ave, Miami
FL 33142. 305/871-1930.

International Total Service
Tampa International Airport,
Tampa FL 33607. 813/870-
0620.

Signature Flight Support
5700 NW 36th Ave, Miami
FL 33142-2714. 305/526-
6344.

UNC Aviation Service
4900 Bayou Blvd, Pensacola
FL 32503-2525. 904/477-
7771.

UNC Aviation Service
Tow Way St, Pensacola FL
32508. 904/455-1801.

United Beechraft
2450 N Westshore Blvd,
Tampa FL 33607-5700.
813/878-4500.

Orlando International Airport
1 Airport Blvd, Orlando FL
32827-4328. 407/825-
2001.

**PASSENGER
TRANSPORTATION
ARRANGEMENT SERVICES**

Dillard Travel
750 Tyrone Blvd N, St
Petersburg FL 33710-7127.
813/384-0202.

Freestyle Cruise & Travel
239 Commercial Blvd, Ft
Lauderdale FL 33308-4428.
954/776-7120.

Hata USA
6000 Airport Circle, Sarasota
FL 34243-2105. 941/358-
9116.

Liberty Travel
8903 Glades Rd, Boca Raton
FL 33434-4019. 407/487-
9997.

**NFT Gulf Coast Travel
Service**
1908 Bay Rd, Sarasota FL
34239-6903. 941/951-
0330.

Oceanair
6301 NW 5th Way, Ft
Lauderdale FL 33309-6139.
954/491-2602.

**Persons-Landsee Travel
Service**
11300 49th St N,
Clearwater FL 34622-4807.
813/572-8800.

Promotional Travel
407 Whooping Loop, Suite
1679, Altamonte Springs FL
32701-3298. 407/339-
1678.

Rosenbluth Travel Agency
1311 N Westshore Blvd,
Suite 310, Tampa FL 33607-
4616. 813/289-7805.

Security Travel USA
11740 N Dale Mabry Hwy,
Tampa FL 33618-3504.
813/961-5006.

The Travel Shoppe
2425 Manatee Ave W,
Bradenton FL 34205-4933.
941/749-1552.

Trans-Mark Travel
3900 Clark Rd, Suite F1,
Sarasota FL 34233-2300.
941/924-2747.

Travel Incorporated
11780 US Highway 1, No
Palm Beach FL 33408-3007.
407/622-9065.

Travel Now International
301 S Solandra Dr, Orlando
FL 32807-1737. 407/380-
0808.

Unique Travel Service
7265 Estapona Circle, Fern
Park FL 32730-2349.
407/767-8100.

Wright Travel Agency
500 Winderley Place,
Maitland FL 32751-7247.
407/660-8008.

Historic Tours Of America
601 Duval St, Key West FL
33040-6554. 305/296-
3609.

Adventure Tours
7677 Dr Phillips Blvd, Suite
200, Orlando FL 32819-
7294. 407/351-5155.

Jetsave
6412 International Dr,
Orlando FL 32819-8268.
407/351-2434.

Kuoni Travel
150 153rd Ave, St
Petersburg FL 33708-1856.
813/392-3047.

Thompson Holiday Services
5260 Bronson Memorial
Highway, Kissimmee FL
34746-5309. 407/397-
9822.

Virgin Holiday Limited
8000 S Orange Ave, Suite
107, Orlando FL 32809-
6747. 407/856-1177.

Wasteels Travel
7041 Grand National Dr,
Suite 207, Orlando FL
32819-8380. 407/351-
2537.

Aly's Dream Travel
8051 NW 36th St, Miami FL
33166-6626. 305/477-
4755.

Aries Travel
2301 Maitland Center Pkwy,
Maitland FL 32751-4128.
407/660-2101.

Carlson Travel Network
2300 Maitland Center Pkwy,
Suite 11, Maitland FL
32751-4129. 407/875-
1440.

Thomas Cook Travel
780 Carillon Pkwy, St
Petersburg FL 33716-1106.
813/573-7688.

Thomas Cook Travel
1390 Main St #10, Sarasota
FL 34236-5687. 941/365-
2520.

USTravel
7650 W Courtney Campbell
Cswy, Tampa FL 33607-
1462. 813/286-2467.

Wright Travel
1511 N Westshore Blvd,
Suite 290, Tampa FL 33607-
4523. 813/289-0027.

SEL Maduro Florida
611 Eisenhower Blvd, Ft
Lauderdale FL 33335.
954/763-8091.

Terminal Services
8410 NW 53rd Terrace,
Miami FL 33166-4531.
305/599-0331.

Transica Interocean Contract
5553 NW 36th St, Miami FL
33166-5873. 305/884-
0711.

PACKING AND CRATING

Total Distribution Systems
1111 Meson Park Blvd,
Jacksonville FL 32218-4907.
904/757-8250.

**La Montana Moving &
Storage**
353 N Ivey Ln, Orlando FL
32811. 407/291-2334.

**WHOLESALE OF
TRANSPORTATION
EQUIPMENT AND SUPPLIES**

**International Airline Support
Group**
8095 NW 64th St, Miami FL
33166. 305/593-2658.

Tri-Star Aerospace
3411 SW 11th St, Deerfield
Beach FL 33442-8138.
954/421-5700.

Rite Hite
890 Northern Way #D-2,
Winter Springs FL 32708-
3880. 407/365-4567.

For more information on career opportunities in transportation:

Associations

AIR TRANSPORT ASSOCIATION OF AMERICA
1301 Pennsylvania Avenue NW, Suite 1100, Washington DC 20004. 202/626-4000.

AMERICAN BUREAU OF SHIPPING
2 World Trade Center, 106th Floor, New York NY 10048. 212/839-5000.

AMERICAN MARITIME ASSOCIATION
380 Madison Avenue, 17th Floor, New York NY 10017. 212/557-9520. A trade association which offers collection and bargaining services.

AMERICAN SOCIETY OF TRAVEL AGENTS
1101 King Street, Suite 200, Alexandria VA 22314. 703/739-2782. For information, send a SASE with $.75 postage to the attention of the Fulfillment Department.

AMERICAN TRUCKING ASSOCIATION
2200 Mill Road, Alexandria VA 22314-4677. 703/838-1700.

ASSOCIATION OF AMERICAN RAILROADS
50 F Street NW, Washington DC 20001. 202/639-2100.

FUTURE AVIATION PROFESSIONALS OF AMERICA
4959 Massachusetts Boulevard, Atlanta GA 30337. 404/997-8097. Publishes monthly newsletter which monitors the job market for flying jobs; a pilot employment guide, outlining what is required to become a pilot; and a directory of aviation employers.

INSTITUTE OF TRANSPORTATION ENGINEERS
525 School Street SW, Suite 410, Washington DC 20024-2797. 202/554-8050. Scientific and educational association, providing for professional development of members and others.

MARINE TECHNOLOGY SOCIETY
1828 L Street NW, Suite 906, Washington DC 20036. 202/775-5966.

NATIONAL MARINE MANUFACTURERS ASSOCIATION
401 North Michigan Avenue, Suite 1150, Chicago IL 60611. 312/836-4747. A partnership of three manufacturer groups: The National Association of Boat Manufacturers; The Association of Marine Engine Manufacturers; and The National Association of Marine Products & Services. Subscription to job listing publication is available for a fee.

NATIONAL MOTOR FREIGHT TRAFFIC ASSOCIATION
2200 Mill Road, Alexandria VA 22314-4654. 703/838-1810. Works towards the improvement and advancement of the interests and welfare of motor common carriers.

NATIONAL TANK TRUCK CARRIERS
2200 Mill Road, Alexandria VA 22314. 703/838-1700. A trade association representing and promoting the interests of the highway bulk transportation community.

Directories

MOODY'S TRANSPORTATION MANUAL
Moody's Investors Service, Inc., 99 Church Street, New York NY 10007. 212/553-0300. $12.95 per year with weekly updates.

NATIONAL TANK TRUCK CARRIER DIRECTORY
2200 Mill Road, Alexandria VA 22314. 703/838-1700.

OFFICIAL MOTOR FREIGHT GUIDE
1700 West Courtland Street, Chicago IL 60622. 312/278-2454.

Magazines

AMERICAN SHIPPER
P.O. Box 4728, Jacksonville FL 32201. 904/355-2601. Monthly.

FLEET OWNER
707 Westchester Avenue, White Plains NY 10604-3102. 914/949-8500.

HEAVY DUTY TRUCKING
Newport Communications, P.O. Box W, Newport Beach CA 92658. 714/261-1636.

ITE JOURNAL
Institute of Transportation Engineers, 525 School Street SW, Suite 410, Washington DC 20024-2797. 202/554-8050. One year subscription (12 issues): $50.

MARINE DIGEST AND TRANSPORTATION NEWS
P.O. Box 3905, Seattle WA 98124. 206/682-3607.

SHIPPING DIGEST
51 Madison Avenue, New York NY 10010. 212/689-4411.

TRAFFIC WORLD MAGAZINE
741 National Press Building, Washington DC 20045. 202/383-6140.

TRANSPORT TOPICS
2200 Mill Road, Alexandria VA 22314. 703/838-1772.

UTILITIES: ELECTRIC, GAS AND SANITATION

With deregulation looming closer and closer, utilities are adjusting by cutting costs and providing better service. This is a good sign for the industry but a bad sign for jobseekers as employment should remain just about flat. Job prospects in the utilities industry are probably best with large electric utilities, water supply facilities, and sanitary services right now. The most common positions with public utilities are precision production workers and operators, fabricators, and laborers.

CLAY ELECTRIC CO-OP, INC.
P.O. Box 308, Keystone Heights FL 32656. 904/473-4911. **Contact:** Personnel Director. **Description:** An electric service.

FPL GROUP, INC.
Golden Bear Plaza, P.O. Box 088801, North Palm Beach FL 33408-8801. 407/694-6300. **Contact:** Employment Coordinator. **Description:** FPL Group is the parent company of Florida Power & Light Company, one of the largest investor-owned electric utilities in the country. Florida Power & Light serves 6.5 million people in an area covering almost the entire eastern seaboard of Florida and the southern third of the state. Other operations of FPL Group include ESI Energy, an independent power company; Turner Foods Corporation, one of the largest citrus producers in Florida; and Qualtec Quality Services, Inc., which provides consulting and training services in quality management.

FPL GROUP, INC.
700 Universe Boulevard, Juno Beach FL 33409-2657. 407/694-3509. **Contact:** Human Resources. **Description:** FPL Group is the parent company of Florida Power & Light Company, one of the largest investor-owned electric utilities in the country. Florida Power & Light serves 6.5 million people in an area covering almost the entire eastern seaboard of Florida and the southern third of the state. Other operations of FPL Group include ESI Energy, an independent power company; Turner Foods Corporation, one of the largest citrus producers in Florida; and Qualtec Quality Services, Inc., which provides consulting and training services in quality management. **Corporate headquarters location:** This Location.

FLORIDA KEYS ELECTRIC COOPERATIVE
P.O. Box 377, Tavernier FL 33070. 305/852-2431. **Contact:** Vivian Burrows, Personnel Director. **Description:** An electric utility company.

FLORIDA POWER AND LIGHT COMPANY
P.O. Box 029100, Miami FL 33102. 305/552-4060. **Contact:** Jim A. King, Manager of Professional Placement. **Description:** Florida Power & Light serves 6.5 million people in an area covering almost the entire eastern seaboard of Florida and the southern third of the state. One of the largest investor-owned electric utilities in the country. **Parent company:** FPL Group, Inc. **Number of employees nationwide:** 12,000.

FLORIDA POWER CORPORATION
3133 Alafaya Trail, Orlando FL 32826. 407/646-8226. **Fax:** 407/646-8232. **Recorded Jobline:** 407/646-8429. **Contact:** Manager of Human Resources. **Description:** A utility company. **NOTE:** Jobseekers need to fill out and submit the company's application form for all positions. **Common positions include:** Customer Service Representative; Draftsperson; Electrical/Electronics Engineer; Line Installer/Cable Splicer. **Educational backgrounds include:** Business Administration; Engineering; Liberal Arts; Marketing. **Benefits:** Disability Coverage; Employee Discounts; Life Insurance; Medical Insurance; Pension Plan; Profit Sharing; Savings Plan; Tuition Assistance. **Corporate headquarters location:** St. Petersburg FL. **Parent company:** Florida Progress Corporation. **Operations at this facility include:** Administration; Divisional Headquarters. **Listed on:** New York

Stock Exchange. **Number of employees at this location:** 1,000. **Number of employees nationwide:** 5,000.

FLORIDA PROGRESS CORPORATION

P.O. Box 33028, One Progress Plaza, St. Petersburg FL 33733-8028. 813/824-6400. **Contact:** Human Resources Representative. **Description:** Florida Progress is a diversified utility holding company with several subsidiaries. The company's principal subsidiary, Florida Power Corporation, is an electric utility involved in the generation, purchase, transmission, distribution, and sale of electricity. Other subsidiaries include Electric Fuels Corporation, an energy and transportation company that serves electric utilities; and Mid-Continent Life Insurance Company, a life insurance company. Florida Progress Corporation continues to withdraw from its other operations in real estate and lending and leasing. **Corporate headquarters location:** This Location. **Other U.S. locations:** Oklahoma City OK. **Listed on:** New York Stock Exchange.

GULF POWER COMPANY
EMPLOYMENT OFFICE

P.O. Box 1151, Pensacola FL 32520-0221. 904/444-5481. **Contact:** Bill Threadgill, Supervisor of Employment. **Description:** A public utility. **Common positions include:** Accountant/Auditor; Customer Service Representative; Electrical/Electronics Engineer; Mechanical Engineer; Systems Analyst. **Educational backgrounds include:** Accounting; Computer Science; Engineering. **Benefits:** Disability Coverage; Employee Discounts; Life Insurance; Medical Insurance; Pension Plan; Savings Plan; Tuition Assistance. **Special Programs:** Training Programs. **Corporate headquarters location:** This Location. **Parent company:** Southern Company Services. **Operations at this facility include:** Regional Headquarters. **Listed on:** New York Stock Exchange. **Number of employees nationwide:** 1,565.

HILLSBOROUGH COUNTY PUBLIC UTILITIES

P.O. Box 1110, Tampa FL 33601. 813/272-6680. **Contact:** Civil Service. **Description:** A water/wastewater utility department.

LEE COUNTY ELECTRIC COOPERATIVE, INC.

4980 Bayline Drive, North Fort Meyers FL 33917. 941/656-2203. **Fax:** 941/995-7904. **Contact:** Human Resources. **Description:** An electric utility. **Common positions include:** Accountant/Auditor; Adjuster; Automotive Mechanic/Body Repairer; Budget Analyst; Buyer; Claim Representative; Computer Operator; Computer Programmer; Computer Systems Analyst; Construction and Building Inspector; Construction Contractor and Manager; Customer Service Representative; Department Manager; Draftsperson; Editor; Electrical/Electronics Engineer; Electrician; Employment Interviewer; Financial Manager; General Manager; Graphic Artist; Human Resources Specialist; Industrial Engineer; Marketing Research Analyst; Mechanical Engineer; Paralegal; Payroll Clerk; Postal Clerk/Mail Carrier; Property and Real Estate Manager; Public Relations Specialist; Purchasing Agent and Manager; Receptionist; Registered Nurse; Systems Analyst; Technical Writer/Editor; Typist/Word Processor. **Educational backgrounds include:** Accounting; Business Administration; Communications; Computer Science; Engineering; Finance; Marketing. **Benefits:** Dental Insurance; Disability Coverage; Leave Time; Life Insurance; Medical Insurance; Pension Plan; Profit Sharing; Savings Plan; Tuition Assistance. **Special Programs:** Apprenticeships; Training Programs. **Corporate headquarters location:** This Location. **Operations at this facility include:** Administration; Service. **Number of employees at this location:** 405.

MASTEC

8600 Northwest 36th Street, Miami FL 33166. 305/599-1800. **Contact:** Human Resources. **Description:** A water, sewer, and power service.

ORLANDO UTILITIES COMMISSION

P.O. Box 3193, Orlando FL 32801. 407/423-9100. **Contact:** Arthur Fenton, Director of Personnel. **Description:** Offers utility services to Central Florida.

PALMER ELECTRIC COMPANY

875 Jackson Avenue, Winter Park FL 32789. 407/646-8700. **Contact:** Tammy Nelson, Director of Personnel. **Description:** Provides electrical services to commercial and residential customers.

PEOPLES GAS SYSTEMS, INC.

P.O. Box 2562, Tampa FL 33601. 813/273-0074. **Contact:** Jim Senk, Personnel Director. **Description:** A distributor of natural gas.

SOUTHEASTERN PUBLIC SERVICE COMPANY
2001 NW 107th Avenue, Miami FL 33172. 305/593-6565. **Contact:** Personnel Department. **Description:** Provides utility and municipal services. **Parent company:** DWG Corporation.

TAMPA ELECTRIC
P.O. Box 111, Tampa FL 33602. 813/228-4111. **Contact:** Human Resources. **Description:** An electric company.

Note: Because addresses and telephone numbers of smaller companies change rapidly, we recommend you call each company to verify the information below before inquiring about job opportunities. Mass mailings are not recommended.

Additional employers with under 250 employees:

ELECTRIC SERVICES

Choctawatchee Electric Coop
P.O. Box 512, Defuniak Springs FL 32433-0512. 904/892-2111.

Florida Power Corp. Eustis District Office
14623 SR 50, Altamonte Springs FL 32716. 904/394-3892.

Florida Power & Light
P.O. Box 2409, Delray Beach FL 33447-2409. 407/265-3104.

Florida Power & Light
1611 Waverly Place, Melbourne FL 32901-4639. 407/727-9495.

Florida Power Corp.
8564 W 7th Rivers Dr, Crystal River FL 32629. 904/795-3145.

Florida Power Corporation
6600 US Highway 19, New Port Richey FL 34652-1739. 813/842-9591.

W Florida Electric Cooperative Association
P.O. Box 127, Graceville FL 32440-0127. 904/263-3231.

Withlacoochee River Electric Coop
5330 W Gulf To Lake Hwy, Crystal River FL 32629. 904/795-4382.

CH Stanton Energy Center
5100 S Alafaya Trail, Orlando FL 32831-2000. 407/658-6444.

Cutler Generating Station
14925 SW 67th Ave, Miami FL 33158-2102. 305/252-3000.

McIntosh Generating Station
3030 E Lake Parker Dr,
Lakeland FL 33805-9513. 941/499-6600.

Northside Generating Station
4377 Heckscher Dr, Jacksonville FL 32226-3099. 904/632-6670.

Putnam Generating Station
P.O. Box 308, East Palatka FL 32131-0308. 904/325-9061.

Turkey Point 1 & 2 Fossil Plant
9700 SW 344th St, Homestead FL 33035-1800. 305/246-6010.

West Palm Beach B 1 & 2
7501 N Jog Rd, West Palm Beach FL 33412-2414. 407/697-8716.

GAS UTILITY SERVICES

City Gas Co. Of Florida
955 E 25th St, Hialeah FL 33013-3403. 305/691-8710.

Enron Corporation
601 S Lake Destiny Rd, Maitland FL 32751-7226. 407/875-5800.

National Propane
855 Talleyrand Ave, Jacksonville FL 32206-6017. 904/355-0501.

Peoples Gas
4040 Phillips Hwy, Jacksonville FL 32207-6875. 904/739-1211.

GAS AND/OR WATER SUPPLY

Florida Cities Water Company
4271 Saint Clair Ave W, Fort Myers FL 33903-4574. 941/997-1861.

Garden Grove Water Co.
3601 Cypress Gardens Rd,
Winter Haven FL 33884-2487. 941/324-4319.

SANITARY SERVICES

Industrial Waste
3840 NW 37th Ct, Miami FL 33142-4296. 305/638-3800.

International Recovery Corporation
700 S Royal Ponciana Blvd 800, Miami Springs FL 33166-6600. 305/884-2001.

Transcor Waste Services
1501 E 2nd Ave, Tampa FL 33605-5005. 813/248-3878.

Western Waste Industries
1334 N Goldenrod Rd, Orlando FL 32807-8333. 407/273-8200.

County Waste Of Broward
2113 NW 58th Ave, Ft Lauderdale FL 33313-3118. 954/764-1900.

Industrial Waste Service An Attwoods Company
1099 W Miller St, Orlando FL 32805-4511. 407/425-6600.

Waste Management Inc. Of Florida
500 W Cypress Creek Rd, Ft Lauderdale FL 33309-6141. 954/771-9850.

Keene Rd Recycle & Disposal
255 W Keene Rd, Apopka FL 32703. 407/886-2920.

Shred-All
11483 Rocket Blvd, Orlando FL 32824. 407/859-9711.

Ohm Corporation Florida Division
P.O. Box 121190, Clermont FL 34712-1190. 904/394-8601.

For more information on career opportunities in the utilities industry:

Associations

AMERICAN PUBLIC GAS ASSOCIATION
Lee Highway, Suite 102, Fairfax VA
22030. 703/352-3890. Publishes a weekly
newsletter.

**AMERICAN PUBLIC POWER ASSOCIATION
(APPA)**
2301 M Street NW, Washington DC
20037. 202/467-2970. Represents
publicly-owned utilities. Provides many
services including: government relations,
educational programs, and industry-related
information publications.

AMERICAN WATER WORKS ASSOCIATION
6666 West Quincy Drive, Denver CO
80235. 303/794-7711.

**NATIONAL RURAL ELECTRIC
COOPERATIVE ASSOCIATION**
1800 Massachusetts Avenue NW,
Washington DC 20036. 202/857-9500.

Directories

MOODY'S PUBLIC UTILITY MANUAL
Moody's Investors Service, Inc., 99 Church
Street, New York NY 10007. 212/553-
0300. Annually available at libraries.

Magazines

PUBLIC POWER
2301 M Street NW, Washington DC
20037. 202/467-2900.

NOTE: *While every effort is made to keep the addresses and phone numbers of these companies up-to-date, employment services often move or change hands and are therefore more difficult to track. Please notify the publisher if you find any discrepancies.*

TEMPORARY EMPLOYMENT SERVICES

ACCUSTAFF INC.
1875 West Commercial Boulevard, Suite 165, Fort Lauderdale FL 33309. 954/928-0699. **Contact:** Rose Holland or Shannon Mile, Branch Managers. Temporary Agency. **Specializes in the areas of:** Clerical.

INTERIM PERSONNEL
7000 Lake Ellenor Drive, Suite 100, Orlando FL 32809. 407/859-6140. **Contact:** Branch Manager. Temporary Agency. **Specializes in the areas of:** Non-Specialized.

INTERIM PERSONNEL
2551 Drew Street, Suite 102, Clearwater FL 34625. 813/797-2171. **Contact:** Manager. Temporary Agency. **Specializes in the areas of:** Non-Specialized.

INTERIM PERSONNEL
2993 Tyrone Boulevard, St. Petersburg FL 33710. 813/341-0000. **Contact:** Manager. Temporary Agency. **Specializes in the areas of:** Non-Specialized.

INTERIM PERSONNEL
10006 North Dale Mabry, Suite 108, Tampa FL 33618. 813/963-0066. **Contact:** Manager. Temporary Agency. **Specializes in the areas of:** Non-Specialized.

KELLY SERVICES, INC.
3300 PGA Boulevard, Suite 330, Palm Beach Gardens FL 33410. 407/694-0116. **Contact:** Manager. Temporary Agency. **Specializes in the areas of:** Clerical; Manufacturing; Technical and Scientific.

KELLY SERVICES, INC.
1700 Palm Beach Lakes Boulevard, Suite 520, West Palm Beach FL 33401. 407/686-2900. **Contact:** Branch Manager. Temporary Agency. **Specializes in the areas of:** Clerical; Manufacturing; Technical and Scientific.

MANPOWER TEMPORARY SERVICES
10750 North 56th Street, Tampa FL 33617-3643. 813/985-8184. **Contact:** Branch Manager. Temporary Agency. **Specializes in the areas of:** Clerical; Industrial; Personnel/Labor Relations.

OFFICE OURS
3300 PGA Boulevard, Suite 625, Palm Beach Gardens FL 33410. 407/691-0202. **Contact:** Office Manager. Temporary Agency. **Specializes in the areas of:** Clerical; Secretarial.

OFFICE OURS
7000 West Palmetto Park Road, Boca Raton FL 33433. 800/925-2955. **Contact:** Jeanne Pardo, Office Manager. Temporary Agency. **Specializes in the areas of:** Clerical; Secretarial.

OFFICE SPECIALISTS
3400 Lakeside Drive, Suite 100, Miramar FL 33027. 954/437-5074. **Contact:** Valencia McDuffy, Recruiter. Temporary Agency. **Specializes in the areas of:** Accounting/Auditing; Clerical; Finance; Legal; Word Processing.

SNELLING PERSONNEL
6555 Northwest 9th Avenue, Suite 203, Fort Lauderdale FL 33309. 954/771-0090. **Contact:** Vicki Hitchinson, Manager. Temporary Agency. **Specializes in the areas of:** Administration/MIS/EDP; Sales and Marketing.

STAFF BUILDERS HOME HEALTH SERVICES
1211 Northwest Shore, Suite 401, Tampa FL 33607. 813/932-7924. **Contact:** Staffing Coordinator. Temporary Agency. **Specializes in the areas of:** Non-Specialized.

STAFF BUILDERS, INC.
3075 West Oakland Park Boulevard, Suite 100, Fort Lauderdale FL 33311. 954/486-5506. **Contact:** Personnel Coordinator. Temporary Agency. **Specializes in the areas of:** Non-Specialized.

TEMP FORCE OF GAINESVILLE
1031 Northwest 6th Street, Suite E, Gainesville FL 32601. 352/378-2300. **Contact:** Carolynn Buchanan, Manager. Temporary Agency. **Specializes in the areas of:** Non-Specialized.

PERMANENT EMPLOYMENT AGENCIES

AAA EMPLOYMENT
4035 South Florida Avenue, Lakeland FL 33813. 941/646-9681. **Fax:** 941/646-9683. **Contact:** Trish MacPeek, Franchise Owner. Employment Agency. **Specializes in the areas of:** Non-Specialized. **Positions commonly filled include:** Accountant/Auditor; Administrative Services Manager; Advertising Clerk; Bank Officer/Manager; Blue-Collar Worker Supervisor; Branch Manager; Brokerage Clerk; Budget Analyst; Buyer; Chemist; Civil Engineer; Claim Representative; Clerical Supervisor; Clinical Lab Technician; Computer Programmer; Computer Systems Analyst; Counselor; Credit Manager; Customer Service Representative; Dental Assistant/Dental Hygienist; Draftsperson; General Manager; Geologist/Geophysicist; Hotel Manager/Assistant Manager; Industrial Production Manager; Insurance Agent/Broker; Licensed Practical Nurse; Management Trainee; Manufacturer's/Wholesaler's Sales Rep.; Mechanical Engineer; Operations/Production Manager; Paralegal; Property and Real Estate Manager; Purchasing Agent and Manager; Quality Control Supervisor; Registered Nurse; Restaurant/Food Service Manager; Services Sales Representative; Software Engineer; Transportation/Traffic Specialist; Travel Agent; Underwriter/Assistant Underwriter; Wholesale and Retail Buyer. Company pays fee.

A CHOICE NANNY
1413 South Howard Avenue, #201, Tampa FL 33606. 813/254-8687. **Contact:** Eleanor Nesbit, Owner/Manager. Employment Agency. **Specializes in the areas of:** Nannies. **Positions commonly filled include:** Nanny. **Number of placements per year:** 100 - 199.

ACCOUNTANTS ON CALL
ACCOUNTANTS EXECUTIVE SEARCH
One Alhambra Plaza, Suite 1435, Coral Gables FL 33134. 305/443-9333. **Contact:** Daniel Perron, Manager. Employment Agency. **Specializes in the areas of:** Accounting/Auditing; Finance.

THE ADDSTAFF NETWORK
101 American Center Place, Suite 203, Tampa FL 33619. 813/621-7700. **Fax:** 813/677-4336. **Contact:** Barbara Franchi, Principal. Employment Agency. **Specializes in the areas of:** Office Support; Personnel/Labor Relations; Secretarial. **Positions commonly filled include:** Claim Representative; Customer Service Representative; Medical Record Technician; Paralegal. Company pays fee. **Number of placements per year:** 1000+.

AVAILABILITY, INC.
P.O. Box 25434, Tampa FL 33622. 813/286-8800. **Contact:** Edgar Hart, Owner. Employment Agency. **Specializes in the areas of:** Clerical; Computer Hardware/Software; Engineering; Legal; Secretarial; Technical and Scientific.

BECKER BENSON PERSONNEL
402 Reo Street, Suite 103, Tampa FL 33609. 813/282-3600. **Fax:** 813/282-3700. **Contact:** Cindee Becker, President. Employment Agency. **Specializes in the areas of:** Administration/MIS/EDP; Personnel/Labor Relations; Secretarial. **Positions commonly filled include:** Administrative Services Manager; Clerical Supervisor; Credit Manager; Customer Service Representative; Human Resources Specialist; Paralegal; Public Relations Specialist; Technical Writer/Editor. Company pays fee.

BENSON AND ASSOCIATES
551 Northwest 77th Street, Suite 102, Boca Raton FL 33487. 407/997-1600.
Contact: Lou Benson, Ph.D., President. Employment Agency. **Specializes in the areas of:** Banking; Construction; Health/Medical.

CAPITAL DATA, INC.
P.O. Box 2244, Palm Harbor FL 34682-2244. 813/784-4100. **Fax:** 800/787-4172.
Contact: Jack Logan, President. Employment Agency. **Positions commonly filled include:** Computer Programmer; Computer Systems Analyst.

CAREEREXCHANGE
220 Miracle Mile, Suite 203, Coral Gables FL 33134. 305/529-0064. **Fax:** 305/577-9460. **Contact:** Sue Romanos, President. Employment Agency. **Specializes in the areas of:** Administration/MIS/EDP; Health/Medical. **Positions commonly filled include:** Administrator; Clerk; Management; Medical Secretary; Receptionist; Secretary; Typist/Word Processor.

CAREERS, INC.
3501 University Drive, Suite 205, Coral Springs FL 33065. 954/341-7100. **Fax:** 954/341-7104. **Contact:** John S. Barton, Manager. Employment Agency. **Specializes in the areas of:** Insurance.

CITY OF HIALEAH
HIALEAH ADULT AND YOUTH EMPLOYMENT SERVICE
240 East 1st Avenue, Hialeah FL 33010. 305/883-6925. **Fax:** 305/883-6910.
Contact: Anthony LaMorte, Placement Specialist. Employment Agency. **Specializes in the areas of:** Electronics; General Labor; Health/Medical; Industrial; Manufacturing; Secretarial. **Positions commonly filled include:** Accountant/Auditor; Architect; Automotive Mechanic/Body Repairer; Blue-Collar Worker Supervisor; Clinician; Customer Service Representative; Draftsperson; Industrial Production Manager; Licensed Practical Nurse; Manufacturer's/Wholesaler's Sales Rep.; Preschool Worker; Quality Control Supervisor; Registered Nurse. **Number of placements per year:** 200 - 499.

COMPU-TECH PERSONNEL
60 2nd Street, Suite 303, Shalimar FL 32579. 904/651-1118. **Fax:** 904/651-2708.
Contact: Jacqueline Giangrosso, Owner. Employment Agency.

COMPUTERPEOPLE DECISIONS
13535 Southern Sound Drive, Suite 220, Clearwater FL 34622. **Contact:** Manager. Employment Agency. **Specializes in the areas of:** Administration/MIS/EDP; Computer Hardware/Software.

DGA PERSONNEL GROUP, INC.
2691 East Oakland Park Boulevard, Suite 201, Fort Lauderdale FL 33306. 954/561-1771. **Contact:** David Grant, President. Employment Agency. **Specializes in the areas of:** Accounting/Auditing; Administration/MIS/EDP; Architecture/Construction/Real Estate; Banking; Clerical; Computer Hardware/Software; Design; Engineering; Finance; Health/Medical; Industrial; Legal; Manufacturing; Real Estate; Sales and Marketing; Secretarial; Technical and Scientific; Transportation.

EXECUTIVE DIRECTIONS INC.
450 North Park Road, Suite 302, Hollywood FL 33021. 954/962-9444. **Fax:** 954/963-4333. **Contact:** Bob Silverman, Director. Employment Agency. **Positions commonly filled include:** Computer Programmer; Computer Systems Analyst; Management Analyst/Consultant. Company pays fee. **Number of placements per year:** 100 - 199.

FIRST EMPLOYMENT CONSULTANTS, INC.
6175 Northwest 153rd Street, Suite 230, Miami Lakes FL 33014. 305/825-8900.
Fax: 305/825-8020. **Contact:** Mark Benson, Vice President. Employment Agency. **Specializes in the areas of:** Architecture/Construction/Real Estate; Engineering. **Positions commonly filled include:** Blue-Collar Worker Supervisor; Buyer; Civil Engineer; Construction and Building Inspector; Construction Contractor and Manager; Cost Estimator; Draftsperson; Electrical/Electronics Engineer; Mechanical Engineer; Purchasing Agent and Manager; Structural Engineer; Surveyor. Company pays fee. **Number of placements per year:** 1000+.

FLORAPERSONNEL, INC.
2180 West State Road 434, Suite 6152, Longwood FL 32779-5008. 407/682-5151. **Fax:** 407/682-2318. **Contact:** Bob Zahra, Manager. Employment Agency. **Positions commonly filled include:** Horticulturist.

FLORIDA JOBS & BENEFITS
5729 Manatee Avenue West, Bradenton FL 34209. 941/741-3030. **Contact:** Manager. Employment Agency. **Specializes in the areas of:** Non-Specialized. **Positions commonly filled include:** Bookkeeper; Clerk; Computer Operator; Construction Trade Worker; Data Entry Clerk; Driver; Factory Worker; Legal Secretary; Light Industrial Worker; Nurse; Receptionist; Secretary; Typist/Word Processor. **Number of placements per year:** 1000+.

FLORIDA JOBS & BENEFITS
609 North Orange Street, Starke FL 32091. 904/964-8092. **Contact:** Jim Wittington, Office Manager. Employment Agency. **Specializes in the areas of:** Non-Specialized.

GIRL FRIDAY
3876 West Commercial Boulevard, Fort Lauderdale FL 33309. 954/735-5392. **Contact:** Nancy Hollins, Manager. Employment Agency. **Specializes in the areas of:** Clerical; Manufacturing; Secretarial.

JANICE HERO MEDICAL RECRUITING
P.O. Box 13194, North Palm Beach FL 33408. **Contact:** Office Manager. Employment Agency. **Specializes in the areas of:** Consumer Sales and Marketing; Industrial Sales and Marketing; Medical Sales and Marketing; Sales and Marketing. **Number of placements per year:** 50 - 99.

IMPACT PERSONNEL
1270 Rogers Street, Clearwater FL 34616. 813/447-2288. **Contact:** Sheila Sliter, Director. Employment Agency. **Specializes in the areas of:** Clerical.

INTERIM SERVICES
2050 Spectrum Boulevard, Fort Lauderdale FL 33309. 954/938-7600. **Contact:** Recruiter. Employment Agency.

INTERNATIONAL INSURANCE CONSULTANTS
1191 East Newport Center Drive, Suite 206, Deerfield Beach FL 33442. 954/421-0122. **Fax:** 954/421-5751. **Contact:** Glenn A. Wootton, CPC, President. Employment Agency. **Specializes in the areas of:** Insurance.

JANUS CAREER SERVICE
525 North Park Avenue, Suite 218, Winter Park FL 32789. 407/628-1090. **Fax:** 407/628-5115. **Contact:** Jan Leach, President. Employment Agency. **Specializes in the areas of:** Non-Specialized. **Positions commonly filled include:** Accountant/Auditor; Administrative Services Manager; Aerospace Engineer; Architect; Attorney; Bank Officer/Manager; Branch Manager; Civil Engineer; Claim Representative; Computer Programmer; Computer Systems Analyst; Construction Contractor and Manager; Cost Estimator; Counselor; Credit Manager; Customer Service Representative; Designer; Draftsperson; Economist/Market Research Analyst; Editor; Electrical/Electronics Engineer; Financial Analyst; General Manager; Hotel Manager/Assistant Manager; Human Resources Specialist; Human Service Worker; Industrial Engineer; Industrial Production Manager; Insurance Agent/Broker; Management Analyst/Consultant; Management Trainee; Manufacturer's/Wholesaler's Sales Rep.; Mechanical Engineer; Metallurgical Engineer; Mining Engineer; Operations/Production Manager; Property and Real Estate Manager; Psychologist; Public Relations Specialist; Purchasing Agent and Manager; Quality Control Supervisor; Reporter; Restaurant/Food Service Manager; Securities Sales Rep.; Services Sales Representative; Software Engineer; Statistician; Structural Engineer; Teacher; Technical Writer/Editor; Transportation/Traffic Specialist; Urban/Regional Planner; Wholesale and Retail Buyer. **Number of placements per year:** 100 - 199.

THE JOB PLACE, INC.
428 Julia Street, Titusville FL 32796. 407/268-2250. **Contact:** Debra Shuler, Owner/Manager. Employment Agency. **Specializes in the areas of:** Non-Specialized.

JOB SERVICE OF FLORIDA
2944 Pennsylvania Avenue, Suite L, Marianna FL 32448. 904/482-9500. **Contact:**
B.K. McDonald, Job Service Office Manager. Employment Agency. **Specializes in the
areas of:** Non-Specialized.

KEYS EMPLOYMENT AGENCY
P.O. Box 1073, Big Pine Key FL 33043. 305/070 0000. Contact: Office Manager.
Employment Agency. **Specializes in the areas of:** Non-Specialized. **Positions commonly
filled include:** Accountant/Auditor; Adjuster; Administrative Services Manager;
Advertising Clerk; Architect; Attorney;· Bank Officer/Manager; Biological
Scientist/Biochemist; Branch Manager; Broadcast Technician; Budget Analyst; Civil
Engineer; Clerical Supervisor; Clinical Lab Technician; Computer Programmer;
Computer Systems Analyst; Construction and Building Inspector; Construction
Contractor and Manager; Cost Estimator; Counselor; Credit Manager; Customer
Service Representative; Dental Assistant/Dental Hygienist; Dental Lab Technician;
Designer; Dietician/Nutritionist; Draftsperson; Education Administrator;
Electrical/Electronics Engineer; Electrician; Emergency Medical Technician; Financial
Analyst; General Manager; Health Services Manager; Human Resources Specialist;
Human Service Worker; Landscape Architect; Librarian; Library Technician; Licensed
Practical Nurse; Management Analyst/Consultant; Management Trainee;
Mathematician; Medical Record Technician; Occupational Therapist;
Operations/Production Manager; Paralegal; Pharmacist; Physical Therapist; Preschool
Worker; Property and Real Estate Manager; Psychologist; Public Relations Specialist;
Purchasing Agent and Manager; Quality Control Supervisor; Radio/TV
Announcer/Newscaster; Registered Nurse; Reporter; Respiratory Therapist;
Restaurant/Food Service Manager; Securities Sales Rep.; Services Sales
Representative; Social Worker; Sociologist; Structural Engineer; Surveyor; Teacher;
Technical Writer/Editor; Transportation/Traffic Specialist; Travel Agent; Urban/Regional
Planner. Company pays fee. **Number of placements per year:** 1 - 49.

LAMORTE SEARCH ASSOCIATES, INC.
3003 Yamato Road, Suite 1073, Boca Raton FL 33434. 407/997-1100. **Fax:**
407/997-1103. **Contact:** William M. LaMorte, President. Employment Agency.
Specializes in the areas of: Insurance.

O'QUIN PERSONNEL/O'QUIN TEMPS
P.O. Box 2263, Lakeland FL 33806. 941/665-6431. **Contact:** Virginia O'Quin,
Owner/Manager. Employment Agency. **Specializes in the areas of:**
Accounting/Auditing; Advertising; Banking; Broadcasting; Clerical; Computer
Hardware/Software; Engineering; Finance; Legal; Manufacturing; Personnel/Labor
Relations; Sales and Marketing; Technical and Scientific; Temporary Assignments.

OLSTEN STAFFING SERVICES
11440 North Kendall Drive, Suite 101, Miami FL 33176. 305/270-2800. **Contact:**
Anthony Herr, Recruiter/Interviewer. Employment Agency. **Specializes in the areas of:**
Administration/MIS/EDP.

PMC&L ASSOCIATES, INC.
328 Banyan Boulevard, Suite K, West Palm Beach FL 33401. 407/659-4523. **Contact:**
Manager. Employment Agency. **Specializes in the areas of:** Accounting/Auditing;
Bookkeeping; Chef; Clerical; Data Processing; Engineering; General Management;
Office Support; Professional. Company pays fee. **Number of placements per year:** 100
- 199.

PERSONNEL ONE, INC.
1109 North Federal Highway, Fort Lauderdale FL 33304. 954/563-8000. **Fax:**
954/561-2736. **Contact:** Kary Capi, Manager. Employment Agency. **Specializes in the
areas of:** Administration/MIS/EDP; Legal; Personnel/Labor Relations; Sales and
Marketing; Secretarial. **Positions commonly filled include:** Accountant/Auditor;
Administrative Services Manager; Administrative Worker/Clerk; Clerical Supervisor;
Computer Programmer; Computer Systems Analyst; Customer Service Representative;
Human Resources Specialist; Paralegal; Services Sales Representative; Technical
Writer/Editor. Company pays fee. **Number of placements per year:** 200 - 499.

PERSONNEL ONE, INC.
770 South Dixie Highway, Suite 200, Coral Gables FL 33146. 305/662-2500. **Fax:**
305/662-6700. **Contact:** Office Manager. Employment Agency. **Specializes in the
areas of:** Accounting/Auditing; Banking; Computer Science/Software; Engineering;
General Management; Legal; Personnel/Labor Relations; Sales and Marketing;

Secretarial; Technical and Scientific. **Positions commonly filled include:** Accountant/Auditor; Bank Officer/Manager; Biological Scientist/Biochemist; Branch Manager; Chemist; Clerical Supervisor; Clinical Lab Technician; Computer Programmer; Computer Systems Analyst; Construction and Building Inspector; Construction Contractor and Manager; Counselor; Credit Manager; Engineer; Financial Analyst; Human Resources Specialist; Human Service Worker; Manufacturer's/Wholesaler's Sales Rep.; Paralegal; Property and Real Estate Manager; Public Relations Specialist; Services Sales Representative. Company pays fee. **Number of placements per year:** 200 - 499.

SHAVER EMPLOYMENT AGENCY
254 West Tampa Avenue, Venice FL 34285. 941/484-6821. **Contact:** Lee Shaver, Owner. Employment Agency. **Specializes in the areas of:** Non-Specialized. **Number of placements per year:** 1 - 49.

EXECUTIVE SEARCH FIRMS

THE BRAND COMPANY, INC.
8402 Red Bay Court, Vero Beach FL 32963. 407/231-1807. **Contact:** Mr. J.B. Spangenberg, President. Executive Search Firm. **Specializes in the areas of:** Engineering; General Management; Industrial; Manufacturing; Personnel/Labor Relations; Sales and Marketing. **Positions commonly filled include:** General Manager; Human Resources Specialist; Operations Research Analyst; Quality Control Supervisor. Company pays fee. **Number of placements per year:** 1 - 49.

THE BUTLERS COMPANY
INSURANCE RECRUITERS
2753 State Road 580, Suite 103, Clearwater FL 34621-3351. 813/725-1065. **Fax:** 813/726-7125. **Contact:** Kirby B. Butler, CPC, President. Executive Search Firm. **Specializes in the areas of:** Insurance; Risk Management. **Positions commonly filled include:** Accountant/Auditor; Actuary; Adjuster; Claim Representative; Computer Programmer; Computer Systems Analyst; General Manager; Insurance Agent/Broker; Loss Prevention Specialist; Underwriter/Assistant Underwriter. Company pays fee. **Number of placements per year:** 50 - 99.

CAREER CHOICE, INC.
1035 South Simmeron, Winter Park FL 32792. 407/679-5150. **Contact:** C.M. Herrick, President. Executive Search Firm. **Specializes in the areas of:** Hotel/Restaurant; Sales and Marketing. **Positions commonly filled include:** Accountant/Auditor; Budget Analyst; Buyer; Chef/Cook/Kitchen Worker; Dietician/Nutritionist; General Manager; Hotel Manager/Assistant Manager; Human Resources Specialist; Insurance Agent/Broker; Physician; Purchasing Agent and Manager; Restaurant/Food Service Manager. **Number of placements per year:** 100 - 199.

THE CHELSEA GROUP
P.O. Box 86647, Madeira Beach FL 33738. 813/593-3005. **Contact:** Office Manager. Executive Search Firm. **Specializes in the areas of:** Health/Medical. **Positions commonly filled include:** Occupational Therapist; Physical Therapist; Physician; Registered Nurse; Speech-Language Pathologist. Company pays fee. **Number of placements per year:** 100 - 199.

COLLI ASSOCIATES OF TAMPA
P.O. Box 2865, Tampa FL 33601. 813/681-2145. **Fax:** 813/661-5217. **Contact:** Benn or Carolyn Colli, Owners/Managers. Executive Search Firm. **Specializes in the areas of:** Computer Science/Software; Engineering; Industrial; Manufacturing. **Positions commonly filled include:** Aerospace Engineer; Biomedical Engineer; Buyer; Chemical Engineer; Designer; Electrical/Electronics Engineer; Human Resources Specialist; Industrial Engineer; Industrial Production Manager; Mechanical Engineer; Metallurgical Engineer; Nuclear Engineer; Operations/Production Manager; Purchasing Agent and Manager; Quality Control Supervisor; Software Engineer; Stationary Engineer; Structural Engineer. Company pays fee. **Number of placements per year:** 1 - 49.

CRITERION EXECUTIVE SEARCH
5420 Bay Center Drive, Suite 101, Tampa FL 33609-3469. 813/286-2000. **Contact:** Richard James, President. Executive Search Firm. **Specializes in the areas of:** Administration/MIS/EDP; Computer Science/Software; Engineering; Insurance;

Manufacturing; Technical and Scientific. **Positions commonly filled include:** Accountant/Auditor; Adjuster; Administrative Services Manager; Aerospace Engineer; Agricultural Engineer; Biological Scientist/Biochemist; Biomedical Engineer; Branch Manager; Chemical Engineer; Chemist; Civil Engineer; Electrical/Electronics Engineer; Human Resources Specialist; Industrial Engineer; Industrial Production Manager; Insurance Agent/Broker; Manufacturer's/Wholesaler's Sales Rep.; Mechanical Engineer; Metallurgical Engineer; Mining Engineer; Nuclear Engineer; Nuclear Medicine Technologist; Operations/Production Manager; Petroleum Engineer; Purchasing Agent and Manager; Radiologic Technologist; Software Engineer; Stationary Engineer; Structural Engineer; Underwriter/Assistant Underwriter. **Number of placements per year:** 100 - 199.

DP SEARCH
7061 South Tamiami Trail, Suite 106, Sarasota FL 34231. 941/925-3503. **Fax:** 941/925-3528. **Contact:** Fred E. Harris, Owner. Executive Search Firm. **Specializes in the areas of:** Personnel/Labor Relations; Technical and Scientific. **Positions commonly filled include:** Computer Operator; Computer Programmer; Computer Systems Analyst; Software Engineer. Company pays fee. **Number of placements per year:** 1 - 49.

DUNHILL OF FLORIDA, INC./LARGO
1915 East Bay Drive, Suite 3B, Largo FL 34641. 813/585-0000. **Contact:** Richard Williams, Owner. Executive Search Firm. **Specializes in the areas of:** Technical and Scientific.

DUNHILL OF TAMPA
4350 West Cypress Street, Suite 814, Tampa FL 33607. 813/872-8118. **Contact:** Mona Kramer, Administrative Assistant. Executive Search Firm. **Specializes in the areas of:** Accounting/Auditing; Health/Medical. **Positions commonly filled include:** Accountant/Auditor; EEG Technologist; EKG Technician; Medical Record Technician; Occupational Therapist; Physical Therapist; Registered Nurse; Respiratory Therapist; Surgical Technician.

F-O-R-T-U-N-E PERSONNEL CONSULTANTS OF SARASOTA
98 Sarasota Center Boulevard, Suite C, Sarasota FL 34240. 941/378-5262. **Fax:** 941/379-9233. **Contact:** Arthur R. Grindlinger, President. Executive Search Firm. **Specializes in the areas of:** Engineering; Industrial; Manufacturing; Materials; Quality Assurance; Transportation. **Positions commonly filled include:** Biomedical Engineer; Chemical Engineer; Electrical/Electronics Engineer; General Manager; Industrial Engineer; Industrial Production Manager; Mechanical Engineer; Metallurgical Engineer; Operations/Production Manager; Purchasing Agent and Manager; Quality Control Supervisor; Software Engineer; Transportation/Traffic Specialist. Company pays fee. **Number of placements per year:** 50 - 99.

GCA/GULF COAST ASSOCIATES
4487 Whisper Drive, Pensacola FL 32504. 904/478-2300. **Fax:** 904/478-2718. **Contact:** Mr. Chris Gordon, Proprietor. Executive Search Firm. **Specializes in the areas of:** Engineering; Heating, Air Conditioning, and Refrigeration; Manufacturing. **Positions commonly filled include:** Electrical/Electronics Engineer; Industrial Engineer; Mechanical Engineer; Metallurgical Engineer; Technical Writer/Editor. Company pays fee.

HR PROFESSIONAL CONSULTANTS, INC.
1975 East Sunrise Boulevard, Suite 604, Fort Lauderdale FL 33304. 954/523-6888. **Fax:** 954/485-6509. **Contact:** Employment Manager. Executive Search Firm. **Specializes in the areas of:** Accounting/Auditing; Engineering; Finance; Manufacturing; Personnel/Labor Relations; Plastics; Secretarial; Technical and Scientific. **Positions commonly filled include:** Accountant/Auditor; Biological Scientist/Biochemist; Biomedical Engineer; Buyer; Chemical Engineer; Chemist; Computer Programmer; Computer Systems Analyst; Electrical/Electronics Engineer; Financial Analyst; Industrial Engineer; Industrial Production Manager; Management; Mechanical Engineer; Operations/Production Manager; Packaging Technologist; Plastics Engineer; Purchasing Agent and Manager; Quality Assurance Engineer; Quality Control Supervisor; Science Technologist. Company pays fee. **Number of placements per year:** 1 - 49.

HEALTHCARE RECRUITERS OF CENTRAL FLORIDA
3000 Gulf To Bay Boulevard, Suite 305, Clearwater FL 34619. 813/725-5770. **Fax:** 813/725-9421. **Contact:** Tom Fleury, President. Executive Search Firm. **Specializes in the areas of:** Health/Medical; Sales and Marketing. **Positions commonly filled include:** Biological Scientist/Biochemist; Biomedical Engineer; Health Services Manager; Manufacturer's/Wholesaler's Sales Rep.; Occupational Therapist; Pharmacist; Physical

Therapist; Respiratory Therapist; Services Sales Representative. Company pays fee. **Number of placements per year:** 1 - 49.

K GROUP
9900 West Sample Road, Suite 300, Coral Springs FL 33065. 954/345-4444. **Contact:** Office Manager. Executive Search Firm. **Specializes in the areas of:** Accounting/Auditing; Banking; Computer Science/Software; Engineering; Finance; General Management; Industrial; Manufacturing; Personnel/Labor Relations. **Positions commonly filled include:** Accountant/Auditor; Attorney; Biological Scientist/Biochemist; Biomedical Engineer; Budget Analyst; Chemical Engineer; Chemist; Civil Engineer; Computer Programmer; Computer Systems Analyst; Credit Manager; Electrical/Electronics Engineer; Financial Analyst; Hotel Manager/Assistant Manager; Human Resources Specialist; Industrial Engineer; Industrial Production Manager; Mechanical Engineer; Public Relations Specialist; Purchasing Agent and Manager; Quality Control Supervisor; Registered Nurse; Software Engineer; Statistician; Technical Writer/Editor. Company pays fee. **Number of placements per year:** 50 - 99.

KELLEY & KELLER
2518 Key Largo Lane, Fort Lauderdale FL 33312. 954/791-4900. **Contact:** Verne Kelley, President. Executive Search Firm. **Specializes in the areas of:** Sales and Marketing. **Positions commonly filled include:** Marketing Specialist. Company pays fee. **Number of placements per year:** 1 - 49.

R.H. LARSEN & ASSOCIATES, INC.
1401 East Broward Boulevard, Suite 101, Fort Lauderdale FL 33301. 954/763-9000. **Fax:** 954/763-9318. **Contact:** Human Resources. Executive Search Firm. **Specializes in the areas of:** Accounting/Auditing; Administration/MIS/EDP; Architecture/Construction/Real Estate; Banking; Computer Science/Software; Engineering; Finance; Food Industry; General Management; Health/Medical; Manufacturing; Personnel/Labor Relations; Printing/Publishing; Sales and Marketing. **Number of placements per year:** 50 - 99.

MANAGEMENT RECRUITERS INTERNATIONAL INC.
3005 26th Street West, Suite C, Bradenton FL 34205. 941/753-5837. **Contact:** Mr. Lynn Moore, Owner. Executive Search Firm. **Specializes in the areas of:** Accounting/Auditing; Administration/MIS/EDP; Advertising; Architecture/Construction/Real Estate; Banking; Chemical; Communications; Computer Hardware/Software; Construction; Design; Electrical; Engineering; Finance; Food Industry; General Management; Health/Medical; Industrial; Insurance; Legal; Manufacturing; Operations Management; Personnel/Labor Relations; Pharmaceutical; Printing/Publishing; Procurement; Real Estate; Retail; Sales and Marketing; Technical and Scientific; Textiles; Transportation.

MANAGEMENT RECRUITERS INTERNATIONAL INC.
603 East Government Street, Pensacola FL 32501. 904/434-6500. **Fax:** 904/434-9911. **Contact:** Ken Kirchgessner, President. Executive Search Firm. **Specializes in the areas of:** Engineering; Industrial; Manufacturing. **Positions commonly filled include:** Chemical Engineer; Electrical/Electronics Engineer; General Manager; Industrial Engineer; Industrial Production Manager; Mechanical Engineer. Company pays fee. **Number of placements per year:** 1 - 49.

MANAGEMENT RECRUITERS INTERNATIONAL INC.
P.O. Box 7711, Clearwater FL 34618-7711. 813/791-3277. **Contact:** Helen G. Lianopoulos, Manager. Executive Search Firm. **Specializes in the areas of:** Health/Medical; Packaging; Sales and Marketing. **Positions commonly filled include:** Accountant/Auditor; Computer Programmer; Computer Systems Analyst; Designer; Dietician/Nutritionist; EEG Technologist; EKG Technician; Health Services Manager; Medical Record Technician; Nuclear Medicine Technologist; Occupational Therapist; Pharmacist; Quality Control Supervisor; Registered Nurse; Respiratory Therapist. Company pays fee. **Number of placements per year:** 50 - 99.

MANAGEMENT RECRUITERS OF CORAL GABLES
2121 Ponce de Leon Boulevard, Suite 940, Coral Gables FL 33134. 305/444-1200. **Fax:** 305/444-2266. **Contact:** Stephanie Anderson, Operations Manager. Executive Search Firm. **Specializes in the areas of:** Biology; Engineering; Manufacturing. **Positions commonly filled include:** Biological Scientist/Biochemist; Biomedical Engineer; Clinical Lab Technician; Electrical/Electronics Engineer; Mechanical Engineer; Quality Control

Supervisor; Software Engineer; Statistician. Company pays fee. **Number of placements per year:** 1 - 49.

MANAGEMENT RECRUITERS OF FORT MYERS
4100 Center Point Drive, #105, Fort Myers FL 33916. 941/939-2223. **Fax:** 941/939-2742. **Contact:** Calvin Beals, Manager. Executive Search Firm. **Specializes in the areas of:** Banking; Engineering. Positions commonly filled include: Actuary; Bank Officer/Manager; Chemical Engineer; Civil Engineer; Electrical/Electronics Engineer; Financial Analyst; Industrial Engineer; Mechanical Engineer; Physical Therapist. Company pays fee. **Number of placements per year:** 50 - 99.

MANAGEMENT RECRUITERS OF LAKE COUNTY, INC.
1117 North Donnelley Street, Mount Doraf FL 32757. 352/383-7101. **Fax:** 352/383-7103. **Contact:** Roger Holloway, President. Executive Search Firm. **Specializes in the areas of:** Engineering; Food Industry; General Management; Industrial; Manufacturing; Sales and Marketing; Transportation. **Positions commonly filled include:** Agricultural Engineer; Aircraft Mechanic/Engine Specialist; Designer; Draftsperson; Electrical/Electronics Engineer; Food Scientist/Technologist; General Manager; Industrial Engineer; Industrial Production Manager; Mechanical Engineer; Operations/Production Manager; Production Coordinator; Quality Control Supervisor; Structural Engineer. **Number of placements per year:** 50 - 99.

MANAGEMENT RECRUITERS OF MELBOURNE
1775 West Hibiscus Boulevard, Suite 215, Melbourne FL 32901. 407/951-7644. **Contact:** General Manager. Executive Search Firm. **Specializes in the areas of:** Accounting/Auditing; Administration/MIS/EDP; Advertising; Architecture/Construction/Real Estate; Banking; Chemical; Communications; Computer Hardware/Software; Construction; Design; Electrical; Engineering; Finance; Food Industry; General Management; Health/Medical; Industrial; Insurance; Legal; Manufacturing; Operations Management; Personnel/Labor Relations; Pharmaceutical; Printing/Publishing; Procurement; Real Estate; Retail; Sales and Marketing; Technical and Scientific; Textiles; Transportation.

MANAGEMENT RECRUITERS OF MIAMI
815 Northwest 57th Avenue #110, Miami FL 33126. 305/264-4212. **Fax:** 305/264-4251. **Contact:** Del Diaz, President. Executive Search Firm. **Specializes in the areas of:** Accounting/Auditing; Administration/MIS/EDP; Architecture/Construction/Real Estate; Computer Science/Software; Engineering; Finance; Health/Medical; Industrial; Manufacturing; Personnel/Labor Relations; Sales and Marketing. **Positions commonly filled include:** Accountant/Auditor; Administrative Services Manager; Aerospace Engineer; Agricultural Engineer; Biological Scientist/Biochemist; Biomedical Engineer; Branch Manager; Buyer; Ceramics Engineer; Chemical Engineer; Chemist; Civil Engineer; Clinical Lab Technician; Computer Programmer; Computer Systems Analyst; Construction Contractor and Manager; Cost Estimator; Customer Service Representative; Designer; EEG Technologist; EKG Technician; Electrical/Electronics Engineer; Financial Analyst; General Manager; Geologist/Geophysicist; Health Services Manager; Human Resources Specialist; Industrial Engineer; Industrial Production Manager; Licensed Practical Nurse; Manufacturer's/Wholesaler's Sales Rep.; Materials Engineer; Mechanical Engineer; Medical Record Technician; Metallurgical Engineer; Mining Engineer; Nuclear Engineer; Nuclear Medicine Technologist; Occupational Therapist; Petroleum Engineer; Physical Therapist; Property and Real Estate Manager; Public Relations Specialist; Purchasing Agent and Manager; Quality Control Supervisor; Radiologic Technologist; Recreational Therapist; Registered Nurse; Respiratory Therapist; Science Technologist; Services Sales Representative; Software Engineer; Stationary Engineer; Structural Engineer; Surveyor; Technical Writer/Editor; Wholesale and Retail Buyer. Company pays fee. **Number of placements per year:** 50 - 99.

MANAGEMENT RECRUITERS OF ST. PETERSBURG
9500 Koger Boulevard, Suite 203, St. Petersburg FL 33702. 813/577-2116. **Contact:** Manager. Executive Search Firm. **Specializes in the areas of:** Accounting/Auditing; Administration/MIS/EDP; Advertising; Architecture/Construction/Real Estate; Banking; Chemical; Communications; Computer Hardware/Software; Construction; Electrical; Engineering; Finance; Food Industry; General Management; Health/Medical; Industrial; Insurance; Legal; Manufacturing; Operations Management; Personnel/Labor Relations; Pharmaceutical; Printing/Publishing; Procurement; Real Estate; Sales and Marketing; Technical and Scientific; Textiles; Transportation.

MANAGEMENT RECRUITERS OF TALLAHASSEE
1406 Hays Street, Suite 7, Tallahassee FL 32301. 904/656-8444. **Contact:** Kitte Carter, Manager. Executive Search Firm. **Specializes in the areas of:** Accounting/Auditing; Administration/MIS/EDP; Advertising; Architecture/Construction/Real Estate; Banking; Chemical; Communications; Computer Hardware/Software; Construction; Design; Electrical; Engineering; Finance; Food Industry; General Management; Health/Medical; Industrial; Insurance; Legal; Manufacturing; Operations Management; Personnel/Labor Relations; Pharmaceutical; Printing/Publishing; Procurement; Real Estate; Retail; Sales and Marketing; Technical and Scientific; Textiles; Transportation.

MANAGEMENT RECRUITERS OF TAMPA
4200 West Cypress Street, Suite 640, Tampa FL 33607. 813/876-1151. **Contact:** Mike Case, Manager. Executive Search Firm. **Specializes in the areas of:** Accounting/Auditing; Administration/MIS/EDP; Advertising; Architecture/Construction/Real Estate; Banking; Chemical; Communications; Computer Hardware/Software; Construction; Design; Electrical; Engineering; Finance; Food Industry; General Management; Health/Medical; Industrial; Insurance; Legal; Manufacturing; Operations Management; Personnel/Labor Relations; Printing/Publishing; Procurement; Real Estate; Retail; Sales and Marketing; Technical and Scientific; Textiles; Transportation.

MANAGEMENT SEARCH INTERNATIONAL, INC.
2170 West State Road 434, Suite 454, Longwood FL 32779. 407/788-7700. **Fax:** 407/682-5372. **Contact:** Steven J. Bohn, General Manager. Executive Search Firm. **Specializes in the areas of:** Engineering; Health/Medical; Manufacturing. **Positions commonly filled include:** Aerospace Engineer; Agricultural Engineer; Biomedical Engineer; Chemical Engineer; Electrical/Electronics Engineer; Health Services Manager; Industrial Engineer; Mechanical Engineer; Metallurgical Engineer; Mining Engineer; Petroleum Engineer; Software Engineer. Company pays fee. **Number of placements per year:** 50 - 99.

McGUIRE EXECUTIVE SEARCH, INC.
1650 San Blake Road, Suite 302, Orlando FL 32809. 407/857-6100. **Contact:** Harry McGuire, Manager. Executive Search Firm. **Specializes in the areas of:** Hotel/Restaurant.

NPF ASSOCIATES, LTD, INC.
1999 University Drive, Suite 405, Coral Springs FL 33071. 954/753-8560. **Contact:** Dave Phillips, Research Associate. Executive Search Firm. **Specializes in the areas of:** Personnel/Labor Relations. **Number of placements per year:** 1 - 49.

OMNI PARTNERS
8211 West Broward Boulevard, Plantation FL 33324. 305/748-9800. **Fax:** 305/452-0800. **Contact:** Marvin A. Cohen, President. Executive Search Firm. **Specializes in the areas of:** Retail. **Positions commonly filled include:** Buyer. **Number of placements per year:** 200 - 499.

PEARCE ASSOCIATES
9116 Cypress Green Drive, Jacksonville FL 32256. 904/739-1736. **Contact:** Frank and Lois Pearce, Owners. Executive Search Firm. **Specializes in the areas of:** Health/Medical; Sales and Marketing. **Positions commonly filled include:** Health Services Manager; Physician; Respiratory Therapist; Services Sales Representative. Company pays fee.

PERFECT SEARCH INC.
2400 East Commercial Boulevard, #702, Fort Lauderdale FL 33308. 954/776-7533. **Fax:** 954/776-7606. **Contact:** Robin D. Newton, President. Executive Search Firm. **Specializes in the areas of:** Health/Medical; Sales and Marketing. **Positions commonly filled include:** Manufacturer's/Wholesaler's Sales Rep.; Medical Record Technician. Company pays fee. **Number of placements per year:** 1 - 49.

PERRY'S PERSONNEL
4900 Bayoa Boulevard, Suite #115, Pensacola FL 32503. 904/479-1202. **Contact:** Chuck Perry, Owner. Executive Search Firm. **Specializes in the areas of:** Engineering; Food Industry; Health/Medical; Manufacturing. **Positions commonly filled include:** Biological Scientist/Biochemist; Biomedical Engineer; Chemical Engineer; Quality Control Supervisor. **Number of placements per year:** 50 - 99.

PHYSICIAN EXECUTIVE MANAGEMENT CENTER
4014 Gunn Highway, Tampa FL 33624. 813/963-1800. **Fax:** 813/264-2207.
Contact: David R. Kirschman, President. Executive Search Firm. **Specializes in the
areas of:** Physician Executive. Company pays fee. **Number of placements per year:** 1 -
49.

RETAIL EXECUTIVE SEARCH, INC.
2550 West Oakland Park Boulevard, Suite 101, Fort Lauderdale FL 33311. 954/731-
2300. **Fax:** 954/733-0642. **Contact:** Manuel Kaye, President. Executive Search Firm.
Specializes in the areas of: Fashion; Retail. **Positions commonly filled include:** Retail
Executive; Retail Manager; Retail Merchandiser. Company pays fee. **Number of
placements per year:** 200 - 499.

JACK RICHMAN & ASSOCIATES
P.O. Box 25412, Tamarac FL 33320. 954/940-0721. **Fax:** 954/389-9572. **Contact:**
Jack Richman, President. Executive Search Firm. **Specializes in the areas of:**
Administration/MIS/EDP; Computer Science/Software; Engineering. **Positions
commonly filled include:** Computer Programmer; Computer Systems Analyst; Technical
Writer/Editor. Company pays fee. **Number of placements per year:** 1 - 49.

MATTHEW ROGALLA & ASSOCIATES
3347 Sandy Ridge Drive, Clearwater FL 34621. 813/786-8143. **Fax:** 813/784-0577.
Contact: Matt Rogalla, CPC, Recruiter. Executive Search Firm. **Specializes in the areas
of:** Engineering; General Management; Industrial; Manufacturing. **Positions commonly
filled include:** Chemical Engineer; Designer; Draftsperson; Electrical/Electronics
Engineer; Human Resources Specialist; Industrial Engineer; Industrial Production
Manager; Mechanical Engineer; Metallurgical Engineer; Operations/Production
Manager; Quality Control Supervisor; Software Engineer; Technical Writer/Editor.
Company pays fee. **Number of placements per year:** 1 - 49.

ROMAC & ASSOCIATES
5900 North Andrews Avenue, Suite 826, Fort Lauderdale FL 33309. 954/928-0800.
Fax: 954/771-7649. **Contact:** Howard Sutter, Vice President. Executive Search Firm.
Specializes in the areas of: Accounting/Auditing; Computer Hardware/Software;
Government. **Positions commonly filled include:** Accountant/Auditor; Computer
Programmer; EDP Specialist; MIS Specialist; Systems Analyst.

ROTH YOUNG OF TAMPA
5201 West Kennedy Boulevard, Suite 409, Tampa FL 33609. 813/289-6556. **Fax:**
813/289-9118. **Contact:** Barry Coishing, President. Executive Search Firm. **Specializes
in the areas of:** Engineering; Food Industry; Health/Medical; Sales and Marketing.
Positions commonly filled include: Buyer; General Manager; Hotel Manager/Assistant
Manager; Medical Doctor. Company pays fee. **Number of placements per year:** 50 -
99.

SALES CONSULTANTS OF FORT LAUDERDALE
100 West Cypress Creek Road, Suite 965, Fort Lauderdale FL 33309. 954/772-5100.
Contact: Jeff Taylor, Manager. Executive Search Firm. **Specializes in the areas of:**
Accounting/Auditing; Administration/MIS/EDP; Advertising;
Architecture/Construction/Real Estate; Banking; Chemical; Communications; Computer
Hardware/Software; Construction; Design; Electrical; Engineering; Finance; Food
Industry; General Management; Health/Medical; Industrial; Insurance; Legal;
Manufacturing; Operations Management; Personnel/Labor Relations;
Printing/Publishing; Procurement; Real Estate; Retail; Sales and Marketing; Technical
and Scientific; Textiles; Transportation.

SALES CONSULTANTS OF JACKSONVILLE
9471 Baymeadows Road, Suite 204, Jacksonville FL 32256. 904/737-5770. **Contact:**
General Manager. Executive Search Firm. **Specializes in the areas of:**
Accounting/Auditing; Administration/MIS/EDP; Advertising;
Architecture/Construction/Real Estate; Banking; Chemical; Communications; Computer
Hardware/Software; Construction; Design; Electrical; Engineering; Finance; Food
Industry; General Management; Health/Medical; Industrial; Insurance; Legal;
Manufacturing; Operations Management; Personnel/Labor Relations; Pharmaceutical;
Printing/Publishing; Procurement; Real Estate; Retail; Sales and Marketing; Technical
and Scientific; Textiles; Transportation.

SALES CONSULTANTS OF ORLANDO
900 Winderley Place, Suite 126, Maitland FL 32751. 407/660-0089. **Contact:** Tom Brown, General Manager. Executive Search Firm. **Specializes in the areas of:** Accounting/Auditing; Administration/MIS/EDP; Advertising; Architecture/Construction/Real Estate; Banking; Chemical; Communications; Computer Hardware/Software; Construction; Datacommunications; Electrical; Engineering; Finance; Food Industry; General Management; Health/Medical; Industrial; Insurance; Legal; Manufacturing; Operations Management; Personnel/Labor Relations; Printing/Publishing; Procurement; Real Estate; Retail; Sales and Marketing; Technical and Scientific; Textiles; Transportation.

SALES CONSULTANTS OF SARASOTA
1343 Main Street, Suite 600, Sarasota FL 34236-5687. 941/365-5151. **Contact:** Rose L. Castellano, Co-Manager. Executive Search Firm. **Specializes in the areas of:** Accounting/Auditing; Administration/MIS/EDP; Advertising; Architecture/Construction/Real Estate; Banking; Chemical; Communications; Computer Hardware/Software; Construction; Datacommunications; Electrical; Engineering; Finance; Food Industry; General Management; Health/Medical; Industrial; Insurance; Legal; Manufacturing; Operations Management; Personnel/Labor Relations; Printing/Publishing; Procurement; Real Estate; Retail; Sales and Marketing; Technical and Scientific; Textiles; Transportation.

SPECIALIZED SEARCH ASSOCIATES
15200 Carter Road, Suite 201, Delray Beach FL 33446. 407/499-3711. **Fax:** 407/499-3770. **Contact:** Leonard Morris, President. Executive Search Firm. **Specializes in the areas of:** Architecture/Construction/Real Estate; Engineering. **Positions commonly filled include:** Architect; Chemical Engineer; Civil Engineer; Construction and Building Inspector; Construction Contractor and Manager; Cost Estimator; Industrial Engineer; Mechanical Engineer; Structural Engineer; Transportation/Traffic Specialist. Company pays fee. **Number of placements per year:** 1 - 49.

THE STEWART SEARCH GROUP, INC.
Four Sawgrass Village, Ponte Vedra Beach FL 32082. 904/285-6622. **Fax:** 904/285-0076. **Contact:** James H. Stewart, President. Executive Search Firm. **Specializes in the areas of:** Biotechnology; Medical Sales and Marketing; Pharmaceutical. **Positions commonly filled include:** Biological Scientist/Biochemist; Biomedical Engineer; Chemist; Economist/Market Research Analyst; Operations/Production Manager; Pharmacist; Physician; Registered Nurse; Respiratory Therapist. **Number of placements per year:** 1 - 49.

TEMPFORCE/DIVACK MANAGEMENT
1111 North Westshore Boulevard, Tampa FL 34683. 813/286-2222. **Fax:** 813/289-0465. **Contact:** Susan Divack, President. Executive Search Firm. **Specializes in the areas of:** Accounting/Auditing; Administration/MIS/EDP; Computer Hardware/Software; General Management; Legal; Manufacturing; Personnel/Labor Relations; Secretarial; Technical and Scientific. **Positions commonly filled include:** Accountant/Auditor; Administrative Assistant; Bookkeeper; Clerk; Computer Operator; Computer Programmer; Customer Service Representative; Data Entry Clerk; EDP Specialist; Factory Worker; Legal Secretary; Light Industrial Worker; Marketing Specialist; Medical Secretary; Operations/Production Manager; Quality Control Supervisor; Receptionist; Secretary; Systems Analyst; Typist/Word Processor. Company pays fee.

TERRY M. WEISS & ASSOCIATES
LEGAL SEARCH
P.O. Box 915656, Longwood FL 32791-5656. 407/774-1212. **Fax:** 407/774-0084. **Contact:** Mr. Terry M. Weiss, Esq., President. Executive Search Firm. **Specializes in the areas of:** Accounting/Auditing; Legal. **Positions commonly filled include:** Accountant/Auditor; Attorney. Company pays fee. **Number of placements per year:** 1 - 49.

CAREER COUNSELING SERVICES

CENTER FOR CAREER DECISIONS
980 North Federal Highway, Suite 203, Boca Raton FL 33432. 407/394-3399.
Contact: Linda Friedman, MA, NCCC, Director. Career/Outplacement Counseling.
Specializes in the areas of: Executives; Professional.

PROFESSIONAL RESUME AND BUSINESS WRITING SERVICE
250 Bird Road, Suite 300, Coral Gables FL 33146. 305/441-1667. **Fax:** 305/441-6459. **Contact:** Joseph P. Garbin, President. Career/Outplacement Counseling.

INDEX OF PRIMARY EMPLOYERS

NOTE: *Below is an alphabetical index of primary employer listings included in this book. Those employers in each industry that fall under the headings "Additional employers" are not indexed here.*

Your Job Hunt
Your Feedback

Comments, questions, or suggestions? We want to hear from you. Please complete this questionnaire and mail it to:

The JobBank Staff
Adams Media Corporation
260 Center Street
Holbrook, MA 02343

Did this book provide helpful advice and valuable information which you used in your job search? Was the information easy to access?

Recommendations for improvements. How could we improve this book to help in your job search? No suggestion is too small or too large.

Would you recommend this book to a friend beginning a job hunt?

Name: _____

Occupation: _____

Which JobBank did you use? _____

Address: _____

Daytime phone: _____

Other Adams Publishing Books

The Adams Jobs Almanac, 1996. (Editors of Adams Publishing)
Updated annually, *The Adams Jobs Almanac, 1996* includes names and addresses of over 7,500 leading employers; information on which jobs each company commonly fills; industry forecasts and geographical cross-references; a close look at over 40 popular professions; a detailed forecast of 21st-century careers; and advice on preparing resumes and standing out at interviews. 5 1/2" x 8 1/2", 928 pages, paperback, $15.95.

The Adams Cover Letter Almanac. (Editors of Adams Publishing)
The Adams Cover Letter Almanac is the most detailed cover letter resource in print, containing over 600 cover letters used by real people to win real jobs. It features complete information on all types of letters, including networking, "cold," broadcast, and follow-up. In addition to advice on how to avoid fatal cover letter mistakes, the book includes strategies for people changing careers, relocating, recovering from layoff, and more. 5 1/2" x 8 1/2", 736 pages, paperback, $10.95.

The Adams Resume Almanac. (Editors of Adams Publishing)
This almanac features detailed information on resume development and layout, a review of the pros and cons of the various formats, an exhaustive look at the strategies that will definitely get a resume noticed, and 600 sample resumes in dozens of career categories. *The Adams Resume Almanac* is the most comprehensive, thoroughly researched resume guide ever published. 5 1/2" x 8 1/2", 768 pages, paperback, $10.95.

The JobBank Series. (Editors of Adams Publishing)
There are now 20 local *JobBank* books, each providing extensive, up-to-date employment information on hundreds of the largest employers in each job market. Recommended as an excellent place to begin your job search by *The New York Times, The Los Angeles Times, The Boston Globe, The Chicago Tribune,* and many other publications, *JobBank* books have been used by hundreds of thousands of people to find jobs. Editions available:

The Atlanta JobBank—The Boston JobBank—The Carolina JobBank—The Chicago JobBank—The Dallas-Ft. Worth JobBank—The Denver JobBank—The Detroit JobBank—The Florida JobBank—The Houston JobBank—The Los Angeles JobBank— The Minneapolis-St. Paul JobBank—The Missouri JobBank—The Metropolitan New York JobBank—The Ohio JobBank—The Greater Philadelphia JobBank—The Phoenix JobBank—The San Francisco JobBank—The Seattle JobBank—The Tennessee JobBank—The Metropolitan Washington JobBank

Each *JobBank* book is 6" x 9 1/4", at least 320 pages, paperback, $15.95.

Available Wherever Books Are Sold

If you cannot find these titles at your favorite retail outlet, you may order them directly from the publisher. BY PHONE: Call 1-800-872-5627 (in Massachusetts 617-767-8100). We accept Visa, Mastercard, and American Express. $4.50 will be added to your total order for shipping and handling. BY MAIL: Write out the full title of the books you'd like to order and send payment, including $4.50 for shipping and handling to: Adams Publishing, 260 Center Street, Holbrook, MA 02343. 30-day money-back guarantee.